José Pagán · Mounir Mokhtari ·
Hamdi Aloulou · Bessam Abdulrazak ·
María Fernanda Cabrera (Eds.)

How AI Impacts Urban Living and Public Health

17th International Conference, ICOST 2019
New York City, NY, USA, October 14–16, 2019
Proceedings

Editors
José Pagán
New York University
New York, NY, USA

Mounir Mokhtari
Institut Mines-Télécom
Paris, France

Hamdi Aloulou
Digital Research Centre of Sfax
Sfax, Tunisia

Bessam Abdulrazak
Université de Sherbrooke
Sherbrooke, QC, Canada

María Fernanda Cabrera
Technical University of Madrid
Madrid, Spain

https://doi.org/10.1007/978-3-030-32785-9

LNCS Sublibrary: SL3 – Information Systems and Applications, incl. Internet/Web, and HCI

Preface

This year we organized the 17th ICOST conference, an event which has succeeded in bringing together a community from different continents for over a decade and half and raised awareness about frail and dependent people's quality of life in our societies.

After 16 very successful conferences held in France (2003, 2009, 2017), Singapore (2004, 2013, 2018), Canada (2005, 2011), Northern Ireland (2006), Japan (2007), USA (2008, 2014), Korea (2010), Italy (2012), Switzerland (2015), and China (2016), we decided to open the conference to public health experts and tackle emerging challenges related to AI technologies for health and well-being. This 17th edition of the International Conference on Smart Living and Public Health (ICOST 2019), was hosted by the College of Global Public Health at New York University (NYU) and the New York Academy of Medicine (NYAM) in New York City, USA, during October 14–16, 2019. The theme of the conference this year was "How Does AI Impact Urban Living and Public Health?"

ICOST 2019 provided a premier venue for the presentation and discussion of research in the design, development, deployment, and evaluation of AI for health, smart urban environments, assistive technologies, chronic disease management, and coaching and health telematics systems. ICOST 2019 aimed to understand and assess how research impacts public health policies when facing emerging social and economic challenges. ICOST 2019 brought together stakeholders from health care, public health, academia and industry along with end users and family caregivers to explore how to utilize technologies to foster health prevention, independent living, and offer an enhanced quality of life. The ICOST 2019 conference featured a dynamic program incorporating a range of technical, clinical, and industrial related keynote speakers, oral and poster presentations, along with demonstrations and technical exhibits. Specific use cases were presented, such as the PULSE European funded project aiming at accelerating the use and vision of Big Data by designing a system to exploit Big Data Value (BDV) in the public health sector. PULSE (Participatory Urban Living for Sustainable Environments) is incorporating several major cities as test beds: Barcelona (Spain), New York City (USA), Paris (France), Birmingham (United Kingdom), Singapore, Keelung (Taiwan) and Pavia (Italy).

ICOST 2019 was proud to extend its hospitality to an international community consisting of researchers from major universities and research centers, representatives from industry and users from 13 different countries. We would like to thank the authors for submitting their current research work and the Program Committee members for their commitment to reviewing submitted papers. The ICOST proceedings have now reached over 150,000 downloads, and are in the top 25% of downloads of Springer LNCS.

We were very pleased to host world-renowned keynote speakers from multiple backgrounds coming from all over the world. We are extremely thankful to our sponsors for their commitment and support to the vision and mission of ICOST.

October 2019

José Pagán
Mounir Mokhtari
Hamdi Aloulou
Bessam Abdulrazak
María Fernanda Cabrera

Organization

General Chair

José Pagán	New York University and the New York Academy of Medicine, USA

Conference Co-chairs

Mounir Mokhtari	Institut Mines-Télécom, France, and Image and Pervasive Access Lab., Singapore
Maria Fernanda Cabrera	University Politecnica de Madrid, Spain

Steering Committee

Mounir Mokhtari	Institut Mines Télécom, France, and Image and Pervasive Access Lab., Singapore
Sumi Helal	Lancaster University (2017–present), UK, and University of Florida (1998–2017), USA
Bessam Abdulrazak	University of Sherbrooke, Canada
Hamdi Aloulou	University of Monastir, Tunisia, and Institut Mines-Télécom, France
Jose Pagan	New York University and the New York Academy of Medicine, USA
Maria Fernanda Cabrera	University Politecnica de Madrid, Spain

Scientific Advisory Board

Daqing Zhang	Institut Mines Télécom, Télécom SudParis, France
Hisato Kobayashi	Hosei University, Japan
Jongbae Kim	Science and Technology Research Center, Yonsei University, South Korea
Christian Roux	Institut Mines Télécom, France
Dong Jin Song	National University of Singapore, Singapore, and Griffith University, Australia
Sungyoung Lee	College of Electronics and Information, Kyung Hee University, South Korea
Timo Jämsä	EAMBES, University of Oulu, Finland
Daby Sow	IBM Research AI, USA

Program Committee

Chairs

Bessam Abdulrazak	University of Sherbrooke, AmI-Lab., Canada
Hamdi Aloulou	University of Monastir, Tunisia, and Institut Mines-Télécom, France

Members

Abdallah M'Hamed	Télécom SudParis - Evry, France
Belkacem Chikhaoui	University of Sherbrooke, Canada
Benoît Encelle	Université de Lyon, CNRS Université Lyon 1, LIRIS, France
Boussada Rihab	National School for Computer Science (ENSI), Tunisia
Charles Gouin-Vallerand	Télé-Université du Québec, Canada
David Menga	EDF R&D, France
Diane Cook	Washington State University, USA
Farah Arab	Université Paris 8, France
Hisato Kobayashi	Hosei University, Japan
Hongbo Ni	Northwestern Polytechnical University, China
Houssem Aloulou	Faculté des Sciences Économiques et de Gestion de Sfax, Tunisia
Ibrahim Sadek	Singapore University of Technology and Design (SUTD), Singapore
Jeffrey Soar	University of Southern Queensland, Australia
Laurent Billonnet	University of Limoges, France
Manfred Wojciechowski	University of Applied Sciences Duesseldorf, Germany
Salim Hima	ESME-SUDRIA, France
Sofia Ben Jebara	Ecole supérieure des communications de Tunis (SUPCOM), Tunisia
Timo Jämsä	University of Oulu, Finland
Victor Manuel Ponce Diaz	Université de Sherbrooke, Canada
Vigouroux Nadine	Institut de Recherche en Informatique de Toulouse (IRIT), France
Yves Demazeau	Laboratoire d'Informatique de Grenoble (LIG), France

Industry Liaison Committee

Peter Wu	ASUS Cloud, Taiwan
Daby M. Sow	IBM Research AI, USA
Vladimir Urosevic	Belit, Serbia
Suzanne Ballard	FCL, UK

Organizing Committee

Chair

Nina Raffio	NYU College of Global Public Health, USA

Members

Elisa Fisher	The New York Academy of Medicine, USA
Hamdi Aloulou	University of Monastir, Tunisia, and Institut Mines-Télécom, France
Antoine de Marassé Enouf	CNRS, Singapore
Valentina Tageo	European Connected Health Alliance, Spain

Sponsors

Institut Mines Télécom, Paris, France
National Center for Scientific Research, France
PULSE H2020 Project, Europe
New York University College of Global Public Health, USA
The New York Academy of Medicine, USA

Contents

E-health Technology Design

Privacy and Security of IoT Based Healthcare Systems: Concerns, Solutions, and Recommendations 3
Ibrahim Sadek, Shafiq Ul Rehman, Josué Codjo, and Bessam Abdulrazak

Designing an ICT Solution for the Empowerment of Functional Independence of People with Mild Cognitive Impairment: Findings from Co-design Sessions with Older People 18
Silvia de los Ríos, Rebeca I. García-Betances, Miguel Páramo, María Fernanda Cabrera-Umpiérrez, Marta Vancells, Maite Garolera, Jakub Kaźmierski, and María Teresa Arredondo Waldmeyer

Deployment of an IoT Solution for Early Behavior Change Detection 27
Hamdi Aloulou, Mounir Mokhtari, and Bessam Abdulrazak

Long Short Term Memory Based Model for Abnormal Behavior Prediction in Elderly Persons 36
Meriem Zerkouk and Belkacem Chikhaoui

Well-being Technology

A Deep Learning Method for Automatic Visual Attention Detection in Older Drivers 49
Belkacem Chikhaoui, Perrine Ruer, and Évelyne F. Vallières

Smart Mat for Respiratory Activity Detection: Study in a Clinical Setting . . . 61
Samuel Otis, Bessam Abdulrazak, Sofia Ben Jebara, Francois Tournoux, and Neila Mezghani

Non-invasive Classification of Sleep Stages with a Hydraulic Bed Sensor Using Deep Learning. 73
Rayan Gargees, James M. Keller, Mihail Popescu, and Marjorie Skubic

Biomedical and Health Informatics

A Convolutional Gated Recurrent Neural Network for Epileptic Seizure Prediction 85
Abir Affes, Afef Mdhaffar, Chahnez Triki, Mohamed Jmaiel, and Bernd Freisleben

Ubiquitous Healthcare Systems and Medical Rules in COPD Domain 97
Hicham Ajami, Hamid Mcheick, and Karam Mustapha

DL4DED: Deep Learning for Depressive Episode Detection on Mobile Devices 109
Afef Mdhaffar, Fedi Cherif, Yousri Kessentini, Manel Maalej, Jihen Ben Thabet, Mohamed Maalej, Mohamed Jmaiel, and Bernd Freisleben

ICT-Based Health Care Services for People with Spinal Cord Injury: A Pilot Study 122
Wanho Jang, Dongwan Kim, Jeonghyun Kim, Seungwan Yang, Yunjeong Uhm, and Jongbae Kim

Smart Environment Technology

An Interconnected Smart Technology System for Individuals with Mental Illness Living in the Community and Transitional Hospital Apartments 131
Cheryl Forchuk, Jonathan Serrato, Abraham Rudnick, Deborah Corring, Rupinder Mann, and Barbara Frampton

Transfer Learning for Urban Landscape Clustering and Correlation with Health Indexes 143
Riccardo Bellazzi, Alessandro Aldo Caldarone, Daniele Pala, Marica Franzini, Alberto Malovini, Cristiana Larizza, and Vittorio Casella

An IoT Architecture of Microservices for Ambient Assisted Living Environments to Promote Aging in Smart Cities 154
Hubert Kenfack Ngankam, Hélène Pigot, Maxime Parenteau, Maxime Lussier, Aline Aboujaoudé, Catherine Laliberté, Mélanie Couture, Nathalie Bier, and Sylvain Giroux

Designing a Navigation System for Older Adults: A Case Study Under Real Road Condition 168
Perrine Ruer, Damien Brun, Charles Gouin-Vallerand, and Évelyne F. Vallières

Short Contributions

User Embeddings Based on Mobile App Behavior Data. 183
Kushal Singla, Satyen Abrol, and Sungdeuk Park

Design, Development and Initial Validation of a Wearable Particulate Matter Monitoring Solution 190
José G. Teriús-Padrón, Rebeca I. García-Betances, Nikolaos Liappas, María F. Cabrera-Umpiérrez, and María Teresa Arredondo Waldmeyer

Cooperative System and Scheduling Algorithm for Sustainable Energy-Efficient Communities 197
Esther Palomar, Carlos Cruz, Ignacio Bravo, and Alfredo Gardel

ForeSight - Platform Approach for Enabling AI-based Services for Smart Living 204
Jochen Bauer, Hilko Hoffmann, Thomas Feld, Mathias Runge, Oliver Hinz, Andreas Mayr, Kristina Förster, Franz Teske, Franziska Schäfer, Christoph Konrad, and Jörg Franke

Mobility Application with Semantic Reasoning 212
Martin Kodyš, Antoine de Marassé, and Mounir Mokhtari

Author Index 223

E-health Technology Design

Privacy and Security of IoT Based Healthcare Systems: Concerns, Solutions, and Recommendations

Ibrahim Sadek[1(✉)], Shafiq Ul Rehman[2], Josué Codjo[3], and Bessam Abdulrazak[3]

[1] Faculty of Engineering, Biomedical Engineering Department, Helwan University, Cairo, Egypt
ibrahim_ibrahim@h-eng.helwan.edu.eg
[2] ST Electronics-SUTD Cyber Security Laboratory, Singapore University of Technology and Design, Singapore, Singapore
[3] Département d'Informatique, Faculté des sciences, Université de Sherbrooke (UdeS), Sherbrooke, Canada

Abstract. Although emerging IoT paradigms in sleep tracking have a substantial contribution to enhancing current healthcare systems, there are several privacy and security considerations that end-users need to consider. End-users can be susceptible to malicious threats when they allow permission to potentially vulnerable or leaky third-party apps. Since the data is migrated to the cloud, it goes over insecure communication channels, all of which have their security concerns. Moreover, there are alternative data violation concerns when the data projects into the proprietor's cloud storage facility. In this study, we present some of the existing IoT sleep trackers, also we discuss the most common features associated with these sleep trackers. As the majority of end-users are not aware of the privacy and security concerns affiliated with emerging IoT sleep trackers. We review existing solutions that can apply to IoT sleep tracker architecture. Also, we describe a deployed IoT platform that can address these concerns. Finally, we provide some of the recommendations to end-users and service providers to ensure a safer approach while leveraging the IoT sleep tracker in caregiving. This incorporates recommendations for software updates, awareness programs, software installation, and social engineering.

1 Introduction

The 2019 "World Economic Forum" global risk report[1] has nominated cyber attacks and data breaches as the fourth and fifth deliberate risks facing the world today. It is the second year in a row that these threats feature in the top five list of risks. Healthcare, among others, was offended with more cybersecurity breaches, in which several situations can lead to these breaches, for example,

[1] World Economic Forum. The Global Risks Report 2019. Retrieved May 29, 2019, from https://www.weforum.org/reports/the-global-risks-report-2019.

J. Pagán et al. (Eds.): ICOST 2019, LNCS 11862, pp. 3–17, 2019.
https://doi.org/10.1007/978-3-030-32785-9_1

credential-stealing malware, an insider who either systematically or accidentally unveils patient data, or lost laptops or other mobile devices. On the illegal market, "Protected Health Information" (PHI) is more important than credit card credentials or even personally identifiable information. Hence, there is a higher motivation for cybercriminals to target medical databases, and so they can sell the PHI or adapt it for their benefits.

Throughout the world, healthcare challenges can exist in different shapes and forms. Subsequently, this presents tremendous pressure on the current system. Even though every society faces various demands and encounters several effects, it is still practicable to determine the overall global risk to current healthcare systems. These demands are a fundamental starting point for the work ahead. Population aging, the prevalence of chronic diseases, shortage of healthcare specialists, and the unpredictable rise of healthcare costs, among other reasons, are the considerable challenges facing today's healthcare systems. For dealing with these issues, public and private sector players should collaborate to find more innovative and affordable methods that can be deployed in out-of-hospital environments [14]. Healthcare IoT based systems are multiples and vary from wearable to mobile sensors going through actuators, that acquire patient biosignals, motion, or contextual information. Amongst those systems, we have Zio Patch depicted in [24] which measures heart rate and electrocardiogram (ECG) and Myo [9] which is a motion controller used in orthopedics for patients who need to exercise after a fracture. None of the above performs in multiple information gathering. Therefore, we have systems, which can combine biosignals, motion, and contextual information such as sleep trackers.

In this paper, we focus on sleep tracking as a significant vector of quality of life. Sleep is crucial to our health and sleep disorders can often be a symptom of a disease; or likewise may be a signal of a subsequent illness such as depression. As a result, assessment of sleep is a fundamental component of any health check. Understanding cardiovascular and respiratory systems are essential for analyzing sleep and sleep cycles. This is because the active processes in the human body are different in sleep and wakefulness.

Nowadays, we can render the Internet of Things (IoT) and Cloud services to improve access to caregiving by remotely strengthen the quality of caregiving and above all cut down the cost of caregiving. As different sleep trackers, i.e., IoT devices are used to collect the user data and transfer it to the cloud. The collected data is later being analyzed by sleep experts to enhance these devices for better results. According to the "ABI Research" report[2] currently, there are over 10 billion wirelessly connected IoT devices, and by 2020, the number will exceed 30 billion devices. Some of these devices will fall within the category of sleep-tracking devices. Nevertheless, these emerging technologies are vulnerable to adversarial attacks because of their design. The data breach can have severe consequences both on individual users and the company's reputation. Moreover,

[2] ABI Research. Over 30 Billion Devices Will Wirelessly Connect to the Internet of Everything in 2020. Retrieved May 29, 2019, from https://www.abiresearch.com/press/more-than-30-billion-devices-will-wirelessly-conne/.

compromised IoT sleep tracking devices can allow intruders to monitor the user's private lives actively.

The main contribution of this study is to highlight the privacy and security concerns of IoT sleep trackers and provide an insight into how precise mechanisms or approaches can be applied to prevent or mitigate such adversarial attempts. We anticipate this research to guide future researchers to use and apply specific solutions for IoT in healthcare problems based on the proposed approaches and mechanisms by security experts.

The rest of the paper is organized as follows: IoT sleep trackers and their types are described in Sect. 2. We state the security and privacy issues that are associated with IoT sleep trackers in Sect. 3. We present some existing solutions in Sect. 4, then we depict an IoT based case study in Sect. 5, while we mention the recommendations in Sect. 6. We outline the conclusion in Sect. 7.

2 IoT Sleep Trackers

The healthcare system desperately needs reform to rein in costs, improve quality, and expand access. Medical diagnosis consumes a large part of hospital bills. Technology can move medical check routines from a hospital (hospital-centered) to the home (home-centered) of the patient. A new paradigm, known as the IoT, widely applies in many areas, including healthcare. The full application of this paradigm in healthcare is a mutual hope, as it enables medical centers to function more efficiently and patients to receive better treatment. There are unique benefits with the use of this technology that could improve the quality and efficiency of treatments and thus improve patient health.

IoT technology permits and facilitates remote monitoring of patients who do not have ready access to adequate health monitoring. Likewise, it helps to thoroughly reduce costs and promote health by increasing the availability and quality of care [12]. The IoT is a network of smart devices and other objects integrated with electronics, software, sensors, and network connectivity that permit these objects to get and exchange data. The concept of IoT provides healthcare professionals and caregivers to access a patient's medical history, vitals, lab results, medical and prescription histories either on-site or remotely via tablets or smartphones. Patients can be observed and notified from anywhere [9]. We can use IoT based solutions to record patient health data securely from several sensors, apply complicated algorithms to analyze the data and then distribute it through wireless connectivity with medical specialists who can make suitable health recommendations [21].

Typically, examining a person's sleep requires an overnight sleep test (Fig. 1) or polysomnography (PSG) that allows the monitoring of several physiological functions besides sleep cycles [4,22]. Although the PSG, or as known as the gold standard for sleep monitoring, provides real-time and accurate information about sleep, it is cumbersome, expensive, and time-consuming. Thus, the healthcare community is inquiring novel nonintrusive solutions that can improve the quality of healthcare for the patient while sustaining the cost of the service provided [19].

Fig. 1. An illustration of the location of the various electrodes and sensors used during the overnight sleep. Adapted from: mattressclarity.com

Actigraph is a very famous example that can be used for sleep analysis. The device is not as accurate as of the PSG. However, its information, which is based on the users' activity, is critical for healthcare professionals to interpret and analyze the sleep behavior of the users. As hardware and software technology is advancing quickly, several devices and mobile apps have been developed for general healthcare monitoring, including sleep. These devices could be wearables such as bracelets, smart-watches, smart-shirts, or smart-rings (Fig. 2) or non-wearable like bed-sensors that can be installed underneath the user's bed mattress (Fig. 3).

Sleep monitoring is described as getting qualitative sleep metrics by monitoring a person's sleep during the night. These serve two functions. One is to formulate an objective view of the quality of a person's sleep, while the other role is to determine the trends in sleep. Respiratory rate and body movements are considered the most detailed measurements for sleep monitoring during the sleeping session. The respiratory rate and respiratory rate variability are used for rapid eye movement (REM) sleep identification, while the movement metrics are utilized to discriminate between deep sleep, light sleep, and then waking stages of sleep. We can also extract several sleep parameters, for example, the duration of a sleep period, the number of awakenings, duration of disturbed sleep periods, and the time required to fall asleep. In recent years, various sensor technologies have been exploited, especially to monitor sleep-wake patterns simultaneously with the gold standard PSG and actigraphy; these sensor technologies are commonly denoted as consumer sleep tracking devices. Consumer sleep tracking devices are just like actigraphs because they allow users to be mobile and sleep as usual while being monitored closely.

Most of the consumer sleep monitors pretend to help provide information about sleep duration and quality of sleep, enabling subjects to awaken only from the light sleep. Typically, the data gained from consumer sleep tracking devices are not intended for routine diagnosis of sleep disorders. However, scientific improvements in hardware and software, accessibility, and ready availability

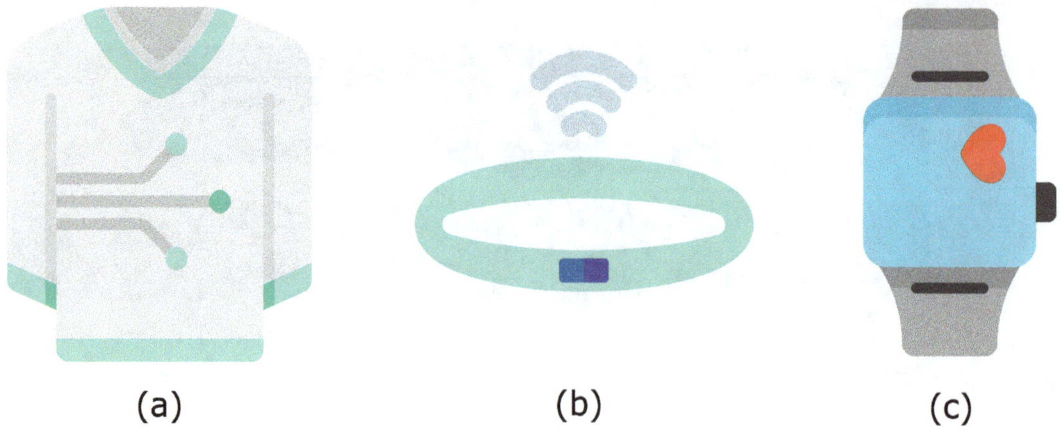

Fig. 2. Illustrations for wearable sleep trackers; (a) smart-shirt, (b) smart-bracelet, and (c) smart-watch. Icons made by Freepik from: flaticon.com

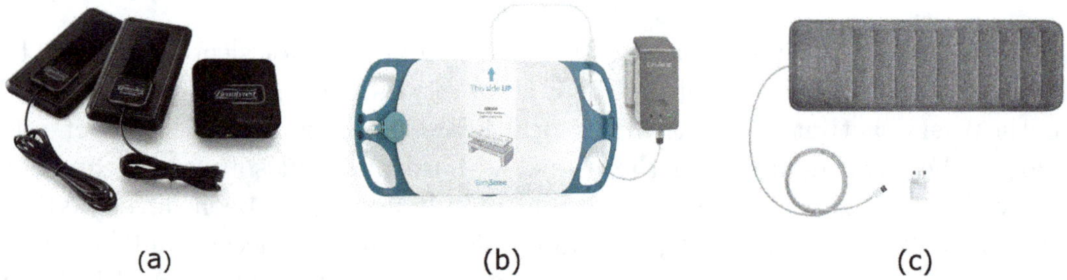

Fig. 3. Some examples of non-wearables sleep trackers; (a) Beautyrest © 2019 Simmons Bedding Company LLC, (b) EarlySense © 2019 Early Sense, and (c) Withings © 2019 Withings.

allow the public to adopt them for clinical purposes. These devices include *Emfit QS*, *Beddit*, *Withings*, *Sleepace Reston*, *Beautyrest*, and *Juvo*. Figure 3 shows three examples of existing bed-based sleep trackers.

These sensors are designed and packaged in a way that makes them invisible to the subjects. For instance, we can easily integrate them into home furniture such as beds, pillows, chairs, or even weighing scales [26]. These sensors technologies are preferred than those popular sensors (e.g., ECG) when we are considering long-term (trend over time, early detection and intervention by sending alarms to family members or caregivers through well-designed user interfaces), mobile, convenient and practical (aging-in-place, senior activity centers). However, in critical situations, gold-standard methods should be considered [20].

Most of the existing products implement the piezoelectric technology for nonintrusive monitoring of vital signs (for example, *Beddit*, *Withings*, *Sleepace Reston*, and *Beautyrest*) which shows the popularity and suitability of the piezoelectric material for measuring the slight vibrations caused by the heart movements that is transmitted through the bed mattress. Another famous sleep tracker sensor using a piezoelectric sensor is *EarlySense*. The system can report information about heart rate, respiration, snoring, coughing, and movement. A recent study showed good agreement between *EarlySense* and the gold standard PSG for sleep staging [23]. The device provided promising results for sleep apnea detection [7].

On the one hand, there are some standard features that these sensors claim to measure, such as heart rate, respiration, sleep and wake-up time, and sleep interruptions. There are several publications in the existing literature that can support these claims, as mentioned in [20].

Insufficient publications are available in existing literature that can support other claims such as sleep efficiency (i.e., the time in bed spent asleep before waking up), sleep score (i.e., summarizes your night's sleep quality and quantity in a single number, it takes your sleep time, sleep efficiency, restfulness, snoring, and heart rate into account), smart alarm (i.e., to awaken the wearer at an optimal time within a time-window that ends in the final alarm setting) and sleep stages. For example, to get accurate results about the different stages of sleep, the patient should undergo a full-night sleep study or as known as polysomnography [25]. It seems that *Emfit QS* is the only device claiming to measure heart rate variability. Similarity, Withings is claiming to measure a breathing disturbance metric that can contribute to identifying abnormal sleep patterns such as apneas. A power supply is required for operating most of these sensors. However, *Sleepace Reston* is a battery-powered. It is worth mentioning that these sensors are only designed to monitor a single person overnight. However, the *BeautyRest* sleep tracker comes with two sensors, so couples can independently track their sleep.

Having said that, although the security and privacy feature of these sensors are essential, most of the end-users might not fully know of weaknesses and potential risks in their existing devices. Therefore, we present in the ensuing sections, the security and privacy features associated with existing IoT sleep trackers.

3 Privacy and Security Concerns

According to Deborah Lupton's report[3], during her Research she found there are risks associated with data collection (a) from IoT tracking devices such as devices' storage, (b) while transmitting it over the network and (c) finally, in the cloud where data is stored for analyses. The same risk applies to the IoT Sleep Tracker Architecture, where these devices are being used for collecting data while users are asleep, later transmitted to cloud via wireless communication.

Sleep tracking devices aid us in practical applications in gaining quality sleep, thus improving our lives by measuring our heart rates and movements as described in Sect. 2. However, they can possess severe security and privacy risks. Since the sleep tracker users can become a victim to malware by downloading the insecure third-party apps and thus gives permission to the potential adversary to access the device remotely, Later, the users operate these sleep

[3] The Irish Times. Fitness trackers run into resistance over data security concerns. Retrieved May 29, 2019, from https://www.irishtimes.com/business/technology/fitness-trackers-run-into-resistance-over-data-security-concerns-1.3119483.

trackers knowingly or unknowingly in their private places, i.e., home, considering their devices are secure enough to be compromised. Mostly IoT sleep-tracking devices communicate over the public networks. As the data is being transferred to the cloud, the adversary can intercept over the communication channel by carrying out various attacks such as Botnet, Denial of Service (DoS) and Man in the Middle (MITM) attacks. Moreover, there are data breach concerns, as the adversary can remotely access the data stored in the cloud by compromising it via malicious software. Once the device/storage is hacked, a hacker can gain the user's confidential data about sleeping habits such as sleep talking, snoring sounds, and sensual activities. Such a data breach can have a severe impact on the user's reputation. Besides, a hacker can induce the noise by speaking or producing some sounds to disturb the user while asleep, which can consequently result in inadequate sleep.

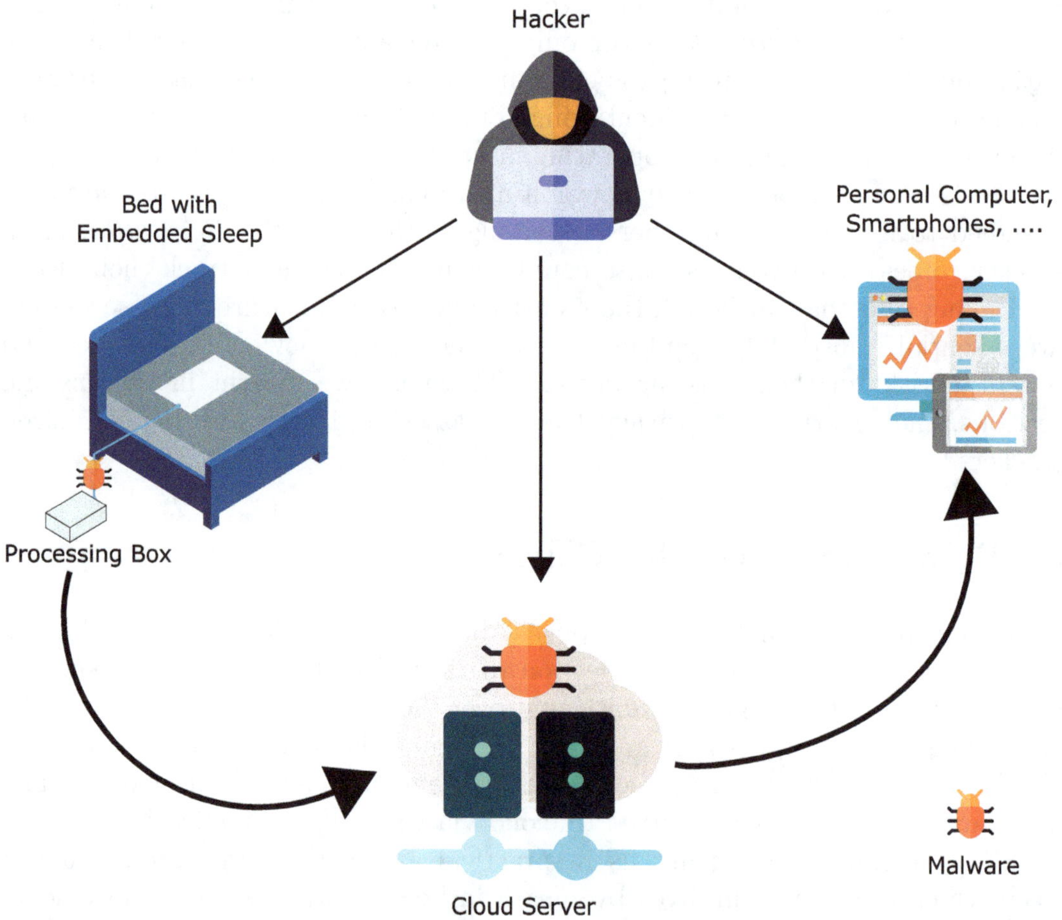

Fig. 4. An illustration of a sleep-tracking mat as an example of an IoT device in a medical setting and how an attacker can exploit the several stages of data processing, i.e., from data acquisition to end-users.

Similarly, there is a risk of data profiling which is defined as "collecting a person's behavior and analyzing psychological characteristics to predict or assess their ability in a certain sphere or to identify a particular group of people." This means the data generated by the sleep tracker devices can be exploited to create profiles of such device users, which can be afterward used for target advertisements. The reason being that an individual's data is collected through wirelessly connected devices means there is a need for advanced measures to ensure the security and privacy of end-users. Research has shown [1], that because of the heterogeneous nature of IoT, it has raised various privacy and security concerns. For instance, data confidentiality, integrity, availability, user authentication, authorization, and anonymity. Figure 4 depicts the different attack scenarios that can affect the remote monitoring of sleep.

4 Existing Security and Privacy Solutions

While considering these IoT privacy and security concerns, the researchers and security experts around the globe from different domains, i.e., academia, industry, and technical backgrounds are attempting to mitigate these flaws in IoT infrastructure by fulfilling the necessary security and privacy measures as mentioned in Sect. 3. Some existing proposed mechanisms that also apply to sleep-tracker architecture are as follows:

Bruening and Waterman [5] introduced a concept of data tagging to ensure data privacy while transferring the sensor data over the network. It appends an additional tag to data transfer to ensure trusted communication, hence can hide the user's identity. Similarly, Chatzigiannakis *et al.* [6] proposed another approach to preserve user identity, which is known as the zero-knowledge proof (ZKP). Based on this concept, the sender can show to receive specific properties of transferred information that can ensure its authenticity without revealing its identity. Moreover, Henze *et al.*, [11] have examined the clustering technique known as the k-anonymity model to hide the location of sensor nodes to protect the sensitive data being transferred over the wireless network (WSN). The idea behind this is to gather the data from these nodes at different positions without being easily traced. Furthermore, Google[4] proposed a solution that is a part of the Google cloud platform. Scalability is the main feature of this platform, which allows connecting the devices, collecting the data, and visualizing them.

Besides, IoT solutions, namely IBM Bluemix Platform offered by IBM, is an IoT-enabled cloud solution. This platform can be used for the development of cloud-based applications managing data generated by several sensors and devices, and it supports secure data transfers.

Moreover, Internet Protocol version 6 (IPv6) [8] is the next-generation Internet protocol, which is being deployed as a communication protocol in the IoT environment. However, because of its nature, it is vulnerable to DoS attacks [17]. Such vulnerability can interrupt the communication between the nodes in a network. To resolve this problem, the Rule-based mechanism [16] and a lightweight, encrypted scheme known as Secure-DAD [18] have been proposed by Rehman

[4] Google Cloud IoT - Fully managed IoT services — Google Cloud. Retrieved May 29, 2019, from https://cloud.google.com/solutions/iot/.

and Manickam. The former technique can detect any attempt of the DoS attack, while a later system can prevent it from occurring. Thus, by deploying such mechanisms, we can ensure a trusted communication between the IoT nodes in a heterogeneous environment.

Recently, Dwivedi *et al.* [10] proposed an IoT framework based on a modified blockchain model. The authors claim that the proposed framework provides a solution that is based on advanced cryptographic primitives for IoT data applications and secure transactions. Also, it can provide anonymity of users over the blockchain-based network.

To complement, in Sect. 5, we present an IoT-based case study (i.e., AMI-IoT platform) to show how these security concerns as aforementioned can be addressed in a real-life scenario.

5 AMI-IoT Deployed Platform

The Ami-lab has been developing several IoT architectures for the past decade and following; we described how we addressed the previously discussed security issues. We have mainly focused on privacy, data profiling, the man-in-the-middle-attack, data corruption, which can undermine the end-to-end communication from the environmental nodes to the database. The AMI-IoT platform as depicted in Fig. 5 is composed of three main components, which are, end-users environment, network, and cloud architecture. Based on the work of Mendonça *et al.* [2], we assume that the three elements, Sensing Approach (SA), Awareness & Security (AS) and Responsibility & Actions (RA), are essentials to address the IoT security concerns.

5.1 Sensing Approach (SA)

The SA element is the entry point of the architecture. It ensures data detection and its migration from environmental nodes to the database. It also represents the listening state of other components as well as the architecture. At this point, making sure of the working state of environmental nodes is crucial. Data gathered by nodes will be sent through a network path built by the node and its peer. This element is the foundation of IoT architecture, enabling endpoint sleep trackers and allowing them to submit information through the entire network, giving the opportunity to experts to process the data. Sleep tracker such as a smart mat has been used, transmitting data to a node that will serve as a broker and publish the information. On the other hand, a unique peer will be subscribing to that broker getting the data in time through a canal. A gateway will be used to monitor and redirect the traffic from the peer to the smart mat. Nevertheless, during the SAP, neglecting the user's privacy, the authenticity of the information sent, and the security of the database on which information is stored does not respect the security standards Raza *et al.* [15]. It's from this perspective that we build the same element.

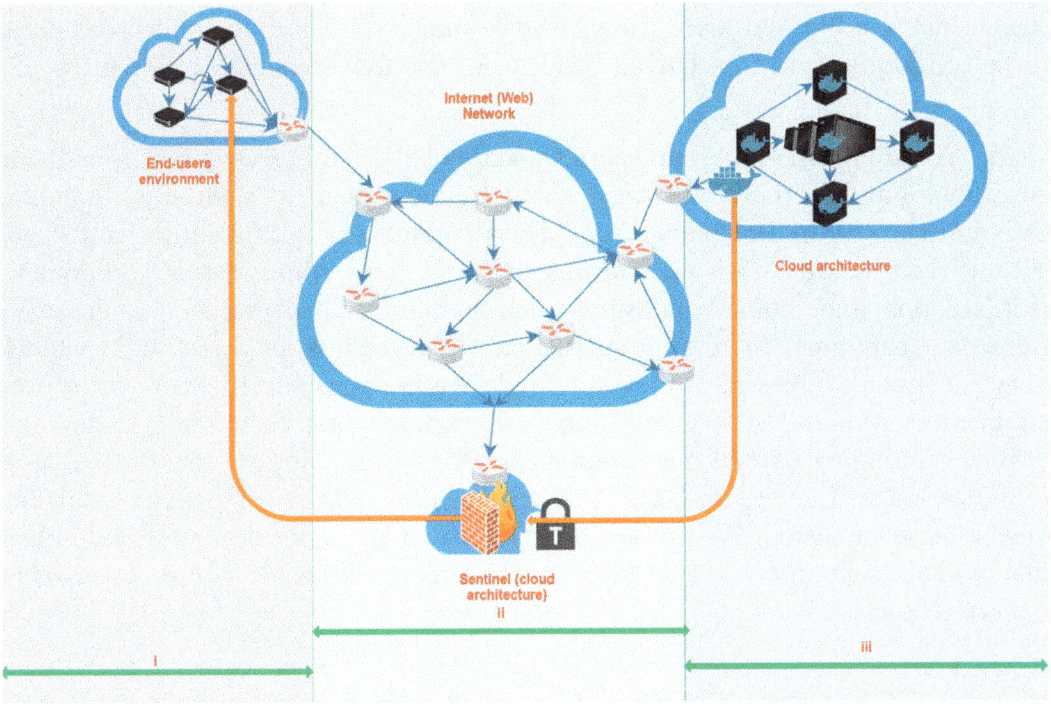

Fig. 5. Ami-IoT Architecture issues addressed (i. Jamming, Flooding, Phishing, Connection Timed out, Battery, Not responsible, Privacy, Data profiling; ii. The sinkhole, Man-in-the-middle, Hello Flood, Connection persistence, Packet loss, Botnet; iii. Flooding, Dos, Data stealing, Data loss, Data modification, privacy)

5.2 Awareness and Security (AS)

This element intends to make the system aware of abnormalities and breaches, which can occur and put the needed security to prevent a possible attack. On this note, a system cannot be protected if we are not aware of the situations and the risks surrounding it. Based on that, the Ami-lab will be relying on the three components of the architecture.

End-User Environment. It regroups all the environmental nodes gathering the data. This component is the favorite spot of attackers due to the negligence of users and their compliance with the attacks mentioned previously. This component is subject to external attacks and faces issues such as privacy, access, data profiling. To face those challenges, Ami-lab implemented firewalls Raza *et al.* [15] in every node deployed on the end-user side. Those firewalls have been added, preventing external attacks and allowing just one communication at a time. Regarding privacy, we concluded that even the node should be identified by their ID and not the users. Thus, yet if the attacker has the identifier, he won't be able to know whose information he has access to. Moreover, rules have also been applied so that the user will have limited access to the node. It will restrict phishing attacks, which can compromise the system. Also, all incoming connections are blocked, accepting just the one responsible for collecting data. These techniques lead to securing the End-users environment component.

Cloud Architecture. It represents the core of the Ami-lab system. It's all the technologies and methods put together to enable a peer for each environmental node and the storing in the database. Data corruption, data stealing, data loss, privacy, data modification are various problems undermining this component. Ami-lab took some countermeasures such as defining a firewall on each server composing this part, to restrict intrusion. Every rule is set carefully, to block every incoming traffics and allowing single traffic from the listener to its peer (environmental node). Every outgoing traffic is controlled. Self-configuration and optimization being part of our architecture, everything adapts itself to the new configuration in our cloud. Thus, we are avoiding "data corruption" and any other kind of intrusion. We are keeping the use of the environmental node identifier and data compression to address the privacy issue. It comes to another concern, the bridge.

Internet (Network). Named in IoT architecture, the weak link, due to its public nature, it can be subject to many attacks mentioned in the previous sections. It relates the end-users environment to the cloud environment serving as a bridge. While an attack cannot reach the first component of the architecture, there is still a chance to intercept the data while it's been sent. Then, botnet attacks, man-in-the-middle attacks, which will block the transaction or worst prevent data from storing in the database. To avoid this weak point, we created a secure tunnel known just by our peers. The Internet will serve to, will be retrieving the certificates and then establishing a secured channel between the environmental node and the cloud node. Every communication has been made to guarantee that each environmental node has its peer and can communicate just with that peer. In case something happened, it won't affect the whole system since we made them independent. To reinforce the security, a high level of encryption has been used as well as data compression.

5.3 Responsibility and Actions (RA)

This element is the last piece conferring "responsibility" feature to a system and is based on Angarita and Kelaidonis *et al.* work [3,13]. Making a system able to take action, depending on the outcome of a situation is the key role of this part. Being part of our future work, Ami-lab strives to achieve a self-healing architecture. The concept of "responsibility" should be transmitted to the architecture enabling its self-management. A responsible environment based on awareness feature should be able to react in time when a situation occurs. A system should be able to define the right action to take and complete it in an optimal way. Indeed, an IoT system, when facing an intrusion issue, should be able to take action and keeps working. For instance, if there is an attack on the environmental node, the node should be able to detect and close all the connections, then re-enable the peer connection. We achieved "the responsibility" feature on the environmental nodes. It allows them to take action against intrusion, connectivity issues, and data transmission issues. Processing information, and creating an adapted virtual object dynamically to decipher the correct information, is also part of our future work. This feature grants autonomy to the applications letting the system creating an environment suited to the end-user. It gives the required access to the user, based on its knowledge and background. Regarding the listening peers for data retrieval, our system can take action upon peers' failure by replacing them in time. A monitoring system such as Prometheus or Zabbix will be listening to applications, environmental nodes, cloud nodes, and servers and networks to transmit the right information, while the nodes themselves will decide the communication state.

6 Recommendations

Apart from the given possible solutions as described in Sects. 4, and 5 certain things need to be considered by both parties, i.e., sleep tracker end-users as well as the healthcare service providers, to ensure a safer approach while leveraging the IoT sleep tracker in caregiving. This section outlines some of these recommendations.

- **Application/Firmware Updates:** Hackers are always in search of finding the weak links to attack victims, which could be via mobile apps, IoT sleep trackers. For instance, outdated mobile apps are the most vulnerable to security threats. Similarly, healthcare system providers rarely provide the latest firmware updates on existing IoT sleep trackers, which open the doors for possible side-channel attacks on end-user devices. Therefore, healthcare service providers should offer the regular updates on mobile apps and ensure availability of sleep tracker device's latest firmware to mitigate the zero-day attacks i.e., latest security threats which are unknown to security systems, while end-users should update their device apps and keep IoT sleep tracker's firmware updated to prevent possible security breaches.
- **Software Installation:** After ensuring the mobile app and IoT sleep tracker are updated. End-users should also refrain from downloading any untrusted third-party software, applications or click on any adware link by doing so, and they are inviting the malware into their mobile devices. For example, end-users receive any health promotion ads by clicking on the link or by downloading a malicious app, IoT sleep tracker users allow the attacker to gain access, thus can monitor their privacy remotely. After compromising the mobile user device, an attacker can secretly get the private information that most of the time, IoT sleep tracker users are unaware of. Therefore, before downloading any app or clicking such links, IoT sleep tracker users should confirm their source or authenticity to prevent malware installation into their mobile devices.

- **Social Engineering:** With the massive impact of social media, end-users share their personal information publicly on social media sites such as Facebook, Instagram, etc. With such a large user-base, these platforms are seen by cybercriminals as a new and lucrative platform to spread malware. Therefore, IoT sleep tracker users should not reveal their personal details with an unknown person over these sites or the phone's calls.
- **Awareness Program:** Moreover, healthcare service providers should conduct awareness programs such as online surveys and workshops to keep educating their IoT sleep tracker customers regularly so that end-users can gain awareness about the latest hacking tactics, cybercrimes, and their possible countermeasures.

By applying these suggestions into practice, the possibilities of privacy and security threats targeted against the IoT sleep tracker environment can be prevented. Thus, to enable a safe and secure remote caregiving.

7 Conclusion

With the rapid advancement and deployment of the IoT in the healthcare domain, these technologies are closely related to people; therefore, privacy and security are major concerns. To highlight these two critical aspects of IoT, we reviewed in this paper the progress of the research works related to IoT sleep trackers and found that these concerns need to be addressed. Moreover, to mitigate such threats, some proposed solutions from researchers and security experts are described. Furthermore, there are certain things that we recommend for both end-users and service providers to deploy a resilient IoT infrastructure to ensure a secured sleep tracker.

References

1. Aldowah, H., Ul Rehman, S., Umar, I.: Security in internet of things: issues, challenges and solutions. In: Saeed, F., Gazem, N., Mohammed, F., Busalim, A. (eds.) IRICT 2018. AISC, vol. 843, pp. 396–405. Springer, Cham (2019). https://doi.org/10.1007/978-3-319-99007-1_38
2. de Almeida, F.M., de Ribamar Lima Ribeiro, A., Moreno, E.D.: An architecture for self-healing in internet of things. In: UBICOMM 2015, p. 89 (2015)
3. Angarita, R.: Responsible objects: towards self-healing internet of things applications. In: 2015 IEEE International Conference on Autonomic Computing, pp. 307–312, July 2015. https://doi.org/10.1109/ICAC.2015.60
4. Boulos, M.I., Jairam, T., Kendzerska, T., Im, J., Mekhael, A., Murray, B.J.: Normal polysomnography parameters in healthy adults: a systematic review and meta-analysis. Lancet Respir. Med. **7**(6), 533–543 (2019). https://doi.org/10.1016/S2213-2600(19)30057-8. http://www.sciencedirect.com/science/article/pii/S2213260019300578
5. Bruening, P.J., Waterman, K.K.: Data tagging for new information governance models. IEEE Secur. Priv. **8**(5), 64–68 (2010). https://doi.org/10.1109/MSP.2010.147

6. Chatzigiannakis, I., Pyrgelis, A., Spirakis, P.G., Stamatiou, Y.C.: Elliptic curve based zero knowledge proofs and their applicability on resource constrained devices. In: 2011 IEEE Eighth International Conference on Mobile Ad-Hoc and Sensor Systems, pp. 715–720, October 2011. https://doi.org/10.1109/MASS.2011.77
7. Davidovich, M.L.Y., Karasik, R., Tal, A., Shinar, Z.: Sleep apnea screening with a contact-free under-the-mattress sensor. In: 2016 Computing in Cardiology Conference (CinC), pp. 849–852, September 2016. https://doi.org/10.23919/CIC.2016.7868876
8. Deering, S., Hinden, R.: Internet protocol, version 6 (IPv6) specification. RFC 8200, RFC Editor, July 2017. https://tools.ietf.org/pdf/rfc8200.pdf
9. Dimitrov, D.V.: Medical internet of things and big data in healthcare. Healthcare Inform. Res. **22**(3), 156–163 (2016). https://doi.org/10.4258/hir.2016.22.3.156
10. Dwivedi, A.D., Srivastava, G., Dhar, S., Singh, R.: A decentralized privacy-preserving healthcare blockchain for IoT. Sensors **19**(2) (2019). https://doi.org/10.3390/s19020326. http://www.mdpi.com/1424-8220/19/2/326
11. Henze, M., Hermerschmidt, L., Kerpen, D., Häußling, R., Rumpe, B., Wehrle, K.: A comprehensive approach to privacy in the cloud-based internet of things. Future Gener. Comput. Syst. **56**, 701–718 (2016). https://doi.org/10.1016/j.future.2015.09.016. http://www.sciencedirect.com/science/article/pii/S0167739X15002964
12. Islam, S.M.R., Kwak, D., Kabir, M.H., Hossain, M., Kwak, K.S.: The internet of things for health care: a comprehensive survey. IEEE Access **3**, 678–708 (2015). https://doi.org/10.1109/ACCESS.2015.2437951
13. Kelaidonis, D., et al.: A cognitive management framework for smart objects and applications in the internet of things. In: Timm-Giel, A., Strassner, J., Agüero, R., Sargento, S., Pentikousis, K. (eds.) MONAMI 2012. LNICST, vol. 58, pp. 196–206. Springer, Heidelberg (2013). https://doi.org/10.1007/978-3-642-37935-2_15
14. Niewolny, D.: How the internet of things is revolutionizing healthcare. Healthcare Segment Manager, Freescale Semiconductor, October 2013. freescale.com/healthcare
15. Raza, S., Wallgren, L., Voigt, T.: SVELTE: real-time intrusion detection in the internet of things. Ad Hoc Netw. **11**(8), 2661–2674 (2013). https://doi.org/10.1016/j.adhoc.2013.04.014. http://www.sciencedirect.com/science/article/pii/S1570870513001005
16. Rehman, S.U., Manickam, S.: Rule-based mechanism to detect denial of service (DOS) attacks on duplicate address detection process in IPv6 link local communication. In: 2015 4th International Conference on Reliability, Infocom Technologies and Optimization (ICRITO)(Trends and Future Directions), pp. 1–6. IEEE (2015)
17. Rehman, S.U., Manickam, S.: Denial of service attack in IPv6 duplicate address detection process. Int. J. Adv. Comput. Sci. Appl. **7**, 232–238 (2016)
18. Rehman, S.U., Manickam, S.: Improved mechanism to prevent denial of service attack in IPv6 duplicate address detection process. Int. J. Adv. Comput. Sci. Appl. **8**(2), 63–70 (2017)
19. Sadek, I., Seet, E., Biswas, J., Abdulrazak, B., Mokhtari, M.: Nonintrusive vital signs monitoring for sleep apnea patients: a preliminary study. IEEE Access **6**, 2506–2514 (2018). https://doi.org/10.1109/ACCESS.2017.2783939
20. Sadek, I., Biswas, J., Abdulrazak, B.: Ballistocardiogram signal processing: a review. Health Inf. Sci. Syst. **7**(1), 10 (2019). https://doi.org/10.1007/s13755-019-0071-7
21. Sadek, I., Demarasse, A., Mokhtari, M.: Internet of things for sleep tracking: wearables vs. nonwearables. Health Technol. (2019). https://doi.org/10.1007/s12553-019-00318-3

22. Shustak, S., et al.: Home monitoring of sleep with a temporary-tattoo EEG, EOG and EMG electrode array: a feasibility study. J. Neural Eng. **16**(2), 026024 (2019). https://doi.org/10.1088/1741-2552/aafa05
23. Tal, A., Shinar, Z., Shaki, D., Codish, S., Goldbart, A.: Validation of contact-free sleep monitoring device with comparison to polysomnography. J. Clin. Sleep Med. **13**(3), 517–522 (2017). https://doi.org/10.5664/jcsm.6514
24. Tung, C.E., Su, D., Turakhia, M.P., Lansberg, M.G.: Diagnostic yield of extended cardiac patch monitoring in patients with stroke or TIA. Front. Neurol. **5**, 266 (2015). https://doi.org/10.3389/fneur.2014.00266. https://www.frontiersin.org/article/10.3389/fneur.2014.00266
25. Tuominen, J., Peltola, K., Saaresranta, T., Valli, K.: Sleep parameter assessment accuracy of a consumer home sleep monitoring ballistocardiograph beddit sleep tracker: a validation study. J. Clin. Sleep Med. **15**(03), 483–487 (2019). https://doi.org/10.5664/jcsm.7682
26. Zaunseder, S., Henning, A., Wedekind, D., Trumpp, A., Malberg, H.: Unobtrusive acquisition of cardiorespiratory signals. Somnologie **21**(2), 93–100 (2017). https://doi.org/10.1007/s11818-017-0112-x

Check for updates

Designing an ICT Solution for the Empowerment of Functional Independence of People with Mild Cognitive Impairment: Findings from Co-design Sessions with Older People

Silvia de los Ríos[1(✉)], Rebeca I. García-Betances[1(✉)], Miguel Páramo[1], María Fernanda Cabrera-Umpiérrez[1], Marta Vancells[2], Maite Garolera[2], Jakub Kaźmierski[3], and María Teresa Arredondo Waldmeyer[1]

[1] Universidad Politécnica de Madrid, ETSI Ingenieros de Telecomunicación, 28002 Madrid, Spain
{srios, rgarcia, mparamo, chiqui, mta}@lst.tfo.upm.es

[2] Grupo de investigación clínica del cerebro, cognición y conducta, Consorci Sanitari de Terrassa, Barcelona, Spain
{mvancells, mgarolera}@cst.cat

[3] Department of Old Age Psychiatry and Psychotic Disorders, Medical University of Lodz, Łódź, Poland
jakub.kazmierski@umed.lodz.pl

Abstract. Mild Cognitive Impairment (MICI) symptoms are one of the main issues that contribute, in older people, to the difficulty to live independently, social isolation and loss of autonomy. INFINITy solution provides a set of services aimed to reinforce and support the daily routines of people with MCI for both indoor and outdoor scenarios. A co-design session with end-users were performed in order to better adapt the INFINITy solution to the needs and characteristics of the target beneficiaries. Results show the feedback received form end-users regarding different aspects of the solution such as: functionalities, use cases, and interfaces. The results were useful to improve the INFINITy solution to better address user's needs and preferences.

Keywords: Co-design · Participatory design · Older users · Functional independence · Mild cognitive impairment · Dementia

1 Introduction

It is estimated that 75 million of people will live with Dementia in 2030 worldwide and this number is expected to double every 20 years, to 132 million in 2050. Due to its widespread high incidence the World Health Organization recommended that Dementia should be treated and handled as a major public health issue [1] and its prevention and treatment currently represent one of the major challenges for researches, health and social services worldwide. Impairments in memory and spatial navigation

J. Pagán et al. (Eds.): ICOST 2019, LNCS 11862, pp. 18–26, 2019.
https://doi.org/10.1007/978-3-030-32785-9_2

associated with aging and, in some cases, to a cognitive condition such as Mild Cognitive Impairment (MCI) or Dementia, are one of the main issues that contribute to the difficulty to live independently, social isolation and a progressive loss of autonomy [1]. Behavioral changes and spatial disorientation that leads to develop a wandering behavior and reduce social activities and interactions, are important early indicators of a potential evolution from normal aging to other more severe cognitive conditions [2]. Different ICT solutions could help to prevent the evolution to these conditions or maintain as long and possible a condition in which people could live independently and continue to perform their daily routines, but most of them do not provide the necessary support and tools while performing outdoor activities [3].

Based on this, the INFINITy project offers a technological solution to cover some of the needs of people with MCI, with the ambition of safeguarding their independence and autonomy while performing their daily routines for as long as possible. The main objective is to have a positive impact on the Quality of Life (QoL) of these people and their main caregiver, while preserving their functionality and extending their autonomy in indoor and outdoor activities by using a technological solution.

Currently there are two main directions collecting data from users with cognitive impairments. Either within the framework of clinical trials which often entails large cohorts of users but rarely focuses on ICT solutions but rather on the medicinal effects, or studies involving the effect of ICT solutions to people with cognitive impairments focused on cognitive impairment as co-morbidity or results because of the primary health condition. The important of QoL metrics and techniques are of vital importance for testing quality of living assessment in older people. The primary INFINITy innovation is to estimate the real-life depiction of the potentially positive effect of ICT solution on cognitive decline in both indoors and outdoors activities of daily living.

The manuscript presents the process followed to design an ICT solution together with potential end users. Section 2 presents the materials used, the sample, and methods followed to conduct the co-design sessions with end-users. Section 3 describe the design of the INFINITy solution showing the use cases defined and the first designs of the solution (i.e. interfaces and NFC tags formats) used as an initial visual material. Section 4 presents the key findings from co-design sessions regarding system designs and defined use cases. Finally, Sect. 5 presents the conclusions.

2 Materials and Methods

The following sub-sections present the materials used and the methods followed to carry out the co-design sessions with end-users. The findings obtained following this approach provide useful information that will be used to define and develop the final INFINITy solution.

2.1 Materials

The main materials used for the co-design sessions were: (1) the questionnaires used to collect user's feedbacks, both standardized and designed for the occasion questionnaires, including questions regarding social and leisure activities, technology use, interfaces look and feel, functionalities and use cases; (2) the interface mock-ups of the INFINITy solution; and (3) the NFC tags presented in different formats.

Technologies used for the INFINITy solution (e.g. NFC, BLE) were selected based on their low costs, easiness to use, availability and compatibility with current smartphones, and communication capabilities that fulfill the main purpose of the features provided by INFINITy.

Specifically, the standardized questionnaires used were: Socioeconomic Subjective Status (SES) [4], Montreal Cognitive Assessment (MoCa) [5], Lawton & Brody test [6], and Memory Failures of Everyday (MFE) [7].

Consent must be obtained from all participants including the individuals who act as their informal caregiver. Participants were provided with the information they need to make an informed decision. In the occurrence of a change in the informal carer during the testbed duration, consent must be obtained from the new carer before they can become involved in the evaluation. A series of Consent Form Sheets were provided in English to all clinical partners, detailing the list of items to be consented. All participants completed the consent before the start of the co-design session.

2.2 Sample

The study involved 20 participants from Spain and Poland (10 participants by site) including people with MCI and their caregivers. Caregivers participated during the co-design sessions as supporters of the MCI participants as well as providing their opinions specifically in the definition of features and use cases. Demographic data collected from MCI participants is the following: age mean of 72.7 (sdv 5.96), 50% of the sample is in the age range from 71 to 80 years old; 8 females and 2 males; schooling level with a mean of 8.4 (sdv 4.06) years of schooling; MoCa mean score of 23.9 (sdv 2.13); a functionality level of 6.8 (sdv 1.03); and SES mean score of 4.7 (sdv 1.159).

2.3 Co-design Sessions Protocol

The co-design sessions aim to design and improve different technical aspects of the application in terms of interface design and workflow of functionalities. The session consists of an interview conducted by a project member of testbed site, where the participant and the caregiver will go through different questions related to interface design and functions of the proposed solution. The questions were defined in an easy and understandable way in order to collect the opinions and suggestions from MCI participants and their caregivers.

Specifically, the objectives of the co-design sessions were:

- Define the format and icons design of NFC tags (using questionnaires and set of NFC cards and media material)
- Assess first set of use cases and get ideas for new use cases (using questionnaires and videos of the Smart Cards)
- Get feedback regarding the mock-ups of the interface (using the mock-ups and the questionnaires)

Each session had an approximate duration of 90 min. A written informed consent was provided to the participant and caregiver in order to be part of the co-design session and to approve video recording of the session to later visualize and analyze the answers. These recordings will only be viewed by members of the project, and subsequently deleted from the system.

Three main phases of the study were defined: (1) socio-demographic assessment; (2) psychometric assessment; and (3) qualitative assessment.

Socio-demographic Assessment: In this phase information regarding age, sex, years schooling, profession, marital status and socioeconomic status (SES questionnaire) were collected from participants.

Psychometric Assessment: The MoCa questionnaire and the Lawton & Brody test were used to collect information about cognitive and functional state. Additionally, the Subjective Cognitive Complaints were measured using the most important items from the MFE questionnaire. The items used are the following: forgetting where you have put something; having to go back to check whether you have done something; forgetting that you were told something yesterday; and getting lost on a place where you have only been once or twice before.

Qualitative Assessment: A questionnaire designed for the occasion questions related to social and leisure activities, technology use, interfaces, functionalities and use cases was provided to participants. The project member guiding the session went through all the specific questions complementing the information provided in the questionnaire with additional materials such as screen shots of the interfaces and NFC tags in different formats.

3 INFINITy Solution Design

The INFINITy solution is aimed to support daily life activities of older people with MCI in indoor and outdoor environments in order to reinforce their functional abilities and safeguard their independence and autonomy while performing daily routines. It is constituted by a smartphone App (on Android) and a set of cards with the contact less technology Near-Field-Communication (NFC). In addition, a set of Bluetooth Low Energy (BLE) beacons located around the city are used to activate automatic messages while walking around.

3.1 Use Cases

3.1.1 Support to Indoor and Outdoor Activities with NFC Cards

Different use cases (UC) with NFC cards were designed in order to support daily life activities in both, indoors and outdoors scenarios. Table 1 shows the description of each defined UC. These use cases were pre-defined in order to assess and refine them during the co-designed session with MCI participants and with their caregivers.

Table 1. Use cases with NFC cards.

Environment	UC name	Description
Indoors	Voice mail	It allows a bidirectional communication between the user and their caregiver by sending (recording) and receiving (listening) voice messages through two paired of NFC cards
	Battery	It provides the battery status of the smartphone
	Pre-fixed message	It sends a predefined message to the caregiver
	Date and time	It provides the current date and time
	Agenda	It allows to create an event on the agenda or consult the existing ones
Outdoors	Go home	It guides the user to go home from wherever he is
	Go to a POI	It guides the user to go to a specific Point of Interest from wherever he is
	Call a contact	It makes a phone call to a contact
	Share a GPS	It sends the GPS location of the user to their caregiver

3.1.2 Automatic Messages to Reinforce Abilities

In addition to the use cases described in the previous section, there is an additional use case related to the reinforcement of the abilities through the stimulation of the declarative memory using associative principles to link two pieces of information by content and context relationships. While the user with MCI is walking around the city, the city sends them messages to their smartphone with the aim to support their daily life activities. Messages are in the form of quick games (or quizzes) and healthy or well-being tips and are launched every time that a user passes nearby a Point of Interest mapped with GPS or with a BLE beacon.

3.2 Interface First Designs

Based on the previous use cases, the INFINITy App was designed as a launcher application that enables the different functionalities of the system. It provides a simple and user-friendly interface, where the caregiver can access to set up the initial configuration of the system and where the user with MCI can access normally their standard applications installed on the phone.

3.2.1 Main Menu (Launcher) Interface

Different mockups of the main interface were designed to offer a variety of options for the co-design sessions: two options in portrait mode (A and B), two options in landscape mode (C and D), two options with soft colors (A and C), and two options with vivid colors (B and D). Figure 1 shows the four design options of the main menu interface.

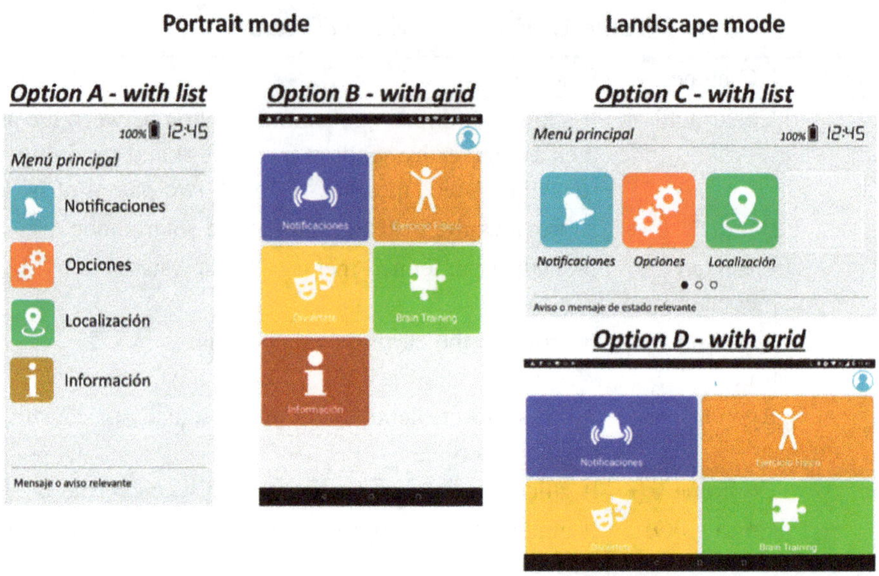

Fig. 1. Four design options for the user interface of the main menu.

In addition, two themes were designed: one with light background (A) and one with dark background (B), as presented in Fig. 2.

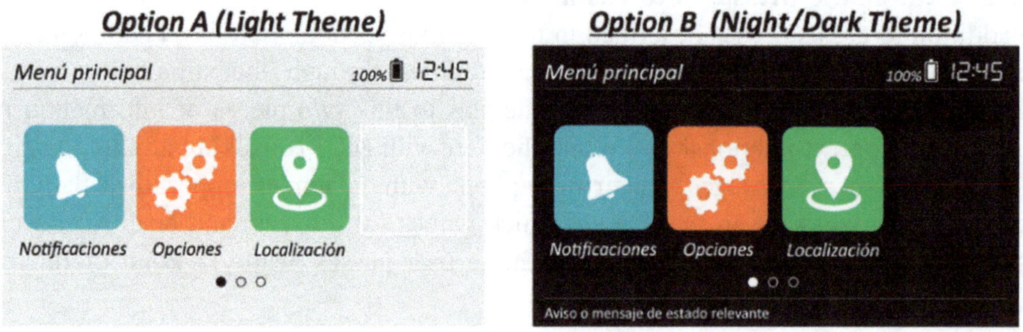

Fig. 2. Two design option with different themes.

3.2.2 Automatic Messages Interface

Three mockups defined to provide the messages to reinforce abilities while the user is walking around the city. The first presents message launched when a user passes nearby a region (POI) mapped with GPS or BLE in the INFINITy system. This screen informs the user that he is walking nearby a concrete type of POI and asks whether a quick quiz can be launched. The second one presents the quiz and provides the user with two options to answer the question proposed. The third provides the tip/recommendation related to the POI.

3.2.3 Other Interface Buttons and Functionalities

In addition, other interface components were designed with the aim to discover what was preferred by the end users according to the font type, status bar, icons and navigation elements. Moreover, a pair of mockups were designed to show the different contrasts proposed, three with light background colors and black font, and three with dark background colors and white font.

3.3 NFC Cards Format

During co-design sessions it was also provided a set of options to understand which is the best format to provide the NFC cards for indoor and outdoor scenarios. Taking into account the wide offer of formats in which an NFC chip can be embedded and presented, the following six were selected as the most appropriate for the proposed use cases: credit card, key chain, pendant, ring, wristband and fridge magnetic.

4 Key Findings from Co-design Sessions

Before analyzing the results obtained regarding the functionalities and interface design of the solution, it is important to analyze the overall general opinion about technologies, perceived level of difficulty of smartphones and technology usage.

Regarding technological level of participants, the majority do not use smartphones (70%). Specific responses of different statements were asked regarding technology use with a liker scale from 1 to 5 where 1 means completely disagree, 2 disagree, 3 neutral, 4 agree and 5 completely agree. Participants reported that they find smartphones hard to use (mean 3.30 SD 1.34), feel that new technologies are not for them (mean 3.50 SD 1.65) and they feel overwhelmed with so much technology (mean 3.10 SD 1.85).

Pre-defined use cases were assess by participants in order to give their opinons about their usefulness. In the case of outdoor use cases, 70% of the participants in general perceive that all use cases presented are very useful for them. Regarding, indoor use cases the 90% of the participants think that the voice mail use case is the most useful for them, followed by send pre-fixed messages, with 70%, and know the battery level with a 60%. The use cases that MCI participants liked the most were: phonebook management, use of calendar, know date and time, outdoors guidance, make calls and send messages.

Specifically, where asked about their opinions regarding the additional use case related to the reinforcement of the abilities through the stimulation of the declarative memory. In this respect, 50% of participants find it useful, the other half thinks that in some cases could represent an additional workload (30%) and could be annoying (40%).

Results regarding the interface designs participants likes more option B (portrait mode with grid) and think it is clean, pretty and that the size of the elements are correct. In terms of screen look and feel (e.g. colors) they think that option A (portrait mode with list) colors will not tire their eyesight (70%). Overall, 80% of participants prefer the list format although they liked more option B with a grid format, they think that having a list would be most simple to them. In the case of other interface buttons and functionalities, users prefered the options that make it more intuitive and readable, for example: icons text in plain instead of italic; navigation bars with buttons and with text; and a good contrast between background colors and font.

Futhermore, participants were asked to choose their prefered format of NFC tags for both types of use cases, indoors and outdoors. In general the most voted was the card format (40%).

5 Conclusions

Co-design sessions were a fruitful experience to start involving end users from the early stages of the prototype definition, in order to better adapt the product to the target beneficiaries of the solution.

After the co-design sessions were carried out, we could conclude that a positive feedback was collected that helped us to understand the user needs and choose their preferred elements when developing the system. Feedback from end-users will be used to improve the first designs of the solutions and to identify potential new use cases and functionalities.

Acknowledgments. This work was financially supported by the EIT Health, a body of the European Union, under the activity code: 19342.

References

1. World Health Organization (WHO): Global action plan on the public health response to dementia 2017–2025 (2017). ISBN 978-92-4-151348-7
2. Alzheimer's Association: 2018 Alzheimer's disease facts and figures. Alzheimer's & Dementia 14, no. 3, pp. 367–429 (2018). https://doi.org/10.1016/j.jalz.2018.02.001
3. Teipel, S., Babiloni, C., Hoey, J., Kaye, J., Kirste, T., Burmeister, O.K.: Information and communication technology solutions for outdoor navigation in dementia. Alzheimer's Dementia **12**(6), 695–707 (2016). https://doi.org/10.1016/j.jalz.2015.11.003
4. Adler, N.E., Epel, E.S., Castellazzo, G., Ickovics, J.R.: Relationship of subjective and objective social status with psychological and physiological functioning: preliminary data in healthy, White women. Health Psychol. **19**(6), 586 (2000). https://doi.org/10.1037/0278-6133.19.6.586
5. Montreal Cognitive Assessment (MoCa). Spanish version. https://www.mocatest.org/pdf_files/test/MoCA-Test-Spanish.pdf. Polish version https://www.mocatest.org/pdf_files/test/MoCA-Test-Polish.pdf

6. Lawton, M.P., Brody, E.M.: Assessment of older people: self-maintaining and instrumental activities of daily living. Gerontologist **9**(3), 179–186 (1969)
7. Montejo, P., Peña, M., Sueiro, M.: The memory failures of everyday questionnaire (MFE): internal consistency and reliability. Spanish J. Psychol. **15**, 768–776 (2012). https://doi.org/10.5209/rev_SJOP.2012.v15.n2.38888

Deployment of an IoT Solution for Early Behavior Change Detection

Hamdi Aloulou[1,2(✉)], Mounir Mokhtari[3], and Bessam Abdulrazak[4]

[1] Centre de Recherche en Numérique de Sfax, Sfax, Tunisia
hamdi.aloulou@isima.u-monastir.tn
[2] Université de Monastir, Institut Supérieur d'Informatique de Mahdia, Mahdia, Tunisia
[3] Institut Mines Télécom, Paris, France
[4] Université de Sherbrooke, Sherbrooke, Canada

Abstract. Today, numerous factors are causing a demographic change in many countries in the world. This change is producing a nearly balanced society share between the young and aging population. The noticeable increasing aging population is causing different economical, logistical and societal problems. In fact, aging is associated with chronic diseases in addition to physical, psychological, cognitive and societal changes. These changes are considered as indicators of aging peoples' frailty. It is therefore important to early detected these changes to prevent isolation, sedentary lifestyle, and even diseases in order to delay the frailty period. This paper presents an experiment deployment of an Internet of Thing solution for the continuous monitoring and detection of elderly people's behavior changes. The objective is to help geriatricians detect sedentary lifestyle and health-related problems at an early stage.

Keywords: Behavior change · Internet of Things · Frailty

1 Introduction

Aging is often related to significant changes in physical activities, mobility, nutrition, social life and cognitive status. These changes considerably affect elderly people quality of life. According to the World Health Organization (WHO) [1], the biggest health risk for seniors is the adoption of a sedentary lifestyle that causes isolation, depression and many other diseases such as cardiovascular disease, obesity, high blood pressure, etc.

In this paper, we present our experience in deploying an Internet of Things (IoT) solution for the continuous monitoring and detection of elderly people's behavior changes. The objective is to help geriatricians detect sedentary lifestyle and health related problems at early stage, without the need to perform classical psycho-geriatric tests that have many limitations like assessment inaccuracies

Supported by H2020 European Project City4Age.

J. Pagán et al. (Eds.): ICOST 2019, LNCS 11862, pp. 27–35, 2019.
https://doi.org/10.1007/978-3-030-32785-9_3

and the difficulty for elderly people to recall past events. The work was performed as part of the European project City4Age based on 6 pilot sites: Athens, Birmingham, Lecce, Madrid, Montpellier and Singapore. In this paper, we will focus and detail the deployment performed in the pilot site of Montpellier.

2 Literature Review and Related Work

Early detection of ageing people behavior change can improve medical assessments and enable proactive intervention. In fact, aging-related health problems generate long-term behavior changes, such as possible instabilities, variations, impairments, declines, increases or improvements [2]. Nowadays, geriatricians use psycho-geriatric scales and questionnaires to analyze behavior and investigate possible changes [3,4]. These psycho-geriatric approaches are insufficient to monitor patients on a daily basis [5]. Thus, geriatricians need technological services to acquire new objective observations that complete their medical observations. Monitoring technologies can help follow-up elderly people at home and in city, in order to early detect possible health changes [6].

Contrary to existing technological solutions that target Short-term Health Change Detection [7], retrospectively investigate possible changes after change occurrence [8] and use intrusive technologies to capture video sequences, collect daily questionnaire-based information and record physical data using body sensors [9], our proposed approach analyzes overall behavior over long periods, in order to detect long-term changes in health status. These long-term changes require weeks and months to emerge, and are difficult to detect due to normal continuous variation in human behavior [10]. In addition, it continuously analyzes monitoring data on a daily basis, in order to early detect possible changes. This proactive change detection provides opportunity for daily assessment and subsequent intervention. Finally, it uses unobtrusive monitoring technologies that are embedded in our real environment or in objects of daily living, do not interfere with natural behavior of elderly people and do not change their daily habits.

3 Montpellier Pilot Setup

Montpellier pilot site goal is to quickly and unobtrusively detect possible aging people's behavior changes. Detected behavior changes are afterwards analyzed and confirmed by collaborating geriatricians to provide adequate intervention.

The pilot site is Coordinated by the French National Center for Scientific Research (CRNS) and is collaborating with local authorities such as Montpellier Metropolis, the ETAPE (health autonomy pole) association and healthcare professionals from Beausoleil Clinic and Saint Vincent De Paul nursing home.

The proposed solution deployed in the pilot site of Montpellier consists of a set of sensors deployed in the participants' homes and in the city as shown in Fig. 1. For indoor monitoring, the pilot uses motion sensors, contact sensors and bed sensors. Outdoor monitoring is based on Smartphones carried by participants and beacons deployed in places of interest of participants in the city. These sensors allow to collect raw data and objective information in real time, which are processed to detect behavior changes.

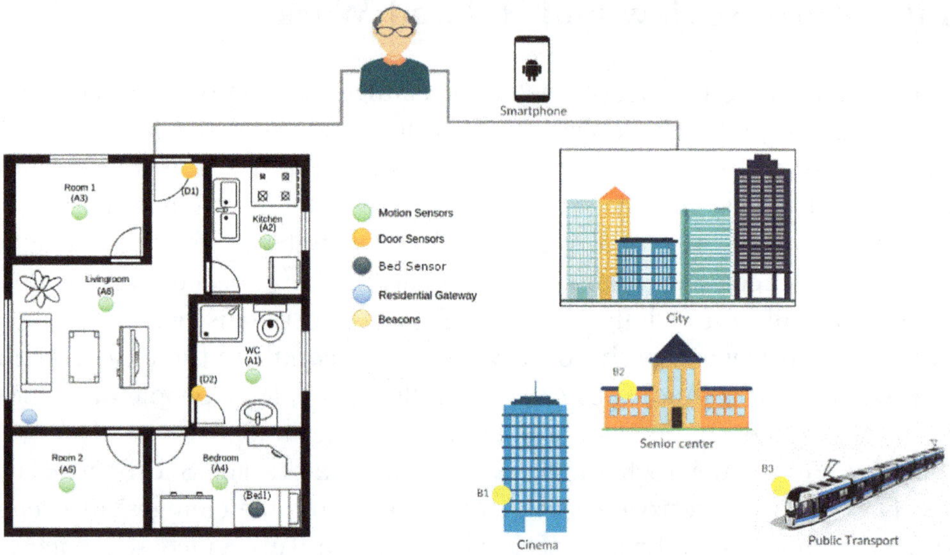

Fig. 1. Montpelier pilot site global setup

4 Recruitment and Engagement

Each of the six pilot sites followed a specific ethical approval process, related to specific countries' regulation, in order to recruit participants. For Montpellier pilot site, the ethical process consists in sending the specifications of the deployment to CNRS's Data Protection Correspondent (Correspondants Informatique et Libertés: CIL). In parallel, an application was also submitted to the Institutional review board (Comités de Protection des Personnes: CPP).

After obtaining the ethical approval, we started the recruitment process. We have approached around 40 potential participants with the help of ETAPE association and Saint Vincent De Paul nursing home. In fact, we have presented the solution in several local events to promote the project and identify interested people to be included in the study. As shown in Fig. 2, briefing and presentation sessions were organized in the Montpellier pilot site to better promote experimentation objectives, quickly launch recruitment process and keep recruited participants involved in the experimentation. These events allowed to have in depth discussions with interested aging people who accepted to visit a demonstration house, see a live demonstration of the system and have their feedback. The demonstration house highlights the unobtrusiveness of the technological solution proposed for the potential participants. Interested people also observe sensor events in real-time and examples of real data over weeks and months indicating significant changes in health status. Potential participants asked for information about employed technological solutions, real benefits of adopting them at home and possible risks.

Local Medical Event "Pass'Sport Santé Séniors"

Local Medical Event "France Parkinson"

Fig. 2. Briefing and involvement sessions

19 participants accepted and have been equipped with the City4Age solution. An initial interview with included participants allowed to collect some indications on their social and health profiles. Participants have diverse medical and social profiles such as educational level, dependence level, habits and health status. Table 1 presents regular habits and health info of some participants.

Table 1. Examples of Montpelier pilot site participants habits and health status

Patient	Regular habits	Health info
98	Wakes up at 8 h. Home aid 4 times per day. Stays most often at home. Sometimes goes out with daughter or caregiver	Alzheimer Diabetes Vision and audition problems
101	Wakes up at 7 h30–8 h. Home aid visits 3 times per day (morning, midday and evening). Niece and neighbor visits during the day. Sleeps earlier than before (at 20 h, and before at 22 h)	Alzheimer Some falls and hospitalizations
102	Wakes up at 6 h–7 h. Home aid visits each day in the morning. Lives alone. Daughter house is nearby. Monthly visits to and from daughter	Heart problems Urinary infection

5 Technologies and Data Collection

The system proposed in Montpellier pilot site uses indoor and outdoor technologies to monitor daily living activities of participants. For indoor monitoring, the pilot is proposing a set of sensors (motion sensors, contact sensors and bed sensors). These sensors operate discreetly and allow to collect raw data and objective information in real time. The objective is to be able to accurately determine the "habitual behaviours" of people by collecting data over time. Outdoor monitoring is based on beacons deployed in the participants' places of interest in the city (e.g. bus and metro stations, cinemas, restaurants, etc.) and smartphones with dedicated mobile application carried by the participants. Thus, it is possible to collect data on the activities of our participants' even when they are in outdoor in the city. Figure 3 showcases some deployed sensors in Montpellier pilot site.

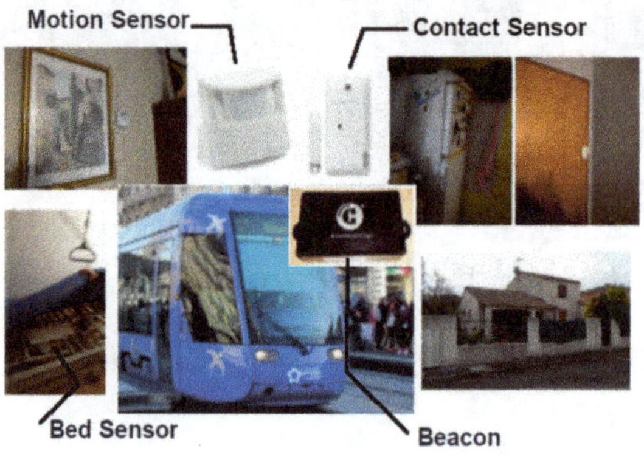

Fig. 3. Indoor and outdoor sensors deployment

All indoor and outdoor data are collected in Montpellier pilot site local server where local treatment for Low Elementary Actions (LEAs) and measures identification is performed. Low Elementary Actions are basic participants' actions which are inferred from received sensors' events (e.g. Start Moving, Stop Moving, Change Room, Visit Restaurant, etc.). Measures are quantified data extracted from LEAs (e.g time in the bedroom/day, number of toilet visits /day, number of shops visits/week, etc.). Later, these information are transferred to the City4Age repository and analytic algorithm where further treatments are performed in order to produce visualisations for the geriatrician. The complete architecture of the City4Age solution and the performed deployment and data analysis in Montpellier pilot site is presented in Fig. 4.

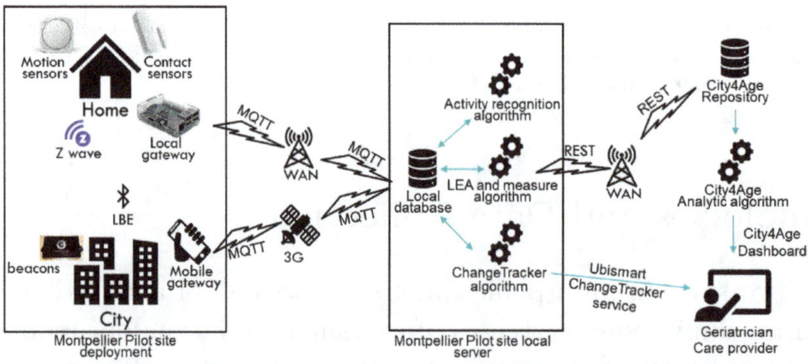

Fig. 4. Complete architecture of Montpellier pilot site's deployment

The deployment of this system in France allowed to collect around two years of real data. We have collected 310.590 of Low Elementary Actions (LEA) and 49.659 of Measures for 19 participants.

6 Data Interpretation

The goal of the system proposed in Montpellier pilot site is to detect possible behavior changes that will be analysed and confirmed by collaborating geriatricians to provide adequate intervention. A behavior change tracker service [11] was developed allowing to detect changes in participants' behavior using statistical algorithms. Collected data are analyzed by this developed algorithm and presented to collaborating geriatricians from clinic Beausoleil. Figure 5 showcases some behavior changes detected by the ChangeTracker service for one of the participants in the pilot site. In Fig. 5, 3 consecutive decreases on 2017-02-15, 2017-06-20 and 2017-10-25 are detected for participant 91. Participant and family doctor confirm mobility impairments and increased risk of dependence in managing activities of daily living. Professional caregiver helps with medication taking and household from 2017-05-04.

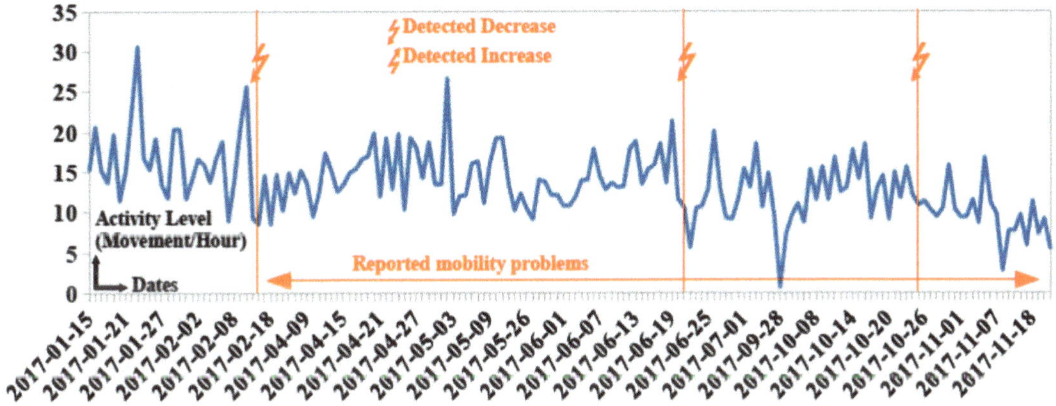

Fig. 5. Detected changes in activity level of participant 91 due to mobility impairments

7 Intervention Process

To perform intervention, the pilot site is providing a framework with visualizations about participants activities and statistics about their daily routines and habits. The ChangeTracker service is integrated in this framework allowing to automatically detect possible changes that can be confirmed by the caregivers and the geriatrician. The caregivers and geriatricians can navigate the data provided by these visualizations and decide on the type and form of intervention when needed. As an example, after detecting a decrease in outdoor and indoor activities for participant 96, nursing home stuff decided to initiate home assistance.

8 Validation

8.1 Detection Process Validation

The ChangeTracker service has being validated with the help of our stakeholders. Detected changes are being correlated with medical observation and health records to validate the used algorithms and their performances.

The ChangeTracker service sends change notifications. Change notifications provide opportunity to confirm that detected changes are really permanent and investigate possible correlations with geriatric observations. Regular review meetings with elderly people, family members and family doctors allow to accurately investigate possible causes of detected changes. Review meetings investigate mutli-dimensional correlations of detected changes, such as identifying parallel decreases in activity level and time out home related to mobility impairments, and consecutive increases in sleep interruptions and toilet entries after treatment change. Figure 6 shows some results of changes detected by ChangeTracker service and their correlation with medical observations and participant feedback.

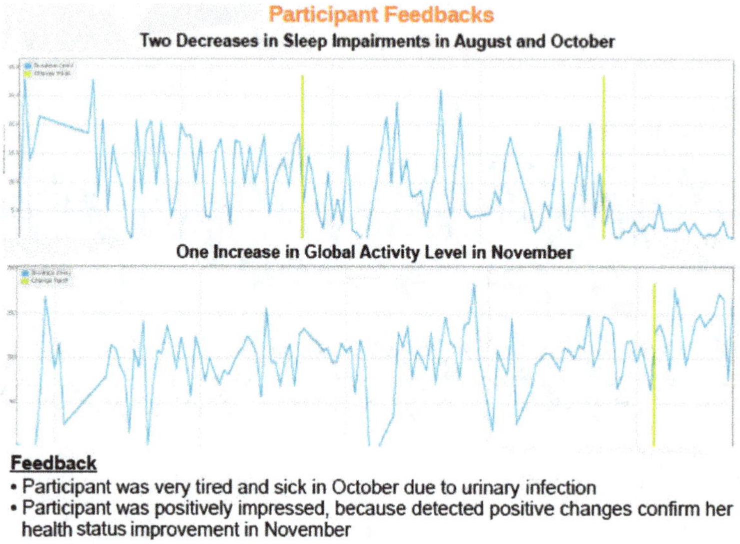

Fig. 6. Detected behavior changes by ChangeTracker and corresponding participant feedback

8.2 Results and Performance

In total, we have detected 340 changes for all participants with an average of 0.97 change per month. Participants show diverse changes in monitoring period that are associate with diverse medical reasons, such as physical problems (45.59% of detected changes), health improvements (36.76%), nutritional problems (8.82%), personal changes (7.35%) and social problems (1.47%).

9 Conclusion

Montpellier pilot site was a proof of concept of our IoT proposed solution for the early identification of behavior changes. In total, 340 changes have been detected for all participants. These changes have been validated and classified with the help of local geriatrician and by correlation with Medical Observations. This solution could be of great value for the geriatricians. In fact, the technological observations provided by the proposed solution enrich their medical observation for better assessments of frailty and MCI. The solution is also valuable for nursing homes. In fact, nursing homes need to maintain independent living at home and identify elderly people at risk who really require entry to nursing home.

Acknowledgment. This work was supported by the European project City4Age that received funding from the Horizon 2020 research and innovation program under grant agreement number 689731. We would like to thank all the participants who accepted to be part of this experimentation and all our collaborating geriatricians and professional and informal caregivers.

References

1. Waxman, A.: Who global strategy on diet, physical activity and health. Food Nutr. Bull. **25**(3), 292–302 (2004)
2. Cao, L.: In-depth behavior understanding and use: the behavior informatics approach. Inf. Sci. **180**(17), 3067–3085 (2010)
3. Tardieu, E., et al.: External validation of the short emergency geriatric assessment (SEGA) instrument on the safes cohort. Geriatrie et psychologie neuropsychiatrie du vieillissement **14**(1), 49–55 (2016)
4. Cockrell, J.R., Folstein, M.F.: Mini-mental state examination. In: Principles and Practice of Geriatric Psychiatry, pp. 140–141 (2002)
5. Lökk, J.: Lack of information and access to advanced treatment for Parkinson's disease patients. J. Multidisc. Healthc. **4**, 433 (2011)
6. Acampora, G., Cook, D.J., Rashidi, P., Vasilakos, A.V.: A survey on ambient intelligence in healthcare. Proc. IEEE **101**(12), 2470–2494 (2013)
7. Aloulou, H., et al.: Deployment of assistive living technology in a nursing home environment: methods and lessons learned. BMC Med. Inform. Decis. Making **13**(1), 42 (2013)
8. Sprint, G., Cook, D.J., Schmitter-Edgecombe, M.: Unsupervised detection and analysis of changes in everyday physical activity data. J. Biomed. Inform. **63**, 54–65 (2016)
9. Avvenuti, M., Baker, C., Light, J., Tulpan, D., Vecchio, A.: Non-intrusive patient monitoring of Alzheimer's disease subjects using wireless sensor networks. In: 2009 World Congress on Privacy, Security, Trust and the Management of e-Business, pp. 161–165. IEEE (2009)
10. Lally, P., Van Jaarsveld, C.H., Potts, H.W., Wardle, J.: How are habits formed: modelling habit formation in the real world. Eur. J. Soc. Psychol. **40**(6), 998–1009 (2010)

11. Kaddachi, F., Aloulou, H., Abdulrazak, B., Fraisse, P., Mokhtari, M.: Long-term behavior change detection approach through objective technological observations toward better adaptation of services for elderly people. Health Technol. **8**(5), 329–340 (2018)

Long Short Term Memory Based Model for Abnormal Behavior Prediction in Elderly Persons

Meriem Zerkouk[1(✉)] and Belkacem Chikhaoui[2(✉)]

[1] Department of Computer Science, USTO-MB University, Oran, Algeria
zerkouk.meriem@gmail.com

[2] LICEF Research Center, Department of Science and Technology, TELUQ University, Montreal, Canada
belkacem.chikhaoui@teluq.ca

Abstract. Smart home refers to the independency and comfort that are ensured by remote monitoring and assistive services. Assisting an elderly person requires identifying and accurately predicting his/her normal and abnormal behaviors. Abnormal behaviors observed during the completion of activities of daily living are a good indicator that the person is more likely to have health and behavioral problems that need intervention and assistance. In this paper, we propose a method, based on long short-term memory recurrent neural networks (LSTM), to automatically predicting an elderly person's abnormal behaviors. Our method allows to model the temporal information expressed in the long sequences collected over time. Our study aims to evaluate the performance of LSTM on identifying and predicting elderly persons abnormal behaviors in smart homes. We experimentally demonstrated, through extensive experiments using a data-set, the suitability and performance of the proposed method in predicting abnormal behaviors with high accuracy. We also demonstrated the superiority of the proposed method compared to the existing state-of-the-art methods.

Keywords: Smart home · ADL · LSTM · Anomaly detection

1 Introduction

Internet of Things (IoT), which is an emerging domain, promises to create a world where all the objects around us are connected to the Internet and communicate with each other with minimum human intervention. The crucial goal is to create a better world for human beings, where objects around us are context awareness, that can respond to questions: what we want, what we need and where we are. Smart homes represent one of the main application domains of IoT that received particular attention from researchers [1].

The smart homes become a safe and secure environment for dependent people. They offer the ability (1) to track residents' activities without interfering in their daily life, and (2) to track residents' behaviors and to monitor their health by using sensors embedded in their living spaces [2]. The data collected from smart homes needs to be

J. Pagán et al. (Eds.): ICOST 2019, LNCS 11862, pp. 36–45, 2019.
https://doi.org/10.1007/978-3-030-32785-9_4

deeply analyzed and investigated, in order to extract useful information about residents' daily routines, and more specifically (specific) activities of daily living.

Activity recognition [3], as a core feature of smart home, consists of classifying data recorded by the different integrated environmental and/or wearable sensors, into well-defined and known movements. However, dependent persons are usually exposed to different types of problems causing them mostly to perform activities of daily living in a wrong way. Therefore, detecting abnormal behaviors is of great importance for dependent people in order to ensure that activities are performed correctly without errors [4]. This will also ensure their safety and well-being.

Detecting an anomaly in the activities of daily living (ADL) of a person is usually performed by detecting nonconformities from their usual ADL patterns. This has been conducted in various works using classical machine learning algorithms [5, 6]. Telehealth care requires systems with high accuracy, less computational time and less user intervention because data are becoming larger and more complex [7]. However, deep learning architectures provide a way to automatically extract useful and meaningful spatial and temporal features of a raw data without the need for data labeling which is time consuming, complex and error prone. This makes deep learning models easily generalizable to different contexts. LSTM is a powerful deep learning model for sequence prediction and anomaly detection in sequential data [8]. LSTM models are able to extract temporal features with long time relationships. This property is of great importance in smart homes in order to understand person's behaviors, they change over time, and particularly any deviations from normal execution of activities of daily living.

In this paper, we propose an LSTM model to identify and predict elderly people's abnormal behaviors. The rationale of using LSTM model in our work is threefold: (1) it is capable of handling multivariate sequential time-series data, (2) it can identify and accurately predict abnormal behavior in time-series data [9, 10], and (3) it can automatically extract features from massive time-series data, which makes it possible to be easily generalizable to other types of data. Therefore, the contributions of our paper can be summarized as follows:

1. Proposing an LSTM model for automatic prediction of abnormal behaviors in smart homes.
2. Managing the problem of imbalanced data by oversampling minority classes.
3. Conducting extensive experiments to validate the proposed LSTM model.

The paper is organized as follows: Sect. 2 presents an overview of anomaly detection models and related work in machine learning algorithms. Section 3 presents Materials and methods to conduct our work and the obtained results. Section 4 gives a comparison of different machine learning algorithms. Finally, Sect. 5 discusses the outcomes of the experiments and perspectives for future work.

2 Related Work

Tracking user behavior for abnormality detection has gain a large attention and becomes one of the main goals for certain researchers [11]. Abnormal behavior detection approaches are based mainly on machine learning algorithms, and more specifically supervised learning techniques [12]. Supervised classification techniques need labelled data points (samples) for the models to learn. This kind of classification requires to train a classifier on the labelled data points and then evaluate the model on new data points. Therefore, in case of normal and abnormal classes, the model learns the characteristics of these data points and classify them as normal or abnormal. Any data point that does not conform to this normal class, will be classified as an anomaly by the model. Various classification techniques have been applied for abnormal behavior detection.

Pirzada et al. [13] explored KNN as a classifier which works well to classify data in categories. They performed a binary classification where they classify activity as good or bad to distinguish the anomaly in the user behavior. Eventually, the proposed KNN applied to predicts whether the class belongs to regular (good) or irregular (bad) class. The performed work monitor health conditions of elderly person living alone using sensors in unobtrusive manner.

Aran et al. [4] proposed a method to automatically observe and model the daily behavior of the elderly and detect anomalies that could occur in the sensor data. In their proposed method, the anomaly relies on signal health related problems. For this purpose, they have created a probabilistic spatio-temporal model to summarize daily behavior. They define anomalies as significant changes from the learned behavioral model and detected, the performance is evaluated by cross-entropy measure. Once the anomaly is detected, the caregivers are informed accordingly.

Ordonez et al. [14] presented an anomaly detection method based on Bayesian statistics that identify anomalous human behavioral patterns. Their proposed method assists automatically the elderly person's with disabilities who live alone, by learning and predicting standard behaviors to improve the efficiency of their healthcare system. The Bayesian statistics are choosen to analyze the collected data, the estimation of the static behavior is based on three probabilistic features that introduce, namely sensor activation likelihood, sensor sequence likelihood and sensor event duration likelihood.

Yahaya et al. [11] proposed novelty detection algorithm known as One-Class Support Vector Machine (SVM) which is applied for detection of anomaly in activities of daily living. The anomaly is situated in sleeping patterns, which could be a sign of Mild Cognitive Impairment (MCI) in older adults or other health-related issues.

Palaniappan et al. [15] interested in detecting abnormal activities of the individuals by ruling out all possible normal activities. Authors define abnormal activities as unexpected events that occur in random manner. Multi-class SVM method is used as classifier to identify the activities in form of a state transition table. The transition table helps the classifier in avoiding the states which are unreachable from the current state.

Hung et al. [16] proposed a novel approach that mix SVM and HMM to a homecare sensory system. RFID sensor networks are used to collect elder's daily activities, Hidden Markov Model (HMM) used to learn the data, and SVMs used to estimate whether the elder's behavior is abnormal or not.

Bouchachia et al. [17] proposed an RNN model to deal the problem of activity recognition and abnormal behavior detection for elderly people with dementia. The proposed method suffered from the lack of data in the context of dementia.

The aforementioned methods suffer from one or more of the following limitations:

1. The presented methods focus on the spatial and the temporal anomalies in user assistance. However, we noted that the abnormal behavior does not treated in the case of the smart home.
2. These methods require feature engineering, which is difficult specifically when data becomes larger.
3. The abnormality identification and prediction lack of good accuracy.

These points motivate us to propose a method, which tries to overcome these limitations and to be useful in smart homes for assistance.

3 Proposed Method

In this section, we present a description of our problem related to the identification and prediction of elderly person's abnormal behaviors.

3.1 Problem Description

Abnormality detection is an important task in health care monitoring, particularly for monitoring elderly in smart homes. Abnormality consists in finding unexpected activities, variations in normal patterns of activities, finding the patterns in data that do not conform to the expected behavior [18] because humans usually perform their ADLs in a sequential manner. According to [19], the abnormality can be categorized into temporal, spatial, and behavioral abnormality. Our work focuses on the behavioral anomaly because this kind of abnormality depends on the same on time (when performing the activity) and location (where performing the activity). Each activity is defined by a sequence of sub-activities and if the person violates the expected sequence then it is an abnormality.

3.2 LSTM for Anomaly Description

LSTMs [20] are a recurrent neural network architecture, the principal characteristic is the memory extension that can be seen as a gated cell, where gated means that the cell decides whether or not to store or delete information, based on the importance it assigns to the information. The assignment of importance happens through weights, which are also learned by the algorithm. This simply means that it learns over time, which information is important.

LSTM architecture consists of three layers: Input layer, hidden layer and output layer. The hidden layers are fully connected to the input and output layers. A layer in LSTM is composed from blocs, and each block has three gates: input, output and forget gates. Each gate is connected to each other. These gates decide whether or not to let new input in (input gate), delete the information because it isn't important (forget gate) or to let it impact the output at the current time step (output gate).

As we mentioned previously, our motivations in using LSTM rely on the fact that it enables to remember their inputs over a long period of time which allows to remember the data sequences. Abnormality detection aims to identify a small group of samples, which deviate remarkably from the existing data. That why, we choose LSTM to identify and accurately predict the abnormality behavior from a long sequential data given that persons perform their ADL in a sequential manner, less human intervention in the identification and prediction process.

The LSTM input layer development requires reshaping the data. It needs the input data to be 3-dimensions as training sample, time step, and features. We add for this layer an activation function (ReLu). To avoid overfitting problem in LSTM architectures, we used the dropout method [24] and improve model performance. In our proposed model, the dropout is applied between the two hidden layers and between the last hidden layer and the output layer. We setup the dropout at 20% as recommended in literature [24].

The last layer (dense layer) defines the number of outputs which represents the different activities and anomaly (classes). The output is considered as vector of integer which is converted into binary matrix. The anomaly prediction is formulated as multi classification problem which requires to create 7 output values, one for each class, Softmax as activation function and categorical_crossentropy is used as the loss function. The Fig. 1 indicate the LSTM architecture development.

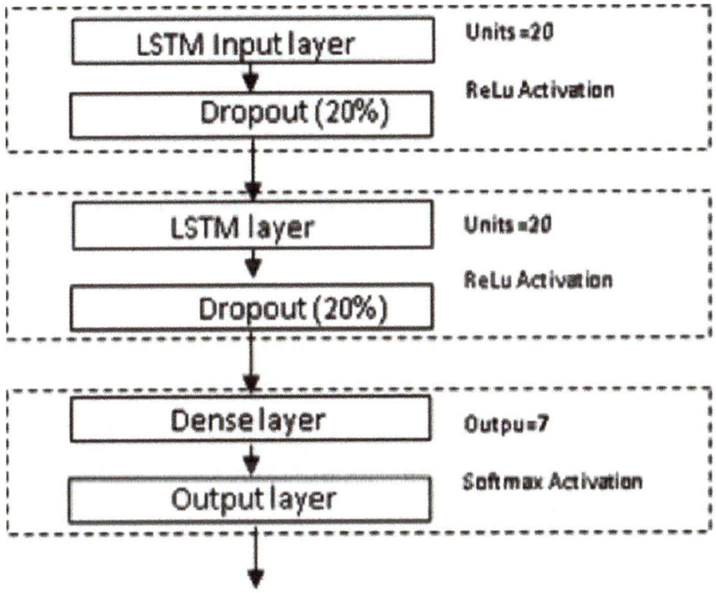

Fig. 1. LSTM development.

4 Experiment Study

In this section, we present our dataset that we want to analyze, overcome to the problem of imbalanced data by oversampling our data with SMOTE. After that, we identify and predict the abnormal behavior based on LSTM model.

4.1 Dataset

This research uses SIMADL [21] dataset generated by OpenSHS [22] which is an open source simulation tool that offered the flexibility needed to generate the inhabitant's data for classification of ADLs. OpenSHS was used to generate several synthetic datasets that includes 29 columns of binary data representing the sensor values, each binary sensor has two states, on (1) and off (0). The sensors can be divided into two groups, passive and active. The passive sensors react without explicitly the participants interact with them. Instead, they react to the participant movements and positions.

The sampling was done every second. Seven participants were asked to perform their simulations using OpenSHS. Each participant generated six datasets resulting in forty-two datasets in total. The participants self-labelled their activities during the simulation. The labels used by the participants were: Personal, Sleep, Eat, Leisure, Work, Other and Anomaly. The simulated anomalies are behavioral and are described in Table 1. Note that each user has his/her own behavioral abnormality to simulate.

Table 1. Anomalies description

Participants	Description
Participant 1	Leaving the fridge door open
Participant 2	Leaving the oven on for long time
Participant 3	Leaving the main door open
Participant 4	Leaving the fridge door open
Participant 5	Leaving the bathroom light on
Participant 6	Leaving tv on
Participant 7	Leaving light bedroom and wardrobe open

4.2 Imbalanced Data

The distribution of the classes (that represent the different ADL) is not uniform, leads to imbalanced classes. This situation appears because of rare abnormal behavior which is clear in the Fig. 2. As shown in Fig. 2, the class anomaly represent a minority. We tackle this problem in order to improve our classification performance. Dealing with imbalanced datasets requires strategies such as oversampling techniques before providing the data as input to the LSTM model. Oversampling strategy consists in augmenting the minority class samples to reach a balanced level with the majority class.

4.2.1 Oversampling

We deal with abnormality, called also anomaly, detection problem as a supervised learning that refers to correctly classifying rare class samples as compared to majority samples.

Therefore, anomalies are a minority in the whole behavior, which create an imbalanced data problem. Therefore, we have to oversample our data and after that, we can classify correctly.

A subset of data is taken from the minority samples as an example and then new synthetic similar data points are created. These synthetic data points are then added to the original dataset. The new dataset is used to train the classification models. The main objective of balancing classes is to either increasing the samples of the minority class or decreasing the samples of the majority class. In oversampling, we increase the minority class samples. This is done in order to obtain approximately the same number of instances for both the classes as demonstrated in Fig. 2. Our motivation in the use of this strategy is to avoid overfitting. We use SMOTE statistical method [23] to oversample our classes as indicated in Fig. 2. We note that the x-axes indicate the number of classes and y-axes indicate the number of input data.

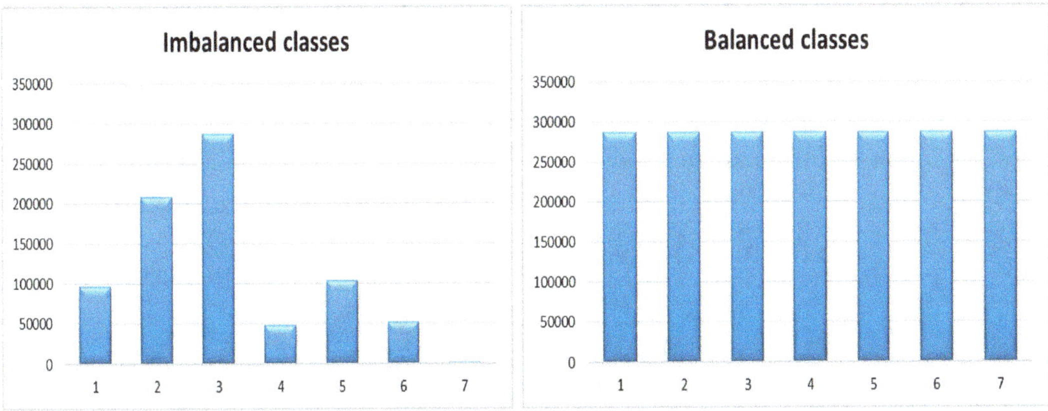

Fig. 2. Imbalanced classes vs Balanced classes

4.3 Network Architecture and Hyper-parameters Tuning

The crucial task is to find a suitable network structure for training the data, specifically to choose the right amount of nodes and layers. Many experiments were run by varying LSTM networks architecture as shown in Table 2 to find the suitable units number. We varied this number from 20, 30, 50, 60, 100 to 200. The number of layers was experimentally fixed to four layers.

To compile and fit the model, we experimentally fixed mini-batch size to 128 samples, with ADAM [25] as optimizer, which is an algorithm that can used instead of the classical stochastic gradient descent procedure to update the network weights iterative based on training data.

Our experiment with LSTM were implemented in Python language using Keras library [26] with Tensorflow [27]. The Fig. 1 shows the development of our LSTM network and the adjusted parameters to obtain the appropriate results.

4.4 Performance Metrics Analysis

High performance system should have less false positive and false negative rates. The performance of our proposed method is evaluated in terms of precision, recall and f-score [28]. Table 2 presents the obtained results.

Table 2. LSTM experiment.

Units	Precision	Recall	F-score
20	0.91	0.91	0.91
30	0.87	0.85	0.86
50	0.90	0.90	0.90
60	0.86	0.86	0.86
100	0.90	0.90	0.90
200	0.90	0.90	0.90

Table 2 refers to the results obtained on SIMADL dataset for abnormal behavior detection and shows that LSTM with 20 units gives the best precision of 0.91%, recall of 0.91% and f-score of 0.91%. The rest of the results is expressed in the Table 2 for which we have varied the unit number to 30, 50, 60, 100 and 200.

To demonstrate the superiority of the proposed method, we conducted comparison with existing state-of-the-art methods. The results are summarized in Table 3.

Table 3. LSTM comparison with the state of the art.

Models	Precision	Recall	F-score
LSTM	0.91	0.91	0.91
SVM	0.90	0.90	0.90
NB	0.79	0.79	0.79
KNN	0.89	0.89	0.89
NN	0.77	0.77	0.77

According to Table 3, we note that LSTM gives a good result by comparing to machine learning methods such as: SVM, NB, KNN and NN.

5 Conclusion

We proposed an LSTM based abnormal behavior prediction method. Our method identifies and predicts abnormal behaviors with a high degree of accuracy and with less user intervention in order to automate the identification and prediction process. We note that before to classify the activities, we have checked the distribution of classes, we detected an imbalanced classes, to deal with this problem we have applied SMOTE for oversampling classes.

The future work can focus on using real dataset from environmental and physiological sensors to understand the health condition of the elderly person's for better wellbeing.

References

1. Perera, C., Zaslavsky, A., Christen, P., Georgakopoulos, D.: Context aware computing for the internet of things: a survey. IEEE Commun. Surv. Tutor. **16**, 414–454 (2014)
2. Lê, Q., Nguyen, H.B., Barnett, T.: Smart homes for older people: positive aging in a digital world, pp. 607–617 (2012). https://doi.org/10.3390/fi4020607
3. Mehr, H.D., Polat, H., Cetin, A.: Resident activity recognition in smart homes by using artificial neural networks (2016)
4. Aran, O., Sanchez-Cortes, D., Do, M.-T., Gatica-Perez, D.: Anomaly detection in elderly daily behavior in ambient sensing environments. In: Chetouani, M., Cohn, J., Salah, A.A. (eds.) HBU 2016. LNCS, vol. 9997, pp. 51–67. Springer, Cham (2016). https://doi.org/10.1007/978-3-319-46843-3_4
5. Omar, S., Ngadi, A., Jebur, H.H.: Machine learning techniques for anomaly detection: an overview. Int. J. Comput. Appl. **79**, 33–41 (2013)
6. Grover, A.: Anomaly detection for application log data (2018)
7. Ismail Fawaz, H., Forestier, G., Weber, J., Idoumghar, L., Muller, P.A.: Deep learning for time series classification: a review. Data Min. Knowl. Discov. **33**, 917–963 (2019)
8. Wang, J., Chen, Y., Hao, S., Peng, X., Hu, L.: Deep learning for sensor-based activity recognition: a survey. Pattern Recognit. Lett. **119**, 3–11 (2019)
9. Chandola, V.: Anomaly detection : a survey, pp. 1–72 (2009)
10. Paudel, R., Eberle, W., Holder, L.B.: Anomaly detection of elderly patient activities in smart homes using a graph-based approach, pp. 163–169 (2016)
11. Yahaya, S.W., Langensiepen, C., Lotfi, A.: Anomaly detection in activities of daily living using one-class support vector machine. In: Lotfi, A., Bouchachia, H., Gegov, A., Langensiepen, C., McGinnity, M. (eds.) UKCI 2018. AISC, vol. 840, pp. 362–371. Springer, Cham (2019). https://doi.org/10.1007/978-3-319-97982-3_30
12. Mukhopadhyay, S.C.: Next generation sensors and systems. Next Gener. Sens. Syst. **16**, 1–330 (2015)
13. Pirzada, P., White, N., Wilde, A.: Sensors in smart homes for independent living of the elderly. In: Proceedings of 5th International Multi-Topic ICT Conference Technology Future Generation, IMTIC 2018 (2018)
14. Ordóñez, F.J., de Toledo, P., Sanchis, A.: Sensor-based Bayesian detection of anomalous living patterns in a home setting. Pers. Ubiquit. Comput. **19**, 259–270 (2015)
15. Palaniappan, A., Bhargavi, R., Vaidehi, V.: Abnormal human activity recognition using SVM based approach. In: International Conference on Recent Trends Information Technology, ICRTIT 2012, pp. 97–102 (2012)
16. Hung, Y.-X., Chiang, C.-Y., Hsu, Steen J., Chan, C.-T.: Abnormality detection for improving elder's daily life independent. In: Lee, Y., et al. (eds.) ICOST 2010. LNCS, vol. 6159, pp. 186–194. Springer, Heidelberg (2010). https://doi.org/10.1007/978-3-642-13778-5_23
17. Arifoglu, D., Bouchachia, A.: Activity recognition and abnormal behaviour detection with recurrent neural networks. Proc. Comput. Sci. **110**, 86–93 (2017)
18. Novák, M., Jakab, F., Lain, L.: Anomaly detection-2013, vol. 3 (2013)
19. Zhu, C., Sheng, W., Liu, M.: Wearable sensor-based behavioral anomaly detection in smart assisted living systems. IEEE Trans. Autom. Sci. Eng. **12**, 1–10 (2015)
20. Hochreiter, S., Schmidhuber, J.: LSTM. Neural Comput. **9**, 1–32 (1997)
21. Alshammari, T., Alshammari, N., Sedky, M., Howard, C.: SIMADL: simulated activities of daily living dataset. Data **3**, 11 (2018)
22. OpenSHS by openshs. https://github.com/openshs/

23. Chawla, N.V., Bowyer, K.W., Hall, L.O., Kegelmeyer, W.P.: SMOTE: synthetic minority over-sampling technique. J. Artif. Intell. Res. **16**, 321–357 (2002)
24. Hinton, G.: Dropout: a simple way to prevent neural networks from overfitting. J. Mach. Learn. Res. **15**, 1929–1958 (2014)
25. Kingma, D.P., Ba, J.L: Adam: a method for stochastic optimization, pp. 1–15 (2014)
26. FAQ - Keras Documentation. https://keras.io/
27. TensorFlow. https://www.tensorflow.org/
28. Hossin, M., Sulaiman, M.N.: A review on evaluation metrics for data classification evaluations. Int. J. Data Min. Knowl. Manag. Process **5**, 1–11 (2015)

Well-being Technology

A Deep Learning Method for Automatic Visual Attention Detection in Older Drivers

Belkacem Chikhaoui[1(✉)], Perrine Ruer[2], and Évelyne F. Vallières[1]

[1] LICEF Research Center, TELUQ University, Montreal, QC, Canada
belkacem.chikhaoui@teluq.ca, Evelyne.Vallieres@teluq.ca
[2] HEC Montreal, Montréal, QC, Canada
pruer.pro@gmail.com

Abstract. This paper addresses a new problem of automatic detection of visual attention in older adults based on their driving speed. All state-of-the-art methods try to understand the on-road performance of older adults by means of the Useful Field of View (UFOV) measure. Our method takes advantage of deep learning models such as Long-short Term Memory (LSTM) to automatically extract features from driving speed data for predicting drivers' visual attention. We demonstrate, through extensive experiments on real dataset, that our method is able to predict the driver's visual attention based on driving speed with high accuracy.

Keywords: UFOV · Deep learning · LSTM · Classification · Divided attention · Older drivers

1 Introduction

Visual and cognitive abilities are important parameters for safe driving. These abilities tend to decrease naturally with aging, and many older adults become unable to drive because of a serious decline in their visual and cognitive abilities. The decline in visual and cognitive abilities may lead to unsafe driving [1].

One of these abilities concerned divided attention, which is defined as the ability to construct information from multiple sources that are critical to the execution of a specific task (e.g., driving) [1], has received particular interest from researchers as a good indicator of driving performance in older drivers [1,2]. In fact, in the context of driving, drivers face multiple stimuli coming from the environment including the car, the road, other drivers, the weather, and driving time of day. These stimuli create a complex context, particularly for older drivers, that requires from them to shift attention between all these stimuli in order to ensure safe driving.

The Useful Field of View (UFOV) [3] is a well known and widely used test to measure visual attention [4]. It consists of three subtests of visual attention: processing speed, divided attention, and selective attention. The first one

J. Pagán et al. (Eds.): ICOST 2019, LNCS 11862, pp. 49–60, 2019.
https://doi.org/10.1007/978-3-030-32785-9_5

is to identify peripheral targets, the second and third subtests are to identify peripheral target presented either in the presence or absence of distractors while completing a central discrimination task [5–7].

The UFOV test has been shown to be highly effective in predicting driving outcomes such as (1) predicting crash risk among older adults [8–10], (2) predicting on-road performance [1,11], (3) predicting driving in the presence of distracters [12].

The overall studies using UFOV focus on driving outcomes and performance based on obtained UFOV test results. In this regard, our work is original and tries to predict the UFOV divided attention results based on older adults performances during driving, more specifically driving speed. To the best of our knowledge, no prior studies have examined the relationship between driving speed and divided attention. Therefore, the present research was initiated as it may have a great potential in developing assistance systems to help older adults drivers improve their safety while driving. In the research presented in this paper, we resort to deep learning models, particularly Long-Short Term Memory model (LSTM), to automatically detect older adult's divided attention based on his/her driving speed. The rationale of using LSTM models is threefold: (1) it allows to analyze raw speed data in order to automatically extract important features to perform predictions, (2) it allows to learn features across time by using their internal memory, and (3) it allows to process arbitrary sequences of inputs (speed data) unlike other existing feedforward neural network models. The major contributions of this paper can be summarized as follows:

- Proposing a LSTM based method to automatically detect older adults drivers' visual attention based on driving speed data.
- Conducting extensive experiments through real data to validate the proposed method.
- Demonstrating the performance and superiority of our proposed method compared to the state-of-the-art methods.

The rest of the paper is organized as follows. First, we give an overview of related work in Sect. 2. Section 3 describes the proposed model in terms of LSTM representation, and divided attention detection. The results of our experiments on a real driving dataset are presented in Sect. 4. Finally, Sect. 5 presents our conclusions.

2 Related Work

Multiple studies have been conducted examining the relationship between UFOV test performance and driving. These studies have used a variety of outcome measures, including on-road driving performance, crashes, simulated driving performance, and self-reported driving performance that assess components of driving ability that are neither exhaustive nor necessarily unique.

Driving performance can be assessed by cognitive tests, simulation, on-road driving tests, or a combination of these. In the driving activity, people have to respond rapidly to risks with good abilities. Previous research has investigated specific functions and/or deficits for any correlation with safe driving and in order to predict on-road driving performance.

Some physical impairments found frequently among older people may have negative impacts on their driving skills. Among them, a deficit in visual-cognitive functions, and more specifically divided attention, which is a good predictor of driving performance for older drivers [13].

Aging is associated with decreased performance on the UFOV test due to the higher prevalence in visual search, attention, speed of deficit treatment [13], poorer vision and mental status [14]. Poor performance on the UFOV test was associated with increased crash risk. Older drivers with UFOV impairments are twice as likely to be involved in a road accident [5]. The utility of the UFOV measure has been investigated in different studies. However, a link between the number of crashes and UFOV has been examined in the research [5]. Results showed a significant link between visual attention measures and a car crash for the older drivers. Authors highlighted that self-reported accident frequency by older drivers is not an accurate measure of their actual accident frequency. Authors said the use of this dependent measure in earlier studies may have led to erroneous conclusions about vision and driving relationships [15].

A number of studies used a variety of outcome measures. Some of them investigated on-road driving performance, particularly with simulated driving performance and they assessed driving performance and UFOV test performance. Results reported that both decreased with age. Older is the driver, the more errors are reported during the on-road driving assessment with a slower performance during the UFOV test [16]. Willstrand et al. [16] also highlighted an increasing number of driving errors seen and correlated with age-related reduced selective attention. The reduction of selective attention has a negative effect on driving speed, that is driving too fast, which was the most common error in the on-road driving assessment [16]. Baldock et al. [17] emphasized the importance of speed adaptation, especially the "approach speed", as it can lead to a delay in the needed braking. The third phase of the UFOV test may be an intervention for older drivers to increase their awareness of attentional problems when driving. Reducing speed when appropriate is an important factor to study with older drivers, as it gives them more time for visual search (processing speed and selective attention [16]).

3 Proposed Method

In order to understand how to detect divided attention based on speed data, firstly we describe the UFOV test in detail. Secondly, we will introduce our proposed method based on LSTM model.

3.1 UFOV Test

The UFOV is a computer-administered and computer-scored test of functional vision and visual attention [18], which can be predictive of ability to perform many everyday activities, such as driving a vehicle. The UFOV test lasts about 15 min and is highly recommended for drivers having an age of 55 years or older, particularly those who suffer from health problems including cognitive deficits [18].

UFOV consists in three subtests for assessing speed of visual processing under complex task demands [18]:

1. The first subtest (T1) consists in identifying a target presented in a centrally located fixation box presented for varying lengths of time.
2. The second subtest (T2) consists in identifying a target and localizing a simultaneously displayed target on the periphery of the computer screen.
3. The third subtest (T3) is identical to the second subtest, except that the displayed target is embedded in distractors to make the test more difficult. Each subtest has a threshold score as shown in Table 2.

Table 1 presents an example of UFOV test results (or score) in milliseconds (ms) obtained in real experiments. The range is 17 to 500 ms [18].

Table 1. Example of UFOV test results obtained in real experiments.

	UFOV results		
Participant	Subtest (T1)	Subtest (T2)	Subtest (T3)
1	17	17	197
2	17	23	110
3	17	87	177
4	83	44	287
5	17	23	203
6	20	93	380

The UFOV results can be categorized in different categories called classes of divided attention as shown in Table 2

Table 2. UFOV test values categories

	Classes		
Subtest	Class 1: healthy	Class 2: moderate	Class 3: severe
T1	≤30	>30, and, ≤60	>60
T2	<100	≥100, and, <350	≥350
T3	<350	≥350, and, <500	≥500

By using this definition of classes, results (from Table 1) are categorized in Table 3.

Table 3. Example of UFOV test results classes.

	UFOV results		
Participant	Subtest (T1)	Subtest (T2)	Subtest (T3)
1	1	1	1
2	1	1	1
3	1	1	1
4	3	1	1
5	1	1	1
6	1	1	2

Once the classes are defined, we will be able to label the dataset accordingly. Therefore, with driving speed data, we try to predict the corresponding class using the LSTM model described in the next section.

3.2 LSTM Model

This section introduces the LSTM deep learning model we used to predict divided attention.

LSTM models are a type of recurrent neural networks (RNN) for processing, classifying and making predictions based on times-series data. In contrast to other deep learning models such as Convolutional Neural Networks [19,20], LSTM models are able to extract temporal features from data. This is a very important characteristic, particularly in driving context where driving speed tend to change over time due to different environmental factors. Moreover, LSTM models have the property of selectively remembering patterns for long durations of time, which make them advantageous compared to basic RNN models.

All recurrent neural networks have the form of a chain of repeating modules of neural network, normally a single tanh layer [21]. In LSTM models, the repeating modules have different structures so that instead of having one single tanh layer, they have four layers as shown in Fig. 1 (this figure is taken from [21]).

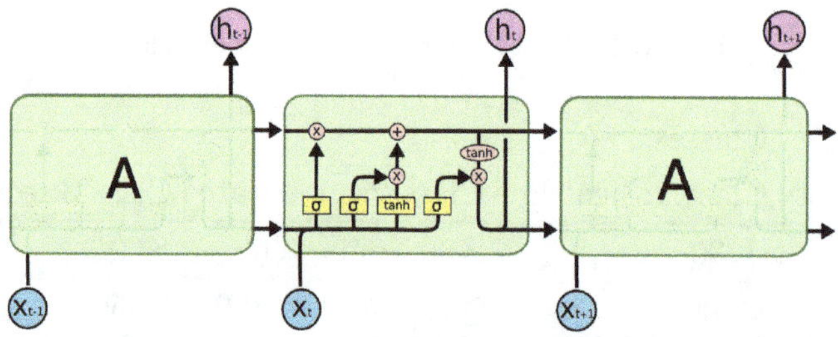

Fig. 1. LSTM structure.

The central component of LSTM model is the cell state presented in Fig. 1 with a horizontal line in the top. Information in the cell state could be added or removed, and this process is regulated by components called gates [21]. In other words, gates have the ability to let or not let information through [21].

To prevent the LSTM model from overfitting, we used the dropout principle [22]. The dropout consists in randomly dropping units with their connections from the neural network during training. Therefore, we randomly dropped 20% of units and their connection after each hidden layer. This percentage is recommended in literature [22]. We experimentally setup the number of units to 256 with a batch size of 128. The number of epochs is experimentally setup to 50. Our LSTM model was implemented in Python programming language using Tensorflow [23].

4 Experimental Study

In this section, we describe our experiments conducted at the University of Montreal for data collection and validation of proposed method.

The UFOV test, as mentioned previously, measures three types of attention: selective, shared and divided attention and detects an attention deficit. It is a 15 min computer test. The requirements increase in complexity between tasks. The purpose is to evaluate the visual processing speed of a person by detecting, identifying and locating targets briefly presented on the screen. This test is recommended to measure driving ability for older drivers [5,18].

Twenty-eight participants (14 women, 14 men) aged between 55 and 79 years old (mean: 63,86 y-o; standard-deviation: 6,20) were recruited. They drive on average five days per weeks. All participants have a valid driving licence and have been driving for several years (mean: 45 y-o, sd: 8,95). Participants did not report sleep disturbance or medication use that may affect driving.

All participants went to the driving simulation laboratory at the University of Montreal. Participants received a financial compensation of 60 CAD. The experiments were carried for 20 days during a two-month period.

The research protocol was to provide participants a consent form followed by a first sociodemographic questionnaire. Then, participants performed the UFOV test before driving in the simulator for about 40 min. Different data were saved with the simulator as speed, acceleration, braking and steering wheel angle. After driving, they answered "a final post-driving questionnaire" regarding their driving experiment.

The driving simulator is an intermediate level simulator. It is interactive with a fixed base, composed of an entire car (Honda Civic) with fully functional pedals, steering wheel and dashboard as shown in Fig. 2.

The simulator is parked in a brightly room in the Department of Psychology at the University of Montreal. The simulator faces a large projection screen (three metres by four metres), which allows a 70- degree view. The road image is computerized and projected by an RGB overhead projector. The location and speed (km/h) of the vehicle on the x, y and z axes are recorded during each simulation. We used these data for our analysis.

Fig. 2. Driving simulator used in our experiments.

5 Classification Results

To evaluate our proposed method for automatic detection of the different classes of drivers' divided attention, we divided the data collected into trainset (70%) and testset (30%). The trainset is used to build and train the LSTM model whereas the testset is used to validate the model. To evaluate the performance of the LSTM model, we used the precision, recall, and F-measure metrics. The classification results obtained are presented in Table 4.

Table 4. Classification results.

	Classification results		
	Subtest (T1)	Subtest (T2)	Subtest (T3)
Precision	0.9645	0.8581	0.8828
Recall	0.9642	0.8559	0.8733
F-Measure	0.9643	0.857	0.8780

As shown in Table 4, our method shows promising results in classifying the three subtests T1, T2 and T3 with high accuracy. More specifically, the highest performance was observed in T1 with an F-measure equals to 0.9645, while T2 represents the lowest performance with an F-measure equals to 0.857. The rational of having lower F-measure for T2 and T3 compared to T1 is the lack of data about the moderate and severe classes in these two categories. More participants should be recruited in the future in order to overcome this limitation. Confusion matrices obtained for the classification of the three subtests are presented in Fig. 3

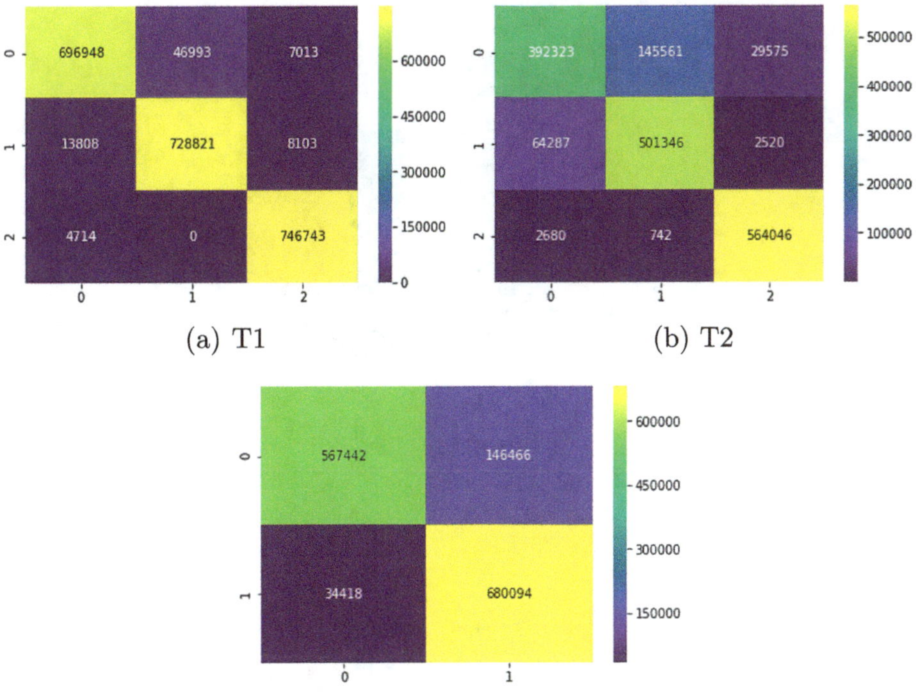

(a) T1

(b) T2

(c) T3

Fig. 3. Confusion matrices.

As shown in Fig. 3(a), some samples of class T3 were misclassified as class T1. This could be explained by the similarity in terms of some driving patterns at the beginning of the driving test as shown in Fig. 4 compared to T2.

We also evaluated the performance of our proposed method compared to the well known state-of-the-art methods of the domain such as decision trees, naive Bayes, Bayesian networks, support vector machines, K-nearest neighbor, and perceptron neural network. The comparison results for the three different subtests are presented in Figs. 5(a), (b), and (c) respectively.

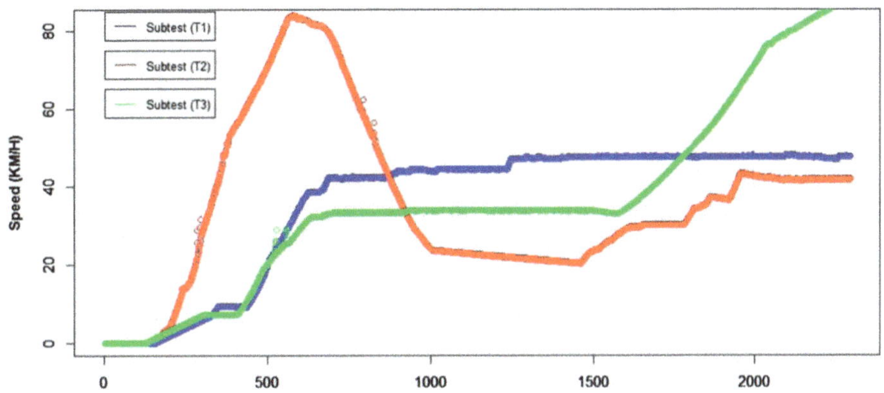

Fig. 4. Speed examples for participants in each class.

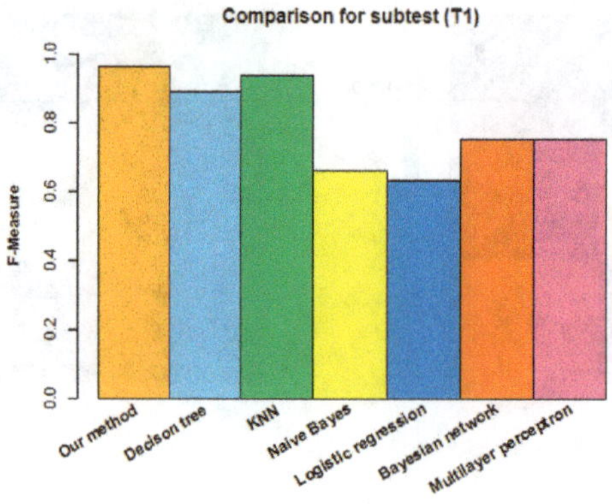

(a) T1

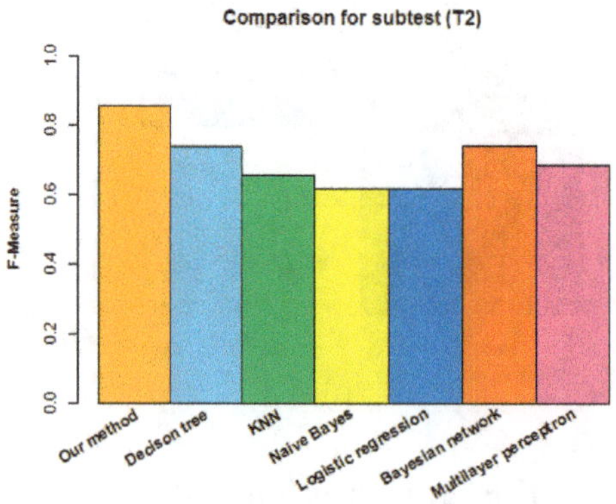

(b) T2

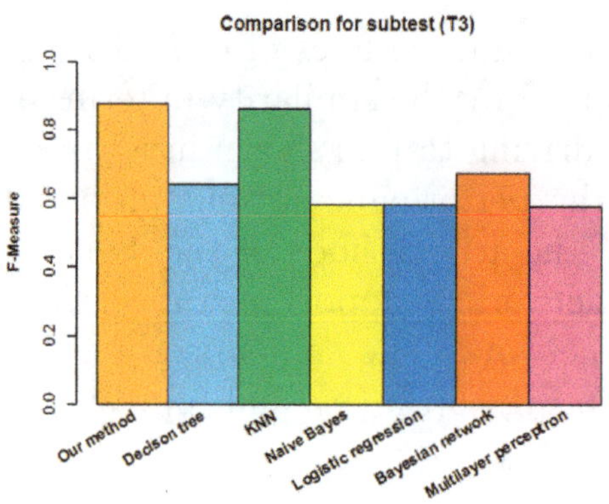

(c) T3

Fig. 5. Classification accuracy using different values of window size.

As shown in Fig. 5, our proposed method outperforms all the existing state-of-the-art methods in terms of classification accuracy followed by the K-NN method and Bayesian networks.

Some limits appear in this study. The first one concerns the number of participants. The sample was convenient with only 28 participants coming from the metropole area of Montreal. A further study has to integrate more participants coming from suburban area or countryside to confirm these results.

Another limit is the age group. We proposed a solution with only one age group (55 to 79 years old). As people is driving older and older, a comparison should be interesting between 'young' older adults and oldest one (55–74 years-old vs 75–100 years-old).

6 Conclusion

In this paper, we demonstrated the possibility of automatically detecting visual attention in older drivers based on driving speed data and their score from the UFOV test. Our method uses a deep learning model based on LSTM to automatically extract features from raw data and to detect with high accuracy the three different subtests of the UFOV test to determine visual attention of older drivers. We empirically demonstrated the suitability of the proposed method and its superiority compared to the state-of-the-art methods. The results of this research are of great importance for vehicle manufacturers who could integrate our finding to improve safety and security of older drivers. Moreover, the outcome of this research could have a great potential in the future to replace UFOV measure which is not easily reachable for everyone and requires human resources and temporal planning because of its time consuming.

Acknowledgement. The authors would like to thank the professors Jacques Bergeron, University of Montreal, and Charles Gouin Vallerand, TELUQ University, to share the data used in this study.

References

1. Crizzle, A.M., Winter, S.M., Lanford, D.N., Sherrilene, C., Wang, Y.: Predicting older driver on-road performance by means of the useful field of view and trail making test part B. Am. J. Occup. Ther. **67**(5), 574–582 (2013)
2. Roenker, D.L., Miller, R.L., Griggs, D.S., Ball, K.K., Beard, B.L.: Age and visual search: expanding the useful field of view. J. Opt. Soc. Am. Opt. Image Sci. **5**, 2210–2219 (1988)
3. Owsley, C., Wood, J.M.: Useful field of view test. Gerontology **60**(4), 315–318 (2014)
4. Sloane, M.E., Roenker, D.L., Bruni, J.R., Ball, K., Owsley, C.: Visual attention problems as a predictor of vehicle crashes in older drivers. Invest. Ophthalmol, Vis. Sci. **34**(11), 3110–3123 (1993)
5. Owsley, C., et al.: Visual processing impairment and risk of motor vehicle crash among older adults. JAMA **279**(14), 1083–1088 (1998)
6. Owsley, C., McGwin, G., Ball, K.: Vision impairment, eye disease, and injurious motor vehicle crashes in the elderly. Ophthalmic Epidemiol. **5**(2), 101–113 (1998)
7. Allman, R.M., Ball, K., Owsley, C., Sims, R.V., McGwin Jr., G.: Exploratory study of incident vehicle crashes among olderdrivers. J. Gerontol. Ser. A **55**(1), 22–27 (2000)
8. Goode, K.T., et al.: Useful field of view and other neurocognitive indicators of crash risk in older adults. J. Clin. Psychol. Med. Settings **5**(4), 425–440 (1998)

9. Vance, D.E., Stavrinos, D., McManus, B., Cox, M.K.: Predicting motor vehicle collisions in a driving simulator in young adults using the useful field of view assessment. Traffic Inj. Prev. **16**(8), 818–823 (2015)
10. Dubinsky, R., McDowd, J.M., Atchley, P.: The role of visual attention in predicting driving impairment in older adults. Psychol. Aging **20**(4), 610–622 (2005)
11. Edwards, J.D., Roth, D.L., Roenker, D.L., Ball, K.K., Clay, O.J., Wadley, V.G.: Cumulative meta-analysis of the relationship between useful field of view and driving performance in older adults: current and future implications. Optom. Vis. Sci. **82**(2), 724–731 (2005)
12. Lacherez, P., Hickson, L., Wood, J.M., Chaparro, A.: Useful field of view predicts driving in the presence of distracters. Optom. Vis. Sci. **89**(4), 373–381 (2012)
13. Roenker, D.L., Miller, R.L., Griggs, D.S., Ball, K.K., Beard, B.L.: Age and visual search: expanding the useful field of view. J. Opt. Soc. Am. Opt. Image Sci. **5**(12), 2210–2219 (1988)
14. Owsley, C., Ball, K.: The useful field of view test: a new technique for evaluating age-related declines in visual function. J. Am. Optom. Assoc. **64**(1), 71–79 (1993)
15. Owsley, C., Ball, K., Sloane, M.E., Roenker, D.L., Bruni, J.R.: Visual/cognitive correlates of vehicle accidents in older drivers. Psychol. Aging **6**(3), 403–415 (1991)
16. Selander, H., Dukic Willstrand, T., Broberg, T.: Driving characteristics of older drivers and their relationship to the useful field of view test. Gerontology **63**(2), 180–188 (2017)
17. Baldock, M.R.J., Berndt, A., Mathias, J.: The functional correlates of older drivers' on-road driving test errors. Top Geriatr. Rehabil. **24**, 204–223 (2008)
18. BrainHQ. Ufov assessment manual. Technical report (2011)
19. Chikhaoui, B., Gouineau, F.: Towards automatic feature extraction for activity recognition from wearable sensors: a deep learning approach. In: 2017 IEEE International Conference on Data Mining Workshops, ICDM Workshops 2017, New Orleans, LA, USA, 18–21 November 2017, pp. 693–702 (2017)
20. Chikhaoui, B., Gouineau, F., Sotir, M.: A CNN based transfer learning model for automatic activity recognition from accelerometer sensors. In: 14th International Conference on Machine Learning and Data Mining in Pattern Recognition, MLDM 2018, New York, NY, USA, 15–19 July 2018, Proceedings, Part II, pp. 302–315 (2018)
21. Olah, C.: Understanding LSTM networks. Technical report (2015)
22. Srivastava, N., Hinton, G., Krizhevsky, A., Sutskever, I., Salakhutdinov, R.: Dropout: A simple way to prevent neural networks from overfitting. J. Mach. Learn. Res. **15**(1), 1929–1958 (2014)
23. Abadi, M., et al.: Tensorflow: a system for large-scale machine learning. In: 12th USENIX Symposium on Operating Systems Design and Implementation (OSDI 2016), pp. 265–283 (2016)

Smart Mat for Respiratory Activity Detection: Study in a Clinical Setting

Samuel Otis[1(✉)], Bessam Abdulrazak[2], Sofia Ben Jebara[3], Francois Tournoux[4], and Neila Mezghani[1,5]

[1] Laboratoire de recherche en imagerie et en orthopédie, CRCHUM, Montreal, Canada
samuel.otis.1@ens.etsmtl.ca

[2] Department of Computer Science, Sherbrooke University, Sherbrooke, Canada
Bessam.Abdulrazak@usherbrooke.ca

[3] COSIM Laboratory, Carthage University, Higher School of Communications of Tunis, Ariana, Tunisia
sofia.benjebara@supcom.tn

[4] Department of Medicine, Centre Hospitalier de l'Université de Montréal, Montreal, Canada
francois.tournoux@umontreal.ca

[5] Centre de recherche LICEF, Université TÉLUQ, Montreal, Canada
neila.mezghani@teluq.ca

Abstract. We discuss in this paper a study of a smart and unobtrusive mattress in a clinical setting on a population with cardiorespiratory problems. Up to recently, the vast majority of studies with unobtrusive sensors are done with healthy populations. The unobtrusive monitoring of the Respiratory Rate (RR) is essential for proposing better diagnoses. Thus, new industrial and research activity on smart mattresses is targeting respiratory rate in an Internet-of-Things (IoT) context. In our work, we are interested in the performances of a microbend fiber optic sensor (FOS) mattress on 81 subjects admitted in the Cardiac Intensive Care Unit (CICU) by estimating the RR from their ballistocardiograms (BCG). Our study proposes a new RR estimator, based on harmonic plus noise models (HNM) and compares it with known estimators such as MODWT and CLIE. The goal is to examine, using a more representative and bigger dataset, the performances of these methods and of the smart mattress in general. Results of applying these three estimators on the BCG show that MODWT is more accurate with an average mean absolute error (MAE) of 1.97 ± 2.12 BPM. However, the HNM estimator has space for improvements with estimation errors of 2.91 ± 4.07 BPM. The smart mattress works well within a standard RR range of 10–20 breaths-per-minute (BPM) but gets less accurate with a bigger range of estimation. These results highlight the need to test these sensors in much more realistic contexts.

Keywords: Smart mattress · Ballistocardiogram · Respiratory rate

This research was supported by the Canada Research Chair on Biomedical Data Mining (950-231214).

J. Pagán et al. (Eds.): ICOST 2019, LNCS 11862, pp. 61–72, 2019.
https://doi.org/10.1007/978-3-030-32785-9_6

1 Introduction

New sensors for the unobtrusive detection of vital signs have to be tested in a clinical setting to assess their potential and limits. These sensors are interesting to propose better treatment and care for subjects having cardiorespiratory problems in an Internet of Things (IoT) context. This is especially important since long term data is required to offer better and more accurate diagnoses [7]. Recently, smart mattresses acquiring the ballistocardiogram (BCG) [24] have proven to be reliable. The BCG is the motion of the body following the mechanical action of the heart. Consequently, the BCG also contains the motion from the respiration. Thus, if a subject rests on a smart mattress, it would be possible to acquire his vital signs in a completely unobtrusive way during in-bed periods.

Still, most studies on a smart mattress are done using a small number of healthy and/or young subjects [10,12–14,20]. Thus, having a few number of subjects or only healthy subjects is not sufficient because the recruited populations are not representative of the targeted users. Most of the potential users of these sensors have contrasted health issues and physiological differences such as being overweight, underweight, young, old, smoker, and non-smoker. All of these parameters have [8] effects on the quality of the acquired BCG. This is an issue since we want to extract important vital signs such as the respiratory rate (RR) from the BCG. The RR has been neglected in the past but is now more and more in use by nurses and doctors. For instance, an abnormal RR is a strong marker of serious illness [6].

In this paper, we test the performance of a smart mattress, the microbend fiber optic sensor (FOS) mattress, during the detection of the RR. This was done through a study, in a clinical setting, involving 100 subjects having a wide range of cardiorespiratory problems. We acquired the BCG and estimated the RRs of the subjects using well-known methods. Maximal Overlap Discrete Wavelet Transform (MODWT) [22] and Continuous Local Interval Estimation (CLIE) [2,4] are the two most used vital signs estimators for the RR in the literature. Although, CLIE hasn't been tested on an unhealthy population and MODWT has limits in the range of frequency phenomenons it can capture. Thus, we propose to enrich the study with a new estimator based on Harmonic plus Noise Models (HNM)[17].

The rest of this paper is organized as follows: In Sect. 2, we will explore in more details the use of the BCG as well as the signal processing tools we selected. In Sect. 3, we detail our experimental methodology study and describe the population that was recruited. In Sect. 4, we present and analyze the results of the study. In Sect. 5, we discuss the relevance of the results and justify the used tools. In Sect. 6, we conclude with a summary of our findings, we show their limits and propose future relevant work in this field.

2 Background

The BCG signal contains vital signs such as the Heart Rate (HR) and Respiratory Rate (RR). It is present in the range of indiscernible motions coming from the human body. The BCG measures the ballistic forces generated by the heart, that is, the mechanical response of the body when the heart ejects the blood into the vascular tree. Notwithstanding the heart activity, it is also possible to retrieve the respiratory activity from the motion of the thorax when a subject inhales and exhales. All other motions present during the sleep also corrupt the signals Fig. 1.

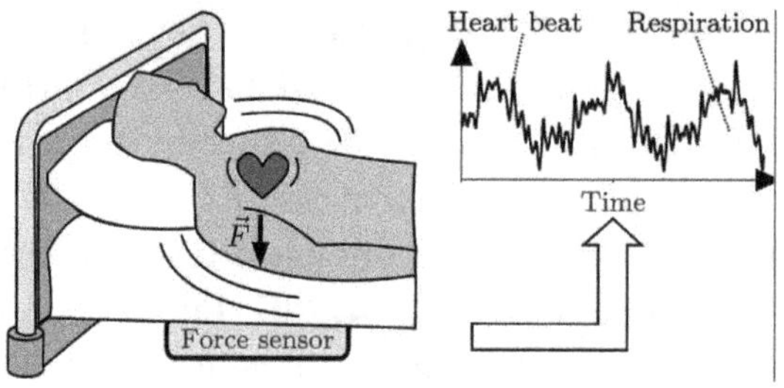

Fig. 1. A raw BCG signal containing heart activity, respiratory activity and general body motions. [5]

To retrieve the respiratory activity from the BCG, we need both a very sensitive force sensor placed under the subject and advanced signal processing techniques to estimate the information. New generations of sensor-based mattress can unobtrusively monitor the BCG by being placed under the sheets or even under the bed mattress.

Recently, an interesting microbend FOS, embedded in a small mattress, has been developed [24]. This microbend FOS provides a new way of acquiring the mechanical activity of the human body. It is achieved through the intensity attenuation of the light passing through an optic fiber in response to a mechanical stimulus on the fiber [26]. Figure 2 shows the principle of the microbend FOS.

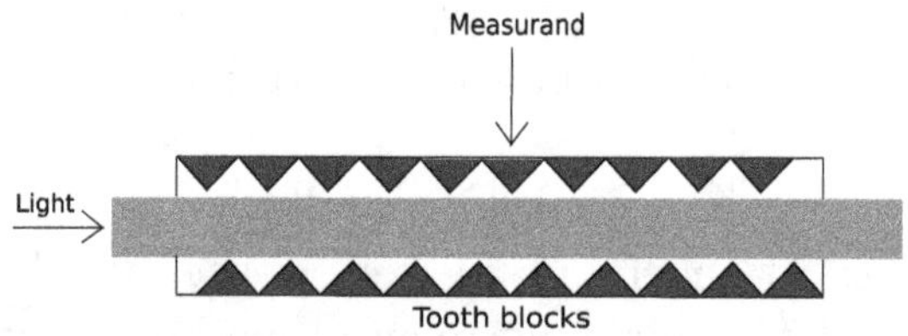

Fig. 2. Microbend FOS principle. The light passing through the microbend FOS is modulated by the deformations in the optical fiber due to the displacement of the micro-benders.

Lau *et al.* [13] used an FOS mattress to monitor the respiration and gait the image in synchrony with said respiration. They obtained high accuracy on the respiration estimation using simple filtering and peak detection on still subjects during functional magnetic resonance imaging (fMRI). Sadek *et al.* [22,28] also used an FOS mattress to acquire the BCG of subjects during headrest on a chair. Research using this sensor has given promising results, showing high accuracy for that technology.

Nevertheless, as it has been mentioned earlier, such sensors also require advanced signal processing algorithms to estimate the vital signs and more precisely the RR from the raw BCG signal. Multiple estimators have been tested like wavelets [22], empirical mode decomposition (EMD) [23], cepstrum analysis [5,27], clustering [3], standard filtering [14], bayesian fusion [4] and fast Fourier transforms (FFT) [11]. Two methods stand out in the literature for having good results on wider groups of subjects: (1) MODWT and (2) CLIE. These algorithms can be considered as reference methods in the literature. We use them not only as a reference to validate the smart mattress on a symptomatic population, but also to validate the new HNM method we developed.

Maximal Overlap Discrete Wavelet Transform (MODWT). It is a method to gain a spectro-temporal representation of studied signal by passing it through multiple and customizable narrow filters at arbitrarily selected levels. It is often used for signal denoising as well as for feature extraction. Jin *et al.* [9] detected the heart rate with a peak searching algorithm and wavelet shrinkage. Sadek *et al.* [22] implemented the Maximal Overlap Discrete Wavelet Transform (MODWT) to extract the BCG signal from a microbend FOS. Previous studies [15,18,22] have shown that wavelets and especially MODWT fare better than other algorithms such as clustering and EMD. DWT's strengths rely on its ability to split the signal into multiple levels of frequency components. It is, however, harder to select the right level of frequency components to represent the desired phenomenons.

Continuous Local Interval Estimation (CLIE). It is developed by Bruser *et al.* [4] and uses the Bayesian fusion of three estimators of the interval between heartbeats. These indicators are respectively *i* a modified version of the autocorrelation method [19], *ii* a modified version of the average magnitude difference function (AMDF) [21] and (3) the maximum amplitude pairs (MAP). Using Bayesian mathematics, the three estimators are fused as seen in Fig. 3. This estimator has also been used in a single [4] and multichannel [2] context. It offers a much more robust and reliable estimation of the interval between heartbeats. It has, however, not been tested for estimating the RR.

Harmonic Plus Noise Models (HNM). It represents a signal as a sum of harmonic parts and a noise part [25]. By using special methods like the one developed by Pantazis *et al.* [17], it is possible to estimate the harmonics of this HNM. This method, known as the iterative estimation of sinusoidal signal parameters, only needs the fundamental frequency of the signal to build a model of it. The goal with HNM is to construct a synthetic representation of the respiration signal. The synthetic signal can be written as follow:

$$\hat{s} = s_h(t) + s_n(t) \tag{1}$$

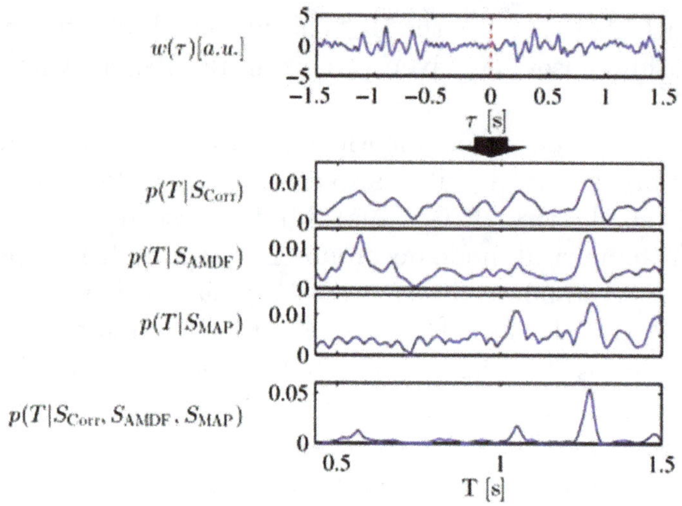

Fig. 3. Example of the fusion of autocorrelation, AMDF and MAP estimators as proposed by Bruser *et al.* [4]. Each of the estimators proposes its probability distribution of the most probable interval between two heartbeats. The fusion of the three of them, in the bottom graph, shows more robustness in the quality of the estimation than the three separate estimators.

The harmonic part is modeled as a sum of harmonics:

$$s_h(t) = \sum_{k=-L}^{L} A_k(t) cos \left(2 * \pi k f_0 t + \phi_k(t) \right), \tag{2}$$

where L denotes the number of harmonics included in the harmonic part, $\phi_k(t)$ is the temporal phase of the kth harmonic, f_0 denotes the fundamental frequency and A_k denotes the amplitude of the sinusoidal components.

The noise part is commonly considered as white Gaussian noise synchronized with the harmonic part.

In the next section, we explain our experimental setup for conducting the study at a hospital as well as the specifics of the population recruited into the study. We also describe the methods we used to extract the RR from an FOS mattress as well.

3 Methodology

Experimental Setup. The study for this work was conducted in the Centre Hospitalier de l'Universite de Montreal (CHUM) at the Cardiac Intensive Care Unit (CICU) in Montreal, Canada. This study was reviewed and approved by the TELUQ, ETS and CHUM institutional review board (IRB). We approached patients already admitted in the CICU who were *i* conscious and able to give informed consent, *ii* french-speaker, *iii* at least the whole night in the CICU and *iv* able to be lightly mobilized for the installation of the smart mattress.

Once patients accepted to take part in the study, we collected data from their health records such as their demographic and anthropomorphic data (age, weight, height, etc.). We then installed the smart mattress directly under the sheets of their bed at the level of their thorax, as visible in Fig. 4. They could still move as they wished during the recording.

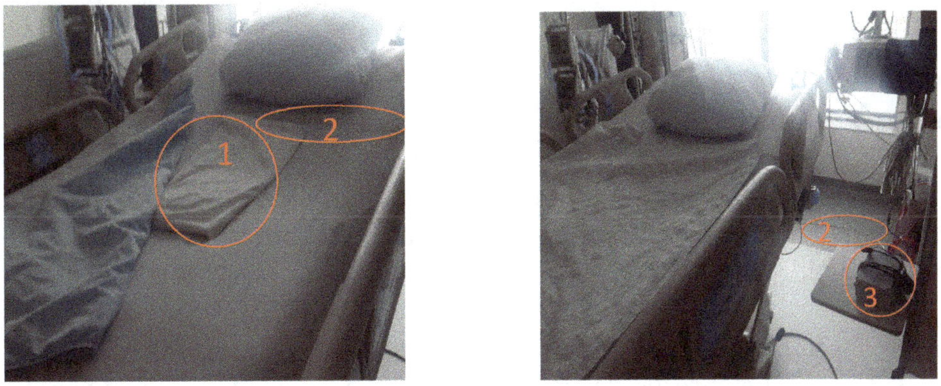

Fig. 4. Positioning of the smart mattress (1) and its acquisition box (3). On the left, we see the smart mattress (1) encased in a waterproof pillowcase. This is to protect it against standard biohazards present in a hospital as well as to meet the sanitary requisites of the hospital. On both images, we see the fiber optic cable (2) going from the smart mattress (1) to the acquisition box (3).

We then started a recording of the movements of the subject which would last more or less 24 h, depending on the length of the stay. After the recording, the smart mattress would be removed from the subject's bed. The data recorded by the system is then extracted on a normal computer as a *.csv file.

The reference values of the hospital, which serve as ground truth for future estimations of our system, were also extracted from the hospital' systems.

Hardware. The microbend FOS technology allowed us to record raw BCGs with their system. The raw data is sampled at 50 Hz by the acquisition module. Through a debug port on the acquisition module, the time serie of the BCG was stored on a Raspberry Pi 3 B+. The reference values of the hospital' systems were acquired through the CARESCAPE Monitor B850 of GE Healthcare. The CARESCAPE monitor recorded, amongst other values, the ElectroCardioGram (ECG), PhotoPlethysmoGraph (PPG) and Impedance PneumoGram (IPG). The CARESCAPE monitor also recorded the time occurrence of anomalous events such as TachyCardia (TC), BradyCardia (BC) and Atrial Fibrillation (AF).

The extracted recordings of the smart mattress and the CARESCAPE monitor were all processed on Intel(R) Core(TM) i7-6700 CPU @ 3.40 GHz computer using Python 3.7.

Dataset. We have recruited 100 patients that were admitted for the night at the CICU. 20 patients were removed from the study because of (1) missing data or (2) unforeseen leave from the CICU. When a patient leaves the hospital, his recordings are automatically deleted from their systems. Thus, it was impossible to compare the recorded BCG with the reference. In total, 80 patients with a maximum of 24 h of recorded data (53 male, 27 female; age 65.58 ± 12.58 years old; height 168.65 ± 9.35 cm; weight 77.94 ± 18.31 kg) are used for RR detection. The available data compiles 1520 h of recordings.

Filtering and Artefacts Removal. The data went first through a bidirectional Butterworth bandpass filter of 5th order with bandpass frequencies of 0.1 to 2 Hz. Moreover, the motions from a subject may quickly decrease the quality of the signal. Therefore, the motions were removed from the raw signals using a simple thresholding technique. We added bottom and upper variance thresholds to remove parts of the recordings where the bed was empty and where there was too much motion. We experimented on the size of the sliding window as well as the values of the thresholds. By looking at samples of performance results, we adjusted these parameters to yield maximal precision during estimations. With a sliding window of 6 s, the bottom threshold was set at 0.01 times the variance of the whole complete recording. The upper threshold was set at 10 times the complete recording. Signal segments with a variance outside of these limits were automatically removed with a mask in the end. These parts of the signal generally include motions like turning over, getting in or out of bed and coughing. Since the sensor is a single motion sensor, it remains hard to detect which position the subject is in. Therefore, we keep every segment of the signal with low variance even if the subject is in an undesirable posture.

3.1 RR Estimation

To estimate the RR, we used each of the RR estimation technique with a sliding window of 800 samples (16 s). Windows overlapped by 50% (8 s). All parameters were optimized, while the others were fixed, by choosing the value yielding the best estimation performance at the end of the processing chain. Optimized parameters, for our study, include the selected wavelet, its coefficient level, the low and high periods of the CLIE method and the number of harmonics used for synthesizing the signal using HNM.

MODWT. It is one of the estimators that yielded good results in the past. The approach we use is similar to that of Sadek *et al.* [22]. We use the Symlet 8 (Sym8) wavelet transform to extract the coefficients of the filtered signal. The 6-th level of the approximation coefficients is selected since it represents best the respiration cycle in the BCG. We then apply a basic peak searching algorithm to extract the mean period between peaks and, thus, the RR.

CLIE. It is implemented as per the work of Bruser *et al.* [4]. Since they used it to detect the heart rate, we adapted some parameters to capture the period range of the RR instead of the HR. The lowest period T_{min} was set to 1 s and the highest period T_{max} was set to 10 s.

HNM. When working with the BCG, the heart, respiration, and noise signals are mixed. It is possible to build a synthetic heart signal from its original version using an HNM. It is critical, though, that we estimate the fundamental frequency f_0 of the heart as close as possible to the truth. We do this using an FFT with Harmonic Artifact Rejection (HAR) as proposed by Beattie *et al.* [1]. A set of heuristics will work to eliminate higher and lower amplitudes harmonics to make sure we extract the true fundamental frequency of the heart. This is more efficient than simply selecting the highest amplitude frequency in the FFT.

We then build an HNM using this frequency by applying the same operations as Pantazis *et al.* [17]. The filtered signal is directly fed to the HNM algorithm and we build an HNM with $L = 6$ harmonics of the fundamental heart frequency. We then subtract this HNM from the original signal. This yielded the estimated true respiration component from which we selected, using the highest spectral peak, the fundamental respiration frequency.

4 Results and Discussion

We extracted the average Mean Absolute Error (MAE), Root Mean Squared Error (RMSE) and Standard Deviation (SD) of the Absolute Error (AE) for every recording on 81 patients. The AE is the absolute difference between an estimate of the RR and the RR from the ground truth. Every metric is expressed in Breaths Per Minute (BPM). This yielded the following results for the HNM, CLIE and MODWT estimators.

Table 1. Performances of estimators in relation to ground truth for different ranges of RR

Estimator	Average MAE (BPM)	RMSE (BPM)	SD (BPM)
All RR estimates			
HNM	6.29	10.29	8.14
CLIE	8.71	12.11	8.37
MODWT	4.57	8.27	6.89
Between 5 and 30 BPM			
HNM	4.64	7.04	5.30
CLIE	7.18	9.17	5.71
MODWT	2.89	4.17	3.01
Between 10 and 20 BPM			
HNM	2.91	5.00	4.07
CLIE	5.38	7.39	5.06
MODWT	1.97	2.89	2.12

We separated the results for 3 ranges of reference values. The top part of Table 1 represents the performances on all possible values of the recorded reference. This allows us to view if the estimators work well for big (>30 BPM) and small (<10 BPM) reference values. The middle part shows results with reference limits between 5 and 30 BPM. Finally, in the bottom part, we look at the performances between 10 and 20 BPM, which are standard values for the RR of healthy subjects. Figure 5 shows the agreement between the methods and the reference equipment using Bland-Altman analyses. Our artifact removal method yielded a mean coverage of 76.62% ± 12.05%.

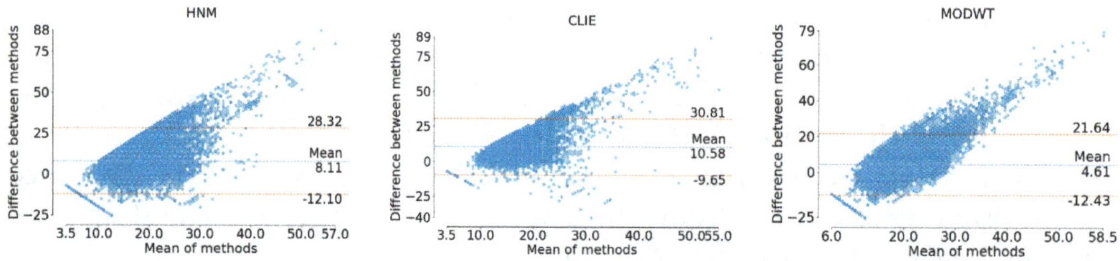

Fig. 5. These 3 Bland Altman graphs represent the agreement of each method during the estimation of the RR. The left graph represents the agreement for HNM, the middle graph is the agreement for CLIE and the right graph is the agreement for MODWT.

It is possible to view the results of Table 1, as good indicators of the caveats of RR and even HR estimators. Most studies preoccupy themselves with performances concerning a healthy population. Thus, the subjects of these studies have vital signs within the standard limits. For instance, Paalasmaa *et al.* [16] had a mean error on the HR of 0.78 BPM for 46 healthy subjects. Our best results, lower than theirs, of 1.97 ± 2.12 BPM is with unhealthy subjects and within a strict range. It drops to 4.57 ± 6.892 BPM with the entire range of RR values. This shows that when facing high variance in the recorded RR values and unhealthy subjects, the quality of the estimations decreases rapidly for estimators that would have similar performances on a similar dataset. An estimator should be able to keep the same performances no matter the reference values and the type of subject. However, we see that previously developed estimators, as well as our HNM estimator, have troubles in finding very high or very low RR values. This especially apparent in every Bland-Altman analyses, where we observe a difference proportional to the mean of the methods. To put it simply, the methods work well between 10 and 20 BPM rates but will overestimate for slower rates and underestimate for faster rates.

Moreover, with every result, we can observe an SD as big or bigger than the average MAE. This means that there are multiple bad estimations but that it is common for the estimator to give results of the right order of magnitude. This is even more apparent with the HNM estimator. Most of the HNM's estimations are directly related to the fundamental frequency estimation, before building the HNM model. The computed fundamental frequency needs to be exactly right if we want to build a high-fidelity model of the respiration. This means that the HAR we used is not as efficient as we thought in finding the right fundamental frequency, thus leading to incorrect models and incorrect true RR estimations.

CLIE is generally seen as the golden standard for estimating the HR. Its performance, however, diminishes in a single channel setup with the RR. It is too sensitive to the heart rate, which we can't remove from the signal perfectly with basic bandpass filtering. With many subjects, the heart signal is often stronger than the respiration signal. In other cases, we see the opposite situation. Thus, during the fusion of the three sub-estimators of CLIE (autocorrelation, AMDF, and MAP), the heart rate will often greatly modify the result. This explains the often very high estimates of CLIE even in the standard RR range.

We also see that MODWT performs the best but gets less and less efficient at very low or very high reference values. For instance, it obtains the same RR estimation precision as Beattie *et al.* [1], but with a simpler algorithm and inside the same range of RR. MODWT was often used within a small range of reference values. With bigger ranges, one level of wavelet coefficient is not enough to represent well lower and higher magnitude RRs. It would be interesting to select the right coefficient to represent the RR during computations. It would lead to much lower RMSE and SD for MODWT.

5 Conclusion

In this work, we discuss a study involving a smart FOS mattress for the detection of the respiratory rate in a clinical setting. This study, including 100 subjects, is done with old subjects having a wide range of cardiorespiratory problems, in opposition with precedent studies using mostly young and healthy subjects. We use previously known methods for estimating the RR from the recordings. These methods were MODWT and CLIE. Since they had shortcomings in their precedent applications, we also proposed a new method based on HNM. Our new HNM algorithm gave good results, but the selection of the fundamental frequency for the computation of the HNM needs to be improved. MODWT gave the best performances, similar to other studies on the RR [1], but only within constrained reference values. It is, however, less accurate than other vital signs tools used in bigger studies [4,16] on the HR. This is most probably due to the subjects of these studies being healthy and younger. It would still be interesting to add a way of selecting the right level of wavelet coefficients to further improve the estimation of the RR with MODWT.

Future work will be on the characterization of this database and its relation to the performances of estimators such as MODWT. We will explore the effects of anthropomorphic parameters on the quality of the estimations.

Acknowledgment. This research was supported in part by the Canada Research Chair on Biomedical Data Mining (950-231214). The authors would like to thank the anonymous reviewers for their valuable comments and suggestions to improve the quality of the paper.

References

1. Beattie, Z.T., Jacobs, P.G., Riley, T.C., Hagen, C.C.: A time-frequency respiration tracking system using non-contact bed sensors with harmonic artifact rejection. In: 2015 37th Annual International Conference of the IEEE Engineering in Medicine and Biology Society (EMBC), pp. 8111–8114, August 2015
2. Brüser, C., Kortelainen, J.M., Winter, S., Tenhunen, M., Pärkkä, J., Leonhardt, S.: Improvement of force-sensor-based heart rate estimation using multichannel data fusion. IEEE J. Biomed. Health Inform. **19**(1), 227–235 (2015)
3. Bruser, C., Stadlthanner, K., Waele, S.d., Leonhardt, S.: Adaptive beat-to-beat heart rate estimation in ballistocardiograms. IEEE Trans. Inf. Technol. Biomed. **15**(5), 778–786 (2011)
4. Brüser, C., Winter, S., Leonhardt, S.: Robust inter-beat interval estimation in cardiac vibration signals. Physiol. Meas. **34**(2), 123–138 (2013)
5. Bruser, C., Antink, C.H., Wartzek, T., Walter, M., Leonhardt, S.: Ambient and unobtrusive cardiorespiratory monitoring techniques. IEEE Rev. Biomed. Eng. **8**, 30–43 (2015)
6. Cretikos, M.A., Bellomo, R., Hillman, K., Chen, J., Finfer, S., Flabouris, A.: Respiratory rate: the neglected vital sign. Med. J. Aust. **188**(11), 657–659 (2008)
7. Donaldson, M.S., Corrigan, J.M., Kohn, L.T., et al.: To Err Is Human: Building a Safer Health System, vol. 6. National Academies Press, Washington, DC (2000)
8. Harrison, W.K., Smith, J.E.: Sex differences in cardiac function of a group of young adults. Cardiology **66**(2), 74–84 (1980)
9. Jin, J., Wang, X., Li, S., Wu, Y.: A novel heart rate detection algorithm in ballistocardiogram based on wavelet transform. In: 2009 Second International Workshop on Knowledge Discovery and Data Mining, pp. 76–79, January 2009
10. Jung, D.W., Hwang, S.H., Yoon, H.N., Lee, Y.J.G., Jeong, D.U., Park, K.S.: Nocturnal awakening and sleep efficiency estimation using unobtrusively measured ballistocardiogram. IEEE Trans. Biomed. Eng. **61**(1), 131–138 (2014)
11. Kortelainen, J.M., Gils, M.v., Pärkkä, J.: Multichannel bed pressure sensor for sleep monitoring. In: 2012 Computing in Cardiology, pp. 313–316, September 2012
12. Kortelainen, J.M., Mendez, M.O., Bianchi, A.M., Matteucci, M., Cerutti, S.: Sleep staging based on signals acquired through bed sensor. IEEE Trans. Inf. Technol. Biomed. **14**(3), 776–785 (2010)
13. Lau, D., et al.: Intensity-modulated microbend fiber optic sensor for respiratory monitoring and gating during MRI. IEEE Trans. Biomed. Eng. **60**(9), 2655–2662 (2013)
14. Mack, D.C., Patrie, J.T., Suratt, P.M., Felder, R.A., Alwan, M.: Development and preliminary validation of heart rate and breathing rate detection using a passive, ballistocardiography-based sleep monitoring system. IEEE Trans. Inf. Technol. Biomed. **13**(1), 111–120 (2009)
15. Otis, S., Mezghani, N., Abdulrazak, B.: Comparative study of heart rate extraction methods for a novel intelligent mattress. In: 2018 9th International Symposium on Signal, Image, Video and Communications (ISIVC), pp. 93–98, November 2018
16. Paalasmaa, J., Toivonen, H., Partinen, M.: Adaptive heartbeat modeling for beat-to-beat heart rate measurement in ballistocardiograms. IEEE J. Biomed. Health Inform. **19**(6), 1945–1952 (2015)
17. Pantazis, Y., Rosec, O., Stylianou, Y.: Iterative estimation of sinusoidal signal parameters. IEEE Signal Process. Lett. **17**(5), 461–464 (2010)

18. Pino, E.J., Chávez, J.A.P., Aqueveque, P.: Noninvasive ambulatory measurement system of cardiac activity. In: 2015 37th Annual International Conference of the IEEE Engineering in Medicine and Biology Society (EMBC), pp. 7622–7625, August 2015
19. Rabiner, L.: On the use of autocorrelation analysis for pitch detection. IEEE Trans. Acoust. **25**(1), 24–33 (1977)
20. Rosales, L., Skubic, M., Heise, D., Devaney, M.J., Schaumburg, M.: Heartbeat detection from a hydraulic bed sensor using a clustering approach. In: Conference Proceedings of IEEE Engineering in Medicine and Biology Society 2012, pp. 2383–2387 (2012)
21. Ross, M., Shaffer, H., Cohen, A., Freudberg, R., Manley, H.: Average magnitude difference function pitch extractor. IEEE Trans. Acoust. **22**(5), 353–362 (1974)
22. Sadek, I., Biswas, J., Abdulrazak, B., Haihong, Z., Mokhtari, M.: Continuous and unconstrained vital signs monitoring with ballistocardiogram sensors in headrest position. In: 2017 IEEE EMBS International Conference on Biomedical Health Informatics (BHI), pp. 289–292, February 2017
23. Sadek, I., Biswas, J., Fook, V.F.S., Mokhtari, M.: Automatic heart rate detection from FBG sensors using sensor fusion and enhanced empirical mode decomposition. In: 2015 IEEE International Symposium on Signal Processing and Information Technology (ISSPIT), pp. 349–353, December 2015
24. Sadek, I.: Ballistocardiogram signal processing: A literature review, July 2018
25. Stylianou, Y.: Concatenative speech synthesis using a harmonic plus noise model. In: The Third ESCA/COCOSDA Workshop (ETRW) on (1998)
26. Udd, E.: An overview of fiber-optic sensors. Rev. Sci. Instrum. **66**(8), 4015–4030 (1995)
27. Zhu, Y., et al.: Heart rate estimation from FBG sensors using cepstrum analysis and sensor fusion. In: 2014 36th Annual International Conference of the IEEE Engineering in Medicine and Biology Society, pp. 5365–5368, August 2014
28. Zhu, Y., Zhang, H., Jayachandran, M., Ng, A.K., Biswas, J., Chen, Z.: Ballistocardiography with fiber optic sensor in headrest position: a feasibility study and a new processing algorithm. In: 2013 35th Annual International Conference of the IEEE Engineering in Medicine and Biology Society (EMBC), pp. 5203–5206, July 2013

Non-invasive Classification of Sleep Stages with a Hydraulic Bed Sensor Using Deep Learning

Rayan Gargees[1(✉)], James M. Keller[1], Mihail Popescu[2], and Marjorie Skubic[1]

[1] Electrical Engineering and Computer Science Department, University of Missouri, 201 Naka Hall, Columbia, MO 65211, USA
{rsgxc9,kellerJ,skubicm}@missouri.edu

[2] Health Management and Informatics Department, University of Missouri, CE707 Clinical Support and Education Building, DC006.00, Columbia, MO 65212, USA
popescuM@missouri.edu

Abstract. The quality of sleep has a significant impact on health and life. This study adopts the structure of hierarchical classification to develop an automatic sleep stage classification system using ballistocardiogram (BCG) signals. A leave-one-subject-out cross validation (LOSO-CS) procedure is used for testing classification performance. Convolutional Neural Networks (CNNs), Long Short-Term Memory (LSTM), and Deep Neural Networks DNNs are complementary in their modeling capabilities; while CNNs have the advantage of reducing frequency variations, LSTMs are good at temporal modeling. A transfer learning (TL) technique is used to pre-train our CNN model on posture data and then fine-tune it on the sleep stage data. We used a ballistocardiography (BCG) bed sensor to collect both posture and sleep stage data to provide a non-invasive, in-home monitoring system that tracks changes in health of the subjects over time. Polysomnography (PSG) data from a sleep lab was used as the ground truth for sleep stages, with the emphasis on three sleep stages, specifically, awake, rapid eye movement (REM) and non-REM sleep (NREM). Our results show an accuracy of 95.3%, 84% and 93.1% for awake, REM and NREM respectively on a group of patients from the sleep lab.

Keywords: Sleep stages · Transfer learning · BCG bed sensor · Deep learning

1 Introduction

Sleep is a critical physiological phenomenon for recovery from mental and physical fatigue. Lately, there has been much interest in the quality of sleep, and research is actively underway. In particular, it is vital to have a repetitive and regular sleep cycle for good sleep. Nevertheless, it takes much time to determine

J. Pagán et al. (Eds.): ICOST 2019, LNCS 11862, pp. 73–82, 2019.
https://doi.org/10.1007/978-3-030-32785-9_7

sleep stages using physiological signals by experts. A person with a sleep disorder such as apnea will stop breathing for a while throughout sleep. If it regularly happens, sleep disorders can be risky for health. An early step in diagnosing these disorders is the classification of sleep stages [4,13].

Unfortunately, sleep disorders have been affecting many people around the world in different ways. Whatever the cause of these disorders, the consequences can be severe. The quality of sleep depends on the number and order of these stages. The names of these stages, are Wake, Non-REM1, Non-REM2, Non-REM3, and REM. Detection of any sleep disorder, such as sleep apnea, insomnia, or narcolepsy, requires a correct staging of sleep [2,18].

Classification of sleep stages is also essential for managing the quality of sleep. Sleep studies depend on manual scoring of sleep stages from raw polysomnography signals, which is a tedious visual task. Thus, research efforts to develop an automatic sleep stage scoring based on machine learning techniques have been carried out in the last several years [19]. Convolutional neural networks (CNN) [14] and Long-Short Term Memory Recurrent Neural Networks (LSTM) [15] provide an interesting framework for automated classification of sleep based on raw waveforms. In the past few years, Deep Neural Networks (DNNs) have accomplished tremendous success for time series tasks compared to traditional machine learning systems. Recently, further improvements over DNNs have been obtained with alternative types of neural network architectures. CNNs, LSTMs, and DNNs are individually limited in their modeling capabilities, and we believe that time series data classification can be improved by combining these networks in a unified framework. The classification of time series signals presents many challenges that make it a uniquely difficult problem in machine learning. Many feature extraction approaches in time series face issues related to the non-stationary nature of the signal when the probability distribution does not change over time. Accordingly, features such as mean and variance will not change. Furthermore, the physiological signals are very noisy, being susceptible to factors such as posture, mood, physical movement, and external noise [8]. Lack of comparability between experiments is another issue that can be faced in this field. Unlike in image classification, there are no standard time series datasets used as performance benchmarks [16,20]. Some approaches use models for individuals, while others try to make a general model, training, and testing with samples from all individuals at one time.

In this paper, we propose a method for classifying sleep stages based on the CNN, LSTM and DNN with the help of transfer learning. More specifically, we use a transfer learning technique to train our network model with sleep posture data for 56 subjects (source dataset) and use it for sleep stage classification (target data). The sleep data was obtained from 5 subjects and it was collected in the Boone Hospital Center (BHC) in Columbia, MO, USA under the University of Missouri IRB approval, project number 2008526. The main contribution of this work is developing a new deep model architecture that utilizes CNNs and LSTMs to classify sleep stage data. The CNNs are trained to learn filters that extract time-invariant features from the BCG signals while the LSTMs are trained to encode temporal information such as sleep stage transition rules.

2 Sensors and Datasets

A home monitoring system using a ballistocardiography (BCG) hydraulic sensor has been developed to monitor sleep at home (see Fig. 1). The hydraulic bed sensor has been developed at the Center for Eldercare and Rehabilitation Technology (CERT) at the University of Missouri. A BCG device provides a noninvasive, low-cost, and robust solution for capturing physiological parameters such as heart rate and respiration rate, during sleep [6,10,11]. The BCG sensor has four transducers. Each transducer is composed of a water tube with a pressure sensor placed at one end. The water tube is 50 cm long and 6 cm wide and it is filled with about 0.4 liters of water. The BCG sensor is placed under the mattress, parallel to the body direction, to provide sleeping comfort and not to disturb a person's normal sleep pattern.

The pressure outputs are coupled to a Maxim MAX7401 which is a filtering circuit that consists of a 741 operational amplifier and an 8th-order integrated Bessel filter [3,9]. The four-channel signal is sampled and quantized to 12-bit precision. The BCG signal acquired from the sensor is superimposed over the respiration signal. The four matching transducers are independent; consequently, the data quality collected by those transducers might vary depending on the subject's sleeping position, type of bed (*e.g.*, material, thickness, *etc.*) and the physical characteristics of the subject such as age and body mass index (BMI). In this study, two kinds of datasets have been collected utilizing our bed sensor: sleep posture and sleep stages.

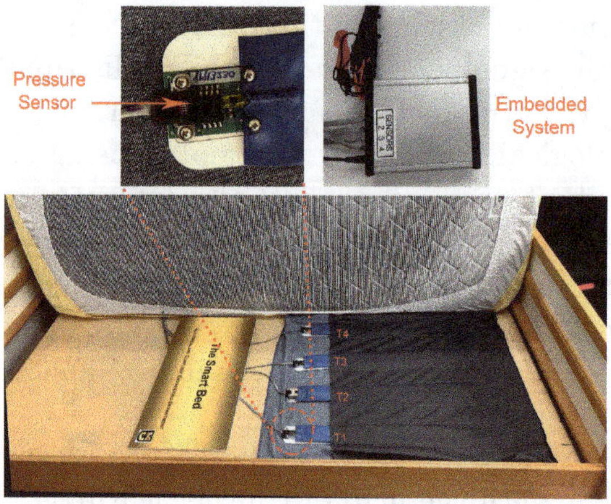

Fig. 1. Hydraulic bed sensor system.

2.1 Posture Dataset

A total of 56 young healthy subjects (About 75.8% of males and 24.2% of females) were asked to lie still in our lab for one minute on each of the four main postures, supine, prone, left lateral and right lateral. The data collection procedure was approved by the University of Missouri Institutional Review Board (MUIRB). The bed sensor produced data sampled at 100 Hz. The subjects age ranged between 18 and 49 years (mean 29.27 years); the weight ranged between 48 and 184 kg (mean 77.40 kg); the height ranged between 100 and 190 cm (mean 173.04 cm); the average body mass index was 27.34 kg/m^2, ranged between 18.1 and 184 kg/m^2.

2.2 Sleep Stage Dataset

Sleep stage data was collected from consenting patients by a sleep-credentialed physician during the regularly scheduled PSG studies conducted in the sleep lab of the Boone Hospital Center (BHC) in Columbia, MO, USA. In addition to the regular PSG equipment, we placed our hydraulic bed sensor under the study bed mattress. The scoring system for staging the sleep was based on the American Academy of Sleep Medicine Manual (AASM) [1], which is the standard for scoring sleep stages and it provides guidelines for associated events during sleep. Sleep stage scoring in 30-second epochs is required for the AASM protocol. A program produced by Natus SleepWorks (Natus Medical Inc., San Carlos, CA, USA) was used in the BHC sleep lab to assist the staff in monitoring a patient throughout the night. SleepWorks not only collects the PSG data but also performs a video recording of the entire night. The technician can view the patient's sleep video if they have any uncertainty about the data. SleepWorks can also provide an initial analysis of the collected data and can generate a report, which helps the sleep physicians who make treatment recommendations.

The BHC sleep lab provides de-identified polysomnography (PSG) data with a sample rate of 256 Hz. PSG is a multiparametric recording method used in sleep labs to monitor physiological changes throughout sleep. It is a consistent tool for diagnosing sleep disorders, and it can similarly help adjust treatment. Moreover, a technician scores each patient's clinical events (e.g., limb movements, respiratory and cardiac events, and arousals) using the American Academy of Sleep Medicine (AASM) standards. PSG is used in this research as ground truth for our bed sensor signals. The hypnogram is one PSG outcome that displays the sleep stages as a function of time (Fig. 2). Sleep stages are annotated in 30-second epochs. From top to bottom, the sleep stages are Wake (W), REM (R), NREM1 (N1), NREM2 (N2), and NREM3 (N3). For the patient shown in Fig. 2, 742 epochs were monitored during sleep. REM sleep happened between epoch 392 and epoch 485, also highlighted in red.

Those who participated in the sleep study are likely to have a sleep disorder. The partial and the complete collapse of the airways are called hypopnea and apnea, respectively. Lack of airflow will affect breathing patterns and then influence sleep stage sequence. The Apnea-hypopnea index (AHI) represents the number of apnea and hypopnea events per hour during sleep. Based on the AASM, the mild sleep apnea AHI is between 5 and 15. In this study, we did not use the data collected from patients with severe apnea symptoms. For this study, we selected five sleep lab patients with a low Apnea-hypopnea index (AHI), so

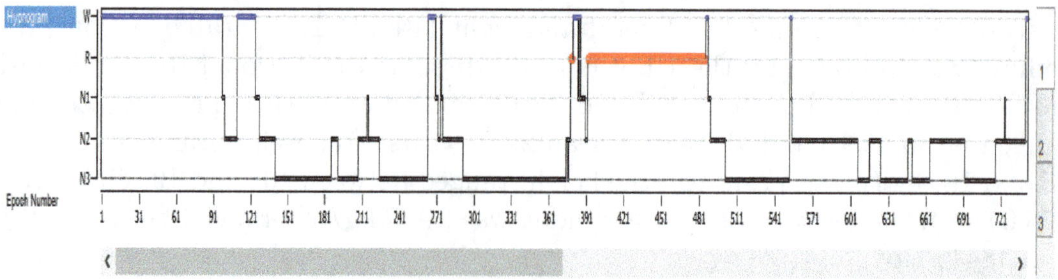

Fig. 2. Hypnogram of an entire night exported from a PSG system. (Color figure online)

that each one has sufficient REM, NREM, and Wake sleep stages during the night.

2.3 Data Preprocessing

We present the preprocessing steps for our data. For the posture data, we truncate the signals utilizing the percentile method [21] to remove any noise that was introduced due to the desynchronization between the time of leaving the bed and stopping recording the signal. After denoising, we normalize the data by utilizing standard score normalization technique. Then we down-sample the data to 100 Hz and shuffle it to prepare it for net training. To account for the varying length of the signals, we divide the preprocessed bed sensor signals into 5-second segments with 80% overlap. Each output label corresponds to a segment of the input. Together the output labels cover the full sequence. The above two algorithms are applied on posture and sleep stage data. Another algorithm is applied for sleep stages only, which are the rules from [22] that help to improve the accuracy about 1%. These rules can be illustrated as followed:

- For three consecutive 30s epochs, if the center one is not the same as the other two and the other two are the same, change the center one to the same stage as the other two epochs. However, the center epoch is not changed if it is an Awake stage.
- For every three 30s epochs, if the sleep stages are all different, the center epoch is removed from the recording. Similarly, this rule does not apply to the Awake stage.
- If REM stages show up in the first hour, these stages are removed from the recording.

3 Architecture Design

We propose a new architecture to classify BCG bed sensor data (see Fig. 3.). The network takes as input the windows of time series of filtered BCG signal and outputs a sequence of label predictions. The basic block is a convolution layer followed by a batch normalization layer [7], Rectified Linear Unit (ReLU) activation layer, and max-pooling layer. We similarly employ shortcut connections to those found in the Residual Network architecture [5] to make the optimization of such a network manageable. The shortcut connections between neural network layers enhance training by permitting by permitting information to propagate well in deep neural networks. The convolutional layers in the first and second blocks have 8 filters; this number of filters doubles in successive blocks until it reaches 32 in the last block. Moreover, the Max Pooling layer helps to subsample the input to become one-fourth of the input sample at the top layer since Max Pool is set to size two. When a block subsamples the input, the corresponding shortcut connections also subsample their input using a Max Pooling operation with the same subsample size. We next pass the CNN block output to LSTM layers with 128 units, which are appropriate for modeling the signal in time.

Regularization techniques are employed in our architecture to reduce overfitting effects during training. Regularization techniques help keep the model from becoming too complex and specific to the training data, thus reducing the tendency to overfit. In this paper, two regularization techniques were used. The first technique was a dropout, which randomly sets the input value to zero with a certain probability [17]. A probability of 0.5 was used in the dropout layer after LSTM, as shown in Fig. 3. The second technique was L2 weight decay, which adds a penalty term into the loss function. L2 regularization is a typical technique used in many optimization methods, in which the squared sum of the weights is applied as a penalty to the optimization function. In essence, this weighs the advantage of increased classification of the training data against model complexity. By preventing the model from becoming too complicated, memorization of the training data is reduced, and a more generalizable model is developed.

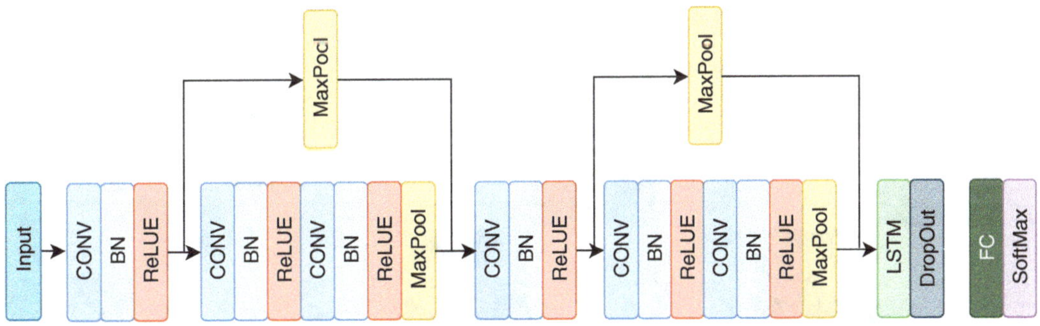

Fig. 3. The proposed architecture of the network

4 Training and Experimental Results

Transfer learning is employed in the experiments of this paper to classify sleep stages. Transfer learning is a technique wherein the knowledge gained from training a model on a dataset (source) can be reused as a starting point, when fine-tuning the model on another dataset (target). This is usually done when the target dataset is not as rich as the source, and hence, a complex deep network would have more trouble training only on the target. Consequently, we split the network model training into two distinct phases. First, our model is trained on the class-balanced training posture dataset of 56 people using five-fold cross-validation. Then, the network weights obtained in the first phase are used as an initialization for the second phase of training on sleep stage data subjects.

We conducted LOSO-CS to fine-tune the sleep stage data. Each time (fold), one patient was left out for testing while the remaining four patients were used to train the DNN networks. In the testing part, we utilize a hierarchical classification scheme for our automatic sleep stage classification system. This structure is composed of two layers. The first layer separates wake from the sleep, which is a union of REM and NREM, in a binary classification problem. Next, all the epochs classified as sleep are fed into the next layer to classify the REM and NREM epochs further. The last block of the architecture, shown in Fig. 3 is used to fine-tune the sleep stage data. In the first phase, the optimal hyperparameters for the model are carefully chosen for a given dataset. The model is at that time fine-tuned on the given dataset with these hyperparameter settings.

Training overnight raw sleep stage data using DNN is time-consuming. Moreover, the ground truth of the posture data is more reliable than the ground truth of sleep stage data. Deep learning models with transfer learning can, however, successfully converge on short-time data (sleep posture data) split across multiple subjects. By training a model over multiple posture data subjects, we obtained an initialization that is then used for fine-tuning our model on the sleep stage data. Based on Williams *et al.* [20], this process is hypothesized to make convergence on an individual's data more likely; it should also provide stronger general filters in the first layers of the neural network.

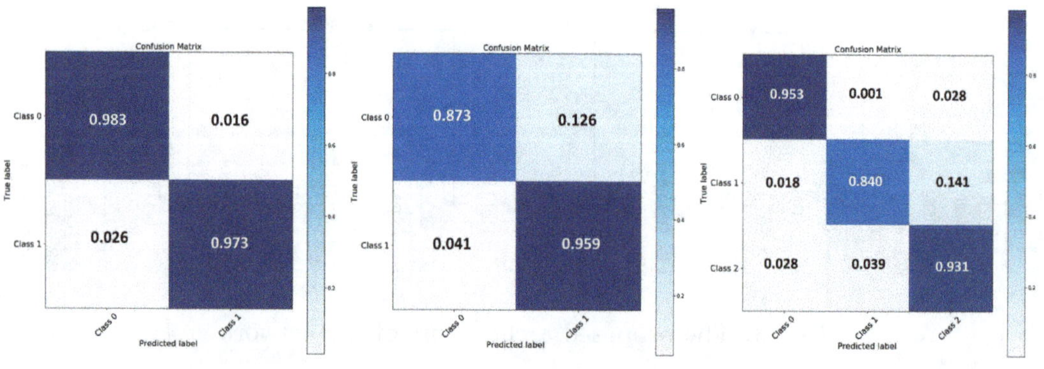

(a) (b) (c)

Fig. 4. Confusion matrix of leave-one-subject-out hierarchical sleep stages classification utilizing posture data knowledge (a) Training phase, Class 0: Wake, Class 1: Sleep (b) Training phase, Class 0: REM, Class 1: NREM (c) Hierarchical testing phase Class 0: Wake, Class 1: REM, Class 2: NREM

Figure 4(a) and (b) show the average of fine-tuned training five-fold LOSO-CS sleep stage data to classify wake from sleep and to classify REM from NREM respectively. Figure 4(c) shows the average of hierarchical fine-tuned testing five-fold LOSO-CS sleep stage data. Clearly, our model was able to classify the sleep stage classes better than the results reported by Yi, *et al.* [23] which were 79.9%, 78.8%, and 88.8% sensitivity for wake, REM, and NREM respectively; the previous work has been done using the same data and the same sensor, but with traditional machine learning algorithms. Table 1 shows the percentage of epochs that are correctly classified for each class Wake, REM, and NREM comparing to the percentage ground truth. The sleep stage agreement was 3.64%, 2.76%, and 8.920% for the Wake, REM, and NREM, respectively. This agreement result is much better than the agreement reported by Rosenberg *et al.* [12], which was 82.6% as the highest agreement averaged for REM and 63.0% as the lowest agreement averaged for NREM. From the results shown in Fig. 4, and Table 4, it is worth to mention the misclassification of the Wake as Sleep in the first layer in the hierarchical method is fed into the second layer, which has a cumulative impact on the second layer classification.

Table 1. Selected five sleep lab patients with a low Apnea-hypopnea index (AHI).

Information			Ground truth			Predicted labels		
Subject	Gender	Age	Wake (%)	REM (%)	REM (%)	Wake (%)	REM (%)	NREM (%)
1	F	69	21.57	14.13	64.29	19.13	11.54	54.32
2	M	66	14.95	16.61	68.44	13.53	13.39	57.14
3	M	68	33.76	12.3	53.94	29.83	10.04	45.03
4	F	66	46.98	7.32	45.7	42.01	6.03	39.07
5	F	62	29.85	19.53	50.63	25.58	15.75	43.74

5 Conclusion

In this paper, we have developed a deep learning-based hierarchical classification method for automatic sleep stage classification based on BCG data. The deep learning model is a state-of-the-art algorithm that consists of a stacked CNN-LSTM model. The proposed model was trained using a transfer learning approach that achieved a significantly improved performance in comparison to similar studies. The results of the leave-one-out cross-validation strategy showed potential in automatically classifying sleep stage epochs. Our sleep monitoring system based on the BCG can indeed provide a more natural way of diagnosing sleep problems, and make long-term sleep monitoring possible. However, to validate our algorithms we used a selected, balanced dataset with a reduced level of noise. We are currently working to increase the robustness of our methodology and validate it for patients with reduced REM and high AHI.

Acknowledgments. We would like to show our gratitude to all staff of Boone Hospital Center Sleep Center at Columbia, Missouri, with a special thanks to Mr. Custer for his patient and helpful advice.

References

1. Berry, R.B., Brooks, R., Gamaldo, C.E., Harding, S.M., Marcus, C.L., Vaughn, B.V., et al.: The AASM manual for the scoring of sleep and associated events. Rules, Terminology and Technical Specifications. American Academy of Sleep Medicine, Darien, Illinois, vol. 176 (2012)
2. Dursun, M., Gunes, S., Ozsen, S., Yosunkaya, S.: Comparison of artificial immune clustering with fuzzy c-means clustering in the sleep stage classification problem. In: 2012 International Symposium on Innovations in Intelligent Systems and Applications, pp. 1–4. IEEE (2012)
3. Gargees, R., Keller, J., Popescu, M.: Early illness recognition in older adults using transfer learning. In: 2017 IEEE International Conference on Bioinformatics and Biomedicine (BIBM), pp. 1012–1016. IEEE (2017)
4. Giri, E.P., Arymurthy, A.M., Fanany, M.I., Wijaya, S.K.: Sleep stages classification using shallow classifiers. In: 2015 International Conference on Advanced Computer Science and Information Systems (ICACSIS), pp. 297–301. IEEE (2015)
5. He, K., Zhang, X., Ren, S., Sun, J.: Deep residual learning for image recognition. In: Proceedings of the IEEE Conference on Computer Vision and Pattern Recognition, pp. 770–778 (2016)
6. Heise, D., Rosales, L., Sheahen, M., Su, B.Y., Skubic, M.: Non-invasive measurement of heartbeat with a hydraulic bed sensor progress, challenges, and opportunities. In: 2013 IEEE International Instrumentation and Measurement Technology Conference (I2MTC), pp. 397–402. IEEE (2013)
7. Ioffe, S., Szegedy, C.: Batch normalization: accelerating deep network training by reducing internal covariate shift. In: Proceedings of the 32nd International Conference on Machine Learning, vol. 37, pp. 448–456 (2015)
8. Kevric, J., Subasi, A.: Comparison of signal decomposition methods in classification of EEG signals for motor-imagery BCI system. Biomed. Signal Process. Control **31**, 398–406 (2017)
9. Lydon, K., et al.: Robust heartbeat detection from in-home ballistocardiogram signals of older adults using a bed sensor. In: 2015 37th Annual International Conference of the IEEE Engineering in Medicine and Biology Society (EMBC), pp. 7175–7179. IEEE (2015)
10. Rosales, L., Skubic, M., Heise, D., Devaney, M.J., Schaumburg, M.: Heartbeat detection from a hydraulic bed sensor using a clustering approach. In: 2012 Annual International Conference of the IEEE Engineering in Medicine and Biology Society, pp. 2383–2387. IEEE (2012)
11. Rosales, L., Su, B.Y., Skubic, M., Ho, K.: Heart rate monitoring using hydraulic bed sensor ballistocardiogram 1. J. Ambient. Intell. Smart Environ. **9**(2), 193–207 (2017)
12. Rosenberg, R.S., Van Hout, S.: The american academy of sleep medicine interscorer reliability program: sleep stage scoring. J. Clin. Sleep Med. **9**(01), 81–87 (2013)
13. Sadek, I., Biswas, J., Abdulrazak, B.: Ballistocardiogram signal processing: a review. Health Inf. Sci. Syst. **7**(1), 10 (2019)

14. Sainath, T.N., Vinyals, O., Senior, A., Sak, H.: Convolutional, long short-term memory, fully connected deep neural networks. In: 2015 IEEE International Conference on Acoustics, Speech and Signal Processing (ICASSP), pp. 4580–4584. IEEE (2015)
15. Sak, H., Senior, A., Beaufays, F.: Long short-term memory recurrent neural network architectures for large scale acoustic modeling. In: Fifteenth Annual Conference of the International Speech Communication Association (2014)
16. Schmidt, S., Eich, G., Hanquinet, S., Tschäppeler, H., Waibel, P., Gudinchet, F.: Extra-osseous involvement of langerhans' cell histiocytosis in children. Pediatr. Radiol. **34**(4), 313–321 (2004)
17. Srivastava, N., Hinton, G., Krizhevsky, A., Sutskever, I., Salakhutdinov, R.: Dropout: a simple way to prevent neural networks from overfitting. J. Mach. Learn. Res. **15**(1), 1929–1958 (2014)
18. Tuominen, J., Peltola, K., Saaresranta, T., Valli, K.: Sleep parameter assessment accuracy of a consumer home sleep monitoring ballistocardiograph beddit sleep tracker: a validation study. J. Clin. Sleep Med. **15**(03), 483–487 (2019)
19. Vilamala, A., Madsen, K.H., Hansen, L.K.: Deep convolutional neural networks for interpretable analysis of eeg sleep stage scoring. In: 2017 IEEE 27th International Workshop on Machine Learning for Signal Processing (MLSP), pp. 1–6. IEEE (2017)
20. Williams, J.M.: Deep learning and transfer learning in the classification of EEG signals (2017)
21. Wu, M.H., Chang, E.J., Chu, T.H.: Personalizing a generic ECG heartbeat classification for arrhythmia detection: a deep learning approach. In: 2018 IEEE Conference on Multimedia Information Processing and Retrieval (MIPR). IEEE (2018)
22. Yang, J., Keller, J.M., Popescu, M., Skubic, M.: Sleep stage recognition using respiration signal. In: 2016 38th Annual International Conference of the IEEE Engineering in Medicine and Biology Society (EMBC), pp. 2843–2846. IEEE (2016)
23. Yi, R., Enayati, M., Keller, J., Popescu, M., Skubic, M.: Non-invasive in-home sleep stage classification using a ballistocardiography bed sensor. In: 2019 IEEE International Conference on Bioinformatics and Biomedicine (BIBM). IEEE (2019)

Biomedical and Health Informatics

A Convolutional Gated Recurrent Neural Network for Epileptic Seizure Prediction

Abir Affes[1(✉)], Afef Mdhaffar[1,2], Chahnez Triki[3], Mohamed Jmaiel[1,2], and Bernd Freisleben[4]

[1] University of Sfax, ENIS, ReDCAD Laboratory, B.P. 1173, Sfax, Tunisia
abir.affes@stud.enis.tn

[2] Digital Research Center of Sfax, 3021 Sfax, Tunisia
{afef.mdhaffar,mohamed.jmaiel}@redcad.org

[3] Department of Child Neurology, Hospital Hedi Chaker, 3029 Sfax, Tunisia
chahnezct@gmail.com

[4] Department of Mathematics and Computer Science, Philipps-Universität Marburg, Marburg, Germany
freisleb@informatik.uni-marburg.de

Abstract. In this paper, we present a convolutional gated recurrent neural network (CGRNN) to predict epileptic seizures based on features extracted from EEG data that represent the temporal aspect and the frequency aspect of the signal. Using a dataset collected in the Children's Hospital of Boston, CGRNN can predict epileptic seizures between 35 min and 5 min in advance. Our experimental results indicate that the performance of CGRNN varies between patients. We achieve an average sensitivity of 89% and a mean accuracy of 75.6% for the patients in the data set, with a mean False Positive Rate (FPR) of 1.6 per hour.

Keywords: Epilepsy · Elecroencephalogram · Spectrogram · STFT · CNN · GRU · Seizure prediction

1 Introduction

Epilepsy is a complex neurological disorder, manifested by unexpected and unprovoked seizures due to abnormally excessive or synchronous neuronal activity in the brain. There are various forms of epileptic seizures, and the symptoms differ from one person to another. Epileptic seizures can be accompanied with a loss of consciousness that leads to serious injuries with residual disabilities and even to death. Also, people with epilepsy are socially discriminated due to a widespread lack of knowledge, negative public attitudes, and misconceptions about the disease that reduce their self-esteem.

Therefore, it is crucial to predict epileptic seizures before they happen. This is a challenging problem attracting researchers from several disciplines. Existing approaches [3,8,10–12,17,19–21,23] can be divided into two categories. The first

J. Pagán et al. (Eds.): ICOST 2019, LNCS 11862, pp. 85–96, 2019.
https://doi.org/10.1007/978-3-030-32785-9_8

category [3,6,8,16,19,20,23] includes seizure detection approaches that are usually used by health professionals to improve diagnostic capabilities. In fact, they do not allow us to prevent the consequences of epileptic seizures. The second category [10–12,17,21] focuses on seizure prediction to improve a patient's quality of life. One approach [17] is based on a combination of a convolutional neural network (CNN) and a long short-term memory network (LSTM). It achieves promising results. Other approaches are essentially based on the use of a single type of deep learning network, such as a CNN or a recurrent neural network (RNN) variant (e.g., RNN vanilla, LSTM, gated recurrent unit (GRU)). GRU networks have shown good results in temporal sequence modeling and especially in the detection of different seizure phases [12,19,22].

In this paper, we present a novel convolutional gated recurrent neural network (CGRNN) to predict epileptic seizures. It is a combination of CNN and GRU. The proposed approach is a patient-specific predictor that allows us to predict epileptic seizures on the basis of the electrical activity of the brain (EEG signals). Our CGRNN takes into consideration the temporal aspect as well as the frequency aspect of the EEG signal. Using a data set collected in the Children's Hospital of Boston, CGRNN can predict epileptic seizures between 35 min and 5 min in advance. Our experimental results indicate that the performance of CGRNN varies between patients. We achieve an average sensitivity of 89% and a mean accuracy of 75.6% for the 13 patients in the data set, with a FPR ranging from 0 to 6.57 per hour.

The paper is organized as follows. Section 2 explains basic concepts of epilepsy disorder. Related work is discussed in Sect. 3. In Sect. 4, we present our proposed approach. Section 5 discusses the experimental setup and our obtained results. Section 6 concludes the paper and outlines areas for future research.

2 Background

2.1 Epilepsy

Epilepsy is a chronic neurological disease that affects people of all ages and has a worldwide distribution [4]. It affects approximately 65 million people in the world [14] and is considered as the fourth most common neurological disease [4]. The cardinal manifestations of epilepsy are epileptic seizures, i.e., recurrent paroxysmal events characterized by stereotyped behavioral alterations reflecting the neural mechanisms involved in the epileptic process [5]. The recurrence of seizures and their unpredictability cause major concerns for patients and their family and have physical and psychological consequences. Therefore, epilepsy is a burdensome neurological disorder. Despite the growing number of antiepileptic drugs, almost 30% of epilepsy cases are intractable with uncontrolled epileptic seizures. These events have several phases that may not be visible or easily distinguishable from each other [4]:

- **The pre-ictal phase** refers to the period just before a seizure [15].
- **The ictal phase** lasts from the initial symptoms of the seizure (including an aura) until the end of the abnormal activity.
- **The post-ictal phase** occurs when the seizure ends. It is the period of recovering from the seizure's symptoms [4].
- **The inter-ictal phase** is the normal state for people with epilepsy (99% of their life). In this phase, these persons have abnormal waveforms in EEG records that are not associated with seizure symptoms [15].

2.2 EEG

Epileptic seizures are related to the electrical activity of the brain. Therefore, electroencephalography (EEG) is the most effective way to determine the epileptogenic cortex. EEG [2] is an electrophysiological exploration method to measure the electrical activity of the brain using electrodes fixed on the scalp. Since EEG can detect any abnormal brain activity, it is mainly used for epilepsy diagnosis and seizure analysis. Figure 1 shows the EEG signal of a patient that has experienced a seizure. It is evident that a seizure can be visually distinguished from a normal brain signal.

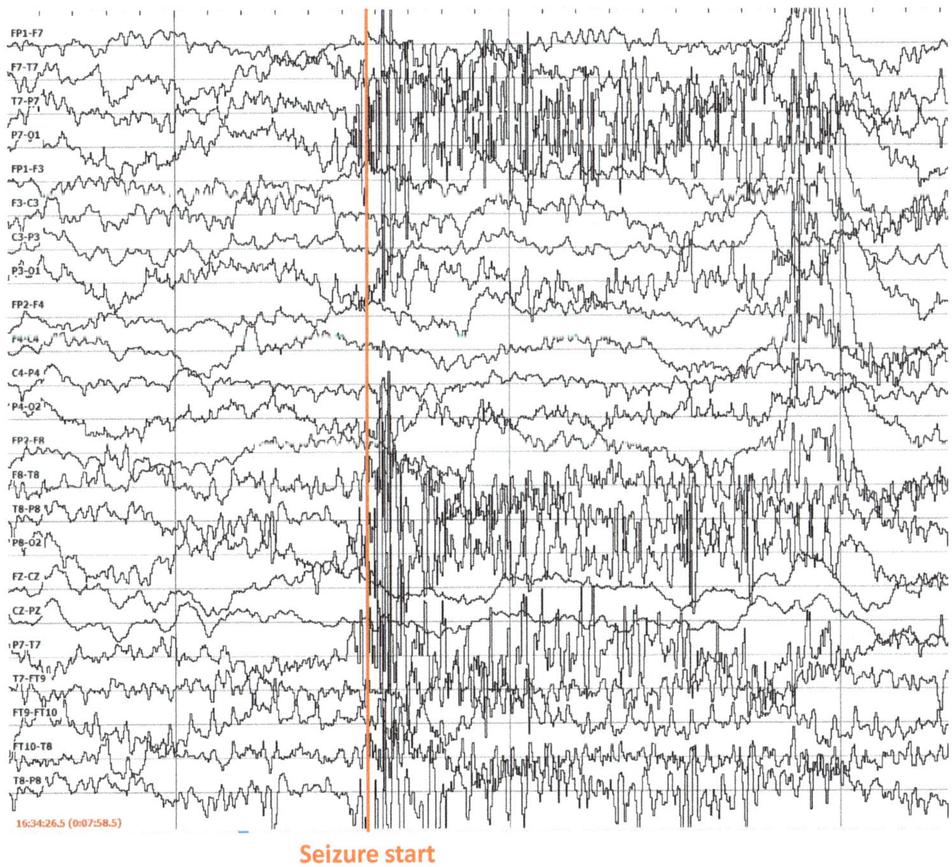

Fig. 1. Exemple of normal and seizure EEG recordings

3 Related Work

In this section, different approaches related to seizure detection and prediction are presented.

3.1 Epileptic Seizure Detection

Thodoroff et al. [20] proposed patient-specific and cross-patient epileptic seizure detectors. Both are based on features extracted from spatial, temporal, and frequency information of the EEG recordings. EEG data was first transformed into an image representation that integrates spatial domain knowledge (i.e., electrode's positions). Then, the data was fed into a recurrent convolutional neural network that combines CNN and LSTM networks.

The method presented by Yuan et al. [23] detects epileptic seizure onsets. It combines features extracted from handcrafted engineering methods and deep learning approaches. The authors used short-time Fourier transforms (STFT) for image based representation and a stacked sparse denoising autoencoders (SSDA) for data classification. An SSDA-based channel selection procedure was adopted to reduce the dimension of features by considering the correlation of EEG channels.

Talathi [19] proposed a deep learning framework for epileptic seizure detection. He developed a RNN with GRU hidden units for the classification task. Raw input data was directly used after a minimal pre-processing step. The model achieved 99.6% accuracy on the validation data set and can detect about 98% of epileptic seizures within the first 5 s of the event.

Golmohammadi et al. [8] presented two RNN variants for seizure detection: LSTM and GRU. Both recurrent variants are based on handcrafted features, and each of them is integrated into a CNN. The experiments revealed that the convolutional LSTM network has slightly better results than the convolutional GRU network. In fact, both networks achieved 30% sensitivity, but with 6 false alarms per day (FA/24h) for LSTM and 21 FA/24h for GRU.

Choi et al. [3] proposed a multi-scale 3D-CNN with a bidirectional GRU model for cross-patient seizure detection. The authors used STFT to get spectral and temporal features from EEG signals. They also considered spatial features extracted from electrode positions. The proposed model [3] was evaluated on two data sets: the Boston Children's Hospital MIT scalp EEG data set (CHB-MIT) and the Seoul National University Hospital (SNUH) Scalp EEG data set. The approach achieved a sensitivity of 89% with a FPR of 0.5/h on the first database and 89% sensitivity with FPR of 0.6/h on SNUH data.

3.2 Epileptic Seizure Prediction

Truong et al. [21] applied a CNN to three databases: (1) the Freiburg Hospital intra-cranial EEG (iEEG) data set, (2) the CHB-MIT data set, and (3) the American Epilepsy Society (AES) Seizure Prediction Challenge data set. They considered only data from 13 patients over 24 cases when considering the CHB-MIT database. These patients have less than 10 seizures per day and at least 3 h of inter-ictal signals. STFT has been applied on raw data to build spectrograms. The proposed model is patient-oriented. It achieved a sensitivity of 81.4%, 81.2%, and 75% and a FPR of 0.06/h, 0.16/h, and 0.21/h, for the 3 data sets mentioned above, respectively.

In the context of the AES Seizure Prediction Challenge organised by Kaggle, Korshunova [11] implemented two models for seizure prediction. She proposed a CNN architecture and also explored a classifier based on logistic regression and linear discriminant analysis. The iEEG data used in the competition was recorded from 5 dogs and 2 humans. It was transformed into spectrograms by applying a discrete Fourier transform (DFT) before being fed to the models.

Larmuseau [12] compared three RNNs for seizure prediction: vanilla RNN, GRU, and LSTM. iEEG data of four subjects was used. He concluded that GRU layers outperform other networks and are also faster than LSTM. RNNs are effective in analyzing the sequential iEEG data, but the results were not better than those of other methods used from the state of the art.

Hosseini et al. [10] proposed a cloud-based approach for real-time seizure prediction. This work followed three main steps: (1) dimensionality reduction to reduce algorithmic computational complexity and get faster response, (2) a stacked autoencoder as a deep learning approach for automatic feature extraction and classification, and (3) a cloud computing system for real-time analysis of iEEG signals. The authors achieved 94% of accuracy and a FPR of 0.05/h.

Shahbazi and Aghajan [17] proposed an approach based on CNN-LSTM and STFT for raw data transformation. A seizure is anticipated only if at least 8 of 10 successive samples are detected as pre-ictal signals. This model was evaluated on the CHB-MIT data set. It achieved an average sensitivity of 98.21% with a FPR of 0.13/h and a mean 44.74 min as the prediction time.

Seizures are events demarcated in time with several successive phases. During this event, EEG segments are correlated. Therefore, the recurrent aspect in a neural network was shown to be important in seizure prediction. In fact, RNNs are usually used when output at time t depends on the previous one. Regarding different proposed networks [3,8,12,19], GRU was demonstrated to be efficient for EEG data analysis.

4 CGRNN

To predict epileptic seizures on the basis of EEG signals in a patient-oriented manner, we propose a deep learning model based on the combination of CNN and GRU networks, called convolutional gated recurrent neural network (CGRNN). As shown in Fig. 2, our approach follows two steps: data preparation and data analysis.

The data preparation step consists of refining the data and transforming raw EEG into spectrograms, which allows us to capture spectral and temporal patterns representing a seizure. The data analysis step includes the deep learning

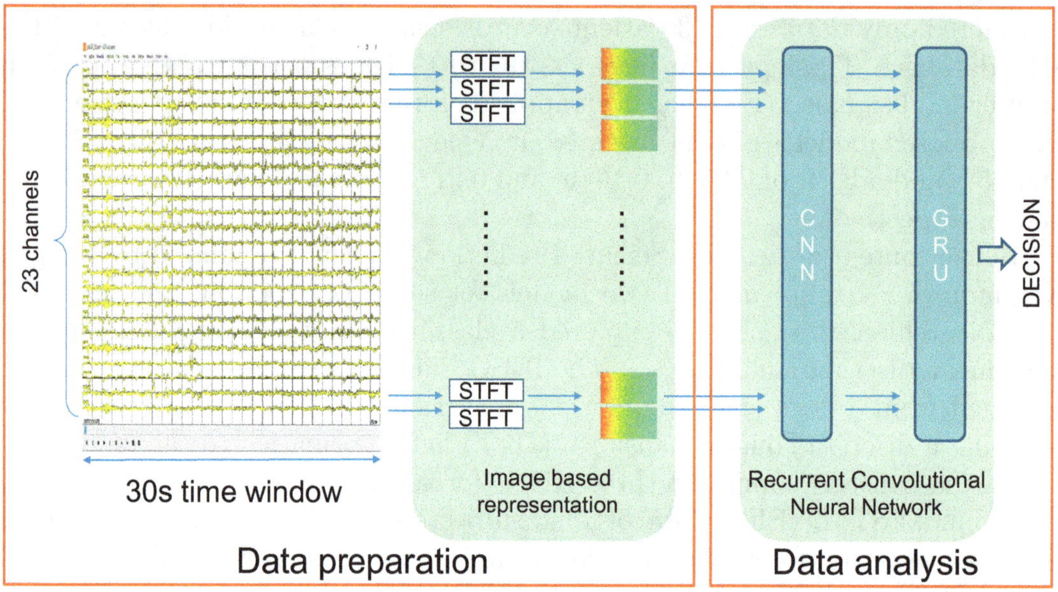

Fig. 2. The proposed approach

model composed of a CNN and a GRU. The convolutional network plays the role of a feature extractor. It takes as input the image-based representation of EEG and reduces the image into an easier form to process, without losing essential features. The GRU learns from the extracted features the epileptic seizure patterns to make the final decision.

4.1 Data Preparation

Epileptic seizure prediction can be modeled as a binary classification problem. Therefore, after introducing the used data set (CHB-MIT Scalp EEG database), we select the two appropriate classes. We also exclude the unused signals from our data set before data transformation.

Database: The CHB-MIT Scalp EEG database is used in this paper. It was collected by an MIT team in partnership with the pediatric hospital in Boston and can be downloaded from the Physionet platform [7]. The data set is composed of approximately 1136 h of brain activity recordings and 198 seizures. It includes many types of seizures and was collected from both genders with different ages. One fifth of the data was recorded from men aged from 3 to 22 years. The remaining data concerns females aged from 1.5 to 19 years [18]. In a few records, other non-EEG signals were also recorded, such as electrocardiogram (ECG) or vagal nerve stimulus (VNS). Furthermore, we used electrode positions and nomenclature different from the International 10–20 system in some records. Consequently, one step to do was data refitting to get the same channels for all files. The data sampling rate is 256 samples per second [7].

Data Refinement: Litt et al. [13] demonstrate that complex epileptiform discharges are common 7 h before seizures and an activity similar to a seizure becomes more frequent 2 h before the actual onset. Also, the accumulated energy increases during the 50 min before the ictal state [13]. Most of the existing studies consider the pre-ictal phase as one hour before a seizure begins. In our work, we consider the inter-ictal and the pre-ictal signals, shown in Fig. 3, as the two most relevant categories to classify. The inter-ictal signal is defined as the period between 1 h after the end of a seizure and 1 h before the onset of the next one. Based on Truong et al. [21], the pre-ictal signal is extracted from 35 min to 5 min before the epileptic seizure, which enables us to take the necessary precautions. Furthermore, considering that seizures can happen very close to each other, we are interested in predicting the leading crisis, which is about less than 30 min away from the next one.

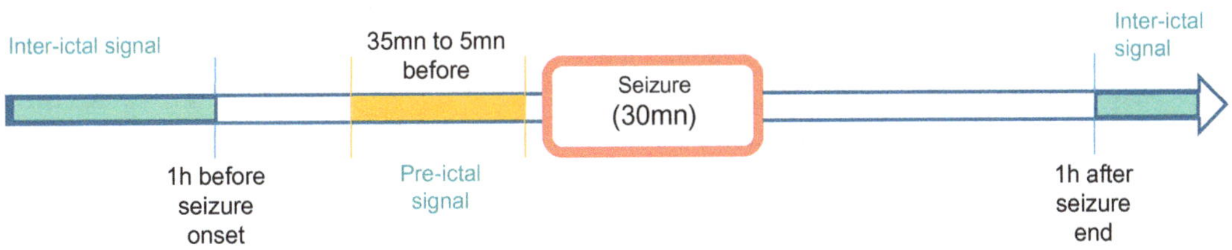

Fig. 3. Inter-ictal and pre-ictal signals as the two classification categories

After considering the two categories, we get different ratios between pre-ictal and inter-ictal data for every patient due to the number of recorded seizures. Considering that seizures are rare events, the number of inter-ictal recordings is higher than the number of pre-ictal ones. Consequently, we get an unbalanced data set for all cases. Most machine learning algorithms assume that data from different classes is equally distributed. If we have unbalanced data, we get biased classifiers towards classes with more instances over other classes [9]. Therefore, to deal with this issue, we use an overlapped sampling technique with the training data to get more pre-ictal segments. For every patient, we calculate the ratio between the pre-ictal and inter-ictal hours. Then, we slide a 30 s window by the calculated factor along the time axis over all the pre-ictal records.

Raw Data Transformation: Abnormal brain activity is detected on the basis of the cerebral rhythms in the EEG recordings. These are classified according to their frequency range hence the importance of the frequency aspect with the temporal aspect in EEG data analysis. Time-frequency features are usually studied using the signal spectrogram [1]. This is a tool used to visualize the change in the frequency spectrum of a signal over time. It represents in one two-dimensional diagram three parameters. The time and frequency are the two axes of the graph. The third parameter indicates the amplitude of a particular frequency at a particular time and is distinguished by the color of each point in

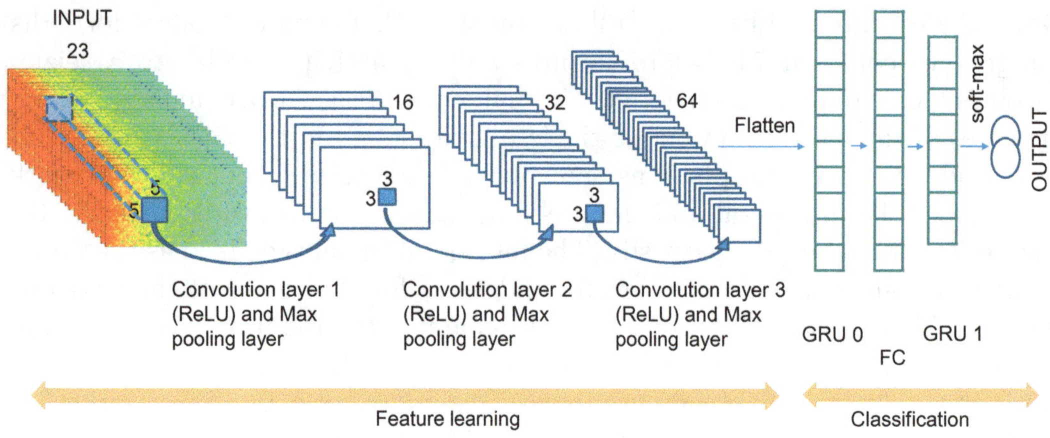

Fig. 4. The CGRNN architecture

the image. Spectrograms are generated using the Fourier transform. In this work, after excluding useless signals, we apply STFT to translate raw EEG signals into a two-dimensional matrix with time and frequency axes, which is a suitable input for a CNN. STFT is a common method for time-frequency analysis. EEG records are contaminated by a 60 Hz power line noise in the American continent. Therefore, a bandpass filter for frequency ranges of 57–63 Hz and 117–123 Hz is used. The 0 Hz component is also excluded.

4.2 Data Analysis

We use our CGRNN model illustrated in Fig. 4 for data analysis. The first part of the model is a CNN with 3 convolution blocks. Each block includes a convolution layer with a rectified linear unit activation (ReLU). Max pooling layers are used to reduce the number of calculations and prevent the model from overfitting during the training. We also use batch normalization between layers to ensure that the input distribution is the same for each layer no matter the changes in the previous one. The data is then flattened and reshaped to be piped into a first gated recurrent layer with 256 units. The next fully connected layer uses a sigmoid activation function. It is followed by a second gated recurrent layer with 100 units. The output of this layer is fed into the softmax layer to predict the class probabilities of the input data. The gated recurrent layer has a dropout rate of 0.5 to reduce overfitting.

5 Experimental Evaluation

The proposed CGRNN was implemented in Python 3.5 using Tensorflow 1.9.0 backend and Keras 2.2. Models for different patients were configured to run on an NVIDIA GeForce GTX 1080 GPU.

We used 25% of the data for validation and 75% for training. Categorical cross-entropy was adopted as our loss function and the ADAM optimization

Table 1. Seizure prediction results obtained with CHB-MIT. CNN is our implementation of the approach of Truong et al. [21]. Sen: percentage of sensitivity, FPR: false positive rate per hour, Acc: percentage of accuracy.

Patient	[21]		CNN		CGRNN		
	Sen	FPR	Sen	FPR	Acc	Sen	FPR
Patient 1	85.7	0.24	87.5	0	94.46	87.59	0
Patient 2	33.3	0	100	0	83.61	100	0
Patient 3	100	0.18	100	0.66	87.72	82.26	0
Patient 5	80 ± 20	0.19 ± 0.03	18.6	0	57.53	92.85	3.6
Patient 9	50	0.12 ± 0.12	100	2.5	73.57	79.13	0
Patient 10	33.3	0.00	53.7	7.428	48.57	59.33	6.57
Patient 13	80	0.14	46.6	2.5	51.67	100	5.5
Patient 14	80	0.40	93.3	9.0	60.79	92.21	3.33
Patient 18	100	0.28 ± 0.02	91.6	3.5	71.83	100	0.5
Patient 19	100	0.00	100	10.0	97.23	100	0
Patient 20	100	0.25 ± 0.05	24.8	0	76.47	96.36	1.33
Patient 21	100	0.23 ± 0.09	84.3	0	87.11	83.98	0
Patient 23	100	0.33	100	0	92.45	84.26	0
Average	80.01	0.18	76.95	2.73	75.6	89.07	1.6

algorithm was used for model optimization. It is an extension of stochastic gradient descent.

To test our model, we consider that one signal clip is preceding a seizure only if at least 8 of 10 successive samples of this sequence are detected as pre-ictal. The calculated metrics are accuracy, sensitivity, and FPR. We also implemented a CNN model with the same architecture as proposed by Truong et al. [21]. This model considers the same defined classes in [21]: the inter-ictal signal which is about 4 h before and after a seizure and the pre-ictal signal as the period from 35 min to 5 min before the ictal phase. Thus, both implemented CGRNN and CNN models can predict epileptic seizures between 35 min and 5 min in advance.

For the seizure prediction task, the most crucial part is to determine all of the positive cases. Missing a patient who has a seizure but goes undetected will be critical. Furthermore, the less we get false alarms, the better will be the solution. Therefore, our model evaluation is mainly based on sensitivity and also FPR values.

The obtained results on the 13 patients considered by Truong et al. [21] are shown in Table 1. The differences between metrics presented by Truong et al. [21] and the results obtained with the implemented CNN is due to data pre-processing step and also to the random initialization of weights in neural networks.

The model performance varies from one patient to another. In fact, for the patients 1, 2, 10, 18 and 19, our CGRNN achieves better classification results. For the three patients 3, 13, and 20, we obtain better sensitivity values than the CNN approach, but we get a higher FPR. Our model achieves comparable results for the patients 14 and 21 and lower sensitivity values for the patients 3, 9, and 23. An average of 75.6% accuracy and an average sensitivity of 89% are reached for the 13 patients. The FPR ranges between 0 and 6.57 per hour, with a mean FPR of 1.6 per hour. The differences in the performance for each patient are related to the characteristics of the available data, namely the number of recorded seizures and the time periods between the events.

6 Conclusion

We presented a novel convolutional gated recurrent neural network (CGRNN) to predict epileptic seizures. The proposed approach is a patient-specific predictor that allows us to predict epileptic seizures on the basis of EEG signals, taking into account the temporal aspect as well as the signal frequency content. The publicly available data set CHB-MIT was used in our experimental evaluation. Our CGRNN can predict epileptic seizures between 35 min and 5 min in advance and achieved an average sensitivity of 89% and a mean accuracy of 75.6% for the 13 patients in the data set, with a mean FPR of 1.6 per hour. This demonstrates the efficiency of the proposed approach in the epileptic seizure prediction task.

There are several areas for future work. First, we want to investigate whether techniques of weight initialization and regularization of the implemented neural network have effects on the evaluation metrics, such as zero and He initializations. Furthermore, we plan to train the model on large-scale data sets to achieve higher performance, such as the Freiburg Hospital iEEG data set and the TUH EEG Seizure Corpus. Also, we plan to build a real database by recording EEG signals from the university hospital of Sfax, Tunisia. Finally, we also intend to investigate channel selection techniques and design neural architectures based on attention mechanisms.

Acknowledgements. This work is supported by the German Academic Exchange Service (DAAD) (Transformation Partnership: Theralytics Project).

References

1. Bashivan, P., Rish, I., Yeasin, M., Codella, N.: Learning representations from EEG with deep recurrent-convolutional neural networks. In: 4th International Conference on Learning Representations, ICLR 2016, San Juan, Puerto Rico, 2–4 May 2016, Conference Track Proceedings (2016). http://arxiv.org/abs/1511.06448
2. Blinowska, K., Durka, P.: Electroencephalography (EEG). American Cancer Society (2006). https://doi.org/10.1002/9780471740360.ebs0418. https://onlinelibrary.wiley.com/doi/abs/10.1002/9780471740360.ebs0418

3. Choi, G., et al.: A novel multi-scale 3D CNN with deep neural network for epileptic seizure detection. In: 2019 IEEE International Conference on Consumer Electronics (ICCE), pp. 1–2, January 2019. https://doi.org/10.1109/ICCE.2019.8661969
4. Fisher, R.S., et al.: Epileptic seizures and epilepsy: definitions proposed by the international league against epilepsy (ILAE) and the international bureau for epilepsy (IBE). Epilepsia **46**(4), 470–472 (2005). https://doi.org/10.1111/j.0013-9580.2005.66104.x. https://onlinelibrary.wiley.com/doi/abs/10.1111/j.0013-9580.2005.66104.x
5. Fisher, R.S., et al.: Operational classification of seizure types by the international league against epilepsy: Position paper of the ilae commission for classification and terminology. Epilepsia **58**(4), 522–530 (2017). https://doi.org/10.1111/epi.13670. https://onlinelibrary.wiley.com/doi/abs/10.1111/epi.13670
6. Fukumori, K., Thu Nguyen, H.T., Yoshida, N., Tanaka, T.: Fully data-driven convolutional filters with deep learning models for epileptic spike detection. In: ICASSP 2019–2019 IEEE International Conference on Acoustics, Speech and Signal Processing (ICASSP). pp. 2772–2776, May 2019. https://doi.org/10.1109/ICASSP.2019.8682196
7. Goldberger, A., et al.: Physiobank, physiotoolkit, and physionet : components of a new research resource for complex physiologic signals. Circulation **101**, E215–E220 (2000). https://doi.org/10.1161/01.CIR.101.23.e215
8. Golmohammadi, M., et al.: Gated recurrent networks for seizure detection. In: 2017 IEEE Signal Processing in Medicine and Biology Symposium (SPMB), pp. 1–5, December 2017. https://doi.org/10.1109/SPMB.2017.8257020
9. Guo, X., Yin, Y., Dong, C., Yang, G., Zhou, G.: On the class imbalance problem. In: 2008 Fourth International Conference on Natural Computation. vol. 4, pp. 192–201, October 2008. https://doi.org/10.1109/ICNC.2008.871
10. Hosseini, M., Soltanian-Zadeh, H., Elisevich, K., Pompili, D.: Cloud-based deep learning of big EEG data for epileptic seizure prediction. In: 2016 IEEE Global Conference on Signal and Information Processing (GlobalSIP), pp. 1151–1155, December 2016. https://doi.org/10.1109/GlobalSIP.2016.7906022
11. Korshunova, I.: Epileptic Seizure Prediction using Deep Learning. Master's thesis, Universiteit Gent, Belgique (2014–2015)
12. Larmuseau, M.: Epileptic Seizure Prediction using Deep Learning. Master's thesis, Universiteit Gent, Belgique (2015–2016)
13. Litt, B., et al.: Epileptic seizures may begin hours in advance of clinical onset. Neuron **30**, 51–64 (2001). https://doi.org/10.1016/S0896-6273(01)00262-8
14. Moshe, S., Perucca, E., Ryvlin, P., Tomson, T.: Epilepsy: new advances. Lancet **385**, 884–898 (2014). https://doi.org/10.1016/S0140-6736(14)60456-6
15. Mula, M., Monaco, F.: Ictal and peri-ictal psychopathology. Behav. Neurol. **24**, 21–25 (2011). https://doi.org/10.3233/BEN-2011-0314
16. Roy, S., Kiral-Kornek, I., Harrer, S.: ChronoNet: a deep recurrent neural network for abnormal EEG identification. arXiv e-prints arXiv:1802.00308, January 2018
17. Shahbazi, M., Aghajan, H.: A generalizable model for seizure prediction based on deep learning using CNN-LSTM architecture, pp. 469–473 (2018). https://doi.org/10.1109/GlobalSIP.2018.8646505
18. Shoeb, A.H., Guttag, J.V.: Application of machine learning to epileptic seizure detection. In: Proceedings of the 27th International Conference on Machine Learning (ICML 2010), Haifa, Israel, 21–24 June 2010, pp. 975–982 (2010). https://icml.cc/Conferences/2010/papers/493.pdf
19. Talathi, S.S.: Deep recurrent neural networks for seizure detection and early seizure detection systems. arXiv e-prints arXiv:1706.03283, June 2017

20. Thodoroff, P., Pineau, J., Lim, A.: Learning robust features using deep learning for automatic seizure detection. In: Doshi-Velez, F., Fackler, J., Kale, D.C., Wallace, B.C., Wiens, J. (eds.) Proceedings of the 1st Machine Learning in Health Care, MLHC 2016, JMLR Workshop and Conference Proceedings, Los Angeles, CA, USA, 19–20 August 2016, vol. 56, pp. 178–190. JMLR.org (2016). http://proceedings.mlr.press/v56/Thodoroff16.html
21. Truong, N.D., et al.: Convolutional neural networks for seizure prediction using intracranial and scalp electroencephalogram. Neural Netw. **105**, 104–111 (2018). https://doi.org/10.1016/j.neunet.2018.04.018. http://www.sciencedirect.com/science/article/pii/S0893608018301485
22. Xu, Y., Kong, Q., Huang, Q., Wang, W., Plumbley, M.: Convolutional gated recurrent neural network incorporating spatial features for audio tagging (2017). https://doi.org/10.1109/IJCNN.2017.7966291
23. Yuan, Y., Xun, G., Jia, K., Zhang, A.: A multi-view deep learning method for epileptic seizure detection using short-time Fourier transform. In: Proceedings of the 8th ACM International Conference on Bioinformatics, Computational Biology, and Health Informatics, ACM-BCB 2017, pp. 213–222. ACM, New York (2017). https://doi.org/10.1145/3107411.3107419. http://doi.acm.org/10.1145/3107411.3107419

Ubiquitous Healthcare Systems and Medical Rules in COPD Domain

Hicham Ajami[1(✉)], Hamid Mcheick[1], and Karam Mustapha[2]

[1] Department of Computer Sciences and Mathematics, University of Québec at Chicoutimi, Chicoutimi, QC G7H 2B1, Canada
{hicham.ajamil,Hamid_mcheick}@uqac.ca

[2] Polytechnic of Montreal, Station Centre-Ville, Montreal H3C 3A7, Canada
Karam.mustapha@gmail.com

Abstract. Chronic Obstructive Pulmonary Disease (COPD) is a severe lung illness that causes a progressive deterioration in the function and structure of the respiratory system. Recently, COPD became the fifth cause of mortality and the seventh cause of morbidity in Canada. The advancement of context-aware technology creates a new and important opportunity to transform the standard shape of healthcare services into a more dynamic and interactive form. This research project design and validates a rule-based ontology-reasoning framework that provides a context-aware system for COPD patients. The originality of the proposed approach consists in its methodology to prove the efficiency of this model in simulated examples of real-life scenarios based on collaborative data analysis, recognized by specialized medical experts.

Keywords: Data analysis · Ontology · Context-aware system · COPD · Healthcare systems

1 Introduction

COPD has a significant impact on individuals and society. Moreover, COPD represents an economic burden on the health care system. Statistics Canada [1], ranked COPD as the fifth cause of death in the country. Studies show that people with COPD are vulnerable to many natural events, environmental factors, and sudden worsening of the common signs and symptoms. Recent years have witnessed a widespread increase in the number of telemedicine projects in this domain. This kind of intervention will help COPD patients to avoid severe problems and lengthy hospital admissions [2]. Most research focuses on post exacerbation reactions, but what if we took a step back, and look for ways to avoid exacerbation as much as possible. This task requires working on three different levels, first, find the safe range of environmental factors, second, adjust the normal limits of relevant biomarkers, and third, figure the external influences (e.g. excessive physical effort, climatic factors) on the patient's body. The originality of this approach resides in the intelligent monitoring and control of persistent changes in the physiological parameters and the ambient environment. This work was part of a concentrated effort to create safe adaptive ranges for the personalized biomarkers where the normal values of these vital signs are often affected by the medical profile, the type

J. Pagán et al. (Eds.): ICOST 2019, LNCS 11862, pp. 97–108, 2019.
https://doi.org/10.1007/978-3-030-32785-9_9

of current exercise, the place, and the weather. Environmental factors are also one of the COPD irritants, where cumulative exposure to the multitude of climate hazards such improper humidity levels or extreme weather temperatures, both indoor and outdoor air pollution, in addition to the abnormal concentrations of oxygen in the atmosphere may threaten patient lung health. Developing dynamic alarm thresholds is an important contribution because that would promote the services provided and increase the value of telemonitoring in self-management. Moreover, a customized threshold will help to decrease the proportion of false alarms and differentiate between true exacerbation and normal variation. To achieve these goals, there is an important need to develop a comprehensive representation of knowledge to capture the real context of the patient to avoid misdiagnosis and allow dynamic reconfiguration of health disorders threshold. Rule-based ontology to support context-aware systems offers potential solutions to the multi-scale nature of COPD. In a previous work [3] we designed an ontological reasoning framework that provides a rules-driven context-aware system for COPD patients. In this article, we will present the validation process of that proposition, proving its results by specialized medical experts, and demonstrating its efficiency in simulated examples of real-life scenarios through empirical data about environment, activities, symptoms and physiological parameters.

2 Related Works

Almost two decades ago, the use of medical ontologies was no longer limited to define medical terminologies such as Systematized Nomenclature of Medicine - Clinical Terms (SNOMED CT) or Unified Medical Language System (UMLS), but also it has become one of the powerful solutions to tackle serious health problems and support the management of complex and large data. The ontologies have been also used in hundreds of research projects concerned with medical issues such as diagnosis, self-management, and treatment [4]. The ontological approach proved its effectiveness in the remote healthcare arena, for instance, Lasierra et al. [5] and Larburu et al. [6] have presented robust examples of ontology usage in the telemonitoring domain for generic and specific chronic diseases. Lasierra proposed an autonomic computing ontology for integrated management at home using medical sensors. Rubio provides a formal representation of knowledge to describe the effect of technological context variations in the clinical data quality and its impact on a patient's treatment. Another example can be found in [7], Benyahia developed a generic ontology for monitoring patients diagnosed with chronic diseases. The proposed architecture aims to detect any anomalies or dangerous situations by collecting physiological and lifestyle data. Hristoskova et al. [8] presented an ontology-based ambient intelligence framework that supports real-time physiological monitoring of patients suffering from congestive heart failure. Ryu [9] proposed a ubiquitous healthcare context model using an ontology; the model extracts the contextual information for implementing the healthcare service taking into consideration the medical references and environments. Kim [10] has designed an interactive healthcare system with wearable sensors that provides personalized services with formal ontology-driven specifications. In the same setting, an ontology-based context-aware framework for customized care has been presented by Ko et al. [11] as a form of wearable biomedical technology. An interesting projection of ontology in this domain can be found in [12] that builds a context-aware mobile service aiming at supporting mobile caregivers and sharing information to improve quality of life of people living with chronic diseases. In addition to this obvious interest in ontology, most of health care projects related to computer-assisted medical decision-making, are often modelled using rule-based approaches. The Semantic Web Rule Language (SWRL) has emerged over existing OWL axioms to promote expressiveness of Semantic Web. In the medical environment, there are several uses of rules, for example, but not limited, the IF-THEN rules can be used for chaining or mapping ontology properties to achieve Knowledge Integration. By applying rules, the pattern of behaviors of all entities can be expressed, which would produce new facts and tailored services. The use of the ontology in COPD is only restricted to certain aspects of patients' lives. For example, authors in [13] developed an ontology inspired by the autonomic computing paradigm that provides configurable services to support home-based care. Authors in [6] proposed a predictive model to extract relevant attributes and enable the early detection of deteriorations but the proposed ontology aims at describing the basic structure of the application. Although a significant amount of research has been done studying the importance of telehealth in COPD, the concept of integrated care services is still in its infancy. The use of semantic mapping between the physiological parameters, environmental factors, symptoms, physical activity and patient-specific data to construct a telemonitoring system for COPD using ontologies was not found in the literature. This work will be the first building block for creating a comprehensive primary e-health care delivery system, capable of organizing various daily life scenarios for COPD patients in a healthy and safe environment.

3 Proposed System

In our previous work, we proposed an ontology-based approach to keep track of the physical status of patients, suggest recommendations and deliver interventions in a timely manner. The proposed system provides an intelligent monitoring infrastructure guided by rules. This process involves observing and controlling the behavior of physiological parameters and the surrounding environment. Consequently, the system adapts the safe ranges for the vital signs in proportion to demographic factors, medical profile, physical activity, and external ambiance. The main contribution of that work consists in proposing a specific domain architecture for COPD. This architecture is designed and implemented in four distinct layers: the acquisition layer is dedicated for collecting and properly transmitting different sorts of data, such as the medical profile of COPD patient, biomarkers and environmental information whether gathered from wearable or fixed monitoring sensors. The semantic layer or the ontological schema has been used to interpret complex information and translate the real context of the patient into machine-understandable and accessible language. At the macro level, the telemonitoring system aims to detect all the possible hazardous events that could influence COPD patient. Since OWL has expressivity limitations on representing many types of contextual information, especially IF-THEN statement, our ontologies have been extended with forward-chaining rules. These rules were expressed in the Semantic Web

Rule Language (SWRL) to describe all implications and consequences. The proposed rules are extracted from data analysis, existing medical guidelines and opinions of pneumologists. Practically, these rules are used by an inference engine to derive new facts, detect events, and predict the potential risk. The novelty of these rules lies in its dynamic structure, which has the capacity to configure and re-configure the secure boundaries according to the current circumstances and contexts.

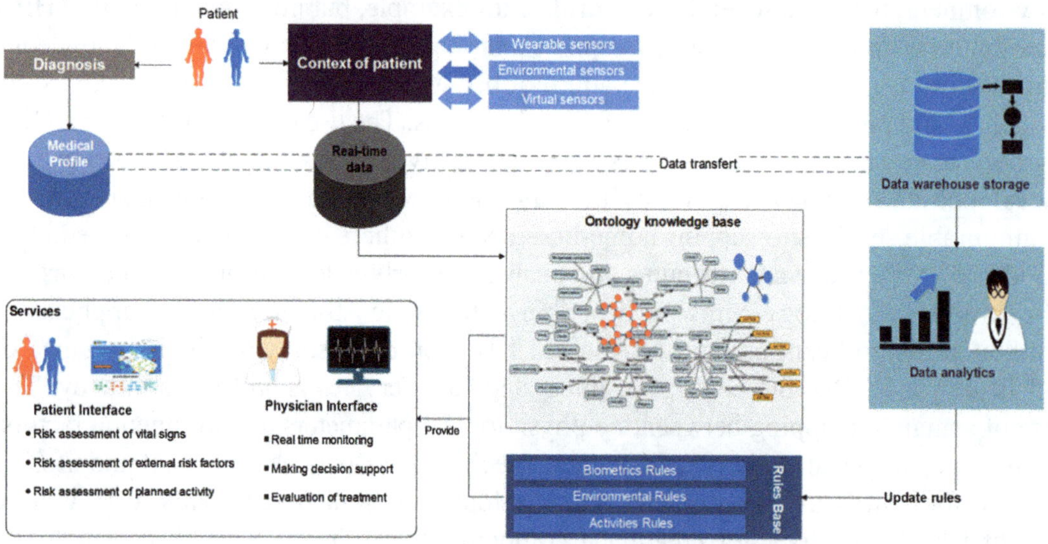

Fig. 1. General architecture

Figure 1 above provides an explanation of the relationships between the constituent entities of the system in a simplified manner. In the next section, we will learn about the methods of extracting the medical rules of COPD.

4 COPD Rules

In preparation for rules extraction, we performed data analysis, reviewed medical guidelines, interviewed experts and examined published sources to map biomarkers of COPD patients to various real-life patterns. A rule, on the other hand, is a description of how a patient is affected by internal bodily characteristics and external environmental factors.

4.1 Biomarkers Rules

In clinical therapy, each patient must be recognized as individuals with a unique health state. However, grouping patients with a similar medical profile is an excellent solution to treat diseases. Unlike previous works and based on this scientific principle, we studied all relevant factors according to the personal and medical profile, which includes the demographic information and the clinical chart of patients. Hurst et al. [14] and Rajeh et al. [15] identified the main physiological parameters and symptoms to be monitored. Understanding the maximum possible extent of change for each variable in different scenarios is a crucial need for the early detection of pulmonary exacerbations. In the next section, we will try to find out how these parameters change with COPD patient in different medical profiles and during common daily life activities. Profile differences help to explain discrepancies in medical care received by COPD patients. Having considered the guidelines, it is recommended dividing the population of patients into groups or quartiles according to age, gender, stage, BMI, smokers, medication, and comorbidity. Identifying factors that may indicate if something is wrong with COPD patients is about to happen was a daunting task and took a long time. This study has established 11 physical parameters must be monitored namely, body temperature, blood pressure, heart rate, partial pressure oxygen (PaO2), oxygen saturation (SpO2), partial pressure carbon dioxide (PaCO2), oxygen consumption (VO2), respiration rate, PH, HCO3, and FEV1. Understanding the role of these biomarkers and their normal ranges in the stable COPD patients with all potential scenarios grants us the ability to sense imminent danger. Patients were separated horizontally by gender, age and stage, these groups have been then reclassified vertically according to the effects of BMI, smoking, medication, and comorbidities on the vital signs. To illustrate this point, we will provide an example to explain changes in heart rate with different profiles.

4.1.1 Heart Rate Rules

Analysis of data obtained from medical records [16, 17, and 18] finds that heart rate in women can be slightly different from men. Figure 2 shows that females have a higher heart rate compared with males at all ages, as this difference increases in the early middle age and decreases in late adulthood. In contrast, the overall analysis shown a remarkable decline in the normal resting heart rate (Fig. 3).

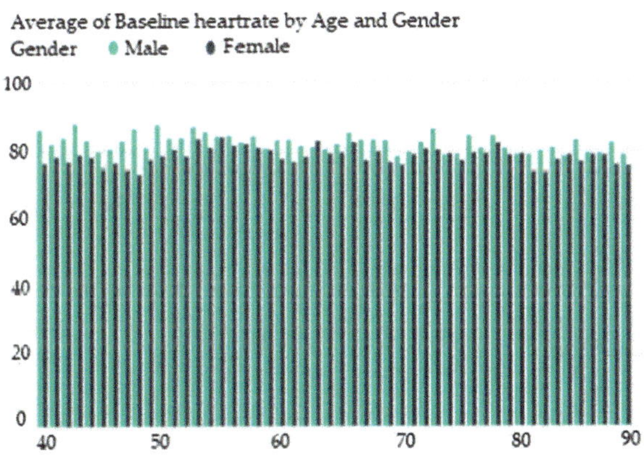

Fig. 2. Heart rates by age and gender

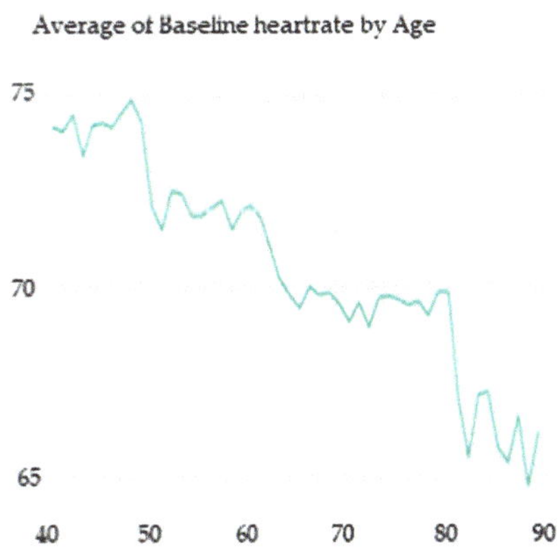

Fig. 3. Heart rates by age

Resting heart rate was also associated with both obese and all inhaler medication across all stages of COPD ($p < 0.004$ and $p < 0.003$). The change in heart rate was only associated with four comorbidities, CHF, anemia, PH, and asthma. One of the key factors that change heart rate is activity. Heart rate differs from person to person during exercise or when doing any physical effort, this variation is determined by mathematical equations with an acceptable degree of accuracy. In summary, this evidence-based analysis proves that heart rate varies depending on the medical profile of the patient, which in turn will affect the stable ranges of this vital sign during physical activities. The same analytical methodology has been used on the other physiological parameters mentioned above.

4.2 Indoor and Outdoor Rules

According to Healthy Environments and Consumer Safety Branch (HECSB), Canadians spend approximately 90% of their life indoors [19] often, due to the extreme nature of the climate conditions. Therefore, it's very important to pay attention to the quality of that indoor air, temperature, humidity, and pressure, especially as COPD patients must fully live in a safe environment, away from any kind of exacerbation irritants. Unlike the internal environment, we cannot control the external environmental factors. There are six main factors that affect the patient outside of the ordinary indoor ambient, these factors must include outdoor temperature, humidity, wind speed, precipitation, atmospheric pressure, and air quality but in terms of air compounds and outdoor pollutants. The proposed rules must provide customized protection against all the inappropriate environmental factors.

5 Dataset

Gatherings such different kinds of data from real sensors are subject to some practical limitations such as ethical approval, financial costs, and deployment time. Hence, researchers suggest an alternative experimental method using intelligent simulation. There are three basic data sources to build such scenarios, (1) medical information, (2) daily life activities, and (3) the environmental conditions.

5.1 Real-Life Activities

There are relatively many published studies about the simulation of activities. Based on previous findings, we attempted to extend the existing indoor scenarios proposed by Mshali [20]. Using the same approach which is built upon Markovian models. Many other scenarios have been built upon the Markovian models, we created new sequences of expected activities including outdoor actions that can be performed by COPD patients. These scenarios took into consideration the levels of severity and disabilities as provided for in the international classification of functioning (ICF). These daily life activities of COPD patients have been divided into six successively sequences associated with six-time periods from sunrise to sunset. Each one of these sequences consists of a set of coordinated activities with a random duration created through transition probabilities matrices.

5.2 Environmental Conditions

Unlike the patient activity dataset, challenges in assembling environmental data were easier, where we found many open sources that describe environmental conditions of indoor and outdoor spaces at long intervals. One of the most interesting outdoor datasets for environmental information is published by the ministry of environment and climate change strategy in British Columbia in Canada [21]. These data sets contain continuous readings of meteorological and pollutants index from air quality monitoring stations across the province from 1980 till the end of 2017. Simulation of the internal environment is also important where the patient spends most of his time at home. The indoor data is tracked via GAMS indoor air quality monitor [22].

5.3 Medical Records

Medical profiles are a vital asset in ensuring the validation process. In this context, we have collected thousands of electronic medical records, hospital admission data, and measures of the outcome in clinical studies from different medical sources ([16] Al-Sahel hospital and MIR clinic [17]).

6 Implementation

The experimental dataset consists of the activities that have been generated using the MATLAB, the environmental conditions which are captured by real sensors and the biomarkers that obtained from medical sources. The simulated scenarios revolve around creating sequential records over 12 months period for COPD patients with different levels of disease severity and autonomy. In this section, we briefly describe the implementation steps of this project using protégé (Fig. 4).

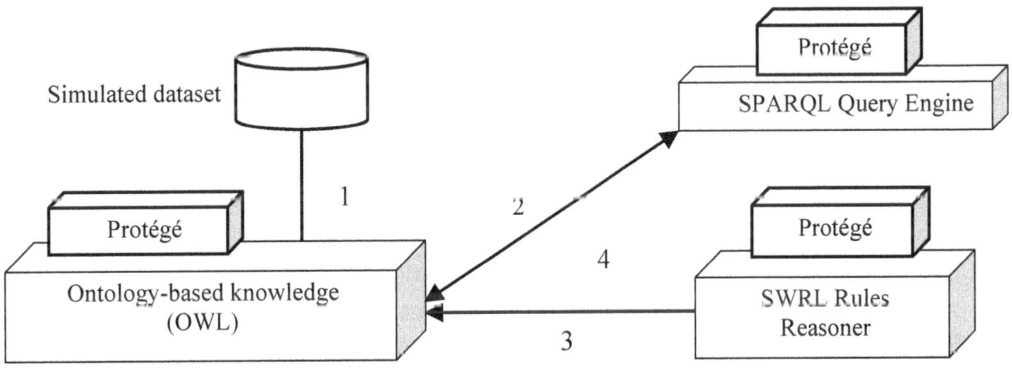

Fig. 4. Flow in the implemented system

The initial implementation of the project will be done in the following manner: (1) the simulated data stored in Excel spreadsheet files will be uploaded directly to Ontology-based knowledge using Cellfie plugin. (2) The SPARQL query engine accesses to the Knowledge Base to retrieve information of patient's profile, current location, and activity, etc. (3) SWRL rule reasoner adds additional information such as normal ranges, and appropriate environment to the Knowledge Base. Moreover, SWRL rule reasoner performs reasoning on the updated Knowledge Base of COPD domain and new inferred facts are added to the Knowledge Base. (4) The SPARQL query engine accesses to the Knowledge Base to retrieve the notifications and the recommendations according to the patient's context. We constructed eight ontologies for monitoring COPD patient to represent machine-understandable Knowledge Base. The developed ontologies consist of concepts related to personal and medical profile, physical examinations, laboratory tests, location, activity, environment, time, recommendations, and disease [3] (Fig. 5).

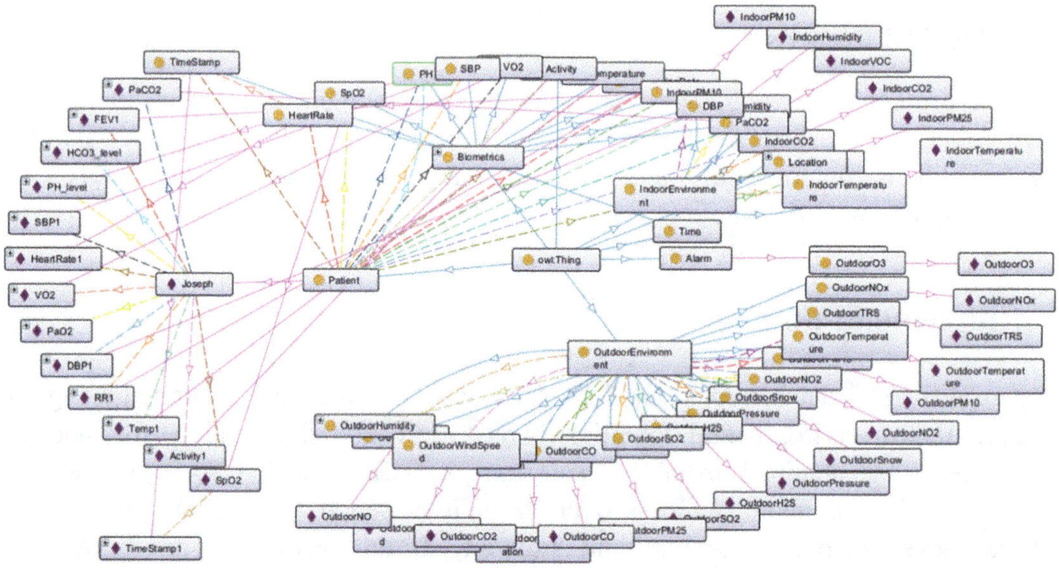

Fig. 5. Part of the ontology

Thousands of SWRL rules were used to manage the safe conditions of almost 600 COPD medical profiles in various circumstances. Based on the medical information found in the guidelines and other information provided by physicians, we created 20,328 rules using forward chaining of inference. These rules use concepts/axioms defined in our ontology. These rules are set to achieve different goals such as (i) verify the profile of patients (ii) detect the location and environment (iii) evaluate the patient's status and surrounding conditions, (iv) provide the corresponding service for patients. For more details, please refer to the reasoning section of our previous work [3]. Having reasoning techniques of ontologies and rules that contain the asserted and inferred statements, we used SPARQL to retrieve, and derive contextual information from the knowledge base. The aim of this query is to retrieve any information relating to an identified instance, such as a sign, symptom, treatment, alarm, recommendation, decision, etc. To illustrate the use of the model, we will present some examples. Let's consider the scenario of a COPD patient being remotely monitored after diagnosis. The patient vital signs, activity, and environmental parameters are continuously monitored (Fig. 6).

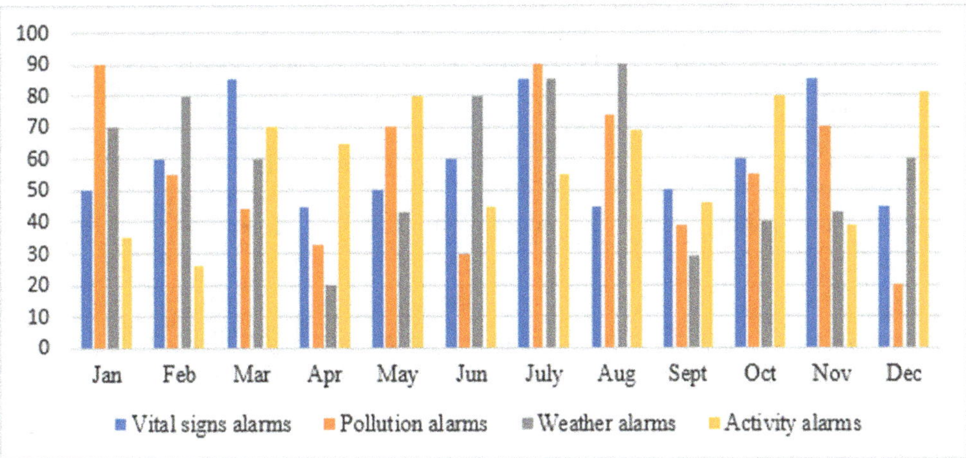

Fig. 6. Number of alarms by months

The presented simulations have handled a great amount of data of possible situations. The generated alarms have been classified into four main categories: vital signs, activity, pollution, and weather. The system applies continuous monitoring and detects a total of 2,817 abnormal situations.

7 Evaluation

This section will explore partially the performance of our system using a confusion matrix. Performance measurement refers to information that quantifies accuracy, sensitivity, specificity, and the probability of predicting a dangerous change in physiological parameters in COPD patients. The purpose of this evaluation is to measure the diagnostic performance of technical and clinical accuracy.

A master file was created in MS Excel® that contains 1200 patients records, biometric readings for each patient have been extracted from the results inferred from ontology in different scenarios. This information was presented to physicians. This data is used to calculate the confusion matrices for the physician's report outcomes. There are four possible outcomes, true positive (TP), true negative (TN), false positive (FP), and false-negative (FN). The confusion matrix contains information about the predicted classifications identified by our ontology and the opinions of medical experts. Categories in this research are defined as follows (Table 1):

1. TP is an alarm with a hospitalization.
2. FN has no alarm with a hospitalization.
3. TN has no alarm and no hospitalization.
4. FP has an alarm with no hospitalization.

Table 1. The confusion matrix

Ontology recommendation	Physicians' recommendation	TP	FP	TN	FN
Hospitalization alarm	Hospitalization	1			
Hospitalization alarm	No hospitalization		1		
No hospitalization alarm	No hospitalization			1	
No hospitalization alarm	Hospitalization				1

The results refer that our system reaches an accuracy of 88% in a set of 1200 clinical cases. Sensitivity and specificity have high values, denoting the ability of the system to detect warning signs. The positive predictive value (PPV) is defined as the probability of intervention for positive test results while the negative predictive value (NPV) describes the probability of being healthy for negative test results (Table 2).

Table 2. Standard reference and results for the clinical decision support system

	Intervention present	Intervention absent	Total
Index test positive	True positive (TP) = 512	False positive (FP) = 88	TP + FP = 600
Index test negative	False negative (FN) = 56	True negative (TN) = 544	TN + FN = 600
Total	TP + FN = 568	TN + FP = 632	
1. Accuracy = 88%			
2. Sensitivity = 91.14%			
3. Specificity = 86.07%			
4. Positive predictive value (PPV) = 85.33%			
5. Negative predictive value (NPV) = (TN)/(FN + TN) = 90.66%			

8 Conclusion

The proposed model involves a qualitative leap in the healthcare systems that supports COPD because it establishes new obligations that will limit many of the potential hazards at different levels, both physiological and environmental. The system can recognize any important changes in biometrics and environment based on a personalized threshold. The protection process aims to adjust the thresholds around the normal state to avoid exacerbation triggers. Our findings proved that dynamic thresholds can enhance the existing telemonitoring systems and make a valuable contribution identify the health status of COPD patients. Many conclusions can be drawn from this experimental simulation. Firstly, the ontology-based system can provide a more efficient way to deal with medical data. Secondly, adding an SWRL layer of experts' rules on top of OWL can handle various types of context and suggest reliable recommendations. Thirdly, the results support the importance of context where it demonstrates that context variables have a strong influence on the accuracy of decisions. For future research, this study will have to be evaluated through real implementation and crossover trial to assess patients' experiences and measure their effectiveness and usability.

References

1. Public Health Agency of Canada Report from the Canadian Chronic Disease Surveillance System: Asthma and Chronic Obstructive Pulmonary Disease (COPD) in Canada, Ottawa (2018). ISBN 978-0-660-09274-4
2. Segrelles, G., Gómez-Suárez, C., Soriano, J.B., Zamora, E., Gónzalez-Gamarra, A., et al.: A home telehealth program for patients with severe COPD: the PROMETE study. Respir. Med. **108**, 453–462 (2014)
3. Ajami, H., Mcheick, H.: Ontology-based model to support ubiquitous healthcare systems for COPD patients. Electronics **7**, 371 (2018)
4. Button, K., van Deursen, R.W., Soldatova, L., Spasić, I.: TRAK ontology: defining standard care for the rehabilitation of knee conditions. J. Biomed. Inform. **46**(4), 615–625 (2013). https://doi.org/10.1016/j.jbi.2013.04.009. [PMID: 23665300]
5. Lasierra, N., Alesanco, A., Guillen, S., Garcia, J.: A tree stage ontology-driven solution to provide personalized care to chronic patients at home. J. Biomed. Inform. **46**, 516–529 (2013)
6. Larburu, R., Bults, R.G., Van Sinderen, M.J., Hermens, H.J.: An ontology for telemedicine systems resiliency to technological context variations in pervasive healthcare. IEEE J. Transl. Eng. Health Med. **3**, 10 (2015). https://doi.org/10.1109/JTEHM.2015
7. Benyahia, A.A., Hajjam, A., Hilaire, V., Hajjam, M.: E-care ontological architecture for telemonitoring and alerts detection. In: 5th IEEE International Symposium on Monitoring & Surveillance Research (ISMSR): Healthcare-Safety-Security (2012)
8. Hristoskova, A., Sakkalis, V., Zacharioudakis, G., Tsiknakis, M., De Turck, F.: Ontology-driven monitoring of patient's vital signs enabling personalized medical detection and alert. In: Nikita, K.S., Lin, J.C., Fotiadis, D.I., Arredondo Waldmeyer, M.-T. (eds.) MobiHealth 2011. LNICST, vol. 83, pp. 217–224. Springer, Heidelberg (2012). https://doi.org/10.1007/978-3-642-29734-2_30
9. Ryu, J.-K., et al.: Ontology based context information model for u-healthcare service. In: 2011 International Conference on Information Science and Applications, pp. 1–6 (2011)
10. Kim, J., Lee, D., Chung, K.: Ontology driven interactive healthcare with wearable sensors. Multimed. Tools Appl. **71**, 827–841 (2012)
11. Ko, E.J., Lee, H.J., Lee, J.W.: Ontology-based context modeling and reasoning for U-HealthCare. IEICE Trans Inf. Syst. **E90-D**(8), 1262–1270 (2007)
12. Paganelli, F., Giuli, D.: An ontology-based system for contextaware and configurable services to support home-based continuous care. IEEE Trans. Inf. Technol. Biomed. **15**, 324–333 (2011)
13. Valls, A., Gibert, K., Snchez, D., Batet, M.: Using ontologies for structuring organizational knowledge in home care assistance. Int. J. Med. Inform. **79**(5), 370–387 (2010)
14. Hurst, J.R., et al.: Susceptibility to exacerbation in chronic obstructive pulmonary disease. New Engl. J. Med. **363**, 1128–1138 (2010)
15. Al Rajeh, A., Hurst, J.: Monitoring of physiological parameters to predict exacerbations of chronic obstructive pulmonary disease (COPD): a systematic review. J Clin. Med. **5**, 108 (2016)
16. AL Sahel Hospital. Beirut, Lebanon (2018)
17. Medical International Research (MIR), clinical laboratory. Beirut, Lebanon (2018)
18. Simulated patient cases, training and validation dataset. https://doi.org/10.1371/journal.pone.0188532.s004

19. Ventilation and the Indoor Environment. Water and Air Quality Bureau Healthy Environments and Consumer Safety Branch, March 2018. http://publications.gc.ca/collections/collection_2018/sc-hc/H144-54-1-2018-eng.pdf
20. Mshali, H., Lemlouma, T., Magoni, D.: Context-aware adaptive framework for e-health monitoring. In: IEEE International Conference on Data Science and Data Intensive Systems, Sydney, Australia, pp. 276–283, December 2015
21. Outdoor air quality dataset. https://catalogue.data.gov.bc.ca/dataset/air-quality-monitoring-verified-hourly-data
22. GAMS Indoor Air Quality Dataset. https://github.com/twairball/gams-dataset

DL4DED: Deep Learning for Depressive Episode Detection on Mobile Devices

Afef Mdhaffar[1,2(✉)], Fedi Cherif[3], Yousri Kessentini[1], Manel Maalej[4], Jihen Ben Thabet[4], Mohamed Maalej[4], Mohamed Jmaiel[1,2], and Bernd Freisleben[5]

[1] Digital Research Center of Sfax, Sfax, Tunisia
afef.mdhaffar@gmail.com
[2] National School of Engineering of Sfax, University of Sfax, Sfax, Tunisia
[3] Geeks Data Consulting, Tunis, Tunisia
[4] Department of Psychiatry "C", Hedi Chaker University Hospital, Faculty of Medicine of Sfax, University of Sfax, Sfax, Tunisia
[5] Department of Mathematics and Computer Science, University of Marburg, Marburg, Germany

Abstract. This paper presents a deep learning approach for depressive episode detection on mobile devices, called DL4DED. It is based on a convolutional neural network and a long short-term memory network to identify the status of a patient's voice extracted from spontaneous phone calls. To run DL4DED on mobile devices, two neural network model compression techniques are used: quantization and pruning. DL4DED protects data privacy, since it can be executed on a patient's smartphone. Our proposal is validated on the DAIC-WOZ database. The obtained results show that the accuracy of DL4DED with model compression is only slightly lower than the accuracy of DL4DED without model compression. Furthermore, our experiments indicate that the power consumption of DL4DED is reasonably low.

Keywords: Deep learning · Mobile application · Depression · Pruning · Quantization · Optimization

1 Introduction

According to the World Health Organization (WHO), 800 000 people die every year due to suicide[1], which is the second leading cause of death in people aged between 15 and 29 years. However, many suicides can be prevented. Indeed, mental disorders, such as depression, contribute to many of them around the world. Hence, early detection and appropriate management are key to ensuring that people receive the care they need[2]. Therefore, patients suffering from Major

[1] https://www.who.int/news-room/fact-sheets/detail/depression.
[2] https://apps.who.int/iris/bitstream/handle/10665/131056/9789241564779_eng.pdf.

J. Pagán et al. (Eds.): ICOST 2019, LNCS 11862, pp. 109–121, 2019.
https://doi.org/10.1007/978-3-030-32785-9_10

Depressive Disorder (MDD) and Bipolar Disorders (BD) should be continuously monitored, since they might experience frequent depressive episodes.

Several mental health monitoring approaches using mobile devices have been proposed. Most of them [1–3,5–11,13,14] are based on (1) collecting and analyzing smartphone features such as activity, localization, and phone calls, and (2) launching interactive questionnaires such as PHQ-9[3] and BDI[4]. "Active" monitoring approaches (i.e., requiring a patient's intervention) are less used and less effective than "passive" ones (i.e., not requiring a patient's intervention) in practice. Actually, patients do not like to answer questionnaires every day, and even if they answer them, we cannot be sure about the honesty of their answers.

Passive monitoring approaches [3,5–8,10,11,13,14] can be divided into two categories. The first category tries to use most of the smartphone's sensors, such as accelerometer and camera, to collect related features [5–7,11,14]. These approaches require special environmental conditions to ensure the precision of collected data. For instance, Maxhuni et al. [11] require the smartphone to be held in a special position to accurately capture the patient's activity. This makes these approaches difficult to use in practice. The second category of approaches [3,8,10,13] focuses on analyzing "only" voice sounds, recorded from phone calls. Indeed, acoustic changes in speech allow us to detect depressive episodes [8]. Most of these approaches are based on the use of complex algorithms for speech analysis, such as deep learning approaches. Typically, these approaches require significant computational resources. Therefore, this category of approaches sends recorded phone calls to an external server for analysis, since running complex algorithms on smartphones is still a challenging task [12]. This reduces the chances of using these mobile applications, because they do not protect data privacy. Actually, many patients do not accept that external servers process their recorded phone calls.

In this paper, we present a novel deep learning approach that can be loaded and executed on a patient's smartphone to allow real-time detection of depressive episodes. Our proposal, called DL4DED (Deep Learning for Depressive Episode Detection), is based on optimizing and compressing a deep learning model to be integrated in our mobile application. DL4DED (1) records phone calls, (2) executes our deep learning model, and (3) triggers alerts if a depressive episode is detected. DL4DED does not send recorded phone calls to an external server and consequently preserves data privacy. To evaluate our approach, two groups of experiments have been conducted. The first one illustrates the efficiency of DL4DED in terms of accuracy. The second one demonstrates that the power consumption of DL4DED is reasonable when compared to baseline approaches.

The paper is organized as follows. Section 2 discusses related work. DL4DED and its implementation are detailed in Sects. 3 and 4, respectively. Section 5 presents experiments and results. Section 6 concludes the paper and outlines areas for future research.

---

[3] Patient Health Questionnaire (PHQ-9).

[4] Beck's Depression Inventory.

2 Related Work

A comprehensive survey reviewing existing mobile applications for mental health diseases (e.g., BD, MDD, schizophrenia) has been published by Cornet et al. [1]. This survey explains different parameters that have been used throughout the years to detect mental health diseases. These parameters are usually extracted from smartphone sensors, such as microphone (i.e., phone calls), accelerometer (i.e., movement data), and GPS (i.e., localization). The authors also describe the used analysis algorithms, where the most advanced ones are based on deep learning networks. Moreover, the authors discuss data privacy issues related to all reviewed approaches, since all extracted smartphone features are sent to an external server for analysis.

Haque et al. [6] present a deep learning model to measure the severity of depression symptoms. The proposed approach is based on analyzing 3D facial expression and spoken language. It has been evaluated on the DAIC-WOZ dataset [4]. The proposed approach requires an active intervention from the patient, which makes it unusable in some cases. Actually, it is hard to ask a patient to daily record videos, due to privacy issues. In contrast, our approach is passive, analyzes spontaneous phone calls, and preserves data privacy.

Su et al. [14] present a diagnosis assistance system that is based on deep learning and fusion techniques. The proposed system makes use of two deep learning models. The first one is used for speech classification, while the second one processes facial expression. This work is aimed at assisting doctors to avoid misdiagnosis in the case of BD. Actually, BD is usually confused with MDD. The results are quite promising, but the system architecture cannot not be applied in a spontaneous manner. Indeed, the system requires special environmental conditions to be applied, such as a camera.

Huang et al. [7] propose an attention-based convolutional neural network (CNN) and long short-term memory (LSTM) approach for distinguishing between MDD and BD. The proposed approach identifies mood disorders on the basis of responses given to 6 video sequences. Consequently, it can be applied to depressive episode detection. The analysis includes speech processing and facial recognition to extract emotional state. In contrast to our approach, this work cannot be applied in a spontaneous manner and does not protect data privacy. Actually, recording responses to 6 particular videos cannot be expected on a daily basis and without the intervention of a psychiatrist.

Grunerbl et al. [5] present a smartphone-based approach for mood status identification in BD. The proposed approach makes use of smartphone features (e.g., location, phone call sounds, phone light) to detect depressive and maniac episodes. Features are extracted manually, and data privacy is not protected.

Maxhuni et al. [11] define an analysis approach that identifies manic and depressive episodes on the basis of activity data and phone calls. To monitor activities, the authors mention that the phone has to be held in a special position. Moreover, phone calls are recorded, stored in the phone's memory card and sent to another server for analysis. This means that this approach does not protect data privacy and requires special environmental conditions to generate accurate results.

Khorram et al. [10] propose a machine learning (ML) approach for depression detection in BD. The proposed approach is based on the analysis of acoustic features of the patient's voice. The paper shows the effectiveness of speech features in detecting depression. However, features are extracted manually due to the use of ML techniques. Moreover, a patient's voice is sent to an external server for analysis, which does not protect data privacy. Therefore, we propose a deep learning model that allows us to automatically extract features and preserve data privacy.

Gideon et al. [3] discuss the impact of a recorded voice on the identification of depressive and manic episodes in BD. Only phone calls recorded during clinical trial are considered. Other phone calls are removed to protect data privacy. This means that this work does not analyze naturalistic and spontaneous voice, which might alter the detection results. However, our work is based on the analysis of spontaneous phone calls (i.e., recorded on a daily basis), thanks to our deep learning model that is locally running on a patient's smartphone.

Huang et al. [8] define two speech features based on speech landmark bigrams (i.e., bigram count and LDA bigram) for depression detection. Both features could be extracted from naturalistic phone calls including 6 elicitation tasks such as measuring the diadochokinetic rate. Landmarks are extracted using the SpeechMark® toolbox[5], which is a Matlab tool that runs under Windows 7, Windows XP, Apple OSX (Lion or Mountain Lion), as mentioned on their web page. This means that the proposed work needs to send recorded phone calls to an external server for feature extraction. However, our work allows us to locally extract features on the smartphone.

Pan et al. [13] propose analysis approaches for detecting manic episodes in BD. The proposed approaches are based on the use of Support Vector Machines (SVM) and Generalized Markov Models (GMM). They record spontaneous phone calls and send them to an external server for analysis. This approach does not protect data privacy.

3 DL4DED

This section presents our novel approach, called DL4DED. It is a mobile voice analysis approach that:

1. monitors patients suffering from BD and MDD;
2. detects depressive episodes by locally analyzing their phone calls without storing them;
3. alerts patients, their family members, and their psychiatrists if a depressive episode is detected.

[5] https://speechmrk.com/speechmark-products-downloads/the-speechmark-matlab-toolbox/.

DL4DED is based on the use of deep learning methods applied to spontaneous speech, recorded from phone calls, to identify depressed voice. The proposed deep learning model is locally running on a patient's smartphone to preserve data privacy. Indeed, recorded phone calls are "temporarily" stored on the smartphone until the analysis is accomplished. Once the decision is sent to our external server, the recorded phone call is discarded. The architecture of DL4DED, the proposed deep learning model, and our optimizations are described below.

3.1 Architecture

Figure 1 shows the architecture of DL4DED. Our approach (1) records spontaneous phone calls, (2) stores them temporarily in a buffer belonging to the local memory of a patient's phone, (3) processes them via our "mobile" deep learning model, (4) identifies the state of the recorded voice (i.e., depressed or not depressed), (5) discards the recorded voice (i.e., phone call), and finally (6) sends and stores the obtained decision to a database that is installed on a cloud server. The communication links between the smartphone and the cloud server are enabled via the HTTP protocol. A web dashboard is available for both patients and psychiatrists. It is used to display the patient's mood on the basis of the voice status.

To identify the status of the voice, we use a novel deep learning model that is described in Sect. 3.2.

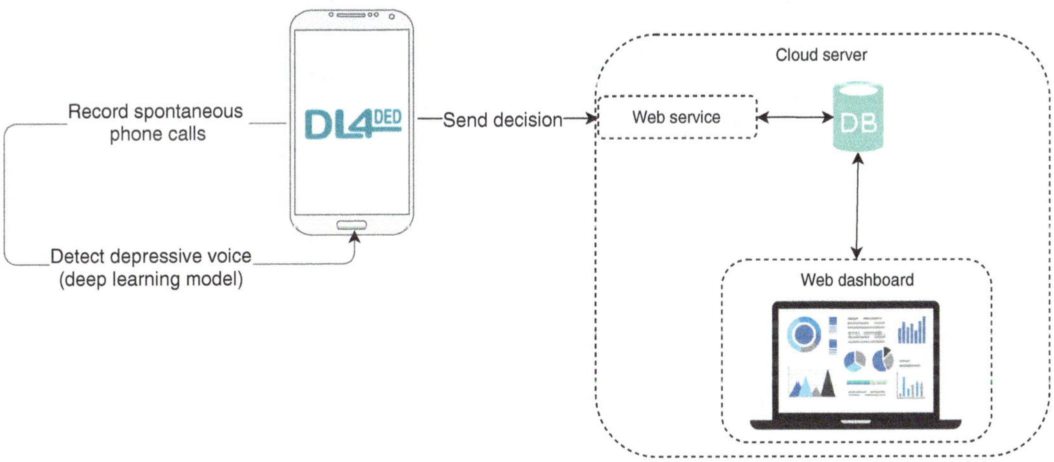

Fig. 1. Architecture of DL4DED

3.2 Deep Learning for Voice Status Identification

Figure 2 shows our deep learning model. It processes recorded phone calls and detects depressed voice. The proposed model takes as input a spectrogram. To obtain a spectrogram, a Short-Time Fourier Transform (STFT) is applied to the recorded phone calls. A spectrogram, also called voiceprint, represents the

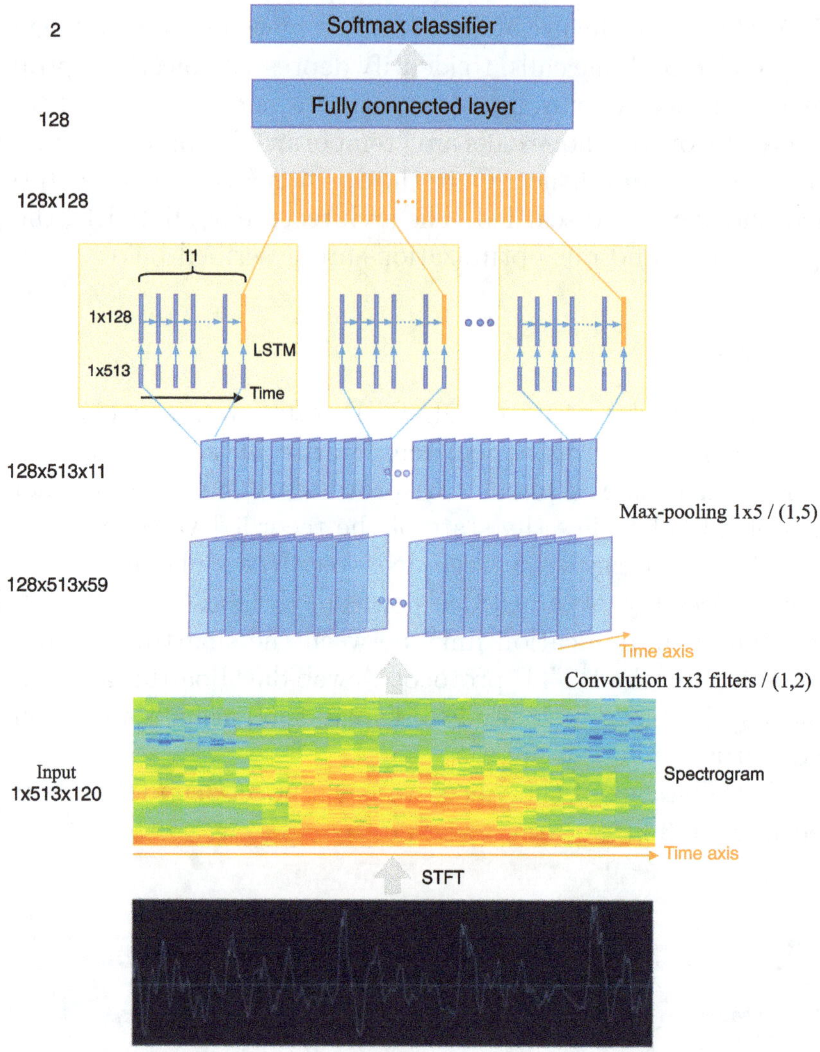

Fig. 2. Deep learning model for voice status identification

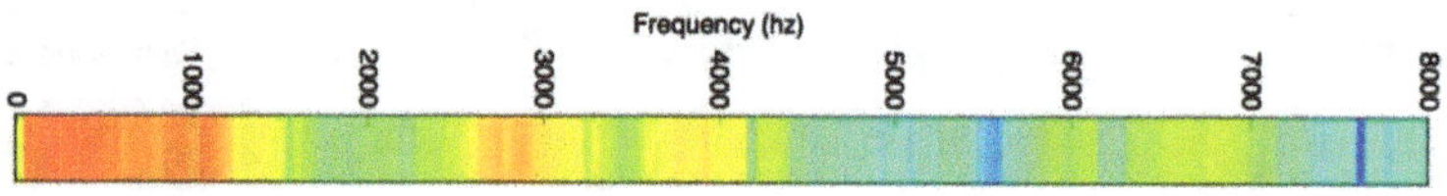

Fig. 3. Energy bar: an audio segment

spectrum of frequencies of the recorded phone call, as a function of time. It is composed of a set of frequency bars. Each bar corresponds to a time-stamp t. It is a vector, having the dimension 513 corresponding to the quantities of energy, expressed in decibels (see Fig. 3).

In our case, the spectrogram is a matrix having the dimensions 513 (frequencies) and 120 (times). The temporal dimension has been experimentally chosen. However, the frequency dimension has been obtained by applying STFT on audio segments, recorded with a frequency of 16 kHz (standard frequency for human voice recording). The intensity of colors represents the intensity of the energy of the recorded voice at the instant t, which might be useful for the identification of the patient's mood. Once the spectrogram is built, it is processed by a CNN network, having one convolution layer and one max-pooling layer. The convolution layer applies a $(1 * 3)$ filter/$(1, 2)$, allowing us to keep all frequencies (i.e., all energy quantities describing the voice) and preserve the temporal continuity. The max-pooling layer applies a $(1 * 5)$ filter $/(1, 5)$, to extract medium-term features, while keeping all frequencies. The output of the max-pooling layer is processed by an LSTM that includes memory cells to save long-term information. A fully connected layer is applied afterwards, to transform the obtained matrix into a 128-dimensional vector. The latter is processed by a softmax classifier allowing a binary classification (i.e., depressed voice or not depressed voice). The parameters of our CNN model have been identified experimentally.

To run the proposed deep learning model on mobile devices, we considered two compression methods: quantization and pruning. These methods allow us to reduce the size of our deep learning model by removing weights or operations that are least useful for prediction.

4 Implementation Issues

Figure 4 shows the technical architecture of DL4DED. The smartphone is in charge of recording and analyzing phone calls, while running our deep learning model that has been implemented using the Keras[6] library. Generated decisions are then sent to a Flask RESTful API 1.0.2, a web service platform that stores received decisions in a RethinkDB 2.3.6 0xenial (GCC 5.3.1) database. A nodeJS v4.2.6 server is installed to build a real-time web application. It is composed of a set of dashboards, displaying analysis results and an estimation of the patient's mood/status.

To predict depressed voice, recorded phone calls are pre-processed first. Afterwards, the deep learning model is loaded into a mobile application to trigger predictions. Implementation details are presented below.

4.1 Data Processing

To process a phone call by a CNN model, a spectrogram is built. For this purpose, the recorded voice (i.e., voice signal) is processed by a pre-emphasis filter. A pre-emphasis filter allows us to (1) improve the Signal-to-Noise Ratio (SNR); (2) avoid numerical problems that might appear during the Fourier Transform operation and (3) balance the frequency spectrum. Actually, high frequencies usually have smaller magnitudes compared to lower frequencies.

[6] https://keras.io.

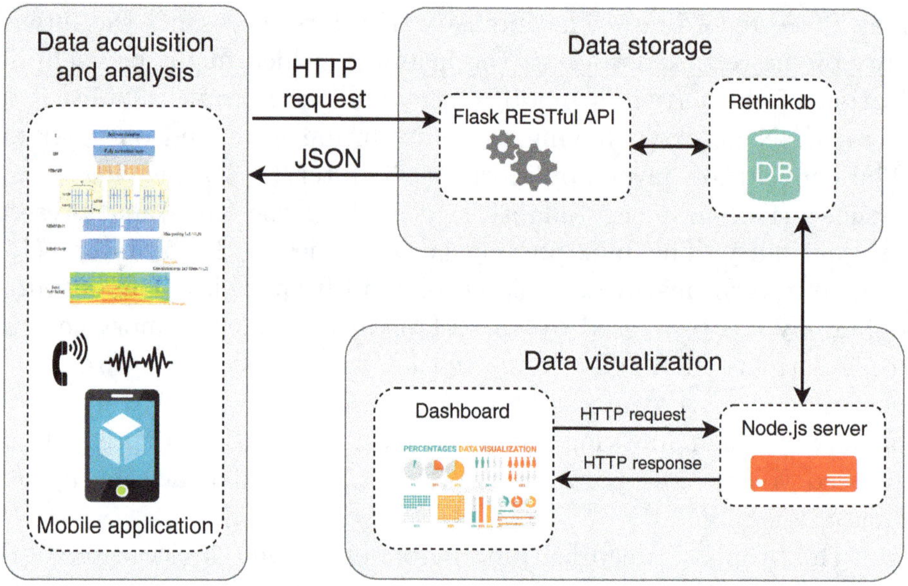

Fig. 4. DL4DED implementation

After applying the pre-emphasis filter, the signal is decomposed into short-time and overlapping frames. This step allows us to avoid applying the STFT across the entire signal and consequently losing the frequency contours of the signal over time. In this case, STFT will be applied on short-term frames allowing us to obtain a good approximation of the frequency contours of the signal by concatenating adjacent frames.

A window function (e.g., Hamming window) and a STFT are applied to each frame. This allows us to compute the power spectrum that is used to extract the frequency bands by applying triangular filters on a mel scale. The mel scale aims to mimic the non-linear human ear perception of sound, by being more discriminative at lower frequencies and less discriminative at higher frequencies.

After applying the filter bank to the power spectrum (i.e., periodogram) of the signal, we obtain the spectrogram that is processed by our CNN.

All steps described above were implemented in Android studio to create our mobile application (see first step of Fig. 5).

4.2 Implementation on Mobile Devices

To implement our deep learning model on mobile devices, we followed three steps (see Fig. 5). First, our Keras-based deep learning model is converted to Tensorflow. Actually, Tensorflow allows an easier integration of deep learning models on mobile devices (i.e., Android or IOS). For this purpose, we use a method called "Keras_to_Tensorflow" provided by the Tensorflow library. This method converts a Keras model file into a Tensorflow file which contains both the network architecture and its associated weights. Second, we optimize the generated model by removing weights and operations that are least useful for predictions by applying pruning and quantization methods. Third, we load our model (i.e.,

*.pb file including weights and architecture) into our mobile application to allow real-time detection of depressed voice.

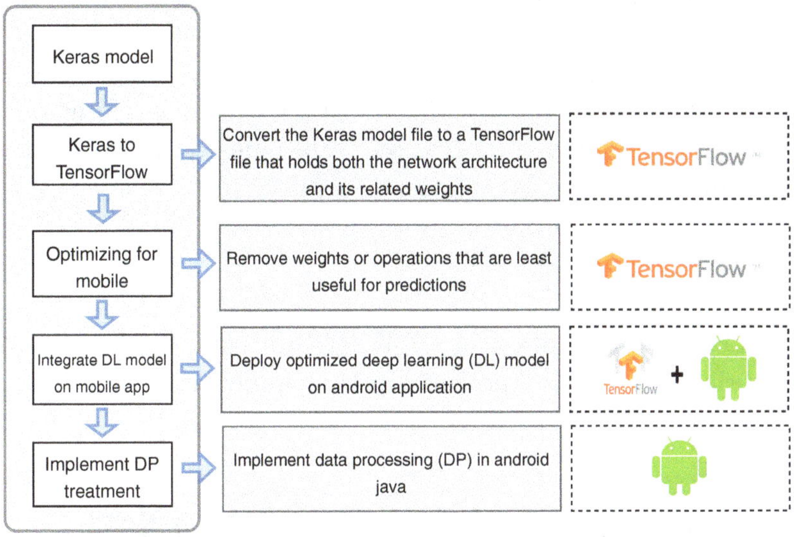

Fig. 5. Implementation of our deep learning model on mobile devices

5 Experimental Results

Our experiments were conducted on (1) an Ubuntu Server 16.04.5 LTS, with 2 GPUs Nvidia GeForce GTX1080 Ti Turbo 11 GB GDDR5X-RAM PCIe x16 HDMI and (2) a OnePlus A6003 Smartphone, running under an Android OS 8.1.0, with 8 GB of RAM and 128 GB of storage. We use the DAIC-WOZ data set[7] to evaluate DL4DED. The DAIC-WOZ dataset was compiled by the USC Institute of Creative Technologies and published as part of the Audiovisual Emotional Challenge 2016 (AVEC 2016). The DAIC WOZ data set includes 189 sessions, with an average duration of 16 min, between a participant and a virtual interviewer, controlled by a human interviewer in another room via a "Wizard of Oz" approach. Prior to the interview, each participant completed a psychiatric questionnaire (PHQ-8), from which a binary classification (depressed, non-depressed) was derived [4]. To evaluate DL4DED, we conducted two groups of experiments. The first group is used to evaluate the performance of our approach in terms of accuracy. The second group aims to assess the power consumption of DL4DED on mobile devices.

5.1 Performance

The main objective of this group of experiments is to compare our "optimized deep learning model" (i.e., with model compression, running on a smartphone)

[7] http://dcapswoz.ict.usc.edu.

and the "original deep learning model" (i.e., the originally created deep learning model without compression and optimization), in terms of accuracy that has been calculated using Tensorflow libraries. This experiment does not depend on the used data since it assesses the accuracy loss related to the use of DL4DED. Therefore, we evaluate both models on the same database (i.e., the DAIC-WOZ dataset). The obtained results demonstrate that the accuracy of DL4DED (0.5) is slightly lower than the accuracy of the original deep learning model (0.52). This means that the applied compression techniques do not significantly alter the analysis results.

5.2 Power Consumption

To assess the power consumption of DL4DED, we used the battery monitoring functionality provided by the Android OS that allows us to measure the power usage of each application in mAh (see Fig. 6).

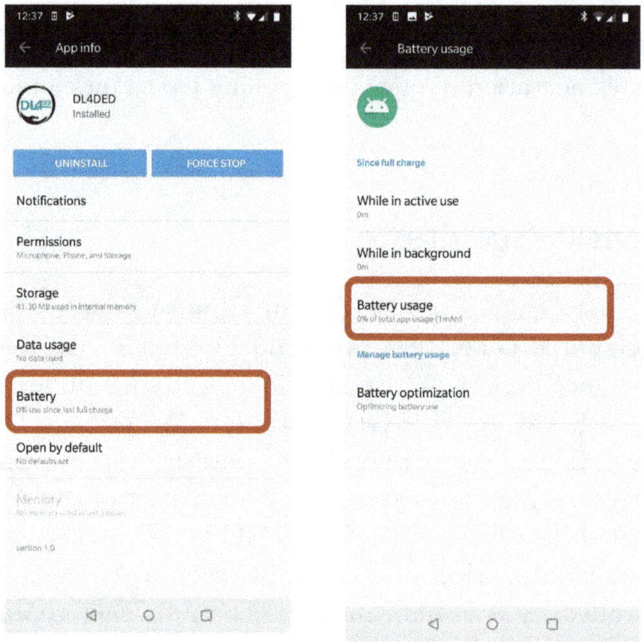

Fig. 6. Power monitoring functionality of Android OS

mAh stands for milli-Ampere-hours and expresses the number of milliampere (i.e., electric charge quantity), the mobile application has used per hour. Actually, the battery capacity is usually expressed in mAh.

We measured the power consumption of (1) DL4DED and (2) a baseline mobile application, while varying the duration of phone calls (from 1 min to 16 min). The baseline mobile application only records phone calls and sends them to an external server that loads and runs our "original deep learning model" (i.e., without compression and optimization) to detect depressed voice. Due to the throughput of our communication links, the baseline approach does not send the whole duration of the phone call. However, DL4DED processes the whole duration of the recorded phone call to allow better classification. The obtained results show that the average power consumption of DL4DED (5 mAh) is higher than the power consumption of the baseline mobile application (1 mAh), for a phone call duration of 4 min. This is quite plausible. Actually, DL4DED records phone calls, saves it to a temporary buffer and loads a deep learning model on the smartphone, to allow real-time prediction of the depressed voice. Loading an optimized deep learning model on a smartphone should logically increase power consumption. Our experiments show that the average difference of power usage (4 mAh) for a phone call of 4 min is reasonably low and therefore acceptable. As shown in Fig. 7, it is clear that the power consumption of DL4DED increases when the duration of the phone call increases. This is related to the fact that we process the whole duration of the phone call in contrast to the baseline approach. This issue will be solved in future work by processing only pertinent parts of the recorded phone call.

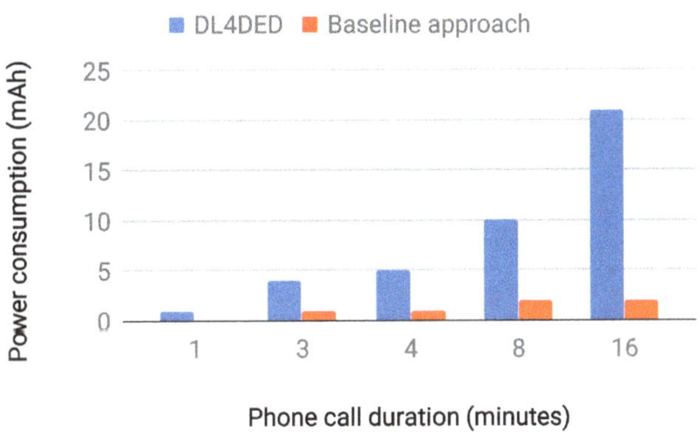

Fig. 7. Power consumption: DL4DED vs. baseline approach

6 Conclusion

We presented a novel mobile deep learning approach for depressive episode detection, called DL4DED. It is a combination of CNN and LSTM networks. The proposed deep learning model was optimized using compression techniques to be loaded onto smartphones. DL4DED records spontaneous phone calls on a daily basis, stores them temporarily locally on a smartphone, and loads our optimized deep learning model to allow real-time detection of depressed voice. DL4DED preserves data privacy since recorded phone calls are not sent to external servers. DL4DED was evaluated on the DAIC-WOZ database. The results demonstrated the efficiency of DL4DED in terms of accuracy and power consumption.

There are several directions for future research. First, we aim to consider the number of recorded phone calls in our study to improve analysis results.

Actually, the absence of phone calls could be seen as a severe sign of depression. Second, we plan to extend our deep learning approach to detect manic episodes in BD. Third, we aim to build a realistic and balanced database to improve the performance of DL4DED. Finally, further optimization methods should be investigated to improve our implementation on mobile devices.

Acknowledgment. This work is supported by the German Academic Exchange Service (DAAD) (Transformation Partnership: Theralytics Project).

References

1. Cornet, V.P., Holden, R.J.: Systematic review of smartphone-based passive sensing for health and wellbeing. J. Biomed. Inform. **77**, 120–132 (2018)
2. Eralp, A., Orhan, Z., Kabil, M.: Psychodroid: a mobile psychological disorder detection application by dynamic question generation and content analysis. Proc. - Soc. Behav. Sci. **159**, 691–696 (2014)
3. Gideon, J., Provost, E.M., McInnis, M.G.: Mood state prediction from speech of varying acoustic quality for individuals with bipolar disorder. In: 2016 IEEE International Conference on Acoustics, Speech and Signal Processing (ICASSP), pp. 2359–2363 (2016)
4. Gratch, J., et al.: The distress analysis interview corpus of human and computer interviews. In: Proceedings of the Ninth International Conference on Language Resources and Evaluation, LREC 2014, pp. 3123–3128. LREC, Reykjavik (2014)
5. Grünerbl, A., et al.: Smartphone-based recognition of states and state changes in bipolar disorder patients. IEEE J. Biomed. Health Inform. **19**(1), 140–148 (2015)
6. Haque, A., Guo, M., Miner, A.S., Fei-Fei, L.: Measuring depression symptom severity from spoken language and 3D facial expressions, pp. 1–7. CoRR abs/1811.08592 (2018)
7. Huang, K.Y., Wu, C.H., Su, M.H.: Attention-based convolutional neural network and long short-term memory for short-term detection of mood disorders based on elicited speech responses. Pattern Recogn. **88**, 668–678 (2019)
8. Huang, Z., Epps, J., Joachim, D.: Speech landmark bigrams for depression detection from naturalistic smartphone speech. In: 2019 IEEE International Conference on Acoustics, Speech and Signal Processing (ICASSP), ICASSP 2019, pp. 5856–5860 (2019)
9. Jiménez-Serrano, S., Tortajada, S., García-Gómez, J.M.: A mobile health application to predict postpartum depression based on machine learning. Telemed. J. E-Health: Off. J. Am. Telemed. Assoc. **21**(7), 567–574 (2015)
10. Khorram, S., Gideon, J., McInnis, M.G., Provost, E.M.: Recognition of depression in bipolar disorder: leveraging cohort and person-specific knowledge. In: INTERSPEECH, pp. 1215–1219 (2016)
11. Maxhuni, A., Muñoz-Meléndez, A., Osmani, V., Perez, H., Mayora, O., Morales, E.F.: Classification of bipolar disorder episodes based on analysis of voice and motor activity of patients. Pervasive Mob. Comput. **31**, 50–66 (2016)
12. Mohammadi, M., Al-Fuqaha, A., Sorour, S., Guizani, M.: Deep learning for IoT big data and streaming analytics: a survey. IEEE Commun. Surv. Tutor. **20**(4), 2923–2960 (2018)

13. Pan, Z., Gui, C., Zhang, J., Zhu, J., Cui, D.: Detecting manic state of bipolar disorder based on support vector machine and gaussian mixture model using spontaneous speech. Psychiatry Invest. **15**(7), 695–700 (2018)
14. Su, M., Wu, C., Huang, K., Yang, T.: Cell-coupled long short-term memory with L-skip fusion mechanism for mood disorder detection through elicited audiovisual features. IEEE Trans. Neural Netw. Learn. Syst. 1–12 (2019)

ICT-Based Health Care Services for People with Spinal Cord Injury: A Pilot Study

Wanho Jang[1], Dongwan Kim[1], Jeonghyun Kim[2], Seungwan Yang[3], Yunjeong Uhm[4], and Jongbae Kim[5](✉)

[1] Department of Occupational Therapy, The Graduate School, Yonsei University, Seoul, South Korea
crewano@gmail.com, dwan3303@naver.com

[2] Usability Center, Enabling Science Technology Research Center, Yonsei University, Seoul, South Korea
otrehab486@gmail.com

[3] Yonsei Enabling Science and Technology Research Center, Seoul, South Korea
shilover0@gmail.com

[4] Department of Ergonomic Therapy, The Graduate School of Health and Environment, Yonsei University, Seoul, South Korea
uyjot@naver.com

[5] Department of Occupational Therapy, College of Health Science, Yonsei University, Seoul, South Korea
jongbae@yonsei.ac.kr

Abstract. People with Spinal cord injuries are having difficulty in health care, and complications cause physical, social and economic losses. In severe cases, complications lead to death and require systematic management. In this study, ICT-based health care service was developed to manage the respiratory function and urinary function of the people with spinal cord injuries and to help adapt to daily living activities and social participation through home visit occupational therapy. A pilot study was conducted with five clients with spinal cord injuries to investigate the effectiveness of the intervention services. As a result, it was confirmed that satisfaction, importance, and difficulty were appropriate. In the future, RCT clinical studies will be needed to diversify intervention services and expand the number of patients.

Keywords: ICT-based health care service · Spinal cord injury · Health · Complication

1 Introduction

People with spinal cord injuries have impaired motor and sensory function and have difficulty in daily activities and social participation [1–3]. They participate in rehabilitation treatment in hospitals, and after discharge, suffer from complications [4]. Pressure ulcers may occur due to sensory impairment, and various complications such as respiratory diseases occur due to respiratory muscle function deterioration [5]. This can lead to difficulties in activity and participation and, in severe cases, to death [6, 7].

J. Pagán et al. (Eds.): ICOST 2019, LNCS 11862, pp. 122–127, 2019.
https://doi.org/10.1007/978-3-030-32785-9_11

Complications, therefore, lead to many losses physically, socially, and economically [8]. In the Republic of Korea, 90.5% of those with spinal cord injuries reported complications. The main complications were cystitis, pressure sores, and pain. Most spinal cord injuries also report that complications are a major detriment to a healthy life [9]. Therefore, it is essential to prevent and systematically manage these complications. Traditionally, complications are managed regularly by a doctor at a hospital. However, people with spinal cord injuries have difficulty in accessing medical services due to the inconvenience of movement due to physical impairment and the economic burden on hospital expenses [10, 11]. Therefore, recently, a service for managing health by using a remote system has been provided [12, 13]. Telerehabilitation using information and communication technology refers to providing comprehensive medical services to patients who have difficulty in moving to medical facilities or who wish to rehabilitate at home [14, 15]. Therefore, this study aims to verify the effectiveness of health management by providing ICT-based health care services for people with spinal cord injuries.

2 Method

2.1 Participants

From June 2019 to July 2019, we visited five families with spinal cord injury in the community and provided an ICT-based complication management system. The characteristics of the subjects were five males, and the mean onset duration was 21.8 years, four thoracic level injury and one lumbar level injury. The level of paralysis is five complete injuries.

2.2 ICT-Based Health Care Services

After using respiratory and urinary devices, and applying home visit occupational therapy, enter the data into a smart device or a desktop computer. If the doctor

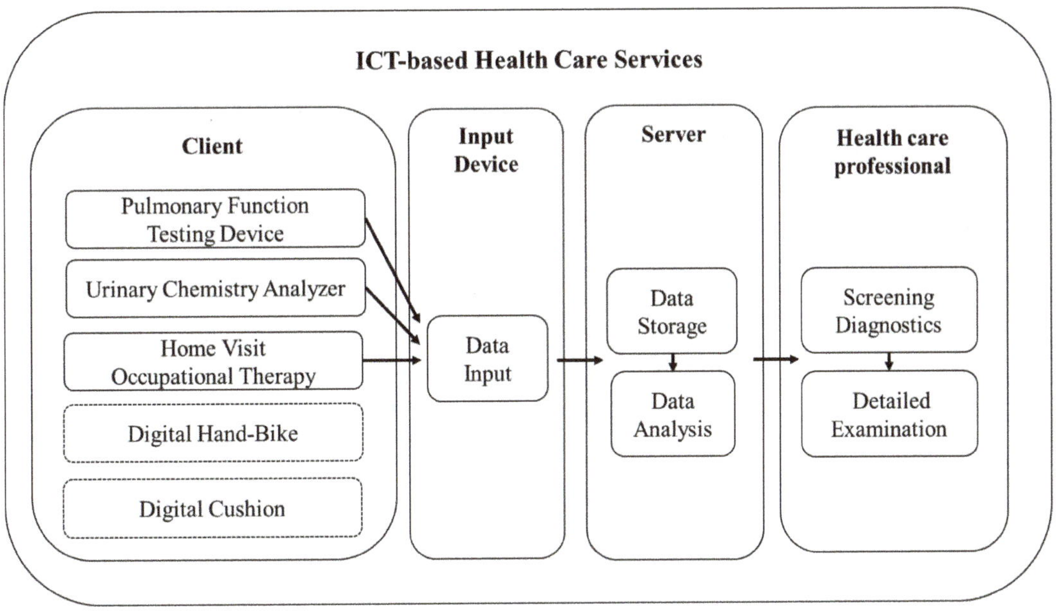

Fig. 1. ICT-based health care services

determines that there is a problem with the patient, he or she will request a hospital visit. Digital hand bikes and digital cushions are currently in development (Fig. 1).

2.3 Pulmonary Function Testing Device

It is a device that can measure FEV1 (Forced Expiratory Volume in one second), PEF (Peak Expiratory Flow), and these are typical indicators of respiratory function [16]. The patient can measure it directly. Occupational therapists can be visited, trained, and assisted with the measurement as needed. This data will be stored on the server. If the doctor or occupational therapist determines that the client have a problem with a pulmonary function, ask to visit the hospital.

2.4 Urinary Chemistry Analyzer

A urine chemistry analyzer can be used to screen a total of 10 components, including glucose, protein, and white blood cells. The client's urine will be examined, or an occupational therapist will be available to help if needed. Data is stored on the server and can be accessed by doctors and occupational therapists. If an outlier is found, the client will be referred for a detailed examination.

2.5 Home Visit Occupational Therapy

The occupational therapist visits the home and performs occupational therapy to the client. Occupational therapy interventions consist of interventions in daily living activities, home environment modifications, self-exercise training, and range of motion exercises, assistive technology services, and community service information. The result data of the evaluation and treatment is input to the smart device, and the data is stored in the server.

2.6 Digital Hand-Bike

There is not much exercise equipment for people with cervical spinal cord injury. Therefore, we are currently developing a hand-bike for them (Fig. 2). Previous studies have reported that hand-bikes for people with spinal cord injuries help improve motor function and health [17]. This was excluded in this pilot experiment.

2.7 Digital Cushion

Pressure ulcers in people with spinal cord injuries are one of the most common complications [18]. The reason is caused by sensory paralysis of the lower extremities. Therefore, they need appropriate seating system intervention. We are making a customized cushion with pressure sensors (Fig. 2). It can monitor the pressure in real-time. This cushion was excluded from the current study.

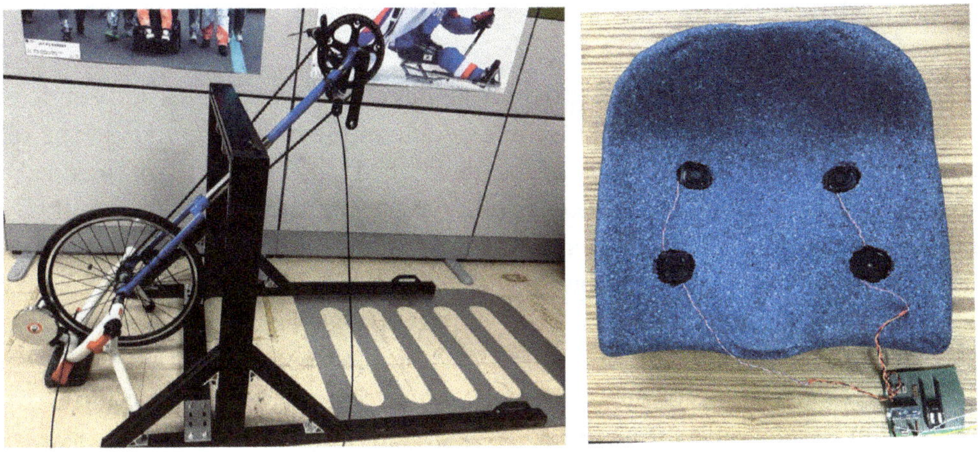

Fig. 2. Digital hand-bike and digital cushion

3 Results

Each intervention was evaluated with satisfaction, necessity, and difficulty, and the scale was 5 points. The results of experiments with five spinal cord injuries are as follows. Satisfaction was high at 4.8 for urinary function test and 4.4 for respiratory intervention and home visit occupational therapy. Necessity was high with interventional function test (4.4), respiratory function intervention (4.2), and home visit occupational therapy (4.2). The difficulty was not severe, all reported as 1.4 (Fig. 3).

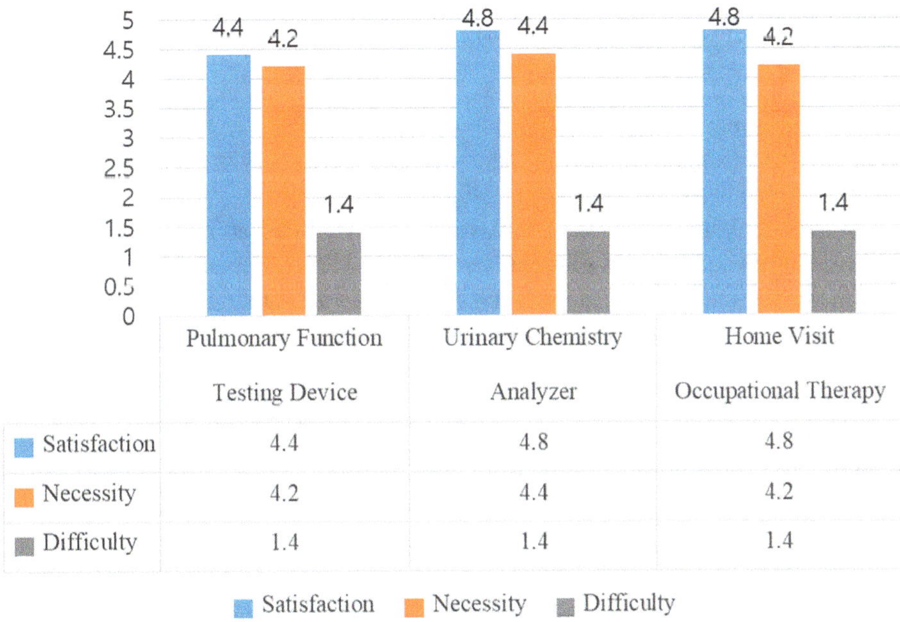

	Pulmonary Function Testing Device	Urinary Chemistry Analyzer	Home Visit Occupational Therapy
Satisfaction	4.4	4.8	4.8
Necessity	4.2	4.4	4.2
Difficulty	1.4	1.4	1.4

Fig. 3. Results

4 Conclusion

World Health Organization (WHO) provides guidance on technologies and services for improving the health of elderly and disabled people in the community [19]. The report recommends that new technologies to be developed and serviced for medical and assistive devices should have good accessibility and usability and that they will be able to use quality and effective services at a low cost. Above all, the emphasis was placed on meeting the needs of local communities and consumers. The ICT-based health care service model for community spinal cord injuries presented in this study shows the appropriate level of satisfaction in both satisfaction and need, as shown in the study results. Based on the results of this pilot study, we recognized the need for further study and are currently preparing for the RCT clinical study. Improvements to products and services will require constant updates. In addition, we are designing exercise equipment to improve body function and developing products to prevent a pressure ulcer. If so, this service could be more helpful in health care and prevention of complications, and it can be expected to be reflected in the health insurance system.

Acknowledgments. The research was supported by a grant of the Korea Health Technology R&D Project through the Korea Health Industry Development Institute (KHIDI), funded by the Ministry of Health & Welfare, Republic of Korea (grant number: HI18C0552).

References

1. Liem, N.R., McColl, M.A., King, W., Smith, K.M.: Aging with a spinal cord injury: factors associated with the need for more help with activities of daily living. Arch. Phys. Med. Rehabil. **85**(10), 1567–1577 (2014)
2. Nas, K., Yazmalar, L., Şah, V., Aydın, A., Öneş, K.: Rehabilitation of spinal cord injuries. World J. Orthop. **6**(1), 8–16 (2015)
3. Dijkers, M.P.: Correlates of life satisfaction among persons with spinal cord injury. Arch. Phys. Med. Rehabil. **80**(8), 867–876 (1999)
4. Amatachaya, S., Wannapakhe, J., Arrayawichanon, P., Siritarathiwat, W., Wattanapun, P.: Functional abilities, incidences of complications and falls of patients with spinal cord injury 6 months after discharge. Spinal Cord **49**(4), 520–524 (2011)
5. Sezer, N., Akkuş, S., Uğurlu, F.G.: Chronic complications of spinal cord injury. World J. Orthop. **6**(1), 24–33 (2015)
6. Jackson, A.B., Groomes, T.E.: Incidence of respiratory complications following spinal cord injury. Arch. Phys. Med. Rehabil. **75**(3), 270–275 (1994)
7. McKinley, W.O., Jackson, A.B., Cardenas, D.D., Michael, J.: Long-term medical complications after traumatic spinal cord injury: a regional model systems analysis. Arch. Phys. Med. Rehabil. **80**(11), 1402–1410 (1999)
8. Krueger, H., Noonan, V.K., Trenaman, L.M., Joshi, P., Rivers, C.S.: The economic burden of traumatic spinal cord injury in Canada. Chronic Dis. Injuries Can. **33**(3), 113–122 (2013)
9. Korea Spinal Cord Injury Association. http://www.kscia.org/board/list/menu03_05?init
10. Hossain, M.S., et al.: A pilot randomised trial of community-based care following discharge from hospital with a recent spinal cord injury in Bangladesh. Clin. Rehabil. **31**(6), 781–789 (2017)

11. White, B.A., et al.: The economic burden of urinary tract infection and pressure ulceration in acute traumatic spinal cord injury admissions: evidence for comparative economics and decision analytics from a matched case-control study. J. Neurotrauma **34**(20), 2892–2900 (2017)
12. Sechrist, S., Lavoie, S., Khong, C.M., Dirlikov, B., Shem, K.: Telemedicine using an iPad in the spinal cord injury population: a utility and patient satisfaction study. Spinal Cord Ser. Cases **4**(1), 71 (2018)
13. Martinez, R.N., et al.: Sociotechnical perspective on implementing clinical video telehealth for veterans with spinal cord injuries and disorders. Telemed. e-Health **23**(7), 567–576 (2017)
14. Wellbeloved-Stone, C.A., Weppner, J.L., Valdez, R.S.: A systematic review of telerehabilitation and mHealth interventions for spinal cord injury. Curr. Phys. Med. Rehabil. Rep. **4**(4), 295–311 (2016)
15. Phillips, V.L., Vesmarovich, S., Hauber, R., Wiggers, E., Egner, A.: Telehealth: reaching out to newly injured spinal cord patients. Public Health Rep. **116**, 94–102 (2016)
16. Tiftik, T., et al.: Does locomotor training improve pulmonary function in patients with spinal cord injury? Spinal Cord **53**(6), 467–470 (2015)
17. Kim, D.I., Lee, H., Lee, B.S., Kim, J., Jeon, J.Y.: Effects of a 6-week indoor hand-bike exercise program on health and fitness levels in people with spinal cord injury: a randomized controlled trial study. Arch. Phys. Med. Rehabil. **96**(11), 2033–2040 (2015)
18. Byrne, D.W., Salzberg, C.A.: Major risk factors for pressure ulcers in the spinal cord disabled: a literature review. Spinal Cord **34**(5), 255–263 (1996)
19. WHO: Consultation on Advancing Technological Innovation for Older Persons in Asia. https://extranet.who.int/kobe_centre/sites/default/files/summary_report_innovation_feb2013.pdf

Smart Environment Technology

An Interconnected Smart Technology System for Individuals with Mental Illness Living in the Community and Transitional Hospital Apartments

Cheryl Forchuk[1,2(✉)], Jonathan Serrato[1], Abraham Rudnick[3], Deborah Corring[2], Rupinder Mann[1], and Barbara Frampton[4]

[1] Lawson Health Research Institute, London, ON, Canada
cforchuk@uwo.ca
[2] Western University, London, ON, Canada
[3] Dalhousie University, Halifax, NS, Canada
[4] CONNECT for Mental Health, London, ON, Canada

Abstract. The overall objective of this research was to develop and test the use of smart technology in delivering safe, effective mental health services before expanding into community homes. A system was created that linked multiple screen devices such as smartphones and tablets and health monitoring devices with a central secure database for data to be funneled and stored for monitoring and tracking. In order to assess the feasibility of this technological innovation, the research team installed equipment in two prototype apartments at two inpatient psychiatric hospitals and in up to eight community homes operated by the Canadian Mental Health Association and London Middlesex Community Housing. The results indicate that most participants found the technology acceptable, and that the system was successfully able to export data securely.

Keywords: Smart technology · Mental illness · Health management · Housing · Data management

1 Introduction

In Canada, the Mental Health Commission of Canada estimates that 20% of the population will experience a mental illness during their lifetime while the remaining 80% will be affected by the mental illness of others [1]. Mood and psychotic disorders have also been linked with polydipsia [2] and cardiovascular disease [3]. It is therefore important for comorbidities to be observed in order to understand the complete health status of the individual. This is of particular importance given the patient-specific issues in Canada such as travel-related barrier for accessing community mental health care as well as long wait-times, lack of information, and stigma [4]. Furthermore, previous research has revealed increased mortality rates among individuals with severe mental illness due to a lack of self-management for acute and chronic illnesses [5]. Impairment in activities of daily living, function (e.g. inability to maintain a healthy diet, lifestyle, etc.) and cognition can result in missed medications, appointments, or self-care activities. Individuals

J. Pagán et al. (Eds.): ICOST 2019, LNCS 11862, pp. 131–142, 2019.
https://doi.org/10.1007/978-3-030-32785-9_12

with these types of impairments may not realize their self-care is declining therefore causing greater declines in mental and physical health. Symptom tracking and monitoring, enhanced awareness of pre-symptoms, and greater access to informational resources through smart technology may also aid patient well-being and beneficence [6].

In previous studies conducted by this research team, correlations between mental health and housing have been demonstrated but housing alone is not enough to promote stabilization [7]. While mental illness is often conceptualized as a problem between the individual and their environment, mental health care is almost entirely focused on "fixing" the individual rather than the environment they are in. To that end, previous research has demonstrated promising findings from the implementation of mobile and web-based technologies in a population of individuals experiencing mood or psychotic disorders [8–11]. Forchuk et al. revealed a 48.6% reduction in hospitalizations and 57% fewer outpatient visits after 18 months using mobile phones for prompts and reminders along with access to a personal health record [12]. This current project therefore reflects a logical extension of these studies by developing a "high-dose" smart technology intervention for those with severe mental illnesses; first by starting in hospital prototype apartments before extending further into community homes. Two reviews have revealed that there is a lack of evaluation of smart technology within a health care context [13, 14]. One of which, a Cochrane review, revealed no health-related smart technology studies that met the Cochrane Handbook criteria for inclusion and none of the identified studies evaluated effectiveness [14].

The groundwork of this project, laid by Corring, Campbell and Rudnick [8], aims to provide supportive systems within an individual's environment, be it within one's home or a hospital transitional apartment to promote community integration, to facilitate chronic illness management, and support independence. Furthermore, this project will attempt to establish the use of smart technology in assisting individuals with mental illness and cognitive impairment in a hospital apartment setting first before progressing and expanding into community homes. The objective of these phases was to develop and test smart technology in delivering safe, effective mental health services. As such, we hypothesize that this smart technology intervention will result in:

1. An increase in participants' level of community integration.
2. An increase in participants' housing stability.
3. A decrease in excessive health and social service utilisation.
4. An improvement in the participants' overall health.

At present, the hospital prototype phase has been ongoing for approximately 7 months. The community phase has seen equipment installed in five homes and is continuing to enroll participants.

2 Materials and Methods

Design

This quasi-experimental project is separated into two phases. The hospital prototype phase is employing a within-group, mixed-methods, descriptive pilot design in order to ascertain the feasibility of the smart technology in a hospital setting as well as testing the system as a whole. Data was collected upon discharge from the hospital apartment and at 6-month follow-up.

As the project moves from the hospital prototype phase, the community phase is adopting a more longitudinal approach in testing the project's hypotheses. This involves a within-group, mixed-methods, repeated-measures design. Data is being collected over three assessments conducted at baseline, 6-month and 12-month follow-ups. Comparisons regarding levels of community integration, health, housing stability and service usage throughout the intervention will be observed. Ethical approval was obtained through Western University's Research Ethics Board and Lawson Health Research Institute.

Description of the Settings

Health Care Providers (HCPs) at two inpatient psychiatric facilities and HCPs in community homes coordinated with the research staff to set up various smart technologies in the apartments for individuals with mental illness. The prototype apartments within the psychiatric facilities are available to individuals who were being discharged into the community in order to provide a transitional experience. The community homes are operated by the Canadian Mental Health Association (CMHA) and London Middlesex Community Housing (LMCH). These include group homes, family homes and individual apartments with staff members providing in-home care and support on a need-to-need basis.

The System

This project has sought to incorporate real-time integration of data in order to provide HCPs with notifications and monitoring capabilities. The system links multiple smart technology devices and funnels the data into one database. This system has been comprised of two software innovations; the Lawson Integrated Database (LIDB) and the Collaborative Health Record (CHR).

The LIDB is an information management platform that collates and manages client health information behind the St. Joseph's Health Care hospital firewall. The LIDB keeps health data segregated in its own database schema but is capable of matching patient data across HCPs. With funds from the Canada Health Infoway, the research team was able to ensure the security of the LIDB through a third-party Privacy Impact Analysis and Threat Risk Assessment. Encrypted incremental data backups are performed on a nightly basis and full backups performed weekly with both stored securely off-site. The LIDB also utilizes virtual servers to move from one server to another to enable continuous operations with no impact to users. Weekly meetings with software engineers and monthly meetings with the hospital I.T. and Privacy departments have been held since the commencement of the project to address any data security concerns and ensure the integrity of the system. HCPs are able to log-in to the LIDB to view data from the health monitoring devices and the CHR, and also to set the reminders to be transmitted to the screen devices.

The CHR allows for both synchronous and asynchronous communication between patients and HCPs to deliver team-based, longitudinal health care. The CHR operates on the screen devices offered to the participants. The specific functions of the CHR include:

1. Access to personal health information and self-assessments to enhance early identification of concerns related to symptoms.
2. A comprehensive patient-record system that provides workflows for a diverse group of HCPs.
3. Prompts and reminders that can support care planning for symptoms and comorbidities (e.g. medication reminders and activity prompts).
4. Secure communication between HCPs and participants including videoconferencing and messaging.

This functionality aids the complex care of people with severe mental illnesses by creating an enhanced secure connection between them and their circle of care. This helps overcome barriers to care such as mobility, transportation, or lack of resources readily available, and reduces the number of in-person appointments necessary. Self-assessments (known in the software as "Qnaires©") are also completed within the CHR by the participant which allows the HCP and care team to monitor changes and potential crises. These self-assessments can include standardised tools used such as Patient Health Questionnaire (PHQ-9) and fully customisable tools created by the HCP within the CHR. The data from these assessments are then backed up to the participant's profile in the LIDB. In the event of a crisis (e.g. a participant indicates suicidal ideation on a Qnaire), an alert is sent to the care team so that they can act accordingly.

Equipment

Participants residing in the hospital prototype apartments can select a variety of screen devices including smartphones, tablets, and touch-screen monitors. These devices provide prompts and reminders generated by the LIDB to assist participants with cognitive deficits and facilitate self-care. The touch-screen monitors are developed in-house by the research team's programmer. The monitor is programmed so that prompts and reminders on the screen can be "acknowledged" by the user by pushing the "Got It" button. This sends an automated message back to the HCP who set the reminder to inform them the reminder was received. Furthermore, a "Help" button was added after initial discussions with HCPs which sends a message to the participant's care team requesting them to provide support. This exhaustive approach of ensuring all devices were able to connect to each other and allowed for ease of data exporting to the LIDB was completed after weekly meetings and thorough testing.

In addition to the screen devices, the participants are offered a choice of adjunct health monitoring devices. In the hospital prototype phase, these include weigh scales, blood pressure monitors, glucometers, and a wearable activity tracker (smartwatch). These devices account for the comorbidities that may be present and will support chronic illness management. Data from these devices is pushed to the LIDB via encrypted authentication keys and SSL connectivity. The weigh scale exports data via WiFi whereas the glucometer, weigh scale and activity tracker utilize Bluetooth connectivity.

The screen devices on offer for individuals residing in the community homes differ slightly. Participants in this phase are offered smartphones and touch-screen monitors only. This was done to further refine the intervention and allow for an additional health adjunct health monitoring device to be offered.

For participants in the community homes, their choice of health monitoring equipment also differs slightly with an automated medication dispenser being made available for selection but the blood pressure monitor and glucometer are not. The medication dispenser was not available for the hospital prototype phase due to medication protocols within the hospital. This addition of a medication dispenser represents the tailoring and refinement of the intervention for individuals living in the community. This was implemented to help participants with self-medication (if appropriate) and save time by reducing the need for participants and/or HCPs to collect medications from the pharmacy.

In both phases, participants are given the choice of devices they can use and are able to refuse any device with which they were not comfortable with. Participants recruited into the study are also allowed to refuse all devices but are still expected to complete a full semi-structured interview in order to acquire their opinions and attitudes as to why.

Recruitment

For all participants in both phases, the research team first recruited HCPs who then referred participants to the research team. For the hospital prototype phase of the project, the study is recruiting up to 20 participants and for the community phase, we are recruiting up to 13 participants. Participants are excluded from the study if they do not reside in the hospital prototype apartment for a minimum of one week.

Additional inclusion criteria for participants to participate in the community phase of the study include:

1. Must be on a caseload of a participating HCP.
2. Able to understand English to the degree necessary to participate.
3. Living in, eligible for, and wanting, housing provided by the CMHA housing program or LMCH.
4. Diagnosed with a psychotic or major mood disorder.
5. Identified by the clinical team to require prompting/reminding to complete activities of daily living and self- assessments as indicated by a score between 70 and 20 on the Social and Occupational Functioning Assessment Scale [15].
6. Must be between the ages of 18–85 years old and able to provide informed consent.

For both phases, this represents an opportunity sample as enrollment entirely depended on whether the participant is currently residing in the hospital or in the community. All participants have provided capable informed consent.

Procedure

The initial hospital prototype phase includes two hospital apartments located in two psychiatric inpatient facilities. Upon consenting to participate in the study, selected equipment was verified and approved by their HCP. The equipment was then delivered to the participant by the research coordinator and the research team's programmer who then sets up the devices and provides training to the participant. Training for usage of the CHR is provided by the research coordinator with the HCP in a one-to-one session. The participant completes their first interview upon discharge from the hospital prototype apartment. The participants complete a second interview at 6 months post-discharge.

The community phase is an expansion of the hospital prototype phase but participants are not crossed over, meaning that those who are discharged from the hospital prototype apartments do not enter the community phase. Upon enrollment into the study, participants for this phase of the project complete a baseline interview consisting of questionnaires pertaining to demographic data, health, housing, community integration and service utilization. Follow-up interviews are then conducted at 6 months and 12 months.

Focus groups are being provided to HCPs for both phases at the study's end allowing them to provide their observations and thoughts on the use of smart technology for the participants. A focus group at the study's end for participants will only be made available for participants in the community phase.

Instruments

In both phases of the study, the participants complete semi-structured interviews that include the following assessment tools: Community Integration Questionnaire - Revised (CIQ-R), Short-Form 36, EQ5D, the Housing History survey, the Health, Social and Justice Service Utilization (HSJSU) questionnaire, and the Perception of Smart Technology Questionnaire, a researcher-developed questionnaire that inquired about participants' attitudes and opinions of the equipment provided to them. Demographic data is also collected during these interviews.

Health data from the health monitoring devices include blood pressure, weight, blood glucose levels and heart rate. This data is backed up to the LIDB and made available to their HCPs for monitoring and tracking. Apps for these devices are preloaded onto the smartphones and tablets so that participants can also monitor their data. Participants could use the devices as and when they wished, or if directed by their HCP.

Data Analysis

Data is entered and stored on REDCap, a secure web-based database application by a research assistant. For quantitative analysis, the research team uses SPSS Statistics Software to generate descriptive statistics. It should be noted that data from the CHR's Qnaires have not, and will not, be analysed. The primary outcome of interest is the total score from the CIQ-R. Further quantitative analyses will investigate the housing history of the participant to assess housing stability, the health status of the participant, and experience with health, social and justice services to evaluate service usage.

Individual interviews are held with all participants enrolled in the study. Focus groups, as described by Krueger [16], are held with HCPs in both phases as well as participants in the community phase. Research assistants will conduct qualitative analyses by applying a thematic grouping of responses by identifying recurrent themes and opinions expressed by the participants and HCPs. Specifically, an ethnographic method of analysis will be used to observe the broader social and cultural contexts surrounding individual experiences as well as the impact on HCPs and how the intervention influenced their practice [17].

A standardised evaluation framework facilitated systematic effectiveness, economic, ethical and policy analysis of outcomes [18].

Effectiveness analyses will utilise the mixed-methods approach of this study by analysing the quantitative data from the instruments provided during the individual interviews to assess for any changes or improvements to the participants' health, service utilization and community integration. Common qualitative items from the focus groups will also assess the usage of the technologies and suggestions for improvement. By using a mixed methods approach, the research team is able to ascertain the participants' experiences with the technology as well as the effects on health, housing stability, and community integration.

The economic analyses will focus on the value for money aspect of the intervention as well as the costs and benefits. Specifically, the health costs of the intervention compared to usual care as well as the costs of hospitalizations, emergency room visits, outpatient visits and home care service.

Quantitative and qualitative findings related to views of fairness, benefits and social inclusion will be compared to ethical standards derived from welfare theory and accepted ethical principles of care providers (i.e. autonomy, beneficence and respect) as part of the ethical analyses.

Finally, policy analyses will address the implications that arise from the issues identified in the interviews such as access to and utilization of services, housing history, impact of severity of illness, and need for personal resources.

3 Results

Data collection and enrollment into the study is currently still ongoing. However, of all the participants approached so far, none have rejected to participate in the study and none have participated in the study without any equipment. All participants so far have met the study with great enthusiasm and eagerness. In terms of acceptability of the devices offered, the participants in the study so far have been positive about having the smart technologies in their home. When asked the question "How do you feel about having these smart technologies in your home/hospital?" on the Perception of Smart Technology questionnaire, preliminary analyses have revealed an average of 6.5 out of 7 demonstrating favorable attitudes towards having the technology.

Participants who have completed their interviews did not indicate any changes to their health after using the smart technologies they had selected. However, the ability to track health changes was seen as a benefit of the health monitoring devices. Number of steps measured by the activity tracker and weight was seen as useful. Furthermore, one participant highlighted that these devices aided them in making healthier choices by checking their weight two to three times per week and reaching their goals for walking. This could therefore reflect an uptake in healthier lifestyle choices as the devices provide an extra level of incentive and accountability. Although screen devices could not be used in the prototype apartment based in a forensic setting, one participant noted they would like to have a screen device in order to use apps for nutrition and fitness.

One of the concerns that arose from an interview with one participant was the issue of using small screens for those with visual impairments. Although the tablet used was 10.1 in. in size, the text on the screen was still too small to accommodate visual difficulties, even when the font size had been increased. The touch-screen monitor however was able to remedy this as the screen size was double that of the tablet and therefore the participant was able to clearly see their prompts and reminders. One suggestion was to use sounds instead of text thereby reducing the need to read prompts and reminders.

Future analyses will be able to provide more in-depth data and knowledge pertaining to changes in community integration, health and housing stability over the course of the study and after discharge from the hospital prototype apartments. We will also be able to perform more detailed analyses of the effects of the smart technology on the participants and to what degree they had an impact on their lives.

Part of this project was also to observe whether a smart technology system would be feasible and whether it could be used in a mental health care environment. This project has demonstrated that this system has been capable of funnelling various forms of data from a number of different sources. Key to mental health care treatment and recovery planning is the ability to tailor the intervention specifically to the participant. This was achieved as participants could pick and choose the devices specific to their care plans with no change or drop in performance from the system.

4 Discussion

Developing a reliable and secure system is a crucial step before community adoption of the intervention and must ensure the privacy of users and their data. This initial testing performed in the hospital prototype apartments allowed for further developments and refinements before going live in community-based environments. The intervention has undergone a number of enhancements from the time of its conception, mostly as a result of the fast-moving pace of technology but also the upgrades and additions to existing software and capabilities that meet the needs of the HCPs and participants.

To the researchers' knowledge, there are no other community-integrated, systems-level research studies underway that leverages novel state-of-the-art smart technology systems in community homes or in transitional hospital apartments. This project will advance the current knowledge of smart homes for individuals with severe mental illness by combining innovative health platforms (LIDB and CHR) and push smart technology to the forefront of mental health care within the home. With the infrastructure now in place, our team of researchers, health technology experts and software programmers are now equipped to support individuals with mental illness living in the community. Furthermore, this research project will have universal design potential across a range of mental illnesses for future research studies and/or interventions where optimal facilitation of healthy lifestyles may require smart technology support.

In terms of usage, the participants expressed they were generally satisfied with their usage of the devices provided to them. It was noted that the smartphone and tablet may be too small for individuals with visual impairments but the touch-screen monitor was able to provide suitable coverage. Training on using the devices was mostly straightforward as the activity tracker simply required the user to wear the device on their wrist and the weigh scale only required the user to stand on it. Similarly, the blood pressure monitor was easy to use, with the user strapping the cuff to their wrist then pushing one button located on the monitor attached to the cuff.

It has been reported so far that the health monitoring devices also helped to encourage weight and steps monitoring, which may be indicative of added motivation for the participants to maintain healthy lifestyles. The devices therefore may have acted as an accountability tool, providing the participants with their measurements and providing valuable feedback through enabling them to track their health. Previous studies have linked frequent observation to weight loss using personal digital assistants (PDAs) and daily feedback messages [19]. Research has also revealed that level of depression has been found to be a prognostic indicator for chronic illness such as coronary heart disease [20] and individuals with schizophrenia or depression have also demonstrated higher rates of diabetes and cardiac disease compared to the general population [3]. Therefore the use of health monitoring devices for individuals with mental illness cannot be understated.

A key benefit of this intervention would be the impacts on housing and economics. This project has allowed for the testing of commercial devices that can be easily purchased in the community or online and installed in community homes as opposed to expensive clinical equipment. This could inform housing policy decision-makers to consider the use of smart technologies for future housing development planning and for individuals with severe mental illnesses returning to the community. It is realistic to consider that future clinicians may prescribe smart devices and personalised health care technologies to support treatment or recovery. As the cost of mental care across Canada has been estimated to cost billions of dollars, this intervention may propose a more cost-effective alternative. At present, the cost of fitting an apartment with the devices plus CHR licensing and setup, and phone plan bills is less than $20,000 per year. St. Joseph's Hospital in London, ON, has estimated the mental health per diem cost as $454 per day ($165,710 per year) with a total of 10,699 patient days per year; which amounts to a net cost of $4,857,346 per year with the most prolonged stays being those with difficulty finding housing due to functional issues. Further costs can be saved by reducing travelling and improving efficiency in managing caseloads through greater monitoring and time-saving communication for HCPs [21].

Challenges

Many smart devices do not meet the security or privacy requirements of such a system or the compatibility requirements to connect with the other selected smart devices. For example, six different activity trackers were reviewed before one met the security and compatibility criteria. Finding a Cloud where it's Application Programming Interface (API) would grant the research team easy access to the data to be exported to the LIDB also proved to be challenging.

A challenge for this project was encouraging HCPs to adopt this technological approach. Although a number of HCPs embraced the technology and efficiency of the software available, others were skeptical. Due to the personal nature of the data being collected, some were concerned about the participants' privacy. However, concerns were allayed during the training sessions with HCPs as monthly meetings had been held between the hospital's IT and Privacy departments and the research team prior to the study's commencement. Some HCPs in the forensic setting felt more comfortable seeing the participant in person due to the close proximity between the prototype apartment and the HCP's office instead of viewing the CHR or the health data exported to the LIDB.

As one of the inpatient psychiatric facilities was a forensic mental health institution, a number of security protocols needed to be addressed. Internet usage specifically was prohibited due to the nature of the institution and the ease of access for harmful, dangerous or offensive materials on the internet. This therefore included the prohibition of screen devices that can connect to the internet. Further, devices with the ability to take photos or videos were also prohibited. The touch-screen monitor was acceptable as it could not be used for web-browsing and was programmed only to receive reminders as well as send acknowledgements back to the LIDB. However, this meant that the functions of a smartphone or tablet were not able to be replicated. The health monitoring devices were allowed as these did not allow for internet web-browsing.

5 Conclusions

Based on the preliminary findings of the current studies, the use of smart technology offers an alternative to traditional mental health care plans by allowing for enhanced connectivity and greater access to resources. The system described in this article is an efficient and reliable form of data management that can allow for tracking and monitoring of physical and mental health data. This intervention could enable mental health care strategies and inform policy decision-makers to adopt more smart technologies into care and treatment plans for individuals with severe mental illness. In addition, if implemented it can be cost-effective for individuals with mental illness living in the community and the lack of access to non-emergency health care services, the latter of which leads to an increase in emergency department usage and therefore funding. In providing a quality-assured smart technology system, individuals experiencing severe mental illness can gain access to mental health services that they may not have been able to access previously. Critical to this was the initial prototype apartment testing to ensure the intervention met the standards of those living in the community and their care teams. Full acceptability of smart technology within mental health care could support quality of care and improve integration for individuals living in the community. This can happen by combining mental health care legislation with public awareness to allay fears of personally identifiable data falling outside of the individual's circle of care, and assuring patients/tenants/HCPs that third parties will not have access to their information as the system is capable of managing electronic medical records.

Acknowledgments. We would like to acknowledge St. Joseph's Health Care, the Canadian Mental Health Association and London Middlesex Community Housing for facilitating the research environment. We would like to thank the participants and HCPs for their voluntary participation. Also, we appreciate the commitment of the research assistants for data collection and auditing to make sure the quality of research is assured. Finally, we would also like to acknowledge the two granting agencies - Canadian Mortgage & Housing Corporation, and Canadian Institutes for Health Research - for making the funding available.

Conflicts of Interest. The authors declare no conflict of interest.

References

1. Mental Health Commission of Canada: Making the Case for Investing in Mental Health in Canada. Mental Health Commission of Canada, Ottawa (2013)
2. Poirier, S., et al.: Schizophrenia patients with polydipsia and water intoxication are characterized by greater severity of psychotic illness and a more frequent history of alcohol abuse. Schizophr. Res. **118**, 285–291 (2010)
3. De Hert, M., et al.: Physical illness in patients with severe mental disorders. I. Prevalence, impact of medications and disparities in health care. World Psychiatry **10**, 52–77 (2011)
4. Dyck, K.G., Hardy, C.: Enhancing access to psychologically informed mental health services in rural and northern communities. Can. Psychol. **54**, 30–37 (2013)
5. Walker, E.R., McGee, R.E., Druss, B.G.: Mortality in mental disorders and global disease burden implications: a systematic review and meta-analysis. JAMA Psychiatry **72**, 334–341 (2015)
6. Ho, A., Quick, O.: Leaving patients to their own devices? Smart technology, safety, and therapeutic relationships. BMC Med. Ethics **19**, 18 (2018)
7. Forchuk, C., Csiernik, R., Jensen, E. (eds.): Homelessness, Housing and Mental Health. Canadian Scholars' Press, Toronto (2011)
8. Corring, D., Campbell, R., Rudnick, A.: A smart apartment for psychiatric inpatients. Psychiatr. Serv. **63**, 508 (2012)
9. Corring, D., Meier, A., Rudnick, A., Forchuk, C.: Using mobile technology to promote independence: an innovation in psychiatric rehabilitation – a feasibility study. Res. Insights **12**, 2–6 (2015)
10. Forchuk, C., et al.: TELEPROM-G: a study evaluating access and care delivery of telehealth services among community-based seniors. In: Future Technologies Conference: Proceedings of Future Technologies Conference, pp. 1346–1348. IEEE, San Francisco (2016)
11. Forchuk, C., et al.: Mental health engagement network (MHEN). Int. J. Adv. Life Sci. **5**, 1–10 (2013)
12. Forchuk, C., et al.: Mental health engagement network: an analysis of outcomes following a mobile and web-based intervention. J. Technol. Soc. **11**, 1–10 (2015)
13. Garafalo, J., Nathan-Roberts, D.: Assessment of the impacts from the addition of novel assistive technologies in mental health care. In: Proceedings of the Human Factors and Ergonomics Society 2016 Annual Meeting, vol. 60, pp. 1245–1248. Sage, Washington DC (2016)
14. Martin, S., Kelly, G., Kernohan, W.G., McCreight, B., Nugent, C.: Smart home technologies for health and social care support. Cochrane Database Syst. Rev. **4** (2008)
15. Goldman, H.H., Skodol, A.E., Lave, T.R.: Revising axis V for DSM-IV: a review of measures of social functioning. Am. J. Psychiatry **149**, 1148–1156 (1992)
16. Krueger, R.A.: Focus Groups: A Practical Guide for Applied Research. Sage Publications, Thousand Oak (1994)
17. Leininger, M.M.: Ethnography and Ethnonursing: models and modes of qualitative analysis. In: Leininger, M.M. (ed.) Qualitative Research Methods in Nursing, pp. 33–72. Grune & Stratton, Orlando (1985)
18. Forchuk, C., Rudnick, A., MacIntosh, J., Bukair, F., Hoch, J.S.: Evaluation framework for smart technology mental health interventions. In: Chang, C., Chiari, L., Cao, Y., Jin, H., Mokhtari, M., Aloulou, H. (eds.) ICOST 2016. LNCS, vol. 9677, pp. 203–210. Springer, Cham (2016). https://doi.org/10.1007/978-3-319-39601-9_18
19. Turk, M.W., et al.: Self-monitoring as a mediator of weight loss in the SMART randomized clinical trial. Int. J. Behav. Med. **20**, 556–561 (2013)

20. Nicholson, A., Kuper, H., Hemingway, H.: Depression as an aetiologic and prognostic factor in coronary heart disease: a meta-analysis of 6362 events among 146,358 participants in 54 observational studies. Eur. Heart J. **27**, 2763–2774 (2006)
21. Wurster, A.E., Archer, N.: Smart home technology and the needs of the aging population in Southern Ontario. Working Paper No. 59. McMaster eBusiness Research Centre (2016)

Transfer Learning for Urban Landscape Clustering and Correlation with Health Indexes

Riccardo Bellazzi[1(✉)], Alessandro Aldo Caldarone[1], Daniele Pala[1], Marica Franzini[2], Alberto Malovini[3], Cristiana Larizza[1], and Vittorio Casella[2]

[1] Department of Electrical, Computer and Biomedical Engineering, via Ferrata 5, 27100 Pavia, Italy
{riccardo.bellazzi, cristiana.larizza}@unipv.it, {alessandroaldo.caldarone01, daniele.pala02}@universitadipavia.it

[2] Department of Civil Engineering and Architecture, via Ferrata 3, 27100 Pavia, Italy
{marica.franzini, vittorio.casella}@unipv.it

[3] IRCCS ICS Maugeri, via S. Maugeri 2, 27100 Pavia, Italy
alberto.malovini@icsmaugeri.it

Abstract. Within the EU-funded Pulse project, we are implementing a data analytic platform designed to provide public health decision makers with advanced approaches to jointly analyze maps and geospatial information with health care data and air pollution measurements. In this paper we describe a component of such platform, designed to couple deep learning analysis of geospatial images of cities and some healthcare and behavioral indexes collected by the 500 cities US project, showing that, in New York City, urban landscape significantly correlates with the access to healthcare services.

Keywords: Transfer learning · Deep learning · Urban landscape · Health indexes

1 Introduction

Recent advances in machine learning and deep learning enable the design and implementation of novel data analysis pipelines that allow fusing heterogeneous data sources to extract novel insights and predictive patterns. These approaches seem particularly suitable to help increasing our insights in the relationships between the urban landscape of cities and the behavior of their residents, with particular focus on well-being and healthcare indexes. In this context, it can be of interest of health care planners and city decision-makers to have instruments able to find clusters of city areas that share similar urban structures and to analyze some behavioral indexes of their residents, in particular to see potential correlations and to plan similar interventions in the different clusters, even if such clusters contain areas that are geographically far. We have applied such approach in the context of the PULSE (Participatory Urban Living

J. Pagán et al. (Eds.): ICOST 2019, LNCS 11862, pp. 143–153, 2019.
https://doi.org/10.1007/978-3-030-32785-9_13

for Sustainable Environment) EU-project[1]. PULSE aims at developing a set of models and technologies to predict and manage public health problems in cities and promote health. It follows a participatory approach where citizen provide data through personal devices that are integrated with information from heterogeneous sources: open city data, health systems, urban sensors and satellites. The project deals with various issues concerning air quality, lifestyle and personal behavior and it aims to investigate the correlations between the exposure to atmospheric pollutants, the citizen habits and the health of the citizen themselves, focusing on asthma and type 2 diabetes. PULSE is being implemented in 5 major cities all over the world. Within PULSE, we are implementing a data analytic platform that will provide public health decision makers with advanced approaches to jointly analyze maps and geospatial information with health care data and air pollution measurements.

In this paper we will describe the results obtained with a prototypical component of such platform, designed to couple deep learning analysis of geospatial images of cities and some healthcare and behavioral indexes, showing that in New York City urban landscape significantly correlates with the access to healthcare services.

2 Deep Learning and Transfer Learning Models

Deep neural models provide flexible instruments to perform non-linear approximation of a variety of multivariate functions and to extract latent variables from a data set. In a nutshell, deep neural models are neural networks with many layers, able to map non-linear functions with a number of parameters that is typically lower than their equivalent models with one layer only. Such models are particularly attractive since they can be used to perform clustering, regression and classification starting from data sets made of images, texts, time series.

In dependence of the nature of the input data set, different architectures can be exploited, ranging from the combination of many Convolutional layers in the case of images to the use of Long-term/Short-term networks in the case of time series and speech/text data.

Recently, an increasing number of papers are using deep learning to examine the relationships between the urban landscape and some environmental or citizens' behavioral data [1–3].

One of the main limits of deep learning models is related to the need of very large data sets in order to be able to gain advantage of their capability of encoding even the finest details that can be important to map input data, without getting trapped into noise and poor parameters estimates.

Rather interestingly, in order to deal with this problem, it is possible to resort to an increasing set of pre-trained deep learning models that can be used for the task of transfer learning [4], i.e. models that are able to represent the input space into a set of latent variables on the basis of a mapping mechanism, usually a deep neural network, learned on a large (external) data set, so that the relationships between such latent

[1] "http://www.project-pulse.eu".

variables and the outcomes can be later learned on a specific and smaller data set. A well-known example is Inception-v3, a convolutional neural network trained on more than a million images from the ImageNet database (http://www.image-net.org). The network has 48 layers and can classify images into one thousand object categories, including trees and many animals. Another interesting example is represented by the Painters [5] networks, developed to automatically classify Paintings of famous artists. In principle, any of those methods can be used following the transfer learning paradigm to represent images coming from urban landscape of New York City.

3 Data and Methods

Our analysis is based on two data sources: NYC high resolution images and healthcare data coming from the 500 cities project [6]. NYC images have been collected by the "The National Agriculture Imagery Program" (NAIP) that acquires aerial imagery during the agricultural growing seasons in the continental United States. In particular, we have downloaded an image having an original resolution of 0.5 m and have downsampled it to 2 m which allows to have a fine-grained representation of the aerial urban landscape (see Fig. 1).

As it will be explained in the following, the reason for the downsampling is that the big image has been subdivided into tiles and the neural network adopted can accept images having maximum size of 299 pixel; we had to tune the ground resolution in order to have meaningful tiles, embracing a sufficiently-sized area.

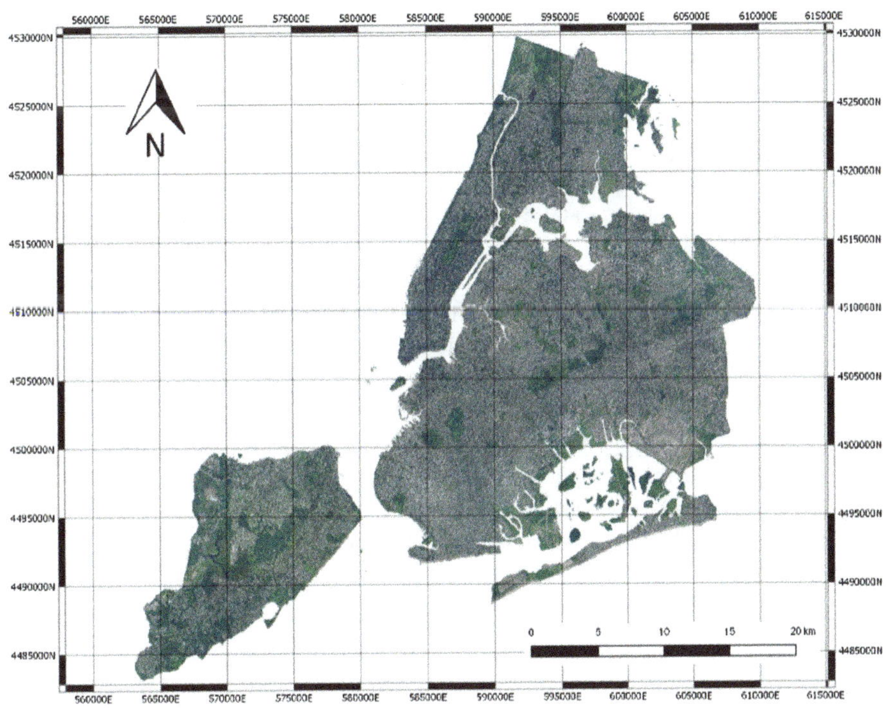

Fig. 1. NAIP image of NYC.

Health care data have been extracted from the repository made available by the 500 Cities project. "500 cities" is a collaboration between CDC, the Robert Wood Johnson Foundation, and the CDC Foundation[2]. The project provides city- and census tract-level small area estimates for chronic disease risk factors (unhealthy behaviors), health outcomes, and clinical preventive service use for the largest 500 cities in the United States. NYC is divided in 2166 census tracts and the latest data available concerns 2017. The 27 chronic diseases measures provided by the project are listed in Table 1.

The measures include major risk behaviors that lead to illness, suffering, and early death related to chronic diseases and conditions, as well as the conditions and diseases that are the most common, costly, and preventable of all health problems.

Table 1. 500 cities measures grouped by category. The 27 measures include 13 health outcomes, 9 prevention practices and 5 unhealthy behaviors.

Category	Measure
Health outcomes	Arthritis among adults aged ≥ 18 years
	Current asthma among adults aged ≥ 18 years
	High blood pressure among adults aged ≥ 18 years
	Cancer among adults aged ≥ 18 years
	High cholesterol among adults aged ≥ 18 years who have been screened in the past 5 years
	Chronic kidney disease among adults aged ≥ 18 years
	Chronic obstructive pulmonary disease among adults aged ≥ 18 years
	Coronary heart disease among adults aged ≥ 18 years
	Diagnosed diabetes among adults aged ≥ 18 years
	Mental health not good for ≥ 14 days among adults aged ≥ 18 years
	Physical health not good for ≥ 14 days among adults aged ≥ 18 years
	All teeth lost among adults aged ≥ 65 years
	Stroke among adults aged ≥ 18 years
Prevention	Current lack of health insurance among adults aged 18–64 years
	Visits to doctor for routine checkup within the past year among adults aged ≥ 18 years
	Visits to dentist or dental clinic among adults aged ≥ 18 years
	Taking medicine for high blood pressure control among adults aged ≥ 18 years with high blood pressure
	Cholesterol screening among adults aged ≥ 18 years
	Mammography use among women aged 50–74 years
	Papanicolaou smear use among adult women aged 21–65 years
	Fecal occult blood test, sigmoidoscopy, or colonoscopy among adults aged 50–75 years
	Older adults aged ≥ 65 years who are up to date on a core set of clinical preventive services by age and sex
Unhealthy behaviors	Binge drinking among adults aged ≥ 18 years
	Current smoking among adults aged ≥ 18 years
	No leisure-time physical activity among adults aged ≥ 18 years
	Obesity among adults aged ≥ 18 years
	Sleeping less than 7 h among adults aged ≥ 18 years

[2] https://www.cdc.gov/500cities/index.htm.

3.1 The Data Analysis Pipeline

The pipeline implemented in our work is described in Fig. 2. The NAIP NYC image has been subdivided into image square blocks having size of 256 × 256 pixels, corresponding to a 512 m edge. Therefore, it was possible to estimate the value of each of the 27 variables collected by "500 Cities" for each block. During this process, blocks out of the tracts or over the sea have been excluded, thus reducing the dataset. The images have been then processed by a pretrained deep model, thus extracting the final features for each image. Images are clustered by resorting to k-means clustering, and the clusters, confirmed with visual inspection, are associated to the healthcare indexes by statistical analysis.

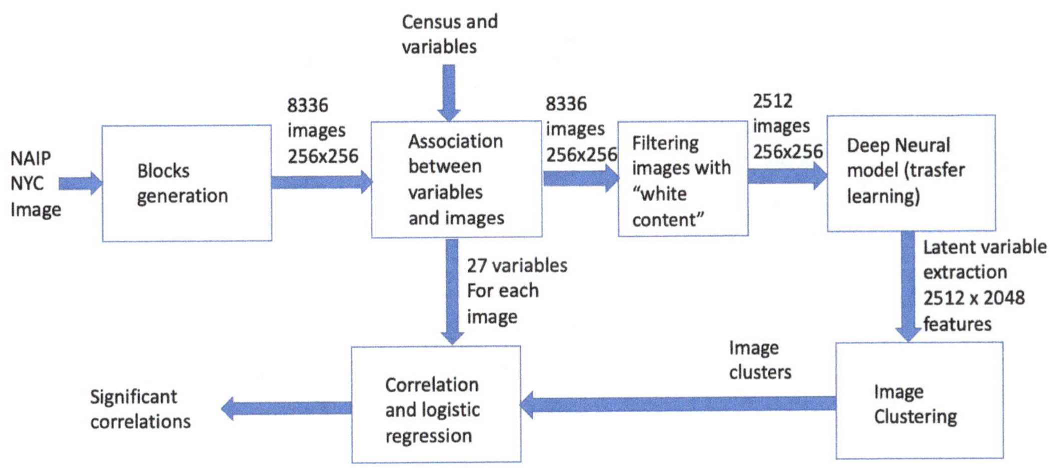

Fig. 2. The data analysis pipeline

3.2 Image Blocks

The NAIP NYC image has been subdivided into 8336 images of 256 × 256 pixels. Each image is a square with edge equal to 512 m. It must be underlined that the original image is georeferenced, meaning that each single pixel is precisely located in space. The small derived tiles are georeferenced as well and can be effectively overlapped to the health and well-being maps. The images have been processed resorting to the Matlab Image Processing and Mapping toolboxes, which are capable of properly managing georeferenced images. Figure 3 shows some examples of the resulting images.

It is possible to note that some of the squares have white areas, corresponding to unmapped zones, due to the irregular borders of the image and to the presence of sea, rivers. Due to the availability of the vector map of the borders of NYC, we have been able to quantify, for each tile, the amount of its surface lying inside the borders of the city; we then filtered the original tile set and maintained only those having a minimal overlapping of 90%.

3.3 Estimation of the Healthcare Indexes for Each Image Block

The healthcare indexes of the 500 Cities database are collected for census tracts and NYC has, as already reported, 2166 census tracts. In order to carry out our analysis, we had to determine the value of the considered variables for each image block. In fact, a given tile overlaps, in general, several tracts. Therefore, we had to implement a simple estimator of the healthcare index of the block, as:

$$hci(block) = \frac{\sum_j w_j hci(j)}{\sum_j w_j}$$

where *hci(j)* is the value of the generic health care index for the j-*th* census tract and w_j is the percentage of the image block covered by the mentioned tract. An example is shown in Figs. 3 and 4.

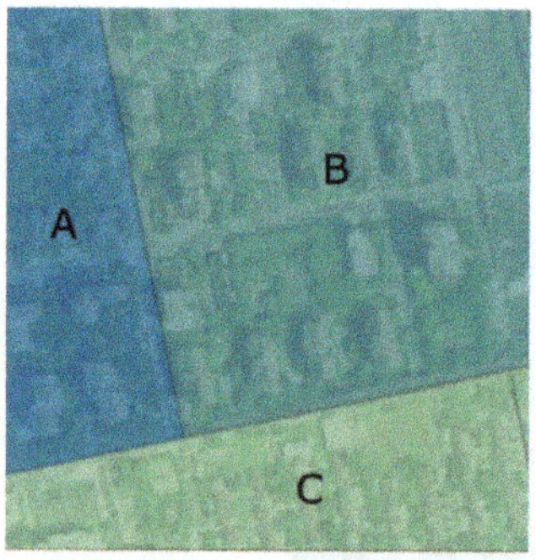

Census tract	SLEEP
A	8.45
B	47.36
C	32.48

w_A = Area of A/Area of image * 100
w_B = Area of B/Area of image * 100
w_C = Area of C/Area of image * 100

SLEEP(block) = (w_A * 8.45 + w_B * 47.36 + w_c * 32.48)/100

Fig. 3. The quantification of the healthcare index value (SLEEP) of a block.

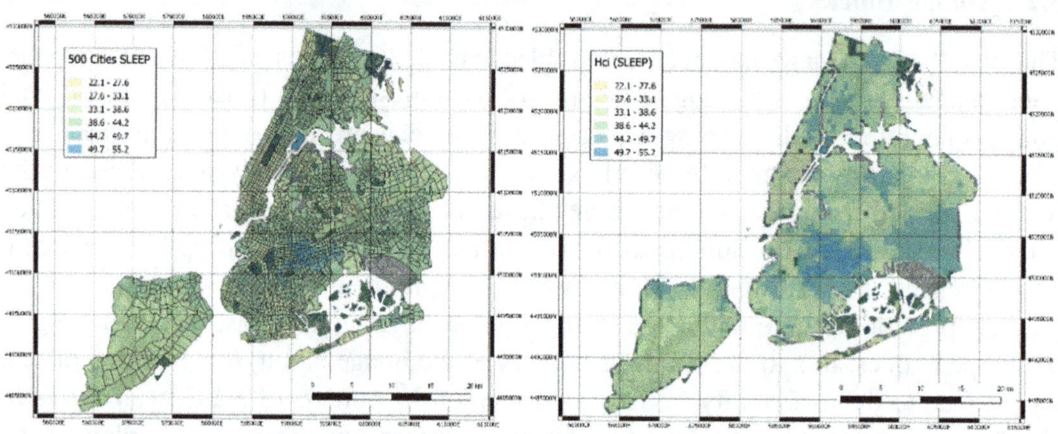

Fig. 4. Original census tracts with the 500 Cities SLEEP index (left hand side) and derived quantification of the healthcare index values for SLEEP variable (right hand side).

In order to properly quantify *hci*s, the blocks with a white area greater than 10% of the image have been removed. The final number of image blocks used for the following analysis has thus lowered to 2512 images. Each image has been then processed by resorting to a deep neural model to extract a set of latent features.

3.4 Deep Neural Networks Processing and Clustering

As a deep neural network model used for transfer learning, we have selected the network developed for the 2016 Painters by number competition [6]. In such competition the goal was to learn how to discriminate the authors of paintings between 1584 unique painters, starting from a training set of 79433 instances; the test set was composed of 23817 instances. In this case, a deep neural network model was learned, with 23 layers, mostly convolutional layers with some max pooling layer. The Painters network computes a layer of 2048 latent variables before the final discrimination layer implemented with a soft-max non-linear function. Those latent variables can be used as a way to embed generic images in the latent space. Therefore, using the software Orange (https://orange.biolab.si) and its Python pipeline, we have processed all image blocks with the Painters model, thus obtaining a final data matrix of 2512 examples with 2048 features.

Such features have been used to cluster the image blocks by resorting to the well-known K-means clustering algorithm. The value of K has been derived with a grid search between 2 and 6 and taking the value that maximize the Silhouette coefficient.

3.5 Correlation and Statistical Analysis

The final step of the data analysis pipeline is represented by the search of statistical correlations between the clusters and their *hci*s. Univariate multinomial logistic regression was applied to estimate the probability to belong to a specific cluster given single variables' values. Multivariate multinomial logistic regression was performed after removal of samples characterized by missing values. A backward stepwise selection procedure based on AIC was applied to identify the most informative set of variables jointly modulating the probability to belong to the clusters. Multinomial logistic regression and the stepwise selection procedure were implemented in the R packages "nnet" and "stats", respectively. Analyses were performed by the R software tool version 3.5.1 (http://www.r-project.org).

4 Results

4.1 Clustering

K-means was run on the 2512 instances with Euclidean distance and 10 reruns. 4 clusters were found to maximize Silhouette coefficient. The output of the clustering algorithm has been validated by analyzing the cluster distribution with the tSNE two-dimensional mapping, as reported in Fig. 5. It is easy to see that the four clusters are in general well separated in the two-dimensional space[3].

[3] It is worthwhile mentioning that this criterion was qualitatively used to assess also other deep neural networks model; Painters turned out to generate the clusters that had the best tSNE spatial distribution of clusters.

Thanks to visual inspection, it is possible to highlight that the four clusters well correspond to different urban landscapes. Cluster C1 corresponds to green areas, Cluster C2 to residential areas with small houses, Cluster C3 to industrial areas and larger buildings, Cluster C4 to residential with larger buildings. Four examples are shown in Fig. 6. Cluster analysis clearly show that the deep neural network model is able to map images in the latent space that share the intuitive notion of similarity that humans may use when they have to classify urban landscape. The method is thus able to automatically cluster similar areas where similar interventions can be planned.

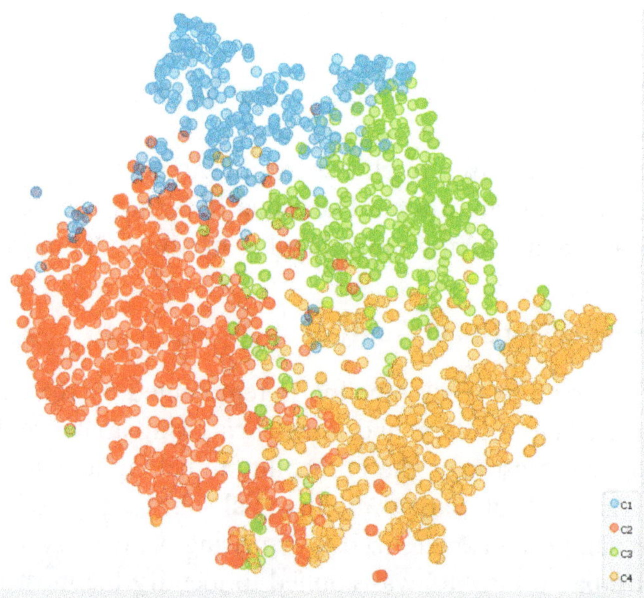

Fig. 5. The tSNE representation of the data with colors identifying the four clusters.

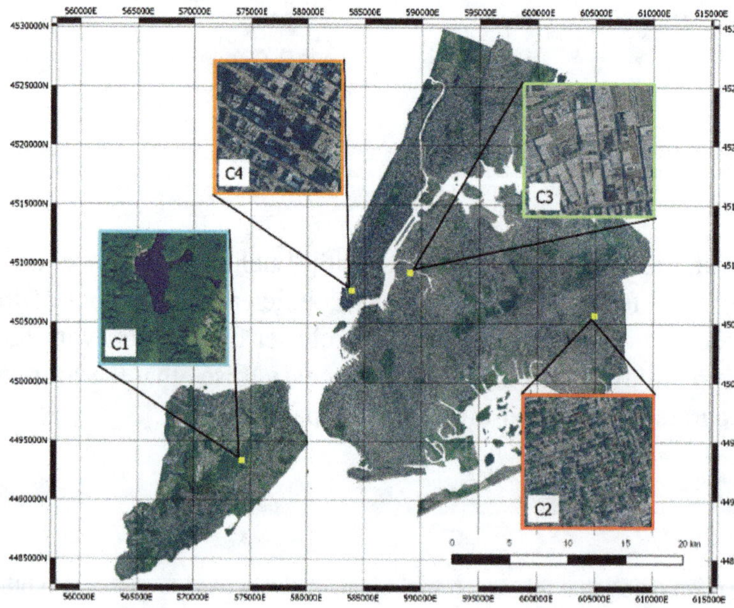

Fig. 6. Four images representing the clusters.

4.2 Correlation and Statistical Analysis

Univariate analysis shows that 22 over 27 variables were significantly correlated with the clusters. This is also confirmed with visual inspection showing the variables distributions after equal frequency discretization against the clusters, as shown in Fig. 7.

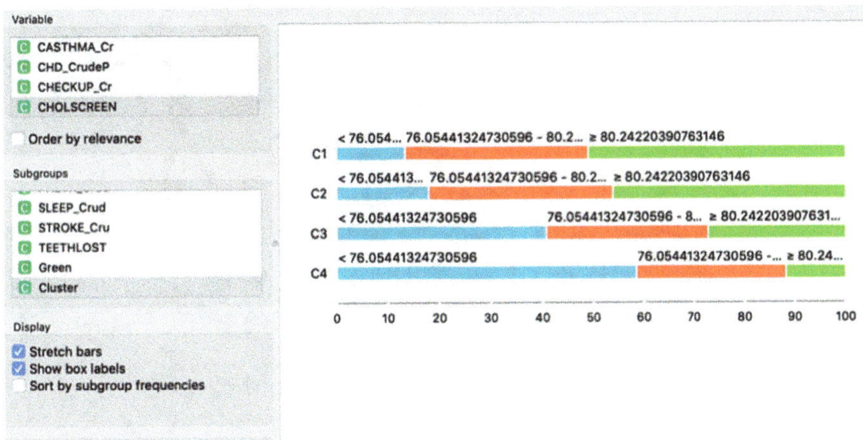

Fig. 7. The different distributions of Cholesterol screening among adults aged ≥ 18 years in the different clusters. Inhabitants of cluster C1 have much higher propensity towards screening than those who live in Cluster C4.

In general, cluster C1, which is the one that groups green areas, has consistently better prevention and health indicators, but worse sleeping indexes and leisure time. Overall, there is a gradient with all indexes moving from cluster C1, to C2, to C3 and finally to C4, which are the residential areas with large buildings.

A multivariate multinomial logistic regression has been performed to assess if significant correlations are present even in the multivariate setting. In this case, after a stepwise feature selection process, 20 variables have been selected. Of those, five variables have been found to be significant ($p \ll 0.01$) in all sub-regressions performed by the multinomial model: Colon screening (Fecal occult blood test, sigmoidoscopy, or colonoscopy among adults aged 50–75 years), Chronic obstructive pulmonary disease among adults aged ≥ 18 years, High cholesterol among adults aged ≥ 18 years who have been screened in the past 5 years, Chronic kidney disease among adults aged ≥ 18 years and finally Stroke among adults aged ≥ 18 years.

4.3 Mapping

The blocks and the clusters have been represented in the original map, confirming the qualitative evaluation of the clusters reported above (Fig. 8).

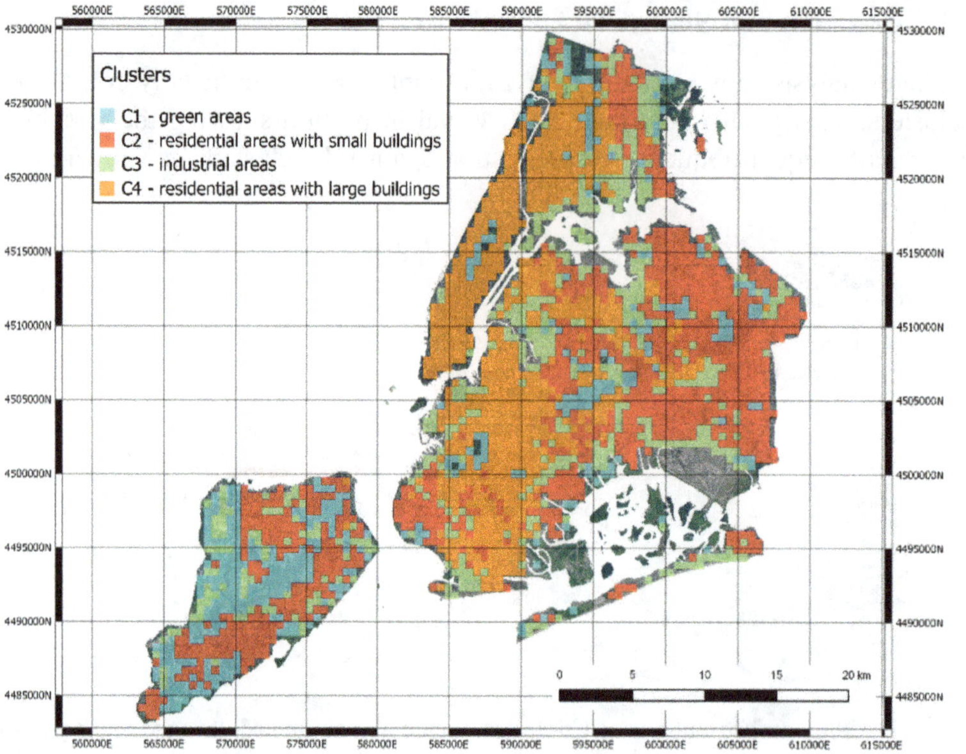

Fig. 8. The clusters remapped in NYC. (Color figure online)

We can find green areas (C1), residential areas with larger buildings (C2), industrial areas (C3) and finally residential areas (C4).

5 Discussion and Conclusions

The data analysis pipeline described in this paper shows that it is possible to automatically correlate urban landscape with healthcare indicators at the whole city level. In the NYC case, such correlation seems particularly strong, probably because of social factors, which, in the US society, makes health indicators related to the urban areas where people live.

Our work has a number of implications.

First of all, it shows that deep neural networks designed to encode image data can be successfully reused within transfer learning approaches. Their application to represent urban landscape seems very effective.

Second, in the context of the PULSE project, the capability of finding clusters of similar urban landscape may allow to profile city areas, in which health care decision makers may plan similar interventions.

Finally, the combination of urban landscape and healthcare indicators is not only useful to hypothesize the intertwining of these two dimensions, but also to further profile urban areas by finding similar areas with similar behaviors of their inhabitants, thus allowing also life style interventions and more “precise” health care policies.

Of course, the analysis has some limitations. First of all, the "quantification" of the health care indexes in the city blocks have been performed by a weighted averaging of the indexes of the census tracts included in the blocks. The weights are computed taking into account only the spatial overlap and not the actual number of inhabitants of the blocks. Second, the results obtained are probably "proxies" of the wealth of the people living in the different areas. For this reason, results may be representative of specific cities and not generalizable to other ones.

Acknowledgement. The work is part of the project PULSE, H2020 - 727816, funded by the European Union.

References

1. Helbich, M., Yao, Y., Liu, Y., Zhang, J., Liu, P., Wang, R.: Using deep learning to examine street view green and blue spaces and their associations with geriatric depression in Beijing. China. Environ Int. **126**, 107–117 (2019)
2. Hong, K.Y., Pinheiro, P.O., Minet, L., Hatzopoulou, M., Weichenthal, S.: Extending the spatial scale of land use regression models for ambient ultrafine particles using satellite images and deep convolutional neural networks. Environ. Res. **30**(176), 108513 (2019)
3. Zewdie, G.K., Lary, D.J., Levetin, E., Garuma, G.F.: Applying deep neural networks and ensemble machine learning methods to forecast airborne ambrosia pollen. Int. J. Environ. Res. Public Health **16**(11), 1992 (2019)
4. Sharma, S., Ball, J.E., Tang, B., Carruth, D.W., Doude, M., Islam, M.A.: Semantic segmentation with transfer learning for off-road autonomous driving. Sensors (Basel). **19**(11), 2577 (2019)
5. Painters by Numbers. http://blog.kaggle.com/2016/11/17/painter-by-numbers-competition-1st-place-winners-interview-nejc-ilenic/. Accessed 21 June 2019
6. Centers for disease control and prevention. National center for chronic disease prevention and health promotion. Division of population health. 500 cities project data (2019). https://www.cdc.gov/500cities. Accessed 21 June 2019

An IoT Architecture of Microservices for Ambient Assisted Living Environments to Promote Aging in Smart Cities

Hubert Kenfack Ngankam[1(✉)], Hélène Pigot[1], Maxime Parenteau[1], Maxime Lussier[2], Aline Aboujaoudé[2], Catherine Laliberté[1], Mélanie Couture[3], Nathalie Bier[2], and Sylvain Giroux[1]

[1] Laboratoire Domus, Université de Sherbrooke, 2500 boul. Université, Sherbrooke, QC J1K 2R1, Canada
{hubert.kenfack.ngankam,helene.pigot,maxime.parenteau, catherine.d.laliberte,sylvain.giroux}@usherbrooke.ca

[2] Centre de recherche de l'Institut de gériatrie de Montréal, 4565, rue Queen Mary, Montréal, QC H3W 1W5, Canada
maximelussier@gmail.com, aline.aboujaoude@mail.mcgill.ca, nathalie.bier@umontreal.ca

[3] Centre for Research and Expertise in Social Gerontology (CREGES), CIUSSS West-Central Montreal, 5800, Cavendish Boulevard, Côte Saint-Luc, QC H4W 2T5, Canada
melanie.couture.cvd@ssss.gouv.qc.ca

Abstract. Ambient Assisted Living (AAL) environments encompass technical systems and the Internet of Things (IoT) tools to support seniors in their daily routines. They aim to enable seniors to live independently and safely for as long as possible when faced declining physical or cognitive capacities. This work presents the design, development and deployment of an AAL system in the context of smart cities. The proposed architecture is based on microservices and software components. We examined the requirements and specifications of AAL systems in smart homes, in efforts to describe and evaluate how they would be transposable in the case of smart cities. The system has been tested and evaluated in the laboratory; it has been deployed in real life settings within city and is still in use by five elderly people.

Keywords: Ambient Assisted Living · Internet of Things · Architecture · Smart homes · Smart cities · Aging in place · Microservices

1 Introduction

As defined by Marsal-Llacuna et al. [1], Smart Cities aim to improve urban performance by using data, information and information technology (IT) to deliver

J. Pagán et al. (Eds.): ICOST 2019, LNCS 11862, pp. 154–167, 2019.
https://doi.org/10.1007/978-3-030-32785-9_14

more efficient services to citizens. IT must satisfy interconnected and smart characteristics. On one hand, city services may be interconnected through a distributed computing platform allowing integration, collection and dissemination of data; on the other hand, to become smart they must integrate information from various sources, analyze model, optimize and help visualization of these complex information to make better operational decisions.

The Centre of Regional Science at the Vienna University of Technology has identified six main components of a smart city: smart economy, smart mobility, smart environment, smart people, smart living, and smart governance [2]. The city of Côte Saint-Luc, Canada, faces an increased number of seniors that forces them to find solutions for promoting aging well at home, within the city. These circumstances leads the city to adopt a smart city approach mainly characterized by smart living for the aging population. Efficient and economical solutions may provide peace of mind, safety and support to limit isolation and promote social participation. Indeed, the administrative team of the city of Côte Saint-Luc believes that its intelligence relies on investments in human and social capital, as well as in technology infrastructure, sustainable growth and the quality of senior's life. These refer to the key components "smart living" of a smart city. The smart cities services must be able to interact with most of the aging population, offering non-complex interfaces that are well adapted to the abilities and preferences of each elder while maintaining functional efficiency in the delivery of services.

The needs of seniors and their state of health change over time as they age and loss of autonomy sets in [3,4]. Thus, as activities of daily living become more and more difficult to perform by the senior, increasing the number of situations of handicaps, institutionalization sometimes becomes the only solution [5]. Moreover, social interactions, community living and communication are factors that have an important influence on quality of life [6,7]. For seniors, interacting with citizens and participating in social activities and entertainment are essential for a good life [6,7]. Generally, seniors can communicate with family and friends by phone, email, and mail. However, seniors with cognitive or physical impairments have difficulty accessing social media and participating in social activities. This leads to social isolation and aggravation of the state of health [8].

To delay institutionalization and limit isolation, Ambient Assisted Living (AAL) systems build smart environment that provides assistance as well as healthcare and especially rehabilitation to seniors with physical or cognitive deficits. AAL systems include technology networks, heterogeneous information, smart devices, products and services. It is an ecosystem of connected objects, medical technologies, sensor networks and software applications for the monitoring and home support of frail people. To make everyday life easier, they propose to automate complex tasks and to monitor activities of daily living for facilitating independence. Above all, they offer continuous assessment of activities carried out, and a reduction in caregiver burden [3,6].

To design AAL system that fulfills the user requirements, the City needs action-oriented approach where research questions emerge through consultation and interaction among several disciplines and sectors to develop socially useful, feasible, practical, effective and sustainable solutions [9]. Stakeholders must work together in a transdisciplinary research approach and methodology. As defined by Harvard transdisciplinary research "Transdisciplinary Research is defined as research efforts conducted by investigators from different disciplines working jointly to create new conceptual, theoretical, methodological, and translational innovations that integrate and move beyond discipline-specific approaches to address a common problem". Indeed, transdisciplinary research provides an opportunity to bring out AAL relevant and appropriate solutions [9]. However, these solutions must be based on a reliable architecture to guarantee efficient services. As the domain of IoT is emerging, lack of standardization leads to a variety of products that provokes communication issues. It is then difficult to propose a coherent AAL system for the users. The goal of this work is twofold: (1) to identify the technical and technological requirements to be met to enable the city to promote aging in place for older residents; and (2) to design a software infrastructure that provides efficient and useful AAL applications that fulfill these requirements.

The rest of the document is structured as follows; Sect. 2 describes background and related works. Section 3 discusses the requirements and challenges an AAL system must satisfy in a smart city context. Section 4 describes the design and the implementation of the AAL architecture. Section 5 shows how the architecture was deployed in five participants home to fulfill their needs. A discussion of the deployment results follows. Finally, Sect. 6 concludes the paper and highlights the future work.

2 Background and Related Works

AAL is a multidisciplinary approach that leverages a wide range of technologies from different fields to deliver personalized services. Deployed AAL systems deal with many contextual information, based on a sensor/actuator information, user actions, user profiles, and ambient information [3]. The different AAL technologies that accompany aging in place are applied in various domains [3,5,6]:

- Facilitate communication between the senior and caregivers;
- Monitor the health parameters of the senior;
- Monitor the environment and the activities of the senior's daily life using sensors to ensure greater comfort and safety;
- Facilitate the mobility of people out of their homes.

To offer adequate services to the seniors, the scope of the AAL systems covers not only the measure, control and connection of the network of sensors and actuators, it also requires understanding the habits and the behavior of the inhabitants in order to react according to their needs, their state of mind and their desires [4]. A user-centered approach is therefore required, involving the elders themselves, as well as a transdisciplinary approach that includes the

City's administrators, computer engineers, geriatric specialists, caregivers and clinicians [9].

Most AAL systems are moving towards the IoT platform paradigm with programs to control devices, display monitoring recordings, adjust ambient settings, lock doors and windows, and so on [10]. The Internet of Things (IoT) is a technological paradigm derived from innovative concepts and developments in information and communication technologies associated with ubiquitous computing, and ambient intelligence [11,12]. Such an approach brings significant improvements to the interaction of users, but is often based on the presence of a monolithic architecture. Monolithic architecture is complex and costly in deployment time, with many limitations in terms of scalability and component reuse [13]. Yet, while connected to a wide range of independent devices and systems, the architecture of today's AAL systems tends to focus on service resiliency and software component integration.

The choice of a general structure has an impact on the reliability, performance, maintainability and therefore lifetime of the AAL systems. It needs a structure that is customizable, that could adapt to various features and react to dynamic changes to devices. Therefore, among the various infrastructure proposed, AAL middleware is mainly preferred to facilitate the homogenization of different technologies and to satisfy the prerequisite characteristics [14]. Also a microservices platform is favored because it makes possible to design an easy-to-scale IoT system that quickly integrates new technological components and allows each instance to be adapted to the profile of the user [13].

3 AAL Systems Requirements and Challenges

Designing AAL systems requires respecting several characteristics and norms. The general architecture of AAL systems must fulfill the following requirements: heterogeneity; interoperability; usability; security; accuracy; reliability; maintainability; efficiency and technological scalability [15]. In a smart city context, the vast number of users reached necessitates to assure effective services delivery. The scalability is then twofold. Its scope covers the increase of the number of users reached and the number of devices to integrate because of the personalization of the services offered to each senior.

The AAL system designed and presented in this paper is part of a transdisciplinary methodological approach, which ensures that the issues emerging from seniors and the city are satisfied. We will show in the following that designing AAL on a middleware architecture that integrates microservices will realize the pre-cited requirements and respond to transdisciplinary approach. These requirements are grouped into four categories:

- Modularity: heterogeneity – interoperability – maintainability;
- Availability of services: scalability of technology – reliability – efficiency;
- Services delivery: scalability for seniors – security;
- Adaptability: adaptation to the senior profile – usability – accuracy.

Indeed, scalability is required for the city to offer services to a large number of citizens. However, modularity is a key requirement for the city to offer multiples services that should evolve according to new services the city desires to offer and new devices the IoT improvements will make available. Citizens expect also that the city will comply with security, reliability and accuracy of the city services.

3.1 Modularity

Modularity is a concept that includes heterogeneity, interoperability and maintainability. Indeed, it expresses the fact that the technological components fit together despite their differences. Due to the rapid evolution of the IoT domain, no standard has yet emerged. Rather, a wide variety of IoT components appears on the market including network connectivity options, proprietary or standards-based protocols, and unknown communication methods. It is expected that for years, new devices, new services and new protocols force IoT systems to accommodate various components and let them interact despite the diversity. Users also ask to get access to IoT services irrespective to the medium used.

This heterogeneity requires interoperability without concession regarding maintainability. Interoperability refers to the ability for the AAL system to propose interfaces that are understood by all the IoT components and to allow access between them. Maintainability guarantees the ability of the AAL system to continue to be interoperable in the future despite the evolution of the technology, the update of each component and the apparition of new components.

To respect heterogeneity, ensure interoperability and maintain it over time, communication protocols as well as data format must be independent. Middleware and software components address this heterogeneity issue. Middleware is a feature that allows several devices to be managed by the platform. In general, middleware can be considered as a software construct mediating between two or more disparate software components [16]. The software components are part of a system or application. It is a web service, a software package, a web resource, or a module that encapsulates a set of functions or data. Components are a way to break down the complexity of the software into manageable parts [14]. Each component hides the complexity of its implementation behind an interface. This mechanism reduces the complexity of software development, maintenance, operations, and support, and allows to reuse the same code in many systems. To preserve this mechanism, the software components and the middleware for AAL must be kept simple and offer broad compatibility and interoperability with most of the IoT components. Excessive duplication of proprietary software must be prevented. Overall, it is better to opt for solutions and initiatives that are open source, easily to install, and quickly maintainable. Moreover, if the middleware is built on microservices, it guarantees flexibility and ease of work in large systems, reducing the amount of communication and coordination between entities [13].

3.2 Availability of Services

AAL systems are intended to change according to the needs of seniors and the configuration of the smart home that must integrate new IoT components. The user profile and his preferences are unique, necessitating the use of personalized sensors and actuators. Sometimes, it also requires to implement new services or modify existing ones. Despite the scalability of the technology induced by the changes, the AAL system must provide reliable and efficient services. This is all the more important given that the final users are not comfortable with technology. The software architecture must then be able to evolve with the senior needs and inspire confidence among the seniors and the city.

Each microservice can be: deployed independently; independently designed, developed and tested. As a result, this architecture style has a greatly increased responsiveness to change. It makes it possible to respond better to the objectives of responsiveness and adaptability of Agile approaches [13]. The individual components can be run across a variety of platforms. A layered and non-monolithic architectural organization makes it possible to promote the scaling up of components and technical requirements in a transparent manner. Indeed, each layer is responsible for the local management of a subset of information, while the overall management lies with all components. To ensure the availability of services, the system must be able to detect, to reason and act on the actions performed in the environment. The ability to communicate and interact with the surroundings is part of the AAL approach.

3.3 Services Delivery

The proposed architecture is intended for an entire city. It must then be able to be deployed to multiple participants. This scalability according to the number of seniors must not affect the quality of services offered. The AAL system must also guarantee security as it covers private issues.

The microservice architecture structures an application as a collection of services that are highly maintainable and testable, loosely coupled, independently deployable and organized around business capabilities. The microservice architecture enables the continuous delivery and deployment of large and complex applications. AAL system can be spread across multiple servers or even multiple databases. The architecture has better fault isolation; if one microservice fails, the others will continue to work. To evolve quickly, the system offers at least one local cache. This is necessary to ensure the resilience of the system. For example, if the microservice of the local user fails or is slow, other microservices will not be affected, they should be able to work independently. In the worst case, the remote information will be empty or classified with a default value. In this case, the microservices will also be faster, because they will not need to join data from a remote source to meet the demands of users.

3.4 Adaptability

To ensure that the smart home fulfills the senior needs, the design of AAL system must be participatory, transdisciplinary and user centered [9]. Interactions with the smart home remain simple and integrated into everyday life to facilitate its use by seniors. AAL systems should be able to anticipate the user's needs as much as possible and provide the necessary assistance in a non-intrusive and subtle manner. The profiles, the health status of seniors and the habitats are mostly different. The system must be organized to effectively manage these differences and offers equal, adapted and accurate services despite the underlying differences and the response of the users.

To ensure adaptability and ease of use, intuitive interfaces through voice control and tangible interfaces must be offered to provide for the seniors, easy ways to control the AAL system. At the reverse, the AAL system must put in place mechanisms to notify caregivers using IoT components that are dispatched into the home. Thus, the AAL architecture must share information between the IoT components to monitor the senior anywhere, at any time, regardless of the kind of action performed and assistance needed. Therefore, the information shared between the IoT components is described at a high level of abstraction in order for the IoT components to avoid specific implementation details and rather exchange semantic information.

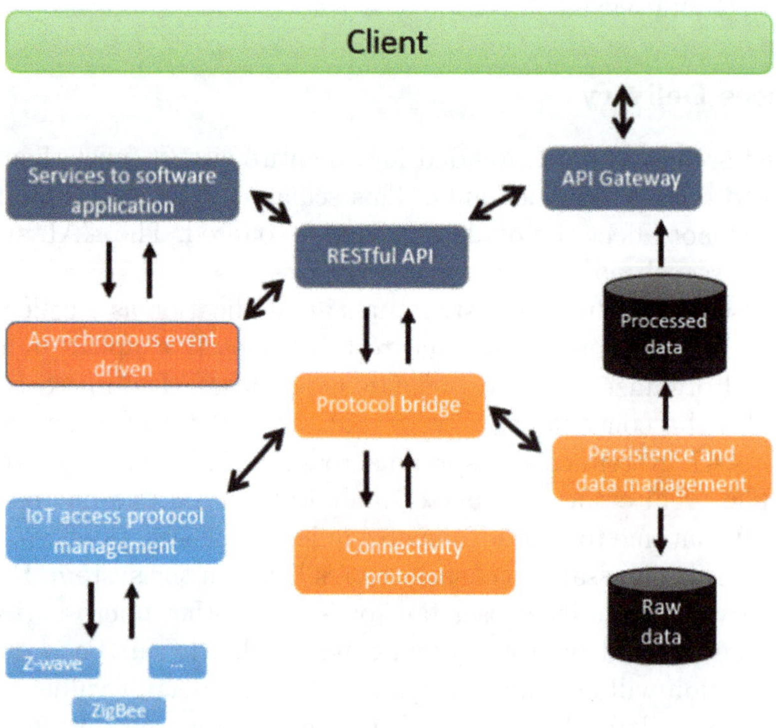

Fig. 1. AAL system logic architecture based on microservices.

4 AAL Systems Design and Implementation

Deriving from the previous requirements, the AAL architecture proposed in the City is based on a middleware that offers microservices described on a high level of abstraction. The microservice architecture ensures interoperability between distinct technologies over time. A microservice architecture is a specific software system design process that structures an application as a collection of loosely coupled services. The services work in cooperation to provide the features defined in the system. With microservices, each application runs independently from the others. Therefore, adding or changing features will affect only the service involved without affecting the others.

4.1 Architecture Design

Figure 1 illustrates the logical architecture of microservices that defines the distribution and relationship between AAL systems, subsystems, and components. This architecture, built as a set of independent microservice modular components, is easy to test, maintain and understand. It enables organizations to increase their agility while improving workflows and the time needed to enhance production.

The access protocol management module provides an interface for the handling of the different communication protocols based on the standard IEEE 802.15.x and 802.11. It usually acts as a driver for connected objects. Typically, this module provides wireless mesh technology designed to carry small amounts of data over short or medium distances.

The connectivity protocol module is designed as an extremely lightweight published/subscribed messaging transport. It is useful for connections to remote sites where a small code footprint is required or a reduced network bandwidth. It implements a channel subscription mechanism. Whenever an event occurs, it notifies all entities registered in the channel. Thus, when a new event occurs all registered components are notified, avoiding an active standby.

The microservice of persistence and data management deals with data backup in the appropriate databases. As part of this architecture, we deployed two database management systems. One deals with raw data and the other with processed data to increase efficiency in some monitoring operations.

The protocol bridge is a microservice that bundles devices and other technologies into a single solution. It provides a uniform user interface and a common approach to automating actions and rules across the system. It communicates electronically with smart and not-so-smart devices, performs user-defined actions, and provides high-level access to connected objects.

The asynchronous event driven is responsible for the web application server, for presenting information and notifications in a client's application. It communicates with the rest API by the PUT, GET, POST and DELETE commands. It spreads the data to the upper layers. The Gateway API manages access, certificates, and security protocols.

Physically, the proposed system is organized in six layers (Fig. 2). The lowest layer is composed of connected objects, including all the sensors, equipment and actuators that transform the habitat into a smart habitat.

Each data, each event, each action generating a stimulus is sent to the upper layer, the layer of controllers. This layer deals with the management of connected objects and the sensor network. It includes Sensors Controllers, Smart Lamp Controllers and Voice Command Controllers. This layer allows bidirectional communication between the connected objects and the middleware. The controller layer is implemented logically in our architecture by the access protocol management module.

Interoperability, subscription, notification, heterogeneity, and command execution are operations performed in the middleware layer. This layer offers mostly an abstraction to handle connected objects. It is just composed of few components: OpenHab and MQTT servers. It is deployed in a server running on a Raspberry Pi. Clients connect to an application server for data access. To ensure security, the Rest API is the only API able to connect to the Rapsberry Pi for data exploitation. All other layers consist of components that allow access and exploitation of data via Rest APIs or rich clients.

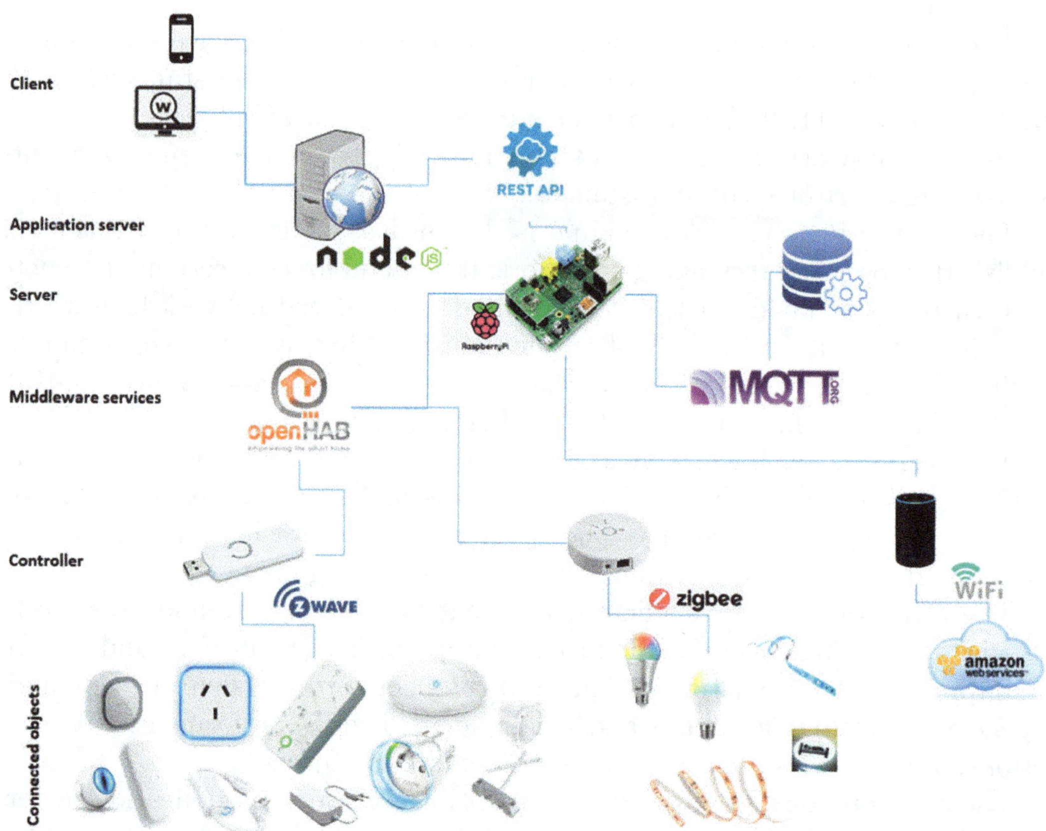

Fig. 2. Physical architecture of the IoT components for AAL system design.

5 Architecture Deployment

The experimental evaluation of the proposed system was performed in two phases. During the first phase, a functional test of the user's system assistance scenarios was run in the laboratory to establish the perceived usefulness of the system. During this phase, we emphasized the robustness and scalability of the system from a user and a technological point of view. During the second phase, we conducted a home experiment. We deployed the AAL architecture in five senior apartments in the city of Côte Saint-Luc, Canada.

The main objective of the proposed AAL system is to provide intelligent assistance and detect changes in the behavior of the occupant. The rest of the document focuses on the second phase experimentation that satisfies the requirements management on the heterogeneity, scalability and adaptation to the senior profile.

5.1 Materials and Method

The five participants involved in the experiment were living alone and showed quite diverse profiles (Table 1). They were between the age of 80 and 95. The proposed architecture of the system did not require any particular configuration for its deployment in different habitats. An installation at the participant's house required between one and two hours, depending on the layout of his apartment. To this must be added two hours of configuration of each kit, then about five minutes to adapt the services to the needs of a participant. The adaptation of the services is done by activation or deactivation of the docker corresponding to microservices.

Table 1. Profile of participants.

Participants	Sex	User profile
Participant 1	M	Rheumatism, uses a cane to get around
Participant 2	M	No physical and cognitive impairments
Participant 3	F	Overweight person, difficulty moving
Participant 4	F	Visual difficulties, poorly sighted
Participant 5	M	Walking with a walker

First in the laboratory, several user experiences and robustness tests were conducted to determine the behavior of software components in the face of profile changes, partial updating and technological scalability. Secondly, during the experience at home, a preliminary interview was conducted with each participant to explain technological tools. The participant was then invited during the usability testing phase to create real-life scenarios. Each situation was accompanied by a possible adjustment of the system, efforts were put to change as less as possible the participants' habitat. To meet the needs of the citizens, four assistance mechanisms were proposed:

- Automatic lighting controlled by voice;
- Automatic lighting when the person comes out of the bedroom and goes to the bathroom during night. A light path is installed between the bedroom and the bathroom;
- Spotlight lighting system to remind activity (It's time to take medication) or objects (Do not forget the keys when going outside);
- Automatic notification of community and social information organized by the town hall.

To illustrate the participation of seniors in the installation process, one of the participants preferred that the light path was installed along the stairs, instead of between the bedroom and the bathroom. He had expressed the need that the path from the garage to the ground floor be lit when needed. Another participant, presenting visual impairments, emphasized the advantage of ordering the turning on of lights by voice, as soon as she entered her home.

At the end of the installation, a summative evaluation of acceptability was requested from participants. Four of the five participants were satisfied with the test and would be curious to go further. They found the use of voice commands appropriate to their context.

The diversity of sensors and actuators used demonstrated the multiplicity of protocols and the technological scalability put in place. The 80 sensors used and distributed in about 20 devices per apartment materialize this part of the scalability. The local cache used for each installation makes it easier to partition the systems so that individual configurations and settings do not affect the entire system.

Figure 3 shows, for each AAL system requirement, the elements used to perform the evaluation.

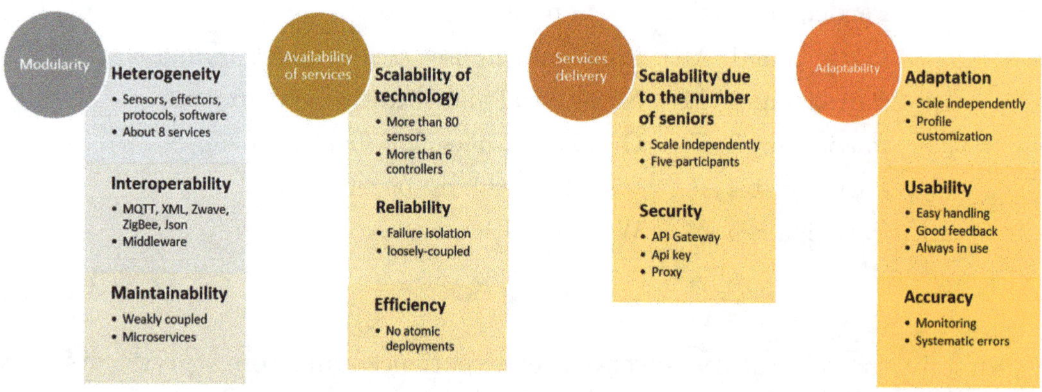

Fig. 3. Elements used by each requirement to make the assessment.

Many factors affect the performance of the AAL system, such as the performance of connected objects, the amount of available memory, the communication mode, the response time, the architecture and operating system of each component, the support of communication between the IoT, the algorithms used and the primary need of the system. In particular, heterogeneity induced by the disparity between IoT components may contribute to other factors, such as additional downtime while some components are waiting for others. It is therefore important to calibrate all relevant IoT components to provide information about events, such as communication time, system time, input output time and idle time. The six communication protocols and the eight services were interoperable to ensure the heterogeneity of the system.

The design of the modules in microservices brings a loosely coupling between component and a fault isolation these translate the reliability. Efficiency translates into the ability to perform non-atomic deployments and individually update components. For the moment, the number of five participants is too small to evaluate the capacity of our AAL infrastructure to support scalability. It is expected to deploy with more than 20 participants for better assessing this requirement.

6 Conclusion

This paper presents the design, development and deployment of an AAL environment which supports independent living in smart home for seniors. The system is based on a middleware that merges many different technologies to build the smart environment. The backbone of the system is its modular architecture based on microservices where different bundles (independent pieces of code) are in charge of providing the required functionalities. It allows adding easily new devices and new features, or replacing some devices without disrupting the system and minimizing the adaptation effort.

Another advantage of the proposed microservice architecture is its insulation quality and resilience. If one of the components fails, if the technology becomes obsolete or the code is out of date, the team can design another one without impacting the rest of the applications, which continue to operate independently.

The installation and evaluation of the AAL system in five seniors' home has shown that the system developed meet seniors needs. The seniors have expressed also how it is easy to use.

Ongoing research is currently conducted for analyzing the collected data and proposing new applications for satisfying new user requests. It has also shown that a middleware architecture based on microservices fulfills the requirements necessary for connecting citizens to smart city services. More technical investigations are planned to evaluate the scalability of the architecture and to deliver city services to the seniors thanks to the connected devices installed at home.

Acknowledgments. The authors want to thank all the partners and participants involved in the project. A special thanks to the Côte Saint-Luc city administrators.

References

1. Marsal-Llacuna, M.-L., Colomer-Llinàs, J., Meléndez-Frigola, J.: Lessons in urban monitoring taken from sustainable and livable cities to better address the Smart Cities initiative. Technol. Forecast. Soc. Change **90**, 611–622 (2015)
2. Giffinger, R., Gudrun, H.: Smart cities ranking: an effective instrument for the positioning of the cities? ACE Archit. Environ. **4**, 7–26 (2010)
3. Cook, D.J., Augusto, J.C., Jakkula, V.R.: Ambient intelligence: technologies, applications, and opportunities. Pervasive Mob. Comput. **5**, 277–298 (2009). https://doi.org/10.1016/j.pmcj.2009.04.001
4. Hwang, A.S., et al.: Co-designing ambient assisted living (AAL) environments: unravelling the situated context of informal dementia care. Biomed Res. Int. **2015**, 1–12 (2015). https://doi.org/10.1155/2015/720483
5. Blackman, S., et al.: Ambient assisted living technologies for aging well: a scoping review (2016). https://doi.org/10.1515/jisys-2014-0136
6. Rashidi, P., Mihailidis, A.: A survey on ambient assisted living tools for older adults. IEEE J. Biomed. Heal. Inf. **PP**, 1 (2013). https://doi.org/10.1109/JBHI.2012.2234129
7. Valkanova, N., Jorda, S., Vande Moere, A.: Public visualization displays of citizen data: design, impact and implications. Int. J. Hum Comput Stud. **81**, 4–16 (2015). https://doi.org/10.1016/j.ijhcs.2015.02.005
8. Li, R., Lu, B., McDonald-Maier, K.D.: Cognitive assisted living ambient system: a survey. Digit. Commun. Networks. **1**, 229–252 (2015). https://doi.org/10.1016/j.dcan.2015.10.003
9. Boger, J., et al.: Principles for fostering the transdisciplinary development of assistive technologies. Disabil. Rehabil. Assist. Technol. **12**, 480–490 (2017)
10. Yachir, A., Amirat, Y., Chibani, A., Badache, N.: Event-aware framework for dynamic services discovery and selection in the context of ambient intelligence and Internet of Things. IEEE Trans. Autom. Sci. Eng. **13**, 85–102 (2016)
11. Gubbi, J., Buyya, R., Marusic, S., Palaniswami, M.: Internet of Things (IoT): a vision, architectural elements, and future directions. Futur. Gener. Comput. Syst. **29** (2013). https://doi.org/10.1016/j.future.2013.01.010
12. Dohr, A., Modre-Osprian, R., Drobics, M., Hayn, D., Schreier, G.: The Internet of Things for ambient assisted living. In: ITNG2010 - 7th International Conference on Information Technology: New Generations, pp. 804–809 (2010). https://doi.org/10.1109/ITNG.2010.104
13. Alshuqayran, N., Ali, N., Evans, R.: A systematic mapping study in microservice architecture. In: Proceedings - 2016 IEEE 9th International Conference on Service-Oriented Computing and Applications, SOCA 2016, pp. 44–51. IEEE (2016). https://doi.org/10.1109/SOCA.2016.15
14. O'Grady, M.J., Muldoon, C., Dragone, M., Tynan, R., O'Hare, G.M.P.: Towards evolutionary ambient assisted living systems. J. Ambient Intell. Humaniz. Comput. **1**, 15–29 (2010). https://doi.org/10.1007/s12652-009-0003-5
15. Memon, M., Wagner, S.R., Pedersen, C.F., Aysha Beevi, F.H., Hansen, F.O.: Ambient assisted living healthcare frameworks, platforms, standards, and quality attributes (2014). https://doi.org/10.3390/s140304312
16. Albano, M.F., Ferreira, L.L., Pinho, L.M., Alkhawaja, A.R.: Middleware for smart grids. Comput. Stand. Interfaces **38**, 133–143 (2015)

Designing a Navigation System for Older Adults: A Case Study Under Real Road Condition

Perrine Ruer[1(✉)], Damien Brun[2], Charles Gouin-Vallerand[3], and Évelyne F. Vallières[4]

[1] HEC Montreal, Montreal, QC H3T2A7, Canada
perrine.ruer@hec.ca
[2] Université TÉLUQ, Montréal, QC H2S3L5, Canada
brund@acm.org
[3] École de Gestion, Université de Sherbrooke, Sherbrooke, QC J1K2R1, Canada
charles.gouin-vallerand@usherbrooke.ca
[4] Centre LICEF, Université TÉLUQ, Montréal, QC H2S3L5, Canada
evelyne.vallieres@teluq.ca

Abstract. Recent research allows envisioning what kind of sensory devices could be used for drivers' navigation in the future, particularly for older adults. Population all around the world is aging, older adults will be more on the road. In this paper, we present a contact-less navigation system dedicated to this category of people based on a mobile head-up display. The aim of this system is to preserve their mobility in order to promote their autonomy and daily social activities. To do so, we interviewed older drivers to design a driving assistance system and we assessed the system under real road conditions (N = 34) with measurement of older drivers' mental workload and the adequacy of users' expectations. We emphasize the need to combine both measures of mental workload. The contribution aims at providing a richer understanding of how older people experience navigation technologies and to discuss the design recommendations of digital devices for older people.

Keywords: Older people · Driving assistance system · Mental workload · Field studies

1 Introduction

Some research in Human-Computer Interaction (HCI) focuses on the kind of sensory devices that could be used for a driver's navigation in the future. That is convenient for the case of older drivers. This category of drivers will be more and more on the road in the next decades as shown from demographics prediction. Many physical and cognitive changes are associated with the aging process and could have negative impacts on driving activity. It is essential to preserve their mobility in order to continue to promote their autonomy and to have daily social activities.

In the last decade, little focus has been given to the driving assistance system focusing on older drivers' mobility that could help them to drive safely in the long

J. Pagán et al. (Eds.): ICOST 2019, LNCS 11862, pp. 168–179, 2019.
https://doi.org/10.1007/978-3-030-32785-9_15

term. To promote the autonomy of older drivers, one suggestion is to design navigation systems for and with the concerned users [1]. Several new cars are equipped with different driving assistance systems that have the potential to help older people to drive more safely as long as they are accepted and perceived as useful by these users with special needs and characteristics. Therefore, the aim of the present research was to propose a driving assistance system to promote driving for older drivers considering their aging impairments.

Usability is something to consider when dealing with older adults. Older people do not have the same familiarity with new technologies that young people [2]. If older drivers question the system, this may cause them to stop using the system. It is necessary to understand their expectations of technologies. In addition, if people are familiar with a system, they are likely to have a more favorable opinion of it [3].

After the definition of needs and expectations with older drivers, we designed a driving assistance system corresponding as closely as possible with these ones. The study involves the assessment of the newly designed driving assistance system from real-world experiments with 34 participants measures of objective and subjective mental workload. Our contributions are (1) to design a driving system assistance for older drivers based on Head-Up Display interactions (2) to assess the value of the system with the assessment of different measures of mental workload.

2 Related Works

The development of transportation technologies makes possible to maintain older drivers' mobility by allowing them to use a personal vehicle to reach their needs. In-vehicle systems support drivers. Their aims are to increase safety and save lives. These systems can help drivers in critical situations or in unfamiliar environments by giving driving information. For example: turn on your left at the next intersection [4]. However, these systems are developed most of the time for all drivers and few of them are assessed with older drivers [4]. Especially since older drivers have their own usability problem with computing systems [2]. They have particular needs and expectations which could differ from other categories of people (for instance, young people) [5].

A bad conception of a driving assistance system leads to the perception of the complexity of the driving task and a higher risk of accidents [6]. Furthermore, a bad conception induces more inconvenience for older drivers, whereas the system's role is to encourage mobility and security of the driver who uses it [6, 7]. User tests allow to assess a system and to verify its credibility [8]. A previous study was made with older drivers to assess a new driving system during user tests. Results indicated the system was positively perceived. Participants were able to better understand the benefits and limits of it [9].

Head-Up Display (HUD) is a recent interesting driving assistance system for older drivers. It is defined as a display mode which is used to present different information to the driver's field view (speed information, warnings or other indicators) [10]. The benefits of HUD are to allow quick reaction time; earlier detection of road hinders or to let more time to scan the traffic scene [10–12]. Most research focuses on the visual canal to provide information during the driving task. Older drivers are more sensitive to visual impairments with aging. Several authors agree that the main beneficiaries of HUD systems are aging people because of their narrower field of vision [11]. HUD is used to limit off-field sightings of the road scene by transmitting information directly into the driver's field of view and allowing a controlled driving task [12, 13]. A study indicated that the use of a head-up display system was assessed by participants as it was easy to use [10]. HUD has great potential to improve comfort for older drivers.

Interaction with driving assistance system can increase task complexity having consequences regarding safety (i.e. distraction or increased fatigue) [13]. Mental workload is a good indicator of distraction during the evaluation of a new driving assistance system [14]. A system should not increase distraction involving a higher mental workload with too much information to process [4, 13]. Mental workload allows assessing if a computing system supports or increases people's cognitive resources needed, particularly when a driving assistance system is added. The system could either assist the drivers or disturb them to drive more safely, especially older drivers [1, 4, 6]. Indeed, older drivers are more sensitive to distraction during dual tasks due to the aging process [15]. Mental workload is not directly observed. Two main measures are generally used to do so: an objective measure and a subjective measure. Objective measure is physiological cues such as heart rate, pupillary diameter, skin temperature, electrodermal activity [16, 17]. To detect these clues, biometric sensors are used to measure the body's reactions reflecting the driver's mental workload [17]. Subjective measures are questionnaires or scales to assess a specific event such as NASA Task Load Index (NASA-TLX). It is a multidimensional assessment tool with six different dimensions: mental demand, physical demand, temporal demand, effort, performance, and frustration [18]. It is strongly recommended to combine these different type of measurements in order to better assess mental workload when using a driving assistance system [14].

During the development of a driving assistance system, it is recommended to offer user tests, particularly for older drivers. The measurement of mental workload makes it possible to predict the influence (positive or negative) of a new driving assistance system during a driving task. The HUD seems to be an interesting system for older drivers, especially with the reduction of their field of view.

3 Methodology

The study consists of an implementation phase (3.1) and an exploratory study under real conditions (3.2).

3.1 Implementation Phase

Driving Assistance System Choice. Among driving assistance systems, HUD is interesting for older drivers. In our study, we used a commercialized system named HudwayGlass. This system consists of a phone holder and a tinted plastic blade covered with a mirror coating to reflect phone screen. This system can easily be purchased by any driver from the company's website[1]. The HudwayGlass HUD has three advantages: (1) the system is universal and can be used in all vehicles, (2) with any smartphone and (3) is customizable, letting the possibility to design any kind of mobile application adapted for this type of display (Fig. 1).

Fig. 1. HudwayGlass HUD

The HudwayGlass company offers specific mobile applications, but for our research, we developed our own mobile application for it to be well tailored for our intended older drivers.

Design of Mobile Applications. Regarding the design process, we assessed expectations of older drivers relative to mobile application interfaces with interviews. In these, we asked participants about pictogram and color for three types of interfaces. We implemented the most preferred interfaces in a mobile application (app.) named "AR Driving Assistant". The mobile app has been divided into two sub-app. The first one presents information to the driver. This sub-app was built with the Unity software and was configured to run on an Android phone. It projects the information to the driver through the HUD interface. The objective was to provide driving notifications with pictograms and colors. These choices are important when designing technology interfaces [19]. Figure 2 presents the three selected interfaces according to expectations collected.

Fig. 2. Interfaces from the first sub-app. (in order of presentation: alert, information and advice)

[1] http://hudwayglass.com.

The second sub-app allows control of notifications sent to the driver and collects data. The objective was to control the first sub-application by collecting data during driving for later analysis (i.e. speed, breaking, position, etc.). The application consists of a scrolling view containing several buttons including a dialog box to configure and start sensor monitoring (Fig. 3).

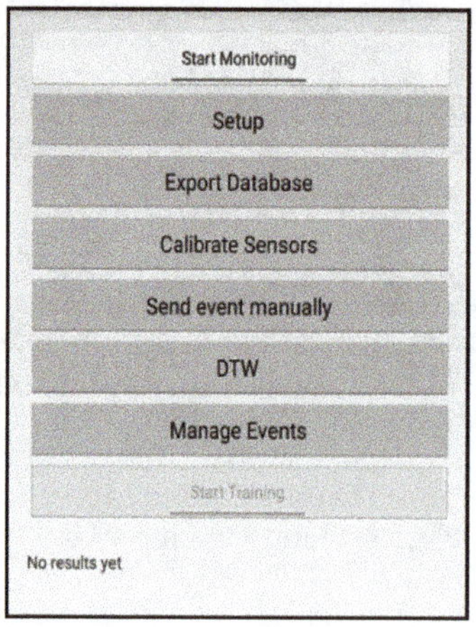

Fig. 3. Interface from the second sub-app.

This application was developed with the Android Studio software and the application code is available on GitHub (https://github.com/limvi-licef/AR-driving-assistant).

3.2 Assessment Under Real-World Conditions

The success or failure of a driving assistance system lies in a design for the targeted drivers.

Participants. Thirty-nine (39) participants were recruited, but only 34 took part in this study (41% of whom were women). Five participants withdrew a few days before their appointment for various reasons (loss of interest in the study, a problem with their personal vehicle or health problem). The sample was composed of older people between 60 and 85 years old (mean age: 68.8 years, standard deviation: 5.91). Participants lived in Montreal area (Quebec, Canada). We recruited participants with a local paper ad and with the university e-journal. Each participant was reached by phone to answer a pre-recruitment questionnaire to verify that they matched with the selection criteria. These criteria were to be 60 years old or more, to hold a valid driving license, to drive each week on a regular basis and to be in good health. To confirm the relevance of our system, we compared several measures by dividing our sample. Two groups were randomly composed: a control group and an experimental group. The experimental group (N = 17) drove with the prototype system, while the control group (N = 17) did not have the prototype system during driving. The control group was used as a reference group for the comparison of the collected measures. They were instructed to perform a routine driving task.

Procedure. Participants were invited to read and fill out a consent form. Once completed, they answered a questionnaire to collect sociodemographic variables, such as age, gender or driving experience. Participants were asked to drive on a highway in the greater Montreal area. The journey distance was a loop of 63 km and was completed in 40 min. All participants must respect traffic laws and driving speed limitations. The route drivers needed to drive was to follow the highway until exit 160. Then, they made a turn back to the outset. The journey was selected to a limited amount of traffic on the highway, with fewer stimuli than in urban road and to have a reproducibility of the scenario during experiments. Highway driving is known not to increase mental workload, unlike an urban road with the presence of less disruptive elements (e.g. pedestrians, parked vehicles, etc.) [14]. We also avoided as much as possible peak hours (8:00 am–9:00 am and 4:00 pm–5:00 pm) and intense traffic. We chose experiments in real-world conditions because they allow assessing variables with dynamic factors coming from the driving context [18]. Finally, they answered a questionnaire about their overall experience and received 30 Canadian dollars for their participation.

Collected Measures. We collected two objective measures: skin temperature and electrodermal activity. These two measures allow the assessment of the driver's mental workload [14, 17, 20]. During the driving task, all participants wore two biometric sensors from the Captiv' Solutions. These sensors are affixed with self-gripping tape and can be positioned at different locations on the body such as wrists or elbows. Each sensor weights 20 grams, measures 52 mm × 25 mm × 14 mm. Their sampling frequency is 32 Hz with a resolution of 16 bits and 0.05 °C. The amount of data collected is 1920 per minute for each sensor. These sensors are conveniently connected to a wireless box. Software is available to synchronize and display the data in real time, then record the data collected and perform subsequent analyses. Sensors were positioned on participants' left-hand fingers and a medical tape was added to hang the wires to the hand. They cause slight discomfort but do not prevent the steering wheel from being grasped or the execution of driving gestures with the right hand [21].

Regarding the subjective measure NASA-TLX, Participants answered it in the car straight after the driving task on the highway and before they got out. The first step of the NASA-TLX was to assess the six dimensions (mental demand, physical demand, time demand, effort, performance, and frustration) on scales ranging from low to high. We presented a definition for each dimension to ensure the participants' understanding. Then, participants carried out a comparison phase and chose from two dimensions that the experimenter said out loud. For example: "indicate the dimension required the most effort while driving between mental demand or performance".

All participants drove the University instrumented vehicle, named LiSA car. They all drove this vehicle to have better comparison and not have a vehicle change that would potentially influence the data collection. This vehicle is a Nissan Versa 2007 equipped with a data logger (AIM Evo4) and a computer embedded on board. An experimenter was placed in the back seat of the vehicle. The experimenter indicated to the participant that he or she could not speak during the whole driving task to not influence the driver. The experimenter could track the collected data in real time and complete the task with a paper-pencil statement with driving information (i.e. traffic, participant comments). The experimenter sent one of the three interfaces with the second sub-application to the first sub-application.

4 Results

As a reminder, our objective is to propose a driving assistance system to promote safe driving for older drivers. We did assessments under real-road conditions in order to confirm if this system meets the expectations of older drivers. First, we present results from the objective mental workload data (skin temperature and electrodermal activity) for control and experimental groups. Then we present the subjective mental workload's results for both groups. We study comparison between objective and subjective mental workload. Finally, we describe system usability assessment results completed by the experimental group.

4.1 Objective Mental Workload

Control group participants had a lower average skin temperature than experimental group participants (31.34 Celsius degree (°C) vs 31.81 °C). There is a small gap between the two groups for the skin temperature. For electrodermal activity, mean is lower for the control group than for the experimental group (2.20 micro-Siemens (µS) vs 3.51 µS). There is a higher variability into the experimental group. Table 1 shows descriptive results for each sensor by group.

Table 1. Descriptive results.

		Group	
		Control group	Experimental Group
Skin temperature	Mean	31.34 °C	31.81 °C
	Sd	2.3 °C	2.02 °C
Electrodermal activity	Mean	2.20 µS	3.51 µS
	Sd	1.59 µS	3.29 µS

A Mann-Whitney U test was used to compare the group's influence on skin temperature and electrodermal activity. There are no significative group's differences neither for skin temperature (U: 136.50; $p = .78$; $n = 34$) nor for electrodermal activity (U: 124; $p = .50$; $n = 34$).

Even if participants in the experimental group show higher skin temperature and electrodermal activity than participants in the control group, the differences are non-significant. Additional experiments should confirm whether there is a difference which can be inferred by the context or the stress induced by experimenting a new driving assistance system.

4.2 Subjective Mental Workload

For the control group, the most relevant dimension was mental demand (mean: 104.6), for the experimental group, it was performance (mean: 152.94). Figure 4 presents descriptive results.

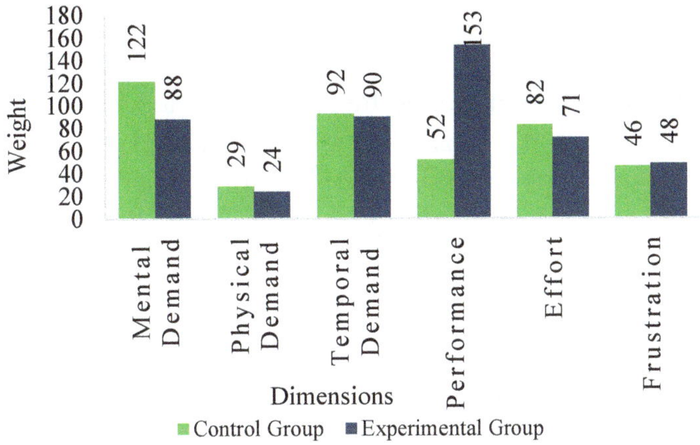

Fig. 4. NASA-TLX descriptive results.

A Mann-Whitney U test was used to compare groups' assessment of NASA-TLX dimensions. The hypothesis was that participants, regardless of group, would answer in the same way. This hypothesis was confirmed for five dimensions: mental demand (U: 121.5; $p = .43$; $n = 17$), physical demand (U: 124; $p = .49$; $n = 17$), temporal demand (U: 134.5; $p = .73$; $n = 17$), effort (U:143.5; $p = .97$; $n = 17$) and frustration (U:125; $p = .52$; $n = 17$). The hypothesis was rejected for performance. There is a significant difference for the performance dimension between control and experimental groups (U: 56; $p < .005$; $n = 17$). Subjective perception of participants mental workload is higher for performance. This result suggests that the system (HUD and driving mobile app.) had an impact on the performance dimension of driving, but not on the other dimensions of the NASA-TLX. It was more demanding for participants who drove with the system than those who drove without it.

4.3 Comparison of Objective and Subjective Mental Workload

Following the results presented above, a comparison was made on the three measures of mental workload (objective and subjective). We wanted to identify an effect between means of skin temperature; mean electrodermal activity; subjective conditions: mean total weight of NASA-TLX dimensions. The inter-subject factor was the group condition (control or experimental). Table 2 indicates no significant effect of objective and subjective mental workload conditions according to the group ($F [30] = .954$, $p < .50$).

Table 2. Multivariate ANOVA test.

Test name	Value	F	Hypoth. Df	Sig. of F	Sum of square	p
Pillais	.09	.95	3.00	.47	.09	.24
Wilks	.91	.95	3.00	.43	.09	.24
Hotelings	.09	.95	3.00	.43	.09	.24
Roys	.09	.95	3.00	.43	.09	.24

This result indicates that both groups did not differ on the measures of objective and subjective mental workload. It appears the system (HUD and driving application) is an interesting modality for a driving assistance system for older drivers.

4.4 System Usability Assessment

After the driving task, participants from the experimental group (N = 17) were asked to answer a questionnaire for assessing the system usability. Measures assessed were the satisfaction of the driving experiment, the strengths and the weaknesses of the system, and to judge the system usefulness. The overall driving experiment was rated satisfactory or very satisfactory for 94% of participants. Participants were surveyed about the strengths and weaknesses of the system (i.e. HUD and interfaces). They had to rate five strengths: reliable, high-quality, useful, singular and ergonomic. Classified in order from best to least strength, the first was its ergonomics, its usefulness, its singularity, its high-quality rate, and the last its reliability. The five weaknesses were: seems too expensive, impractical, ineffective, poor quality and unreliable. Amongst these, the first is its poor quality, its unreliability, its inefficiency, its impracticality, and it seems too expensive. These strengths and weaknesses allow us to determine what was considered interested and what has to be improved.

Most participants indicated that the system did not interfere during the driving task (70%). It means that the system in the participants' field of view is not perceived as a visual discomfort. About usefulness, 47% of participants considering the system useful or somewhat useful compared to 53% who considered it useless or rather useless. Subsequently, a question was asked about the benefit of the system to help driving safely. The system was rated as very beneficial or beneficial for 41% of participants. After testing the system, a quarter of participants would be interested in purchasing the system (24%). And the system did not seem like other computer systems with which participants were familiar (58%). The system was considered different from other known computing systems. These different aspects assessed allow us to know which ones need to be improved or preserved.

5 Discussion - Conclusion

Driving assistance systems are a solution to support the older drivers in their task. However, this type of assistance must be adapted and designed to meet the real needs of drivers. The assessment of the system influenced the subjective driving performance of older drivers, but not the objective mental workload where results did not indicate a significant difference between the two groups. Results of this work confirm the usefulness of measuring the mental workload of older drivers objectively and subjectively. Results of objective mental workload suggested there is no increased for the experimental group who assessed the system. Comparing both groups (control and experimental), mean skin temperature and mean electrodermal activity was slightly higher for drivers who had to assess the system. It means that the system tested would cause a slight increase in mental workload during driving activity, although there is no significant difference between groups. Objective mental workload measurements do not always correspond to the participants' feelings. It is the reason that we added to our objective measurements a subjective measure (NASA-TLX scale). This combination of mental workload measures should be encouraged in future research of older drivers. Our results indicated only one significant difference between the experimental and control groups: the performance dimension. The experimental group appears to have found it more difficult to drive than the control group. One explanation may be due to the novelty of the task, rather than the fact of driving with the system per se. Experimenting with a new system may have caused more anxiety. Combining mental workload measures is therefore recommended [14].

This study proposed to develop and assess new material based on expectations of older drivers in Quebec province (Canada). When a driving assistance system is designed with the intended users, it meets the expectations of users and will tend not to increase mental workload. The whole study provides new knowledge to think about improving driving for older drivers. A practical contribution is a development of HUD with adapted mobile applications which can be deployed quickly on the market and offered to older people by insurance companies.

In this study, the time to assess the system is a limitation. Participants discovered the system and drove with it for less than one hour. Since familiarity encourages opinion and system use [3], a longitudinal study is a proposal for future research in order to assess the system several times to encourage its usefulness.

As we wanted to validate the different interfaces with older drivers, it depended on the driving habits of each driver. Some would not have had as much information from the mobile app. while driving as they received during the experiments. It is necessary to propose a new study with the presentation of interfaces according to the context of the driving task through the analysis of data in real time. In the current mobile app., it is possible to collect contextual data (speed, brakes, acceleration, localization, etc.). It might be interesting to also include a data mining technique (e.g. decision tree) for real-time analysis of driving data. Future research could follow this direction and offer a personalized interface to the driver based on the driving context in real time.

Acknowledgments. This work was supported by MITACS. We thank all the participants from the user study and staff who wrote and provided helpful comments.

References

1. Reimer, B.: Driver assistance systems and the transition to automated vehicles: a path to increase older adult safety and mobility? Public Policy Aging Rep. **24**(1), 27–31 (2014)
2. Fisk, A.D., et al.: Designing for Older Adults: Principles and Creative Human Factors Approaches. CRC Press, Washington, DC (2009)
3. Duncan, M., et al.: Enhanced mobility for aging populations using automated vehicles (2015)
4. Eby, D.W., Molnar, L.J.: Has the time come for older driver vehicle? J. Ergon. (2014)
5. Williams, D., et al.: Considerations in designing human-computer interfaces for elderly people. In: 2013 13th International Conference on Quality Software. IEEE (2013)
6. Simões, A., Pereira, M.: Older drivers and new in-vehicle technologies: adaptation and long-term effects. In: Kurosu, M. (ed.) HCD 2009. LNCS, vol. 5619, pp. 552–561. Springer, Heidelberg (2009). https://doi.org/10.1007/978-3-642-02806-9_64
7. Davidse, R.J.: Older drivers and ADAS: which systems improve road safety? IATSS Res. **30** (1), 6–20 (2006)
8. Castillejo, E., Almeida, A., López-de-Ipiña, D.: User, context and device modeling for adaptive user interface systems. In: Urzaiz, G., Ochoa, Sergio F., Bravo, J., Chen, L.L., Oliveira, J. (eds.) UCAmI 2013. LNCS, vol. 8276, pp. 94–101. Springer, Cham (2013). https://doi.org/10.1007/978-3-319-03176-7_13
9. Reimer, B., Mehler, B., Coughlin, J.F.: An evaluation of driver reactions to new vehicle parking assist technologies developed to reduce driver stress. New England University Transportation Center, Massachusetts Institute of Technology, Cambridge (2010)
10. Tretten, P., et al.: An on-road study of head-up display: preferred location and acceptance levels. In: Proceedings of the Human Factors and Ergonomics Society Annual Meeting. Sage Publications, Los Angeles (2011)
11. Pauzie, A.: Head up display in automotive: a new reality for the driver. In: Marcus, A. (ed.) DUXU 2015. LNCS, vol. 9188, pp. 505–516. Springer, Cham (2015). https://doi.org/10.1007/978-3-319-20889-3_47
12. Tufano, D.R.: Automotive HUDs: the overlooked safety issues. Hum. Factors **39**(2), 303–311 (1997)
13. Kim, S., Dey, A.K.: Augmenting human senses to improve the user experience in cars: applying augmented reality and haptics approaches to reduce cognitive distances. Multimedia Tools Appl. **75**, 1–21 (2015)
14. Schneegass, S., et al.: A data set of real world driving to assess driver workload. In: Proceedings of the 5th International Conference on Automotive User Interfaces and Interactive Vehicular Applications. ACM (2013)
15. Lemercier, C., Cellier, J.-M.: Les défauts de l'attention en conduite automobile: inattention, distraction et interférence. Le travail humain **71**(3), 271–296 (2008)
16. Collet, C., Salvia, E., Petit-Boulanger, C.: Measuring workload with electrodermal activity during common braking actions. Ergonomics **57**(6), 886–896 (2015)
17. Solovey, E.T., et al.: Classifying driver workload using physiological and driving performance data: two field studies. In: Proceedings of the SIGCHI Conference on Human Factors in Computing Systems. ACM (2014)
18. Hart, S.G.: Theory and measurement of human workload. Hum. Prod. Enhanc. **1**, 396–456 (1986)
19. Leung, R., McGrenere, J., Graf, P.: Age-related differences in the initial usability of mobile device icons. Behav. Inf. Technol. **30**(5), 629–642 (2011)

20. Shi, Y., et al.: Galvanic Skin Response (GSR) as an index of cognitive workload. In: ACM CHI Conference Work-in-Progress (2007)
21. Clarion, A.: Electrodermal indices for mental workload analysis in car driving. Université Claude Bernard - Lyon I (2009)

Short Contributions

User Embeddings Based on Mobile App Behavior Data

Kushal Singla[1(✉)], Satyen Abrol[1], and Sungdeuk Park[2]

[1] Samsung R&D Institute, Bangalore, India
{kushal.s, satyen.abrol}@samsung.com
[2] Samsung Electronics, Suwon, Korea
sdeuk.park@samsung.com

Abstract. We consider a smart phone scenario with a number of apps used by a user. The app usage data provides information about the user behavior, which can be used to identify the user demographics and interest and in turn is used to find similar users. In this paper, we propose a method to generate a latent space user embedding using the user app usage data, which is a dense low-dimensional representation of the user. This representation is used for low latency user similarity computation and acts as the user feature representation in user demographics prediction models.

Keywords: User2vec · AutoEncoder · User embedding

1 Introduction

User Modeling and User Profiling are well-studied areas of Computer Science finding applications in broad range of areas including recommendation systems and expert systems. Understanding the user preferences, interests and characteristics allows service providers to serve more personalized content to user resulting in improved user experience and increased success (engagement, purchases, etc.) for the business. In the domain of smartphones, a potential approach for building the user profiles is based on either developing a predictive model that map the user to a pre-defined taxonomy or creating user segments based on the app installation or app usage. In this paper, we present a novel approach to map a user to a latent space embedding which implicitly captures user behavior. In our work, we make several contributions in the field of user modelling based on app usage. First, we propose a user modelling method for creating a user embedding using Auto encoders. Second, we show the effectiveness of user embedding for different use cases such as demographics prediction. Thirdly, we show that this user representation can be used for user segmentation using vector operations.

2 Related Work

User modelling and Personalization has been studied extensively, especially since the advent of smartphones. Zolna et al. [1] present a method to build LSTMs to model user behavior on a website, with applications in e-commerce domain. The approach looks at

J. Pagán et al. (Eds.): ICOST 2019, LNCS 11862, pp. 183–189, 2019.
https://doi.org/10.1007/978-3-030-32785-9_16

user's browsing pattern and maps it into a fixed-size vector. Amir et al. [2] describe a method to create user embedding from text to capture latent user aspects. App2Vec [3] and AppDNA [4] are two such papers, which present methods to create embedding which captures semantic relationship between apps. The work done by us presents a novel unified method to compute user embedding based on the apps of the user instead of deducing user embedding from the app embedding. [5] Shows that usage of user embedding for the gender prediction task where the social context of the user is available but the social context is not readily available in all cases so in the absence of social context, the proposed approach doesn't require the user relations. Mannan [6] shows the use of artificial neural network for the user similarity computation but it is computationally expensive to compute the similarity between all the set of users and it cannot perform vector-based operations using this approach but the autoencoder fills this gap.

3 User Embeddings Model

User embedding can be used for finding similar user. The app space cardinality is very high but it is very sparse per user whereas dense user embeddings are usefull in this case. User embedding can be used as a feature for predictive analytics like classification of user into various categories extracted in an unsupervised manner. User embedding can be used to perform vector operations like addition, subtraction etc. This can be used to perform user analogy tasks. Our method is based on autoencoder. Autoencoder is a neural network model, which was developed for unsupervised learning and is used for feature extraction. [7] explains the usage of autoencoder for reducing the dimensions using a multi-layer neural network, which is proven to be better than the standard PCA approach. Amiri [8] presents a method to compute similarity between text pairs using autoencoder.

3.1 Method Explanation

In this subsection, we explain the architecture of the user-embedding model based on the autoencoder architecture. The layers of the encoder model are explained below (Fig. 1).

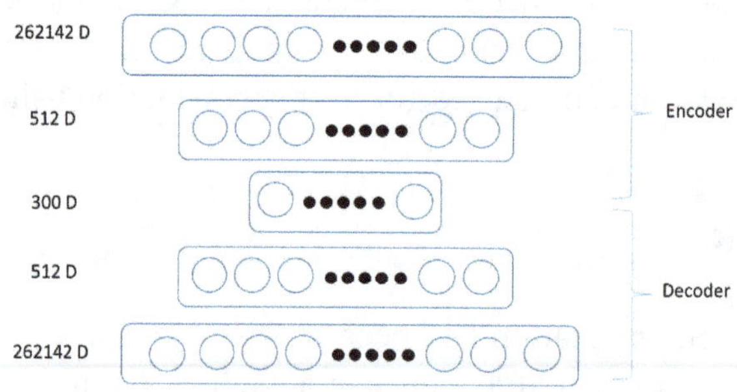

Fig. 1. Architecture for the autoencoder

(1) Input Layer – The input layer is 262,142 dimensional which is equal to the vocabulary of the app space.
(2) Hidden later – This layer is 512 dimensional which is followed by Relu, batch-norm, dropout respectively.
(3) Output later – This layer is 300 dimensional. Tanh computation is applied on the output layer

The layers of the decoder model are in the reverse order until the input layer. Sigmoid operation is applied to the output layer. Loss is optimized using the Adam optimizer and BCELoss. Number of epoch is equal to 6. Variable learning rate is employed per epoch- [0.1, 0.05, 0.025, 0.01, 0.005, 0.0001]. We ran the experiment on Amazon AWS p2.xlarge which has 12 GB of GPU memory which influences the autoencoder design (Table 1).

Table 1. Algorithm to compute the user embedding using the mobile app usage data

ALGORITHM: Algorithm to compute the user-embedding model using app usage

Input: User app usage vector for the app $A_1\ A_2\ A_{3\ldots\ldots}\ A_n$
Output: User embedding vector for the user $U_1\ U_2\ U_{3\ldots\ldots}\ U_n$

1. Pre-process the app usage vector and one-hot encode the vector
2. Train the auto encoder model using the user one-hot encoded vector.
3. Generate the user embedding from the output layer of the encoder section of the auto encoder.
4. *exit*: end procedure

4 Experiments

We evaluate the user-embedding model using a private dataset collected from a survey of the user app usage. We collected the app usage data of the users over a period of 2 months. The User set is composed of both the male and female users within the age group from 16 to 80. App usage data consists of the app ids (For example - com. whatsapp) of the apps used by the users within this period in the csv format. This dataset is used to evaluate the user embedding using various tasks. The app usage data is preprocessed using Spark to create the one hot encodings of the user app usage vector.

4.1 User Embedding Use Cases

4.1.1 Gender Clustering

In this sub section, we try to find the relation between the embedding and the user gender. In this case, we sampled 1000 user randomly from the two classes and generate the user embedding using the model training earlier and generate t-sne plots.

4.1.2 Age Clustering

In this sub section, we try to find the relation between the embedding and the user age. In the case of the age attribute based clustering of the user, we divider the user into two groups based on different point of age as the separation point and observe that the distinct clusters are formed at various age separation points. Figure 3 shows the user clusters based on different age threshold point. Equal numbers of users are sample from the two sets and t-sne plot are computed for the various threshold ages. This shows that distinct clusters are observed under various age thresholds (Fig. 2).

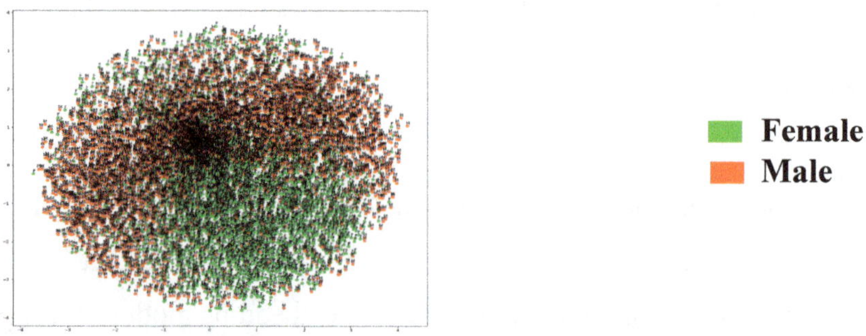

Fig. 2. T-SNE based gender plot of the users based on the autoencoder embedding

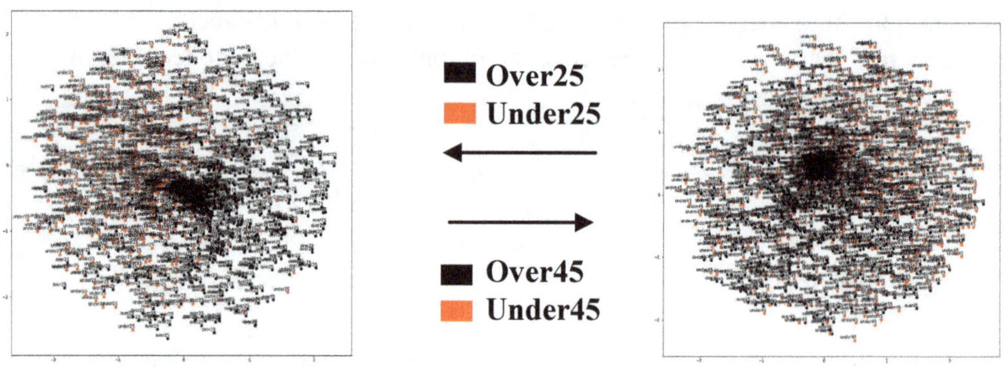

Fig. 3. T-SNE based age plots of the users based on the autoencoder embedding

4.1.3 Embedding for User Similarity Task

In this sub section, we evaluate the quality of finding users with similar attributes.

Figure 4a shows the quality of the user similarity task. In this experiment, we sampled a subset of users from the two age groups. This figure shows the probability of finding a user within the same age group by using the cosine distance between the user embedding lies within the range of 0.6 to 0.8. The app usage behavior of the people in the age group under 35 and over 35 is the least non-distinguishable in the experiment as it can be shown in lowest cosine distance of 0.6 whereas it's most distinguishable in the age-group under 75 and over 75 as shown by the cosine distance of 0.8. Figure 4b shows the quality of the user similarity task on dividing the user sample into two sets based on the age threshold.

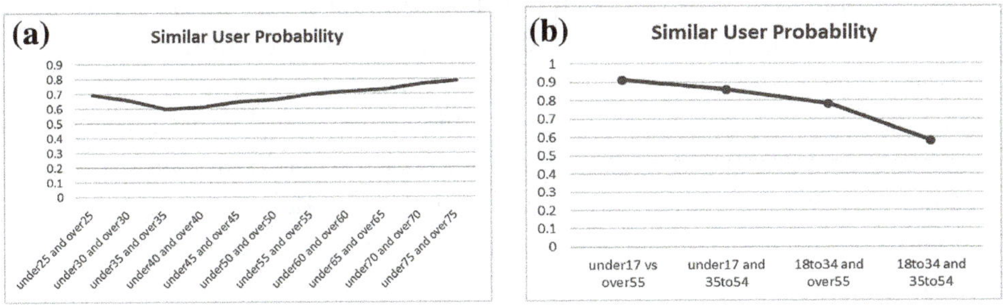

Fig. 4. (a) Probability of similar user in various age groups (b) Probability of similar user in various age groups

4.1.4 Validation Using Analogy Tasks

In this sub-section, we try to derive relationships based on multiple attributes. For e.g. the deduced semantic relation between an old woman user group and old man user group is similar to the semantic relation between young girl user group and young boy user group. These multi-attribute semantic relations can be evaluated by performing vector operation on the embedding. For example - To compute the semantic relation old_woman - old_man = young_girl - X, we sample 1000 users randomly from the each user group, compute the average of the vectors, perform this process for the old_woman, old_man, young_girl user groups and then search the vector space for the user_group vector closest to X using the cosine distance method and found that the closest vector is equal to the young_boy user group. We performed eight more experiments like this and the results are shown in the Table 2.

Table 2. Analysis of the classification quality for gender prediction using user embeddings and shallow network

Analogy	Actual test case
old_woman-old_man = young_girl-young_boy	60 to 65_F-60 to 65_M = 20 to 25_F-25 to 30_M
old_woman-young_girl = old_man-young_boy	70 to 75_F-20 to 25_F = 70 to 75_M-25 to 30_M
young_girl-young_boy = old_woman-old_man	20 to 25_F-20 to 25_M = 70 to 75_F-65 to 70_M
young_girl-old_woman = young_boy-old_man	20 to 25_F-70 to 75_F = 20 to 25_M-65 to 70_M
old_man-old_woman = young_man-young_girl	60 to 65_M-60 to 65_F = 20 to 25_M-25 to 30_F
old_man-young_boy = old_woman-young_girl	60 to 65_M-20 to 25_M = 60 to 65_F-25 to 30_F
young_boy-old_man = young_girl-old_woman	20 to 25_M-70 to 75_M = 20 to 25_F-65 to 70_F
young_boy-old_woman = young_girl-old_man	20 to 25_M-70 to 75_F = 20 to 25_F-60 to 65_M
young_boy-young_girl = old_man-old_woman	20 to 25_M-20 to 25_F = 70 to 75_M-65 to 70_F

4.1.5 User Embedding for Classification Task

In this sub-section, we use the embedding as feature for user attribute prediction and compare its performance with a shallow prediction model with manual feature engineering. The shallow prediction model is based on SVM [9] model with the following parameters: gamma = 1 and C = 0.1. Input data to the embedding based model is the app-based user embedding whereas the shallow network is build using the tf-idf features of the metadata of the app ids used by the user. Table 3. shows that the embedding based binary prediction model achieves accuracy similar to the shallow model without hand engineered features and this method helps to build the solutions faster. Table 4. shows the quality of the age prediction model. The recall of the classes 0 to 17 and over 55 is higher using the embedding approach because of the generalization aspect of embedding.

Table 3. Analysis of the classification quality for gender prediction using user embeddings and shallow network respectively

		precision	recall	f1-score	support
	F	0.8889	0.889	0.889	5083
	M	0.8853	0.8851	0.8852	4917
weighted	avg	0.8871	0.8871	0.8871	10000

	precision	recall	f1-score	support
F	0.8872	0.869	0.878	89299
M	0.8961	0.9109	0.9034	110701
avg/total	0.8921	0.8922	0.8921	200000

Table 4. Analysis of the classification quality for age prediction using embedding vector feature and shallow network

	precision	recall	f1-score	support
0to17	0.684211	0.537931	0.602317	145
18to34	0.767632	0.740511	0.753827	4189
35to54	0.693874	0.766928	0.728574	4711
over55	0.65047	0.434555	0.52103	955
avg	0.720486	0.7208	0.717502	10000

	precision	recall	f1-score	support
0to17	0.734463	0.463954	0.568679	1401
18to34	0.761585	0.759016	0.760298	41206
35to54	0.694594	0.774033	0.732165	46945
over55	0.695152	0.381508	0.492646	10448
avg / total	0.722815	0.722490	0.716442	100000

5 Conclusion and Future Work

In this paper, we have proposed a method to create user embedding for a smartphone user based on their app usage. Our experiments highlight the usefulness of such an embedding in capturing user behavior and for binary prediction tasks and vector operations. In future, we plan to evaluate the use of the user embedding for the recommendation task.

References

1. Zołna, K.: User modeling using LSTM networks (2017)
2. Amir, S., Coppersmith, G., Carvalho, P., Silva, M.J., Wallace, B.C.: Quantifying mental health from social media with neural user embeddings. arXiv preprint arXiv:1705.00335 (2017)

3. Ma, Q., Muthukrishnan, S., Simpson, W.: App2vec: vector modeling of mobile apps and applications. In: Proceedings of the 2016 IEEE/ACM International Conference on Advances in Social Networks Analysis and Mining, pp. 599–606. IEEE Press (2016)
4. Xue, S., Zhang, L., Li, A., Li, X.Y., Ruan, C., Huang, W.: Appdna: app behavior profiling via graph-based deep learning. In: IEEE INFOCOM 2018-IEEE Conference on Computer Communications, pp. 1475–1483. IEEE (2018)
5. Chen, L., Qian, T., Zhu, P., You, Z.: Learning user embedding representation for gender prediction. In: 2016 IEEE 28th International Conference on Tools with Artificial Intelligence (ICTAI), pp. 263–269. IEEE (2016)
6. Mannan, N.B., Sarwar, S.M., Elahi, N.: A new user similarity computation method for collaborative filtering using artificial neural network. In: Mladenov, V., Jayne, C., Iliadis, L. (eds.) EANN 2014. CCIS, vol. 459, pp. 145–154. Springer, Cham (2014). https://doi.org/10.1007/978-3-319-11071-4_14
7. Hinton, G.E., Salakhutdinov, R.R.: Reducing the dimensionality of data with neural networks. Science **313**(5786), 504–507 (2006)
8. Amiri, H., Resnik, P., Boyd-Graber, J., Daumé III, H.: Learning text pair similarity with context-sensitive autoencoders. In: Proceedings of the 54th Annual Meeting of the Association for Computational Linguistics, Long Papers, vol. 1, pp. 1882–1892 (2016)
9. Boser, B.E., Guyon, I.M., Vapnik, V.N.: A training algorithm for optimal margin classifiers. In: Proceedings of the Fifth Annual Workshop on Computational Learning Theory, pp. 144–152. ACM (1992)

Design, Development and Initial Validation of a Wearable Particulate Matter Monitoring Solution

José G. Teriús-Padrón(✉), Rebeca I. García-Betances, Nikolaos Liappas, María F. Cabrera-Umpiérrez, and María Teresa Arredondo Waldmeyer

Universidad Politécnica de Madrid, ETSI Ingenieros de Telecomunicación, 28002 Madrid, Spain
{jterius, rgarcia, nliappas, chiqui, mta}@lst.tfo.upm.es

Abstract. Air pollution in one of the main problems that big cities have nowadays. Traffic congestion, heaters, industrial activities, among others produce large quantities of Particulate Matter (PM) that have harmful effects on citizens' health. This paper presents the design, development and initial validation of a wearable device for the detection of PM concentration, with communication capacity via WiFi and Bluetooth Low Energy and an end user interface. The results are promising due to the high accuracy of measurements collected by the developed device. This solution is a step forward in empowering citizens to prevent being exposed to high levels of air pollution and is the beginning of what could be a macro-network of air quality sensors within a Smart City.

Keywords: Air pollution · Wearable sensor · Smart cities · Particulate matter

1 Introduction

Air pollution affects the quality of life (QoL) of people in large cities [1]. Vehicular traffic, heaters and lack of clean transport alternatives are some of the causes of this problem [2]. According to the World Health Organization, only 20% of cities worldwide comply with the required air quality standards [3].

Among the most dangerous pollutants, the Particulate Matter (PM) is one of the air pollutants that causes most damage to people's health due to its characteristics of size and composition [4]. PM_{10} or Coarse Particles have a diameter of less than 10 µg, $PM_{2.5}$ or Fine Particles less than 2.5 µg, and PM_1 less than 1 µg/m^3 [5].

Due to the long-term exposure to air pollutants, especially $PM_{2.5}$, the mortality of people with chronic diseases is increasing [6]. Cardiovascular, respiratory and neurodegenerative diseases are directly affected by the effects of these pollutants [7, 8]. One of the ways to reduce exposure to pollution is by providing awareness about the pollution levels within the cities. Smart Cities offer data that come from the air quality stations installed in the city from which different services and applications (e.g. PulsAir application [9]) could gather data to empower citizens with urban, environment and

J. Pagán et al. (Eds.): ICOST 2019, LNCS 11862, pp. 190–196, 2019.
https://doi.org/10.1007/978-3-030-32785-9_17

health recommendations. However, the data currently available come from fixed sensor stations, and do not necessary cover the entire city.

On the other hand, there are few wearable devices available in the market that seek to provide the user with the necessary information about the pollution levels in a precise location of the city. These solutions present certain weaknesses like the Sparrow [10] and ATMO sensors [11] only focus on $C0_2$ detection, and The Plume Flow [12] only uses Bluetooth as a communication protocol which limits the possibility to scale-up this solution to other services within a Smart City.

This manuscript presents the design, development and initial validation of a wearable real-time Air Quality (AQ) monitoring device based on PM concentration detection, with a user-friendly interface to show AQ levels, and to report warnings, alerts and recommendations based on the pollution levels detected. The device allows to send the gathered data to other devices or services through WiFi and Bluetooth Low Energy (BLE) and can be programmed to use different communication protocols. This solution is presented as the initial step for a result applicable to large Smart Cities in order to increase the granularity of air quality information that allows the public authorities to develop the appropriate policies to improve the QoL of the citizens.

The next sections are organized as follows: Sect. 2 presents the methodology and material used to develop the proposed solution; Sect. 3 includes the design, develop and evaluation of the system; and finally, Sect. 4 presents discussions, conclusion and future steps to extend this work.

2 Materials and Methods

The proposed solution includes the design development and initial validation of the wearable device for air quality measurement, with a user-friendly interface and multiple communication capabilities. The materials used throughout this work are the following:

- PMS7003 Air Quality Sensor (Plantower, Co.): this device can measure concentrations of PM_1, $PM_{2.5}$, and PM_{10}. It has a built-in flow system that allows air circulation through the device enabling to measure pollution levels.
- ESP32 microcontroller (Espressif Systems, Co.): it can establish communication via Serial, WiFi and BLE protocols, which gives great versatility when transmitting or receiving data to/from sensors, actuators and services.
- Sketch-Up software (Trimble, Inc.): is the software used to design the 3D case of the wearable device to be printed in the Ultimaker 3 extended (Ultimaker BV).
- Air Visual Pro Air Quality device (IQAir, Inc): a commercial fixed air quality device, capable to measure PM_1, $PM_{2.5}$, and PM_{10}. The device has a test configuration, that allows to run tests and extract the data collected.
- Arduino Integrated Development Environment (IDE): is an open-source development software to program multi-platform microcontrollers boards [13].

The following methodology has been established:

1. *First Phase, state of the art study of AQ sensors and protocols:*

In this phase, a research of the main air pollutants and their impact on the people health was carried out. Additionally, air quality protocols were studied in order to select the one to be applied in our system, based on current regulations and standards. Finally, a study of air quality sensors available in the market and comparisons were done in terms of size, accuracy communication and energy consumption. Findings of this phase were used to design the proposed device.

2. *Second Phase, design and development of the solution:*

Once the AQ sensor was selected the design and development of the electronics necessary for the operation of the device were conducted. As a final stage, the wearable case, where all the technology developed is built in, was designed with the 3D design sketch tool and produced in the 3D printer.

3. *Third Phase, initial validations:*

This phase consisted on analysing the operation of the device according to the established design, making the necessary adjustments and comparisons with a commercial device to study its accuracy.

Tests were carried out following two stages to analyse the measured quality of the solution developed compared with the Air Visual Pro air quality monitor. In the first stage, the PM sensor was placed without any encapsulation. In the second stage, the same test was conducted with the final design (including the case) in order to verify that the design of the 3D encapsulation did not affect the sensor accuracy. The devices were placed in a home kitchen and synchronized to measure $PM_{2.5}$, PM_1 and PM_{10}, every five minutes. These tests were carryout for a total of six days, three continuous days in each test.

3 Results

This section presents the results obtained from the design, development and initial validations according to the methodology described in Sect. 2.

3.1 Main Components and Design

The designed solution has been conceived with the purpose of being wearable, easy to use and with multiple communication capacity. There are 5 main components: (1) a microcontroller, that mange the sensor, actuators and interface, makes the necessary calculations, and establishes the communications via BLE or WiFi to other devices. It has a lithium battery port and an embedded charger module, which guarantees the portability of the solution; (2) a sensor, that detects the $PM_{2.5}$, PM_1 and PM_{10} concentration and sends it to the microcontroller via serial communication; (3) a screen to show the levels of air quality detected by the sensor; (4) a button which has the functionality to activate the screen. In this way, battery consumption is decreased by not activating the screen unless the user decides to do so; and (5) a sound emitter, which is activated in case of any health risk due to high pollution levels.

3.2 Development

For the development of the firmware, the Arduino IDE has been used taking advantage of the compatibility with the ESP32 microcontroller.

The Air Quality Index (AQI) has been calculated with the data received through the sensor, based on the Environmental Protection Agency standard [14], where 6 levels of pollution are established according to the concentration level of PM. The system will respond in different ways, depending on the AQI value, as presented in Fig. 1.

Three functionalities have been established: to sense the pollution levels, to show the data collected, and to present the information through a user-friendly interface. The measurements are later sent to other devices or services. The functionalities established are the following:

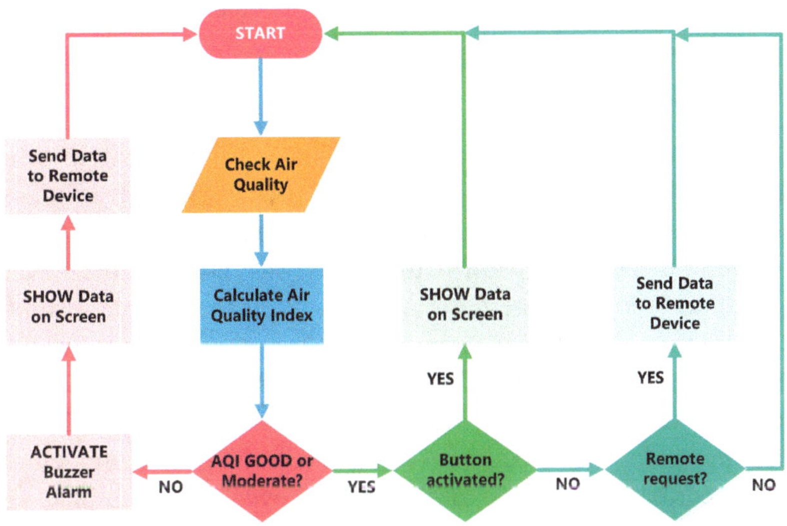

Fig. 1. Flow diagram of the solution.

1. *Activation by button:* when the button is pressed the device calculates the AQI and shows on the screen the AQI levels, taking into consideration the colour scale described by the AQI standard.
2. *Remote communication:* the device measurements and the calculated PM concentration are sent, via BLE, to another device (e.g. smartphone) or service. This functionality allows to present the historical data in a mobile application or to be used by other services.
3. *Pollution levels*: the device reacts autonomously depending on the AQI calculated. When the levels are in a safe range for health ($PM_{2.5}$ concentration between 0 and

12 μg/m^3), the device remains in passive mode. However, when the detected levels are harmful ($PM_{2.5}$ concentration above 35.5 μg/m^3), the system proceeds to alert the user by emitting an alarm sound and showing on the screen the appropriate icon. Furthermore, if a device or service are connected, the information is sent in order to have a historical record of the event.

Each of the functionalities described above were developed individually, and later assembled and incorporated into the case.

4 3D Case Design

Taking into account that the users of this device can have different needs, the case has one top cover, were all the components developed are embedded, and then includes three exchangeable lower caps, describes as follows: (1) lower cap with a clip to attach the device on the side of the pants or belt; (2) lower cap with a hole in one side to hang it on bags or purses; (3) lower cap with two holes to be used with an arm band, designed for people who do physical activities.

4.1 Initial Validations

As described in Sect. 2, the validation was carried out in 2 phases in order to ensure that the design of the 3D encapsulation did not affect the sensor accuracy. The first, with the prototype developed not embedded in the designed case, and the second, with the final prototype inside the case. In both phases was calculate the mean of the PM concentration the accuracy and the correlation between the designed solution and the Air Visual Pro monitor.

As a result of the first phase, the $PM_{2.5}$ mean obtained had an accuracy of 91.42% and a positive correlation of 0.86, which shows that the PMS7003 sensor has an excellent performance for the detection of $PM_{2.5}$. Regarding measurements of PM_1 and PM_{10}, a similar correlation can be observed however, the accuracy decreases but remains over 75%.

On the second tests, the measurement of $PM_{2.5}$ concentration has an accuracy of 92.69% and a correlation of 0.87. In the case of PM_1 and PM_{10} measurements, the data collected show a high accuracy, over 70%, and a positive correlation.

5 Discussions and Conclusion

The system developed represents a novel monitoring device that will help improving the quality of life of people within a smart city environment. Thanks to its small design and wearability, users can have air quality information when moving around city areas where the monitoring stations do not cover. Big cities have insufficient air quality monitoring stations, hence there is no granularity in the provided air pollution data, so that the impact that public policies have on pollution levels cannot be measured with total accuracy.

The proposed solution can be useful to implement a macro network of distributed air quality sensors, monitoring the pollution levels in every corner of the city and thus implement more efficient and effective public policies that will impact positively in the quality of life of the citizens. Taking advantage of the portability and communication capabilities of both BLE and WiFi technologies, the developed sensor can be easily scalable and adaptable to other communication systems and protocols such as Web of Things [15]. The initial validation demonstrates that there are no differences in the measures made by the proposed solution and the commercial device Air Visual Pro monitor.

Future research lines include: (1) the conduction of usability tests in order to improve the design of the final product; (2) largest validations of the device with respect AQ monitoring stations in major cities; and (3) the incorporation of this technology as part of an innovative distributed sensor network for large Smart Cities.

Acknowledgment. This work has been funded by the European Union Horizon 2020 research and innovation program under the Marie Skłodowska- Curie grant agreement ACROSSING No 676157.

References

1. Kelly, F., Fussell, J.: Air pollution and public health: emerging hazards and improved understanding of risk. Environ. Geochem. Health **37**, 631–649 (2015)
2. Ambient air pollution: Pollutants. www.who.int/airpollution/ambient/pollutants/en
3. Health, environment and sustainable development: Air Pollution. https://www.who.int/sustainable-development/cities/health-risks/air-pollution/en/
4. Kim, K., Kabir, E., Kabir, S.: A review on the human health impact of airborne particulate matter. Environ. Int. **74**, 136–143 (2015)
5. Zhang, L., Ninomiya, Y., Yamashita, T.: Formation of submicron particulate matter (PM1) during coal combustion and influence of reaction temperature. Fuel **85**, 1446–1457 (2006)
6. Cohen, A., Brauer, M., Burnett, R., Anderson, H., Frostad, J., et al.: Estimates and 25-year trends of the global burden of disease attributable to ambient air pollution: an analysis of data from the global burden of diseases study 2015. Lancet **389**, 1907–1918 (2017)
7. Zaheer, J., Jeon, J., Lee, S., Kim, J.: Effect of particulate matter on human health, prevention, and imaging using PET or SPECT. Prog. Med. Phys. **29**, 81 (2018)
8. Underwood, E.: The polluted brain. Science **355**, 342–345 (2017)
9. Ottaviano, M., Beltrán-Jaunsarás, M., Teriús-Padrón, J., et al.: Empowering citizens through perceptual sensing of urban environmental and health data following a participative citizen science approach. Sensors **19**(13), 2940 (2019)
10. Sparrow Sense. https://www.sparrowsense.com/
11. AMTO. https://atmotube.com/?view=es
12. Plume Labs. https://plumelabs.com/en/flow/
13. Boxall, J.: Arduino Workshop: A Hands-on Introduction with 65 Projects. No Starch Press (2013)

14. US Environmental Protection Agency, US Environmental Protection Agency, Office of Air Quality Planning and Standards, Outreach and Information Division. Air Quality Index: A guide to air quality and your health. EPA-456/F-14-002 (2014)
15. Teriús-Padrón, J., et al.: Autonomous air quality management system based on Web of Things standard architecture. In: The 5th IEEE Smart World Congress (In press)

Cooperative System and Scheduling Algorithm for Sustainable Energy-Efficient Communities

Esther Palomar(✉), Carlos Cruz, Ignacio Bravo, and Alfredo Gardel

Department Electronics, University of Alcala, Madrid, Spain
{esther.palomar,carlos.cruzt,ignacio.bravo,alfredo.gardel}@uah.es

Abstract. The High connectivity among devices within the Internet-of-Things facilitates two-way flow of information throughout the infrastructure reaching homes and the consumers targeting broader energy goals. Our proposal encompasses consumers cooperating in response to utility supply conditions, i.e., electricity available from renewable sources. Such a smart and green community of consumers autonomously adapts its energy consumption by enabling a local aggregator to (1) integrate their demand into a common view and, (2) re-schedule the community demand given the renewable energy supply and the consumers' demand time preferences. In this paper, we evaluate the developed scheduling algorithm using benchmark data to validate our proposal implementation over existent technology.

Keywords: Cooperative demand response · Scheduling algorithm · Consumer time preferences · Renewable supply

1 Introduction

Information and communication technologies (ICT) are essential tools for enabling energy efficiency as well as establishing new energy services and solutions [4]. In particular, the Internet of Things (IoT) [2] and the Smart Grid [3] together can provide the foundational infrastructure and use of advanced information, control and communication technologies to save energy, reduce cost and increase reliability and transparency. Connected devices (e.g, household items, machines, or gadgets) can automatically influence each other so increasing the overall potential for energy savings and the range of management systems' involvement. ICT can also play an important role in shaping consumer behaviour [5]. Furthermore, the real exploitation of renewable sources for energy supply presents multiple challenges not only for utilities, grid and system operators, but also for the consumers who do not see this type of information on their utility bills [6].

Supported by Comunidad de Madrid (Spain) under the grant Talent Attraction with reference 2017-T1/TIC- 5184.

J. Pagán et al. (Eds.): ICOST 2019, LNCS 11862, pp. 197–203, 2019.
https://doi.org/10.1007/978-3-030-32785-9_18

Demand response (DR) programmes appear to bolster not only energy efficiency but also renewable energy resource management initiatives as to handle their sophisticated planning and operation scheduling requirements [1,7]. In this short paper, we present a cooperative DR system model which is designed to promote behavioural changes in small or large communities of electricity consumers. The community will target common interests (i.e., to be green) that create the need for involved entities to reach binding agreements and coordinated behaviour. We implement and analyse the resource (i.e., the renewable supply) allocation process, initially conceived in a centralised way by means of a data collector called the *Aggregator*. This entity provides the community with the scheduling of the total demand taking into account both the renewable supply available from the local utility providers and the costumers' consumption time preferences. Experimentation with estimated values and benchmarks throws feasible performance cost that validates the viability of the system implementation over existent technology (i.e., Z-Wave or IEEE 802.11i standards).

2 System Model

Figure 1 illustrates the main roles and processes within the adopted cooperative demand response framework. In our proposal, Consumers adapt their energy consumption cooperatively on a centralised way; that is, they share their demand schedule with a data collector called **Aggregator**. The **Aggregator** facilitates the integration of the energy consumption information and implements an optimised resource allocation algorithm in response to the Utility's supply conditions, in particular, targeting renewable sources.

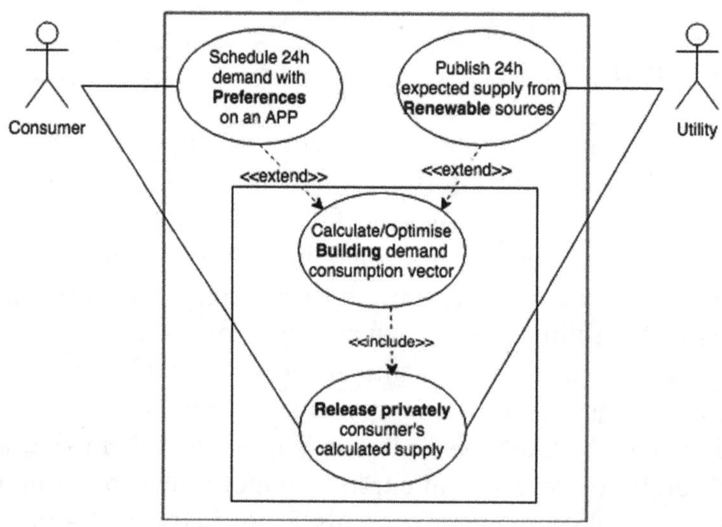

Fig. 1. A user (or household) equipped with an energy consumption scheduler or home energy manager on a portable device (i.e., an app on a smartphone or tablet) that is connected to a communication network. A community consists of a set of Consumers sharing electricity supplier or substation.

2.1 Consumer System Design

Let $\mathcal{N}$ denote an ordered set of Consumers that are willing to cooperate in the pursuit of global community targets (i.e., become greener), sending their data to the *Aggregator*. Each Consumer $i \in \mathcal{N}$ has a set of household appliances $\mathcal{A}_i = \{\text{washer, dryer, coffee makers, cooker, fridge, TV, alarm, light controller, water heating, AC system,}\ldots\}$. Each consumer then pre-allocates[1] a certain amount of fixed demand[2] as well as variable consumption resulting from their utilisation planned for the upcoming 24 h. The daily fixed demand for consumer $i \in \mathcal{N}$ is denoted by $f\mathcal{D}_i = \sum_{t=0}^{23} \sum_{a_{ij} \in \mathcal{A}_i} fx_{i,a_{ij}}^t$ as the aggregated load of non-shiftable local consumption of the appliances and frequent behaviours. Variable energy demand is considered *flexible* since consumer preference for an appliance to start within a particular time interval is also taken into account. For each appliance, there is a execution window (i.e., a closed interval) denoting a minimal starting time and a maximal ending time. In other words, Consumer i will keep/set the following data for his/her appliance $a_{ij} \in \mathcal{A}_i$ as in Table 1.

Table 1. Appliance configuration

Consumption (KW/h)	Fixed consumption (KW/h)	Duration (hours)	Time ON	Time OFF

2.2 Aggregator System Design

A centralised system with aggregation tasks communicates with the Utility as well as with the Consumers as shown in Fig. 1. An algorithm is originally built to optimise the allocation of the expected electricity supply from renewables amongst the community's Consumers and according to the their expressed preferences. We denote by $\mathcal{RW}^t$ the energy supply generated from a set of renewable sources at a time slot $t \in \{0, \ldots, 23\}$. The *Aggregator* can easily compute the daily fixed demand for the whole community of consumers at a time t as $f\mathcal{D}^t = \sum_i^N f\mathcal{D}_i^t$, which should not reach the worst case such that $\sum_i^N \sum_{t=0}^{23} f\mathcal{D}_i^t \gg \sum_{t=0}^{23} \mathcal{RW}^t$. By contrast, aggregation of the variable consumption is an optimisation problem given the consumers' time preferences.

---

[1] We consider a discrete time slot system, which granularity is one hour of the day. We have developed an energy consumption scheduling app (or home energy manager) that connects via a home area network (HAN) and/or lower power wireless such as ZigBee, with all the appliances at home and the Aggregator. The app provides the Consumer with an interface to control, monitor, visualise and program the functioning of appliances.

[2] Formulae and benchmarks can be used to estimate appliance and home electronic energy use in kilowatt hours (kWh) as well as household local records.

Algorithm 1. Demand Calculation Function ($\mathcal{DCF}$)

1: **for** iappliance 1 to size of appliances configuration ($\mathcal{A}_i$) **do**
2: $\mathcal{RW}^t = \mathcal{RW}^t - \mathcal{A}_i(f\mathcal{D}_i^t)$
3: **end for**
4: $\mathcal{A}_i(v\mathcal{D}_i^t) = \mathcal{A}_i(v\mathcal{D}_i^t) - \mathcal{A}_i(f\mathcal{D}_i^t)$
5: $\mathcal{A}_i(\mathcal{D}_i^t(\mathcal{D}_i^t < 0)) = 0$
6: $\mathcal{A}_i(f\mathcal{D}_i^t) = \mathcal{A}_i(f\mathcal{D}_i^t) - \mathcal{A}_i(f\mathcal{D}_i^t)$
Objective Function $\mathcal{F}(\mathcal{A}_i, \mathcal{RW}^t, t_{osi})$
Require: $\mathcal{A}_i$ configuration: $v\mathcal{D}_i^t, f\mathcal{D}_i^t, \mathcal{L}_i^t, st_i, et_i$
Ensure: $st_i < et_i$
7: $\mathcal{HC}$ initialisation (consume Hourly Energy)
8: **for** iappliance 1 to size of appliance configuration **do**
9: Set t_{sti}
10: Set t_{eti} based on $\mathcal{L}_i$ and t_{sti}
11: **for** ihour time to the total number of hours **do**
12: **if** ihour belongs to interval $[st_i, et_i]$ **then**
13: $\mathcal{HC}(ihour) \leftarrow \mathcal{HC}(ihour) + \mathcal{A}_i(v\mathcal{D}_i^t)$
14: **else**
15: $\mathcal{HC}(ihour) \leftarrow \mathcal{HC}(ihour) + \mathcal{A}_i(f\mathcal{D}_i^t)$
16: **end if**
17: **end for**
18: **end for**
19: $\mathcal{RW}^t s = \mathcal{RW}^t - \mathcal{HC}^t$
20: $\mathcal{RW}^t s(\mathcal{RW}^t s < 0) = 0$
21: $Demanded\_\mathcal{RW}^t \leftarrow min(\mathcal{RW}^t, \mathcal{HC}^t)$
22: $\mathcal{R}1 = sum(\mathcal{RW}^t s)$; $\mathcal{R}2 = max(\mathcal{HC})$
23: $Result = sum(\mathcal{R}1 + \mathcal{R}2)$
24: **return** $Result, Demanded\_\mathcal{RW}^t, \mathcal{HC}^t(t_{osi}, t_{oei})$

The *Aggregator* will execute a scheduling of the community's requested variable demand per hour $v\mathcal{D}_i^t$ when the aforementioned worst case does not apply, and aiming at $\forall t \in \{0, \ldots, 23\}, \sum_i^N (f\mathcal{D}_i^t + v\mathcal{D}_i^t) \leq \mathcal{RW}^t$. We face here a global centralised optimisation problem to which there exists a unique *Nash bargaining solution* such that: $\forall i \in \{1 \ldots \mathcal{N}\}, \mu_i^t = f\mathcal{D}_i^t + min\{\mathcal{F}(v\mathcal{D}_i^t)\} \leq \mathcal{RW}^t$, where $\mathcal{F}(\cdot)$[3] is in charge of shifting the variable demand given Consumers' appliance preferred activation time. Algorithm 1 displays a round-robin strategy over the matrix of all appliances' operation preferences and the remnant of the *RW* supply vector after deducting the total fixed demand (Algorithm 1 – lines 1–3). Upon reaching the optimisation objective, the *Aggregator* will notify the community that an agreement has been reached and privately release the reallocated demand vector $\overrightarrow{\mu}_i, \forall i \in \mathcal{N}$.

[3] The *Aggregator* can apply different strategies to the aggregated load vector $v\mathcal{D}$ by shifting appliance's demand within their preferred activation time frame as well as by selecting one or another appliance to serve first.

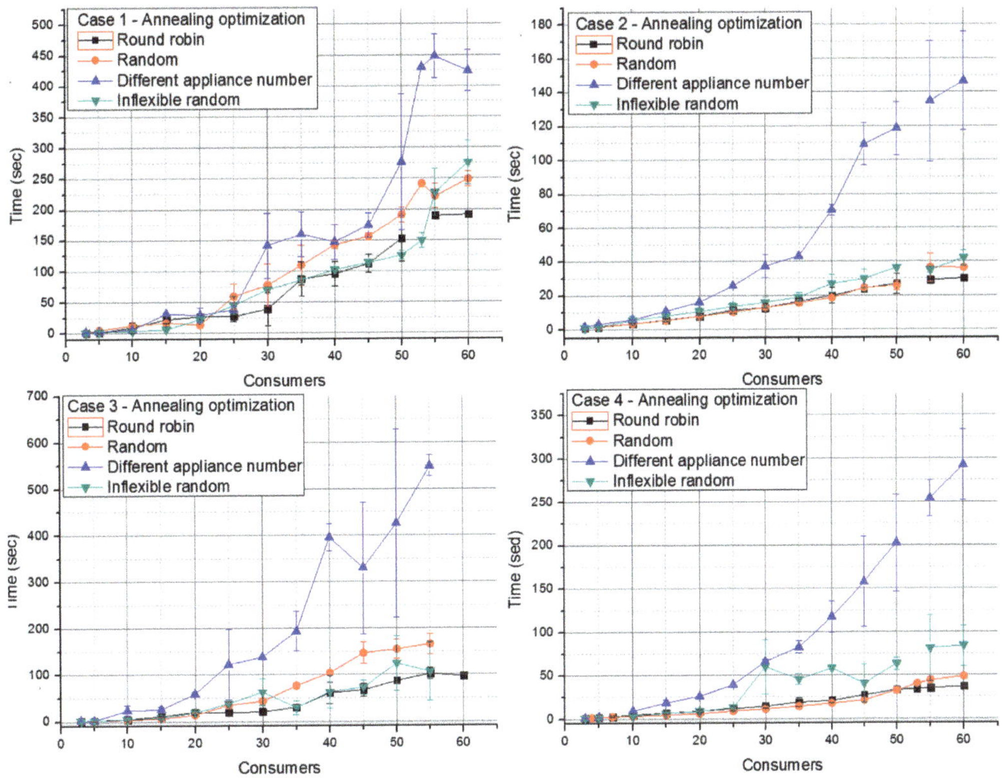

Fig. 2. Computational cost in Cases 1–4 using SA and strategies RR, randomness and consumers with heterogeneous/homogeneous number of appliances.

3 Algorithm Validation

We evaluate the performance of Algorithm 1 with simulated[4] data of consumers' fixed and variable consumption demands at different case scenarios for appliances' fixed and variable consumption, i.e., Case 1 for high consumptions, Case 2 for high fixed expends, Case 3 when variable is high and, Case 4 for low consumption communities.

Figure 2 illustrates the reallocation processing cost of communities with up to 60 consumers with up to 4 appliances, which is taking 3 min in the worst case. In fact, worst case occurs when appliances demand high variable consumption (Cases 1 and 3) and the algorithm performs a random strategy. On the other hand, we found that the factor incurring the highest performance cost on our algorithm is consumers holding a different number of appliances to schedule; 6 min in the worst case (triangle-up line in Fig. 2) and applying a sequence with the first player being the same every time. Figure 3 throws best outcomes over communities with low variable demand and the same number of appliances per consumer.

[4] Simulation run on a computer with the following specifications: CPU: 2.3 GHz Intel Core i5; Memory: 8 GB 2133 MHz LPDDR3 and MATLAB R2018b. Data is estimated by applying manufactures' benchmarks.

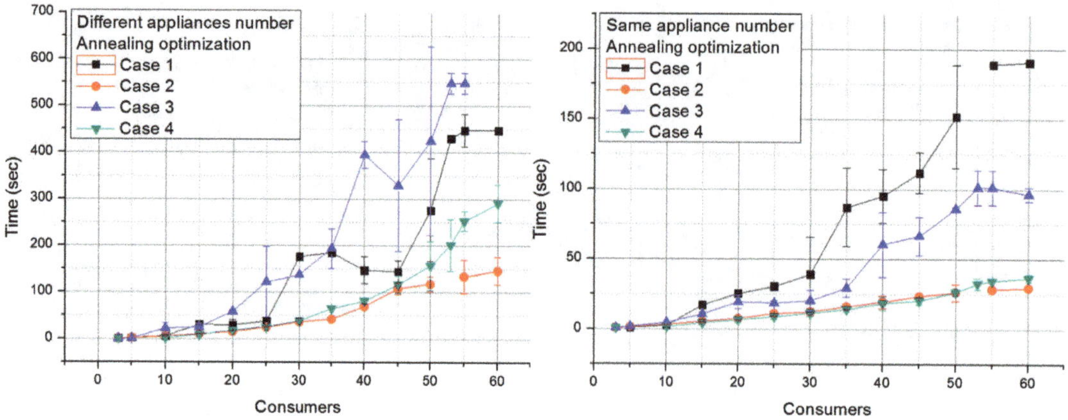

Fig. 3. Performance at the four case scenarios with consumers holding (left) different number of appliances, and (right) the same number of appliances.

4 Conclusions

Smart communities, capable of identifying patterns in energy consumption, will be able to reduce or shift their use of the utility resource, making the overall consumption more sustainable and efficient. Unlike the majority of previous Demand Response strategies that focus on pricing and aim at reducing the energy cost and the peak-to-average ratio, our solution tends to promote a transformation of the whole energy value chain by making consumer communities cooperate targeting the available renewable energy supply. In this paper, we have shown the performance cost of a centralised scheduling algorithm (less than 1 min cost) for different size of communities and consumption patterns. Immediate future work relates to the algorithm testing with real traces from the Birmingham Living Lab and the real implementation of both algorithm and home controllers on a pilot testbed, paying special attention to the system and network security.

References

1. Aghaei, J., Alizadeh, M.I.: Demand response in smart electricity grids equipped with renewable energy sources: a review. Renew. Sustain. Energy Rev. **18**, 64–72 (2013)
2. Gubbi, J., Buyya, R., Marusic, S., Palaniswami, M.: Internet of Things (IoT): a vision, architectural elements, and future directions. Future Gener. Comput. Syst. **29**(7), 1645–1660 (2013)
3. Ipakchi, A., Albuyeh, F.: Grid of the future. IEEE Power Energ. Mag. **7**(2), 52–62 (2009)
4. Lui, T.J., Stirling, W., Marcy, H.O.: Get smart. IEEE Power Energ. Mag. **8**(3), 66–78 (2010)
5. Mattern, F., Staake, T., Weiss, M.: ICT for green: how computers can help us to conserve energy. In: Proceedings of the 1st International Conference on Energy-Efficient Computing and Networking, e-Energy, pp. 1–10. ACM (2010)

6. Palensky, P., Dietrich, D.: Demand side management: demand response, intelligent energy systems, and smart loads. IEEE Trans. Ind. Inform. **7**(3), 381–388 (2011)
7. Qayyum, F., Naeem, M., Khwaja, A.S., Anpalagan, A., Guan, L., Venkatesh, B.: Appliance scheduling optimization in smart home networks. IEEE Access **3**, 2176–2190 (2015)

ForeSight - Platform Approach for Enabling AI-based Services for Smart Living

Jochen Bauer[1(✉)], Hilko Hoffmann[2], Thomas Feld[3], Mathias Runge[4], Oliver Hinz[5], Andreas Mayr[1], Kristina Förster[1], Franz Teske[1], Franziska Schäfer[1], Christoph Konrad[1], and Jörg Franke[1]

[1] Institute for Factory Automation and Production Systems, Friedrich-Alexander-University Erlangen-Nürnberg, Egerlandstraße 7-9, 91058 Erlangen, Germany
jochen.bauer@faps.fau.de

[2] Deutsches Forschungszentrum für Künstliche Intelligenz GmbH, Stuhlsatzenhausweg 3, 66123 Saarbrücken, Germany

[3] Strategion GmbH, Albert-Einstein-Straße 1, 49076 Osnabrück, Germany

[4] IoT connctd GmbH, Hardenbergstraße 32, 10623 Berlin, Germany

[5] Faculty of Economics and Business Administration, Goethe University Frankfurt, Theodor-W.-Adorno-Platz 4, 60323 Frankfurt am Main, Germany

Abstract. In future, smart home and smart living applications will enrich daily life. These applications are aware of their context, use artificial intelligence (AI) and are therefore able to recognize common use cases reliably and adapt these use cases individually with the current user in mind. This paper describes a concept for such an AI-based platform. The presented platform approach considers different stakeholders, e.g. the housing industry, service providers and tenants.

Keywords: Artificial intelligence · Ecosystem · Platform · Smart home · Smart living

1 Motivation

The term "Smart Living" comprises several areas that are separated today: energy management, health and home automation [1]. Furthermore, smart home is a core element in a connected world. There is need for intelligent applications, which fulfil cross-domain use cases. Smart buildings, which include smart homes and commercial buildings, will take an important role to enable smart grid [2] and smart city related approaches. Such approaches can only be realised with intelligent, situation-adaptive control opportunities and building related services [3]. This leads to more comfort, better assistance and increased safety and security as well as improved resource efficiency and reduced overall costs. The reason

Supported by German Federal Ministry for Economic Affairs and Energy.

J. Pagán et al. (Eds.): ICOST 2019, LNCS 11862, pp. 204–211, 2019.
https://doi.org/10.1007/978-3-030-32785-9_19

for such advanced opportunities is the intense usage of AI. This paper describes a concept for a platform approach to enable such an intense AI usage in smart living.

The economic relevance of connected homes or buildings is proven by several key figures [4,5]. In Germany there are currently approximately 19 million residential buildings and around 42 million households. The residential buildings have a share of approximately 98% of the total building stock. 57% of all Germans and 72% of single households lived for rent in 2015. [6] The 23 million rental housing units are managed by about 68,000 companies. Due to the situation described above, it is demanded at government level that the topic of digitisation and connectivity for the housing industry will be addressed. For other European countries, the situation seems not exactly the same, but similar.

2 State of the Art

There are currently various stand-alone smart home systems on the market. Some of these are based on wired or wireless technologies, e.g. KNX [7], Homematic [8, S. 231], Z-Wave [8, S. 216], free@home or digitalSTROM [9]. Moreover, most of the systems offer cloud-based remote access possibilities as an additional option for controlling the building from abroad. Of course, the biggest value proposition for the tenant is if he is able to add various devices from different vendors and consume third party services in his system. There are various middleware systems, which follow this idea like the openHAB system [10] or ioBroker.

Middleware systems usually provide an abstraction layer for devices. Thus, these systems are able to ensure data transfer between such systems and therefore achieve interoperability. In smart homes and for assistance systems in general, privacy and security issues [11] play an important role in Europe. This means that each data record should be extended with the information, who is allowed to do what actions at what time with it.

According to the paragraph before, it becomes obvious that available semantic information is useful to include domain knowledge in suitable data structures. For this purpose the concept of ontologies exists. Ontologies are semantic orders of domain related terms and their relationships [12]. Due to ontologies it is possible to start semantic search operations, combine two knowledge bases or test data for inconsistencies [13]. In the domain of smart living the SAREF ontology [14], BRICK [15] and Web of Things [16] are ontologies or approaches which should be investigated. The world of ontologies and knowledge representations lost some importance in recent years because solutions for numerous challenges were delivered by another part of AI, so-called machine learning (ML). In ML, algorithms and statistical methods are used to find solutions for optimization problems, e.g. more and more pre-trained neural networks offer robust high-quality answers to related questions [21]. In the context of smart living, speech recognition [22], object identification or energy management are relevant examples, where ML is used successfully.

3 Challenges

Requirements are rapidly increasing in the smart building context, i.e. for achieving the energy transition flexible control and monitoring mechanisms need to be offered. Another challenge for German society is to assist elderly people and enable them to live in their preferred environment as long as possible. To achieve this, AI-based smart living technologies can help to extend this period of time. Thus, it is necessary to increase the amount of connected devices and enable energy consumption measurement and localisation technologies to create individual adaptable use cases. Currently, systems lack this functionality and do not offer such individually profile-based approaches. Future smart home systems need to have the specific user in mind, detect users' behaviour and make the correct conclusions. Smart speaker can help here to locate and identify persons. Moreover voice user interfaces (VUI) can bring smart home technology to people who are not used to smartphones. The first numbers of sold smart speakers show that VUIs are a game changer. Anyway, there are lots of people who are still reluctant, because they do not know what happens to their data. Summing up, promising smart home platforms should offer a VUI and address privacy issues as well.

Existing middleware systems are slowly beginning to ensure interoperability [18,19]. In addition to automating tasks, smart home systems begin to offer authentication options based on OAuth. This is pretty common for social media websites, i.e. signing in with your Google or Facebook account to another website [20]. On the one hand, this is quite comfortable for the user but on the other hand it will be even more advanced to sign in with your preferred service and avoid sharing data to lots of different servers abroad. Current platforms and eco systems lack organizational interoperability. This interoperability level should be persuaded, because only then it will be possible to create a flexible eco system with different partners, who are able to include their specific services and corresponding business models. The ideal place to store semantic information is in an ontology, e.g. the SAREF ontology. Ontologies can be extended [17], hence this should be considered by almost any platform project in the smart living domain.

Furthermore, concepts are needed which enable the transition from hard-coded if-else-statements towards context aware, dynamic and situation adaptive, self-learning approaches, which consider future trends as well. These new approaches need to add to current best practice approaches, e.g. plug-and-play mechanisms like the OSGI-based openHAB system. Changing the perspective from system to device, it is possible to speak from "Thinking Objects".

4 Approach

The following ForeSight platform approach was initiated from members of the German Smart Living Business Initiative, a network of smart home and smart building experts. The goal of the ForeSight platform is to create a significant contribution to the further development of smart buildings and homes by providing cross-domain AI-based solutions in combination with established building automation technologies.

In the past, there have been various platform approaches, most of these were not able to conquer the market. There are technical, legal and economic challenges to deal with. In a first step core partners were allowed to found ForeSight. In this six months lasting project a useful platform concept needs to be created and relevant partners have to be identified, so that the value added chain is completed. In addition to that, established research institutes and organisations are added to the consortium to develop the concept further and further.

Due to literature research and experience, possible partners were detected. Afterwards, the team decided to start the working phase by founding a matrix based organisation, composed of several working groups (WG) (see Fig. 1). The figure shows WGs with domain specific focus and groups with cross-sectoral topics. The WG coordinators need to collect relevant data of their WG and interconnect with other WGs.

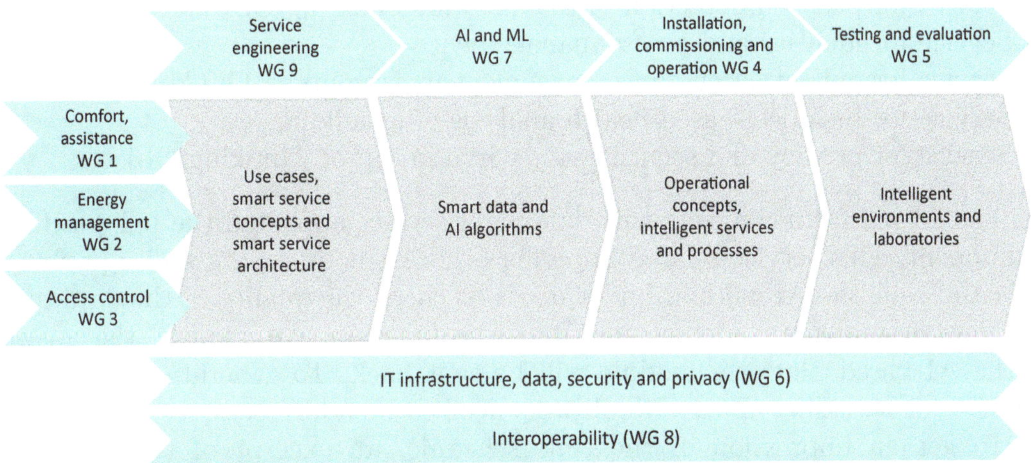

Fig. 1. The consortium created working groups to start an efficient process to push the ForeSight concept creation.

The created ForeSight platform concept should be evaluated and verified in laboratories and real world environments. Therefore, possible user stories and use cases need to be identified and implemented. There are several user story catalogues but usually there is no direct combination with AI, which is one of the core elements of this platform approach. Therefore, a new template for user stories was created and given to the members of the different WGs. This template considers relations to AI services, which are necessary for the specific use case.

With reference to the challenges section, ForeSight wants to reach a high level of interoperability, i.e. that service providers with different business models can replace their services without much effort. The resident focuses on one use case and the platform takes care of necessary processes in the background. To identify users is one of ForeSight's basic features and the key to enable user specific use case adaptions. Horizontal interoperability ensures that the manufacturers and cross-domain interchangeability of devices works. Vertical interoperability considers that interoperability between two services is available, i.e. energy management use cases are interchangeable, although tenants are clients from different energy providers. Following the thinking objects approach it is necessary to offer the most appropriate AI method in relation to a client's use case. It makes sense to offer three subsystems: first, the AI method platform module; second, an IoT platform module to make sure that all commands can be transported to several vendor-independent devices and third, service-related apps which can be built and ran on the IoT platform module and are allowed to connect to the AI module. Several AI base services are necessary and will be made available in ForeSight:

- Service for activity recognition of tenants
- Service for object identification
- Service for predictive maintenance related to Thinking Objects
- Service for self-configuration of Thinking Objects
- Service for position detection of tenants and Thinking Objects
- Service for identity and access management
- Service for optimized energy management in a group of Thinking Objects
- Service for technical-based health analysis of a building
- Service for privacy and security issues in a group of Thinking Objects

The AI platform connects with ForeSight service apps and the IoT platform component. This service-related app offers the AI module data and a preferred use case. Now the AI method finder needs to check the quality of the data, pick the most appropriate AI tool and start the function. Afterwards, the answer of the AI based platform module will be sent back. To generate high quality answers for accessing apps, several tasks need to be addressed (see Fig. 2).

To get an impression of the time schedule, an excerpt of the ForeSight roadmap is shown below.

- 2019, 2020: creation of the ForeSight platform concept and identification of all project partners
- 2020, 2021: implementation of reference architecture and AI-based context sensitive services
- 2021, 2022: realization of service layer to achieve interoperability on business model layer
- 2023, ... : ForeSight entering the market for third party service providers

In addition to the time schedule we defined some milestones and evaluation steps:

- 2019: Partners are able to contribute to all steps of the value added chain.
- 2020: Partners are willing and able to run the platform from 2020 to 2030.

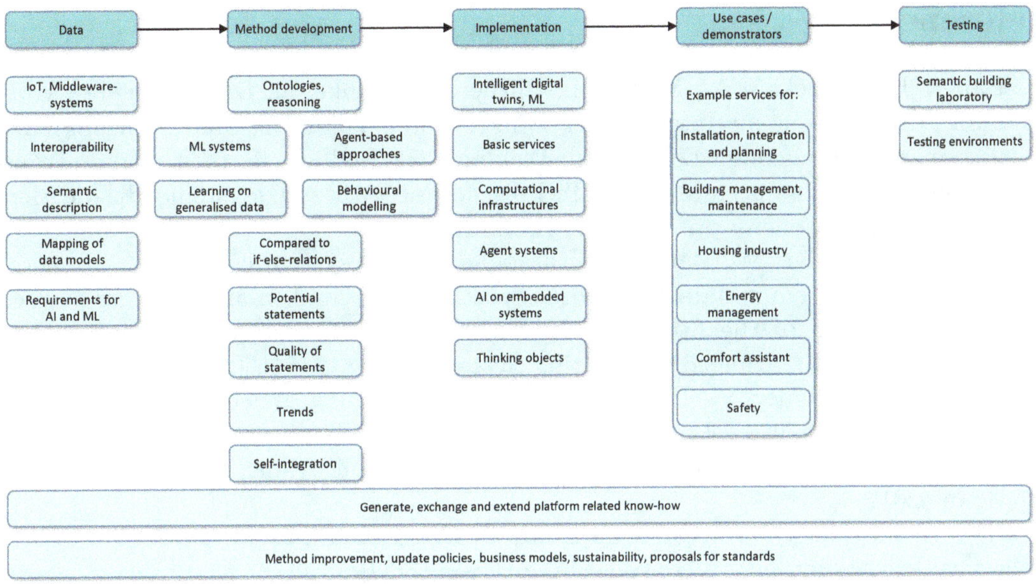

Fig. 2. The AI method platform offers different components to fulfil the needs of accessing service apps.

- 2021: Tests in labs and real world scenarios achieve satisfactory results and robustness.
- 2022: 10 third-party companies connect to the ForeSight platform with their own services.
- 2023: More than 80% of existing smart living systems are using a ForeSight platform service.

5 Discussion

When designing a platform, one of the first questions which arises is who wants to operate such a platform. The ForeSight consortium consists of several companies, which are experienced in running platforms. A flexible service-based approach for running the platform seems to outperform a monolithic approach, as first interviews showed.

Numerous use cases from the ML area require high quality data in order to train the ML models, e.g. neural networks. Such data is often not available and must be generated, which usually takes an enormous amount of time. It will be hard to consider such soft facts in the AI method finder function to answer the service-based apps.

In the past, several critical factors for smart home platforms were identified, i.e. IT security, privacy and economic beneficial business models for all stakeholders. The appropriate treatment of these topics needs to be considered from the very beginning to avoid major concept changes later, which results in high costs.

References

1. Bauer, J., Kettschau, A., Michl, M., Bürner, J., Franke, J.: Die intelligente Wohnung als Baustein im Internet der Dinge: Potenzialanalyse und Konzept einer domänenübergreifenden Lösung. In: Weidner, R., Redlich, T. (eds.) Erste Transdiziplinäre Konferenz zum Thema Technische Unterstützungssysteme, die die Menschen wirklich wollen., pp. 298–307. Hamburg (2014)
2. Kunold, I., Kuller, M., Bauer, J., Karaoglan, N.: A system concept of an energy information system in flats using wireless technologies and smart metering devices. In: Proceedings of the 6th IEEE International Conference on Intelligent Data Acquisition and Advanced Computing Systems, pp. 812–816 (2011)
3. Bakakeu, J., Schäfer, F., Bauer, J., Michl, M.: Building cyber-physical systems - a smart building use case. In: Song, H., Srinivasan, R., Sookoor, T., Jeschke, S. (eds.) Smart Cities: Foundations, Principles, and Applications, pp. 605–640. Wiley, Bonn (2017)
4. IDC Worldwide: Quarterly Smart Home Device Tracker, 29 March 2019. https://www.idc.com/getdoc.jsp?containerId=prUS44971219
5. MarketsandMarkets: Smart Home Market by Product (Lighting Control, Security & Access Control, HVAC, Entertainment, Smart Speaker, Home Healthcare, Smart Kitchen, Home Appliances, and Smart Furniture), Software & Services, and Region - Global Forecast to 2024. https://www.marketsandmarkets.com/Market-Reports/smart-homes-and-assisted-living-advanced-technologie-and-global-market-121.html
6. Statista: Übersicht Wohnen. https://de.statista.com/themen/51/wohnen/. Accessed 16 June 2019
7. Kriesel, W., Sokollik, F., Helm, P.: KNX/EIB für die Gebäudesystemtechnik in Wohn- und Zweckbau. Hüthig Verlag, Heidelberg (2014)
8. Heinle, S.: Heimautomation mit KNX, DALI, 1-Wire und Co. Rehinwerk Computing, Bonn (2016)
9. Dickmann, G.: DigitalSTROM®: a centralized PLC topology for home automation and energy management (2011)
10. Spiller, M.: Smart Home mit openHAB 2. Rheinwerk Computing, Bonn (2018)
11. Zibuschka, J., Nofer, M., Zimmermann, C., Hinz, O.: Users' preferences concerning privacy properties of assistant systems on the internet of things. In: American Conference on Information Systems (AMCIS 2019) (2019, forthcoming)
12. Gruber, T.R.: A translation approach to portable ontology specification. Knowl. Acquis. **5**, 199–220 (1993)
13. Sabou, M.: An introduction to semantic web technologies. Semantic Web Technologies for Intelligent Engineering Applications, pp. 53–81. Springer, Cham (2016). https://doi.org/10.1007/978-3-319-41490-4_3
14. Daniele, L., den Hartog, F., Roes, J.: Created in close interaction with the industry: the Smart Appliances REFerence (SAREF) ontology. In: Cuel, R., Young, R. (eds.) FOMI 2015. LNBIP, vol. 225, pp. 100–112. Springer, Cham (2015). https://doi.org/10.1007/978-3-319-21545-7_9
15. Balaji, B., et al.: Brick: towards a unified metadata schema for buildings. In: ACM Proceedings of the 3rd ACM International Conference on Systems for Energy-Efficient Built Environments, New York, pp. 41–50 (2016)
16. Guinard, D., Trifa, V.: Towards the web of things: web mashups for embedded devices. In: Workshop on Mashups, Enterprise Mashups and Lightweight Composition on the Web (MEM 2009), In Proceedings of WWW (International World Wide Web Conferences) Madrid (2009)

17. Daniele, L., Solanki, M., den Hartog, F., Roes, J.: Interoperability for smart appliances in the IoT world. In: Groth, P., et al. (eds.) ISWC 2016. LNCS, vol. 9982, pp. 21–29. Springer, Cham (2016). https://doi.org/10.1007/978-3-319-46547-0_3
18. Kreuzer, K.: Semantic modelling of smart buildings with the open source software openHAB smart public building website. http://www.hft-stuttgart.de/Forschung/i_city/Handlungsfelder/Explorative-Projekte-i-city/Exploratives-Projekt-SPUB/de/. Accessed 16 June 2019
19. Broering, A., et al.: Enabling IoT ecosystems through platform interoperability. IEEE Softw. **34**(1), 54–61 (2017)
20. Rossnagel, H., Zibuschka, J., Muntermann, J., Hinz, O.: Users' willingness-to-pay for web identity managment. Eur. J. Inf. Syst. (EJIS) **23**, 36–50 (2014)
21. Bauer, J., et al.: Camera-based fall detection system with the service robot sanbot ELF. In: Uckelmann, D., (ed.) Smart Public Building 2018 Conference Proceedings, Stuttgart, DE, pp. 15–28 (2018)
22. Pan, Y., Shen, P., Shen, L.: Speech emotion recognition using support vector machine. Int. J. Smart Home **6**(2), 101–108 (2012)

Mobility Application with Semantic Reasoning

Martin Kodyš[1,2](✉), Antoine de Marassé[1,3], and Mounir Mokhtari[1,3]

[1] Image and Pervasive Access Laboratory (IPAL), CNRS UMI 2955, Singapore, Singapore
martin.kodys@univ-grenoble-alpes.fr
[2] Université Grenoble Alpes, Grenoble, France
[3] Institut Mines-Télécom, Paris, France

Abstract. Active mobility is a way of keeping oneself in a good health, although it may cause some discomfort. Globally, and specifically in Singapore context, several elements can influence our decisions. The choice of the right time for active mobility depends not only on available vehicles but also on the weather and the air quality. Popular fitness trackers motivate users by a daily step count goal. At the same time, open data, bus arrival times or shared bicycles availability help optimise the planning of the active mobility. Given these elements, a personalised mobile application was designed in order to facilitate the mobility choice. The paper describes how this application was constructed. It focuses on the use of semantic web reasoning for the integration of all factors and the recommendation inference. The outcome of the ongoing deployment with 36 participants is presented.

1 Introduction

It is well known that physical exercise enhances blood circulation, which in turn has additional health benefits [5]. Even in advanced age, it is not too late to start even a simple exercise, such as a walk, to notice improvements [1]. Walking, a light physical activity, has been recommended to cope with type 2 diabetes [2].

We consider *active mobility* to be one or a combination of the following activities: walking, jogging, cycling and, to a certain extent, using a scooter or even taking public transportation as there is an additional physical effort compared to use of a private car or a motorcycle.

Getting physical exercise through active mobility is convenient. It has the potential to decrease the cost of commute if it can replace some parts of one's journey. It can save time as well – time that would be needed to get to an activity-specific environment like a gym. Although active mobility is essentially an outstanding way of improving one's health, the outdoor environment is an important risk factor. For instance, air pollution, noise, and risk of accidents [3]. Air pollution becomes dangerous due to increased respiration rate during a physical activity. For that reason, the authorities usually discourage people from performing them if the concentration of particles reaches defined thresholds.

J. Pagán et al. (Eds.): ICOST 2019, LNCS 11862, pp. 212–221, 2019.
https://doi.org/10.1007/978-3-030-32785-9_20

At the same time, other research evidence suggests that the benefits of physical activity due to walking and cycling outweigh the detrimental effects of air pollution exposure and the risk of traffic incidents [4].

Our aim is to promote active mobility by making it more accessible and preferable to other kinds of transportation, such as personal vehicles, taxis and or other similar services. The focus is thus on maintaining and enhancing the health of our users. This has to be done with respect to their profiles and the potential environmental impact of the chosen mobility solutions. Other useful indicators include current daily progress, e.g. using step count, as well as other real-time and near real-time data.

We approached it by providing a unified interface for services that have been already made available by local companies or government agencies. In the back-end, we used semantic technology to facilitate the evolution of the application in order to integrate new features. We also made it modular and allow administrators to create new content that are directly visible to our participants.

Context in Singapore. As in other cities, in Singapore, public transportation faces the problem of the first and the last mile; the distance between the starting point of the commuter's journey and the most convenient transportation node (bus stop, interchange or Mass Rapid Transit (MRT) station) and similarly, the exit point of the network and their real destination.

The city-state allows bicycles-riding on both walkways and roads (unlike, for example, France where riding a bike on a walkway is tolerated but not officially allowed). In 2016, shared bicycles became very popular and the trend is now decreasing. Meanwhile, the use of personal mobility devices (PMDs), mainly electric scooters is rising. In the latest legislation in effect since February 2019, the maximum riding speed on walkways is 10 km/h for all devices. Shared paths (bicycles, rollers, walking) and park connector network allow 25 km/h.

2 Research Problem

This paper presents an approach to tackle the issue of sedentary life-style in a non-intrusive way, that is suitable to everyone regardless of age or health conditions.

The main interest of ours is to motivate the user while ensuring maximum convenience given the space we have. This means we need to push our message without too much pressure in order to retain the user's attention and interest. From the layout point of view, all necessary information should be provided without overwhelming the user.

In the back-end side of the application, which is our main focus in this paper, we ought to provide the aforementioned services in a dynamic way, transparent to the user, having a lot of flexibility as the parameters might need to evolve over time. New sources can be added and discontinued sources must not affect the functionality of the technological solution. Therefore, the proposed solution is expected to be modular.

Semantic web technologies provide interesting tools to create knowledge-based systems. They provide modularity and flexibility when removing or inserting the information. However, the main difficulty is that the logical inference may produce unexpected results and therefore, verification mechanisms have to be implemented (Fig. 2).

From the point of view of semantic technologies in mobile applications surveyed in [7], we position our software as a client-server architecture where the reasoning is performed in a remote server. In this setting, the client only formats and displays the information. The application would belong to several categories: health, recommendation, map-based.

To the best of our knowledge, no holistic application focused on mobility solution was available. We believe that a way of merging the heterogeneous data is a valuable contribution to possible uses of the semantic web technologies.

For instance, Google Maps application, offers different mobility solutions (public transport, walk, taxi). It even offers a travel time estimation. However, the mobility offer is not adapted to the user's profile nor to the current weather. On the other hand, "fitness" applications (Fitbit, Google Fit, Apple Health) are oriented more on achieving better values, being competitive. Therefore, we believe this fusion of multiple functionalities has an added value for the user.

3 Application Design

The resulting Android application data flow is depicted in Fig. 1. Upon opening, our application sends a geo-located request to our server. The server interacts with necessary APIs to obtain the data: the current *physical activity* progress rate from the fitness tracker, e.g. 90 %; the weather 2 h *forecast*, e.g. rain,and current *temperature*, e.g. 26 °C; and the current *air quality* index (AQI), e.g. 140. From the **profile** stored in the database, information about one's personal condition is retrieved: *asthma*, e.g no; *disability*, e.g. yes. All the information is injected into a semantic graph structure using an ontology model in which the parameters fit: the knowledge base. The reasoning process applies our set of rules on this knowledge base. The rules keep producing new knowledge until a "desirability" of modelled mobility solutions is obtained. This information is returned to the client and along with environmental factors (forecast, temperature, AQI). The mobile application then presents this information to the user using colour codes for each mobility solution.

3.1 User Interface

This part of the design process was performed by our industrial partner, having a user-centred approach in mind. The design of the system started with an overview of applications currently offered for major operating systems in sections concerning mobility, well-being and physical activity. Opinions of potential users and other stakeholders were collected in a workshop setting, using questionnaires and brainstorming techniques.

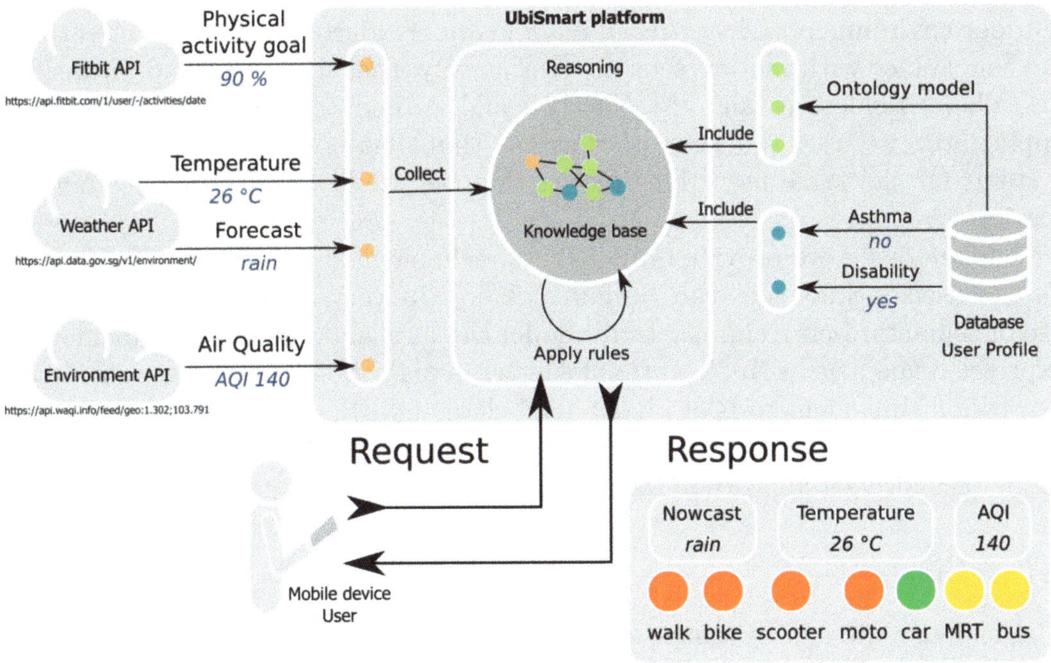

Fig. 1. On a request from the application, platform UbiSmart (designed according to [6]) injects available information from multiple sources into the semantic structure of the knowledge base, applies rules and serves a comprehensive decision and its context.

The outcome showed that a most adapted application would have a very simple interface so that it could be used without a lot of interaction, with few indicators. Then, incrementally complex view was defined for each indicator and service integrated onto the application (Fitbit integration, API for bus arrivals, points of interest, bike-sharing integration).

We defined the simple interface as a three-level indicator according to a colour level: green, yellow and red with the intuitive meaning of the traffic lights or gauges indicating a measure of danger.

Around this basic indicator, we developed an algorithm that aggregates available dimensions and projects them in a one dimensional variable "desirability", having value between 0 and 1, for each of the selected mobility solutions. It represents to what extent we recommend the given mobility solution provided the available information. The interval was divided into three segments, one for each colour.

[0, 1/3]: red – mobility solution is discouraged given the circumstances;
(1/3, 2/3]: yellow – not recommended;
(2/3, 1]: green – recommended.

4 Reasoning

The core of the application was the engine for decision process about each mobility solution. Our reasoning processes has already been deployed in indoor and outdoor environments. *Activities of daily living* of elderly people were monitored in their homes with motion sensors. In this way, their caregiver had an insight into global tendencies and the elderly could extend their autonomy. For this application, we used the same platform so that it is possible to integrate both systems for the same user. This means that we would be able to offer holistic services.

For reference, we provide only a short technological description, and details on the used technologies can be found in [6]. In very simple terms, we make use of semantic web technologies to model the user and their environment. The expression language is N3, Notation3 which is a dialect of Turtle language, a terse expression equivalent to RDF, itself a subclass of XML. The language describes information organised in triples of concepts: subject, predicate, object. A set of the triples forms a knowledge base.

4.1 Model

The main component of semantic web technologies is the knowledge base (KB) that contains all pieces of information. This information is structured in triples. A triple has a form of a three-term sentence, e.g. "hom:aqi qol:hasValue 105". Each term is either a concept or a literal. Each concept is identified by a unique identifier – URI that points to its definition. A literal is a value of one of usual data types: string of characters, numerical value, boolean value, ... The dictionary of the terms and a "grammar" are defined in an *ontology*. An ontology describes what can exist in the world described by our knowledge base. In simple words, it defines the hierarchy of concepts. For instance, "cycling" is a "mobility solution", which translates to concept of "cycling" being a subclass of the concept of "mobility solution".

4.2 Rules

Rules define the mechanics of our world and are also expressed as a special kind of triples - subject is a formula, i.e. zero or more triples, enclosed in curly braces, predicate is the string "=>", object is another formula written in curly braces. Formulas can contain special terms beginning with a question mark, e.g. "?weather". They are similar to variables in imperative programming languages. Their scope is limited to the rule.

A set of rules applied on the current knowledge generates new information. Depending on the evaluation of the output, appearance of some specific triples may trigger actions on the outside world (notification), removal of the information from the KB. Rules can be used to perform arithmetic operations, aggregation or simple inference "if ..., then ...".

The following is an excerpt of the rule set used in our application to determine the coefficient of air pollution from the measure of AQI obtained from a public source.

Soundness of the manually generated rules must be verified and along with the rules a table of all combinations was generated and is presented in Fig. 2.

```
# 100 < AQI < 150
# For all users that do not have asthma, if (100 < AQI < 150) then aqiFactor equals 0.8
{hom:aqi qol:hasValue ?v. ?v math:lessThan 150. ?v math:notLessThan 100.
  []e:findall((){hom:johndoe qol:hasMedicalCondition qol:asthma}()).
  (hom:walk hom:bike hom:scooter hom:moto hom:mrt hom:bus hom:car)  list:member ?mode}
=> {?mode hom:aqiFactor 0.8}.

{hom:aqi qol:hasValue ?v. ?v math:lessThan 150. ?v math:notLessThan 100.
 hom:johndoe qol:hasMedicalCondition qol:asthma.
 (hom:scooter hom:moto) list:member ?mode}
=> {?mode hom:aqiFactor 0.6}.
```

4.3 Reasoner

Once the description of our universe (knowledge base) and its laws (rules) is ready, we apply a reasoner. A reasoner is an application that takes our triplets in input, along with the rules to be applied and a query that defines a selection of the knowledge base that is of interest for us. The reasoner we use is called "eye" shorthand for "Euler yet another proof Engine". The choice of this tool is discussed in [6]. Eye is accessed via a Javascript interface inside our NodeJS application. Components of our application can add, remove and update the knowledge base.

4.4 Implementation of a Decision Table

For this application, we defined basic statements and implemented the rules. However, the most useful was the enumeration of all possible states in a table. It is automatically generated from a list of conditions for each dimension and their combinations. It was very helpful during verification process.

For the proof of our concept, the we integrated 6 dimensions with the segmentation as follows. The full table contain 5 weather conditions $\times$ 2 temperature cases $\times$ 4 AQI intervals $\times$ 1 scalar goal measure $\times$ 2 disability $\times$ 2 asthma = 160 cells (each having a value for every mobility solution).

The visualisation of this space is presented in Fig. 2. This matrix of 16×10 cells represents the different cases taken into account. Each cell contains a combination of digits that denote conditions in order weather (1–5: unknown, rain, fair, danger, wind), AQI (1–4: from better to worse), asthma (0 no or 1 yes), disability (0 no or 1 yes), temperature (0: under 36 °C or 1: over 36 °C).

There are 8 coloured segments, each of them represents a specific configuration of the aforementioned binary parameters. They are coded in RGB 3-dimensional colour space with following attributions: temperature = red, asthma = green, disability = blue. Their combinations give a colour combination: e.g. *black* (gray background) is at all values are 0, *cyan* has blue and green components so it depicts disability and asthma.

Within the coloured cluster, horizontal position indicates 4 cases of air quality indicator AQI with healthiest lowest values on the left and in this order: under 50, up to 100, up to 150, over 150. Vertical position within each coloured block are 5 cases of weather condition in this order: unknown, rain, good weather (fair, overcast, cloudy), dangerous (heavy rain, thunderstorm), and windy.

Inside each cell, 7 mobility solutions are indicated in order: walk, bicycle, scooter, motorbike, car, MRT, bus. Their vertical position within the cell is a measure of recommendation which also defines the colour according to their appearance in the application: red, yellow or green. The lower the mobility is placed, the lower is the score.

The indicated values are the *maximum score* the mobility can obtain in the configuration, and passive mobilities are weighted with current progress in goals. This means that "car" will be *red* if there was no physical activity progress in the day, even if it appears *green* in the cell.

In the case of non-use of the fitness tracker, we decided to show the results as if the daily goal was achieved (we show the colour as in this table).

The current progress is adapted to the time of the day – 100% score is obtained if at 50 % of the day, the user completed 50 % of their goal.

The importance of explicitly drawing this table is for validation of the approaches to make sure that all cases are covered with values that make sense. We made use of it during the verification process and it helped to discover issues with the model.

Product of all values is the measure of desirability of given mobility solution for the currently known situation.

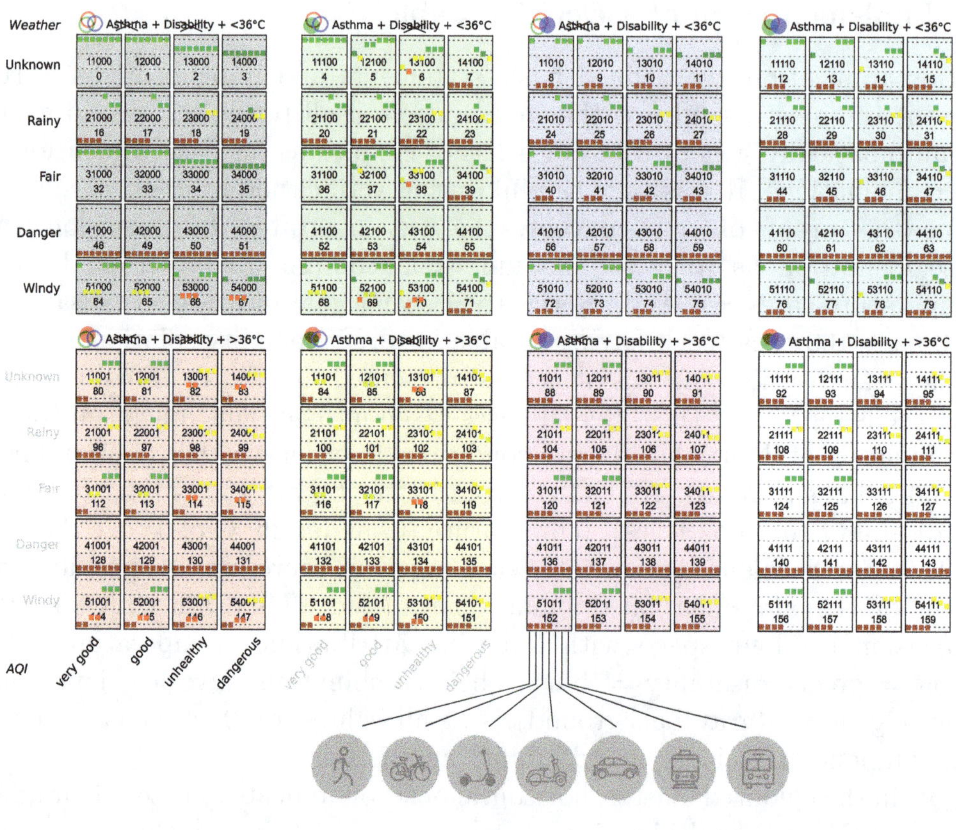

Fig. 2. Six dimensions for each mobility solution as implemented in our application

4.5 Deployment

The application was distributed to participants along with an optional Fitbit device. We were interested in the usage rate of the application and in gathering feedback from the users. Users own a smartphone and know at least basic interactions. In order to encourage users' feedback, the participants were invited to a lucky draw where two participants would win an upgrade of their Fitbit device to a newer model.

5 Results

The application was deployed to 36 very heterogeneous group of users. In the latest phase, of 4 months, we monitored application start, reasoning cycle trigger, and Fitbit synchronisation time-dates.

Very few participants used the application extensively. We recognise that the installation was cumbersome due to the necessity to connect user's Fitbit account to our application and several runtime errors in the application linked to the use of the GPS that need to be addressed in future versions. However the idea of a mobility application with these features seems appreciated. The deployment shows that 15 out of 36 users downloaded the application but needed a guided help to set it up with Fitbit or make the reasoning work (e.g. not activated geolocation services and hence, the application couldn't operate).

According to 17 valid profiles, the age of participants ranged from 22 to 59 years, with an average of 31.5 years and median of 30.

The feedback from our active users include following categorised statements:

Data Empowerment. "The great power of data is when you can communicate it to people at an individual level that makes sense for them, for example: at a neighbourhood level . . . this is what air pollution looks like around you; what it means for you; and what the advice is."

Near Geolocated Data. "Using the mobile App together with the wearable device is motivating, this is my one-stop-app for my personal data activity crossed with impactful Urban data. Those data are geo-located and enhance the use of the public space for citizens."

About the Concept of Service. "Encouraging the people to be physically active and crossing this data with urban data makes sense to empower individuals in their daily lifestyle."

Behaviour Change. "The mobile app enables to track your physical activity, it is very motivating. For instance, I will more likely try to walk or run more, also simple changes have an important impact on our daily lives, for example I take the stairs instead of the escalators to exit the subway. The sport side of the project, improving my physical activity is my main motivation."

We also asked participants about the application's ease of use and their feedback was used to solve technical issues. The need of providing a walk-through of the application was noted but scheduled for a further release.

6 Conclusion

We presented a functional concept application for mobility solutions based on symbolic reasoning. It combines the data from an activity tracker (Fitbit), publicly available environmental data (weather forecast, local temperature and air quality), and private profile data (asthma, disability). We described the functioning and the design, and in particular, the implementation of a 6-dimensional table used for validation of the rules.

Our solution was implemented and as an Android application deployed to 36 users. We are continuing the data collection in order to understand their use of the application. A positive user feedback shows that the application is able to fulfill new needs and it is encouraging us to enhance the interface and performances.

Acknowledgements. The work presented in this paper was supported by the PSA Group.

References

1. DeSouza, C., et al.: Regular aerobic exercise prevents and restores age-related declines in endothelium-dependent vasodilation in healthy men. Circulation **102**, 1351–1357 (2000)
2. Duclos, M., et al.: Physical activity and type 2 diabetes recommandations of the SFD (francophone diabetes society) diabetes andphysical activity working group. Diab. Metab. **39**(3), 205–216 (2013). https://doi.org/10.1016%2Fj.diabet.2013.03.005
3. Johansson, C., et al.: Impacts on air pollution and health by changing commuting from car to bicycle. Sci. Total Environ. **584–585**, 55–63 (2017)
4. Mueller, N., et al.: Health impact assessment of active transportation: a systematic review. Prev. Med. **76**, 103–114 (2015). http://www.sciencedirect.com/science/article/pii/S0091743515001164
5. Nystoriak, M.A., Bhatnagar, A.: Cardiovascular effects and benefits of exercise. Front. Cardiovasc. Med. **5**, 135 (2018). https://doi.org/10.3389/fcvm.2018.00135
6. Tiberghien, T.: Strategies for context reasoning in assistive livings for the elderly. Ph.D. thesis, Institut National des Télécommunications (2013)
7. Yus, R., Pappachan, P.: Are apps going semantic? a systematic review of semantic mobile applications. In: MoDeST@ISWC (2015)

Author Index

Abdulrazak, Bessam 3, 27, 61
Aboujaoudé, Aline 154
Abrol, Satyen 183
Affes, Abir 85
Ajami, Hicham 97
Aloulou, Hamdi 27

Bauer, Jochen 204
Bellazzi, Riccardo 143
Bier, Nathalie 154
Bravo, Ignacio 197
Brun, Damien 168

Cabrera-Umpiérrez, María F. 190
Cabrera-Umpiérrez, María Fernanda 18
Caldarone, Alessandro Aldo 143
Casella, Vittorio 143
Cherif, Fedi 109
Chikhaoui, Belkacem 36, 49
Codjo, Josué 3
Corring, Deborah 131
Couture, Mélanie 154
Cruz, Carlos 197

de los Ríos, Silvia 18
de Marassé, Antoine 212

Feld, Thomas 204
Forchuk, Cheryl 131
Förster, Kristina 204
Frampton, Barbara 131
Franke, Jörg 204
Franzini, Marica 143
Freisleben, Bernd 85, 109

García-Betances, Rebeca I. 18, 190
Gardel, Alfredo 197
Gargees, Rayan 73
Garolera, Maite 18
Giroux, Sylvain 154
Gouin-Vallerand, Charles 168

Hinz, Oliver 204
Hoffmann, Hilko 204

Jang, Wanho 122
Jebara, Sofia Ben 61
Jmaiel, Mohamed 85, 109

Kaźmierski, Jakub 18
Keller, James M. 73
Kessentini, Yousri 109
Kim, Dongwan 122
Kim, Jeonghyun 122
Kim, Jongbae 122
Kodyš, Martin 212
Konrad, Christoph 204

Laliberté, Catherine 154
Larizza, Cristiana 143
Liappas, Nikolaos 190
Lussier, Maxime 154

Maalej, Manel 109
Maalej, Mohamed 109
Malovini, Alberto 143
Mann, Rupinder 131
Mayr, Andreas 204
Mcheick, Hamid 97
Mdhaffar, Afef 85, 109
Mezghani, Neila 61
Mokhtari, Mounir 27, 212
Mustapha, Karam 97

Ngankam, Hubert Kenfack 154

Otis, Samuel 61

Pala, Daniele 143
Palomar, Esther 197
Páramo, Miguel 18
Parenteau, Maxime 154
Park, Sungdeuk 183

Pigot, Hélène 154
Popescu, Mihail 73

Rehman, Shafiq Ul 3
Rudnick, Abraham 131
Ruer, Perrine 49, 168
Runge, Mathias 204

Sadek, Ibrahim 3
Schäfer, Franziska 204
Serrato, Jonathan 131
Singla, Kushal 183
Skubic, Marjorie 73

Teriús-Padrón, José G. 190
Teske, Franz 204
Thabet, Jihen Ben 109
Tournoux, Francois 61
Triki, Chahnez 85

Uhm, Yunjeong 122

Vallières, Évelyne F. 49, 168
Vancells, Marta 18

Waldmeyer, María Teresa Arredondo 18, 190

Yang, Seungwan 122

Zerkouk, Meriem 36

www.ingramcontent.com/pod-product-compliance
Lightning Source LLC
LaVergne TN
LVHW082224200926
848484LV00008B/2302

7 State Control, Bureaucracy, and the National Interest from the Second World War to the 1960s 169

8 Conclusion 195

Chronology of Events 203

Bibliography 207

Index 209

About the Author

A.W.H. Bates is a Coroner's Pathologist, Honorary Senior Lecturer at University College London, and Fellow of the Oxford Centre for Animal Ethics. His other books include *Emblematic Monsters* (2005) and *The Anatomy of Robert Knox* (2010).

Abbreviations

AAMR	Association for the Advancement of Medical Research
ADAVS	Animal Defence and Anti-Vivisection Society
AFS	Animals Friend Society
BBC	British Broadcasting Corporation
BMA	British Medical Association
BMJ	British Medical Journal
BUAV	British Union for the Abolition of Vivisection
COS	Charities Organization Society
FRS	Fellow of the Royal Society
ICRF	Imperial Cancer Research Fund
LDAVS	London and District Anti-Vivisection Society
LMA	London Metropolitan Archives
LRCP	Licentiate of the Royal College of Physicians
MP	Member of Parliament
MRC	Medical Research Council
MRCS	Member of the Royal College of Surgeons
NCDL	National Canine Defence League
OGA	Order of the Golden Age
RDS	Research Defence Society
(R)SPCA	(Royal) Society for the Prevention of Cruelty to Animals
UCL	University College London

UFAW	Universities Federation for Animal Welfare
ULAWS	University of London Animal Welfare Society
VSS	Victoria Street Society
Well	Wellcome Library, London

Abstract

This book provides an introduction to the social history of the anti-vivisection movement in Britain from its nineteenth-century beginnings until the 1960s. Its focus is on the ethical principles that inspired the movement and the sociopolitical background that explains its rise and fall. Opposition to vivisection began when medical practitioners complained it was contrary to the compassionate ethos of their profession. Christian anti-cruelty organizations took up the cause out of concern that callousness among the professional classes would have a demoralizing effect on the rest of society. As the nineteenth century drew to a close, the influence of transcendentalism, Eastern religions and the spiritual revival led new age social reformers to champion a more holistic approach to science, and dismiss reliance on vivisection as a materialistic oversimplification. In response, scientists claimed it was necessary to remain objective and unemotional in order to perform the experiments necessary for medical progress.

1

Introduction

In Britain, the great majority of vivisection—I use the term not just in its literal sense of cutting up living animals but in the broader one of experimenting on them to the extent that they suffer and perhaps die—has been performed in the name of medicine.[1] It is of historical interest, therefore, that, in the mid-nineteenth century, when vivisection was introduced into British laboratories and medical schools from the Continent, much of the opposition to it came from doctors. Their motives in resisting it were complex, but can be boiled down to a conviction that vivisection was not something that a doctor ought to do.

Inspired by their example, this account of the history of the British anti-vivisection movement from its beginnings until the 1960s will focus on the character, or virtue, of the experimenter. This is not being done for the sake of finding a novel perspective on a topic that has been fairly well studied, but because I believe the virtue-centred approach was one of the nineteenth century's most significant contributions to the debate, and that it might profitably be revisited by present day animal ethicists. It may be no coincidence that the massive increase in animal experimentation in the twentieth century coincided with the rise of utilitarianism in medical ethics. As medical scientists assumed greater ethical autonomy, their emphasis was on results, eschewing

A.W.H. Bates, *Anti-Vivisection and the Profession of Medicine in Britain*,
The Palgrave Macmillan Animal Ethics Series, DOI 10.1057/978-1-137-55697-4_1

conventional virtues on the one hand, and sentiment and feeling on the other, with dire consequences for laboratory animals.[2]

In writing a book for a series on animal ethics, I am labouring under a disadvantage in not being an ethicist. Most doctors are in the same position, and in the past 20 years or so a cadre of professional medical ethicists has arisen to guide our thinking. This has not been unproblematic, since few are trained in medicine and almost none practice it. While clinicians have benefited from the input of academic ethicists, some of their contributions have proved controversial, and occasionally shocking, such as the recent paper in a leading British journal of ethics that seemed, certainly to the readers who contacted the journal to complain, to be advocating infanticide. Its perspective was, needless to say, utilitarian.[3] The resulting outcry apparently surprised some members of the academic community, especially since, as the journal's editor observed, arguments in favour of infanticide had previously been put forward by 'the most eminent philosophers and bioethicists in the world…'.[4] Of course, it is not to be supposed that these luminaries would be anything other than horrified if their theorising actually led to children being killed, but the furore does reveal the gulf between ethical theory and practice, and, since the latter is influenced by the former, serves as a reminder that how ethics is taught matters. Bioethics as currently taught in British medical schools is unlikely to stress the importance of the physician's humane character[5]: as anyone who works in a teaching hospital will know, medical students and junior doctors are trained to seek the greatest benefit for the largest number; and to their utilitarian hammer, everything looks like a nail.

The physician's ethical grounding, or lack thereof, is important to the history of vivisection because, since the nineteenth century, by far its commonest defence has been that it saves human lives. It was on this basis that, in 1941, an English court made the landmark ruling that anti-vivisection was no longer to be considered a charitable cause because, as experiments on animals had been shown to be of benefit to humankind, anti-vivisectionists would be harming their fellow humans by banning them. This utilitarian judgement assumed that medics were justified in performing such experiments as were necessary to alleviate human suffering. Apart from a few conscientious objectors, most people working in British biomedicine today subscribe to this view, and will say, if asked, that they dislike experiments on animals, and hope alternatives will be found in time, but are currently obliged to accept them as the only way to develop life-saving treatments. Of course, since the publication of Peter Singer's influential *Animal Liberation* (1975), the interests of animals are less likely to be omitted from the utilitarian calculus, but few if any experimenters value animal lives on a level with human ones. Singer's own commitment to their interests did not extend to calling for the abolition of vivisection, and the balanced position he expressed in 1980 is very close to the view of the medical research community today:

> The knowledge gained from some experiments on animals does save lives and reduce suffering. Hence, the benefits of animal experimentation exceed the benefits of eating animals and the former stands a better chance of being justifiable than the latter; but this applies only when an experiment on an animal fulfils strict conditions relating to the significance of the knowledge to be gained, the unavailability of alternative techniques not involving animals, and the care taken to avoid pain. Under these conditions the death of an animal in an experiment can be defended.[6]

There is very little in this book on the subject of animal rights, since while the concept has a long history, going back at least as far as Thomas Tryon (1634–1703),[7] and while parallels between the rights of man and the rights of animals helped put animal welfare on the political agenda at the end of the eighteenth century, rights-based arguments were seldom used by the anti-vivisection movement before the 1970s. It was only after the publication of the Oxford philosophers' collection of essays, *Animals, Men and Morals* in 1971, followed by *Animal Liberation* (in which Singer himself does not take a rights-based position), that the anti-cruelty movement regrouped under the banner of 'animal rights', and began to appeal primarily 'to reason rather than to emotion or sentiment', a significant departure from what had gone before.[8] Rights-based arguments have certainly caught the public imagination, to the extent that non-specialist publications typically refer to anti-vivisectionists as 'animal rights activists' as though the two are synonymous, with the result that the principles on which the movement was founded are prone to be overlooked.

As Andrew Linzey has written, an idea that has generated as much scholarly activity as animal rights cannot be unimportant, but merely respecting any rights that animals are deemed to have falls far short of the ideal of treating them humanely, an ideal that was at the heart of the original anti-vivisection movement.[9] This history will explore the ethical arguments that sustained that movement from its beginning and throughout its heyday: namely, that it is socially irresponsible to permit cruelty, that Christianity, and other faiths, require animals to be treated as more than means to an end, and that a balanced, holistic approach to medicine must draw on emotional and spiritual insights as well as on the results of experiment.

It is possible that some will turn to this book for an answer to the question of whether animal experimentation has in fact resulted in significant medical advances. In this, as in other aspects of the debate, the propaganda has been extreme: supporters of vivisection have laid claim to almost every major medical advance of the twentieth century, while their opponents argue that nothing useful has been learned. The truth lies in between, though it is difficult to say precisely where, as just because a particular advance *was* made through vivisection does not mean that it could *only* have been thus made. Since vivisection has been normative, or even compulsory, in laboratories for over a century, it has necessarily played a part in most of the important discoveries made during that time, but whether they would have been made without it is as difficult to answer as any question in hypothetical history, and I shall not attempt to do so here. It is notable that historically, while the claim that vivisection has resulted in key advances in medicine has been a critical one for its supporters, for many anti-vivisectionists it was irrelevant, since the issue for them was whether vivisection benefited society as a whole, the answer to which depended on a sophisticated socio-political value judgement of what makes for a good society.

So prominent was the culture of the laboratory in the late-nineteenth century that trials on 'suffering human beings' were dismissed by the *British Medical Journal* (BMJ) as inferior to experiments on animals.[10] Like human dissection half a century earlier, vivisection was controlled by legislation, restricted to professionals, confined to licensed premises, and performed out of the public gaze, and though its practitioners were disliked and sometimes feared by the public, they were also admired for their fortitude and commitment to the pursuit of science. If medical progress required experiments on animals, then the scientist's cool indifference to vivisecting them signified dedication and self-mastery rather than callousness or cruelty. By the early-twentieth century, vivisection had come to be seen as an indispensable weapon in medicine's unending 'fight' against disease: to be pro-vivisection was to be for science, progress, and the relief of human suffering, while anti-vivisectionists were enemies of science, whose sentimentality and squeamishness were obstacles to be overcome.

To understand the motives of anti-vivisectionists, one must first appreciate the fundamental differences over the nature and goals of science that lay (and perhaps still lie) at the heart of the debate. I have laid particular emphasis on the thesis that vivisection was the expression of a particular view of science—objective, dispassionate, materialistic—which has now become so familiar it is largely taken for granted, but which was contentious in its time. Anti-vivisectionists also regarded themselves as scientific—they tried to test their position through experiments such as anti-vivisection hospitals—but their idea of what constituted scientific sources extended beyond results acquired in the clinic and laboratory to encompass less palpable forms of knowledge. To them, a scientist's duty was not simply to investigate physical phenomena but to seek a deeper appreciation of their significance and, by paying attention to ethical and social considerations, to increase the sum of human wellbeing.

The spiritual revival, and 'new age' utopianism, deeply influenced the anti-vivisection movement. While the most important motives for early anti-vivisectionists were probably their commitment to Christian values and personal virtue, it is striking how many later ones were theosophists, vegetarians, pacifists, and members of various socio-religious orders, unions and groups. For these reformers, vivisection was unscientific because it treated animals as mere matter and ignored the spiritual, aesthetic and moral aspects of life that, though intangible, had to be heeded if humankind's harmony with nature was to be restored. The idea that the vivisectionists' mask of objectivity hid their inability to understand the real consequences of their actions, or even accept their own feelings, persisted in animal welfare writing until at least the late-twentieth century, when Air Chief Marshal Lord Dowding (1882–1970) dismissed them as 'so-called scientists'.[11]

As fascinating and revealing as the history of vivisection and its opponents can (I hope) be, the writings on both sides are voluminous, repetitive, and, for the modern reader, wearisome to plough through. There quite possibly never was a contest in which the disputants failed so comprehensively to grasp one another's point of view. John Simon, speaking at the International Medical Congress in London in 1881, summed it up thus:

> Our own [*i.e.* the experimenters'] verb of life is εργαζεσθαι [to work], not αισθανεσθαι [to perceive]. We have to think of usefulness to man. And to us, according to our standard of right and wrong, perhaps those lackadaisical aesthetics [of anti-vivisectionists] may seem but a feeble form of sensuality.

Of course, not even Mr Simon could entirely numb himself to suffering: he went on to say, without irony, that he found vivisection 'painful'.[12] For all their talk of objectivity, many experimenters found themselves in a similar position: according to Rob Boddice, Victorian physiologists used anaesthetics to spare their own sensibilities, rather than out of consideration for the animals.[13] Fearful of a public outcry, the pioneers of animal experimentation imagined potential anti-vivisectionists around every corner, though, as with most other moral issues then and since, the majority of people remained stubbornly indifferent. It took histrionics to break through their complacency, and both sides obliged. Rather than repeat these recurring diatribes in every chapter, it will suffice to summarise them here.

Vivisectionists, according to their critics, were cruel, sadistic, and even diabolical in their wickedness. There are, of course, no facts to support this; in reading many accounts, I have found nothing to suggest that any British vivisectionist derived perverse pleasure from his work.[14] So far as one can tell, all thought they were doing something that needed to be done, and many genuinely disliked doing it. As for the accusations that they were cold, heartless and indifferent, this they did not dispute, though they wrote cool, objective and scientific instead.

For them, the whole point of the scientific method was that one was supposed to be dispassionate.

In turn, experimentalists dismissed anti-vivisectionists as soft, sentimental, and womanish, accusing them of valuing other animals above their own species and hampering life-saving research because they were too weak to stomach the necessary experiments. They knew, in their hearts, that medical science must progress, but were too cowardly, or hypocritical, to help: no wonder some were also pacifists. Personally, I would consider most of the comments directed at anti-vivisectionists quite flattering if applied to me, and reassuring if applied to the doctor about to treat me. Some anti-vivisectionists acknowledged the same, but the culture of masculinity was strong in medicine and this, along with the high importance accorded to laboratory work, explains the otherwise surprising fact that many members of this quintessentially caring profession were driven to regard sentimentality as a weakness of character.

In Chap. 2, I suggest that the vivisection debate in the early-nineteenth century was more about virtue than utility, and that much of the opposition to vivisection in Britain came from medical men who felt it would bring their profession into disrepute by linking them with cruelty. In contrast to more recent debates, the question of what results vivisection was expected to yield was less important than whether a virtuous person ought to do it. This concern about the vivisector's character was particularly germane to doctors, upon whom there rested a professional obligation to behave with compassion. For the anti-vivisection movement, the spectre of 'human vivisection', their alarmist term for experimentation on hospital patients, proved a good recruiting sergeant, since the poor could be convinced that doctors who vivisected animals might well regard the sufferings of their charity patients with similar indifference. The medical profession's defence was that any 'inhumanity' on the part of doctors who experimented was not a failing of character but a deliberately cultivated cold-bloodedness, which was, as John Hunter famously put it, 'necessary'.[15]

Chapter 3 considers the importance of the theological and metaphysical status of animals for the anti-vivisection movement, particularly the question, now somewhat neglected but frequently raised in the nineteenth century, of whether animals have souls. Changes in praxis in Victorian Britain indicate that popular faith moved ahead of 'official' theology, as people mourned the deaths of animals and speculated on the possibility that humans and non-humans might share a common afterlife. It would be almost a century before most Christian denominations would seriously address this and other issues related to animals, and though many animal welfare projects were initiated with Christian intent, no mainstream church had much to say about the subject, and some defended vivisection.

A perception of greater spiritual kinship between humans and animals arose, I suggest, through the influence of a variety of non-Christian sources, including classical paganism, esoteric philosophy, transcendentalism, and Western interpretations of so-called 'Eastern' religions, the same influences that, channelled through the utopian 'new age' organisations that sprang up around the turn of the nineteenth century, would eventually inspire the environmental movement. The connection between what I shall call 'new age' thinking and anti-vivisection stemmed from a shared rejection of the agenda of scientific materialism in favour of a holistic worldview, in which intuition and feeling were as important as observation and experiment.

Chapter 4 looks at the 'new age' programme through the work of Josiah Oldfield, the founder and medical director of Britain's first vegetarian and anti-vivisection hospitals, and secretary of the Order of the Golden Age—a Christian organisation committed, amongst other things, to health reform and pacifism. Oldfield was a campaigner for fruitarianism and anti-vivisection, and his career provides a case study of how medical opposition to cruelty was linked to aspirations for social and spiritual reform. His anti-vivisection hospital, a converted South London town house with only eleven beds was, as its critics eagerly noted, not intended solely for the benefit of its patients. Indeed, there were more vice-presidents than patients, the object being to attract sufficient public support to prove that an anti-vivisection hospital was a financially viable venture.

Chapter 5 surveys the work of the National Anti-Vivisection Hospital, which opened in 1903 and continued Oldfield's project on a larger scale, challenging the state-sponsored 'vivisecting' hospitals and acting as a showcase for compassionate medicine. While it is likely that no animals were directly saved by the hospital's existence, it did spare the anxieties of the local poor, who feared hospitals that permitted vivisection would not scruple to experiment on their patients. As a propaganda exercise it was a victim of its own success: advertised as the only hospital to which anti-vivisectionists were able to donate with a clear conscience, it was seen as a threat to the funding of other voluntary hospitals, and the King's Fund, Research Defence Society and others instigated a financial boycott that forced it to close.

Chapter 6 looks more closely at the vivisectionists' response, particularly as mediated through the work of the Research Defence Society. Founded in the early-twentieth century by a group of physiologists who advised the government on granting vivisection licenses under the 1876 Cruelty to Animals Act, it had far fewer members, and less funds, than any of the main anti-vivisection groups, but managed to exert disproportionate influence. Through astute political manoeuvring it blocked anti-cruelty legislation in parliament, curtailed advertising by anti-vivisection societies, and arranged for their charitable status to be revoked. Anti-vivisectionists complained that shadowy vested interests were conspiring against them, but it was their own links with fascist groups and their opposition to wartime research and vaccination programs that cost them sympathy and led the government and public to see their activities as unpatriotic and even treasonable.

Chapter 7—After the Second World War, anti-vivisection languished as other untarnished social causes competed for money and support. This was the era of the National Health Service, and government control of medicine was also extended to drug testing. Lethal dose testing in particular led to a large increase in the number of animals used, mostly as part of standard drug testing protocols, which left experimenters no longer personally responsible for deciding what procedures they carried out. The deaths of animals specifically bred for the laboratory, in experiments reported only through the publication of official statistics, lacked the emotive impact of the public vivisections of companion animals that had given the anti-vivisection movement its early impetus. While most of the suffering was now hidden, a few well-publicised animal experiments in high tech contexts, such as the field of space exploration, accustomed the public to equate them with prosperity and progress.

While I have tried to include in this book all the major events in the history of anti-vivisection in Britain from the nineteenth century until the 1960s, I have favoured some aspects that are less well covered in the classic studies by John Vyvyan, Richard French, and Nicolaas Rupke (to which the reader may wish to refer), and have focussed on the underlying ethical concepts and social trends at the expense of providing detailed histories of the major anti-vivisection groups and their leaders, as these are, happily, becoming quite well known.[16] I have not described vivisection experiments in detail, because it is not my intention to write a scientific history of vivisection, nor to turn the reader's stomach. Vyvyan's work has been a particular inspiration, and I have followed his lead in that, while striving to be accurate and to do justice to the arguments on both sides, I have not pretended to be dispassionate about the events I describe. Indeed, it would be wilfully obtuse to write so much about the virtues of sympathy and compassion and then affect indifference to the infliction of so much suffering over so many years.

Notes

1. Throughout the text, 'animals' is used for 'non-human animals', lest repeated iterations of the latter phrase become wearisome.
2. Justin Oakley, 'Virtue ethics and bioethics', in Daniel C. Russell (ed.) *The Cambridge Companion to Virtue Ethics* (Cambridge: Cambridge University Press, 2013), 197–220 (Oakley 2013).
3. Alberto Giubilini and Francesca Minerva, 'After-birth abortion: why should the baby live?', *Journal of Medical Ethics, 39* (6), 261–263 (Giubilini and Minerva 2013).
4. Julian Savulescu, '"Liberals Are Disgusting": In Defence of the Publication of "After-Birth Abortion"', http://blogs.bmj.com/medical-ethics/2012/02/28/liberals-are-disgusting-in-defence-of-the-publication-of-after-birth-abortion/, viewed 5 March 2016 (Savulescu 2016).
5. The Oxford English Dictionary defines 'humane' as 'such behaviour or disposition towards others as befits a man', the sense in which it is used in this book.
6. Peter Singer, 'Animals and the Value of Life', in Tom Regan (ed.) *Matters of Life and Death: New Introductory Essays in Moral Philosophy* (New York: Random House, 1980), 218–259, on p. 254 (Singer 1980).

7. Tristram Stuart, *The Bloodless Revolution: A Cultural History of Vegetarianism from 1600 to Modern Times* (New York, W.W. Norton, 2007, 71–72 (Stuart 2007).
8. Stanley Godlovitch, Roslind Godlovitch and John Harris (eds) *Animals, Men, and Morals: An Enquiry into the Maltreatment of Non-Humans* (New York: Taplinger, 1972); Peter Singer, *Animal Liberation* (London: Pimlico, 1995), 270 (Godlovitch et al. 1972; Singer 1995).
9. Andrew Linzey, Animal Theology (London: SCM Press, 1994), 20, 41–42 (Linzey 1994).
10. 'The non-alcoholic treatment of disease' *BMJ, 1* (1878), 830–831 (The Non-alcoholic Treatment of Disease 1878).
11. John Vyvyan, *In Pity and in Anger: A Study of the Use of Animals in Science* (London: Michael Joseph, 1969), 7 (Vyvyan 1969).
12. John Simon, 'An Address delivered at the opening of the Section of Public Medicine', *BMJ, 2* (1881), 219–223, on p. 223 (Simon 1881).
13. Rob Boddice, 'Species of compassion, aesthetics, anaesthetics, and pain in the physiological laboratory', *Interdisciplinary Studies in the Long Nineteenth Century, 15* (2012), 19 (Boddice 2012).
14. As there were apparently no female vivisectionists in nineteenth-century Britain, I have employed the male pronoun, as to do otherwise would be to accord women a false equality as ahistorical as it is unflattering.
15. See Ruth Richardson, 'A necessary inhumanity?', *Medical Humanities, 26* (2001), 104–106 (Richardson 2001).
16. R.D. French, *Antivivisection and Medical Science in Victorian Society* (Princeton, NJ: Princeton University Press, 1975); Nicolaas A. Rupke (ed.), *Vivisection in Historical Perspective* (London: Routledge, 1990) (French 1975; Rupke 1990).

References

Boddice, R. (2012). Species of compassion, aesthetics, anaesthetics, and pain. *Interdisciplinary Studies in the Long Nineteenth Century, 15,* 19.

French, R. D. (1975). *Antivivisection and medical science in victorian society.* Princeton, NJ: Princeton University Press.

Giubilini, A., and Minerva, F. (2013). After-birth abortion: Why should the baby live? *Journal of Medical Ethics, 39*(6), 261–263.

Godlovitch, S., Godlovitch, R., & Harris, J. (Eds.). (1972). *Animals, men, and morals: An enquiry into the maltreatment of non-humans.* New York: Taplinger.

Linzey, A. (1994). *Animal theology*. London: SCM Press.

Oakley, J. (2013). Virtue ethics and bioethics. In D. C. Russell (Ed.), *The Cambridge companion to virtue ethics* (pp. 197–220). Cambridge: Cambridge University Press.

Richardson, R. (2001). A necessary inhumanity? *Medical Humanities, 26*, 104–106.

Rupke, N. A. (Ed.). (1990). *Vivisection in historical perspective*. London: Routledge.

Savulescu, J. (2016). "Liberals Are Disgusting": In Defence of the Publication of "After-Birth Abortion". Retrieved March 5, 2016, from http://blogs.bmj.com/medical-ethics/2012/02/28/liberals-are-disgusting-in-defence-of-the-publication-of-after-birthabortion/.

Simon, J. (1881). An address delivered at the opening of the section of public medicine. *British Medical Journal, 2*, 219–223.

Singer, P. (1980). Animals and the value of life. In T. Regan (Ed.), *Matters of life and death* (pp. 218–259). New York: Random House.

Singer, P. (1995). *Animal liberation*. London: Pimlico.

Stuart, T. (2007). *The bloodless revolution: A cultural history of vegetarianism from 1600 to modern times*. New York: W.W. Norton.

The Non-alcoholic Treatment of Disease. (1878). *BMJ, 1*, 830–831.

Vyvyan, J. (1969). *In pity and in anger*. London: Michael Joseph.

2

Vivisection, Virtue, and the Law in the Nineteenth Century

The history of vivisection is inseparable from that of medical science. Without animal experimentation, the course of medicine would have been radically different (one can admit as much without making any presumption about the validity of animal models). Since the nineteenth century, laboratory experimentation has become the gold standard of academic medicine, shaping not only its approach to solving problems, but also the moral conduct and education of doctors. To experimentalists, it was axiomatic that medical science must be objective, rational, and dispassionate: if its advancement required the infliction of pain on laboratory animals, then it was unprofessional, even unethical, to allow squeamishness or sentiment to get in the way. Thus there arose a tension in medicine between the scientific spirit of cool indifference to suffering and the clinical tradition of compassion and caring. When the Continental fashion for vivisection first touched Britain in the 1820s, many doctors chose to distance themselves from it for the sake of their reputation, and the few who did undertake it felt the need to defend a choice that seemed at odds with the ethos of their profession.

Though 'anti-vivisection' became, in the course of the nineteenth century, so familiar a term of self-description that it would be obtuse to call organized opposition to animal experimentation by any other

A.W.H. Bates, *Anti-Vivisection and the Profession of Medicine in Britain*,
The Palgrave Macmillan Animal Ethics Series, DOI 10.1057/978-1-137-55697-4_2

name, its use has perhaps distorted the way that both the individuals and organizations involved have been understood, implying as it does protest, negativity and perhaps even rejection of progress—a campaign by some out of step luddites and radicals to halt the march of science, or to make a heavy-handed moral point about the abuse of power within society. It would, however, be no less apt to view vivisectionists as the protesters and their opponents as the conservative majority. There was never a time in Britain when there were more people active in support of vivisection than against it, and in the nineteenth century the antis raised petitions with hundreds of thousands of signatures, more than for any other cause of the time. A key question for the historian is why, considering the level of popular support and money at their disposal, anti-vivisectionists made so little progress in curbing, still less ending, experiments on animals. The remarkable success of experimentalists in winning over the government, legislature, and universities, and in carrying through their objectives in a nation of reputed animal lovers, which proved critical in shaping the course of medical science and ethics, also calls for an explanation.

During the nineteenth century, the anti-cruelty lobby went from being largely unaware of vivisection to passionately opposing it, largely due to a few high-profile incidents. By the century's end, anti-vivisection had become a humanitarian *cause celebre*, a mainstream issue with great public support and many societies dedicated to it, despite vivisection being responsible for only a tiny fraction of the vast amount of suffering inflicted on animals by human hands. Vivisection was seen as different from other forms of cruelty, such as the mistreatment of farm and draught animals, partly because those responsible were linked with the healing and academic professions, whose morality was supposed to be beyond reproach, and also because it had implications beyond animal welfare: for the way society made ethical choices, for how science should be conducted, and for how humans saw themselves in relation to the rest of creation. Because of the multiplicity of moral problems that vivisection raised, the anti-vivisection movement attracted people with all sorts of religious, political, and social principles to defend, and with such disparate views that, according to Vyvyan, anti-vivisection was often the only thing they had in common.

Legislating Against Cruelty

The resurgence of interest in animal protection in the 1970s prompted historians to revisit its history, and pioneering studies such as those of Richard French set early-nineteenth century anxieties over cruelty to animals in the context of post-Revolutionary concerns about the damage that a culture of violence might do to human society.[1] According to French and to Anita Guerrini, calls for laws to protect animals were primarily a form of social self-defence, requiring the government, with the cooperation of middle class activists, to legislate to control the violent impulses of an underclass who lacked the wherewithal to regulate themselves, and who, if permitted to acquire a taste for blood, might soon become ungovernable. At the other end of the spectrum of anthropocentric concern for mistreated animals there were radicals, particularly feminists and socialists, who saw animals as surrogates for disempowered humans.[2] If one adds to these British doctors who resented the introduction of novel, Continental experimental methods that challenged their tradition of observational bedside medicine, it can be seen that there were plenty of people calling for a ban on vivisection who were concerned with their own interests rather than those of animals.

Walter Bagehot famously said that one cannot make men good by act of parliament, but early-nineteenth century anti-cruelty legislation was an attempt to do just that. The sight of bloodthirsty crowds at cock-fights and bull-baitings was especially disturbing for an urban bourgeoisie still unsettled by the French Revolution. If casual cruelty to animals led to, or at least stoked a propensity for, violence against humans (a link, incidentally, that is now well established[3]), then its elimination would be in society's interest. Parliament, however, was slow to act, partly because its members could not decide if blood sports were incitements to cruelty or safe outlets for high spirits.[4]

Attempts by private members to put legislation through parliament finally met with success in Richard Martin's (1754–1834) Cruel and Improper Treatment of Cattle Act (3 George IV. c. 71), which became law in 1822. Martin—an Irish politician, duelist and gambler on whom George IV bestowed the nickname 'Humanity Dick'—had been elected to the UK parliament at the time of the Act of Union, but his bill was of little interest to most of its members, who greeted it with mocking laughter.[5] That there was enough support for it to be passed at all was mostly due to London's changing demographic: in the crowded capital, the well to do could not avoid witnessing the brutal treatment of draught animals and livestock. Prior to Martin's Act, it had been against the law to harm an animal only if it were someone else's property, an offence equivalent to criminal damage, but the Act criminalized cruelty to one's own 'cattle' (though not domestic animals). Since there was no funding to enforce it, the law's effectiveness depended upon private citizens being willing to report acts of cruelty and prosecute those responsible in the magistrates' courts.[6]

Voluntary associations such as the Society for the Prevention of Cruelty to Animals (SPCA), founded in 1824, were set up to help gather evidence and bring prosecutions.[7] Their founders hoped this would improve the 'moral temper' of the populus,[8] but the legal requirement for an offender to have acted 'wantonly and cruelly' made convictions for cruelty rare, since any rational act, however heartless, was not 'wanton' in a court of law. For example, a man who whipped a goat pulling a cart was found not guilty because he said he had beaten the animal in order 'to make it go'.[9] A far-reaching consequence of this, and subsequent, anti-cruelty legislation was that people focused on staying within the law rather than doing what was right, turning cruelty from a moral to a legal problem. The best that anti-cruelty societies could hope for was that fear of prosecution would make the urban poor, who they considered to be the chief offenders, take greater responsibility for their own actions, and thus 'compel them to think and act like those of a superior class'.[10]

Martin's Act did not mention vivisection, probably because he was unaware of it. It was a sign of their rarity in Britain that even someone as concerned as he about animal welfare does not seem to have known about experiments on animals until 1824, when the French physiologist François Magendie (1783–1855) gave a widely-reported demonstration at London's Windmill Street anatomy school.[11] The published accounts of Magendie's experiment, in which he nailed a greyhound to the dissecting-table before cutting it open, provoked a vociferous anti-French outcry that marked the start of the organized anti-vivisection movement in Britain.[12] Thereafter, Martin spoke out against Magendie in particular and vivisection in general, but his own law was powerless to stop it because scientific experiments were performed in a deliberate, calculated manner and not 'wantonly', and so could not, by definition, be cruel under the law.[13] The need to show they were compliant with anti-cruelty law inclined future experimenters to favour utilitarian arguments, because anticipated benefits to human health provided a clear, rational justification for their work.

Medical Opposition to Vivisection

At the time of Magendie's arrival in England, vivisection was 'proverbially rare'.[14] It has been estimated that in the 1820s fewer than a thousand experiments on animals were performed each year in the whole of the British Empire, and English medical men were said to have a particular 'horror' of them.[15] At this time, the medical 'profession' was a loosely defined group with no common licensing or regulatory body, so there was no 'official' position on animal experimentation, but groups of practitioners, concerned that physiological experiments would give medicine a 'bad name', signed up to anti-vivisection testimonials.[16]

Particularly worrying for medics was the rumour that Magendie found experimentation pleasurable, a shocking claim, though not an unreasonable one, as according to a medical eyewitness who attended his demonstrations in Paris: '...he really likes his business... when loud screams are uttered, he sometimes laughs outright'.[17] Magendie's supporters seem to have been aware of the damage that a reputation for callousness could do to his medical career, since they published a testimonial to his kindly bedside manner, presumably aimed at reassuring patients and others that his heartlessness in the laboratory did not extend into his clinical practice.[18]

In the wake of the Magendie scandal, the secretary of the SPCA seized the opportunity to solicit the support of prominent medical men for 'a board ... of the profession, to whom all proposed experiments must be submitted'.[19] The medical dignitaries to whom he wrote all declared themselves against unrestrained vivisection, and a selection of their replies, calling for curbs on animal experiments, was published in the national press.[20] The SPCA wanted a panel of distinguished doctors to decide what experiments should be permitted, but to Lewis Gompertz (1783/1784–1861), who founded the rival Animals' Friend Society (AFS) in 1833 after resigning from the SPCA, this was unacceptable. Gompertz, who rejected scientific 'necessity' as a justification for cruelty, and wanted the wording of Martin's Act changed to read 'wantonly *or* cruelly', had no faith in medical self-regulation. He offered a cash reward for evidence leading to the conviction of surgeons or medical students who 'cut up Dumb Animals Alive',[21] though it was never claimed because, as Thomas Wakley (1795–1862), the outspoken editor of the medical journal the *Lancet*, complacently pointed out, anti-cruelty law did not apply to medical experiments.[22] In a misguided attempt to remedy this, the AFS campaigned for, and got, an extension of Martin's law to include the domestic animals experimenters usually used, but this made no difference as experiments on them would still not be judged 'wanton' by a magistrate.[23]

The Character of the Vivisector

One London medical journal accused doctors who opposed vivisection of trying to 'curry favour' with patients, which suggests that patients were known to prefer doctors who were not vivisectionists.[24] Some people were afraid that the vivisectors' real objective was to experiment on humans, and as charity patients were thought to be their most likely victims, anti-vivisection became a popular cause in poor districts of London.[25] Paying patients had less reason to fear being used as experimental material, but they tended, as patients still do, to choose their doctor on the basis of personal attributes such as compassion, kindness and humanity rather than on purely technical ability, which made anti-vivisection a pragmatic position for medics in private practice to adopt.[26]

There was a longstanding, though apocryphal, tradition that anatomists and butchers were banned from serving on coroners' juries because their trades destroyed their moral competence, and vivisection was presumed to have a similar effect, especially on impressionable young students.[27] According to the Irish physician and naturalist James Lawson Drummond (1783–1853), 'little was to be expected' of medical students who became habituated to vivisection, a concern echoed by the SPCA's president Lord Carnarvon, who claimed that it was because they knew that the vivisector's 'feelings of compassion for suffering [could become] entirely obliterated', that the majority of medics wanted it restricted by law.[28]

There is no official record of how many experiments on animals were performed in Britain before the 1876 Vivisection Act, but few were reported in medical journals (most of the experiments published in British journals were performed in France or Germany) and they do seem to have been truly rare. Concerns within the medical profession were probably instrumental in keeping them so, though the few British doctors who did vivisect met with less criticism in the press than their Continental counterparts, partly because there was an element of nationalism behind protests against French physiologists, but also because the English tended not to carry on their work in public.

Opponents of Continental style vivisection demonstrations feared that these open displays of cruelty by professional people would lead to a general moral decline.[29] A well-known account by French physiologist Claude Bernard (1813–1878) of a Quaker who berated Magendie in his own laboratory provides a concise summary of public concerns:

> Thou performest experiments on living animals. I come to thee to demand of thee by what right thou actest thus and to tell thee that thou must desist from these experiments, because thou hast not the right to cause animals to die or make them suffer, and because thou settest in this way a bad example and also accustomest thyself to cruelty.[30]

A review of the case against vivisection by the AFS in 1833 grouped objections to it under five headings: to inflict pain on animals was a moral failing, it engendered public animosity against scientists, encouraged cruelty towards humans, distracted charitable efforts away from human suffering, and offended God.[31] Significantly, even this most committed of anti-vivisection groups relied on anthropocentric arguments: the suffering experienced by animals and their rights or interests were of lesser importance than the effects of vivisection on the experimenter and on society.[32]

British medical practitioners in search of moral guidelines had no governing body to turn to and no written code of conduct to help them; the word 'ethics' was seldom mentioned in medical writing, and there was no specific legislation governing medical practice until the Medical Act of 1858. There was, however, a widely-accepted code of etiquette and personal morality, which, though it included some rules of conduct specific to doctors, such as not stealing a colleague's patients, was largely that of their social group. A medical man was expected to be, or at least act like, a gentleman, a class whose 'honour and humanity are unimpeachable'.[33] For those to whom gentility did not come by birth or upbringing, guidebooks known as gentlemen's manuals provided instruction on correct manners and behaviour: the proper treatment of animals was neither cruel and heartless nor overly emotional, since brutality on the one hand and sentimentality on the other fell short of gentlemanly standards.[34]

I have argued elsewhere that the ideal of gentlemanly medical conduct was, in modern terms, an expression of virtue ethics, a system first described in Aristotle's *Nicomachean Ethics* and distinguished by its focus on motives and character rather than actions.[35] In the eighteenth century, in what has been termed 'the decline of virtue', character-based ethics began to lose ground to utilitarianism and deontology, but medicine still retained an old-fashioned attachment to the virtues and a strong emphasis on the good character of its practitioners.[36] For example, in the *Fortnightly Review* of (1882), the physician William Benjamin Carpenter (1813–1885) wrote that the morality of a pain-giving act lay not in the act itself (deontological ethics), nor in its result (utilitarianism), but in the motive for the act, a test that was also applied to vivisection.[37]

How patients and professionals interpreted the motives behind vivisection was therefore crucial in shaping their response to it. Not a few thought that vivisectors must be callous—like Magendie, they were thought to ignore, or even laugh at, animals' screams—a particularly damning charge for those who treated patients.[38] As long ago as 1758, Samuel Johnson (1709–1784) had fulminated against vivisectionists in his periodical the *Idler*, writing that '[i]t is time that a universal resentment should arise against these horrid operations, which tend to harden the heart and make the physician more dreadful than the gout or the stone'.[39] A century later, a similar sentiment was being quoted with approval by the *British Medical Journal*: 'Let there be no mistake about it: the man who habituates himself to the shedding of blood, and who is insensible to the sufferings of animals, is led on into the path of baseness'.[40]

Virtue ethics did not, however, offer a decisive argument against vivisection. To shun it, as the controversial and outspoken anatomist Robert Knox (1793–1862) did, might be taken as a sign of 'humanity', but others claimed that vivisectionists were prompted by worthy motives such as the desire to alleviate human suffering and to acquire knowledge.[41] The challenge lay in deciding which personal qualities to favour: what Charles Darwin (1809–1882) called the 'virtue' of 'humanity to the lower animals', or the laudable wish to advance medical learning.[42] Virtue ethics did not offer a glib solution: the ideal medical character was a balanced one, and it was 'proverbial' that medics ought to be neither unduly sentimental, lest squeamishness made them shrink from their work in order to spare their own feelings, nor so insensitive that they became callous.[43]

A degree of fortitude and resolve was expected of all well-bred men, and anti-vivisectionists and others who were thought to be deficient in these manly, Christian virtues were criticised as 'effeminate'. As some seventy percent of anti-vivisectionists were women, some of whom used the abuse of animals as a metaphor for their own perceived vulnerability, the cause itself came to be seen as feminine, and men who took it up were subject to accusations of unmanliness.[44] One critic called anti-vivisectionists 'old ladies of both sexes', the implication being that their opinions were formed by emotion rather than intellect and were therefore out of place in a scientific debate.[45] Experimenters faced the opposite criticism, that they were so dispassionate as to be wanting in normal human feeling. That medical practitioners who made *public* statements about vivisection predominantly opposed it, while those who supported it maintained a low profile, suggests that sensitivity was a quality more attractive to potential patients than fortitude and commitment to medical science.

Bad Science

The often-asked question of why most people who objected to vivisection nevertheless ate meat (or wore leather, or hunted) shows that experimenting on animals was seen as a separate moral issue from eating them, wearing them or chasing them, a distinction sometimes lost on the more logically minded: George Bernard Shaw (1856–1950) was shocked to find himself sharing a platform with hunters and fur-wearers when he spoke at an anti-vivisection meeting.[46] From a historical perspective we are not concerned with whether theirs was a coherent or defensible position, but with why they thought as they did. One explanation of why vivisection seemed to be of a different order from other cruelties was that those who performed it were neither the ignorant poor nor the feckless rich but scientists and doctors, precisely the sort of educated, professional people from whom society expected exemplary standards of conduct.[47]

Nineteenth century science was as much an attitude of mind as a field of study, an objective discipline where feelings did not intrude, and whose practitioners cultivated detachment and self-control. But their duty to suppress any feelings of compassion whilst working was problematic: quite apart from the difficulty of arguing that it was virtuous to suppress a virtue, how was an individual who steeled himself to perform vivisection for altruistic motives to be distinguished from someone so morally indifferent as to give no thought to the suffering he was about to inflict? According to the President of the British Association for the Advancement of Science, an organization whose remit was to defend experimentation, the fact that vivisectionists were 'men of science' meant that, unlike 'persons in the lower order', there was no question of their being unthinkingly cruel, not least because their experiments were too 'tedious and toilsome' to be performed unthinkingly.[48]

One could, however, be heartless without being reckless, and the argument that vivisectionists could control their finer feelings at will did not convince even some doctors, who thought that anyone prepared to inflict pain on helpless animals must be seriously lacking in emotional sympathy. Dr Robert Hull, writing against vivisection in the *London Medical Gazette*, agreed with the surgeon John Abernethy (1764–1831) that any doctor who vivisected was unfit to attend a family, and the *Protestant Magazine* concurred, printing a 'caution to parents' advising them to shun the services of any practitioner who carried out vivisection.[49] This was not a 'slippery slope' argument, since it presumed that vivisectionists were already deficient in empathy: as Immanuel Kant had written, 'we can judge the heart of a man by his treatment of animals'.[50]

The controversy over vivisection shows many parallels with that over human cadaveric dissection that took place in the early 1830s, to the extent that the arguments for and against both were regarded as interchangeable (the public also assumed that anatomists were all vivisectionists, despite their protests to the contrary).[51] Both practices were criticised not because of the suffering they caused but because of the supposed cold-heartedness and self-indulgence of the perpetrators, and both became the subject of public scandals that gave rise to regulatory legislation: the much-publicized murders for dissection in Edinburgh and London between 1829 and 1831 led to the 1832 Anatomy Act that legalized pauper dissection, while the shocking experiments performed by the French physiologist Éugène Magnan on a visit to Britain in 1874 led to the introduction of licensing for vivisectionists through the 1876 Cruelty to Animals Act. Vivisectionists and anatomists alike defended themselves with utilitarian arguments (vivisecting animals and dissecting cadavers were necessary to train doctors and develop new treatments), and also tried to show that their motives were virtuous. The 'heroic anatomist', who set aside any personal feelings and stoically endured the horrors of the dissecting-room, was a prototype of the 'imperturbable scientist' who when experimenting on animals in the laboratory was 'callous for the sake of what he deemed the greater compassion'.[52]

Believing that vivisection might be performed by virtuous people still did not make it good science. Experimenters claimed their work would 'place the art of healing upon a firmer basis', and they certainly obtained objective, quantitative data from animals that could not easily have been got from humans, but there were plenty of methodological objections.[53] A somewhat facile criticism, dating back to the seventeenth century, was that normal function could not reliably be investigated in living animals because their responses under vivisection did not represent a normal state (facile because no interventional experiment can ever study a truly 'normal' state). In the nineteenth century, however, it was subtly modified: animal experiments were bad science because they were a crude and clumsy attempt to wrest Nature's secrets from her by force, rather than through skillful philosophical enquiry, and so they reflected badly on the judgement and finesse of those who resorted to them.[54] Drummond compared vivisection to judicial torture in that it both yielded untrustworthy information and discredited the inquirer, and Karl Marx thought it of doubtful value, and an affront to 'humanity'.[55]

Another common methodological criticism was that animal physiology differed so greatly from the human that results could not be extrapolated.[56] In theory, this was difficult for experimenters to counter because if animals were physiologically similar to humans, they likely felt as humans did and so it was cruel to make them suffer, while if they lacked human sensitivity to pain, they were significantly different from us physiologically: so an experiment was 'criminal' if an animals' physiology was like ours and 'objectless' if it was not.[57] Though this might seem a powerful argument against experimentation, it was unusual for nineteenth-century vivisectors to concern themselves with animal pain at all: like Darwin, they could accept that '[t]he lower animals, like man, manifestly feel pleasure and pain, happiness and misery' and still consider vivisection justifiable.[58] We will consider in the following chapter whether the categorical difference between humans and animals that left the latter vulnerable to experiment was primarily spiritual rather than physiological.

Necessity and Humanity

Though British medical practitioners generally disliked the showy displays by Continental physiologists that had 'drawn odium' upon their profession, they were more sympathetic to experimentation done by their own countrymen, provided it was 'necessary' to medical progress: William Harvey's (1578–1657) work on the circulation of blood and John Hunter's (1728–1793) on aneurysms were the most often cited examples. Writing in the 1860s, the physician and author Andrew Wynter (1819–1876) declared that Hunter's work alone had been worth 'the destruction of a whole hecatomb of dogs', and though few vivisectionists made discoveries of the same magnitude as Hunter's, they all anticipated benefits to humankind and used this to justify their work.[59] Their self-assessment of utility was, of course, subjective: in his monograph *Vivisection Investigated and Vindicated*, the English physician George Etherington described among the animal experiments he thought medically important one in which it was shown that creosote, when injected into dogs, acted as a poison, precisely the kind of obvious but apparently pointless result that opponents thought constituted a strong argument against such experiments.[60]

In despair of ever bringing a successful prosecution against a vivisectionist, Gompertz complained that their being allowed to justify their own experiments on the basis of predicted benefits rendered the law 'nugatory'. Naturally, everyone anticipated that their own work would yield vital results, and so 'necessity' had become 'the cheat of humanity'.[61] Even Etherington agreed that the law was rendered powerless by the stipulation that the offender must act 'wantonly': 'the worst moral character, never performs an act without thinking upon and having a motive in performing it…'.[62] Throughout the nineteenth century, anti-cruelty groups such as the London Anti-Vivisection Society would continue to complain that medical experiments were being performed 'needlessly, and therefore cruelly', but there was no prospect of a successful prosecution as long as the experimenters themselves were the arbiters of necessity.[63]

British vivisectionists were, however, prepared to accept that many Continental experiments were unnecessary, and they criticized the French, in particular, for an excess of speculative studies and public demonstrations. The relatively few British doctors who did vivisect—most notably Marshall Hall (1790–1857), James Blundell (1791–1878), James Hope (1801–1841) and Charles J.B. Williams (1805–1889)—were prudent and discrete, working privately, publishing in professional journals, and following prearranged lines of investigation. Overall, they were successful in avoiding public scrutiny. Hall, for example, repeated some of Magendie's experiments in the 1820s, including one in which he opened the chest of a dog and then made him vomit, whereon, according to Hall's own account, 'a portion of lung was driven through the thoracic opening with violence and a sort of explosion'.[64] Though he was criticized in the medical press for this work, there was no public outcry, probably because lay people were simply unaware of it.[65] Shortly afterwards, Hall published his own 'objective' criteria for deciding whether experiments on animals were justified: the information sought must not be obtainable by observation alone, the experiment must have a distinct and definite object, it must not be a repeat, it must cause the least possible suffering to the least sentient animal, and must be properly witnessed and recorded.[66] Though they made little impact at the time, his rules would influence the drafting of the Antivivisection Act 40 years later.

The stimulus for legislation, when it came, was not the protests of anti-cruelty campaigners, but the continued animus towards French physiologists on the part of British doctors. When Éugène Magnan visited London in 1874, his medical audience, led by Thomas Jolliffe Tufnell (1819–1885), the President of the Irish College of Surgeons, intervened to stop a particularly unpleasant experiment.[67] Magnan promptly returned to France, forestalling an attempt by the now Royal Society for the Prevention of Cruelty to Animals to prosecute him, but, while the British organisers of his demonstration were acquitted of any wrongdoing, the magistrates made it clear what they thought by refusing to award the defendants' costs.[68] This was the closest a vivisectionist in Britain would ever come to being convicted. The case, along with the publication in 1873 of John Burdon-Sanderson's (1828–1905) *Handbook for the Physiological Laboratory*, a *vade mecum* for the 'beginner' that made scant reference to anaesthesia, raised such concerns that continental-style vivisection might become acceptable in Britain that in 1875 the government set up a Royal Commission on the matter, the result of which would be the 1876 Cruelty to Animals Act.[69]

The Vivisection Act and the Victoria Street Society

The 1876 Act (39 and 40 Vict. c. 77), known as the Vivisection Act, mandated that vivisection be performed only for an original, useful purpose. This put an end to the sort of public demonstrations that

Queen Victoria and many of her subjects so disliked, but left open the private use of animals for medical research and teaching.[70] The word 'wantonly' was dropped from the definition of cruelty but as, in the expert opinion of Mr Justice Day (Sir John Day, 1826–1908, a judge well known for sentencing felons to flogging), 'cruelty must be something which cannot be justified', the legal requirements for a conviction remained substantially unchanged.[71] Ironically, it was said that the Royal Commission was convinced of the need for regulation not by anti-vivisectionists, but by the testimony of experts such as the German bacteriologist Emanuel Klein (1844–1925), whose candid admission that he used anaesthesia only for his own convenience—to make the animals easier to handle—spoke volumes about the difference in outlook between scientists and the public:

> When you say that you use them [anaesthetics] for convenience sake, do you mean that you have no regard at all for the sufferings of the animals?
>
> No regard at all.
>
> You are prepared to establish that as a principle of which you approve?
>
> I think with regard to an experimenter, a man who conducts special research, he has no time, so to speak, for thinking what the animal will feel or suffer.[72]

Like the Anatomy Act, the Vivisection Act was permissive rather than regulatory. It required all vivisectionists to hold a license but these were liberally bestowed: by 1891, 676 people had been granted one, a large proportion of whom were given 'special' certificates dispensing them from the need to use anesthesia. To acquire an ordinary license, one needed the signatures of two referees who were professors of physiology, medicine, anatomy, or a related discipline; this kept animal experiments 'in the family', so to speak—most licensees worked in the 'golden triangle' of London, Oxford and Cambridge, and enjoyed the support of the universities and medical royal colleges—as well as giving recognition and authority to the new discipline of experimental physiology, whose professional body, the Physiological Society, was founded in the same year the Vivisection Act became law.[73]

The surviving correspondence from the London-based Association for the Advancement of Medical Research, which advised the government on licensing, makes no mention of a licence application being refused, and it is quite possible that none ever was: in 1954, when the Home Secretary was asked how many applications had been turned down since 1876, he told the Commons the information was 'not available'.[74] There was no successful prosecution during the 110 years the Act remained in force.[75]

Medical practitioners opposed to vivisection, some of whom were critical of the Act, were not involved in the licensing process, and ordinary doctors were said to be 'afraid' to speak out because the system was now overseen by the leaders of their profession.[76] The Act also excluded the public from any involvement in decision making, and made it difficult for them to find out where experiments were taking place, as the licensees' names and addresses were not published. The reason for keeping their identities and locations secret was not fear that they would be intimidated (direct action against vivisectionists was unheard of), but concern that the information might deter patients and donors, and encourage unwelcome efforts by members of the public to gain admittance to demonstrations.[77]

It would be difficult to overestimate the importance of the rise of experimental physiology following the Vivisection Act in shaping the narrative of 'modern medicine', of which Claude Bernard was, in the 1930s, already being called the 'father'. Bernard's influence on George Hoggan (1837–1891), an English doctor who briefly worked in his laboratory, would, however, give life to a very different project. In 1875, Hoggan published a harrowing account of the sufferings of the dogs that Bernard vivisected, though without mentioning him by name. He concluded: '…having drunk the cup to the dregs, I cry off, and am prepared to see not only science, but even mankind, perish rather than have recourse to such means of saving it'.[78]

Hoggan suggested to the Irish writer and social campaigner Frances Power Cobbe (1822–1904) that they form a society to campaign against animal experiments, and in 1875, with the support of Lord Shaftesbury (Anthony Ashley-Cooper, 7th Earl of Shaftesbury, 1801–1885) and the Archbishop of York, William Thomson (1819–1890), they formed the Society for the Protection of Animals Liable to Vivisection, better known as the Victoria Street Society (VSS); in 1897, it would become the National Anti-Vivisection Society (NAVS), with Shaftesbury as its president. The Society's goals included preventing the kind of extreme experiments for which Bernard was notorious from being sanctioned in Britain and trying to get the 1876 Act repealed.[79] In the opinion of the VSS, the Act had led to more experimentation than if vivisection had remained unlicensed, and allowed experimenters to use their 'professional esprit de corps... to secure for themselves prolonged immunity from state interference with their atrocities'.[80]

Horrible, Brutalising, Unchristianlike

Rather than continuing with futile attempts to prosecute vivisectionists, pragmatic campaigners tried to instil compassion into the young through anti-cruelty clubs such as the Band of Mercy movement.[81] It is apparent from the voluminous and sometimes tedious polemics published at this time that enthusiasts for, and critics of, vivisection were now relying on very different arguments. For vivisectionists, the justification of their experiments was a utilitarian one, since the predicted benefits to medicine outweighed any suffering, and they saw their opponents, as the ageing Darwin penned to *The Times* in 1876, as tender-hearted but profoundly ignorant.[82] For their part, anti-vivisectionists laboured the point that anyone who experimented on living animals was callous and insensitive, character traits typically associated with the unthinking lower classes, and certainly undesirable in a medical practitioner or scientist. By the end of the nineteenth century, the sentiment was common among the public that, as Queen Victoria had put it, animal experimentation was: 'horrible, brutalising, unchristianlike', and 'one of the worst signs of wickedness in human nature'. With its focus on reducing the pain experienced by animals and licensing scientists, the Vivisection Act had done nothing to address fears that vivisection 'saps our moral sense', 'blunts our sympathy', and promotes 'ruthlessness and oppression'.[83]

In fact, only a small minority of doctors was ever actually involved with animal experiments, and most preferred to avoid them. Despite their stereotypical portrayal in literature as callous and undisciplined, medical students generally shunned vivisection, and it was little used in British medical schools, where many of the teachers shared anatomist Josef Hyrtl's (1810–1894) view that anyone who could look calmly on vivisection would not make a good physician.[84] The VSS, claiming that the new cadre of licensed, professional vivisectors would become so indifferent to suffering that experimentation would be 'the simple, natural thing to do to any helpless creature in their hands', stoked fears that it would be extended to human subjects.[85] Of course, patients were not tied to tables and cut up except in the pages of sensational fiction, but there were other ways of experimenting. The microbiologist Robert Koch (1843–1910) actually did experiment on paupers; Louis Pasteur (1822–1895) proposed experimenting on prisoners, and the dermatologist Jonathan Hutchinson (1828–1913) delayed the treatment of a patient with a painful disease the better to demonstrate the signs to his students, all actions, according to the VSS, to which no vivisectionist could logically object.[86] Though doctors who vivisected may not have treated patients themselves, they could still set a bad example to those who did: if even the most distinguished scientists, wrote Lewis Carroll (Charles Dodgson, 1832–1898), were careless of the suffering they caused, 'what will be the temper of mind of the ordinary coarse, rough man… of whom the bulk of the medical profession… is made up?'[87]

Wary of being thought at best heartless and at worst dangerous, experimental physiologists liked to emphasise that their chosen work was disagreeable to them. According to one sympathetic account, the real sacrifices were being made not by the animals but the experimenters: 'we have heard a considerable number of physiologists declare unanimously, that all vivisection tires them exceedingly; sometimes so shatters them, that it requires all their power of will to carry the process through to the accomplishment of the aim…'.[88] This at least indicates they were aware of the importance of character and sensibility in determining how others judged their actions. From a utilitarian perspective, the case for vivisection would have been stronger if, in addition to acquiring knowledge from it, physiologists enjoyed their work rather than enduring it; by stating that they undertook experiments reluctantly and at great emotional cost to themselves, they were defending their personal virtue by taking on the persona of the heroic scientist who suffers emotional difficulty through being obliged to transgress normal moral boundaries for the sake of science.

George Romanes (1848–1894), Darwin's disciple, stressed that students of physiology must be none the less gentlemen because they were men of science, though the attitudes characteristic of genteel conduct could be difficult to square with what went on in the laboratory.[89] Burdon-Sanderson's private admission that 'emotional and sentimental states' such as sympathy were an experimenter's 'greatest enemies' implies a more heartless attitude than that typically expected of a gentleman, though some physiologists may have thought privately what Queen Victoria's physician Sir William Gull (1816–1890) declared openly: that gentlemen-scientists were above the law, and that anti-cruelty legislation was 'for the ignorant, and not for the best people in the country'.[90]

For the antis, Cobbe memorably asked if:

> … advancement of the 'noble science of physiology' is so supreme an object of human effort that the corresponding retreat and disappearance of the sentiments of compassion and sympathy must be accounted as of no consequence in the balance?[91]

How people answered such questions would determine whether they gave their money, and trusted their health, to vivisectionists, and whether they saw the rise of laboratory medicine as a major advance or a wrong turning.

Notes

1. French, *Antivivisection and Medical Science* (French 1975).
2. Anita Guerrini, 'Animal experiments and anti-vivisection debates in the 1820s', in C. Knellwolf and J. Goodall (eds.), *Frankenstein's*

Science: Experimentation and Discovery in Romantic Culture, 1780–1830 (Aldershot: Ashgate, 2008), 71–86; Coral Lansbury, *The Old Brown Dog: Women, Workers, and Vivisection in Edwardian England* (Madison, WI: University of Wisconsin Press, 1985); Mary Ann Elston, 'Women and anti-vivisection in Victorian England, 1870–1900', in Rupke, *Vivisection in Historical Perspective*; Hilda Kean, 'The "smooth, cool men of science:" the feminist and socialist response to vivisection', *History Workshop Journal, 40* (1995), 16–38; Hilda Kean, *Animal Rights: Social and Political Change since 1800* (London: Reaction, 1998); Ian Miller, 'Necessary torture? Vivisection, suffragette force-feeding, and responses to scientific medicine in Britain *c.* 1870–1920', *Journal of the History of Medicine and Allied Sciences, 64* (2009), 333–372 (Guerrini 2008; Lansbury 1985; Elston 1987; Kean 1995, 1998; Miller 2009).

3. Andrew Linzey (ed.), *The Link between Animal Abuse and Human Violence* (Brighton: Sussex Academic Press, Linzey 2009) (Linzey 2009).
4. Charles D. Niven, *History of the Humane Movement* (London: Johnson Publications, 1967), 57–58; Kean, *Animal Rights*, 33–34 (Niven 1967).
5. Niven, *History of the Humane Movement*, 61 (1967).
6. Gordon Hughes and Claire Lawson, 'RSPCA and the criminology of social control', *Crime, Law and Social Change, 55* (2011), 375–389 (Hughes and Lawson 2011).
7. SPCA, *Sixth Report and Proceedings* (London: W. Molineux, 1832) (SPCA 1832).
8. Kean, *Animal Rights*, 36 (1998).
9. Anon., *Animals Friend, 7* (1839), 51.
10. 'Society for the prevention of cruelty to animals', *Evangelical Magazine and Missionary Chronicle, 2* (1824), 357–358.
11. 'On experiments on living animals', *London Medical Gazette, 20* (1837), 804–808.
12. J.M.D. Olmsted, *François Magendie: Pioneer in Experimental Physiology and Scientific Medicine in Nineteenth-Century France* (New York, NY: Schuman, 1944), 137 (Olmsted 1944).
13. 'Vivisection per se cannot be ranked among acts of cruelty': see, 'The ethics of vivisection', *Lancet*, 2 (1860), 143–144.
14. George F. Etherington, *Vivisection Investigated and Vindicated* (Edinburgh: P. Richard, 1842), 17 (Etherington 1842).
15. François Magendie (transl. E. Milligan), *An Elementary Compendium of Physiology; for the use of Students* (Philadelphia: James Webster, 1824), 261; Etherington, *Vivisection Investigated*, 80 (Magendie 1824).

16. 'Physiology', *Medico-Chirurgical Review, 3* (1825), 198–200; Etherington, *Vivisection Investigated*, 111.
17. Olmsted, *François Magendie* (1994), 221–222 (Olmsted 1944).
18. 'Bills to prevent cruelty to animals', *Parliamentary History and Review* (1826), 756–775.
19. David Mushet, *The Wrongs of the Animal World* (London: Hatchard and Son, 1839), 209 (Mushet 1839).
20. 'Society for preventing cruelty to animals', *Morning Chronicle*, June 1825, 3 (Society for preventing cruelty to animals 1825).
21. Lewis Gompertz, *Moral Inquiries on the Situation of Man and Brutes; On the Crime of Committing Cruelty on Brutes, and of Sacrificing Them to the Purposes of Man* (Fontwell: Centaur Press, 1992), 147 (Gompertz 1992).
22. J. Chippendale, 'Experiments on animals', *Lancet, 1* (1839), 357–358 (Chippendale 1839).
23. 'Amendment of the laws to prevent cruelty to animals', *Animals Friend, 2* (1834), 11–15. The bill (5 and 6 William IV. c. 59) was passed with the help of Quaker MP Joseph Pease.
24. 'Physiology', *Medico-Chirurgical Review, 3* (1825), 198–200.
25. 'Correspondence on field sports and surgical experiments on living animals', *Animals Friend, 6* (1838), 21.
26. Trevor Stammers, 'The NHS—no place for conscience', *Catholic Medical Quarterly, 63* (2013), 12–14 (Stammers 2013).
27. Lloyd G. Stevenson, 'Religious elements in the background of the British anti-vivisection movement', *Yale Journal of Biology and Medicine, 29* (1956), 125–157. No such restriction on jurors ever existed: Leigh Hunt, *Essays* (London: Edward Moxon, 1841), 47–48 (Stevenson 1956; Hunt 1841).
28. James Lawson Drummond, 'On humanity', *London Medical Gazette, 24* (1838/1839), 160–163 (Drummond 1838/1839).
29. A.W. Bates, '"Indecent and demoralising representations": public anatomy museums in mid-Victorian England', *Medical History, 52* (2008), 1–22 (Bates 2008).
30. Quoted in: Mary T. Phillips and Jeri A. Sechzer, *Animal Research and Ethical Conflict: An Analysis of the Scientific Literature: 1966–1986* (New York: Springer-Verlag, 1989), 7 (Phillips and Sechzer 1989).
31. Anon. 'Five reasons against cruelty to animals', *Animals Friend*, 1 (1833), 14 (Anon 1833).
32. Rob Boddice, *A History of Attitudes and Behaviours toward Animals in Eighteenth- and Nineteenth-Century Britain: Anthropocentrism and*

the Emergence of Animals (Lampeter: Mellen, 2007); Anita Guerrini, 'Animal experiments' (Boddice 2007).

33. 'Surgical experiments on living animals', *Animals Friend, 7* (1839), 61–62.
34. Anon., *The Young Gentleman's Book* (London: Baldwin and Cradock, 1832), 249.
35. A.W. Bates, 'Vivisection, virtue ethics, and the law in 19th-century Britain', *Journal of Animal Ethics, 4* (2014), 30–44 (Bates 2014).
36. Thomas Percival, *Medical Ethics, or a Code of Institutions and Precepts Adapted to the Professional Conduct of Physicians and Surgeons* (Manchester: S. Russell, 1803) (Percival 1803).
37. William Benjamin Carpenter, 'The ethics of vivisection', *Fortnightly Review, 31* (1882), 237–246 (Carpenter 1882).
38. Olmsted, *François Magendie* (1944), 221–222 (Olmsted 1944).
39. Samuel Johnson, *Idler, 17* (1758), 64.
40. Anon., 'Vivisections in France', *BMJ, 2* (1863), 215.
41. 'Dr Knox, of Edinburgh', *Medical Times, 10* (1844), 245–246; William Hamilton Drummond, *The Rights of Animals, and Man's Obligation to treat them with Humanity* (London: John Mardon, 1838), 23, 148. (Knox 1844; Drummond 1838).
42. Charles Darwin, *The Descent of Man* (London: John Murray, 1871), 2 vols, 1, 101 (Darwin 1871).
43. 'Body-snatchers', *Church and State Review*, July 1862, 87; James A. Steintrager, *Cruel Delight: Enlightenment Culture and the Inhuman* (Bloomington, IN: Indiana University Press, 2004), 64, 124 (Steintrager 2004).
44. Andreas-Holger Maehle, 'The ethics of experimenting on animal subjects', in Robert B. Baker and Laurence B. McCullough (eds), *The Cambridge World History of Medical Ethics* (Cambridge, Cambridge University Press, 2014), 552–557 (Maehle 2014).
45. Andrew Wynter, *Subtle Brains and Lissom Fingers: Being Some of the Chisel-Marks of Our Industrial and Scientific Progress, and Other Papers* (London: Robert Hardwicke, 1863), 66 (Wynter 1863).
46. George Bernard Shaw, *Prefaces* (London: Constable, 1934), 257 (Shaw 1934).
47. Hayley Rose Glaholt, 'Vivisection as war: the "moral diseases" of animal experimentation and slavery in British Victorian Quaker pacifist ethics', *Society and Animals, 20* (2012), 154–172 (Glaholt 2012).

48. 'The British Association for the Advancement of Science', *Medical Times and Gazette, 2* (1863), 258–260.
49. Robert Hull, 'On vivisection', *London Medical Gazette, 32* (1842/1843), 864. 'A caution to parents', *Protestant Magazine, 6* (1844), 57–58 (Hull 1842/1843).
50. Tom Regan and Peter Singer (eds.), *Animal Rights and Human Obligations* (Englewood Cliffs, NJ: Prentice-Hall, 1989), 24 (Regan and Singer 1989).
51. Wynter, *Subtle Brains*, 67 (1863); Brayfytte, 'Experimental physiology: what it is, and what it asks', *Animals Guardian, 2* (1891/1892), 39–42.
52. Simon Chaplin, 'The heroic anatomist: dissection and the stoic ideal' (2008), retrieved from http://www.rcpe.ac.uk/library/listen; A.W. Bates, *The Anatomy of Robert Knox: Murder, Mad Science and Medical Regulation in Nineteenth-Century Edinburgh* (Brighton: Sussex Academic Press, 2010), 21; Boddice, 'Species of compassion' (Bates 2010; Chaplin 2008).
53. 'Vivisection at Alford', *Lancet*, 2 (1860), 395–396.
54. Rupke, *Vivisection in Historical Perspective*, 22.
55. Drummond, *The Rights of Animals*, 145; 'Christianity and its effect upon man's treatment of animals considered', *Church of England Magazine, 6* (1839), 294–296; K.F.H. Marx (transl. J. Mackness), *The Moral Aspects of Medical Life* (London: John Churchill, 1846), 121 (Marx 1846).
56. 'F. Lallemand, Observations pathologiques propres à éclairer plusieurs points de physiologie' (review), *London Medical and Physical Journal, 53* (1825), 238–245; Robert Knox, 'Some observations on the structure and physiology of the eye and its appendages', *Lancet, 1* (1839), 248–251 (Lallemand 1825; Knox 1839).
57. M. Lordat, Mental dynamics in relation to the science of medicine', *Journal of Psychological Medicine and Mental Pathology, 7* (1854), 252–263 (Lordat 1854).
58. Regan and Singer, *Animal Rights*, 27 (1989).
59. Wynter, *Subtle Brains*, 68 (1863).
60. Etherington, *Vivisection Investigated.*
61. 'Necessity the cheat of humanity', *Animals Friend, 9* (1841), 16.
62. Etherington, *Vivisection Investigated*, 72.
63. 'Our programme', *Animals Guardian, 1* (1890), 2.
64. Marshall Hall, 'On the mechanism of the act of vomiting', *Lancet, 2* (1828), 600–602 (Hall 1828).

65. Diana E. Manuel, 'Marshall Hall (1790–1857): vivisection and the development of experimental physiology', in Rupke, *Vivisection in Historical Perspective*, 78–104 (Manuel 1990).
66. Marshall Hall, *A critical and Experimental Essay on the Circulation of the Blood* (London: R.B. Seeley & W. Burnside, 1831), 2–7 (Hall 1831).
67. 'Prosecution at Norwich', *British Medical Journal, 2* (1874), 751–754.
68. Sarah Wolfensohn and Maggie Lloyd, *Handbook of Laboratory Animal Management and Welfare* (Oxford: Blackwell, 2003), 8 (Wolfensohn and Lloyd 2003).
69. French, *Antivivisection and Medical Science*, 112–158; M.A. Finn and J.F. Stark, 'Medical science and the Cruelty to Animals Act 1876: a re-examination of anti-vivisectionism in provincial Britain', *Studies in the History and Philosophy of Biology and Biomedical Science*, 49 (2015), 12–23 (Finn and Stark 2015).
70. E.M. Tansey, '"The Queen has been dreadfully shocked:" Aspects of teaching experimental physiology using animals in Britain, 1876–1986', American Journal of Physiology, *274* (1998), S18–S33 (Tansey 1998).
71. G. Candy, 'The legal definition of cruelty in relation to the animal world', *Animals Guardian, 1* (1890), 5 (Candy 1890).
72. Quoted in Vyvyan, *In Pity*, 87.
73. Finn and Stark, 'Medical science' (2015).
74. Wellcome Library, London (hereinafter Well) SA/RDS A3; 'Do they ever say "no"?' (editorial), *Animals' Defender*, March 1954, 46.
75. Cobbe tried and failed to prosecute David Ferrier in 1881.
76. F.L.O. Morris, *The Curse of Cruelty. A Sermon [on Ps. Xxxvi. 6] Preached in York Minster* (London, England: Elliot Stock, 1886), 80 (Morris 1886).
77. Anon., *Animals Guardian, 2* (1891/1892), 33.
78. Vyvyan, *In Pity*, 28, 77–78.
79. Amongst other tortures, Bernard employed an 'apparatus for determining the effects of heat upon live animals'. He wrote: 'The animals exhibit a series of symptoms always the same and characteristic. At first the creature is a little agitated. Soon the respiration and circulation are quickened. The animal opens its mouth and breathes hard. Soon it becomes impossible to count its pantings; at last it falls into convulsions, and dies generally uttering a cry': Frances Power Cobbe, *Light in Dark Places* (London: VSS, n.d.), 20.
80. 'Our programme', *Animals Guardian, 1*, (1890), 2; G. Candy, 'Should the vivisection act of 1876 be repealed?', *Animals Guardian, 1*

(1891), 49–50; '"Plain truth" past and present', *Animals Guardian, 2* (1891/1892), 6–9 (Candy 1890, 1891).

81. Chien-hui Li, 'Mobilizing literature in the animal defense movement in Britain, 1870–1918', *Concentric: Literary and Cultural Studies* 32.1 (2006), 27–55 (Li 2006).
82. Charles Darwin, *Times*, 23 June 1876: Darwin Correspondence Project, Letter no. 10,546, viewed 12 July 2016, http://www.darwinproject.ac.uk/DCP-LETT-10546 (Darwin 1876).
83. Samuel L. MacGregor-Mathers, 'The roots of cruelty', *Animals Guardian, 1* (1890), 27 (MacGregor-Mathers 1890).
84. 'Hyrtl, prof. of anatomy, Vienna, on vivisection as demonstration to students', *Zoophilist, 1* (1881/1882), 145 (Hyrtl 1881/1882).
85. Glaholt, 'Vivisection as war'; editorial, *Zoophilist, 1* (1881/1882), 190 (Glaholt 1881/1882).
86. Anon., *Zoophilist, 1* (1881/1882), 244; 'Items of interest', *Animals Guardian, 1* (1890), 34–35 (Anon 1881/1882, 1890).
87. Lewis Carroll, 'Some popular fallacies about vivisection', *Fortnightly Review, 23* (1875), 847–854 (Carroll 1875).
88. 'Two views of the vivisector', *Zoophilist, 1* (1881/1882), 194.
89. *Times*, 25 April 1881, 10.
90. Lady Burdon Sanderson, *Sir John Burdon-Sanderson: A Memoir* (Oxford: Clarendon Press, 1911), 157; Parliamentary Papers, *41* (1876), Q5482 (Sanderson 1876).
91. Quoted in Boddice, 'Species of Compassion'.

References

Anon. (1833). Five reasons against cruelty to animals. *Animals' Friend, 1,* 14.

Anon. (1881/1882). *Zoophilist, 1,* 244.

Anon. (1890). Items of interest. *Animals Guardian, 1,* 34–35.

Bates, A. W. (2008). Indecent and demoralising representations: Public anatomy museums in mid–Victorian England. *Medical History, 52,* 1–22.

Bates, A. W. (2010). *The anatomy of Robert Knox: Murder, mad science and medical regulation in nineteenth-century Edinburgh.* Brighton: Sussex Academic Press.

Bates, A. W. (2014). Vivisection, virtue ethics, and the law in nineteenth-century Britain. *Journal of Animal Ethics, 4,* 30–44.

Boddice, R. (2007). *A history of attitudes and behaviours toward animals in eighteenth- and nineteenth-century Britain: Anthropocentrism and the emergence of animals*. Lampeter: Mellen.

Bills to Prevent Cruelty to Animals. (1826). *Parliamentary History and Review*, 756–775.

Candy, G. (1890). The legal definition of cruelty in relation to the animal world. *Animals Guardian, 1,* 5.

Candy, G. (1891). Should the vivisection act of 1876 be repealed? *Animals Guardian, 1,* 49–50.

Candy, G. (1891/1892). "Plain truth" past and present. *Animals Guardian, 2,* 6–9.

Carpenter, W. B. (1882). The ethics of vivisection. *Fortnightly Review, 31,* 237–246.

Carroll, L. (1875). Some popular fallacies about vivisection. *Fortnightly Review, 23,* 847–854.

Chaplin, S. (2008). The heroic anatomist: Dissection and the stoic ideal. Retrieved from http://www.rcpe.ac.uk/library/listen.

Chippendale, J. (1839). Experiments on animals. *Lancet, 1,* 357–358.

Christianity and its Effect Upon Man's Treatment of Animals Considered. (1839). *Church of England Magazine, 6,* 294–296.

Darwin, C. (1871). *The descent of man and selection in relation to sex*. London: John Murray.

Darwin, C. (1876, June 23). Darwin correspondence project. *Times*, Letter no. 10,546. Retrieved July 12, 2016, from http://www.darwinproject.ac.uk/DCP-LETT-10546.

Drummond, J. L. (1838/1839). On humanity. *London Medical Gazette, 24,* 160–163.

Drummond, W. H. (1838). *The rights of animals, and man's obligation to treat them with humanity*. London: John Mardon

Elston, M. A. (1987). Women and antivivisection in Victorian England, 1870–1900. In N. A. Rupke (Ed.), *Vivisection in historical perspective* (pp. 259–273). London: Croom Helm.

Etherington, G. (1842). *Vivisection investigated and vindicated.* Edinburgh: P. Richard.

Finn, M. A., & Stark, J. F. (2015). Medical science and the cruelty to animals act 1876: A re-examination of anti-vivisectionism in provincial Britain. *Studies in the History and Philosophy of Biology and Biomedical Science, 49,* 12–23.

French, R. D. (1975). *Antivivisection and medical science in Victorian society.* Princeton, NJ: Princeton University Press.

Glaholt. (1881/1882). Vivisection as war; editorial. *Zoophilist, 1,* 190.

Glaholt, H. R. (2012). Vivisection as war: The "Moral Diseases" of animal experimentation and slavery in British Victorian Quaker pacifist ethics. *Society and Animals, 20,* 154–172.

Gompertz, L. (1992). *Moral inquiries on the situation of man and brutes…* Fontwell: Centaur Press.

Guerrini, A. (2008). Animal experiments and antivivisection debates in the 1820s. In C. Knellwolf, & J. Goodall (Eds.), *Frankenstein's science: Experimentation and discovery in romantic culture, 1780–1830* (pp. 71–86). Aldershot: Ashgate.

Hall, M. (1828). On the mechanism of the act of vomiting. *Lancet, 2,* 600–602.

Hall, M. (1831). *A critical and experimental essay on the circulation of the blood.* London: R.B. Seeley & W. Burnside.

Hull, R. (1842/1843). On vivisection. *London Medical Gazette, 32,* 864.

Hughes, G., & Lawson, C. (2011). RSPCA and the criminology of social control. *Crime, Law and Social Change, 55,* 375–389.

Hunt, L. (1841). *Essays* (pp. 47–48). London: Edward Moxon.

Hyrtl. (1881/1882). Prof. of anatomy, Vienna, on vivisection as demonstration to students. *Zoophilist, 1,* 145.

Kean, H. (1995). The "smooth, cool men of science:" The feminist and socialist response to vivisection. *History Workshop Journal, 40,* 16–38.

Kean, H. (1998). *Animal rights: Social and political change since 1800.* London: Reaktion.

Knox, R. (1839). Some observations on the structure and physiology of the eye and its appendages. *Lancet, 1,* 248–251.

Knox of Edinburgh. (1844). *Medical Times, 10,* 245–246.

Lallemand, F. (1825). Observations pathologiques propres à éclairer plusieurs points de physiologie (review). *London Medical and Physical Journal, 53,* 238–245

Lansbury, C. (1985). *The old brown dog: Women, workers, and vivisection in Edwardian England.* Madison, WI: University of Wisconsin Press.

Li, C. H. (2006). Mobilizing literature in the animal defense movement in Britain, 1870–1918. *Concentric: Literary and Cultural Studies, 32*(1), 27–55.

Linzey, A. (2009). *The link between animal abuse and human violence.* Brighton: Sussex Academic Press.

Lordat, J. (1854). Mental dynamics in relation to the science of medicine. *Journal of Psychological Medicine and Mental Pathology, 7,* 252–263.
MacGregor-Mathers, S. L. (1890). The roots of cruelty. *Animals Guardian, 1,* 27.
Maehle, A. H. (2014). The ethics of experimenting on animal subjects. In R. B. Baker & L. B. McCullough (Eds.), *The Cambridge world history of medical ethics* (pp. 552–557). Cambridge: Cambridge University Press.
Magendie, F. (1824). *An elementary compendium of physiology; for the use of students* (E. Milligan, Trans.). Philadelphia, PA: James Webster.
Manuel, D. E. (1990). Marshall Hall (1790–1857): Vivisection and the development of experimental physiology. In N. A. Rupke (Ed.), *Vivisection in historical perspective* (pp. 78–104). London: Rutledge.
Marx, K. F. H. (1846). *The moral aspects of medical life* (J. Mackness, Trans.). London: John Churchill.
Miller, I. (2009). Necessary torture? Vivisection, suffragette force-feeding, and responses to scientific medicine in Britain *c.* 1870–1920. *Journal of the History of Medicine and Allied Sciences, 64,* 333–372.
Morris, F. O. (1886). *The curse of cruelty. A sermon [on Ps. xxxvi. 6] preached in York Minster.* London: Elliot Stock.
Mushet, D. (1839). *The wrongs of the animal world.* London: Hatchard and Son.
Niven, C. D. (1967). *History of the humane movement.* London: Johnson Publications.
Olmsted, J. M. D. (1944). *François magendie.* New York: Schuman.
Percival, T. (1803). *Medical ethics, or a code of institutions and precepts adapted to the professional conduct of physicians and surgeons.* Manchester: S. Russell.
Phillips, M. T., & Sechzer, J. A. (1989). *Animal research and ethical conflict: An analysis of the scientific literature: 1966–1986* (p. 7). New York: Springer.
Regan, T., & Singer, P. (Eds.). (1989). *Animal rights and human obligations.* Englewood Cliffs, NJ: Prentice-Hall.
Sanderson L. B. (1911). *Sir John Burdon-Sanderson: A Memoir.* Oxford: Clarendon Press.
Shaw, G. B. (1934). *Prefaces* (p. 257). London: Constable.
Society for preventing cruelty to animals. (1825, June). *Morning Chronicle,* 3.
SPCA. (1832). *Sixth Report and Proceedings.* London: W. Molineux.
Stammers, T. (2013). The NHS—No place for conscience. *Catholic Medical Quarterly, 63,* 12–14.
Steintrager, J. A. (2004). *Cruel delight: Enlightenment culture and the inhuman.* Bloomington, IN: Indiana University Press.

Stevenson, L. G. (1956). Religious elements in the background of the British anti-vivisection movement. *Yale Journal of Biology and Medicine, 29,* 125–157.

Tansey, E. M. (1998). The queen has been dreadfully shocked: Aspects of teaching experimental physiology using animals in Britain, 1876–1986. *American Journal of Physiology, 274,* S18–33.

Wolfensohn, S., & Lloyd, M. (2003). *Handbook of laboratory animal management and welfare*. Oxford: Blackwell.

Wynter, A. (1863). *Subtle brains and lissom fingers: Being some of the chisel-marks of our industrial and scientific progress, and other papers* (p. 66). London: Robert Hardwicke.

3

Have Animals Souls? The Late-Nineteenth Century Spiritual Revival and Animal Welfare

Although many of the nineteenth-century arguments against vivisection were based on its supposed adverse effects on those who performed or witnessed it, the status of its animal subjects was not inconsequential. One could not be cruel or heartless to a Cartesian automaton that lacked feeling, and perhaps not to animals that had, as some Christians claimed, been put on earth solely to provide for human needs. The art critic and social reformer John Ruskin (1819–1900), addressing the Oxford branch of the Victoria Street Society in 1884, said that: 'It is not the question whether animals have a right to this or that in the inferiority they are placed into mankind, it is a question of what relation they have to God…'.[1] To see animals from a divine perspective, it was necessary to decide whether they possessed rational souls, and what happened to those souls after death.

For most of the nineteenth century, the idea that animals might have afterlives was a decidedly unchristian one. The epitaphist of Lord Byron's dog Boatswain (d. 1808) derided the sort of Christians who disapproved of memorialising a dead dog for trying to keep 'a sole exclusive heaven' for themselves. Almost a century later, when the following lines in memory of Rocket the hunting dog were published, the poetic

A.W.H. Bates, *Anti-Vivisection and the Profession of Medicine in Britain*,
The Palgrave Macmillan Animal Ethics Series, DOI 10.1057/978-1-137-55697-4_3

conceit that dogs would be reunited with their keepers in paradise still had a decidedly heathen ring to it:

> Is a man a hopeless heathen if he dreams of one fair day
> When, with spirit free from shadows grey and cold.
> He may wander through the heather in the 'unknown far away',
> With his good old dog before him as of old?[2]

What became of one's canine companion after death was not a trivial matter; for some Christians, the idea that animals' souls could exist apart from their bodies seemed 'absurd in the extreme' or even 'dangerous'[3]: the divine spark of immortality was the one incontrovertible barrier between humans and other animals, however many biological resemblances scientists might go on to discover.

It is sometimes claimed that science, and Darwinism in particular, improved the lot of animals by replacing the traditional Christian model of a static created order with humans at its earthly summit (just below the angels) with a dynamic model in which higher forms were continually evolving from lower.[4] To put it crassly, people were less likely to ill-treat animals to which they were distantly related. Darwinism certainly made many people think about their kinship with animals, although the idea of a serial affinity between different species (the 'ladder of creation' or 'great chain of being'), and even of species change itself, had been current long before the publication of *The Origin of Species* in (1859).[5] For anatomists, the human–animal boundary had been blurred since at least a century earlier, when the great taxonomist Carl Linnaeus (1707–1778) wrote that he was unable to discover 'the difference between man and the orangoutang, although all of my attention was brought to bear on this point'.[6] By the 1840s, there seemed no prospect of anatomists finding any structure that would categorically distinguish humans from apes in terms of morphology: the popular press responded with sensational tales of ape–human hybrids and mocked the 'siantificle' vogue for dissecting monkeys 'to see … whether like our own specius inside as well as out'.[7]

The most obvious distinction between apes and humans in the nineteenth century was the Christian claim that humans alone had souls made in the image of their Creator, and even this was being challenged, in a religious and philosophical setting rather than a scientific one, through ideas gleaned from classical paganism, Hinduism and transcendentalism. This nineteenth-century re-evaluation of the spiritual status of animals would have profound consequences for animal welfare, by bringing to the theological debate, as evolution did to the scientific one, a changed understanding of the relationship between humans and animals.

It would be a mistake, as some freethinkers did (and some still do), to blame cruelty to animals on the low status accorded them in the Judaeo-Christian tradition before Darwinists, orientalists and humanists managed to knock humans off their pedestal: Christian anti-cruelty campaigners were instrumental in giving Britain the most comprehensive animal protection laws in Europe, which they did for the most part without questioning their God-given dominion over the animals they were protecting.[8] As Coral Lansbury (1929–1991) wrote in *The Old Brown Dog* 'the debate between Singer and [Tom] Regan over the moral status of animals would have bemused the Victorians…'[9]: what mattered to them were the moral consequences of inflicting pain on creatures inferior to themselves. Though they did not owe animals a duty of care, they were bound to pity them, and to avoid any imputation of callousness. Rod Preece comments that Christians were more concerned for animals than were Darwinians, and while it might be more accurate to say they were concerned about the dangers to society of allowing cruelty to animals to go unchecked, they turned out, nonetheless, to be the nineteenth-century laboratory animal's best friends.[10]

Christians and Anti-Vivisection in the Nineteenth Century

Most of the groups active in animal welfare, from the Society for the Suppression of Vice, with its emphasis on saving the working classes from being demoralized by alcoholic drink and cruel sports, through the SPCA and its drive to civilise manners, to the VSS with its ethos of compassion, saw themselves as doing the Lord's work.[11] The SPCA, for example, declared that its programme was 'entirely based on the Christian faith', and they denounced vivisection as 'unchristian'.[12] Insofar as the practice of vivisection repudiated the Christian virtues of mercy and compassion, anti-cruelty campaigners saw it as 'evil', 'fiendish', 'blasphemous', and even 'Satanic'.[13] Furthermore, unlike other cruelties such as hunting or meat eating, it was performed by an educated élite, and there was a risk this would lead those less principled to think it was acceptable to be 'cruel' and 'inhumane' out of expediency, so spreading throughout society a heartlessness that was fundamentally 'unchristian'.[14]

Lord Shaftesbury, arguing in 1879 for a total ban on vivisection, said that, for the sake of one's soul, it would be better to be the vivisected than the vivisector, an attitude that, like Shaftesbury himself, exemplified Christian compassion (the famous memorial to him in Piccadilly represents the Angel of Christian Charity).[15] Caring for animals out of Christian charity had the practical advantages that the intellectual or spiritual status of the animals (so long as they were sentient) was of little consequence, while as a motive for action it was readily comprehensible to most people. Defenders of vivisection might dismiss what they derisively termed a 'Brahminical' love for one's fellow creatures as un-British, sentimental, and heterodox, but it was difficult for them to say the same about mercy and compassion towards the weak.[16] The title of the VSS's journal the *Zoophilist* betokened a love of animals, but the Society declared that the main inspiration for its work was 'a conviction that the spread of mercy was the great cause of civilization'.[17]

Cardinal Henry Manning's (1808–1892) outspoken opposition to vivisection, conspicuous among a general Catholic indifference to animals, also appealed to the most basic of Christian virtues:

> Vivisection is a detestable practice.... Nothing can justify, no claim of science, no conjectural result, no hope for discovery, such horrors as these. Also, it must be remembered that whereas these torments, refined and indescribable, are certain, the result is altogether conjectural—everything about the result is uncertain, but the certain infraction of the first laws of mercy and humanity.[18]

The RSPCA, failing to appreciate that Manning's views were not representative of Rome, tried unsuccessfully to get anti-vivisection adopted as official Catholic policy, but Pius IX supposedly rejected plans for an office for the Protection of Animals on the grounds that it would send a misleading message that animals had rights.[19] Anglicans were rather more sympathetic to the cause: the Archbishops of York and Dublin signed the 1875 'Memorial Against Vivisection', and though the Church of England remained officially non-committal, by the end of the century some four thousand of its clergy had declared their disapproval of it.[20]

Very few Christians justified their opposition to vivisection by appealing to the unconventional possibility that animals, like humans, had souls that survived death, though there were exceptions, such as Robert Hull, who remarked that '[t]he vivisectors cannot, of course, enter into the depths of that well-grounded suspicion, that there may be a future existence for the brute creation'. For Hull, who hoped that vivisectors would, in some future existence, meet with recompense from those they had tormented, no one who believed in animal afterlives could possibly experiment on them.[21] Robert Browning's (1812–1889) poem *Tray*, published in 1879, imagined the nightmarish possibility of vivisectors deliberately setting out to study the soul of a dog, but this was deliberate exaggeration to shock the reader (Browning was a vice-president of the VSS); no real-life vivisectionist mentioned animals' souls, and some felt vindicated by the conventional Christian teaching that animals had no existence beyond their earthly lives.

The physiologist James Blundell, for example, defended his use of animals in research by claiming that, since an animal's death was an eternal sleep, it was less grave to kill an animal than a human.[22] His reasoning is not entirely clear, but seems to have been based on the presumption that killing becomes murder only if the victim has a soul: in the Old Testament the blood of humans, not animals, cries to heaven for vengeance, as do the souls of martyrs in the Book of Revelation.[23] Others, however, saw the lack of a future life for animals as all the more reason to be compassionate towards them in this one; according to James Lawson Drummond: '[the brute] has no heaven to look to, no bright anticipation of a period when misery shall cease.... Its life is its little all', an allusion to these lines by the humanitarian poet Anna Laetitia Barbauld (1743–1825):

> Or, if this transient gleam of day
> Be *all* of life we share,
> Let pity plead within thy breast,
> That little *all* to spare.[24]

Animal Afterlives

The question of whether animals had souls was in one sense trivial: an animal, as the name implied, possessed what is known in the Aristotelian tradition as a vital soul (*anima*). The Cartesian notion of animals as automata had little currency outside philosophy schools, and no British vivisector ever adopted this position: they sometimes argued that animals did not feel pain in the context of a particular experiment, but none claimed they were incapable of feeling at all.[25] Indeed, it would have been difficult for a physiologist to make such a claim, because the validity of experiments on animals depended on their anatomy and physiology being similar to our own: nervous systems organized and functioning like ours could scarcely be found in animals incapable of feeling the pain they so evidently reacted to.[26] The real question was not whether animals had souls, but how closely comparable they were to the souls of humans. Were they rational? Did they experience emotions? And did they, as the poets fancied, share the promise of immortality?

The Christian doctrine of the immortality of the human soul had its roots in the thirteenth century, when Thomas Aquinas had modified Aristotle's position that human beings were a composite of 'form' (*i.e.* soul) and 'matter' by adding that the human soul was incorruptible and persisted after bodily death.[27]Aquinas thus brought Aristotle into line with the Christian promise of eternal life, though at the cost of leaving disembodied souls, unable to act or experience, in a kind of intellectual limbo until the resurrection.[28] These incorruptible souls were unique to humans: other animals possessed 'sensitive' souls but not rational ones, and were blessed with neither reason nor immortality.[29]

In Britain, the Thomist position that the souls of animals perish at death went largely unchallenged by the reformed churches, though the less contentious issue of their rationality was up for debate. In the seventeenth century, Lord Chief Justice Sir Matthew Hale (1609–1676), an advocate of responsible treatment of animals based on a model of stewardship rather than dominion, attributed to them the faculties of memory, reason and imagination (which he called 'phantasies'), but still denied them immortality—the souls of even 'perfect brutes' would die with them.[30] In the eighteenth century, the never easily defensible position that only humans could reason was assailed from both sides: pigs, horses and dogs could apparently be taught to perform calculations and use language, while feral children, brought up without human society, seemed to lack these capabilities.[31] By the nineteenth century, animals' ability to reason was widely accepted, and it was commonplace for magazines and periodicals to entertain their readers with remarkable accounts of animal sagacity.

Although no major Christian church expressed an official view, many individual clergy were happy to admit that animals had rational souls: according to the evangelical missionary Daniel Tyerman (1773–1828), '[t]o deny that brute animals have souls, is virtually to allow that matter can think; and to put an argument into the mouths of materialists that it will not be easy to rescue from them'.[32] For the Catholic Church, Fr John Worthy, a priest in Liverpool, wrote that the rationality of animals was evident from their actions: even bees, Fr Worthy claimed, were intelligent and acted on reason as well as instinct, and many other species appeared from their actions to be 'highly gifted'. Worthy collected numerous accounts from the press in which animals seemed to display social traits such as kindness, gratitude, and affection, or to use imagination and language. However, despite his obvious admiration for these animals' abilities, and his credulity with regard to some rather far-fetched tales, Worthy apologised to any of his readers who thought he had 'lowered the dignity of man's soul and reason, by representing the souls and reason of animals as having any degree whatever of similitude with man...' There was, he concluded, an absolute difference between the souls of animals and humans, namely that only the latter survived death.[33]

Most protestants concurred, taking the Biblical reference to mankind having been made 'in the image of God' to mean that the human soul was uniquely able to exist apart from the body. The majority of British divines accepted this position, though there were, as Preece has shown, not a few distinguished exceptions, including the Cambridge Platonist Henry More (1614–1687), the Quaker George Fox (1624–1691), the Civil War pamphleteer Richard Overton and the founder of Methodism John Wesley (1703–1791), all of whom entertained the idea that animals' souls persisted after bodily death.[34] A few Anglican theologians such as Bishop Joseph Butler (1692–1752) can be added to this list, but animal immortality remained largely a nonconformist position.[35]

In the secular literature, however, there was free speculation that companion animals would have a share in the afterlife. Poets who put forward the idea found a ready audience: indeed, so many toyed with it that the anthologist J. Earl Clauson could devote the whole concluding section of his *Dog's Book of Verse* to 'The Dog's Hereafter'.[36] Of course, this poetical vogue for animal immortality was rooted in sentiment rather than solid theological opinions—one might indeed dismiss it as whimsical, a common critical verdict on poems about animals—but it does suggest there was a mood of popular dissent from the 'official' doctrine of an exclusively human afterlife.

Transmigration

One non-Christian path that the souls of animals might follow after death was familiar to anyone versed in the classics. Usually attributed to Pythagoras and his school, the theory of transmigration of souls, or metempsychosis, postulated that the soul or mind was able to survive periods of incorporeal existence between successive incarnations in humans and animals. Though British classicists had 'flirted' with Pythagoreanism since the 1600s, it did not come to general notice until the mid-eighteenth century, when the surgeon and Orientalist John Zephaniah Holwell (1711–1798) published some notes on the subject along with his sensational best-selling account of the Black Hole of Calcutta, of which he was a survivor.[37]

Transmigration seems first to have been used in print as an argument against cruelty to animals in Barbauld's *The Mouse's Petition*:

> If mind, as ancient sages taught,
> A never dying flame,
> Still shifts thro' matter's varying forms,
> In every form the same,
> Beware, lest in the worm you crush
> A brother's soul you find;
> And tremble lest thy luckless hand
> Dislodge a kindred mind.[38]

Twenty years later, transmigration featured prominently in Thomas Taylor's seminal but idiosyncratic *A Vindication of the Rights of Brutes*, published anonymously in 1792. Despite being one of the earliest contributions to animal rights theory, Taylor's pamphlet is now seldom quoted, in part because his claim that 'brutes' had rights was deliberately hyperbolic, but mostly because the principal object of his writing, as the title suggests, was to satirise Mary Wollstonecraft's (1759–1797) *A Vindication of the Rights of Women* by showing that a parallel argument could be made for the rights of animals.[39] Taylor found Wollstonecraft's proto-feminism ridiculous: he did not acknowledge the rights of men, women, or animals, though he firmly believed that animals were capable of reason and intelligence, which he thought was obvious from their behaviour, and in particular from their capacity to communicate intelligently with one other. From their ability to reason, Taylor concluded that animals had feelings, rejecting Jeremy Bentham's (1748–1832) argument that reason and feeling were distinct, and asserting that 'sense cannot at all operate without intelligence'.[40]

Despite his obvious appreciation of the intellectual abilities of animals, Taylor insisted that compassionate treatment was not their right but a voluntary expression of human virtue, though his work may have inspired subsequent calls for animals to be granted legal rights. When the Lord Chancellor, Lord Erskine (1750–1823) unsuccessfully introduced a Cruelty to Animals bill in the House of Lords in 1809, he complained that: 'Animals are considered as property only: to destroy or to abuse them, from malice to the proprietor, or with an intention injurious to his interest in them, is criminal; but the animals themselves are without protection; the law regards them not substantively; they have no rights!'[41]

Taylor's pseudo argument for the rights of brutes drew not only on their intellectual capacities but also on various traditions concerning the transmigration of souls. A distinguished translator of Plato and Aristotle, Taylor supplemented his classical sources with examples of transmigration collected from non-European traditions, including those of ancient Egypt, Persia and India. Though his writings give the impression he was more attuned to Hellenistic philosophy than Christianity, he did not profess transmigration as a personal belief, but treated the traditions as '[f]ables [which] indicate that brute animals accord with mankind in the nature of the soul'. In other words, the fact that learned people from so many different cultures accepted transmigration revealed a widespread belief that humans and animals were animated by souls of a similar kind.

Pythagoreanism proved to be an inspiration for two influential nineteenth-century anti-cruelty campaigners: Lewis Gompertz and Thomas Forster (1789–1860). Gompertz, who we encountered in the previous chapter, had been secretary of the SPCA until forced to resign in 1833, probably because, as a Jew and a Pythagorean, he did not fit in with the committee's Christian ethos. After a period running the rival, more radical, Animals' Friend Society, he was readmitted after protesting his 'innocence' of Pythagoreanism, but any change of heart in this regard must have been temporary, since in 1852 he wrote in *Fragments in Defence of Animals* that the souls of animals continued to exist after death in a state of limbo, without thought or feeling, until they were united with a new body. Thus, it was possible to be reincarnated, perhaps as a different species, without having any memory of one's previous lives.[42]

Gompertz's interest in Pythagoreanism was shared by his correspondent and fellow member of the AFS, Thomas Forster. A medical practitioner and convert to Roman Catholicism, Forster's eclectic interests included phrenology, vegetarianism, and 'oriental' philosophy, including 'the holy doctrine of Pythagoras and the Indian school, which ascribes to every living creature an eternal existence'.[43] Transmigration was an important part of Forster's idiosyncratic theodicy: 'Metempsychosis implies the future life and everlasting happiness of all living creatures, we must observe that there is plenty of room in this wide universe for all of them… further, without admitting that Animals will live hereafter, we could not reconcile the universal suffering of the brute Creation with the Divine Goodness'. Forster's mix of Catholic purgatory and Pythagorean rebirth allowed cruelty to be punished and suffering recompensed: those who ill-treated animals would find themselves reincarnated in animal bodies, where they would experience for themselves the sufferings they had once meted out, while the merciful would receive 'some light purgatory in the body of some fortunate and beautiful bird or beast'.[44]

Transcendentalism

Apart from evangelicals, who saw medicine as a Christian vocation, and some Anglican Tories among the profession's leaders, medical practitioners had something of a reputation for scepticism and worldliness. Unlike the universities, medical schools did not require their students to profess the Christian faith in order to matriculate, and a lack of pastoral supervision, combined with the materialistic focus of their training, was thought to incline those whose faith was already weak towards atheism.[45] Medical students were certainly encouraged to examine the relationship between humans and animals with a critical eye: comparative anatomy was a key part of their studies, and the problem of why many species, including apes and humans, had similar body plans was, in pre-Darwinian times, accorded high importance. In the 1830s, students frustrated by Professor Granville Sharp Pattison's (1791–1851) '*total ignorance of* and *disgusting indifference* to new anatomical views and researches' forced him from his post at University College London.[46] The students were not, of course, motivated solely by their scientific curiosity: excited by the July Revolution in France, they wanted to hear the radical new Continental ideas on species change and extinction, known as transcendental anatomy, which seemed to carry a particular resonance in those politically unsettling times.

Transcendentalism, also known as philosophical anatomy, was, in its biological sense, a holistic theory of the interconnectedness of all living things that had its roots in German *Naturphilosophie*, which was in turn based on Goethe's concept of nature as a 'vast musical symposium'. It was introduced into Britain by a small number of influential anatomy teachers, who included the surgeon Joseph Henry Green (1791–1863, a friend of Samuel Taylor Coleridge) and the anatomists Robert Knox, Robert Grant (1793–1874) and Richard Owen (1804–1892). Transcendentalism's appeal to students lay in its potential to transform the rather obscure field of comparative anatomy by supplying a coherent, universal theory that would not only account for species change, but also provide a model in nature for abrupt social changes and political revolutions. This potential to upset the status quo gave transcendentalism a radical appeal that ensured its popularity with undergraduates.

Transcendentalism may be defined (not an easy task) as an attempt to discover, through observation and deduction, the fundamental laws and patterns that govern the dynamic, self-organising processes of nature. It thus resembles the Platonic theory of forms in that generalized patterns or archetypes may be deduced from the appearance of objects in the natural world.[47] For example, that most eloquent, and effusive, of transcendentalists, Robert Knox, wrote of the vertebra as: 'the type of all vertebrate animals, of the entire skeleton … of the organic world …. It possesses the form of the primitive cell; of the sphere; of the universe'.[48]

Critics found this sort of thing vague and mystical, but to Knox, one of the finest comparative anatomists of his day, transcendentalism had the potential to revolutionize his discipline. Anatomists were no longer confined to *describing* morphology, but could speculate on its phylogenetic and even social significance. For example, from observing, measuring, and dissecting human bodies, a set of ideal proportions could be derived, which corresponded to those seen in classical Greek statues such as those of Apollo and Venus.[49] According to Knox, it was no coincidence that the ideal form discovered through modern anatomical studies was the same as that created by ancient Greek sculptors, who had arrived at it intuitively through their refined appreciation of beauty. Transcendentalists thought it legitimate to employ the aesthetic sense in scientific study; for example, those individuals that most closely resembled the ideal type of a species would be considered by a practised observer to be the most beautiful. The transcendental method involved a combination of detailed observation and intuition: knowledge of the structure of different species could only come through careful dissection, but intuition was required to discern the unifying pattern of which each was a variation.

Using transcendental methods, Knox developed a complex theory of evolution, according to which new species arose through differential development (what we might now call mutations) of a common embryo. According to this, pre-Darwinian, proposal, the pattern of every potential species, including humans, was inherent in the multipotent embryo, from which new forms ('hopeful monsters') were constantly being generated, though they would flourish only if external conditions happened to be favourable.[50] As one of the French founders of the movement, Étienne Geoffroy Saint-Hilaire (1772–1844) put it, 'philosophically speaking', there was 'but a single animal', or, in the words of the literary transcendentalist Ralph Waldo Emerson (1803–1882), 'Each creature is only a modification of the other; the likeness in them is more than the difference, and their radical law is one and the same'.[51]

The effect of British transcendentalism on biological thinking was complex and has yet to be fully explored by historians of science. From the perspective of vivisection, however, it proved a deterrent. Firstly, the transcendental method was essentially observational: careful dissection of animal and human bodies was preferred to vivisecting the living; Knox refused to allow any vivisection in his anatomy schools, a pragmatic as well as a humane attitude because students reluctant to dissect living animals would be attracted to transcendentalism as 'a substitute for vivisection'.[52] Secondly, transcendentalism called for a subjective response to nature: an appreciation of beauty helped students to discern the ideal types that lay behind the imperfect forms they encountered, so they needed to cultivate their feelings rather than suppressing them. Thirdly, the transcendental teachings that all species, animal and human, were derived from a common embryo, that all were equally well suited for the environment in which they lived, and that all might become extinct if conditions changed, underlined the essential unity, and transience, of all creatures. Humans were not lords of creation but part of an interdependent, self-sustaining biological system whose life force could be conceptualised as a collective soul, *anima mundi*.[53]

Much of transcendentalism's wider appeal was due to its being not only descriptive of how nature was organised but also prescriptive of the proper way to live. If nature sanctioned abrupt changes (which was how transcendentalists thought new species evolved), then human revolutions might be part of the natural order, and if that order was, as Goethe had expressed it, part of a vast symphony of nature, then humans ought, as far as possible, to live in harmony with it. Transcendental notions of the harmonies of nature were conducive to a philosophy of 'nature mysticism' or pantheism, the followers of which, as Lloyd G. Stevenson (1918–1988) observed, tended to be 'on the side of the animals'.[54]

Though there was never a prominent transcendentalist movement in Britain like that which flourished in New England around Harvard and the Unitarians, the themes of living in 'harmony with nature' and of animals as our 'brothers' did began to appear in British letters from the late 1830s, the most celebrated writers to show a transcendental influence being Samuel Taylor Coleridge (1772–1834) and William Wordsworth (1770–1850). Its appeal was particularly strong for romantics, who sought an escape from the cruelties of metropolitan living in an idealized pastoralism in which animals were helpers, friends and companions.[55]

Transcendentalism in Britain effectively ended as a scientific movement with the publication of *The Origin of Species*, as Darwin's elegantly simple proposal of natural selection made transcendentalism's complex, esoteric explanations of why so many different creatures showed such striking anatomical parallels seem redundant. In contrast to revolutionary transcendentalism, Darwin's modest proposal that change could only occur by gradual small steps was considerably more congenial to the Victorian political establishment.[56] There remained, however, an undercurrent of transcendentalism in biological thought, difficult to trace and sometimes surfacing in unexpected places: the concept of natural harmonies, for example, may have been the inspiration for what are now known as ecosystems. Encounters with transcendentalism during medical training may also have motivated some young British doctors to look more closely into the spiritual aspects of biological phenomena, and to become more open to accepting intuition and emotions as evidence, an approach that would find expression in the *fin-de-siècle* spiritual revival. The theosophists, occultists, new age thinkers and others, within and outside medicine, who became involved in this idealistic movement to unite science and spirituality, some of whom we will encounter in subsequent chapters, might be seen as continuing what was begun by the transcendental anatomists.

Animals' Souls and Anti-Vivisection in the Nineteenth Century and After

The waning of the influence of Christianity on the anti-cruelty movement in the twentieth century coincided with a greater focus on animals themselves. Despite accepting, and even admiring, animals' rationality and learning, the mainstream Christian denominations never bridged the gulf between animals and humans: only the latter were made in God's image and could expect a place in the hereafter. By the late-nineteenth century, however, the British people had already granted them one. Those middle class (for the most part) late Victorians who looked forward to being reunited with their companion animals in the world to come, and mourned their passing in this, probably felt neither hopeless nor heathen. They developed rituals, resembling human funeral practices, to mark the passing of their animal companions: post-mortem photographs, a popular means of preserving memories of deceased family members by posing them for the last time within the family group, were taken of animals and those who mourned them, and there were animal funeral services, cemeteries, gravestones, elegies, and mourning cards.[57] To some, this seemed an excessive indulgence in sentimentality, and to others, anthropomorphism, but it was also the expression of a popular, inclusive theology of animals that, in defiance of orthodoxy, granted them souls that survived death, and opened to them the gates of heaven. Paradoxically, perhaps, it was easier to mourn lives when there was some prospect of reunion, and to lay flowers on the grave of a favourite dog in anticipation of a shared life to come:

> Not hopeless, round this calm sepulchral spot,
> A wreath presaging life we twine;
> If God be love, what sleeps below was not
> Without a spark divine.[58]

Vivisectionists, of course, took a different view, and while they did not often discuss such matters, it seems that no-one who believed that animals had souls made a practice of vivisecting them. Perhaps some who vivisected did not believe in souls at all, for the conflict between vivisection and anti-vivisection was beginning to align itself with that of materialism versus anti-materialism (or spiritualism, if you prefer). Many of the most controversial and well publicised animal experiments involved the brain, an organ that vivisectionists treated as a mechanism, but whose subtle workings anti-vivisectionists such as Cobbe did not feel could ever be revealed by the physiologist's knife:

> The common passion for science in general and for physiology in particular, and the prevalent materialistic belief that the secrets of the Mind can be best explored in matter, undoubtedly account in no small matter for the vehemence of the new pursuit of original physiological investigations.[59]

At the turn of the century it remained a matter of great controversy whether evolution could have been responsible for the emergence of the most complex cognitive faculties, including the human capacity for love, imagination, and feeling, or whether there were some transcendent aspects of thought and consciousness that could never be explained in biological terms.[60] The two great founders of evolutionary theory disagreed: Darwin thought that evolution could account for these mental phenomena, Alfred Russel Wallace (1823–1913) that it could not.

For Christians who felt their humanity threatened by talk of the evolution of rationality, one solution was to emphasise the spiritual uniqueness of humankind, allowing that animals were rational and capable of feeling and suffering, but according humans alone the 'spark divine' of an immortal soul. It was presumably a conviction that humans were in some spiritual way ontologically different from animals that led many Christian clergy in early-twentieth century Britain to sign up for the pro-vivisection Research Defence Society (on which, see Chap. 6): they saw human lives as of intrinsically greater value to God than those of brute creation, because God had imparted something to us that mere biology could not. From a mundane perspective, most Churches had no wish to deny the theory of evolution, forcing the faithful to choose between religion and science, so they pragmatically confined the divine likeness in humankind to the immaterial part, leaving animals as mere matter, physically kin to humans, but spiritually inconsequential.

Conclusion

We have seen that, in nineteenth-century Britain, the Christian view of animals as rational but unspiritual was challenged by claims that they were either ensouled individually or were part of a collective world soul, and thus were not, as mainstream churches taught, categorically distinct from humans in a spiritual or metaphysical sense. When a few advanced followers of Pythagorean and Eastern thought proposed that the souls of animals might subsist after death, and that transmigration of souls between animals and humans might occur, this introduced a concept of the soul that was fundamentally different from that of the Christian tradition: a life-force that was constantly changing, reforming and repeating, rather than an artefact eternally linked to the human body for which it had been created.

Transcendentalism inculcated a similar, non-Christian, perspective, according to which humans were only one expression of a universal creative force of nature—arising, developing, and becoming extinct like all living things. For transcendentalists, neither humans nor animals could expect an individual afterlife, but the dynamic system in which all participated could be said to be endowed with a common soul, and death could be seen not as an end, but a return to the source that all life shared.[61] This holistic view of life on earth, the concept of mankind as transient, and the notion of a life-force common to humans and animals, were strong arguments against vivisection for those who accepted them. Though transcendentalists were sometimes condemned in the nineteenth century as atheists, their position was much closer to that of pantheism. Along with other non-Christian faiths, elements of their thinking influenced the development of the spiritual revival, and it is to this movement and its consequences for the welfare of animals in the twentieth century that we shall now turn.

Notes

1. Quoted in Rod Preece, 'Darwinism, Christianity, and the great vivisection debate', *Journal of the History of Ideas*, 64 (2003), 399–419 (Preece 2003).
2. H. Knight Horsfield, 'Old Rocket', in *The Dog in British Poetry*, ed. R.M. Leonard (London: D. Nutt, 1893), 197 (Horsfield 1893).
3. 'Have animals souls?' (editorial), *Leeds Times,* 17 May 1856, 6. (Have animals souls? 1856)
4. Preece, 'Darwinism, Christianity'; Chien-hui Li, 'An unnatural alliance? Political radicalism and the animal defence movement in late Victorian and Edwardian Britain', *EurAmerica,* 42 (2012), 1–43 (Li 2012).
5. Darwin himself took a nuanced position on vivisection, and never suggested that evolutionary theory could resolve the ethical problem.
6. Nancy Stepan, *The Idea of Race in Science: Great Britain 1800–1960* (London: Macmillan, 1982), 7 (Stepan1982).
7. Susan Merrill Squier, *Liminal Lives: Imagining the Human at the Frontiers of Biomedicine* (Durham NC: Duke University Press, 2004), 94; James Baycroft, 'Suspended animation', *Comic Annual* (London: Henry Colburn, 1842): 323–336 (Squier 2004; Baycroft 1842).
8. Li, 'An Unnatural Alliance?' (Li 2012).
9. Lansbury, *The Old Brown Dog*, ix.
10. Preece, 'Darwinism, Christianity'. For the opposing view that Darwinism 'confirmed the kinship between man and animal' see Niven, *History of the Humane Movement*, 79, and French, *Antivivisection and Medical Science.*

11. Chien-hui Li, 'An Unnatural Alliance?'; Chien-hui Li, 'A union of Christianity, humanity and philanthropy: the Christian tradition and prevention of cruelty to animals in nineteenth-century England', *Society and Animals, 8* (2000), 265–285 (Li 2000).
12. Minute book, 1832, RSPCA Archive, Southwater, CM/20, 40, 45–46, 53. (RSPCA Archive 1832)
13. Li, 'An Unnatural Alliance?' (Li 2000).
14. Drummond, *The Rights of Animals*, 15, 17; 'Society for the Prevention of Cruelty to Animals' (editorial*), Evangelical Magazine and Missionary Chronicle* 2 (1824): 357–358; Bates, 'Vivisection, virtue ethics'. (Society for the Prevention of Cruelty to Animals 1824)
15. The charitable angel's arrow was aimed, appropriately, at Parliament.
16. 'The forthcoming ass show' (editorial), *Saturday Review*, 16 (1863), 213–215. (The forthcoming ass show 1863)
17. Craig Buettinger, 'Antivivisection and the charge of zoophil-psychosis in the early twentieth century', *Historian*, 55 (1993), 277–288 (Buettinger 1993).
18. Quoted in Rod Preece, *Animal Sensibility and Inclusive Justice in the Age of Bernard Shaw* (Vancouver: UBC Press, 2011), 121 (Preece 2011).
19. Brian Harrison, 'Animals and the state in nineteenth-century England', *English Historical Review*, 88 (1973), 786–820 (Harrison 1973).
20. Li, 'An Unnatural Alliance?' It is probably no coincidence that the two English cardinals who were anti-vivisectionists, Manning and Newman, were both Anglican converts. Manning was much influenced by his wife, who died before he converted to Catholicism.
21. Robert Hull, 'On vivisection', *London Medical Gazette*, 33 (1843/1844), 219–220 (I Iull 1843/1844).
22. 'Dr. Blundell's introductory physiological lecture' (editorial), *Lancet*, 9 (1825/6), 113–118; Stevenson, 'Religious elements'.
23. Revelation 6: 9–10.
24. James Lawson Drummond, 'On humanity to animals', *Edinburgh Philosophical Journal*, 12 (1831): 172–183 (Drummond 1831).
25. Anita Guerrini, 'The ethics of animal experimentation in seventeenth-century England', *Journal of the History of Ideas,* 50 (1989), 391–407 (Guerrini 1989).
26. Vyvyan, *In Pity*, 23–24.
27. Aristotle, *Metaphysics*, 1037a6.
28. Aquinas, Summa Contra Gentiles II, 68; Anthony Kenny, *Aquinas on Mind* (London: Routledge, 1993), 126 (Kenny 1993).

29. Catholic doctrine as laid down by the Council of Vienne in 1312 was, however, that '… anyone who presumes henceforth to assert defend or hold stubbornly that the rational or intellectual soul is not the form of the human body of itself and essentially, is to be considered a heretic', which appears to have excluded the possibility of a soul without a body, or a person without a soul. The heresy that the Council was trying to prevent was monopsychism: the view that all human beings shared a common intellect: Robert Pasnau, *Thomas Aquinas on Human Nature: A Philosophical Study of Summa Theologiae 1a 75–89* (Cambridge: Cambridge University Press, 2002), 159–160 (Pasnau 2002).
30. Matthew Hale, *The Primitive Organization of Mankind, considered and Examined According to the Light of Nature* (London: William Godbid for William Shrowsbery, 1677), 304, 321 (Hale 1677).
31. G.E. Bentley, 'The freaks of learning', *Colby Library Quarterly*, 18 (1982): 87–104; Douglas K. Candland, *Feral Children and Clever Animals: Reflections on Human Nature* (Oxford, Oxford University Press, 1993) (Bentley 1982; Candland 1993).
32. Daniel Tyerman, *Essays on the Wisdom of God* (London: R. Clay, 1818), 266 (Tyerman 1818).
33. J. Worthy, 'Souls and instincts of animals', *Catholic Institute Magazine* (1856): 143–149, 175–180 (Worthy 1856).
34. Richard Graves, *On the Four Last Books of the Pentateuch* (London: Henry G. Bohn, 1850), 294 (Graves 1850).
35. Preece, 'Darwinism, Christianity' (Preece 2003).
36. J. Earl Clausen (ed.), *The Dog's Book of Verse* (Boston: Small, Maynard and Co., 1916), 145–174 (Earl Clausen 1916).
37. Peter Harrison, 'Animal souls, metempsychosis, and theodicy in seventeenth-century English thought', *Journal of the History of Philosophy*, 31 (1993): 519–544; J.Z. Holwell, *Interesting Historical Events Relevant to the Provinces of Bengal, and the Empire of Indostan…* (London: T. Becket and P.A. De Hondt, 1767); see also Chi-Ming Yang, 'Gross metempsychosis and Eastern soul', in Frank Palmeri (ed.) *Humans and Other Animals in Eighteenth-Century British Culture…* (Ashgate: Aldershot, 2006), 13–30 (Harrison 1993; Holwell 1767; Yang 2006).
38. Anna Laetitia Aikin [Barbauld], 'The Mouse's Petition', *Poems* (London: Joseph Johnson, 1773), 37–40 (Barbauld 1773).
39. Peder Anker, 'A vindication of the rights of brutes', *Philosophy and Geography*, 7 (2004), 259–264 (Anker 2004).

40. Thomas Taylor, *A Vindication of the Rights of Brutes*, ed. R. Urban St Cir (Sequim, WA: Holmes, 2009), 8 (Taylor 2009).
41. House of Lords debate, *Hansard*, 15 May 1809, 14, c554.
42. Lewis Gompertz, *Fragments in Defence of Animals, and Essays on Morals, Soul, and Future State* (London: W. Hornell, 1852), 191–206; Lucien Wolf, 'Gompertz, Lewis' (rev. Ben Marsden) *Oxford Dictionary of National Biography* (Oxford: Oxford University Press, 2004), viewed 4 August 2014, http://www.oxforddnb.com/view/article/10934, (Gompertz 1852; Wolf and Lewis 2004).
43. Forster visited India, and was impressed by the animal hospitals he saw there: Thomas Forster, *Philozoia, or Moral Reflections on the Actual Condition of the Animal Kingdom* (Brussels: Deltombe and Co., 1839), viii–ix, 28, 63 (Forster 1839).
44. Thomas Forster, *An Apology for the Doctrine of Pythagoras as Compatible with that of Christianity with an Account of a New Sect of Christians* (Boulogne sur Mer: Charles Aigre 1812), 4, 7. The 'sect' was the short-lived New Christian Society of Metempsychosians (Forster 1812).
45. 'Aesculapius', The *Hospital Pupil's Guide: being Oracular Communications Addressed to Students of the Medical Profession* (London: E. Cox and Sons, 1818), 39 (Aesculapius 1818).
46. *Lancet*, 1 (1829/30), 749–753.
47. For an introduction to transcendental philosophy see Philip F. Rehbock, *The Philosophical Naturalists: Themes in Early-Nineteenth Century British Biology* (Wisconsin: University of Madison Press, 1983), 15–30 (Rehbock 1983).
48. Robert Knox, *The Races of Men: a Fragment* (London: Henry Renshaw, 1850), 426 (Knox 1850).
49. Robert Knox, *A Manual of Artistic Anatomy, for the use of Sculptors, Painters and Amateurs* (London: Henry Renshaw, 1852) (Knox 1852).
50. Bates, *Robert Knox*, 113, 132–135.
51. Ralph Waldo Emerson, *Nature and Other Essays* (Mineola, NY: Dover, 2009 [1836]), 18 (Emerson 2009).
52. Adrian Desmond, *The Politics of Evolution: Morphology, Medicine, and Reform in Radical London* (Chicago: University of Chicago Press, 1989), 183 (Desmond 1989).
53. Michael Hagner, 'The soul and the brain between anatomy and Naturphilosophie in the early-nineteenth century, *Medical History*, 36 (1992), 1–33 (Hagner 1992).

54. Bates, Robert Knox, 21, 146; Evelleen Richards, 'The "moral anatomy" of Robert Knox: the interplay between biological and social thought in Victorian scientific naturalism', *Journal of the History of Biology*, 22 (1989): 373–436; Stevenson, 'Religious elements' (Richards 1989).
55. David Mushet, *Wrongs of the Animal World* (London: Hatcher and Son, 1839), 79. Shelley thought the Ancient Greeks experienced beauty through living 'in harmony with nature': Percy Bysshe Shelley, *Essays, Letters from Abroad…* (London: Edward Moxon, 1840), 2 vols. 2, 190 (Mushet 1839);(Shelley 1840).
56. See, for example, Gerard M. Verschuuren, *Darwin's Philosophical Legacy: the Good and the Not-So-Good* (Lanham: Lexington Books, 2012), 93–100 (Verschuuren 2012).
57. Teresa Mangum, 'Animal angst: Victorians memorialize their pets', in Deborah Denenholz Morse and Martin A. Danahay (eds), *Victorian Animal Dreams: Representations of Animals in Victorian Literature and Culture* (Aldershot: Ashgate, 2007), 15–34 (Mangum 2007).
58. Francis Doyle, 'Epitaph on a Favourite Dog', in *The Return of the Guards, and Other Poems* (London: Macmillan, 1883), 264 (Doyle 1883).
59. Frances Power Cobbe, *The moral aspects of vivisection* (London: VSS, 1875), 288 (Cobbe 1875).
60. Finn and Stark, 'Medical science'.
61. Knox, *Artistic Anatomy*, 5.

References

Aesculapius. (1818). *The hospital pupil's guide: Being oracular communications addressed to students of the medical profession* (p. 39). London: E. Cox and Sons.

Anker, P. (2004). A vindication of the rights of brutes. *Philosophy and Geography, 7,* 259–264.

Barbauld, A. L. A. (1773). The mouse's petition. *Poems* (pp. 37–40). London: Joseph Johnson.

Baycroft, J. (1842). Suspended animation. *Comic annual* (pp. 323–336). London: Henry Colburn.

Bentley, G. E. (1982). The freaks of learning. *Colby Library Quarterly, 18,* 87–104.

Buettinger, C. (1993). Antivivisection and the charge of zoophil–psychosis in the early twentieth century. *Historian, 55,* 277–288.

Candland, D. K. (1993). *Feral children and clever animals: Reflections on human nature*. Oxford: Oxford University Press.

Clausen, J. E. (Ed.). (1916). *The dog's book of verse* (pp. 145–174). Boston: Small, Maynard and Co.

Cobbe, F. P. (1875). *The moral aspects of vivisection*. London: VSS.

Darwin, C. (1859). *On the origin of species by means of natural selection, or, the preservation of favoured races in the struggle for life*. London: John Murray.

Desmond, A. (1989). *The politics of evolution: Morphology, medicine, and reform in radical London*. Chicago: University of Chicago Press.

Doyle, F. (1883). Epitaph on a favourite dog. In *The return of the guards, and other poems* (p. 264). London: Macmillan.

Dr. Blundell's Introductory Physiological Lecture (Editorial). (1825/1826). Stevenson, 'Religious elements'. *Lancet, 9,* 113–118.

Drummond, J. L. (1831). On humanity to animals. *Edinburgh Philosophical Journal, 13,* 172–183.

Emerson, R. W. (2009 [1836]). *Nature and other essays* (p. 18). Mineola, NY: Dover.

Forster, T. (1812). *An apology for the Doctrine of Pythagoras as compatible with that of Christianity with an account of a new sect of Christians* (pp. 4,7) . Boulogne sur Mer: Charles Aigre.

Forster, T. (1839). *Philozoia, or moral reflections on the actual condition of the animal kingdom* (pp. viii–ix, 28, 63). Brussels: Deltombe and Co.

Gompertz, L. (1852). *Fragments in defence of animals, and essays on morals, soul, and future state*. London: W. Hornell.

Graves, R. (1850). *On the four last books of the Pentateuch* (p. 294). London: Henry G. Bohn.

Guerrini, A. (1989). The ethics of animal experimentation in seventeenth century England. *Journal of the History of Ideas, 50,* 391–407.

Hagner, M. (1992). The soul and the brain between nature and Naturphilosophie in the early-nineteenth century. *Medical History, 36,* 1–33.

Hale, M. (1677). *The primitive organization of mankind, considered and examined according to the light of nature* (pp. 304, 321). London: William Godbid for William Shrowsbery.

Harrison, B. (1973). Animals and the state in nineteenth-century England. *English Historical Review, 88,* 786–820.

Harrison, P. (1993). Animal souls, metempsychosis, and theodicy in seventeenth-century English thought. *Journal of the History of Philosophy, 31,* 519–544.

Have Animals Souls? (Editorial). (1856, May 17). *Leeds Times,* 6.

Holwell, J. Z. (1767). *Interesting historical events relevant to the provinces of Bengal, and the Empire of Indostan…* London: T. Becket and P.A. De Hondt.

Horsfield, H. K. (1893). Old rocket. In R. M. Leonard (Ed.). *The dog in British poetry* (p. 197). London: D. Nutt.

Hull, R. (1843/1844). On vivisection. *London Medical Gazette, 33,* 219–220.

Kenny, A. (1993). Aquinas, summa contra Gentiles II, 68. *Aquinas on mind* (p. 126). London: Routledge.

Knox, R. (1850). *The races of men: A fragment* (p. 426). London: Henry Renshaw.

Knox, R. (1852). *A manual of artistic anatomy, for the use of sculptors,painters and amateurs.* London: Henry Renshaw.

Li, C. (2000). A union of Christianity, humanity and philanthropy: The Christian tradition and prevention of cruelty to animals in nineteenth-century England. *Society and Animals, 8,* 265–285.

Li, C. (2012). An unnatural alliance? Political radicalism and the animal defence movement in late Victorian and Edwardian Britain. *EurAmerica, 42,* 1–43.

Mangum, T. (2007). Animal angst: Victorians memorialize their pets. In D. D. Morse & M. A. Danahay (Eds.), *Victorian animal dreams: Representations of animals in Victorian literature and culture* (pp. 15–34). Aldershot: Ashgate.

Mushet, D. (1839). *The wrongs of the animal world.* London: Hatchard and Son.

Pasnau, R. (2002). *Thomas aquinas on human nature: A philosophical study of summa theologiae 1a 75–89* (pp. 159–160). Cambridge: Cambridge University Press.

Percy Bysshe Shelley. (1840). *Essays, Letters from Abroad…* (Vol. 2, p. 190). London: Edward Moxon.

Preece, R. (2003). Darwinism, Christianity, and the great vivisection debate. *Journal of the History of Ideas, 64,* 399–419.

Preece .R (2011). *Animal sensibility and Inclusive justice in the age of Bernard Shaw* (p. 121). Vancouver: UBC Press.

Rehbock, P. F. (1983). *The philosophical naturalists: Themes in early-nineteenth century British biology.* Wisconsin: University of Madison Press.

Richards, E. (1989). The "moral anatomy" of Robert Knox: The interplay between biological and social thought in Victorian scientific naturalism. *Journal of the History of Biology, 22,* 373–436.

RSPCA Archive. (1832). *Minute book* (CM/20, pp. 40, 45–46, 53). Southwater.

Society for the Prevention of Cruelty to Animals (Editorial). (1824). *Evangelical Magazine and Missionary Chronicle, 2,* 357–358.

Squier, S. M. (2004). *Liminal lives: Imagining the human at the frontiers of biomedicine.* Durham, NC: Duke University Press.

Stepan, N. (1982). *The idea of race in science: Great Britain 1800–1960* (p. 7). London: Macmillan.

Taylor, T. (2009) *A vindication of the rights of brutes.* R. Urban St Cir (Ed.). Sequim, WA: Holmes.

The Forthcoming Ass Show (Editorial). (1863). *Saturday Review, 16,* 213–215.

Tyerman, D. (1818). *Essays on the wisdom of God* (p. 266). London: R. Clay.

Verschuuren, G. M. (2012). *Darwin's philosophical legacy: The good and the not-so-good* (pp. 93–100). Lanham: Lexington Books.

Wolf, L. (2004). *Oxford dictionary of National Biography* (G. Lewis, rev. M. Ben). Oxford: Oxford University Press. Retrieved August 4, 2014, from http://www.oxforddnb.com/view/article/10934.

Worthy, J. (1856). Souls and instincts of animals. In*Catholic Institute Magazine* (pp. 143–149, 175–180).

Yang, C.-M. (2006). Gross metempsychosis and Eastern soul. In F. Palmeri (Ed.), *Humans and other animals in eighteenth-century British culture...* (pp. 13–30). Ashgate: Aldershot.

4

A New Age for a New Century: Anti-Vivisection, Vegetarianism, and the Order of the Golden Age

To Josiah Oldfield (1863–1953) belongs the distinction of having founded Britain's, and quite possibly the world's, first anti-vivisection hospital, the short-lived Hospital of St Francis, which opened in 1898 at 145 New Kent Road in South London. Oldfield is now remembered, if at all, as a pioneering dietary reformer; a bearded, Bible-quoting, besmocked prophet of fruitarianism who devoted his considerable intellectual energy to a raft of utopian projects: a vegetarian hospital, a fruitarian colony, a programme of dietetics. To his critics he was a crank, but it was not easy to dismiss the arguments of a Middle Temple barrister, medical graduate and Oxford Doctor of Law. Oldfield's medical career was an unusual one, pursued outside conventional hospital circles and devoted to a health reform programme whose principles included a cruelty-free diet, a more natural lifestyle, and an emphasis on spiritual as well as physical health. His work is considered here for the light it sheds on a broader health and spiritual reform movement that drew on influences as diverse as Eastern philosophy, transcendentalism and Darwinism to promote a worldview of 'universal kinship' and harmony with nature.[1] This movement, which included vegetarians, anti-vivisectionists and other social improvers, approached the new century in anticipation of a new age in which materialism would be tempered

A.W.H. Bates, *Anti-Vivisection and the Profession of Medicine in Britain*,
The Palgrave Macmillan Animal Ethics Series, DOI 10.1057/978-1-137-55697-4_4

by spiritualism and true science would flourish, heralding an age of prosperity in which violence and oppression, including the abuse of animals, would no longer have a place.

Oldfield set about building this utopia by establishing 'healthian' colonies in the South East of England—the warmest region and thus the best suited to the outdoor work, fruitarian diet, nudity and sun baths that his followers were encouraged to enjoy. The locals regarded these communes of free-living fruitarians with suspicion, but Oldfield's strategy also included vegetarian and anti-vivisection hospitals that he hoped would demonstrate the practical benefits a meat- and cruelty-free lifestyle. His projects were typical of the new age movement in that, while attractive to a minority, they failed to win enough support among people of influence or achieve the necessary level of popular acceptance to bring about significant social change. The first world war undermined public confidence in the prospect of creating a cruelty-free utopia, but the final straw for the back-to-nature movement was the subsequent co-option of 'green' ideology by British fascists, which, along with its links with German National Socialism, made its values seem subversive and treasonable as Britain once more prepared for war.

The Food Reform Movement in Britain

The antecedents of the back-to-nature movement lay in social vegetarianism, of which Oldfield was a lifelong champion. In Britain, organized vegetarianism had been linked from the outset with Fabianism and, in particular, the Concordium (1838–1848), a utopian socialist community that collectively sought the inspiration of the 'Triune Universal Spirit', and whose journal, the *New Age, Concordium Gazette, and Temperance Advocate*, placed health at the centre of an idealistic programme of anti-militarism, temperance and 'vegetarianism' (veganism in modern terminology), which was extoled as the 'beginning and end of all true reforms'.[2] The Concordium, in turn, traced its roots to the American transcendentalist movement—which had a much broader social emphasis than the scientific transcendentalism taught in British medical schools—and named its Surrey headquarters after the New England transcendentalist philosopher Amos Bronson Alcott (1799–1888).

The ethical socialists of the Concordium were concerned about animal welfare for different reasons than the anti-cruelty societies. While the latter were worried that working class cruelty, left unchecked, would spread and threaten the stability of society, socialists thought that cruelty was imposed from above, and that the harsh dominance of mankind over animals both mirrored and encouraged the exploitation of the poor by the rich. Though the Concordium lasted only 10 years, after its demise other socialist groups took up the cause. One of these was the Humanitarian League, founded in 1891 by Henry Stephens Salt (1851–1939), who became its General Secretary and editor of its journals. The League opposed the infliction of avoidable suffering on any sentient being, campaigning against corporal and capital punishment and blood sports as well as vivisection. Salt himself was an ethical vegetarian, an anti-vivisectionist and a pacifist—a not uncommon combination among socialists—who believed that the new-found kinship with animals that had been revealed by Darwin's theory of evolution warranted the extension of rights to the non-human 'races'. Animal rights was something of a surrogate cause among socialists, because they assumed, with reasoning the reverse of Thomas Taylor's, that if animals were recognised as having rights, humans could not possibly be denied them:

> [The] notion of the life of an animal having 'no moral purpose', belongs to a class of ideas which cannot possibly be accepted by the advanced humanitarian thought of the present day—it is a purely arbitrary assumption, at variance with our best instincts, at variance with our best science, and absolutely fatal (if the subject be clearly thought out) to any full realization of animals' rights. If we are ever going to do justice to the lower races [*i.e.*, animals], we must get rid of the antiquated notion of a 'great gulf' fixed between them and mankind, and must recognize the common bond of humanity that unites all living beings in one universal brotherhood.[3]

Perhaps the most prominent of the organizations that carried on the Concordium's work after its closure were the Vegetarian Society and the Order of the Golden Age, both of which aimed to improve health and morals by introducing a lifestyle that was less cruel and more in harmony with the natural world, and to both of which Oldfield would make a significant contribution.

Oldfield joined the Vegetarian Society in the 1860s while he was a theological student at Oxford. The Society had been founded in 1847, primarily to promote vegetarianism on health grounds, but from the beginning it had political and religious overtones. Its membership, which was never more than a few hundred, included ex-members of the Concordium, doctrinally vegetarian Christians such as Cowherdites, and a handful of undergraduates prepared to sign up to a somewhat controversial cause. The Oxford branch served as a kind of club for left-leaning social crusaders, and joining it was a particularly provocative move for a theological student, since ethical vegetarianism seemed to run counter to the conventional Christian wisdom that animals had been placed on earth for the benefit of mankind.[4]

Oldfield's motivation, however, seems to have lain primarily in social concerns: he hoped that vegetarianism would combat poverty and ill health (by encouraging the poor to spend more on vegetables and less on strong drink[5]), and that putting a stop to the cruel slaughter of animals would lead to a more peaceful and humane society. He carried his desire for social improvement into practice after finishing his theological studies, declining to take holy orders as expected and instead pursuing a career first in law and then in medicine, but he also did his best to relieve the sufferings of animals, publishing *A Groaning Creation*, a characteristic blend of logical argument and impassioned rhetoric, followed by *A Tale of Shame and Cruelty*, in which he described the torments to which animals were subjected as they were transported and slaughtered for food, and advocated vegetarianism, 'a natural and humane diet', as the way to avoid it.[6]

Towards the end of the nineteenth century, Oldfield also joined the Order of the Golden Age, a Christian dietary reform movement founded in 1882 with four grades of membership: the lowest required members to believe in the Apostles' Creed, rise early, dress soberly, and be 'humane', while the higher grades required progressive abstinence from meat, fish and alcohol.[7] The Order organized vegetarian banquets and lectures 'for the furtherance of our propaganda',[8] its stated aims being '[t]o proclaim a message of Peace and Happiness, Health and Purity, Life and Power', and '[t]o hasten the coming of the Golden Age when Love and Righteousness shall reign upon earth… by proclaiming obedience to the laws of God'.[9]

Membership was more controversial than it might appear, to the extent that the family of one early member suspected (wrongly, as it turned out) that her link with the Order had been the cause of her being committed to a lunatic asylum.[10] To the uninitiated, vegetarianism seemed an irrational practice, and the Order's mission to live in peace and harmony with the animal kingdom, ridiculous: one newspaper suggested that mad dogs, runaway bulls and tigers should be allowed to join.[11] Those people who did enlist saw themselves as misunderstood pioneers, even revolutionaries, and hoped eventually to convert millions to the 'simpler habits of life', and so transform society by ending food shortages and ushering in a 'Reign of Plenty' that would put an end to war and disease.[12]

As a lawyer, Oldfield accepted that animals had some rights, such as 'the inherent right of the non-human races to be exempted from the infliction of pain...',[13] and he campaigned actively for human rights, founding the Society for the Abolition of Capital Punishment, touring India to study the workings of its legal system, and publishing *Hanging for Murder* (1908) in a bid to get the law on judicial execution changed. It is significant, therefore, that he never called for legislation to protect laboratory animals, presumably because he expected to end vivisection not in the courts, but by bringing about a cultural change that would restore humankind to a more natural and compassionate relationship with the animal world—a cause to which he would devote his life.

The Oriolet Vegetarian Hospital

Having abandoned law for medicine, and while still a medical student, Oldfield set himself up as 'warden' of a pioneering vegetarian hospital that proved popular with patients, though it did not escape the controversy that consistently dogged his endeavours. The Oriolet Hospital, a converted villa with spacious gardens in Loughton on the Eastern outskirts of London, opened in 1895 with an endorsement from the Order of the Golden Age.[14] With the assistance of a visiting medical officer, Oldfield admitted a total of 190 patients in its first year: men, women and children suffering from everything from eczema to varicose veins to paraplegia, all of whom received 'dietetic treatment'. So optimistic was Oldfield that he could also cure carcinoma, sarcoma and epithelioma with a vegan diet that he advertised for patients with these conditions, who were to be admitted for free.[15]

The meat- and alcohol-free diet was apparently well tolerated, as it was never found necessary to vary the rule that no 'fish, flesh, or fowl' was served. What started as the complaints book was soon filled with compliments from patients who showed a suspiciously good grasp of the hospital's purpose: one saw it 'as a proof of what the Vegetarian diet and Hygienic principles properly carried out, will do for suffering humanity', while another hoped that vegetarianism would become 'widely known and recommended… as I am sure it will be by all who have given it a fair trial'. Oldfield's local appeals for his 'pioneer hospital in humane dietetics' attracted gifts of everything from fruit and vegetables to framed Bible verses, but the hospital relied for financial support primarily on its chairman, the shipbuilder Arnold Frank Hills (1857–1927), himself an ardent vegetarian and teetotaller, who kept the it afloat by contributing hundreds of pounds a year.[16]

The medical profession of the time generally disapproved of dietary therapy, and though Oldfield graduated LRCP, MRCS in 1897 and was duly entered in the medical register, he was not welcomed into the fold. According to a critical piece in the BMJ, aimed at the Oriolet, hospitals that relied on 'some special fad or other as to diet…' tended to do well only because they attracted likeminded patients who had faith in the treatments they received there, but they were actually a kind of 'medical sack racing', because patients got better in spite of the restrictions rather than because of them. The British Medical Association (BMA), which published the BMJ, was essentially a trade union, whose defence of its members' interests included opposing 'faddism' wherever they found it: 'Abstinence from animal food is one of these fads, abstinence from alcohol is another. We have not yet heard of a hospital founded on the principle of abstaining from the use of opium…'. They admitted that the results from the Oriolet seemed 'perfectly good', but concluded that '[a]ll these one-legged institutions are tarred with the same brush in this respect, that the patient in choosing his hospital chooses his treatment, which is ethically wrong'.[17]

The same might have been said of any hospital, but vegetarianism troubled the BMA because they thought doctors were recommending it on religious or socio-political grounds rather than medical ones. Whether a regime worked in practice was immaterial if it was chosen for the wrong reasons: what the BMA was opposed to was ideological medicine, insisting that the individual patient's best interests must be addressed disinterestedly in every case. Of course, one could find many examples where mainstream medicine was as ideological as any of the alternatives, but the principle that doctors should not impose their own moral values on patients left vegetarians and anti-vivisectionists vulnerable to accusations that they were pushing their own ethical agenda. The Master of the Rolls (Chief Justice of the Court of Appeal) did, however, dismiss an objection from the profession's leaders that a vegetarian hospital should not operate as a charity because its primary purpose was 'the propagation of a fad' rather than the treatment of the sick, though the courts later came to the opposite conclusion with regard to anti-vivisection charities, with dire consequences for their funding.[18]

The Hospital of St Francis

In March 1897, Oldfield announced a plan to open an anti-vivisection hospital:

> In commemoration of the Queen's Jubilee, the anti-vivisectionists of this country and the Continent have decided to found a hospital on what they call purely humanitarian lines. It is meant to be a protest against 'all forms of cruelty and especially of vivisection'. It is proposed to call it 'The Hospital of St. Francis', in memory of Saint Francis of Assissi [*sic*]. It will be built in the south of London, where the need for a general hospital is very pressing.[19]

Although he was, at the time, a member of the Executive Committee of the Victoria Street Society, and despite the lofty allusion to international anti-vivisectionists, St Francis's was Oldfield's personal initiative. As such, the plan was characteristically both idealistic and shrewd:

a South London Hospital would fly the flag for anti-vivisection at the same time as helping the poor who, in a district desperately short of hospital beds, would gladly accept any treatment offered to them. In such a deprived area, suitable (or, as it turned out, unsuitable) premises could be acquired relatively cheaply, and as St Francis's was the only anti-vivisection hospital in Britain, there would be no alternative for donors who wished to support a hospital while being certain they were not funding vivisection.

Oldfield was a persuasive and determined fundraiser who cast his nets widely. Public feeling against 'vivisecting hospitals' was running high after a pamphlet campaign against them by the leading anti-vivisectionist Stephen Coleridge (1854–1936), and Oldfield appealed to potential donors' religious fervour, exhorting them to '... rise in your millions and pour into the crucible of healing your golden rings...', in order to '... build a fair and beauteous temple of healing'.[20] This was a time when devout ladies were known to give up their jewels to adorn the sacred vessels in Anglo-Catholic churches, and St Francis's, as its name proclaimed, was manifestly a Christian institution, 'an aspiration after the gentleness of the divine' that could 'brook no delay' because those who supported it were 'On the King's [i.e., Jesus Christ's] business'.

Although Oldfield's own faith was idiosyncratic and barely containable even within the very broad limits of Anglicanism, it had every appearance of being heartfelt. He spoke, wrote and even looked—white-bearded, white-suited, and white-coated—like a prophet charged with bringing God's message of compassion to the world. 'No man having the Christ-Spirit within his heart, can see animals ill-treated without a protest!',[21] he thundered, but though he made every oratorical effort to persuade local people to support the hospital out of generosity of spirit, he shrewdly threw in an appeal to self-interest, promising humane treatment, in contrast to the abuses and indifference he cleverly implied awaited any patients of limited means who found themselves in a teaching hospital bed at the mercy of experimentalists:

> Let no demand for 'material' [as teaching hospitals sometimes tactlessly described their patients] ever sully the beauty of [the Hospital's] teaching. Let every patient be looked upon as a casket of priceless worth.... Let no

shadow of inflicted pain upon compulsory victims shut out the sunlight of God's grace… the dying hours shall be sacred, and the body, though the gentle spirit has passed on, shall still be a thing of reverence.

For potential donors, the alternative was stark: money given to the Prince of Wales's Fund (later the King's Fund), the principal charity that distributed money to London's voluntary hospitals, would, according to Oldfield, 'go to strengthen the state that exists and to perpetuate things as they are'.[22]

This did not endear him to the charity fraternity, and as early as 1898, before his hospital had even opened, the Charity Organization Society (COS), a semi-official watchdog, stepped into investigate his fundraising efforts. Their inspector, Charles Carthew, was unimpressed by Oldfield's London office, where his representative, 'a young man got up á la Bohemian', seemed to know little about the proposed hospital, even mixing up anti-vivisection with anti-vaccination (the two were not yet linked, though they would become so).[23] When Carthew finally met Oldfield he came away with the impression, as many others did, that he was 'not altogether straight', though his investigations discovered only that Oldfield was a barrister with chambers in Mitre Court, resident medical officer to the Oriolet Hospital in Loughton, and the author of monographs on 'Tuberculosis' and 'Starch as a food in nature'.[24] The COS concluded he was acting in 'good faith', but advised donors not to support his hospital on the grounds that it was likely to prove of scant public benefit.[25] More candidly, they told Walter Vaughan Morgan (1831–1916), a potential donor who would later become a committee member of the National Anti-Vivisection Hospital (as well as Lord Mayor of London and a baronet), that St Francis's was being set up for Oldfield's 'private purposes', and that he had a bank account jointly in his own name and that of the hospital. This disclosure cost Oldfield Vaughan Morgan's support, and the COS presumably gave similarly discouraging replies to other enquirers.[26]

That the hospital would be of little public benefit was true in so far as it had too few beds to make an appreciable difference to the sick of South London, but Oldfield intended it primarily as propaganda for the anti-vivisection cause, and even a small but flourishing hospital would have sufficed to show that cruelty-free medicine was a viable prospect. Regrettably, the official opening of the hospital, in April 1898, went almost unnoticed, and when the COS inspector arrived unannounced shortly afterwards, he found there were no patients.[27] Oldfield was still busy seeking sponsors, having already persuaded Stephen Coleridge to become the hospital's chairman, and having recruited an impressive number of vice-presidents, including the Duke of Beaufort, Lords Llangattock (1837–1912) and Harberton, and the Dowager Countess of Portsmouth (1834–1906).

The number and quality of the hospital's patrons, most of whom probably never even visited it, was conspicuously disproportionate to its facilities: after it had been open for two years there were still only eleven beds, amply served by three medical officers in addition to Oldfield, and overseen by a matron.[28] The medical officers were obliged to forswear vivisection but the converted town house in which the hospital was located—an unimposing, narrow, redbrick building next door to a bicycle factory—possessed no laboratories; the purpose of the pledge was to demonstrate their humane principles.[29] There was barely enough money to keep the tiny anti-vivisection hospital open, but it could claim the distinction of being Britain's first.

Unfortunately, the haste with which St Francis's was set up probably did its cause more harm than good. The wards were cramped and shabby, a failing not lost on its critics, foremost among whom was the financier and doyen of the voluntary hospital system, Sir Henry Burdett (1847–1920), who published a damning report in his journal, *The Hospital*, which described St Francis's as a 'wretched, grubby little house' with fittings of a 'poverty-stricken character'. It was obvious to him that this 'curious excrescence on London charity' was run 'not for the benefit of the patients' but so that 'the possibility of treating disease on a non-meaty diet might be demonstrated'.[30] Burdett seems to have confused it with the Oriolet, an understandable mistake since Oldfield was best known as a vegetarian, a rare thing for a doctor at the time, though the staff of St Francis's were, as Burdett himself noted, permitted to order meat if their patients wanted it. It is difficult to dissent from Burdett's judgement that: '… the prospects of the institution have been sacrificed to the ambition of those in power on its council to be able to say that there is at least one hospital in London which definitely excludes vivisection', but it is telling that, although only dedicated anti-vivisectionists would have been likely to give to St Francis's, Burdett, London's greatest hospital fundraiser, was concerned about the precedent that might be set by diverting even this tiny amount of charity from the many hospitals that came under his financial control.

Burdett's attack on a hospital with fewer than a dozen beds was as disproportionate as the support the hospital attracted: its ten vice-presidents and thirteen patronesses lent their aristocratic names rather than their money, but their social cachet helped draw attention to Oldfield's project. If donations from philanthropists opposed to vivisection could fully support this one, independent, cruelty-free hospital, then there might be scope for more, and the voluntary hospitals would begin to find themselves poorer. The signs were worrisome for the orthodox: the vicar of St John's church in Westminster, a supporter of the anti-vivisection cause, held his usual collection for the Hospital Sunday Fund, which went to London's voluntary hospitals, followed by a separate collection just for the Hospital of St Francis, which raised over five times as much.[31] The OGA's periodical, *The Herald of the Golden Age*, probably the most widely circulated vegetarian magazine in the English-speaking world, urged its readers to 'let your church collection plate pass by if you are doubtful whether they are sound on vivisection'.[32] It did not matter that most hospitals that received money from the Sunday Fund did not experiment on animals and had no facilities to do so, in the eyes of the scrupulous they were all tarred with the same brush.

Oldfield sent out begging letters to everyone from Dukes to Aldermen, some of whom passed them on to the COS, whose inspector concluded that 'On the whole I do not think there is anything very definite that can be said against Dr Oldfield.... He is a qualified Doctor and the mere fact that he is a rabid vegetarian is not in itself to his discredit', thought the COS did its best to discourage donors, advising them to '...leave Dr Oldfield and all his works entirely alone'. Between them, Burdett and the COS succeeded in stifling Oldfield's struggling venture; in 1904 he announced a last-ditch plan to relocate the hospital to Camberwell Green, but the £2000 needed for the move was not forthcoming and it closed, the remaining funds being transferred to the newly opened National Anti-Vivisection Hospital in Battersea.[33] According to a press report, St Francis's had treated over 100,000 out-patients and 428 in-patients in just under six years.[34]

Back to Nature

Oldfield next turned his attentions to creating a hospital in the country where patients could receive dietary treatment in healthy natural surroundings. The Lady Margaret Hospital in Kent offered fresh air and 'dainty fruitarian meals', but the more esoteric aspects of its programme began to arouse suspicions.[35] Oldfield's links with the Order of the Golden Age were well known, and an anonymous correspondent, perhaps confusing it with the esoteric Order of the Golden Dawn, told the COS that Oldfield had connections with Swami Laura and Theodore Horos, a husband and wife team of serial fraudsters whose Theocratic Unity Temple had been the subject of a financial and sexual scandal two years earlier.[36] In search of evidence, the COS approached the Medical Defence Union, a mutual insurance society for medical practitioners, of which Oldfield does not seem to have been a member. Nevertheless, their representative, Dr Bateman, had apparently heard of him by reputation and was more than happy to pass on a torrent of gossip: Oldfield was married but his wife refused to live with him because he was a 'crank' and a 'sexual pervert [in this context, a womaniser]', and in Kent he had 'got hold of a lot of silly, foolish women and could do just what he liked with them'. For good measure, Bateman told the COS: 'You can't trust a fellow who lives on nuts … it only makes them more and more earthly'.[37]

By this time, Oldfield had antagonised the medical profession not only by using a meat-free diet as therapy and campaigning against vivisection, but also by flouting professional and social standards. The *Lancet* complained that he arranged for favourable news stories about himself to appear in popular newspapers such as the *Daily Mirror* and *Penny Magazine* in order to publicise his hospitals, which was almost, but not quite, the cardinal medical sin of self-advertising.[38] It appears, however, that Oldfield, as one might expect of a barrister, was adept at sailing close to the wind. That he was never reported to the General Medical Council (GMC), still less investigated by them, despite his unpopularity with some sections of the profession and their paymasters, who were presumably watching hawk-like for him to slip up, surely indicates that there was no substance to the rumours of misconduct. As the GMC would not have ignored complaints from Oldfield's patients, it can be confidently stated that they made none.

Lady Margaret's was scarcely a hospital in the medical sense at all, since its regime relied mostly on healthy living rather than therapeutics. Though it retained a link to the more conventional Margaret dispensary in London, by 1908, the 400-acre site was known as Margaret Lodge Colony, and its proprietor not as 'Dr Oldfield' but 'Mr Warden'. A representative from the COS found 'bareness, cleanliness & want of comfort'. Though there was a farm that kept residents supplied with fresh milk, butter and eggs, the spartan, meatless regime came as a surprise to some new residents: one described the communal accommodation as a 'cowshed' (it was actually a former oast house), and another found the food 'very nasty'.[39] Children brought from the London slums to spend a summer helping on the farm left with their health apparently improved by clean air and fresh food, though it did not always appear so, since after roaming freely in the fields and woods for months they arrived home more ragged than ever.[40]

Heralding the Golden Age

Oldfield's work in promoting vegetarianism, anti-vivisection, and health reform was all part of his commitment to bringing in a golden age, to which all these other causes contributed. Vegetarianism and anti-vivisection in particular were close allies: when, in 1880, the anti-vivisection campaigner Anna Kingsford (1846–1888) submitted her thesis for a Paris medical degree (which she had scrupulously completed without recourse to vivisection), she chose to write it on vegetarianism, a less inflammatory choice than anti-vivisection, though still sufficiently controversial for her to be refused the customary public defence of her work. As Vyvyan observed, Kingsford probably intended her anti-vivisection message to be read between the lines of her argument for vegetarianism, since the objections to vivisection and meat-eating (cruel, brutalising, spiritually coarsening) were essentially the same.[41] When it came to fundraising, anti-vivisectionists and vegetarians often worked together: the committee appointed by the VSS to raise funds for an anti-vivisection hospital included the President of the Vegetarian Society, Ernest Bell (1851–1933).

According to one disgruntled Medical Officer of Health, writing in 1902, there was a distinctive personality type, which he called 'the anti', that was common to, among others, anti-vivisectionists, vegetarians, teetotallers and advocates of artificial contraception: '[he] is frequently a nonconformist in religion, usually a supporter of the Opposition in politics, and his chief recreations are crusading and the smashing of idols'.[42] The 'anti' was not confined to a particular social group—he, or she, was as likely to be found among the aristocracy as the working classes—but most were radicals in the true sense of the word, that is to say, they believed that human priorities needed to be re-evaluated and reformed from the ground up. The 'antis' included socialists, feminists, pacifists, and others disenchanted with a culture of industrialisation, urbanisation, and capitalism, whose calls for a return to a more natural way of living—the inspiration for the twentieth century back-to-nature movement—included a boycott of vivisection and meat-eating, not merely because these things were harmful to animals, but because a society preoccupied with the flesh—whether consuming it for food or vivisecting it in search of answers—was thought unlikely to grow spiritually, which the reformers thought an essential prerequisite for the desired social transformation.

It was to this end that the Order of the Golden Age was 'reconstituted' in 1904 under the presidency of Sidney Hartnoll Beard (1862–1938), with Oldfield on its six-strong General Council.[43] Beard saw the fight for more humane treatment of animals both as part of the new age programme and his Christian duty: 'the supremacy of Love and Gentleness, Spirituality and Mercy' proclaimed by Jesus ought to be extended, he argued, to 'sub-human' creatures, who were to be treated with 'beneficence'.[44] Oldfield agreed, writing that Christians should eschew all forms of killing, including butchering animals to celebrate

Christmas.[45] Ending the ill-treatment of animals in the farm, the slaughterhouse, and the laboratory was a precondition for realizing the Golden Age because cruelty, killing, and carnivorism were inherently unspiritual:

> Is it any wonder that our spirituality is at such a low ebb; that we are floundering in a slough of materialistic agnosticism and nescience; that we are in bondage to disease and the fear of death; that the barrier which separates us from the spiritual world is an opaque wall rather than a transparent veil; that the angels and ministering spirits of the higher spheres, either cannot, or will not, commune with such a carnal race of beings; that genuine spiritual experience and conscious realization of the Divine Presence and Influence, are so rare amongst us that such things are scarcely ever mentioned in our Churches ...[46]

The *Herald of the Golden Age* tried to mobilise opposition to medical vivisection, publishing a condemnation by the surgeon Robert Howell Perks (1855–1929), who wrote that it should be 'regarded as a criminal offense upon Earth—as it already is in Heaven', and an editorial which said that the reported 'indifference' and 'laughter' of students at University College was proof that vivisection demonstrations led to 'hardening of heart and searing of sensitive feeling'.[47] Its suggestion for stemming animal experiments was 'closer inquisition into the [disposition of the] hospital funds'.[48]

The OGA's opposition to vivisection alone would have been enough to earn it the disapprobation of the medical profession, had they not already been hostile to its vegetarianism. To members of the OGA, it was necessary, in order to reach the higher spiritual levels, to abjure the flesh-eating habits of wild animals and primitive men.[49] The orthodox medical view, however, was that meat eating was essential to sustain physical health, and that vegetarianism was a dangerous trend. In 1853, the *Lancet* had reported the 'recovery' of a vegetarian opium-eater ('a little, withered creature') after the restoration of an animal diet.[50] Over 50 years later, that journal still considered vegetarianism incompatible with vigorous health, suggesting in an editorial that its prevalence among 'oriental' peoples, a point often positively adverted to by its supporters, might explain 'the marked superiority of the European', and the fact that 'men have often to be employed in India for work that women will do in England…'.[51]

Vegetarianism was condemned as un-British, un-Christian, and disloyal to one's fellow humans, for placing their interests and those of animals on almost the same level. The OGA declared itself 'above all things a society of Christians', but rather than claiming the traditional 'dominion' over animals, took its inspiration from the Old Testament prophecy of a 'Messianic Age' (the 'peaceable kingdom') in which all creatures would live in harmony and killing for food would cease. The Golden Age would be achieved when this perfect state of living, the desire for which remained latent in the human psyche,[52] was finally restored:

> The wolf also shall dwell with the lamb, and the leopard shall lie down with the kid; and the calf and the young lion and the fatling together; and a little child shall lead them. And the cow and the bear shall feed; their young ones shall lie down together: and the lion shall eat straw like the ox. And the sucking child shall play on the hole of the asp, and the weaned child shall put his hand on the cockatrice' den. They shall not hurt nor destroy in all my holy mountain: for the earth shall be full of the knowledge of the Lord, as the waters cover the sea.[53]

This divinely-mandated state could only be relaized after an extensive programme of social reform had swept away vivisection, meat-eating and human conflict. At present, the labourers were few, but the work was God's will; as Oldfield wrote in a flyer for his anti-vivisection hospital: 'The whole creation is groaning and travailing in anguish, and praying to be delivered from the body of death…. Now is the epoch moment to stamp the coming century for Humanity'.[54]

Harmony with Nature

In common with the wider new age movement of the late-nineteenth and early-twentieth century, the OGA's goal was to restore the pre-eminence of the spiritual in all aspects of life. With regard to science, this meant not protesting against it but working towards a closer union between scientific and spiritual thought. Medical science in particular, they felt, had become too wedded to materialism; its practitioners might follow a personal religion, but their faith and their experiments occupied different worlds; they were, to borrow a modern phrase, 'non-overlapping magisteria'. There was a crucial distinction to be made between 'so-called' science, practised mostly in the laboratory and constrained within narrow parameters, and 'true science', which understood the world holistically by combining observation and experiment, faith and feeling.[55]

Darwin's theory of species change, for example, had helped many people to understand what transcendentalists and others claimed to have known intuitively: that 'all life is *one*'. This principle was central to the OGA's mission, and one way for its Christian membership to affirm it without compromising their status as adoptive children of God was to reconceptualize non-human animals as 'living souls' with their own hopes, joys and sorrows, 'similar to our own', and a similar capacity for virtue: according to one contributor to the *Herald*, a dog that licked the hand of a vivisector was as good a moral exemplar as any of the 'imaginary saints'.[56]

The reformers' call for faith and sentiment to guide science in all its aspects, including medicine, was of course ignored by most experimentalists, who preferred to keep external interference to a minimum. According to Oldfield, however, medical scientists already allowed their beliefs to influence their work, though without admitting it: 'it is absolutely unscientific', he wrote, 'to talk about the necessity of sacrificing a thousand dogs or guinea-pigs if need be to save one human life, because we do not know the comparative values about which we are pretending to dogmatize'. Vivisectionists, he claimed, assumed a priori that animals' lives had a lower value than human ones, but had no scientific justification for their position; it could be challenged, and Oldfield did so: 'I have seen a semi-human dog and I have seen a semi-reptilic imbecile man, and ... I should have estimated the life of that so-called dog to be of more value than the life of that so-called man'. A few pages later, he spelled it out even more bluntly: 'Some non-humans may be of more value than some humans...'. His characteristically immodest but ingenious argument was that, as the value of animals' lives could only be judged intuitively and not scientifically, those best able to do so were those, like himself, who had attained a 'higher' awareness of nature:

> The higher science … is always reverent in the presence of the mystery of life…. The higher the man the more nearly he approaches to those heights of scientia and gnosis, which are the crowning stamp of the true scientist, the more reverence he has for his fellow traveller – a true brother in the eyes of science – on the same spiral pathway of vitality, towards a perfection of evolution.[57]

The key question was how to acquire this profound understanding: the Golden Age was gnostic in the sense that the deeper knowledge that Oldfield and others laid claim to could not be grasped by all, at least not in the current state of the world, but was achievable only after long study and reflexion, and with the benefit of spiritual insight. One way to obtain the latter was to study other spiritual and religious traditions, and in practice the OGA's theology tended towards syncretism, with some of its members anticipating that the future would see the establishment of a 'world religion'.[58] These theological developments had possible benefits for animals: it was suggested that the failure of Christians to recognise that animals had souls that survived death placed them 'on a lower spiritual plane' than Buddhists, and that by making a leap of faith and accepting the possibility of human and animal reincarnation, Christians could begin to strive for a better life for all creatures on Earth, rather than selfishly working towards their own salvation.[59]

The influence of Eastern philosophy and religion was also mediated through theosophy, which was closely linked with anti-vivisection. The Theosophical Society and the Victoria Street Society were founded in the same year, and had common purposes and supporters to the extent that, according to Vyvyan, they were practically sister movements. The anti-vivisection and vegetarian doctor Anna Kingsford was instrumental in converting the prominent theosophist Annie Besant to the humane movement, and in turn was herself converted to theosophy, becoming president of the Theosophical Society's London branch in 1883, and launching a psychic war against the vivisectionists Paul Bert (1833–86), Claude Bernard and Louis Pasteur, a campaign in which she claimed some success.[60]

Many other prominent vegetarians were active theosophists, including the Vegetarian Society's London secretary (and ex Concordium member), George Dornbusch (1819–1873); Constance Wachtmeister (1838–1910, a close friend of Blavatsky), and the homoeopath Dr Leopold Salzer (d. 1907), author of *The Psychic Aspect of Vegetarianism*.[61] Vyvyan quotes Kingsford's 1883 speech welcoming the author and theosophist A.P. Sinnett from India: 'Some of us have dreamed that our English Branch of the Theosophical Society is destined to become the ford across the stream which so long has separated the East from the West, religion from science, heart from mind, and love from learning…'.[62] The same objectives were shared by the Order of the Golden Age and the anti-vivisection movement.

Theosophical, vegetarian and anti-vivisection societies tended, like the OGA, to attract people who had become disenchanted with materialism and scientific 'progress'—it is difficult to imagine them flourishing in pre-industrial Britain—but they were more than just refuges for intellectual refuseniks who yearned for a bucolic utopia that had never existed. They preached a gospel of peace, compassion and spiritual awareness that they hoped would make the new century the beginning of a new age, an age inspired by the Old Testament prophecy of the Messianic Kingdom, and foretold by astrologers as the Age of Aquarius, which was the 'Sign of the Son of Man'.[63] In the years leading up to the Great War, it seemed that the OGA's conciliatory and harmonious ideals might prevail: minor royals, members of the nobility and senior army officers all attended its fundraising concerts, which had a pastoral theme, and enjoyed music and readings extolling the glories of creation, even if they were not sufficiently moved by them to give up meat eating.[64] An unlikely late enthusiast for the Order's objectives of combating 'physical deterioration, disease, and intemperance' was Edward VII, who sent them a message of support as he lay dying in Buckingham Palace.[65]

New Age Politics

Vegetarianism and anti-vivisection did not, of course, fulfil their promise to convert humanity to a more peaceful way of life. The Golden Age never dawned, and the dreams of a peaceable kingdom were shattered by the Great War. Materialism and patriotism became the default positions, and advocates of holistic science, natural living, and international peace were relegated to a marginal counterculture along with dress reformers, naturists, homoeopaths, occultists and sexual liberators, most of whom were linked in the public mind with the politics of Liberalism, Socialism, or even Anarchism, and were thought of at best as eccentrics, and at worst as traitors to their country.[66] According to the *Lancet*, the typical vegetarian was a seditious malcontent who '…cultivates a number of what may be called anti-isms. He is anti-alcoholist, anti-vivisectionist, anti-vaccinationist, anti-capitalist, anti-bellumist, anti-patriotist. He is anti-penalist, and … anti-restraintist, and would abolish all lunatic asylums, rightly from his own point of view, for so he would escape the risk of losing his own liberty'.[67] This was 1916, and a psychiatrist was publicly stating in a leading medical journal that vegetarians and anti-vivisectionists were lunatics who deserved to be locked up.

During the Great War, Oldfield (a pacifist, of course) temporarily abandoned his hospitals to command a casualty clearing station, a service for which he was promoted Lieutenant Colonel and mentioned in dispatches.[68] He was said never to have had a day's illness, but was invalided out of the army in 1918 after being thrown from his horse.[69] He then purchased Margaret Manor near Sittingbourne, which he set up as a fruitarian colony with cottages for adults and communal accommodation for children. According to the advertising, girls were taught fruitarian cookery, and boys, farming, but the children sent there from the slums were left largely unsupervised to roam, and sometimes get lost, in the surrounding countryside.[70] There was little use of medicines: 'epileptics' and 'mental cases' were the commonest types of patients treated there, and those with infectious diseases were banned. Oldfield did, however, take up obstetrics with some success, and acquired an orchard by the characteristically shrewd strategy of inviting all new parents to pay for the planting of a commemorative tree.[71] On Sundays, he would attend divine service in the Manor's private chapel, where Sister Francesca, the mother of his illegitimate daughter, played the organ.[72] In the three years from 1920, Margaret Manor received just £190 in subscriptions, most of which were spent on postage stamps for further charity appeals, but it now had enough long-term residents, who paid up to three guineas a week, to enable Oldfield to close his other establishments and concentrate on running the Manor as a new age retreat.[73]

The OGA attracted fewer members after the First World War, and survived on legacies as ageing spiritualists and animal-loving widows died off—in 1927, for example, Edith Annie Douglas-Hamilton (1871–1927) left £25,000 to the Theosophical Society, £10,000 to anti-vivisection and £5000 to the OGA.[74] By this time, Margaret Manor was far from being the only option for people who wished to pursue a more natural lifestyle. Popular outdoor organizations such as the Scout Movement, the Order of Woodcraft Chivalry, and the Kibbo Kift (archaic Cheshire dialect for 'proof of great strength') all encouraged their members to spend time living in, learning about, and respecting nature. Though this fondness for outdoor pursuits, folkloric traditions and clean living seemed (and sometimes was) the epitome of pastoral innocence, it was not a great step from respecting nature to worshipping it (the rituals of Woodcraft Chivalry and Kibbo Kift influenced those of modern Wicca), or from escaping from capitalist society to rebelling against it.

In 1932, the Kibbo Kift allied itself with the Social Credit movement, a scheme for redistributing wealth, whose founder Major C.H. Douglas (1879–1952) blamed Britain's economic problems on 'international Jewry' and hoped to solve them by paying the British poor for not working. The result was the Green Shirt Movement for Social Credit, an anti-capitalist, anti-government and anti-Semitic group whose aggressive greenness fortunately went no further than minor acts of civil disobedience such as throwing green-painted bricks through government windows.[75] Had things gone their way, they might have started a radical back-to-nature movement in Britain, but no right wing, or green, party ever came close to power. The only European regime officially to endorse natural living, promote spiritual harmony with nature, and ban vivisection, was National Socialist Germany.[76]

For British fascists, hoping to bring in an age of national prosperity by breaking the power of 'international financiers' (for which, read 'Jews'), a 'natural' mode of living was that which corresponded to their own ideology. Even their promise that a natural lifestyle would improve physical and mental health had a dark side, which was that a multitude of problems afflicting the British people, from cancer to criminality, and idiocy to unemployment, could be blamed on malign, and implicitly unnatural, influences such as meat eating, alcohol drinking, and moral and physical degeneracy.[77] In his old age, Oldfield became increasingly concerned that fresh air and cruelty-free living would not be enough to reverse the problem of human degeneration, which could only be confronted by enforcing standards of racial health and purity. In 1944, he wrote in *Healing and the Conquest of Pain,* that '…the crossing of a negro with a white woman is fraught with many curious genetic problems…', and advocated euthanasia for 'idiots'.[78]

While interest in back-to-nature living on the part of British fascists temporarily boosted recruitment, and legacies, to the OGA (one Herbert Jones of Liverpool divided his estate between, among others, the OGA, the RSPCA, the Vegetarian Society, the Malthusian League, and the British Fascisti), it went into terminal decline following the death of Beard in 1938. In Britain on the eve of war, the Order's fascist links were a humiliating liability, and it decamped to South Africa, where it survived until 1959.[79] The continuation of the humane movement in the post-war period will be the subject of chapter seven, but we will first consider the successor to Oldfield's anti-vivisection hospital, and the medical profession's response to it.

Notes

1. J. Howard Moore, 'Universal kinship', *Herald of the Golden Age, 11* (1906), 38–42 (Moore 1906).
2. *Vegetarian Advocate*, March 1850, cited in Kathryn Gleadle, '"The age of physiological reformers:" rethinking gender and domesticity in the

age of reform', in Arthur Burns and Joanna Innes (eds) *Rethinking the Age of Reform: Britain 1780–1850* (Cambridge: Cambridge University Press, 2003), 213. Vegetarianism based on Hinduism had been promoted in print as long ago as 1791, in John Oswald's *The Cry of Nature.* Some early vegetarians eschewed all animal products and others, 'fruitarians', avoided killing living things (Gleadle 2003).

3. Henry Stephens Salt, *Animals' Rights Considered in Relation to Social Progress* (New York, Macmillan, 1894), 8 (Salt 1894).
4. Stuart, *Bloodless Revolution*, 422–423. In 1850, 16 of 478 Vegetarian Society members were medics: Julia Twigg, *The Vegetarian Movement in England: 1847–1981: A Study in the Structure of its Ideology.* PhD, London School of Economics (1981), 87 (Twigg 1981).
5. Dellar, *Josiah Oldfield*, 19.
6. Josiah Oldfield. *A Groaning Creation* (London: Ideal Publishing Union, n.d.); *A Tale of Shame and Cruelty* (Paignton: Order of the Golden Age, n.d.) (Oldfield n.d.; A Tale of Shame and Cruelty n.d.).
7. 'A new guild', *Dundee Courier*, 27 July 1882, 3 (A New Guild 1882).
8. 'Vegetarian banquet', *Bristol Mercury*, 30 March 1883, 6; editorial, *Herald of the Golden Age, 12* (1908), 12 (Vegetarian Banquet 1883).
9. *Herald of the Golden Age, 10* (1903), inside front cover.
10. 'General News', *Derby Daily Telegraph*, 27 January 1883, 4 (General News 1883).
11. Editorial, *Aberdeen Evening Express*, 17 November 1883, 2 (Editorial 1883).
12. Josef Francis Charles Craven, *Redskins in Epping Forest: John Hargrave, the Kibbo Kift and the woodcraft experience.* PhD, University College London (1998), 13; *The Order of the Golden Age* [flyer], n.p., [1904], 2, http://www.ordergoldenage.co.uk/page34.html, viewed 20 June 2016 (Craven 1998).
13. Josiah Oldfield, *The Claims of Common Life, or, The Scientific Relations of Humans and non-Humans* (London: Ideal Publishing Union, 1898), 17 (Oldfield 1898).
14. 'A vegetarian hospital', *Herald of the Golden Age, 1* (1896), 150 (A Vegetarian Hospital 1896).
15. The Order of the Golden Age taught that cancer was curable by a vegan diet: 'A dietetic cure of cancer' (editorial), *Herald of the Golden Age, 8* (1903), 114 (A Dietetic Cure of Cancer 1903).
16. Oriolet Hospital, *Annual Report* (1896), 9–11.
17. 'A medical sack race', *BMJ, 2* (1897), 1115–1116.
18. 'Ireland', *Times*, 29 January 1898, 12 (Ireland 1898).

19. London Metropolitan Archives (hereinafter LMA) A/FWA/C/D330/1; *Morning Star*, 23 March 1897.
20. Flyer appealing for 'Hospital of St. Francis', April 1897, LMA A/FWA/C/D330/1.
21. *A Tale of Shame*, back cover.
22. 'Hospital of St. Francis', LMA A/FWA/C/D330/1. Anti-vivisectionists made much of the supposed link between vivisection and experiments on the poor: see, for example, Mark Thornhill, *Experiments on Hospital Patients* (London: Hatchards, 1889) (Thornhill 1889).
23. Statement by Charles Carthew, 21 February 1898, LMA A/FWA/C/D330/1.
24. Oldfield was born at Ryton, Shropshire, on 28 February 1863 and graduated BA in theology in 1885. He then trained as a barrister at Lincoln's Inn and practised on the Oxford circuit. For a fascinating history of his life, see Rosemary Dellar, *Josiah Oldfield: Eminent Fruitarian* (Raynham: Rainmore Books, 2008) (Dellar 2008).
25. Letter, COS to Rev'd A.G. Deedes, 20 May 1898, LMA A/FWA/C/D330/1.
26. Letter, W. Vaughan Morgan to COS, 8 December 1898, LMA A/FWA/C/D330/1.
27. COS report, 25 April 1898, LMA A/FWA/C/D330/1.
28. *Medical Directory* (1900), 459.
29. Dellar, *Josiah Oldfield*, 97 (2008) (Dellar 2008).
30. 'The institutional workshop: the Hospital of St Francis', *The Hospital*, *32* (1902), 296–7.
31. 'Hospital Sunday Fund', *Times*, 17 June 1902, 8 (Hospital Sunday Fund 1902).
32. Dellar, *Josiah Oldfield*, 96.
33. COS memorandum, 7 April 1904, LMA A/FWA/C/D330/1.
34. Flyer for Lady Margaret Hospital, reprinted in *South London Press*, 29 August 1904, LMA A/FWA/C/D330/1 (Flyer for Lady Margaret Hospital 1904).
35. 'Lady Margaret Hospital', *Herald of the Golden Age*, *12* (1908), 14; 'The Fruitarian Hospital', *Herald of the Golden Age*, *11* (1906), 35 (Lady Margaret Hospital 1908; The Fruitarian Hospital 1906).
36. 'Brother pain and his crown' (editorial), *Herald of the Golden Age*, *11* (1906), 14; Anon., letter to COS, n.d., LMA A/FWA/C/D330/1 (Brother Pain and His Crown 1906).

37. Note by Hugh Fickling, 25 April 1910, LMA A/FWA/C/D330/1.
38. Anon., 'The Lady Margaret Hospital, Bromley', *Lancet, 1* (1906), 1088. He was equally controversial in promoting his legal practice: Dellar, *Josiah Oldfield*, 55–56 (Anon 1906).
39. Letter, M. Michael to E.S. Kemp, 13 August 1913; COS notes on Margaret Manor, LMA A/FWA/C/D330/1.
40. COS notes, 22 April 1908, LMA A/FWA/C/D330/1.
41. Vyvyan, *In Pity*, 133–4 (Vyvyan 1969).
42. Killick Millard, 'The rôle of the "anti": an apology and an appeal', *Public Health, 15* (1902), 212–222 (Millard 1902).
43. Anon., *The Order of the Golden Age: Its Aims, Its Objects and Its Rules* (n.p., 1904), 1 (Anon 1904).
44. Sidney H. Beard, 'The festival of the Christians', *Herald of the Golden Age, 8* (1903), 133–134 (Beard 1903).
45. Josiah Oldfield, 'The Christmas feast: an indictment', *Evening News*, 11 December 1912 (Oldfield 1912).
46. Beard, 'The festival of the Christians'. The moral opposition of flesh and spirit was influenced by Pauline theology, e.g., Romans 8.
47. Robert H. Perks, *Why I Condemn Vivisection* (Paignton: OGA, 1992) (Perks 1992).
48. 'The vivisection libel suit', *Herald of the Golden Age, 8* (1903), 190: 'funds' refers to state-controled charities such as the King's Fund (The Vivisection Libel Suit 1903).
49. *Herald of the Golden Age*, *passim*, inside back cover.
50. S.L. Gill, 'Case of an opium-eater and vegetarian becoming bedridden: recovery on taking animal food', *Lancet, 2* (1853), 95 (Gill 1853).
51. 'Vegetarianism and physique' (editorial), *Lancet, 2* (1908), 1537.
52. Craven, *Redskins in Epping Forest*, 113 (1998) (Craven 1998).
53. Isaiah 11: 6–9.
54. Flyer for Hospital of St Francis, 1897, LMA A/FWA/C/D330/1.
55. Josiah Oldfield, *Claims of Common Life*, 7–13.
56. 'From "Realization"', *Herald of the Golden Age, 8* (1903), 119; Moore, 'Universal kinship'.
57. Oldfield, *Claims of Common Life*, 49, 51, 54, 70–72.
58. Edward E. Lond, 'A world religion', *Herald of the Golden Age, 11* (1906), 20–221. Ecumenism had received a boost from the 1893 *World's Parliament of Religions* in Chicago (Lond 1906).

59. Kate Cording, 'A talk with the children', *Herald of the Golden Age, 8* (1903), 137; *The Order of the Golden Age*, 3; Sidney H. Beard, 'Our national peril', *Herald of the Golden Age, 10* (1903), 108–111 (Cording 1903; Beard 1903).
60. She wrote, 'I have killed Paul Bert, as I killed Claude Bernard; as I will kill Louis Pasteur, and after him the whole tribe of vivisectors … it is a magnificent power to have, and one that transcends all vulgar methods of dealing out justice to tyrants': Alan Pert, *Red Cactus: the Life of Anna Kingsford* (Watsons Bay New South Wales: Books and Writers, 2007), 200 (Pert 2007).
61. James R.T.E. Gregory, '"A Lutheranism of the table": religion and the Victorian vegetarians', in Rachel Muers and David Grumett (eds), *Eating and Believing: Interdisciplinary Perspectives on Vegetarianism and Theology* (London: T. and T. Clark, 2008), 135–151 (Gregory 2008).
62. Vyvyan, *In Pity*, 140, 145.
63. Nina A. Hutteman Hume, 'The higher aspects of the simple life', *Herald of the Golden Age, 12* (1908), 6–9; Sidney H. Beard, 'The prevention of pain', *Herald of the Golden Age, 12* (1908), 1–3 (Hume 1908; Beard 1908).
64. 'Order of the Golden Age', *Times*, 1 November 1910, 16 (Order of the Golden Age 1910).
65. 'Court Circular', *Times*, 5 May 1910, 13. A formal expression of support from the sovereign did not necessarily indicate personal interest, but it is significant that the OGA was deemed worthy of royal endorsement (Court Circular 1910).
66. Craven, *Redskins in Epping Forest*, 43–44 (1998) (Craven 1998).
67. Chas. Mercier, 'Diet as a factor in the causation of mental disease', *Lancet, 1* (1916), 565 (Mercier 1916).
68. Virginia Smith, 'Oldfield, Josiah (1863–1953)', *Oxford Dictionary of National Biography* (Oxford: Oxford University Press, 2004), http://www.oxforddnb.com/view/article/40999, viewed 20 June 2016 (Smith 2004).
69. 'Ashford', *Whitstable Times and Herne Bay Herald*, 25 May 1918, 6 (Ashford 1918).
70. M.J. Ferrers to the COS, 19 November 1919, LMA FWA/C/D330/1.
71. *Truth*, 26 May 1926, cutting in LMA FWA/C/D330/1.
72. COS report, September 1913, LMA A/FWA/C/D330/1.

73. 'An obnoxious nursing home' (editorial), *Truth*, 30 December 1925, 1221–1222. One resident was the editor of the Journal of the League for the Abolition of Cruel Sports, Henry Brown Amos (1869–1946) (An Obnoxious Nursing Home 1925).
74. 'Woman millionaire's bequests', *Fife Free Press*, 15 October 1927, 9 (Woman Millionaire's Bequests 1927).
75. According to the Greenshirt newsletter, *Attack!*, published in the early 1930s, they aimed to break the power of 'a handful of power-mad money lenders': 'We attack the bankers!', *Attack!*, *9* (1933), 1.
76. On the links between environmentalism and Nazism, see Anna Bamwell, *Blood and Soil: Richard Walter Darre and Hitler's 'Green Party'* (Buckinghamshire: Kensall Press, 1985); *Ecology in the 20th Century: A History* (New Haven: Yale University Press, 1989) and *The Fading of the Greens* (New Haven: Yale University Press, 1994) (Bamwell 1985, 1989, 1994).
77. Alex Haag, 'The true cause of physical degeneracy', *Herald of the Golden Age*, *11* (1906), 73 (Haag 1906).
78. Dellar, *Josiah Oldfield*, 299–300. Oldfield continued to be active until well over the age of eighty. Though he unfortunately fell out of a rocking chair and broke his leg during a trip to the West Indies, he did not lose a chance to promote vegetarianism, telling the press that 'Since all of nature's common diseases to kill people off are powerless against fruitarianists, she takes a mean advantage of fruitarian veterans by increasing the fragility of old people's bones, so that even a fruitarian runs a danger of a broken bone if he frolics on polished staircases or marble floors or goes mountain climbing', and giving his age as 97: 'Nature's "mean trick" on oldest doctor', *Hull Daily Mail*, 11 March 1950, 5.
79. 'Deaths', *Times*, 21 October 1938, 1; Wills and bequests', *Times*, 28 January 1937, 10 (Deaths 1938; Wills and bequests 1937).

References

A Dietetic Cure of Cancer (Editorial). (1903). *Herald of the Golden Age*, 8, 114.

A New Guild. (1882, July 27). *Dundee Courier*, 3.

A Vegetarian Hospital. (1896). *Herald of the Golden Age*, 1, 150.

An Obnoxious Nursing Home (Editorial). (1925, December 30). *Truth,* 1221–1222.
Anon. (1904). *The Order of the Golden Age: Its Aims, Its Objects and Its Rules* (n. p.), 1.
Anon. (1906). The lady Margaret hospital Bromley. *Lancet, 1,* 1088.
Ashford. (1918, May). *Whitstable Times and Herne Bay Herald, 25,* 6.
Bamwell, A. (1985). *Blood and soil: Richard walter darre and Hitler's 'green party".* Buckinghamshire: Kensall Press.
Bamwell, A. (1989). *Ecology in the twentieth century: A history.* New Haven: Yale University Press.
Bamwell, A. (1994). *The fading of the greens.* New Haven: Yale University Press.
Beard, S. H. (1903a). The festival of the Christians. *Herald of the Golden Age, 8,* 133–134.
Beard, S. H. (1903b). Our national peril. *Herald of the Golden Age, 10,* 108–111.
Beard, S. H. (1908). The prevention of pain. *Herald of the Golden Age, 12,* 1–3.
Brother Pain and His Crown. (Editorial). (1906). *Herald of the Golden Age,* 11, 14.
Cording, K. (1903). A talk with the children. *Herald of the Golden Age, 8,* 137.
Court Circular. (1910, May 5). *Times,* 5, 13.
Craven, J. F. C. (1998). *Redskins in Epping Forest: John Hargrave, the Kibbo Kift and the woodcraft experience.* Ph.D, University of London.
Deaths. (1938, October 21). Times, 1.
Dellar, R. (2008). *Josiah Oldfield: Eminent fruitarian.* Raynham: Rainmore Books.
Editorial. (1883, November 17). *Aberdeen Evening Express,* 2.
Flyer for Lady Margaret Hospital. (1904, August). Reprinted in *South London Press,* 29.
General News. (1883, January 27). *Derby Daily Telegraph,* 4.
Gill, S. L. (1853). Case of an Opium-Eater and vegetarian Beoming Bedridden: Recovery upon Taking Animal Food. *The Lancet, 62*(1561), 95.
Gleadle, K. (2003). "The age of physiological reformers:" Rethinking gender and domesticity in the age of reform. In A. Burns & J. Innes (Eds.), *Rethinking the age of reform: Britain 1780–1850* (p. 213). Cambridge: Cambridge University Press.
Gregory, J. R. (2008). "A Lutheranism of the table": religion and the Victorian vegetarians. (2008). In R. Muers, & D. Grumett (Eds.), *Eating and believing: Interdisciplinary perspectives on vegetarianism and theology.* London: T & T Clark.

Haag. A. (1906). The true cause of physical degeneracy. *Herald of the Golden Age, 11*.
Hospital Sunday Fund. (1902, June 17). *Times,* 8.
Hume, N. A. H. (1908). The higher aspects of the simple life. *Herald of the Golden Age, 12,* 6–9.
Ireland. (1898, January 29). *Times,* 12.
Lady Margaret Hospital. (1908). *Herald of the Golden Age,* 12, 14.
Lond, E. E. (1906). A world religion. *Herald of the Golden Age, 11,* 20–22.
Mercier, C. (1916). Diet as a factor in the causation of mental disease. *The Lancet, 187*(4827), 510–513.
Millard, C. K. (1902). The rôle of the "anti": An apology and an appeal. *Public Health, 15,* 212–222.
Moore, J. H. (1906). Universal kinship. *Herald of the Golden Age, 11,* 38–42.
Oldfield, J. (1898). *The claims of common life, or, the scientific relations of humans and non-humans*. London: Ideal Publishing Union.
Oldfield, J. (1912, December 11). The Christmas feast: An indictment. *Evening News*, 11.
Oldfield, J. (n.d.). *A groaning creation.* London: Ideal Publishing Union.
Oldfield, J. (n.d.). *A tale of shame and cruelty.* Paignton: Order of the Golden Age.
Order of the Golden Age. (1910, November 1). *Times,* 16.
Perks, R. H. (1992). *Why i condemn vivisection.* Order of the Cross. Paignton.
Pert, A. (2007). *Red cactus: The life of Anna Kingsford.* Watsons Bay: Books and Writers.
Salt, H. S. (1894). *Animals' rights considered in relation to social progress.* New York: Macmillan.
Smith, V. (2004). Oldfield, Josiah (1863–1953). *Oxford Dictionary of National Biography*. Oxford: Oxford University Press. Retreived June 20, 2016, from http://www.oxforddnb.com/view/article/40999.
The Fruitarian Hospital. (1906). *Herald of the Golden Age,* 11, 35.
The Vivisection Libel Suit. (1903). *Herald of the Golden Age,* 8, 190.
Thornhill, M. (1889). *Experiments on hospital patients.* London: Hatchards.
Twigg, J. (1981). *The vegetarian movement in England: 1847–1981: A study in the structure of its ideology.* PhD, London School of Economics.
Vegetarian Banquet. (1883, March 30). *Bristol Mercury,* 6.
Vyvyan, J. (1969). *In Pity and in Anger*. London: Michael Joseph.
Wills and bequests. (1937, January 28). *Times,* 10.
Woman Millionaire's Bequests. (1927, October 15). *Fife Free Press,* 9.

5

The National Anti-Vivisection Hospital, 1902–1935

What exactly was an anti-vivisection hospital? The question arose at an inquest into the death of a child, Mabel Florence Jones, in 1908. She had been treated at the National Anti-Vivisection Hospital in Battersea, South London, for 'a clean-cut wound in her head'; a few weeks later, she suddenly became ill and was taken to St Bartholomew's Hospital, where it was discovered that her skull was fractured. According to the house surgeon at St Bart's, the fracture would have been discovered sooner if the child had been 'properly examined' at Battersea, but Dr Ronald da Costa, the Anti-Vivisection Hospital's resident medical officer, told the court he had examined the child thoroughly and that the fracture must have been the result of 'a subsequent accident'. The background to the case suggests parental neglect: the child had been dirty when taken to hospital, and at Bart's the surgeon had found it 'extremely difficult to get a history' from the mother, who first said that Mabel had been hit by a pickaxe carelessly thrown over a wall, and then that she had 'knocked her head against the table'. Unfortunately, poor record-keeping left the Anti-Vivisection Hospital struggling to defend itself. Dr da Costa, a former Indian Army surgeon with 30 years' experience, admitted his hands had been 'pretty full', as in addition to the hospital's in-patients, he attended out-patients from six-thirty until

A.W.H. Bates, *Anti-Vivisection and the Profession of Medicine in Britain*,
The Palgrave Macmillan Animal Ethics Series, DOI 10.1057/978-1-137-55697-4_5

eleven in the evening, seeing scores of patients who paid four pence each. Battersea, the court heard, was one of the poorest suburbs of London, and in Henley Street, where the Joneses lived, slum-dwellers were 'huddled together like sheep'.[1]

The Coroner tried to clarify the objects of the hospital that was treating so many poor South Londoners: 'I see in your hospital's annual report the words, "No experiments on patients". What do they mean?' he asked da Costa, who replied: 'I don't know. I don't suppose any hospital has experiments on patients. We perform every kind of operation'. The hospital's secretary (chief administrator), G.W.F. Robbins, explained that it meant no interventions for the sake of knowledge rather than the benefit of patients. To the Coroner's suggestion that this implied other hospitals *did* experiment, Robbins answered 'Not in the least'.[2] It seemed, however, that local people thought otherwise: one of the medical men present had heard that some people were afraid to go into hospital in case they were experimented on. The accounts of 'human vivisection' that sometimes appeared in British newspapers referred to therapeutic experiments in European hospitals rather than patients being dissected alive in Britain, but they probably stoked fears that London's medical men did not willingly confine their researches to animals.[3] The Anti-Vivisection Hospital, by requiring its staff to sign a personal pledge not to experiment on animals or humans, was deliberately presenting itself as a safer alternative to Bart's and other London teaching hospitals where vivisectionists worked.

Thanks to the indefatigable Stephen Coleridge, everybody thought they knew where London's vivisectionists were. In 1901, he had published a list, *The Metropolitan Hospitals and Vivisection*, with a 'blood-red band' of 'fearsome appearance' against the names of the offending hospitals and schools. This caused serious concern to London's teaching hospitals, which feared that the 'stream of charity' might be diverted away from them if donors thought they were paying for vivisection, and there ensued a convoluted public argument over how much, if any, charitable giving actually found its way into the laboratories of vivisectionists. To add insult to financial injury, Coleridge used the familiar anti-vivisection argument from the nineteenth century—that vivisectionists were, or became, callous and were thus unfit to attend patients—to imply that teaching hospital staff were blasé about using their patients for research: the London School of Tropical Medicine's boast of 'an adequate supply of clinical material for purposes of instruction' was a circumlocution, he told his readers, for 'the prostrate bodies of the sick'.[4] He knew that money was being raised for a new hospital that would promise freedom from experimentation, and to which donors would be able to give with the assurance that they were not supporting animal research.

Josiah Oldfield's tiny, shabby, hastily conceived Hospital of St Francis (discussed in the previous chapter) was, though ground-breaking, scarcely a flagship for the cause, and Coleridge, its chairman, had plans to open a larger hospital once the money had been raised to buy suitable premises. St Francis's had at least shown that it was possible for an anti-vivisection hospital to survive without the support of the medical establishment. Furthermore, it seemed to have caused them some anxiety: the great Sir Henry Burdett had taken the trouble to attack Oldfield's 'little hospital in the New Kent Road run on the cheap and simple plan of giving its patients no meat', professing to find it 'somewhat amusing … that Mr Coleridge, who poses as an opponent of experiments on animals, should be the chairman of a vegetarian hospital which exists for the very purpose of trying a very doubtful experiment on human beings'. Burdett's financial acumen and blustering philanthropy were invaluable to the voluntary hospital system, and he was chary of anyone or anything that threatened its funding, particularly '[t]hose peculiar people who have chosen to associate themselves with the National Anti-Vivisection Society [of which Coleridge was secretary] and to set themselves in opposition to such great charitable movements as the [Metropolitan] Hospital Sunday Fund and King Edward's Hospital Fund'.[5]

The NAVS had been raising money for a hospital since the 1890s, when it set up a charitable trust with Lords Coleridge (1820–1894, Stephen's father) and Hatherton (1842–1930), Dr Abiathar Wall (treasurer of the London Anti-Vivisection Society), Ernest Bell (1851–1933, later president of the Vegetarian Society and chairman of the NAVS) and the Rev'd Augustus Jackson as trustees. Helped by rich anti-vivisectionists (particularly the Dowager Countess of Portsmouth, who replaced Coleridge as a trustee), who donated as an alternative to supporting the 'vivisecting' teaching hospitals such as Bart's, Guy's, the London, Mary's and St Thomas's, the fund grew rapidly.[6] As usual among anti-vivisectionists, there were personality clashes—according to the hospital's first medical director, Dr Alexander Bowie, 'there were two sections who differed about it for a time and the money went into Chancery'—but in 1900 they agreed to buy, for seven thousand pounds, a large private house, known as Lock's Folly, in Battersea, where, two years later, an out-patient department was opened in the former stables.[7]

In-patients followed in 1903: there were 'eight beds, three cots, and four medical officers, one of whom is also chairman of the hospital'. Its prospectus promised 'No Vivisection in its Schools. No Vivisectors on its Staff. No Experiments on Patients', and listed eleven 'honorary' medical staff who, as in all voluntary hospitals, were consultants who did not receive salaries but had the kudos of being associated with a London hospital, albeit in this case an obscure one, which supposedly helped their private practice.[8] In common with most voluntary hospitals, the Anti-Vivisection charged patients a small fee—which might have been paid by one of the hospital's subscribers, an employer, or a provident association—but the bulk of the running costs were met by donations. South London was notoriously short of hospital beds and the local poor, who made up ninety per cent of the new hospital's patients, had few alternatives; nevertheless, Robbins boasted that '[t]he special effect of our principles upon the sick poor is to attract them to our Hospital in which they seem to have complete confidence, as is proved by the rapid increase in our work'.[9]

In an effort to entice patients, and donors, away from other institutions, the hospital spent some three hundred pounds a year advertising in anti-vivisection periodicals.[10] Its annual report described it as 'a standing protest against cruel experiments on animals, and a concrete demonstration that these are not necessary for the succour of the maimed or the healing of the sick'. Its patients were reassured that 'the whole of the medical surgical and administrative staff are pledged against vivisection', that treatments such as Pasteur's vaccines that were prepared using live animals were 'absolutely shut out', and that, except in an emergency, no operation would be performed without the written consent of the patient, a novel undertaking for the time, though no records survive to show whether or not it was adhered to.[11]

The Anti-Vivisection Hospital and the King's Fund

In 1906, Lord Lichfield (1856–1918) and the surgeon Sir William H. Bennett (1852–1931) visited the Hospital on behalf of King Edward's Hospital Fund (the King's Fund). They noted the 'steadily increasing amount of work done', which showed that 'this Institution supplies a want', and found it tolerably well equipped, with modern electrical fittings, though they thought the medical staff were 'gentlemen who are hardly of the status of those who usually occupy positions on the staffs of Hospitals of repute in London'. They submitted a detailed report to the Fund, but the outcome was apparently a foregone conclusion, and the Fund ruled that further visits would be 'a thankless task, which can be productive of no good', since, 'the anti-vivisection basis upon which the Institution is founded is in itself considered a sufficient reason for withholding help'.[12]

The King's Fund was one of three funds that distributed public donations to London's voluntary hospitals, the others being the Sunday and Saturday Funds, which administered church and workplace collections, respectively.[13] The King's Fund was the largest of the three, controlling an £140,000 annual distribution, which gave it great influence over practices and standards. It refused to tell the Anti-Vivisection Hospital why it had refused it a grant, but Sydney Holland (1855–1931), an outstanding fundraiser, founder of the Research Defence Society (see Chap. 6), and chairman of the London Hospital (one of the King's Fund's biggest beneficiaries), was more forthcoming. At a charity dinner in 1908, he called the Anti-Vivisection 'a miserable hospital, miserably built and miserably equipped' (perhaps not the soundest of reasons for *not* giving it money), and he later told Robbins that both the King's Fund and the Sunday Fund were refusing to help because it was unfit, as a building, to be a hospital.[14] This was wrong both in fact—the hospital continued in the same premises until 1972—and as an explanation for the King's Fund's decision, and it appears that Holland, whose hospital had been among those accused of using charitable donations to pay for experiments on animals, was attempting to discourage him from seeking funds in future.

The Anti-Vivisection Hospital's continued existence was, as it was intended to be, an irritation to the funds and the hospitals they supported: at the Sunday Fund's annual meeting in the Mansion House (the official residence of the Lord Mayor of London) the self-congratulatory speeches were interrupted by the Rev'd Lionel Lewis (1867–1953), Vicar of St Mark's Whitechapel, complaining, not for the first time, that the Anti-Vivisection had not received a grant. When the former Lord Mayor Sir John Bell (1843–1924), a wealthy brewer, responded that he would not bandy words with someone whose church had only contributed 3s 6d the Fund, the vicar replied, 'Yes, my parish is a poor one'.[15] This vignette shows something of the patrician distain for anti-vivisectionists among the philanthropists of the City of London, whose liverymen controlled much of the capital's charity.

The conservative *Medical Times* defended the Anti-Vivisection, which it described as 'a small hospital for the treatment of the indigent sick', against Holland's criticisms, on the grounds that 'Patients are not bound to go to the hospital…', and noted that '[t]here are lots of hospitals in London doing excellent work which are 'miserably equipped', adding, 'we are unable to understand why such a dead set has been made against the hospital. Enormous influence is being brought to bear to crush this modest attempt … with such success that the Distribution Committees of the great Hospital Funds in London have been induced to refuse … funds'. The *Medical Times* proposed that, as with the Homoeopathic and Temperance hospitals, the experiment should be allowed to proceed, the result being determined by whether the hospital proved viable or not.[16]

The management of the Anti-Vivisection Hospital seemed genuinely unable to understand why the funds had refused them support, and continued to solicit inspections in the hope of getting the decision reversed. In the 1890s, when the hospital was being planned, it would have been reasonable to have anticipated that the Prince of Wales's Fund (as the King's Fund then was), instituted to commemorate the jubilee of Queen Victoria, would be sympathetic towards anti-vivisection; indeed, had the hospital opened during Victoria's lifetime, she may well have become its patron. Unfortunately, neither the future Edward VII nor the future George V, who as Princes of Wales chaired the King's fund, shared Victoria's anti-vivisection principles, and the medical men who made up the Fund's committee all sympathised with vivisection even if they did not, like its chairman Lord Lister (1827–1927), practise it themselves.[17]

At a public meeting to discuss the Hospital's funding, Stephen Coleridge, an agreeable man in private life, was characteristically forthright: 'these great funds had got into the hands of persons who deliberately disposed of them to forward the views they personally held'.[18] However, since the Anti-Vivisection Hospital had initially been put up as an alternative to supporting the funds, to allow anti-vivisection donors who wanted to give to a hospital to do so directly without 'sacrificing their consciences', its trying to claim from the funds as well looked like an attempt to have one's cake and eat it, and it is not surprising that the funds were indignant.[19]

The funds were, however, supposed to be impartial, and could not risk openly stating they were on the side of vivisection, so the Sunday Fund disingenuously said they had refused the Anti-Vivisection a grant because 'the best treatment known' (presumably antisera) was not given and the 'Governing Body dictates the forms of treatment to be used by its medical staff'.[20] However, the latter was true of most of the voluntary hospitals supported by the fund, including the Homoeopathic and Temperance, and the National Anti-Vivisection actually had more medical board members than most, three doctors and a dentist in 1910, though these were all committed anti-vivisectionists like Lizzy Lind af Hageby (1878–1963), founder of the Animal Defence and Anti-Vivisection Society (ADAVS), whose infiltration of the laboratories at University College London in 1903 had paved the way for the notorious Brown Dog affair. The prominence of women in anti-vivisection circles meant that they too were well represented (five out of eighteen) on the hospital's board.[21]

The Hospital informed the Sunday Fund that its rules banning vivisection and treatments derived from it were no different 'to those which in a Homoeopathic Hospital prevent the appointment of Allopaths, and in a Temperance Hospital the appointment of alcohol drinkers, and which prohibit any alcoholic treatment'.[22] The Sunday Fund, however, said the difference was that patients understood what a homoeopathic hospital was, but not an anti-vivisection one,[23] to which the Hospital's committee replied: 'the poorer class in Battersea, who appreciate our Hospital … well understand its title. Possibly the statue of the dog erected there conduces to this knowledge'.[24]

The reference was to an episode that the people of Battersea would have found hard to ignore: the Brown Dog affair (1907–1909), an anti-vivisection *cause célèbre* that prompted rioting on the streets as medical students attempted to demolish Battersea Council's provocative—the British Medical Association thought libellous—bronze statue of a terrier allegedly 'done to death' in the laboratories of University College. Battersea's menfolk came out in force to defend the dog and 'guard' the hospital; one perhaps rather fanciful account of the riots has them forcibly preventing an injured medical student—whose objection to the hospital had conveniently evaporated when he needed its help—from passing through its doors.[25] These 'town against gown' fights were clearly about more than just vivisection: they channelled the 'pent-up hatred felt by certain classes towards medical science and medical men', who, 'brutalised by vivisection', would not hesitate to experiment on the poor. The students' reaction to hearing that their efforts to learn their trade were brutalising them was, with presumably unintended irony, to start a riot.[26] Whatever the rights and wrongs of the disturbances, the Sunday Fund's claim that potential patients did not know about anti-vivisection was incredible; Battersea people would have seen and heard the riots, they were widely reported in London's papers, and the dog's statue close by the hospital served as a constant reminder.

Sentiment and Science

Some commentators have seen the Brown Dog affair as damaging to anti-vivisection because it overtly politicised it. By defending the dog, Battersea's poor were fighting for more than their right not to be experimented on without their consent; they were using the fate of the dog as a symbol for the exploitation of working class men and women in ways that had nothing to do with vivisection.[27] Medical students were a particular target of the workers' animosity because they represented the sort of unsympathetic middle class parvenus who, unlike the aristocracy, could not be relied upon to treat those who came under their authority with any decency. The students' behaviour, which was tolerated, or even encouraged, by their professors, only reinforced these concerns: rowdyism in defence of science suggested that doctors who insisted upon experimenting on animals were indeed uncaring. One anti-vivisectionist who was present at a meeting disrupted by students shouting and breaking up the furniture wrote to the King's Fund: 'the disgraceful scene at Caxton Hall made by the medical students fills one with the utmost contempt and loathing for these cowardly "butchers" … if these creatures are our coming medical men, then I say—God help their unfortunate patients!'[28] 'Butchers' was a common slur against unpopular medics, since butchers were proverbial for their lack of compassion (and thus reputedly banned from serving on juries), and to compare medics to them, as Lind af Hageby did in *The Shambles of Science*, was to deny medicine its claim to moral and ethical superiority.

The riots show that the medical exponents of vivisection were indifferent to public expectations that they ought to approach their work with compassion, and failed to take seriously concerns that there was a slippery slope from vivisection to experiments on patients. In their crudest form, these concerns were, indeed, no more than fantasies fed by popular fiction, in which mad surgeons with 'elastic' consciences, their appetites for cruelty 'whetted' by experimenting on animals, easily overcame their 'natural prejudice against inflicting suffering' and took to vivisecting humans.[29] However, not only impressionable folk who took such tales literally (they are reminiscent of the mid-nineteenth century tales of paupers dissected and made into 'anatomy pie') would have felt safer in the Anti-Vivisection Hospital, but also those who thought that medics prepared to sign an anti-cruelty pledge would probably treat their patients more sympathetically than most.

To be anti-vivisection was to reject the cold, rational, science on which the teaching hospitals based their reputation for excellence, and be guided by emotion: Lind af Hageby claimed she converted to the cause after the look of suffering on the face of a laboratory dog went, as she put it, 'straight to my heart'. Medical men (and they were always men) complained about womanish emotionality (the American medical profession accused anti-vivisectionists of being literally mad with a mental condition called 'zoophil-psychosis'[30]) but potential patients seem to have agreed with the National Anti-Vivisection Society that for a doctor to be called sentimental was an accolade.[31]

To sign the pledge made, after all, no practical difference to animals—only a tiny minority of medical practitioners ever conducted laboratory experiments, and no busy district hospital had time for them—its purpose was to affirm the commitment of the Hospital's staff to compassionate medicine, and it would have reassured not just patients with strong views on animal experimentation, but also those concerned that charitable hospitals were no longer the benevolent institutions they had once been, but testing-grounds, run for the convenience of an increasingly powerful and self-interested medical profession.[32]

Even though it helped attract patients, for a doctor to sign the anti-vivisection pledge was professionally hazardous: an act of public dissent from the dogmas of the metropolitan medical élite that marked one out as a medical protestant. It was rumoured that 'no one with pronounced anti-vivisectional principles would be elected to the Medical Staff of the larger London Hospitals', and '[t]he retention of his appointment by anyone opposing vivisectional teaching would be difficult, if not impossible and his promotion unlikely'.[33] In view of this, it seems that some, perhaps most, medics who had qualms about vivisection did not voice them. As Walter Hadwen (1854–1932), a Gloucester GP who took over from Cobbe as president of the British Union for the Abolition of Vivisection (BUAV), told an audience of anti-vivisectionists in 1907, anyone prepared to made a stand 'had to learn what it meant to be heterodox',[34] and not all had the courage of their convictions: one anti-vivisection doctor described how 'A young Doctor told a lady that he hated Vivisection, but did not dare express it, or he would have been hooted out of the Profession'.[35]

The British Medical Association, the doctors' trade union, treated anti-vivisectionists as enemies of the profession and smugly observed each year in its journal that the Anti-Vivisection Hospital had once more received nothing from the funds. As the size of each hospital's grant was roughly proportionate to the number of patients seen and the cost of any new buildings, it served as an indicator of a hospital's achievements, so the persistent withholding of an award might embarrass a hospital even if it did not bother it financially. In 1908, the Anti-Vivisection received a one-off payment of £440 from the Sunday Fund, given, according to Burdett, in the hope that 'the [hospital] authorities would mend their ways, purge their methods, and, in fact, fall into line…' It also gave him another opportunity to state in his journal that it was 'pretentious humbug' to employ modern methods that had been developed from experiments on animals and then boast of an anti-vivisection commitment, in response to which, Robbins challenged him to name a treatment whose development *had* depended on vivisection, an invitation to an argument that, though popular over the years with both pro- and anti-vivisectionists, was always unproductive, since even if it were agreed that a particular medical advance had resulted from vivisection (which it never was), it was practically impossible to prove that it could *only* have been made in this way and not by some other means.[36] Burdett also repeated the accusation he had previously made about the Hospital of St Francis, that 'No experiments on hospital patients' was nonsense since 'the whole hospital is an experiment', though he seemed disinclined to wait, as the *Medical Times* had suggested, for its outcome.

The King's Fund's concern that 'anti-vivisection propaganda' would lead to a drop in their income appears to have been justified: one irate correspondent cited 'the devilish abomination called vivisection' as the reason that '[m]y sister and I, together with several of our friends, therefore, do not intend to give one farthing to any other hospital; all the money we can spare we will send to the Battersea Hospital', adding, [w]e also believe that where hospitals practise vivisection upon helpless animals they, naturally, will not stop there, it is not reasonable to expect them to do so'.[37] In 1907, the Fund's committee, with the Prince of Wales in the chair, had discussed the problem and agreed 'that [the Anti-Vivisection] Hospital should not be visited in future in consequence of its work being based on considerations which are not exclusively directed to the welfare of the patients', and that this decision should be kept secret because 'if communicated to the hospital it would at once involve a discussion'.[38]

Their aversion from discussion suggests a lack of confidence in their ability to convince the public that an anti-vivisection hospital was not in the interest of patients. The statistics routinely returned by voluntary hospitals showed the Anti-Vivisection performing at least as well as its peers, with growing patient numbers and a low death rate, but, significantly, neither side showed any interest in comparing the results of cruelty-free versus conventional treatment (for example the Pasteur treatment of rabies versus vapour baths), which indicates that the dispute was not clinical but ideological: were patients best served by animal research to produce better treatments, or by making medicine more compassionate?

Burdett warned the King's Fund that anti-vivisectionists 'are difficult people to tackle, because they always evade the point', though he did not say, and there was no consensus on, what the point actually was.[39] For experimentalists, what mattered most was that vivisection produced results, and they cited the work of Harvey, Pasteur and other medical celebrities to support their case. However, since the outcome of an experiment could not be known in advance, present-day researchers had to rely on anticipated benefits (and what scientist did not anticipate great discoveries?) to justify their continuing use of animals. While some hard-line anti-vivisectionists refused to admit that vivisection had ever led to any useful discovery in human medicine, most accepted that important information had been gained from it in the past, and took the Anti-Vivisection Hospital's pragmatic line that all existing treatments developed through vivisection might still be used, but that no morc animals ought to suffer for medicine.

It still took determination, and perhaps a dose of hypocrisy, to take the moral high ground and say of treatments, such as antisera, that were prepared using live animals: 'I had rather die a hundred deaths than blacken my soul by consenting that such deeds should be done for *my* benefit'.[40] If, however, sick anti-vivisectionists lacked the courage of their convictions and accepted antiserum, this did not, as their opponents liked to argue, nullify their position: as the liberal politician Sir Robert Reid (1846–1923) wrote when asked whether he would permit vivisection to save his own family: 'to save them, we might set fire to the nearest cathedral, though we knew it was wrong. Under strong emotion, good men do bad things'.[41]

For anti-vivisectionists, it was, however, better to give into strong emotion than disdain it. The 'forcible suppression of natural feelings of compassion' that vivisection required was 'a ruinous price to pay for knowledge'; ruinous both to the vivisector and to society, since the example of inhumanity was quickly spread. The consequences were particularly hazardous for medical men, since if their sense of compassion were allowed to atrophy they might become as callous to the suffering of patients as they were to that of dogs in the laboratory.[42] Vivisectionists, however, argued that it was they, by forcing themselves to do unpleasant but necessary experiments, who were truly 'on the side of humanity', while anti-vivisectionists selfishly spared their own feelings.[43] The crux of the matter was whether compassion and sympathy were more important attributes for a doctor than detachment and self-control. It was axiomatic that doctors should be caring and compassionate, but self-discipline and fortitude—for example, the 'cool' hand of the surgeon and the persistence of the anatomist during unpleasant dissections—were also essential qualities.[44] Were doctors and their patients forced to choose between sentimentality and science, or was the dichotomy a false one?

Defenders of animal research muddied the waters by pointing out that many anti-vivisectionists seemed indifferent to non-scientific exploitation of animals, such as meat-eating, hunting, and fur-wearing.[45] The British Medical Association, for example, had berated the Welsh landowner Lord Llangattock, a prominent anti-vivisectionist and vice-president of the Hospital of St Francis, for allowing shooting on his estate.[46] Though the BMA was mistaken in this case, there were other anti-vivisectionists who hunted and/or wore fur. In view of these apparent double standards, experimentalists complained that anti-vivisectionists only affected to sympathise with animals, while their true agenda was anti-science and anti-progress.[47] Though this was not entirely true—Oldfield, for example, seems to have been genuinely upset by the suffering he witnessed in slaughterhouses—the New Age movement certainly did aim to reverse the materialistic direction in which science was being taken, and anti-vivisection was an important strategy for doing so. Vivisection too had a socio-political agenda: the controversial nineteenth-century public vivisection displays had been a 'protest on behalf of the independence of science as against interference by clerics and moralists',[48] and formed part of a 'successful struggle by doctors to free themselves and the practice of medicine from older moral and religious concepts and constraints'.[49]

This separation of science from faith and morality proved highly controversial. In *The Perfect Way, or, The Finding of Christ* (1882), Anna Kingsford and Edward Maitland (1824–1897) wrote of a 'falsely so-called' science that concentrated on superficial forms while ignoring the intellectual, moral and spiritual essence of things.[50] To Kingsford, vivisection's brutal materialism was a 'pseudo-scientific inquisition',[51] and vivisectionists, 'black magicians', whose spreading of amorality would 'work havoc' with human souls. The vivisection controversy thus became the new battleground for two divergent views of science, whose proponents had been in conflict since the bodysnatching scandals a century earlier: must science be subservient to the moral codes that governed other human activities, or did its flourishing justify, or even require, setting the old morality aside?[52]

Rallying to the Cause

When the Anti-Vivisection Hospital was incorporated (registered as a business) in 1910, it took a motto that expressed its wider purpose: *Delenda est Crudelitas*—'Cruelty Must Be Destroyed'.[53] In its early years, the hospital sent representatives to anti-vivisection congresses, but the secretary became concerned that this might give the misleading impression they were anti-research. After some of his staff participated in the 1911 BUAV March against vivisection, Robbins went so far as to write to the anti-vivisection journals and popular press to explain that the hospital, which now had twenty-eight beds—twelve medical and sixteen surgical—did not oppose 'legitimate and beneficent forms of laboratory research unconnected with Vivisection such as microscopical investigation of pathological specimens and bacteriological examinations necessary to the interests of medical progress'.[54] In the same year, a new twelve-bedded 'cancer research department', furnished with the latest electric 'light and colour bath', was opened under the direction of Dr Robert Bell (1845–1926).[55] The hospital board was fond of buying such novel pieces of apparatus, probably to show that they were engaging with the latest developments: the out-patient department boasted 'the Buisson Institute for hydrophobia', but no cases of this rare condition ever turned up, and when the inspectors called they found the cupboard in which the Buisson vapour bath was located full of rubbish.[56]

The hospital's death rates were 'exceedingly low'—4.2% compared with the London Hospital's 9.5%—though Robbins prudently told the King's Fund this was not 'a statistic which we would wish to press or labour', presumably because the nature and complexity of the procedures performed in different hospitals would have to have been taken into account.[57] There were a few inquests at which the hospital was censured for poor practice, though it is unclear whether mistakes were more common there or whether its anti-vivisection policy earned it closer scrutiny. Following the death, in 1910, of a woman brought in after an illegal abortion, Dr da Costa was forced to admit in court that they were still not keeping any records, though the jury found the hospital blameless of her death.[58]

Sloppy record keeping and other failings suggest that capable junior staff were hard to obtain, probably because many were unwilling to compromise their careers by linking themselves with anti-vivisection. The resident medical officer was often the only doctor in the hospital, and struggled to cope with its demands: on 4 July 1911, Dr James Hamilton Stuart left the hospital after luncheon, saying he would be back in half an hour, and returned a month later in 'a deplorable condition having been in the East End'. The penniless medic was given breakfast and told to collect his things.[59] Standards among non-medical staff also left something to be desired: the hospital trained its own nurses and was justifiably proud when they passed their examinations, but once qualified they were often left unsupervised, and their work could be 'casual', as was that of the dispenser, who was found to be using an 'extraordinarily large amount of Cocaine'.[60]

Despite such lapses, Battersea's 'working men and women' valued their hospital and organized dances, concerts and boxing tournaments to pay for it, with pro- and anti-vivisectionists working together for 'so worthy a cause in helping the very poor'.[61] In spite of its earlier resolution, the King's Fund did send more visitors, who noted that patients were being treated according to the latest principles, and that no attempt was being made to exclude treatments developed by experiments on animals, but they still refused to make a grant, explaining in an internal memo that: 'The Distribution Committee decided not to give the arguments—which were that the ~~principles~~ restrictions at the Temperance and Homoeopathic hospitals are adopted because they are believed to be in the interests of the patients: those at the Antivivisection Hospital in the interests of the animals'.[62] The anti-vivisectionists response, had they seen the memo, would presumably have been that the principle of humanity *was* in the interests of patients. What the patients themselves thought would have depended on their views on vivisection, but it seems unlikely the average person would have considered a ban on animal experiments as a restriction, or else why would teaching hospitals have tried to conceal the presence of vivisectionists in their schools?

Whatever one thought of its principles, the Anti-Vivisection Hospital took them seriously: in 1912 an extraordinary meeting was convened to discuss why the resident medical officer, Dr Maurice Beddow Bayly (who by the time of his death in 1962 would be one of Britain's leading medical anti-vivisectionists), had performed a major operation for breast cancer on a terminally ill patient who had shortly afterwards succumbed to surgical shock. There was no suggestion that the patient, who was unconscious throughout, had suffered, and her family did not make a complaint, but Bayly admitted he had not operated for the patient's benefit, but because he had been 'anxious to perform the operation': in other words, he had practiced on a dying woman. This was the kind of 'experiment' that led patients to lose confidence in hospitals, and Bayly, whose conduct had been otherwise excellent, was severely reprimanded for failing to meet the hospital's standards, and left shortly afterwards.[63] In 1926, a nurse was dismissed for 'callous and brutal' treatment of patients, and a visiting doctor was not allowed to demonstrate an Abram's machine because he refused to sign the anti-vivisection pledge; later, a would-be honorary surgeon who tried to water down the pledge by inserting the word 'unnecessary' into the clause about not inflicting pain was not appointed, and a doctor who gave antisera to two patients was asked to resign.[64] Though the hospital was not anti-vaccinationist in the wider sense, vaccines and antisera prepared from live animals were specifically banned under its regulations.

The hospital's supporters argued that it was the funds' boycott, rather than hospital's principles, that was harming patients. In 1914, Mary Culme-Seymour (1871–1944) wrote to the King's Fund: 'It can hardly be right that solely on account of the question for or against vivisection, the poor of a populous district should be left without the aid of a Hospital'.[65] Fortunately, the hospital had sufficient income from legacies and donations to remain solvent and even to expand, leaving the King's Fund's obdurate refusal to contribute looking increasingly ineffectual. In 1922, Richard Morris (1859–1956), the MP for Battersea North, called at the Fund's headquarters to ask why they would not assist an institution that was 'doing the work of a general hospital': were they, he asked, 'prejudiced by the views of orthodox medical men on the fund'?[66] That year, the hospital applied to the Fund once again, and was again refused.

It was typical of an anti-vivisection charity that many different kinds of people supported its work.[67] The hospital's chairmen came from varied professional and political backgrounds, and included the libertarian economist Joseph Hiam Levy (1838–1913, chairman until 1905), John Prince Fallowes, Rector of Heene (d. 1941, chairman 1905–1911), the Liberal politician Sir George William Kekewich (1841–1921, chairman 1911–1914), hereditary peer Lord Tenterden (1865–1939, chairman 1914–1926), solicitor Alderman Robert Tweedy Smith (d. 1948, chairman 1926–1927), insurance broker S.C. Turner (chairman 1927–1928) and MP, novelist, theologian and sometime fascist Lord Ernest Hamilton (1858–1939, chairman 1928–1935).

From the beginning, the hospital enjoyed good relations with local trades unions: they thought it was doing 'good work in Battersea' and its committee was 'indebted' to them for helping to raise funds, repaying their support by insisting that hospital contracts went to local firms who paid their men the higher, union-approved wages.[68] There were also strong links with the Progressive Party borough council, which were cemented during the Brown Dog affair, when anti-vivisectionists found common cause with working-class activists. Most of the hospital's funds came, however, from a few wealthy benefactors, notably, in its early years, Lady Portsmouth, whose death in 1906 deprived it of its most generous supporter.[69] Between 1900 and 1914, twenty-four individuals gave over £100 each, including £600 from Viscount Harberton and £500 each from Countess de Noailles and Maynard Geraldine Wolfe. In comparison to this, local street collections and donations from groups with anti-vivisection sympathies, such as the Ancient Order of Druids, brought comparatively little into the hospital's funds, though they helped maintain good relations with the community.[70]

The stereotype of the anti-vivisection donor as a wealthy widow with animals for company was not without foundation: more than two-thirds of the hospital's governors were women, and at one point the hospital planned a charity appeal to ten thousand widows.[71] The preponderance of female supporters led to its becoming known as a women's hospital, despite a lack of female doctors, which led to a costly misunderstanding over the will of a Miss Constance Edith Guerrier of Boulogne, who died in 1926 leaving her entire estate to 'the Women's Hospital, Battersea'. Her executors wrote to the 'Women's Hospital' but as there was no hospital of that name, the letter was delivered to the borough council (now no longer under radical control), which claimed the legacy for its maternity hospital, though this had not existed when the will was written in 1919. The South London Hospital for Women, which was not in the borough of Battersea, then took legal proceedings against the council and won, which alerted the Anti-Vivisection Hospital's Chairman Lord Tenterden, who put in his own claim for the money. Though it emerged during the proceedings that Guerrier, a woman of strong anti-vivisection views, had written to the South London Hospital for Women asking 'if they carried on the Hospital on Anti-Vivisection principles', and had been told they did not, the court ruled that this was the institution to which she had intended to bequeath her fortune, thus depriving the National Anti-Vivisection of £37,000.[72]

In 1922, an inspection of the hospital, which by then was claiming to have fifty-two beds, found only nine beds and two cots occupied: one male ward, one female ward and the children's ward had been closed since the war, along with the private beds in the cancer wing. A new out-patients building, completed in 1915 at a cost of £15,000, remained empty for want of equipment, and the old one was looking run down and antiquated; a faded card on the wall still proclaimed 'RABIES SCARE BUISSON BATH TREATMENT', but the bath had never been used and its gas pipe was not even connected to the mains.[73]

The post-war period was difficult for many voluntary hospitals as there was less money available for charitable giving, and the Anti-Vivisection also suffered from declining interest in its cause. The anti-vivisectionists' ageing demographic was, however, a rich source of legacies, which, typically for a voluntary hospital, were not always listed in its accounts, or even in the minute books. A bequest of £7361 in 1921 wiped off the debt under which the hospital had been labouring since the war, allowing the committee to begin a large building programme to accommodate the 'ever-increasing applications for admission', and to renovate, redecorate and reequip it 'with every essential modern appliance' until it had been 'made as perfect as possible'.[74] 1929 brought a further windfall of over £38,000 in the form of three large bequests.[75]

Crisis and Compromise

In the 1920s, the hospital was treating over four hundred in-patients and forty thousand out-patients a year, but its reputation was damaged by a dispute that began in 1927 when a former honorary surgeon, J.F. Peart, author of 'Foreign bodies in the rectum', made a number of complaints. The hospital's ban on antisera was well known, and Peart claimed that one of his patients had died of tetanus as a result. Furthermore, he told the King's Fund, the hospital 'more than discouraged' the use of vaccines, two patients had died after straightforward operations owing to the use of infected cat-gut, and 'there were two unqualified persons on the Staff'.[76] In addition, he sent letters, accusing 'the women members of the board of management' of interfering with medical affairs, to the *Lancet* and *British Medical Journal*, which printed detrimental reports. In reply, the hospital maintained that Peart had been aware of an arrangement for giving antiserum—by sending patients who asked for it to other hospitals—since 1922.

There are reasons to be sceptical about Peart's allegations. He had been in bad odour with the hospital since 1924, when the 'large fees' he was charging private patients were brought to the attention of its committee.[77] The hospital minutes state he was dismissed after an argument with the matron, though he claimed it was 'because I endeavoured to get the Board of Management to make reforms which the entire qualified Honorary Staff considered necessary'.[78] His claim that the hospital was anti-vaccination is not substantiated by any other sources, the board's interference with clinicians does not seem to have been greater than at other hospitals, and deaths due to infected cat-gut were more likely the result of poor surgical technique than hospital policy. Peart apparently wanted to cause as much damage as possible: he was directed by the King's Fund to stop the hospital receiving ambulance cases, and so decrease its patient numbers and prestige, and this he did by writing to London County Council, which immediately removed the hospital from its ambulance list on the grounds that it 'prohibits the use of serums and discourages the use of vaccines'.[79]

In response, the hospital board told the Council 'that in cases of tetanus and diphtheria and all else medical officers are authorized to take all steps necessary for the preservation of life'.[80] It is not clear how long this compromise had been going on, but it was a damaging admission, as the hospital appeared either unsafe or hypocritical, depending on whether patients had actually been allowed to have antiserum. Some of its supporters, such as the abolitionist BUAV, deplored this concession to expediency, and resignations of governors followed. The County Council took 4 years to reinstate the hospital on the ambulance list, at which time the hospital secretary told the King's Fund that 'In the opinion and practice of the medical staff there is nothing in our constitution or Articles of Association which limits them in treating patients under their care in any way different from that which they practice in other hospitals in which they work. They maintain that sera are not the products of Vivisection'.[81] This removed any pretence that the hospital's practices were different from the norm, which further alienated its core supporters, while making no difference to the King's Fund's boycott.[82]

By the early 1930s, the hospital's financial shortfall had become unmanageable. Eight board members resigned, and the sale of £4300 in investments failed to clear its debts.[83] Late in 1934, the mortgaged hospital received an ultimatum from Barclays Bank, and Lord Ernest made a desperate appeal to the King's Fund: 'My suggestion is that … you, as custodians of the largest British hospital fund, should take the hospital over as the Battersea General Hospital, without the objectionable title of "Antivivisection"'. He added: 'Personally I should welcome relief from my position as Chairman which is burdensome and which occupies much of my time which could be more profitably employed'. The medical and nursing staff were, he wrote, 'second to none' and the building 'modern and up to date in every respect'; it would be a 'calamity' for Battersea if it ceased to operate.[84] In February 1935, Sir Herbert Lush-Wilson (1850–1941) persuaded the Goldsmiths' Company to give the hospital £100 in the expectation that it would soon abandon its anti-vivisection charter, though this was 'not to be mentioned outside the Board Room'. Meanwhile, Lord Ernest continued secretly to negotiate with the King's Fund, which accepted that the hospital was 'geographically' essential.[85]

The Fund agreed to help only if 'Anti-Vivisection' were removed from the hospital's title and charter, which required winding up the company. Realising that this was the Fund's goal, Coleridge tried to press them into assisting immediately on compassionate grounds, but they refused.[86] The board tried to change the hospital's name by a simple vote but this was blocked by the governors, and would in any case not have satisfied the King's Fund, which complained that 'the Hospital's practice was not in accordance with its principles'.[87] Lord Ernest also appealed to various other medical charities, but without success:

> The Battersea General Hospital is the only Anti-Vivisection Hospital in the London District and, because of its principles, it is debarred by the prejudice of those in authority from participation in King Edward's Hospital Fund, The Metropolitan Hospitals Sunday Fund, the Charitable bequests of the City Livery Companies and other distributing bodies who generously contribute to the expenses of other London Hospitals. This attitude is unreasonable and unjust because the Battersea Hospital serves a large and very poor district and, by general consent, serves it admirably. … THIS IS PRACTICALLY IN THE NATURE OF AN S.O.S.[88]

Then, in what was either an egregious act of disloyalty or an inept attempt at dissimulation, Lord Ernest told the King's Fund that the governors 'consisted mainly of fanatical women', and the press that '[t]he "anti-vivisection" part of the name of the hospital is a meaningless term pinned to it many years ago, and is a great handicap'.[89] As the *Lancet* noted, this was 'not easily reconciled with the provocative policy for which Battersea has stood in the past'.[90]

Once the situation became publicly known, the King's Fund started to receive complaints about its intransigence. As the Fund was entirely reliant on public money, it seems strange that they so readily ignored public opinion with regard to vivisection, though they may rightly have assumed that committed anti-vivisectionists were unlikely to be among their most generous supporters: they ignored a letter from Coleridge after a check of their records showed he had last made a donation in 1920. They were certainly aware of the problem, as their postbag included letters from exasperated members of the public accusing them of using their influence to 'distort' clinical practice, of failing to honour the memory of Queen Victoria—'whose utter detestation of Vivisection was expressed in perfectly definite terms'[91]—of ignoring the fact that some of their £240,000 annual income must have come from people who were 'suspicious' of vivisection, and of failing to point out when they collected money 'that the Fund was only for the orthodox'.[92] A medical charity had never been less popular: H.R. Maynard, the Fund's long-serving secretary, urged its members to refrain from making any comment about the Anti-Vivisection Hospital, as they 'might not realise the dangers of talking about it outside'.[93] The Mayor of Battersea, a far cry from the outspoken radicals of the early part of the century, refused to allow a public meeting to discuss the crisis, fearing that local people would only use it 'to ventilate grievances'.[94]

The hospital's nurses gave up their holidays to raise money and some local people gave their savings; there was talk of a 'giant' petition asking the Prince of Wales personally to intervene as the Fund's chairman, and Lord Ernest wrote to tell him that 'all Battersea is in a ferment'.[95] The King's Fund sent its representatives to meet the Prince at Ascot races, and after hearing their reassurances, His Royal Highness 'fully realised that it would have been impossible to go back on the previous decisions of the Council, which are based on logical reasons'.[96] There was now only one remaining option, and Lord Ernest told the press that 'If we do not change our name we are dead'.[97] In an internal memo to the King's Fund's distribution committee, its Chairman, Edwin Cooper Perry (1856–1938), wrote: 'Let it die, as it will of inanition if we go on saying nothing'. The ambiguous 'it' may have referred to the bad publicity, but he might just as easily have meant the hospital.[98] Cooper Perry was knighted later that year, for services to charity.

The End of the Experiment

In defeat, Lord Ernest vented his spleen to the press, condemning as 'absolutely outrageous' the 'fanatical bigotry' that had 'killed' the hospital. His outburst made good copy: it was a 'blow for poor people', he said: 'If this hospital was in one of the smart well-dressed districts of London there would be no difficulty at all ... But we are situated in a poor district on the wrong side of the river for fashionable sympathy'. When the hospital finally closed at the beginning of June, there were reports of 'sad-eyed' locals watching as ambulances 'whisked' the fifty remaining patients off to other hospitals. Dr John Robert Lee initiated the longwinded process of changing the hospital's charter, informing the high court that in view of the general advance in medical knowledge it was no longer possible to run a hospital on anti-vivisection lines. Mr Justice Lee (no relation) replied that, while he sympathised with the hospital's original aims, he agreed they were no longer practical.[99]

A King's Fund inspection at the end of 1935 found the reopened hospital fit for its purpose and concluded that it had come to grief because of overspending.[100] A number of factors, they felt, had conspired to prevent the hospital paying its debts: declining interest in anti-vivisection in general, disillusionment with the Hospital's equivocation about the antiserum policy, and higher taxation that left the middle classes with less to spare for charitable purposes.[101] In addition, the hospital's policy of paying local people fair wages had kept running costs high, and the anti-vivisection remit made it hard to recruit junior staff and necessitated paying more for those prepared to sign up.[102]

Lord Ernest stepped down as chairman in favour of Sidney Parkes, a London builder and sports promoter, who disconcertingly promised that his strategy to restore the hospital's fortunes would be 'absolutely legal'.[103] Five board members resigned within a year of his appointment, and though he effected 'every possible economy'—reducing the use of X-ray film, requiring attendees at board meetings to pay sixpence for tea and cake, and even accepting a legacy of £100 bequeathed to the (now non-existent) 'Anti-Vivisection Hospital', debts continued to grow.[104] Parkes had personally guaranteed a £6500 bank loan, but there seemed no prospect of repaying it and he resigned in January 1936, 'anxious to be relieved of this responsibility', and having discovered the hard way that 'the Hospital had lost a great deal of income through abandoning anti-vivisection'.[105]

Once its charter had been changed, the hospital's honorary staff were obliged to resign and renew their contracts without the anti-cruelty clause. One who did not do so was Alexander Bowie, the hospital's first chairman, who wrote to the board: 'I remember that we began with one little girl patient. But it soon grew till the number was 100. I appointed the first house physician, a woman, the first nurse and the first medical staff. The hospital was obviously needed, and it has been successful so far as the treatment of patients is concerned…'.[106]

Conclusion

The National Anti-Vivisection Hospital was a thirty-year experiment in putting anti-vivisection principles into practice. It did not directly save a single animal from vivisection, but as a standing protest against cruelty, it became a flagship of the anti-vivisection cause, providing a visible, viable alternative to conventional, 'vivisecting' hospitals and medical schools. For the first time, philanthropists, women's rights activists, socialists, trade unionists, evangelical Christians and other champions of underdogs could help the sick poor without having to compromise their opposition to animal experiments. Like the short-lived but iconic statue of the Brown Dog nearby, the hospital was a rallying point for defenders of humane science, and a provocation to medical orthodoxy. If its efforts to look state-of-the-art by purchasing the latest gadgets looked unconvincing, it at least managed to provide facilities to match those of most conventional district hospitals. Its finances were intentionally kept complex, as like all hospitals dependent on charity it tried to appear needier than it was, but until the 1930s it remained solvent without the help of any of the state-apportioned funds that bolstered the rest of the voluntary system. The fact that there was enough anti-vivisection money to keep even one hospital going was an embarrassment for the medical establishment, and helped convince them that anti-vivisection had great public sympathy and almost unlimited financial support.[107]

In its early years, the hospital made greater efforts to win South Londoners' hearts than their money: 'Give us your help', read a flyer, 'but, above all, give us your sympathy'. Sympathy was an old-fashioned virtue, out of step with the medical profession's push towards dispassionate science, which anti-vivisectionists tried to block by preaching the populist message that knowledge won at the cost of cruelty was not worth the price paid. Experimentalists dismissed such views as sentimentalism or hypocrisy, and tried to shift the focus to what science could achieve rather than the character and methods of those who achieved it. As the twentieth century progressed, the old ideal of the humane, compassionate physician went the way of the honourable soldier and the *noblesse oblige* politician, supplanted by the utilitarian pragmatist who sought the best outcome for the greatest number by any means necessary. By the 1930s, medical scientists had put their case so insistently that it was widely, though perhaps regretfully, accepted among most educated Britons that, as the judge who revoked the hospital's charter put it, medical advances were no longer possible without experiments on living animals. An Anti-Vivisection Hospital could never show that vivisection yielded no benefits: only that a hospital could be run effectively without it, and that there were sufficient conscientious objectors to keep it solvent.

In theory, nothing could have been fairer than the voluntary hospital system: each institution relied on personal philanthropy and received nothing from the public purse; each was governed by a committee answerable to its subscribers, and staffed by consultants who received no salaries. In practice, however, the interposition of the King's Fund and other semi-official charity administrators between donors and recipients led to a system of state-approved patronage. The Fund was what would later be called a QUANGO (Quasi-Autonomous Non-Governmental Organization), answerable in theory to the Crown but in practice to no one outside its own board room (which was the dining room of Marlborough House). Burdett had a talent for getting his own way, but he had no need to persuade a committee that included the Lord Mayor, the Bishop of London, Lords Rothschild and Lister, the Governor of the Bank of England, the President of the Royal Society and the Presidents of the medical and surgical Royal Colleges to refuse support for a hospital that opposed vivisection.[108] The result was that, between 1897 and 1948, the London (later Royal) Homoeopathic Hospital received a total of £70,793, the National Temperance £127,595, and the Anti-Vivisection, nothing,[109] although of the twelve million pounds collected by the fund over that time, thousands must have been given by anti-vivisectionists.

Measured against the criteria used to assess other voluntary hospitals, the Anti-Vivisection held its own. In fact, its work as a hospital was perhaps too successful, since the board pursued their ambitions for growth at the cost of compromising their principles. There was truth in the King's Fund's allegation that by the late 1920s the hospital's management were hypocritically preaching what they sometimes failed to practice, and it was this moral circumlocution, as much as the boycott by the funds, that killed the hospital by alienating its supporters. In 1935, the hospital's board chose to abandon its ideology in order to survive as an institution: a betrayal for its staunch anti-vivisection supporters, but an act of compassion to the sick poor of Battersea, who had been caught up, willingly or otherwise, in an extraordinary and bitterly contested ideological conflict. Even after the board agreed to abandon anti-vivisection, the King's Fund declined to intervene for the sake of the remaining patients, having determined to force the hospital's closure to drive home its point that anti-vivisection was not a viable option.

Shorn of its anti-vivisection trappings, the revived hospital served the people of Battersea until 1972, when it finally succumbed to a National Health Service reorganization. It had been unique in the British hospital system in having been set up and run entirely with anti-vivisection money, but in later years its origins and ethos were purposefully forgotten: the *British Medical Journal's* obituaries of doctors who had worked there in the early days never mentioned the word 'anti-vivisection'. The Hospital's message, that medicine could be practised with compassion, and that some patients preferred this to the cold hand of science, had been so radically unsettling that the establishment wanted it silenced—perhaps the clearest indication of its importance to the anti-vivisection movement.

Notes

1. 'The case of Mabel Florence Jones', *Lancet*, *173* (1909), 124–126; 'Hospital Treatment', *Times*, 31 December 1908, 10 (Hospital Treatment 1908).
2. '"No experiments on patients," but "every kind of operation"', *Nottingham Evening Post*, 31 December 1908, 8 (No experiments on patients," but "every kind of operation 1908).
3. 'Child's death', *Sheffield Evening Telegraph*, 31 December 1908, 2. Many press cuttings on 'human vivisection' are preserved in a scrapbook in Well SA/LIS/E8 (Child's death 1908).
4. Stephen Coleridge, *The Diversion of Hospital Funds: A Controversy between the Hon. Stephen Coleridge and the 'British Medical Journal'* (London: National Anti-Vivisection Society, 1901) (Coleridge 1901).
5. 'Anti-vivisection methods', *The Hospital*, *32* (1902), 244–245.
6. FRCS, 'A guide for the charitable', *Times*, 9 January 1902, 10 (FRCS 1902).
7. Extract from the register of unreported charities, LMA A/KE/245/04; 'Hospital in a lawsuit', *Evening News*, 28 December 1936.
8. Anti-Vivisection Hospital flyer (1903), LMA A/KE/260/001.
9. Letter, G.W.F. Robbins to H.R. Maynard of the King's Fund, 11 November 1907, LMA A/KE/260/001.
10. Hospital board minutes, September 1927, LMA H6/BG/A1/4, p. 137.
11. King's Fund memorandum, *c.* 1912, LMA A/KE/260/001.
12. Extract from visitors' report (1906), LMA A/KE/260/001.
13. On the history of the funds, see F.K. Prochaska, *Philanthropy and the Hospitals of London: The King's Fund, 1897–1990* (Oxford: Clarendon Press, 1992) (Prochaska 1992).

14. Letter, Robbins to Sydney Holland, 18 December 1907; Holland to Robbins, 23 December 1907, LMA A/KE/260/001.
15. 'Ex-Lord Mayor and vicar', *Lancashire Evening Post*, 17 December 1908, 2 (Ex-Lord Mayor and vicar 1908).
16. 'The National Anti-Vivisection Hospital', *Medical Times*, 11 January 1908, 24 (The National Anti-Vivisection Hospital 1908).
17. Prochaska, *Philanthropy and the Hospitals of London*, 53.
18. *Gloucester Citizen*, 24 September 1907, 4; *Times*, 1 October 1907, 10.
19. *Exeter and Plymouth Gazette*, 13 June 1904, 3.
20. Letter, Edmund Hay Currie of the Sunday Fund to Robbins, 15 July 1907, LMA A/KE/260/001.
21. LMA A/KE/245/04.
22. Memorandum, March 1930, quoting a reply from the hospital in 1912, LMA A/KE/260/002.
23. *Exeter and Plymouth Gazette*, 13 June 1904, 3.
24. Letters: Currie to Robbins, 15 July 1907; E.A.G. Pomeroy and Alex Bowie to Currie, 27 August 1907, LMA A/KE/260/001.
25. Peter Mason, *The Brown Dog Affair: the Story of a Monument that Divided the Nation* (London: Two Sevens Publishing, 1997), 55. See also Lansbury, *The Old Brown Dog*; Margo DeMello, *Animals and Society: an Introduction to Human-Animal Studies* (New York: Colombia University Press, 2012), 183–186 and Joe Cain, *The Brown Dog in Battersea Park* (London: Euston Grove Press, 2013) (Mason 1997; Lansbury 2012; Cain 2013).
26. 'The "brown dog" disturbances', *Medical Press and Circular, 85* (1907), 593.
27. Lansbury, *The Old Brown Dog*, 188; Debbie Tacium, 'A History of Antivivisection from the 1800s to the Present: Part I (mid-1800s to 1914)', *Veterinary Heritage, 31*, (2008), 1–9 (Tacium 2008).
28. Letter, Rose M. George to the Treasurer, King's Fund, 22 May 1930, LMA A/KE/260/002.
29. 'Under the seat', *Chambers's Journal, 50* (1873), 147–149; A Citizen, 'Vivisection', *Sheffield Daily Telegraph*, 18 May 1899, 7.
30. Buettinger, 'Antivivisection'.
31. Mason, *The Brown Dog Affair*, 8; R.T. Reid, *On Vivisection* (London: National Anti-Vivisection Society, 1902), 6. On anti-vivisection and feminine sentiment see Rob Boddice, 'Equanimity in the Laboratory? The Sentimentalists versus the Sufferers in America *c.*

1900', *History of Emotions—Insights into Research*, October 2013, doi:10.14280/08241.10 (Reid 1902).
32. French, *Antivivisection and Medical Science*.
33. Letter, Pomeroy and Bowie to Currie, 27 August 1907, LMA A/KE/260/001.
34. 'Anti-vivisection meeting in Cheltenham', *Cheltenham Looker-On*, 23 November 1907, 15 (Anti-vivisection meeting in Cheltenham 1907).
35. T. Waldron Bradley. *Torture in Laboratories and Hospitals* (Broadsheet, n.d.), Well SA/RDS A3.
36. Hospital board minutes, 6 August 1908, LMA H6/BG/A1/1; 'The anti-vivisection hospital', *The Hospital*, 25 September 1909, 677.
37. Letters: Savile Crossley to Davis, 21 December 1909, LMA A/KE/260/001; Rose M. George to the Treasurer, King's Fund, 22 May 1930, LMA A/KE/260/002.
38. King's Fund notes, 16 December 1907, LMA A/KE/260/001.
39. Letter, Burdett to Maynard, 28 September 1909, LMA A/KE/260/001.
40. J. Stratton, 'Anti-vivisection and sport', *Medical Press and Circular, 83* (1907), 48 (Stratton 1907).
41. Reid, *On Vivisection*, 5.
42. Edward Berdoe, 'Human vivisections', *Bristol Mercury*, 4 June 1894 (Berdoe 1894).
43. 'Anti-vivisection', *Medical Press and Circular, 69* (1900), 276–277; 'Anti-vivisectionists take note!', *Medical Press and Circular*, (1901), 247–248.
44. Vivisection, like anatomy, was presented as a heroic exercise in self-discipline: see Bates, 'Vivisection, virtue ethics' and Simon Chaplin, 'The heroic anatomist'.
45. This was true of many, though a significant minority were ethical vegetarians: Twigg, *The Vegetarian Movement*, 183–185.
46. F.R.S., 'Lord Llangattock and the anti-vivisection society', *BMJ, 1* (1901), 1239 (F.R.S. 1901).
47. J. Keri Cronin, '"A mute yet eloquent protest": visual culture and anti-vivisection activism in the age of mechanical reproduction', in John Sorenson (ed.), *Critical Animal Studies: Thinking the Unthinkable* (Toronto: Canadian Scholars' Press, 2014), 284–297, on p. 290. For a dissenting view see Anne DeWitt, *Moral Authority, Men of Science and the Victorian Novel* (Cambridge: Cambridge University Press, 2013), 127 (Cronin 2014; DeWitt 2013).

48. Edward Maitland, *Anna Kingsford: Her Life, Letters, Diary and Work* (London: George Redway, 1896), 340 (Maitland 1896).
49. Twigg, *The Vegetarian Movement*, 175.
50. Anna Bonus Kingsford and Edward Maitland, *The Perfect Way; or, the Finding of Christ* (Cambridge: Cambridge University Press, 2011), 31, 184 (Kingsford and Maitland 2011).
51. Mrs Algernon Kingsford, *Violationism: or Sorcery in Science* (Bath: 1887), 1; *Pasteur, His Method and Results* (Hampstead: 1886), 28; MA Cambridge, 'The pseudo-scientific inquisition', *Ethics*, 3 October 1903, quoted in *Zoophilist, 23* (1903/1904), 155 (Kingsford 1887).
52. Legally there was no cruelty where there was justification: Bates, 'Vivisection, virtue ethics'.
53. Hospital and general purposes committee minutes, 13 September 1910, LMA HO6/BG/A/01/002.
54. Hospital board minutes, 6 December 1911, LMA HO6/BG/A/01/002, p. 151.
55. Special board minutes, 14 June 1911, LMA HO6/BG/A/01/002, pp. 99–102; Hospital board minutes, June 1914, LMA HO6/BG/A/01/002, p. 423. On the light and colour bath see J. Stenson Hooper, 'A new light and colour bath', *Lancet, 2* (1903), 434 (Hooper 1903).
56. Visitors' report, 1908, LMA A/KE/260/001.
57. Ibid. To this day, politicians and public fail to understand that a high death rate is a consequence of treating the sickest patients.
58. 'Hint to hospital' (newspaper cutting), n.d., LMA A/KE/260/001. It was not unusual at the time not to keep case notes, particularly for out-patients.
59. Hospital board minutes, 5 July 1911, LMA HO6/BG/A/01/002, pp. 110–118.
60. Hospital board minutes, 5 September and 3 October 1907, LMA H6/BG/A1/1.
61. Hospital board minutes, May 1922, LMA H6/BG/A1/3, pp. 344–346; Letter, J. Bench to King's Fund, 26 March 1912, LMA A/KE/260/001.
62. Letter, Maynard to Robbins, 24 May 1912, LMA A/KE/260/001.
63. Emergency committee minutes, 21 August 1912; Hospital board minutes, September 1912, LMA HO6/BG/A/01/002, pp. 215–219, 224.
64. Hospital board minutes, March 1926, April 1926, March 1927, LMA H6/BG/A1/4, pp. 28, 33, 37–38, 106.

65. Letter, M.E. Culme-Seymour to Maynard, 1 June 1914, LMA A/KE/260/001. Mary, one of the two daughters of Admiral Sir Michael Culme-Seymour, was known for the scandal in which it was claimed she had secretly married the young George V.
66. Memorandum, 1922, LMA A/KE/260/001.
67. John Vyvyan, *The Dark Face of Science* (London: Michael Joseph, 1971), 95 (Vyvyan 1971).
68. Hospital board minutes, June 1914, LMA HO6/BG/A/01/002, pp. 415–422.
69. Hospital board minutes, 4 October 1906, LMA H6/BG/A1/1.
70. Hospital and general purposes committee minutes, September 1925, LMA H6/BG/A3/1.
71. There were 247 in total: list of governors, LMA H6/BG/A9/1; Hospital board minutes, June 1933, LMA H6/BG/A1/5, p. 244.
72. Hospital board minutes, May 1928, LMA H6/BG/A1/4, pp. 198–199.
73. Report of Sir Cooper Perry and Sir Frederick Fry following a visit to the Anti-Vivisection Hospital, 22 July 1922, LMA A/KE/260/001.
74. Memorandum, LMA A/KE/245/04.
75. Hospital and general purposes committee minutes, June 1929, LMA H6/BG/A9/1, p. 105. These were estimated residues of estates and may exceed the amounts actually received.
76. Letter, J.F. Peart to Maynard, 28 February 1927, LMA A/KE/260/001.
77. Hospital and general purposes committee minutes, Oct 1924, LMA H6/BG/A3/1.
78. Letter, Peart to Maynard, 28 February 1927, LMA A/KE/260/001.
79. Letter, Cox to the Secretary, Anti-Vivisection Hospital, 12 August 1927, LMA A/KE/260/001.
80. Hospital board minutes, 12 July 1928, LMA A/KE/260/001.
81. Letter, Cox to the Medical Superintendent, 17 March 1932, LMA A/KE/260/001.
82. Letter, Harry W. Woolven to Maynard, 18 July 1932, LMA A/KE/260/001.
83. King's Fund papers, LMA A/KE/245/04; Hospital finance committee minutes, April 1933, LMA A6/BG/A4/1.
84. Letter, Lord Ernest Hamilton to Maynard, 19 December 1934, LMA A/KE/260/002.
85. Hospital board minutes, February 1935, LMA H6/BG/A1/6, pp. 26–27.

86. Letter, Thos H.D. Hogg to the Treasurer, King's Fund, 28 May 1934, LMA A/KE/260/002.
87. Memorandum, 28 April 1932, LMA A/KE/260/002.
88. Letter, Aston Charities Trust to King's Fund, 14 April 1934, LMA A/KE/260/002.
89. Memorandum of meeting between Sir Cooper Perry and Hamilton, 15 January 1935, LMA A/KE/245/04; 'Hospital "killed" by a name', *Morning Post*, 30 May 1935 (Hospital "killed" by a name 1935).
90. 'The name of a hospital', *Lancet*, 8 June 1935.
91. Letter from James Blackwood to Maynard, 9 July 1935, LMA A/KE/245/04.
92. 'Closing a hospital', *Star*, 7 June 1935.
93. Letter, Maynard to Sir Harold Wernher, 19 June 1935, LMA A/KE/245/04.
94. Memorandum of telephone enquiry from A. Bailey, 19 June 1935, LMA A/KE/245/04.
95. 'Battersea General Hospital', *South Western Star*, 23 June 1935; 'Battersea General Hospital fighting for life', *Star*, 15 June 1935, 9; Letter, Sir Godfrey Thomas to Maynard, 11 June 1935, LMA A/KE/245/04.
96. Letter, Wernher to Maynard, 22 June 1935, LMA A/KE/245/04.
97. 'Chance of life for hospital', *Morning Post*, 31 May 1935 (Chance of life for hospital 1935).
98. Memorandum from E. Cooper Perry, 30 May 1935, LMA A/KE/245/04.
99. 'Alteration of a hospital's objects', *BMJ*, *2* (1935), 1055.
100. Distribution committee minutes, December 1935, LMA A/KE/245/04.
101. 'Boycotted Hospital: Battersea ceases to be anti-vivisectionist', *News Chronicle*, 20 November 1935 (Boycotted Hospital 1935).
102. Memorandum of interview with Parker, January 1936, LMA A/KE/245/04; Report of inspection, February 1938, LMA A/KE/512(5).
103. 'Hospital board', June 1935, LMA H6/BG/A1/6, pp. 41–44.
104. LMA A/KE/245/04.
105. Hospital finance committee minutes, December 1937, LMA A6/BG/A4/1, pp. 84–91.
106. 'Hospital in a lawsuit', *Evening News*, 28 December 1936 (Hospital in a lawsuit 1936).

107. Letter, Medical Secretary, BMA to Secretary, MRC, 11 March 1927, Well SA/BMA/C86.
108. Prochaska, *Philanthropy and the Hospitals of London*, 19. The presence of even one woman on the committee might have helped the Anti-Vivisection Hospital.
109. Prochaska, *Philanthropy and the Hospitals of London*, 290.

References

Anti-vivisection meeting in Cheltenham. (1907, November 23). *Cheltenham Looker-On*, 15.

Berdoe, E. (1894, June 4). Human vivisections. *Bristol Mercury.*

Bradley, T. W. (n.d.). *Torture in Laboratories and Hospitals* (Broadsheet).

Boycotted Hospital: Battersea ceases to be anti-vivisectionist. (1935, November 20). *News Chronicle.*

Cain, J. (2013). *The brown dog in Battersea park.* London: Euston Grove Press.

Chance of life for hospital. (1935, May 31). *Morning Post.*

Child's death. (1908, December 31). *Sheffield Evening Telegraph,* 2.

Coleridge, S. (1901). *The diversion of hospital funds: A controversy between the Hon. Stephen Coleridge and the 'British medical journal'.* London: National Anti-Vivisection Society.

Cronin, J. K. (2014). "A mute yet eloquent protest": visual culture and anti-vivisection activism in the age of mechanical reproduction. In J. Sorenson (Ed.), *Critical animal studies: Thinking the unthinkable* (pp. 284–297 on p. 290). Toronto: Canadian Scholars' Press.

DeWitt, A. (2013). *Moral authority, men of science and the victorian novel* (p. 127). Cambridge: Cambridge University Press.

Ex-Lord Mayor and vicar. (1908, December 17). *Lancashire Evening Post,* 2.

F.R.S. (1901). Lord llangattock and the anti-vivisection society. *BMJ, 1,* 1239.

FRCS. (1902, January 9). A guide for the charitable. *Times,* 10.

Hospital Treatment. (1908, December 31). *Times,* 10.

Hospital "killed" by a name. (1935, May 30). *Morning Post.*

Hospital in a lawsuit. (1936, December 28). *Evening News.*

Kingsford, A. (1887). *Violationism: Or sorcery in science* (Vol. 1). *Bath.*

Kingsford, A. B., & Maitland, E. (2011). *The perfect way; or, the finding of Christ.* Cambridge: Cambridge University Press.

Lansbury. (2012). *The old brown Dog*; margo demello, *animals and society: An introduction to human–animal studies* (pp. 183–186). New York: Colombia University Press.
Maitland, E. (1896). *Anna kingsford: Her life, letters, diary and work*. London: George Redway.
Mason, P. (1997). *The brown dog affair: The story of a monument that divided the nation*. London: Two Sevens Publishing.
"No experiments on patients," but "every kind of operation". (1908, December 31). *Nottingham Evening Post, 8*.
Prochaska, F. K. (1992). *Philanthropy and the hospitals of London: The king's fund, 1897–1990*. Oxford: Clarendon Press.
Reid, R. T. (1902). *On Vivisection* (p. 6). London: National Anti-Vivisection Society.
Stenson H. J. (1903). A new light and colour bath. *Lancet, 2*, 434.
Stratton, J. (1907). Anti-vivisection and sport. *Medical Press and Circular, 83*, 48.
Tacium, D. (2008). A history of antivivisection from the 1800s to the present: Part I (mid-1800s to 1914). *Veterinary Heritage, 31*, 1–9.
The National Anti-Vivisection Hospital. (1908, January 11). *Medical Times*, 24.
Vyvyan, J. (1971). *The dark face of science*. London: Michael Joseph.

6

The Research Defence Society: Mobilizing the Medical Profession for Materialist Science in the Early-Twentieth Century

At the end of the nineteenth century, medical experimenters were on the defensive. Although the 1876 Act had done nothing to reduce animal use, and Britain's physiologists were confident they could ensure it was 'harmlessly administered' by putting 'effectual pressure upon officials…',[1] it was still more restrictive than the laws of any other European nation, and more intrusive than any of them wanted: one American observer thought it 'significantly handicapped the teaching (if not the practice) of British physiology'.[2] Anti-visectionists naturally claimed the Act did not go far enough, and used initiatives such as anti-vivisection hospitals and pamphlet wars to raise doubts over whether experiments on animals were necessary, and fears that they would inevitably lead on to human experimentation.

The nineteenth-century medical profession had been able to extract some positive publicity from the bitter dispute over vivisection by presenting it as a difficult and demanding task that required great fortitude and commitment to science. Flouting conventional sensibilities had, after all, served medics well in the recent past, when body snatching scandals had introduced the trope of the 'mad' scientist, a heroic figure who transgressed moral boundaries not for personal gain but to win

A.W.H. Bates, *Anti-Vivisection and the Profession of Medicine in Britain*,
The Palgrave Macmillan Animal Ethics Series, DOI 10.1057/978-1-137-55697-4_6

valuable knowledge for the benefit of mankind. The public were willing to be persuaded that the anatomist's noble ends might justify the base and sometimes illegal means used to obtain corpses, though their response was strangely ambivalent: angry crowds called for body-snatchers to be hanged, while anatomy shows became so popular that the subject 'turned to gold'.[3] The furore certainly made it clear to everyone that, after the Anatomy Act, doctors enjoyed privileged access to a body (of course) of knowledge that was denied to laymen, who had neither the opportunity nor the stamina to attend the dissections necessary to obtain it.

In the late-nineteenth century, vivisection assumed a similar function, and vivisectionists, like anatomists before them, enjoyed an ambiguous reputation as both perpetrators of atrocities and pioneers of science. In the twentieth century, however, when vivisection was set up as one of the pillars of experimental medicine, it could hardly remain the prerogative of a few eccentric, taboo-breaking innovators. It had to be normalized within a medical culture that based its intellectual and moral authority on the intimate relationship between professional knowledge and laboratory experimentation.

An obvious obstacle to this was the steady growth of anti-vivisection organizations, which kept up the pressure on experimenters by publically questioning their judgement in using animals to study human disease.[4] According to Tansey, it was the antis persistence that led to the setting up of another Royal Commission in 1906.[5] By this time, the use of laboratory animals was far greater than when the first commission had reported 30 years earlier: the nationally-funded Imperial Cancer Research Fund (ICRF) alone, founded in 1902, was already performing 8,600 experiments a year.[6] Although these were all carried out in accordance with the 1876 Act, large increases of this kind would probably not have commanded public support, and so vivisectionists tended not to publicise them. A new anti-vivisection strategy arose of publishing details of how many experiments were being performed in the hope of shaming vivisectionists into stopping: the *Anti-Vivisection Review* called this publicity 'The Light dreaded by all Vivisectors'.[7]

The second Royal Commission offered an important opportunity for experimenters to launch a 'counter-attack' in the propaganda war. The medical community initially coordinated their response through the Association for the Advancement of Medical Research (AAMR), a working group that had been formed in the wake of the Cruelty to Animals Act, to advise the Home Office on granting licenses. Concerned that the Commission planned to tighten up the regulations, a number of leading physiologists decided to found a new group, the Research Defence Society (RDS), whose inaugural meeting on 27 January 1908 in London's Harley Street saw Lord Cromer elected as President and Stephen Paget (1855–1926) as Secretary. It consisted of a small but distinguished all-male group of physiologists, most of whom had links with UCL, which, thanks to the Brown Dog riots, was the best-known centre for animal experimentation in the country. Among those present at the first meeting were Professor Cushny,[8] Sir Victor Horsley (1857–1916), Dr Charles Edward Beevor (1854–1908), Dr Leonard Hill (1866–1952), Lord Justice Fletcher Moulton (1844–1921) and Sydney Holland. The RDS received a start-up grant of £185 jointly from the Physiological Society (another pro-vivisection group, founded in 1876 'for mutual benefit and protection') and Professor Ernest Starling's (1866–1927) UCL working group, which was busy preparing evidence for the Commission.[9]

The Earl of Cromer, a diplomat and banker, had very little to do with the day to day running of the Society. That task fell to Paget, who was also Secretary of the AAMR, many of whose members joined the fledgling RDS, the two organizations eventually amalgamating in 1917.[10] Paget, whose role was somewhat akin to that of Stephen Coleridge in the anti-vivisection movement, was not himself a vivisectionist and had no connection with UCL. He was medically qualified, but had given up practice altogether in 1910 to devote his professional energies to justifying vivisection, writing frequent articles and letters, and lecturing widely on the topic, despite his worsening health.[11]

Most of the other RDS members were active researchers. Sir Victor Horsley, FRS, who had trained at UCL before becoming Professor of Surgery there, was a man of strong social principles—a temperance reformer and supporter of women's suffrage—and was particularly noted for his kindness to patients. In writings such as 'The Morality of Vivisection', he argued that excessive feeling for animals was displacing proper concern for humans. His own concern for humanity led him to vivisect over 3000 animals (his work on gunshot wounds in dogs involved shooting them in the head), a record hotly criticised in the correspondence columns of *The Times*. He had every reason to resent anti-vivisectionists, having been professor at the notorious Brown Institute in London's Vauxhall (a post previously held by Burdon-Sanderson, author of the vivisectors' handbook), an institution the BUAV and others had strenuously, though unsuccessfully, campaigned to close.[12] It was Horsley who had helped persuade his colleague Bayliss to bring the so-called 'Brown Dog' libel action against Stephen Coleridge in 1903 for reading out an extract from *The Shambles of Science* at a public meeting—UCL men were particularly riled by the chapter entitled 'Fun', in which Lind af Hageby described their 'jokes and laughter' during experiments.

Despite being a dog owner himself (a photograph shows him holding an understandably nervous looking Jack Russell), Horsley was spokesman for the Society for the Prevention of Hydrophobia, and a leading advocate of compulsory dog muzzling—the Society's answer to Britain's periodic outbreaks of 'hydrophobia'. These epidemics took the form of a rash of press reports about 'mad' dogs, at least some of which were probably suffering from common canine diseases such as distemper, or simply misbehaving, rather than carrying the dreaded disease.[13] How much genuine rabies there was in early-twentieth century Britain remains an unanswered question, but scare tactics from the Society for the Prevention of Hydrophobia, such as recommending that all dogs had to be kept muzzled in public in order to prevent a national rabies epidemic, were certainly expedient for vivisectionists, for whom unwelcome and unwanted strays were an easy source of low cost experimental subjects.[14]

Another two UCL men at the inaugural RDS meeting were Leonard Erskine Hill, a physiologist working on decompression sickness, and who held a high view of research ('the path which saves the millions when found'),[15] and Beevor, an associate of Horsley.[16] An important non-medical supporter was Moulton, a barrister who gave evidence to the Royal Commission; he 'preferred not to be a member', in case this was thought to conflict with his legal work, but after he became an Appeal Court judge in 1912, and the first chairman of the Medical Research Council (MRC) the following year, he used his influence to help the RDS 'again and again'.[17]

The second Royal Commission's report was a foregone conclusion given its skewed composition: naturally enough, there were several vivisectors on the panel, but the BUAV's attempt to have Walter Hadwen appointed was rejected on the grounds that as an anti-vivisectionist, he would be biased. Between 1906 and 1912 the commission sifted a large amount of evidence, before unsurprisingly endorsing the status quo. Their major recommendation was the usual one for a public enquiry desirous of seeming to act while in fact doing nothing: they set up a committee to take over the AAMR's role of advising on licensing, which in the BUAV's view made no difference. While the Commission was still pondering the evidence, vivisection had received a boost from the 1911 National Insurance Act, which set aside state (i.e., taxpayers') money to fund medical research.[18] Two years later, the Medical Research Committee and Advisory Council (later the MRC) was formed to control how the money was allocated.

The Early Years

Membership of the RDS was by invitation only and within a month of its foundation almost three hundred experimenters had joined, only six of those approached having declined. The annual subscription was 5 s and life membership £10: since one would have had to live another 40 years for life membership to work out cheaper, the Society apparently had young experimenters in its sights, but as there are no extant membership lists, we cannot be sure who joined. The secrecy was not because members would have faced any direct threat—violence against vivisectionists was unknown until the 1970s—but because being known as a vivisectionist might have deterred some donors, and patients. After only a few months there were over a thousand members, including eighty-four women, plus many hundreds of associates, mostly medical students, who paid half a crown.[19]

The RDS quickly acquired a list of distinguished vice-presidents to rival those of the anti-vivisection societies: these included Elizabeth Garrett Anderson, Lord Curzon, the Duke of Devonshire, Edward Elgar, M.R. James, Rudyard Kipling, Ray Lankester, William Osler, and Henry Wellcome.[20] To the dismay of the anti-vivisection camp, sixteen Anglican bishops signed up, perhaps desirous of demonstrating, as the Bishop of Edinburgh had stressed at a church congress 20 years earlier, that the Church was not 'anti-science'.[21] RDS meetings were, and remained, ticket only, despite being described as 'public', but interested laypeople could, and did, attend; at a meeting of the Kensington branch, more than half the audience were women.[22]

The initial strategy was to hold educational meetings and provide speakers for public debates. The society kept itself abreast of the times and locations of anti-vivisection meetings, and accepted 'challenges' to send along a speaker. These were competitive debates, with a vote taken at the end, and the RDS minutes record that they 'won' in Winchester and Bow, but lost in Bath and Oxford. However engaging these sessions were to those present, the small numbers voting—usually less than a hundred—suggests they did not have a very wide appeal. Recognising that competitive debating was unlikely to achieve its objects, the RDS decided not to accept any further invitations from anti-vivisection societies, though they continued to provide public speakers into the 1920s.[23]

Both the RDS and their opponents were, however, willing to continue the argument at a less intellectual level. In January 1909, the committee was shown a circular, signed 'M. Cowan', outlining 'a plan of prayer for the sudden death of this or that person making experiments on animals'. This echo of Anna Kingsford's notorious campaign of psychic assassination, which she claimed had brought about the deaths of Claude Bernard and Paul Bert, was the sort of anti-vivisection excess that the RDS quite reasonably thought would help their cause. Unfortunately, their own tactics were scarcely more subtle; they accused Lord Llangattock of being 'addicted' to stag hunting, a libel that Dr Morgan Jones for the RDS was foolish enough to try to defend, leaving the Society with no choice but to publish an apology in order to avoid being sued, though Paget churlishly limited it to 'a purely formal expression of regret'.[24]

The task of the RDS was made easier by the anti-vivisectionists' inherent disunity. A major schism had occurred in 1898 when the National Anti-Vivisection Society passed the following resolution by 29 votes to 23:

> The Council affirms that, while the demand for the total abolition of vivisection will ever remain the ultimate object of the National Anti-Vivisection Society, the Society is not thereby precluded from making efforts in Parliament for lesser measures, having for its object the saving of animals from scientific torture.[25]

As a result, Frances Power Cobbe had set up the British Union for the Abolition of Vivisection, which demanded a total and immediate ban on all animal experiments, while the NAVS, under Stephen Coleridge's leadership, was prepared to accept lesser measures in the interim. The choice between principled total abolition and pragmatic gradualism was to prove an enduring source of tension for the movement.

In 1909, two rival international anti-vivisection congresses were held in England, one organised by Lizzy Lind af Hageby's gradualist Animal Defence and Anti-Vivisection Society, and the other by the World League Against Vivisection, which was committed to total abolition. While the latter's position was perhaps logically more coherent (if vivisection were morally wrong, there could be no excuse for tolerating it), it seemed to the pragmatists that those demanding 'all or nothing' were liable to end up with nothing. For the World League, however, total abolition seemed achievable, not least because they had the support of several prominent Labour MPs, whose party was a rising force in parliament.[26]

When engaged in debate, the RDS favoured the time-honoured utilitarian position that vivisection saves human lives, which they backed up by providing facts about the important discoveries that Pasteur and other famous medical scientists had made through animal research. It could be difficult for their some of their speakers to appreciate why the audience remained unconvinced by such powerful evidence. In 1910, the distinguished astronomer Sir David Gill (1843–1914), speaking for the Society, was involved in the following exchange:

Gill: 'Let any mother whose child is suffering from that dangerous disease diphtheria be asked how many dogs' lives she would give for the life of her child'

A lady in the audience: 'None'

Gill: 'God help humanity! (Applause and a few hisses) One lady says she would not give one'
Lady: 'Not one'.[27]

The RDS undertook direct action against anti-vivisectionists with more success. They asked railway companies not to display anti-vivisection posters on their stations, with the result that the District Railway stopped accepting them, while the canny Great Western continued to take the anti-vivisectionists' money but placed the posters in obscure positions.[28] The RDS also persuaded railway bookstalls not to sell anti-vivisection pamphlets, asked the publisher Sir Frederick Macmillan to drop anti-vivisection publications from his list, convinced the Postmaster General to ban anti-vivisection advertisements in post offices, and induced the organisers of Cruft's dog show to stop hosting a BUAV stall there.[29] They even planned to break up a 'monster procession' in the anti-vivisectionists' home territory of South London, until they discovered there would be 'a large contingent of Battersea roughs, to protect the banners from medical students…'.[30]

A common means of promoting the anti-vivisection message was to rent display space in a shop window and hand out leaflets outside. The RDS hired men with sandwich boards to March up and down in front of the ADAVS's 'anti-vivisection shop' in London's bustling Piccadilly and hand out leaflets of their own, a tactic that was successful insofar as the shop closed after a year, though it probably did little to spread a positive message about research. Passers-by found these aggressive pamphleteers, who came to blows on one occasion, a nuisance, and Westminster Council complained about the resulting litter of leaflets that beleaguered pedestrians threw away as soon as they could: a salutary reminder that most people had no interest in the vivisection question one way or the other.[31] In 1910, the BUAV opened shops in Wimbledon, Newcastle, Southport, Liverpool and Worcester, and the minutes of the RDS note that '[e]ach of these shops had been duly besieged with the leaflets of the Research Defence Society, and had been closed'. The contents of their leaflets was as disingenuous as those of the antis: when George Robbins of the Anti-Vivisection Hospital wrote to Paget complaining about a pamphlet entitled 'Fighting the Invisible', Paget admitted that it was untrue to state that animals were always killed immediately after experimentation, because that 'would defeat the objects of enquiry', but said the RDS was not responsible for the contents of the pamphlets they distributed.[32]

The fuss stirred up by the second Royal Commission and the ensuing pamphlet wars died down with the outbreak of the First World War. The public had other concerns, and newspapers had little space to report domestic spats. Civilian medical research and education were stepped down as universities focussed on training extra doctors quickly, and many anti-vivisection groups suspended their activities,[33] though their work was not done, as military experiments replaced civil ones. As the conflict escalated into an industrial and technological race to manufacture weapons faster and in greater numbers than the enemy, science was enlisted to come up with new ones: in 1915, the Ministry of Munitions acquired six thousand acres in Wiltshire that became the War Department Experimental Ground, better known as Porton Down, and commandeered a nearby farm to breed animals for the chemical and other weapons tests that were set to take place there.[34]

Wartime statistics were presented in such a way as to obscure the large increase in the number of animals being used; for example, in 1916, the *Lancet* noted that the latest Home Office return showed 2771 experiments had been performed the previous year, 'other than those of the nature of simple inoculations, hypodermic injections, or similar proceedings…'.[35] While this sounded reasonable enough, these 'simple' injections included inoculations with tuberculosis, anthrax, rabies and bubonic plague, and there were many thousands of them.[36] National newspaper proprietors were bound to keep the government's secrets, and were provided with positive stories about how research on animals was leading to major advances in the fight against disease amongst the troops. The anti-vivisection lobby unfortunately chose to counter what they saw as the government's increasingly authoritarian attitude to medicine by campaigning against compulsory vaccination, with the result that they were denounced in the House of Commons as 'unpatriotic' for trying to stop soldiers from receiving life-saving inoculations.[37] Since this could be construed as interfering with the war effort, a crime under the Defence of the Realm Acts, the anti-vivisection movement found itself effectively boycotted by the press.[38]

Inter-War Politics

After the war, the RDS claimed that experiments on animals had saved the lives of many wounded men by helping surgeons to understand 'the violences offered in modern warfare to the human body…'[39], and they branded the anti-vivisection movement 'an enemy of the people'.[40] The Society resumed its course of blocking anti-vivisection initiatives whenever it could while eschewing open debate, but Paget, whose health was deteriorating, became concerned that, although public opinion was turning in their favour, it would be impossible for them to overcome opponents who had many times more money to spend than they did (in 1921, the RDS's annual income was under £750—less than one anti-vivisection society was spending on stationery).[41] 'We cannot follow them everywhere', he wrote despairingly, painfully aware that many local RDS branches were 'half-dead'.[42]

Fortunately for the RDS, the war had sapped support for anti-vivisection also. Appalling though the suffering inflicted upon animals during the conflict had been, it was lost in the shadow of the human tragedy. It was also believed that animal experimentation carried out in secret had helped the war effort. The BUAV made the best of it, asking donors to recall that animals too had served their country by performing military service, but in the post war years many people were poorer, taxation had increased, and there was little money to spare for animal charities. Most of the anti-vivisection movement's charismatic founders were now dead or aged, and the societies they had founded, like all protestants, had proved fissiparous, and, rather than pooling their resources, tended pursue separate agendas. Consequently, most of the anti-vivisection work undertaken in the inter-war period was uncoordinated, and met with scant success. High-profile researchers such as the UCL physiologists were still subjected to attacks in print, which was how Lizzy Lind af Hageby and Leisa Schartau had begun their campaign at the turn of the century, but perhaps the only new tactic of note was a 'van campaign' to transport posters and pamphlets to far-flung parts of the country and collect signatures for petitions.[43]

Within the medical profession, the growing reliance on animal experiments seemed to have gained unstoppable momentum: animal research had come to be regarded as the gold standard and so scientists who wanted their work to be taken seriously by their peers more or less had to use animals. Of the Nobel prizes in physiology or medicine awarded in the hundred years from 1901, only thirteen did not involve research on non-human vertebrates. This pattern was reflected by lesser prize- and grant-giving bodies, and so animal research became linked in the public mind with reports of acclaimed new discoveries, while the details of what actually went on in the privacy of the laboratory were usually glossed over.[44]

There were some attempts by the anti-vivisection lobby to have Porton Down closed, but they came to nothing as the government was keen to continue its research in anticipation of another conflict. Curiosity about this secret establishment led to speculation in the press and questions in parliament, where the answers given only hinted at what might still have been going on there. In May 1923, the Under Secretary for War admitted in the House of Commons that over 700 animals, including 23 monkeys, had been used in 'gas poisoning' experiments the previous year, and the number of animals acknowledged to have been used in such testing continued to rise until 1925, when the Geneva protocol banned chemical warfare.[45]

Ironically, peace initiatives such as the League of Nations, formed in 1920 to prevent future conflicts, tended to lead to more experiments on animals, since improvements in 'modern medicine' were hyped as a means to alleviate the social hardships that led to war.[46] The post-war conflict in which Europe was now engaged was a war against poverty and disease, and it was being fought with modern, scientific weapons developed in the clinic and laboratory. Pro-vivisection literature made increasing use of this military imagery, with the RDS reporting what had been learned from the 'sacrifice' of laboratory animals in a series of pamphlets entitled *The Fight Against Disease*. Like any war, it needed large sums of money to be raised at a national level: to this end, the British Empire Cancer Campaign was founded in 1923, to supplement the work of the ICRF and MRC, who initially considered it a rival.

The idea that science held the keys to health, prosperity and peace naturally fostered a positive attitude on the part of the public towards laboratory research: at the Efficiency Exhibition in Olympia there were long queues at the Middlesex Hospital stall as people waited to look down the microscopes.[47] The British experienced nothing like the reaction to laboratory-based work that had been seen in Germany, where a so-called 'crisis of medicine' occurred as many ordinary people lost their trust in 'mechanistic' medicine and turned instead to heterodox practitioners of alternative medicine, whose treatments seemed more natural and whose methods appeared more patient-centred.[48] In Germany, vivisection became a symbol of the failure of scientific medicine to respect the ideals of the traditional healer, and the public responded enthusiastically when the rising National Socialist Party adopted an anti-vivisection policy.

In Britain, those parts of society that were most outspoken with regard to vivisection failed to hold the government to account when they were able to, presumably because they felt there were more important issues to vote on. Anyone who had predicted that the government would be forced to ban vivisection once women and the non-landed classes were enfranchised turned out to be badly mistaken.[49] The first Labour government, formed in 1924, included no fewer than four cabinet ministers—Ramsay Macdonald (1866–1937), Philip Snowden (1864–1937), Arthur Henderson (1863–1935) and J.R. Clynes (1869–1949)—who had been pre-war supporters of the World League Against Vivisection, but all of them failed to put their purported principles into practice now that they were able to do so. Clynes confessed his hypocrisy in the most elegant of phrases, writing that in the matter of vivisection he found it impossible 'to harmonise his public duties with his private opinion'.[50]

With support for anti-vivisection groups on the wane, the RDS turned its attention to ensuring that the income derived from legacies as wealthy anti-vivisectionists died off was minimised. In a landmark legal case in 1928, the RDS appealed against a legacy of £200,000 being used to set up a trust to fund the Beaumont Animals Benevolent Society.[51] The bequest was as bizarre as it was generous, but the Court of Appeal ruled that its purpose—to create a sanctuary where all kinds of animals could live undisturbed by humans—was not charitable, since the Court reckoned that this would provide no benefit to the public.[52] Although this so-called Grove-Grady case was not related to anti-vivisection, the judgement did establish a valuable principle, from the RDS's perspective, that money given *for the benefit of animals alone* could not be considered charity. Had the court decided otherwise, wrote its secretary, it 'would have given us endless trouble',[53] as it was, the decision paved the way for a future ruling that anti-vivisection too could not be a charitable cause.

For veterinary hospitals where research on animals took place, Grove-Grady meant that charity must be given for the benefit of the hospital rather than the animals. In 1931, the RDS took legal action against the BUAV on behalf of the Tail Waggers Club, a fundraising scheme for the Royal Veterinary School that the BUAV had tried to block on the grounds that it subsidised animal experimentation. The RDS's action was successful, winning for Captain Hobbs, the only human member of the Tail Waggers, £500 in damages.[54] The following year, the School found themselves less grateful for principle that charity could not be given solely to help animals when the RDS threatened legal action to prevent them accepting £25,000 from an anti-vivisectionist, though the Society relented after School promised 'that none of the sum be devoted to anti-vivisection propaganda'.[55]

The RDS did not receive government assistance, remaining essentially a private lobby group for vivisectionists. New license holders received a letter inviting them to join, but neither the identities of those who did, nor the total number of members, was made public, though there must have been far fewer than even the smallest anti-vivisection society, and the RDS's annual income was less than a thousand pounds. Considering its modest budget, the influence it was able to exert was impressive. In 1934, the honorary secretary, G.P. Crowd, summarised its principal achievements: the defeat of the Dogs Protection Bill, the defence of University College in the dog stealing case, changing the attitude of the RSPCA to research, blocking the Grove-Grady bequest, and protecting research at the Royal Veterinary School.[56] A closer examination of the first of these, the long and frustrated progress of the Dogs Protection Bill in its various forms, shows how the RDS was able to influence parliament and collaborate effectively with the BMA and other pro-vivisection groups.

Stopping the Dogs Protection Bill

The Dogs Protection Bill was conceived as a means to break down the vivisectionists' defences at their weakest point, necessarily forgoing the support of total abolitionists (though the BUAV backed it) in the hope of winning a tactical victory on behalf of the species most adept at appealing to human sympathy. The popularity of dogs as domestic companions as well as their usefulness as working animals made their use as experimental subjects seem particularly objectionable; as Lord Dowding put it, 'the dog has no aim in life other than to love and serve humanity', and the relationship between dogs and humans was often assumed, with good reason, to be a special one.[57] Dogs had had their own anti-cruelty lobby since 1891, when the National Canine Defence League was founded by the breeders of show dogs, to protect dogs from all kinds of cruelty, from vivisection to muzzling.

The advocates of dog-specific anti-vivisection legislation left themselves open to the criticism that they were acting on an irrational, sentimental bias towards a favourite pet, and indeed the positions of both sides in the dogfight were not far removed from hypocrisy. Experimenters pretended there was nothing special about dogs, but then admitted they preferred them because they were particularly cooperative and biddable, even under torture, an admission condemned by anti-vivisectionists as the heartless betrayal of a friend and helper. Dog lovers, however, had little to be proud of; one reason that dogs were such a popular laboratory animal being that they were readily obtainable: Britain was home to a large underclass of strays and mongrels which, though legally protected from vivisection by the 1906 Dogs Act, were, in reality, like pauper cadavers a century before, worthless to all except experimenters, who could easily acquire them for money.

In 1906, when the BUAV sought support for a dogs protection bill (not an entirely novel idea, since a 'Dog Protection Bill' had been contemplated as long ago as the 1840s to prevent the theft of 'fancy dogs' for export),[58] the public, understandably averse from the idea of anyone experimenting on what they saw as pets, responded enthusiastically, and the BUAV was able to present the Home Secretary with a petition weighing a quarter of a ton, nine miles long, and with over 400,000 signatures.[59] Although the size and weight of this monster petition were obviously inflated for dramatic effect, it still stands as one of the largest written petitions in English history.

The BUAV had appealed to the public because a similar bill introduced in the House of Commons the previous year had failed to progress.[60] For those unversed in the labyrinthine complexities of the British parliamentary system, bills receive a nominal 'first reading'—in which the title is read out and the bill is ordered to be printed—followed by a second reading when they are debated and voted on. If they are passed, there follows a committee stage at which amendments are made and voted on, before the bill may proceed, time permitting, to a third reading and another vote. Once a bill has been passed by the Commons, it must then undergo a similar process in the House of Lords, and only when this is finally complete is the bill passed for royal assent, at which point it becomes law. Few private member's bills, i.e., those not sponsored by the government, ever become law, unless the government aids their passage.

The medical profession, through the BMA, responded to the huge petition by releasing a strongly worded manifesto opposing the bill,[61] which suffered the fate of most unsupported bills, reaching its second reading but then running out of parliamentary time. It was reintroduced in 1907 by the radical liberal barrister Ellis Griffith (1860–1926), but met with the same outcome. Sir Frederick (later Lord) Banbury (1850–1936) tried again in 1908, to loud cheers from the backbenches, but despite the support of the fifty or so MPs who were members of the BUAV-sponsored Parliamentary Anti-Vivisection Committee, the bill was blocked by members representing medical and university interests. In 1911, after the BUAV's parliamentary question on the legality of selling dogs for experimentation received an 'evasive and unsatisfactory' answer from the government,[62] Banbury vowed to reintroduce the dogs bill in every session until it was passed. The bill passed its second reading in 1913, but was 'wrecked' at the committee stage, when it was decided, by thirteen votes to twelve, to amend it to allow experiments performed under anaesthesia,[63] thereby, quipped one newspaper, ensuring that the bill was 'painlessly killed'.[64] Perhaps the most quotable contribution in this debate came from the G.G. Greenwood (1850–1928), a supporter of the bill, who, when asked by the committee whether he would vivisect a dog to save his own child, replied: 'to save my child, I should, very possibly, be prepared to vivisect the honourable Member who asked [that question], But that would hardly be accepted as proof that I was morally right in so doing'.[65]

The Bill returned again in 1914, to the dismay of the BMA, and 350 physicians and surgeons wrote to *The Times* in protest.[66] This was sufficient to mobilise enough MPs to block it as, apart from the parliamentary anti-vivisection group, most had no strong opinions on the fate of stray dogs. Accused of being motivated by sentimentality, the anti-vivisection MP Colonel E.S. Sladen said he was 'proud' of being sentimental about dogs, and would welcome 'the advent of sentiment into the house of commons'.[67]

The tenacious Banbury ('a grim old Tory, but he has a very soft heart for a dog') tried again in 1919 and the bill 'slipped through' its second reading in spite of the efforts of the Commons medical committee, who were 'caught napping', and whose best argument seemed to be that the bill was against the national interest, since research on dogs during the war had led to the development of gas masks.[68] The bill got through to the committee stage but was amended to make it, in the words of the RDS, 'absurd' and then defeated on a three line whip (i.e., the government compelled its MPs to vote against it on pain of expulsion from the party).[69] It did not help that an 'epidemic' of 'rabies' broke out while the bill was before the house, a coincidence that looked to one newspaper like 'a political dodge' to deprive stray dogs of public sympathy.[70] *The Times*, which opposed the Bill, took the opportunity to remind readers that the cure for 'this most awful disease' had been discovered by Pasteur's experiments on animals.[71]

The medical lobby continued to present vivisection as both essential and innocuous. A deputation from the Royal Society of Medicine told the Home Office that 'in the absence of infection the wounds [of vivisected dogs] were not painful', but it is inconceivable that anyone with medical experience actually believed this; the point was well made by anti-vivisectionists that scientists were never willing to have these 'painless little operations' performed on themselves.[72] The deputation also appealed to the national interest by claiming that 'success in war or in industry was bound up in experimental research', which gave the government a political and financial excuse for permitting as many experiments as possible, while making anti-vivisection seem to go against the national interest.

The established church, or at least those in authority within it, sided with the RDS. The (Protestant) Archbishop of Dublin, who was president of the RDS's Dublin branch, complained that the bill would 'retard the advance of medical knowledge and hinder the work of surgeons for the benefit of suffering mankind'. He told an RDS meeting that, compared with human needs, the interests of animals were morally negligible: 'Man has a dignity of his own which he does not share with the lower creatures. He is an "end in himself", as the philosophers say: you cannot say that of any other animal'.[73] Pro-vivisection bishops earned the disapproval of some members of their flocks, but their lordships held firm in their views: the Church Anti-Vivisection League told Bishop Frodsham of Queensland that his involvement with the RDS, 'having nothing to do with his sacred office, is a scandal and cause of offence to manifold members of his flock', but the bishop replied that vivisection was a work of mercy to alleviate human suffering,[74] which his critics thought a poor sort of humanity:

> If not a sparrow fillets to the ground,
> Without the notice of Almighty God,
> What will not be required of those who give
> Their sanction and support to such a crime
> As vivisection?
>
> Not a throb or groan
> Of martyred animals strapped down in torture troughs
> (Within those 'cruel habitations' planned by cowards
> And human monsters known as lab'r'tries,
> Where 'science'—falsely called—holds unchecked sway,
> And cruelty un-masked stalks rampant in the midst
> Of dumb defenceless victims dazed with fear,
> And turning piteous eyes on the mean wretch
> Who stands, with Knife upraised, to make the gash
> Which is 'to benefit humanity'!)...[75]

If one can penetrate their execrable style, these verses neatly encapsulate the main argument against vivisection: it was inhumane and so could not benefit humanity, or be a path to knowledge, as only the morally ignorant would perform it.

The RDS seldom responded to religious or philosophical arguments, at times seeming genuinely baffled by them, and certainly did not rely on them to defeat the Dogs Protection Bill, arranging instead for their supporters in the House of Commons deliberately to prolong the proceedings so the bill would run out of time, a not uncommon parliamentary tactic.[76] The Bill, however, showed no signs of going away, and had yet another first reading in 1921.

At a public meeting of the London and Provincial Anti-Vivisection Society, one of its founders, the Irish suffragette Mrs Norah Dacre-Fox (later Norah Elam, 1878–1961), read out twenty letters from Members of Parliament in support of the Bill. As she knew that 'a large majority of the [female] public were strongly in favour of the measure', she felt sure it would pass 'if women made proper use of their new political power'.[77] There was, however, more power in influence than numbers, and the BMA's parliamentary subcommittee collaborated with the Commons medical committee to get the bill 'talked out' again, this time by the medical MP Francis Fremantle (1872–1943), who was acting 'on behalf of the [Research Defence] Society'.[78]

To forestall further attempts at legislation, Viscount Knutsford (the philanthropist Sydney Holland) requested that the BMA produce a definitive statement in favour of vivisection and they duly obliged, declaring in a memorandum of 1926 that any interference with it would 'impede advancement of knowledge'.[79] The following year, another Dogs Protection Bill, this time backed by the National Canine Defence League, was laid before parliament. By this time, public support had grown stronger, and the petition had a million signatures, including three thousand medical practitioners, coincidentally the same as the number of medical signatories on a petition in favour of vivisection that had led the Home Secretary to water down the provisions of the 1876 Act.[80]

The cardiologist Sir Thomas Lewis (1881–1945), who was said to have coined the term 'clinical science', hastily arranged for the BMA to convene a conference on research and animal experimentation, which predictably concluded that experiments on dogs were essential to 'the progress of medical science', and the bill was voted down at its second reading.[81] It did not help that the National Canine Defence League had overstated their case by claiming that physiologists were still staging 'demonstrations of a prolonged and agonising nature' for the benefit of their students, though such demonstrations were the one thing that public pressure had succeeded in curbing. The NCDL's out-dated caricature of medical teaching offended the physiologist J.B.S. Haldane (1892–1964), a humane man who became a vegetarian in later life and who maintained that scientists should avoid causing suffering to animals unless prepared to volunteer as experimental subjects themselves: he offered £100 reward for evidence of a cruel physiological demonstration having taken place within the last ten years, with no claimants.[82] The Dogs Bill was brought up again in 1925, only to be blocked in the Lords by peers representing the combined interests of the MRC, Royal College of Surgeons, Royal College of Physicians, and BMA.[83]

Throughout the inter-war period, the BMA staunchly opposed all parliamentary measures aimed at restricting vivisection.[84] In 1922, 1924 and 1930 Joseph Kenworthy MP (1886–1953) tried to introduce a bill on behalf of the BUAV to prevent National Insurance money (a form of income tax) being spent on vivisection, but the leaders of the BMA (without consulting their membership) rallied medical MPs to deny the bill parliamentary time.[85] Later in the year, the BMA's Secretary asked local branches to lobby their parliamentary candidates not to give the anti-vivisection pledge that some voters wanted. Included with the request was a list of MPs—67 out of a total of 615—whose anti-vivisection views were so well known that it was thought not worthwhile to approach them. All but six were members of the labour party.

One well-known socialist who did not agree with them was H.G. Wells (1866–1946), a graduate of the Royal College of Science in Kensington and sometime Labour parliamentary candidate for the University of London, who weighed in with a newspaper article denouncing anti-vivisectionists' 'fanatical illusions' and arguing that their real battle was not against cruelty but the scientific quest for knowledge.[86] Bernard Shaw replied for the antis that Wells's vision was the 'science' of imbeciles, since it would lead not to a better understanding of the world but to more and more introverted experimentation. The two writers personified the orthodox and alternative attitudes to science. To Wells's argument that the medical profession was 'massively in support of vivisection', Shaw replied that they had been taught to defend it as a 'tenet of faith', though they did not 'massively practice it'.[87] Though the RDS made much of the overwhelming support for vivisection amongst doctors, it was unsurprising given that no one could go through medical school without being indoctrinated in the importance of animal research.[88] Furthermore, for a doctor publically to support the anti-vivisection lobby was tantamount to professional suicide. The BUAV president Dr Walter Hadwen was barred from joining the BMA, and was subjected to what appears to have been a vexatious trial for medical manslaughter after the death of a patient in 1924.[89]

The repeated thwarting of the Dogs Protection Bill shows the strategic effectiveness of mobilising medical and parliamentary influence in support of animal experimentation. The RDS had less money to spend than the anti-vivisectionists, no donations from the public, and little popular support: it would have been impossible for them to muster a substantial petition *in favour* of experimenting on dogs, stray or otherwise.[90] However, they were able to persuade most of the few dozen medically and scientifically trained members of the House of Commons to oppose anti-vivisection bills whenever they arose. That these elected representatives had no qualms about ignoring public opinion reflects the paternalistic nature of medical science, as well as politics, at the time. Perhaps they decided that animal experimentation was for the good of the British people, whether they wanted it or not, though those MPs with connections in the research industry might be suspected of self-interest. Whatever their motives, pro-vivisection parliamentarians had the distinction of ignoring some of the largest petitions ever presented to the British government.

The involvement of the BMA was important in persuading both politicians and public that the nation's health and prosperity depended upon animal research. Led by a generation of doctors trained to accept laboratory experiments as the basis of medical knowledge, the

Association treated any threat to vivisection as a threat to their profession, which they countered by producing, on demand, pro-vivisection statements to suit the RDS's purposes.[91] In common with the RDS and the anti-vivisection lobby, the BMA did not limit its statements to answering questions of fact, but gave strong ideological support to a position that it regarded as non-negotiable.

'Dog Burke and Hare'

In a 1927 memorandum, the MRC stated 'There is no medical practitioner who does not use in his daily work information which he owes to experiments on dogs', and went on to say that, in many respects, the dog's anatomy was the nearest 'available' to that of man.[92] Whether this latter statement can be regarded as true depends on the significance of the word 'available'. It was certainly not the case that, as Viscount Knutsford told the House of Lords in 1924, the dog 'is more closely allied to man in what I may call its internal arrangements than is any other animal'.[93] Apes are obviously more closely related, and even if we charitably suppose his lordship meant British, domesticated animals, for a closer match he would have had to look no further than the pig. The truth was that experimenters preferred to use dogs because they were a convenient size to work with, relatively compliant, and so numerous they could be obtained cheaply and easily. The BMA went beyond defending the sale of dogs for experimentation, by demanding, in an echo of anatomists' calls for pauper dissection a century earlier, that the law be changed so that all strays that were 'unclaimed and obviously unwanted' were automatically made available.[94]

University College London was among the dog dealers' best customers. Its professors included some of Europe's most distinguished physiologists, whose students were exposed to a diet of experimental physiology far in excess of anything they needed to learn medicine: by the 1940s they were receiving a total of over 300 h of practical teaching in experimental physiology, around ten times more than in any present day medical school.[95] Obtaining sufficient animals for research and teaching on this scale was challenging, and while London, like any big city, had plenty of stray dogs, it was illegal under the 1906 Dogs Act to give or sell them to a laboratory. Dogs for vivisection had to be purchased from dealers, though as the provenance of any given dog was almost impossible to establish, the dealers found it easy to flout the law.

University College was first linked with dog stealing in 1913, when Professor Starling was summoned to the High Court to give evidence in a case.[96] Starling was a robust defender of the use of stray dogs for experimentation, arguing that as they were commonly euthanised anyway, they may as well be employed for useful purposes first.[97] On this occasion, the College was acquitted of any wrongdoing, and its physiologists continued to source dogs from local dealers. Thirteen years later, when sentencing a dog-stealer to six months hard labour for receiving and ill-treating two Irish terriers, a London magistrate alluded to the College's continuing involvement:

> You [Hewett the dog seller] are no doubt a cruel and unscrupulous man, and anything I can do to stop this sort of thing I will. I must not say too much because the people who employ you are not here and are not represented. Anyone who has heard this case must have a feeling of considerable uneasiness as to what is taking place. I have been told that a dog-stealer is employed by this school [University College] to supply them with dogs for physiological experiments.… It has been often said in these Courts that if there were no receivers there would be no thieves. At 8 a.m. two valuable pedigree dogs are missed from outside a house. At 9 o'clock they are taken to this school in a sack under circumstances of great cruelty, and in 24 h they would have been dead. No questions would have been asked. It must raise a feeling of considerable alarm among animal lovers to find that this has been going on for some time.

It certainly raised alarm, but it was impossible to prove that the physiologists knew the dogs they were buying were stolen. In their defence, the College pointed out '[t]hat the man Hewett has never been an employé … [t]hat the professor of physiology had no means of ascertaining that Hewett had been convicted [in the past] of dog stealing', and that the professor had always '… required a written guarantee that all the animals so delivered by Hewett and by the other dealer with whom he traded were legitimately obtained'. The National Canine Defence League was suspicious: if the College was obtaining the dogs legally, why were they being brought there 'in sacks, as if they were potatoes'?[98] Lord Banbury thought the insistence on a written guarantee was also incriminating, since only a person who suspected they might be buying stolen goods would be sure to obtain one.[99] Moreover, the dogs showed signs of having been injured, as if their captors had found it necessary to subdue them.[100]

Rumours persisted, and University College soon found itself in the police news again, after one George Phipps was charged with stealing a wolfhound from outside its own home. The dog's 76-year-old owner tellingly went straight to UCL, where he inquired for Professor Ernest Verney (1894–1967). The Professor had the cages checked and the old man was reunited with his dog, which apart from a bump on the head was 'none the worse for his adventure'. At Phipps's trial (which the dog attended) there was more bad publicity for the College:

> A boy of fourteen, who said he was 'animal attendant' at University College, said he had known the defendant for about four weeks. He (the defendant) helped a man named Jackson to fetch dogs to the college.
>
> Counsel: Mr. Jackson often supplies dogs for the college?—Yes.
>
> He brought two on November 19?—Yes'.
>
> I would remark here that it is curious that a boy of fourteen should be employed to look after animals. I do not suppose any of your Lordships would give the charge of your animals solely into the hands of a boy of fourteen. But this is what emerges from those two statements, that within a fortnight two cases of stolen dogs are brought forward and in both of those cases these dogs were going to University College.[101]

The 'University of London Animal Welfare Society', set up by Starling to demonstrate that UCL took a responsible approach to research,[102] sometimes had to arrange for dogs to be nursed back to health to make them fit enough for vivisection, but had never questioned the vendors about why they were delivered in such a poor state.[103] Lord Banbury's allegations of a cover-up seem to have been warranted. When one medical MP commended the use of dogs in research on the grounds that they were cheap, this suggested, said Banbury, that they were being supplied illegally: 'Of course if you steal the dogs you do not pay much for them'.

In 1926, the BUAV decided there was enough evidence to fund an action against Verney, and while they were no doubt gratified when the sensational news that a University Professor had been summoned for 'receiving' was splashed across the newspapers, it soon became obvious that there was no chance of a conviction.[104] At Clerkenwell Police Court, Verney's innocence seemed to be assumed from the outset: he was allowed to sit at the solicitors' table rather than in the dock, and although the court was told the BUAV had paid for the plaintiff's lawyer, there was no mention that Verney's defence was supported by the RDS.[105] Dismissing the case, the magistrate said it should never have been brought, and ordered the prosecution to pay costs, though he did add that the College (which was buying over five hundred dogs a year) should make more stringent enquiries in future.[106] A spokesman for the College told the press: 'I am speaking for a large body of opinion which is tired of this slobbering by people who have nothing better to do than look after pups, parrots and pigeons'.[107] For the public, the message was simple: 'Watch Your Dog'.[108]

The parallels with body-snatching are extensive: the clandestine but widely-known market for 'subjects', the legal ambiguities, the professional denial of any suspicion, and the prosecution of middle men while the doctors went free. The defence of the physiologists who purchased dogs was the same as that of the anatomists who had purchased cadavers: they did not *know* that any crime had been committed to supply their needs, and were not responsible for the actions of others. Their shady deals were only possible with the complicity of a public most of whom simply did not care where scientists obtained their *materiel*. The animal victims, like the human victims of Burke and Hare (a comparison made in the press), were worth more dead than alive; they were, as one dog stealer told Starling's protégé Professor Lovatt Evans (1884–1968; his contribution to the war effort included working on poison gas at Porton Down), 'not worth a penny as dogs',[109] and like the victims murdered for dissection, they came mostly from the lowest classes, and nobody missed them. 'We want only mongrel dogs', said Evans,

'...valuable dogs would be too delicate for us': it required hybrid vigour to be vivisected.[110]

The BUAV would scarcely have been so naïve as to have expected a conviction; their motive was presumably to cause a scandal, and in this they succeeded, for even after Verney was acquitted on the legal technicality that he had not actually been in possession of the dog whilst it was in a cage in his department, the name of University College was still in the news for all the wrong reasons.[111] Questions were asked in the House of Commons and it made headlines that the College had 'used' 1,147 dogs in the past two years.[112] The inevitable public reaction followed, and the College received a flurry of letters: from anti-vivisection ladies, berating them for callousness and threatening divine retribution ('I am sorry for all vivisectors when their time comes to leave this world!'); from the owners of lost dogs, pleading for the professors to look in their laboratory cages; from people offering to sell unwanted dogs to the physiologists; and even one from a lady offering to sell her own body for research. One man who had sent a puppy to the vet to be destroyed only to discover that the lad who had taken it had sold it to a dealer 'for the sake of the money he gets from the Hospitals for vivisection' pleaded to be allowed to buy the dog back, to spare her further 'misery'.

Such compassion was lost on most experimenters: why, asked the RDS, did the anti-vivisectionists not simply accept the use of strays and so put an end to dog-stealing?[113] The fate of strays was, after all, a grim one. The RSPCA, the largest provider of homes for stray dogs, refused to sell them for vivisection, but could not cope with the numbers and destroyed tens of thousands every year by 'painless' electrocution.[114] Was not selling them to laboratories instead the logical thing to do? When Walter Hadwen, one of the few doctors still campaigning against anti-vivisection in the inter-war years, challenged the RDS about the vivisection of strays, they denied any knowledge of it.[115] They were in fact trying to get it legalised, and used their influence to plant a parliamentary question on the subject, having already supplied the Home Secretary with 'the necessary facts to provide an answer'. According to Lovatt Evans, assisting with a scheme to make stray dogs available for vivisection was 'the best opportunity that the RDS has ever had to render us [UCL physiologists] real service'.[116]

Conclusion

One of the most frequent criticisms of anti-vivisectionists between the wars was that they were motivated by sentiment and not logic; a criticism based, I have argued, on a paradigm of dispassionate, amoral science which, though prevalent, was still far from commanding universal assent. It might have been expedient to vivisect strays, as it had been to dissect paupers, but was it right? There were many in the anti-vivisection lobby whose feelings told them it was not. Vivisectionists, however, wielded influence where it counted. It was practically impossible to join the staff of a large teaching hospital if one was opposed animal experiments, and it was from this metropolitan élite that the leaders of the medical profession—presidents of the medical royal colleges and directors of research institutes—were drawn. They pronounced with authority that vivisection was necessary for medical progress, and it was difficult for laypeople or rank-and-file doctors to gainsay them.

Despite its influential supporters, the RDS saw itself as outnumbered and beleaguered by anti-vivisection campaigners with superior numbers and resources. The antis certainly had more money to spend, though any advantage was partially nullified by divisions within the movement, and winning the moral argument proved easier than winning the battle. It is significant that the RDS quickly abandoned their tactic of sending speakers to public meetings and engaging in competitive debates because discussion seemed to be getting them nowhere. It was easier to rely on bullying and intimidation: at a meeting in 1927, in the wake of the UCL dog-stealing scandal, Shaw was unable to make himself heard over the din of two hundred medical students, and in 1929, rowdy students literally broke up the annual general meeting of the BUAV.[117]

The fight for effectively unrestricted vivisection was won in the courts and parliament by clever tactics and collusion between those with vested interests. It is a moral certainty that the staff of University College knew that some of the dogs they purchased were stolen, but the RDS's lawyers correctly argued that as the physiologists had not technically been in possession of the dogs, they could not be guilty of receiving stolen goods. Parliamentarians knew that the public was opposed to vivisection, but the RDS and BMA could count on the support of enough members with medical interests to ensure that legislation to curb it was blocked at every stage, in the knowledge that, since animal experimentation was believed to contribute to national prosperity and security, no government would want anti-vivisection legislation to become law.

With legal challenges to vivisection blocked by parliament and the courts, and a mood of optimism that looked to scientific progress to bring peace and prosperity, anti-vivisection was beginning to look like a lost cause whose supporters were reactionary and selfish, putting their personal feelings before the interests of their own species and their own country. It would take the great depression of the 1930s to revive the link between radical politics and animal welfare, as the state's (mis)treatment of animals once more became a surrogate for its failure to protect its own citizens.

Notes

1. 'A member of the Provisional Committee' (letter), *BMJ*, *1* (1882), 599.
2. A. Flexner, *Medical Education in Europe: A Report to the Carnegie Foundation for the Advancement of Teaching* (New York: Carnegie Foundation, 1912), 120–7 (Flexner 1912).
3. A.W.H. Bates, 'Anatomy on trial: itinerant anatomy museums in mid-nineteenth century England', *Museum History Journal*, *9* (2016), 188–204 (Bates 2016).
4. Emma Hopley, *Campaigning Against Cruelty: the Hundred Year History of the British Union for the Abolition of Vivisection* (London: BUAV, 1998), 12–13 (Hopley 1998).
5. Tansey, 'The Queen'.
6. 'The Home Office report on experiments on living animals performed in 1906', *Lancet*, *1* (1907), 1502.
7. Kean, *Animal Rights*, 104.

8. Sometimes misreported as Harvey Cushing of the Johns Hopkins Hospital in Baltimore, who was a great friend of the RDS and wrote in 1913 that 'I may have said more than was necessary in regard to experimentation upon animals and the handicap which has been put upon British medicine by ill-advised legislation, but the subject is not one for silence if speech can in any measure lend encouragement and support to the work of the Research Defence League…' Harvey Cushing, *Realignments in Greater Medicine…* (London: Henry Frowde, 1914), 5 (Cushing 1914).
9. Minute book, 27 January 1908, Well SA/RDS/C1.
10. Memorandum from Paget, 21 May 1917, Well SA/RDS/C1.
11. C.S. Sherrington, 'Paget, Stephen (1855–1926)', rev. M. Jeanne Peterson, *Oxford Dictionary of National Biography* (Oxford: Oxford University Press, 2004). http://www.oxforddnb.com/view/article/35360, viewed 9 Aug 2015 (Sherrington 2004).
12. Hopley, *Campaigning Against Cruelty*, 10.
13. Kean, *Animal Rights*, 93.
14. The best history of hydrophobia in England dodges the question by refusing to countenance retrospective diagnosis, but the work of Pasteur and others cannot be properly evaluated without considering whether their diagnoses of hydrophobia were rabies or something else: Neil Pemberton and Michael Worboys, *Mad Dogs and Englishmen: Rabies in Britain, 1830–2000* (Basingstoke: Palgrave Macmillan, 2007) (Pemberton and Worboys 2007).
15. Austin Bradford Hill and Brian Hill, 'The life of Sir Leonard Erskine Hill FRS (1866–1952)', *Proceedings of the Royal Society of Medicine, 61* (1968): 307–316 (Hill and Hill 1968).
16. 'Obituary: Charles Edward Beevor, MD, FRCP Lond', *BMJ, 2* (1908), 1785–1786.
17. *The Fight Against Disease*, n.d. [1921], 11.
18. Hopley, *Campaigning Against Cruelty*, 23–5.
19. Minute book, 21 May 1908, Well SA/RDS/C1. In 'old' money there were 12 pence (d) in a shilling and 20 shillings (s) in a pound. Half a crown was 2s 6d.
20. Well SA/RDS/D1.
21. Chen-hui Li, 'Mobilizing Christianity in the anti-vivisection movement in Victorian Britain', *Journal of Animal Ethics, 2* (2012), 141–61 (Li 2012).

22. Kensington branch Minute book, 17 May 1910, Well SA/RDS/C16.
23. Minute book, 23 June, 19 August, 20 October 1908, Well SA/RDS/C1; RDS, *The Fight Against Disease*, n.d. [1921], 12.
24. Minute book, 5 and 11 January 1909, Well SA/RDS/C1.
25. *Animals Defender and Zoophilist, 20/21* (1900), 165.
26. Richard D. Ryder, *Victims of Science: The Use of Animals in Research* (London: Davis-Poynter, 1975), 22 (Ryder 1975).
27. 'Anti-vivisection scene', *Daily Mail*, 6 October 1910 (Anti-Vivisection Scene 1910).
28. Minute book, 22 March, 17 May 1909, Well SA/RDS/C1.
29. Minute book, 19 July 1909, 24 October 1928, p. 119, 24 October 1934, p. 159, Well SA/RDS/C1; SA/RDS/C2; Kean, *Animal Rights*, 149.
30. Minute book, 1 February, 5 July 1909, Well SA/RDS/C1.
31. Minute book, 18 July 1910, Well SA/RDS/C1; Niven, *History of the Humane Movement*, 89.
32. Minute book, 19 July and 14 November, 1910.
33. Hopley, *Campaigning Against Cruelty*, 16.
34. Ulf Schmidt, 'Justifying chemical warfare: the origins and ethics of Britain's chemical warfare programme, 1915–1939', in David Welch and Jo Fox (eds) *Justifying War: Propaganda, Politics and The Modern Age* (Basingstoke: Palgrave Macmillan, 2012), 129–158, on pp. 140–141 (Schmidt 2012).
35. 'Experiments on living animals', *Lancet, 2* (1916), 440.
36. 'Experiments on living animals', *Lancet, 1* (1902), 1617–1618.
37. M. Beddow Bayly, 'The ill-effects of vaccines', *Animals' Defender, 60* (1941), 95 (Bayly 1941).
38. 'Anti-Vivisection in the war', *The Fight Against Disease* (1930), 10–11; Hopley, *Campaigning Against Cruelty*, 26.
39. 'Physiology during the war', *The Fight Against Disease*, January 1922, 2.
40. 'Anti-Vivisection: an enemy of the people', *The Fight Against Disease* (1927), 1–3.
41. RDS minutes, 19 February 1924, 59, Well SA/RDS/C2; *The Fight Against Disease* (1923), 1.
42. Letter from Paget to the RDS, 20 October 1920, Well SA/RDS/C2.
43. 'Notes and comments', *The Fight Against Disease* (1925), 11.
44. Debbie Tacium, 'A history of anti-vivisection from the 1800s to the present: part II (1914–1970)', *Veterinary Heritage, 31* (2008), 21–5 (Tacium 2008).

45. Schmidt, 'Justifying chemical warfare' (Schmidt 2012).
46. Hopley, *Campaigning Against Cruelty*, 27.
47. *The Fight Against Disease*, n.d. [1921], 2–3.
48. Carsten Timmermann, *Weimar medical culture: Doctors, Healers, and the crisis of medicine in interwar Germany, 1918–1933*. PhD, University of Manchester (1999) (Timmermann 1999).
49. Hopley, *Campaigning Against Cruelty*, 9.
50. Ryder, *Victims of Science*, 221.
51. RDS minutes, 24 October 1928, p. 119, Well SA/RDS/C2.
52. Robert Pearce and Warren Barr, *Pearce & Stevens' Trusts and Equitable Obligations*, 6th edn (Oxford: Oxford University Press, 2015), 404–405. It is interesting to speculate on whether this decision would be upheld today, now the importance of wilderness is better appreciated (Pearce and Barr 2015).
53. Memo from G.P. Crowd, honorary secretary RDS, 9 October 1934, Well SA/RDS/C2.
54. RDS minutes, 19 March 1931, p. 135, Well SA/RDS/C2.
55. RDS minutes, 11 March 1932, p. 145, Well SA/RDS/C2.
56. Memo from G.P. Crowd, 9 October 1934, Well SA/RDS/C2.
57. Vyvyan, *In Pity*, 9. Recent evolutionary theories suggest that the relationship is a biologically special one. For an overview of the coevolution of humans and dogs, see Raymond Coppinger and Lorna Coppinger. *Dogs: A Startling New Understanding of Canine Origin, Behaviour, and Evolution* (New York: Scribner, 2001) (Coppinger and Coppinger 2001).
58. 'Exportation of stolen dogs', *Bell's Life in London and Sporting Chronicle*, 28 May 1843, 1 (Exportation of Stolen Dogs 1843).
59. 'Dog's protection bill', *Nottingham Evening post*, 13 December, 1906, 6 (Dog's Protection Bill 1906).
60. House of Commons debate, 17 March 1905, *Hansard*, *143*, c395.
61. 'The vivisection controversy', *Sheffield Evening Telegraph*, 28 March 1906, 4 (The Vivisection Controversy 1906).
62. Hopley, *Campaigning Against Cruelty*, 16–17.
63. 'Problem for speaker', *Manchester Courier and Lancashire General Advertiser*, 17 July 1913, 5; 'Protection of dogs from vivisection', *Times*, 17 July 1913, 3 (Problem for Speaker 1913; Protection of Dogs from Vivisection 1913).
64. *Derby Daily Telegraph*, 24 July 1913, 2.

65. G.G. Greenwood, 'Sympathy and practice', *Times*, 24 July 1913, 14 (Greenwood 1913).
66. 'Experiments on dogs: medical protest against the prohibition bill', *Times*, 21 April 1914, 3 (Experiments on Dogs: Medical Protest Against the Prohibition Bill 1914).
67. 'Operations on dogs', *Aberdeen Journal*, 11 May 1914, 6.
68. 'London letter', *Western Daily Press*, 22 March 1919, 4; 'The vivisection of dogs: a reply', *The Fight Against Disease* (1924), 9; 'Medical research and the war', *Aberdeen Journal*, 28 June 1919, 5 (London Letter 1919).
69. 'The vivisection of dogs: a reply'; 'Dogs' protection bill', *Yorkshire Evening Post*, 27 June 1919, 8 (The Vivisection of Dogs: A Reply; Dogs' Protection Bill 1919).
70. *Western Daily Press*, 17 March 1920, 6.
71. 'The outbreak of rabies', *Times*, 23 April 1919, 13 (The Outbreak of Rabies 1919).
72. 'The dogs' protection bill', *BMJ*, *1* (1919), 613–4; Letter from Arthur H. Jona, *Hastings and St Leonard's Observer*, 12 May 1928, 10 (Jona 1928).
73. Well SA/RDS/D1.
74. 'Bishop and science: reply to anti-vivisectionists', Kensington branch minute book, 27 May 1910 [press cutting pasted in], SA/RDS/C16.
75. 'A new sort of postcard', *The Fight Against Disease* (1922), 9.
76. RDS minutes, 15 March 1920, 3, Well SA/RDS/C2.
77. Founded as the London Anti-Vivisection Society in 1876, it became the LPAVS in the early twentieth century, though there were never any branches outside London.
78. RDS minutes, 21 March 1923, 47; 22 May 1928, 113, Well SA/RDS/C2; *The Fight Against Disease*, n.d. [1921], 4.
79. BMA files, Well MP214 SA/BMA/C87.
80. Charles R. Johns, 'Petition to parliament', *Cornishman*, 9 March 1927, 7; Hopley, *Campaigning Against Cruelty*, 5; Theodore A. Cook, 'Dogs for research', *Times*, 7 March 1927, 20 (Johns 1927; Cook 1927).
81. Arthur Hollmann, *Sir Thomas Lewis: Pioneer Cardiologist and Clinical Scientist* (London: Springer-Verlag, 1997) (Hollmann 1997).
82. Ronald Clark, *J.B.S: The Life and Work of J.B.S. Haldane* (London: Bloomsbury Reader, 2011) (Clark 2011).
83. 'House of Lords, March 31st, 1925', *The Fight Against Disease* (1925), 13–14.
84. In 1927, the Secretary of the RDS wrote to the MRC to reassure them that, every year, the BMA had 'taken active steps in Parliament'

to prevent the passage of the various Dogs Protection bills, Well SA/BMA/C86.

85. 'Anti-vivisection bill', *Gloucester Journal*, 6 December 1930, 12; 'Vivisection bill opposed in public interest', *Western Daily Press*, 15 December 1930, 5 (Vivisection Bill Opposed in Public Interest 1930).
86. H.G. Wells, 'The way the world is going', *Sunday Express*, 24 July 1927 (Wells 1927).
87. George Bernard Shaw, 'These scoundrels!', *Sunday Express*, 7 August 1927 (George Bernard Shaw 1927).
88. 'Notes', *The Fight Against Disease* (1927), 30–1.
89. Hopley, *Campaigning Against Cruelty*, 37–42.
90. Letter from the medical secretary to the MRC, 11 March 1927, Well SA/BMA/C86.
91. In some cases, BMA members obviously did not support their Council's position: John Round was both honorary physician to the Anti-Vivisection Hospital and chairman of the BMA's Greenwich division: Obituary, *BMJ*, *1* (1937), 1234.
92. 'What mankind owes to dogs', *Daily Chronicle*, 8 June 1927, 4.
93. House of Lords debate, 25 March 1924, *Hansard*, *56*, c988.
94. Letter from the medical secretary to the MRC, 11 March 1927: Well SA/BMA/C86.
95. Tansey, 'The Queen'.
96. UCL archives, Kew (hereinafter, UCL) MSS add. 273.
97. Ernest Starling, 'On the use of dogs in scientific experiments', n.d., Well SA/RDS C1.
98. 'Echo of dog-stealing case', *Dundee Evening Telegraph*, 2 December 1926, 6; 'Vivisectors and dog-thieves', *The Abolitionist*, 1 December 1926, 139.
99. House of Lords debate, 8 December 1926, *Hansard*, *65*, cc1346–7.
100. 'Magistrate on sales in the Caledonian market', (newspaper cutting), UCL Bayliss papers, MSS add. 273.
101. Hansard, 8 December 1926, *65*, c1345.
102. 'Who sups with the Devil…', *Anti-Vivisection Journal*, June 1926, 71.
103. M.R. Ellinger, 'Antivivisection' (newspaper cutting), 24 December 1926, UCL MSS Add 273.
104. 'Vivisection: professor charged with receiving', *Johannesburg Star*, 9 December 1926.
105. 'Dogs for college experiments', *Dundee Evening Telegraph*, 22 December 1926, 5.

106. 'Summons against a professor dismissed', *Western News*, 23 December 1926, 2; 'Dogs for experiments', *The Star*, 14 December 1926 (Summons Against a Professor Dismissed 1926; Dogs for Experiments 1926).
107. 'Alarm among dog lovers', *Daily Herald*, 23 November 1926 (Alarm Among Dog Lovers 1926).
108. 'Watch your dog', *John Bull*, 4 December 1926.
109. 'Dog Burke and Hare', *Evening Standard*, 22 November 1926; Robert Blatchford, 'Betraying dumb friends', *Sunday Chronicle*, 28 November 1926, 10 (Burke and Hare 1926; Blatchford 1926).
110. 'The dogs a college bought from a thief', *Evening News*, 22 November 1926 (The Dogs a College Bought from a Thief 1926).
111. 'The dogs' case', *The Fight Against Disease* (1927), 3–11.
112. 'Dogs for experiments: 1,147 used at University College in two years', *Star*, 14 December 1926.
113. 'A challenge to anti-vivisectionists', *The Fight Against Disease* (1927), 15–16.
114. 'Stolen dogs case', *Daily Mirror*, 23 November 1926 (Stolen Dogs Case 1926).
115. RDS minutes, 7 December 1927, p. 107, Well SA/RDS/C2.
116. Memo from Lovatt Evans, November 1926, Well SA/RDS/C2.
117. 'Speakers howled down: uproar at anti-vivisection meeting', *Daily Mail*, 17 June 1927; Hopley, *Campaigning Against Cruelty*, 43.

References

Anti-Vivisection Scene. (1910, October 6). *Daily Mail.*

Alarm Among Dog Lovers. (1926, November 23). *Daily Herald.*

Bates, A. W. H. (2016). Anatomy on trial: Itinerant anatomy museums in mid-nineteenth century England. *Museum History Journal, 9,* 188–204.

Bayly, M. B. (1941). The ill-effects of vaccines. *Animals' Defender, 60,* 95.

Blatchford, R. (1926, November 28). Betraying dumb friends, *Sunday Chronicle,* 10.

Burke, D., & Hare. (1926, November 22). *Evening Standard.*

Clark, R. (2011). *J.B.S: The life and work of J.B.S. Haldane.* London: Bloomsbury Reader.

Cook, T. A. (1927, March 7). Dogs for research. *Times,* 20.

Coppinger, R., & Coppinger, L. (2001). *Dogs: A startling new understanding of canine origin, behaviour, and evolution.* New York: Scribner.

Cushing, H. (1914.). *Realignments in greater medicine...* (p. 5). London: Henry Frowde.
Dogs for Experiments. (1926, December 14). *The Star.*
Dog's Protection Bill. (1906, December 13). *Nottingham Evening post,* 6.
Flexner, A. (1912). *Medical education in Europe: A report to the carnegie foundation for the advancement of teaching* (pp. 120–127). New York: Carnegie Foundation.
Experiments on Dogs: Medical Protest Against the Prohibition Bill. (1914, April 21). *Times,* 3
Exportation of Stolen Dogs. (1843, May 28). *Bell's Life in London and Sporting Chronicle,* 1.
George Bernard Shaw. (1927, August 7). These scoundrels! *Sunday Express.*
Greenwood, G. G. (1913, July 24). Sympathy and Practice. *Times,* 14.
Hill, A. B., & Hill, B. (1968). The life of Sir Leonard Erskine Hill FRS (1866–1952). *Proceedings of the Royal Society of Medicine, 61,* 307–316.
Hollmann, A. (1997). *Sir Thomas Lewis: Pioneer cardiologist and clinical scientist.* London: Springer.
Hopley, E. (1998). *Campaigning against cruelty: The hundred year history of the British Union for the abolition of vivisection.* London: BUAV.
Johns, C. R. (1927, March 9). Petition to parliament. *Cornishman,* 7.
Jona, A. H. (1928, May 12). *Hastings and St Leonard's observer,* 10.
Li, C. (2012). Mobilizing Christianity in the antivivisection movement in victorian Britain. *Journal of Animal Ethics, 2,* 141–161.
London Letter. (1919, March 22). *Western Daily Press,* 4
Pearce, R., & Barr, W. (2015). *Pearce & Stevens' Trusts and Equitable Obligations* (6th ed., pp. 404–405). Oxford: Oxford University Press.
Pemberton, N., & Worboys, M. (2007). *Mad dogs and Englishmen: Rabies in Britain, 1830–2000.* Basingstoke: Palgrave Macmillan.
Problem for Speaker. (1913, July 17). *Manchester Courier and Lancashire General Advertiser,* 5.
Protection of Dogs from Vivisection. (1913, July 17). *Times,* 3.
Ryder, R. D. (1975). *Victims of science: The use of animals in research.* London: Davis-Poynter.
Schmidt, U. (2012). Justifying chemical warfare: The origins and ethics of Britain's chemical warfare programme, 1915–1939. In D. Welch & J. Fox (Eds.), *Justifying war: Propaganda, politics and the modern age* (pp. 129–158, on pp. 140–141). Basingstoke: Palgrave Macmillan.
Sherrington, C. S. (2004). Paget, Stephen (1855–1926), rev. Jeanne Peterson M., *Oxford dictionary of National Biography.* Oxford: Oxford University

Press. Retrieved August 9, 2015, from http://www.oxforddnb.com/view/article/35360.

Stolen Dogs Case. (1926, November 23). *Daily Mirror.*

Summons Against a Professor Dismissed. (1926, December 23). *Western News,* 2.

Tacium, D. (2008). A history of antivivisection from the 1800s to the present: part II (1914–1970). *Veterinary Heritage, 31,* 21–25.

The Dogs a College Bought from a Thief. (1926, November 22). *Evening News.*

The Outbreak of Rabies. (1919, April 23). *Times,* 13.

The Vivisection Controversy. (1906, March 28). *Sheffield Evening Telegraph,* 4.

The Vivisection of Dogs: A Reply; Dogs' Protection Bill. (1919, June 27). *Yorkshire Evening Post,* 8.

Timmermann, C. (1999). *Weimar medical culture: Doctors, healers, and the crisis of medicine in interwar Germany, 1918–1933,* PhD. University of Manchester.

Vivisection Bill Opposed in Public Interest. (1930, December 15). *Western Daily Press,* 5.

Wells, H.G. (1927, July 24). The way the world is going. *Sunday Express.*

7

State Control, Bureaucracy, and the National Interest from the Second World War to the 1960s

In 1935, Norah Elam, the former Mrs Dacre-Fox—separated from her husband and now using the surname of her lover, Edward Elam—having recently joined, and risen to prominence in, the British Union of Fascists, published *The Medical Research Council, What It Is and How It Works*, a distillation of the information she had gleaned while working in the MRC typing pool during the Great War. In this pamphlet, she questioned whether animal research could safely be extrapolated to humans, and why so many experiments were either repeats, or else yielded results apparently obvious to anyone with common sense. She was not alone in thinking that the use of animal models for human disease had gone too far: some among the medical profession were complaining that laboratory experimentation had become the master rather than the servant of medicine, to the detriment of clinical studies.[1] Elam laid the blame at the door of 'powerful vested interests' (which, in the context of her political views, meant Jewry) that had managed to 'entrench' themselves behind 'State-aided research', where they could exercise control without being accountable to the public.[2]

A.W.H. Bates, *Anti-Vivisection and the Profession of Medicine in Britain*,
The Palgrave Macmillan Animal Ethics Series, DOI 10.1057/978-1-137-55697-4_7

British Fascists and Anti-Vivisection

In the political climate of the depression years, right wing activists found common cause with anti-vivisectionists, exploited animals being to fascists, as they had once been to socialists, a symbol for the fate of downtrodden workers in a society where profit came before people, and where a shadowy oligarchy manipulated the poor for its own commercial ends. In Germany, to which other European proto-fascists looked to see their principles put into practice, the Nazis had banned vivisection in 1933, soon after coming to power, a popular move in a country enthusiastic for *Lebensreform*, and also with British anti-vivisectionists, who were of course unaware that the Nazi government would not scruple to sanction experimentation, on animals or humans, when it suited their purposes.

Putting an end to vivisection was for British fascists, as it had been for socialists and the new age movement, part of a utopian plan for liberating the oppressed and re-establishing the natural order, the latter being, as for all ideologues, the state of existence most congruent with their own politico-religious views. Elam was not the only animal welfare campaigner to embrace fascism—Maidie Dudley Ward (d. 1945) was active in the RSPCA, the Animal Defence and Anti-Vivisection Society, the Nordic League, and Oswald Mosley's January Club.[3] For anti-vivisection's critics, the link with fascism showed that the movement's supporters were fundamentally misanthropic: in trying to bring animals closer to the level of humans they were in fact reducing the lowest humans to the level of animals.[4]

British fascists were, however, a vocal minority who never came close to gaining power, though their involvement did bring some new life to organised anti-vivisection. Elam invited the former director of propaganda for Mosley's Blackshirts, Wilfred Risdon (1896–1967), to join her at the LPAVS, thereby introducing to the movement one of its most capable leaders, as well as drawing down upon it increased government scrutiny.[5] Soon after the outbreak of the Second World War, both Elam and Risdon were arrested by Special Branch, an action the police claimed was justified after a search of the LPAVS offices uncovered 'a list containing the names of eight members of the B[ritish] U[nion of Fascists] and a letter from Oswald Moseley [*sic*]'.[6]

It was partly on the basis of this evidence that the historian Richard Thurlow described the LPAVS as 'a known fascist front organisation'.[7] This was certainly how it was perceived by the authorities, and Elam made no secret of her political views in Society meetings (at least one other committee member was an active fascist), but to call the LPAVS a 'front' is an overstatement. The Society had been active in defence of animals since the beginning of the twentieth century, and Elam had been involved from the earliest days, for most of the time while a member of the Conservative party. As her politics became more extreme, she began to proselytise for the Blackshirts as a personal initiative, and found some fellow anti-vivisectionists sympathetic to the cause, but the LPAVS's anti-cruelty mission was genuine enough.[8]

As 'Nazi sympathisers', Elam and Risdon were imprisoned without trial under Defence Regulation 18B, but Risdon swiftly disowned the British Union of Fascists and was promptly released to return to his work at the LPAVS, of which he became secretary in 1942. In this capacity, he exchanged ideas with Air Chief Marshall Sir Hugh Dowding, the former head of RAF Fighter Command, and certainly no sympathiser with the enemy, whose innovative mind, freed from wartime responsibilities by premature retirement, found an outlet in various new age causes. Elam, however, remained in detention, casting a shadow over the LPAVS and rekindling the suspicion fomented during the First World War that anti-vivisectionists were incipient traitors. The LPAVS did their best to distance themselves from embarrassing political links by putting a notice on the front page of their news sheet assuring readers that none of their committee was a member of any 'suspect organisation'.[9]

An even greater problem for them was that, now war had broken out, vivisection seemed a comparatively trivial issue. In an editorial, they defended their continued activity on the grounds that firm moral principles were more important than ever in wartime, and that denunciations of Nazi cruelty would be hypocritical on the lips of those who were cruel themselves, though as Germany had stronger legislation to protect animals that any other country in Europe, the argument that anti-vivisectionists were never cruel seemed rather flimsy.[10] The LPAVS chairman, Captain Guy Coleridge, RN (1884–1941), patriotically tried to show that National Socialism was not the panacea for animals that it seemed, but the best he could come up with was a bizarre story that Hitler had personally given orders that all dogs in Germany should be killed.[11]

The LPAVS's efforts to show they were not assisting the enemy were unfortunately nullified by their campaign against compulsory vaccination, to which their own and the BUAV's publications devoted an increasing amount of space. There had always been some opposition to vaccination from anti-vivisectionists on animal welfare grounds, for example the Anti-Vivisection Hospital's prohibition of vaccines prepared from live animals, but anti-vivisectionists were now opposing vaccination for libertarian reasons. Hadwen had always been an anti-vaccinationist—Cobbe had recruited him to the BUAV after hearing him speak at an anti-vaccination rally—as he felt that patients ought not to be forced into accepting scientific 'progress'.[12] The outbreak of war had given the government an excuse to impose vaccination on servicemen, but anti-vivisection groups failed to appreciate that, in objecting to what they saw as an experiment on unwilling soldiers they appeared to be interfering with the war effort and showing disloyalty to the national government, an unfortunate impression for a movement linked with pacifism and fascism to give.

The War Years

The impact of the War on laboratory animals was largely negative. There was an initial reduction in animal use as peacetime research projects were shelved for lack of funding, and in July 1944, German bombs achieved what anti-vivisectionists had long failed to do, closing down the infamous Brown Institute, but many additional animals were being sacrificed in military tests, and with private members' bills banned there was no chance of anti-vivisection MPs preventing this.[13] The last peacetime Home Office returns, in 1939, reported a total of 908,846 experiments in the previous year, but during the war only simplified reports were issued and the secrecy surrounding experimentation was increased, making it difficult to discover how many animals were used and what experiments were being performed on them. In the absence of reliable information, rumours abounded: the Ministry of Agriculture was said to be seeking ‘unlimited numbers’ of hedgehogs to ‘help to win the war’, while ‘pet stores’ advertised for ten thousand guinea pigs, whose contribution to the war effort remains a mystery.[14]

As the war progressed, reports of research carried out in government facilities began to appear in the medical press. The LPAVS reacted critically to a paper by Solly (later Lord) Zuckerman (1904–1993) in the *Lancet* describing a study of the effects of blast injuries on unanaesthetised mice, rats, guinea pigs, rabbits, cats, monkeys and pigeons, which had been placed as little as thirteen feet from seventy pounds of high explosive. Predictably, those that were not blown to bits mostly died from traumatic haemorrhage of the lungs.[15] In retrospect it is difficult to see what purpose these experiments served, since the animals chosen were generally too small for their injuries to be comparable to those of humans, and in wartime there were plenty of human fatalities in which the effects of blast injuries could have been studied at autopsy.

Many other experimenters sought to reproduce in the laboratory the traumas experienced by humans in war: researchers in the anatomy department at Oxford crushed guinea pigs’ legs with metal rods and introduced bacteria into the wounds to make them suppurate; at University College Hospital, they burned goats and killed the survivors at intervals to study the pathology of their skin; and in the physiology department of King’s College Hospital they administered fifty blows to the thigh bones of cats with a mallet, fracturing them in every case.[16] In all these experiments the animals were anaesthetised when their injuries were inflicted, but they were allowed to regain consciousness later, and some were subsequently experimented upon again. Though these researches were openly reported in medical journals in 1943 and 1944, it was 10 years before the LPAVS ventured to criticise them in print.[17] Other casualties of war included animals of various species that were exposed to poison gas, in anticipation of a gas attack on the British mainland that never occurred, and eighty sheep, infected during the secret testing of an anthrax bomb on the remote Scottish island of Gruinard.[18]

Many of the LPAVS's wartime initiatives were uncontroversial: Risdon designed an ingenious air raid shelter for domestic pets, and they continued to campaign against cruelty in the meat industry.[19] It was, predictably, their denunciation of the government's policies on vaccination and military experimentation that led to confrontation: the RDS reported the LPAVS to the Parliamentary Medical Committee as a 'malevolent influence', and asked the Committee chairman, Sir Francis Fremantle, to put 'pressure' on them.[20] The Army Director of Pathology concurred: having to answer questions about experiments and deal with complaints about compulsory vaccination (the government grudgingly had to admit that soldiers were free to refuse the vaccines if they chose) was a waste of army time and delayed more important work. 'In addition to jeopardising the safety of the individual soldier', he wrote, 'the activities of these [anti-vivisection] societies are a menace to the national effort at this time, I am, therefore of opinion that the strongest possible action should be taken at once to restrain their further activity'.[21]

Despite these forewarnings, six anti-vivisection societies rashly came together in 1942 to oppose compulsory diphtheria inoculation of troops.[22] This ill-timed move gave the treasury the excuse it needed to revoke their charitable status, a change to which Fremantle and the RDS lent their support.[23] The public had grown tired of anti-vivisectionists stirring up dissent in the ranks, and the RDS was pleased to note that 'our society has never done anything more popular'. They swiftly arranged for anti-vivisection societies to be removed from all published lists of charities.[24] When the war was over, there was no public appetite for reversing the decision: the House of Lords rejected a final appeal by the NAVS in 1947.[25]

The judgement was a severe blow for anti-vivisection, whose charitable status had been accepted since the foundation of the VSS in 1875, and upheld in court in 1895. Though it was unusual for charitable status to be granted to any organization whose objects included changing the law, the court ruled that the VSS's overarching purpose was to end what it saw as 'a cruel and immoral practice',[26] a goal it believed would benefit humans as well as animals (whether it would actually do so was not for the court to decide, it sufficed that the charity believed it would). In 1947, however, when the NAVS, as it then was, tried to get its charitable status restored, the Tax Commissioners argued that any benefit to public morals from the abolition of vivisection would be negligible in comparison to the damage to public health. According to the appeal court judge Lord Wright, 'the calamitous detriment of appalling magnitude' that would be suffered by medical science if vivisection were stopped greatly outweighed any 'vague and problematical moral elevation' that society might gain.[27] In their judgement, the Law Lords also adverted to the political nature of the Society's objective. It was a judgement based on materialistic utilitarianism, and it is difficult to see how anyone of this turn of mind could have dissented from it, but it totally disregarded the century-long debate about the nature and purpose of science, which had by, this time become so passé as to elicit little interest outside the dwindling ranks of committed anti-vivisectionists.

Post-War Problems

In the immediate post-war period, civil experimental programmes were resumed with such enthusiasm that the price of laboratory animals rose sharply owing to shortage of supply. In Bristol, physiologists were prepared to pay up to 17 shillings, a labourer's daily wage, for a cat, which suggests they were no longer being offered sufficient numbers of unwanted or stolen domestic animals and strays, probably because many of them had been euthanized during the war, purportedly in the national interest: 400,000 cats and dogs had been massacred in London alone in 1939 as the result of unfounded fears of wartime food shortages to come.[28]

As the already illicit supply of 'strays' to laboratories was insufficient to meet their demands, major consumers such as the pharmaceutical company Burroughs Wellcome found themselves purchasing, perhaps inadvertently, stolen pets. In a notable case in 1945, one Mr Bailey located his 'lost' dog, Digger, when he heard his distinctive barking coming from a crateful of dogs bound for the Wellcome laboratories in Bradford. An attempt by the BUAV to use this incident to publicise the illegal dog trade was blocked by threats of a libel action, and newspaper reports elicited remarkably little public concern: the argument that medical progress was impossible without vivisection was now generally accepted, and anti-vivisection groups had lost their political and charitable credibility.[29]

Details of Nazi medical experiments, when they emerged, only made things worse. Although Vyvyan has argued that all experiments on humans in Nazi Germany 'were in continuation of, or complementary to, experiments on animals',[30] the obvious interpretation of the fact that the most outspokenly anti-vivisection government in history had the worst record on human rights was that ostentatious concern for animals masked an underlying misanthropy in which the value of human lives was debased.[31] The priority in post-war Europe was to strengthen human rights, and the 1948 Universal Declaration of Human Rights concentrated the attention of moral reformers on issues such as judicial corporal punishment and the death penalty. Animals were not mentioned in the Declaration at all, and a comparable declaration of rights for them is still awaited.[32] In some respects, human rights and animal rights had become competing interests: it was apparent that improvements in living standards and health would be critical in preventing future conflicts, and state-sponsored medicine and animal research were seen as vital for achieving this.

In Britain, the National Health Service Act of 1946 was initially welcomed by anti-vivisectionists because they thought it would make it easier for patients to opt out of vaccination, although any who chose to do so were probably more concerned about potential side effects than the use of live animals. In fact, by reducing patient choice, state-run medicine tended to restrict patients' ability to exert moral influence. Although the right of patients to choose their doctor and doctors to choose their patients was enshrined in the Act, it was meaningless in practice because both groups had their freedoms curtailed under the nationalized system.

In 1948, anti-vivisection organizations, concerned that experimentation had become routine, regulation a formality, and dispensations from anaesthesia the norm, requested that the government set up another Royal Commission to revise the 1876

Act, but their plea was ignored.[33] The BMA staunchly defended experimentation and opposed any changes, insisting that all necessary safeguards were in place.[34] Clearly, however, the Act's effectiveness as a regulatory agent was highly questionable: when the BUAV asked in 1954 if the government had ever turned down a licence application, the Secretary of State replied that the information was not available, which suggests that they had not.[35] It was rumoured that the government's secret animal research programme was still going on, but questions in the House of Commons about whether animals were being used in American-style atomic weapons testing met with a wall of silence, as it was deemed 'not in the public interest' to answer them.[36] The director of Britain's atomic research establishment at Harwell did, however, admit that animals had been exposed to radiation, and apparently told a BUAV supporter that 'the end justifies the means'.[37]

LD50

The major change for laboratory animals in the 1950s was the same as that for the medical profession and the population as a whole: they became increasingly subject to state control. The great majority of research on animals was now a matter of bureaucratic necessity rather than, as it had been when the anti-vivisection movement began, the personal initiative of a few ground-breaking physiologists. Until the 1920s, research had been mostly qualitative, directed at determining how animals functioned and how they reacted to disease, either for academic interest or, more often, to provide a model for human pathophysiology. The total number of animals used in qualitative studies was comparatively small: the antis criticised unnecessary repeat experiments and demonstrations done purely for teaching purposes, but their main complaint was that vivisection was demoralising to those who performed it, to the profession of medicine, and to society as a whole.

Paradoxically, opposition to vivisection in the post-war period, when quantitative testing predominated, became less vocal although the number of animals used increased. This was due in part to experimenters having won the propaganda battle by convincing the public that they were saving lives and helping their country to prosper, while anti-vivisectionists were sentimental, reactionary, and disloyal to their own species. Also, Joseph Stalin's apocryphal dictum probably applied: 'a single death is a tragedy; a million deaths is a statistic'. A solitary physiologist choosing to vivisect a stolen dog in a private laboratory was more likely to provoke an emotive response than any number of routine tests carried out by white-coated technicians on anonymous animals that would never see life outside a laboratory.

Chief among these bureaucratised consumers of animals was the lethal dose test, which had originated in 1921, when Dr A.J. Eagleton (1891–1925) of the Wellcome Physiological Research Laboratories proposed a method to standardise the potency of tuberculin by measuring its 'minimum lethal dose' in guinea pigs.[38] It was the potency rather than toxicity of the vaccine that was in question, but the latter was a convenient proxy for the former, since it was harder to test the strength of a vaccine than to find the lowest dose that would cause death. The test was seriously flawed, because susceptibility to toxins varies both between and within species, and it took only one idiosyncratic result to skew the findings. This problem seemed, however, to have been resolved in 1927, when the Dr J.W. Trevan (1887–1956), who had taken up laboratory work because he 'found clinical medicine too difficult',[39] proposed measuring the dose necessary to kill half the population to which it was given, to so-called *dosis letalis* 50% or DL50, which was soon anglicised to LD50.[40] Trevan intended his method to be used for standardizing drugs such as digoxin and insulin that varied from batch to batch and were dangerous in overdose. He appreciated that this would require 'much larger' numbers of animals than minimum lethal dose testing, and made some suggestions for 'economy', though probably with financial rather than humane considerations in mind.

The potential for using animals to test the safety of medicines caught the attention of the BMA, who raised it during a debate on Joseph Kenworthy's bill to stop public money being spent on vivisection, arguing that animal testing was necessary to guarantee that medicines were safe, and that 'effective control of therapeutic substances can only be ensured by the state…'.[41] Though officially apolitical, the BMA, as we saw in the previous chapter, wielded significant parliamentary influence, not by 'retaining' (i.e., paying) MPs, but by persuading the medical men among them to ask planted questions, or block legislation by 'talking out' or delaying bills, in the knowledge that no government would give anti-vivisection extra parliamentary time.[42]

LD50 testing was little used—or at least little reported—in Britain until the Second World War. The first research published in the *Lancet* that employed the technique was a 1943 study, jointly funded by the MRC and Boots Pure Drug Company, into the toxicity of an unknown substance that had been extracted from dead muscle (the object being to investigate the systemic effects of soft tissue injuries).[43] The mystery compound was variously fed to, or injected into, the veins or abdominal cavities of unspecified numbers of cats, rabbits, rats, mice and guinea pigs. Not surprisingly, there were 'wide differences' in response, both within and between species. The 'extreme variability' of the rabbit, the investigators concluded, rendered it 'quite unsuitable for biological assays', a recommendation that the pharmaceutical industry would, in decades to come, comprehensively ignore.

A few weeks later, the professor of morbid anatomy at UCL published a report into the LD50 of tannic acid, a substance of interest to the War Office as it was being tried out in the treatment of burns. The experimenters used of a total of 250 goats, rabbits, guinea pigs and rats, a tenth of whose skin surface was burned off under anaesthesia before they were sprayed with the acid.[44] Wartime necessity allowed such experimentation to escape public censure, as it was intended to alleviate the sufferings of wounded combatants. Another paper in the *Lancet* in 1945 reported the efforts of the biochemistry department at Oxford to develop an antidote to arsenical gases, which, it was feared, might be deployed in a last-ditch German attack. Their LD50 was determined by applying them to the skin of rats, presumably causing considerable pain, since a human 'volunteer' who had as little as one milligramme rubbed onto his arm experienced oozing and redness.[45]

One reason that lethal dose testing did not generate a significant public reaction despite the large quantities of animals used and the suffering it caused was that rodents soon became the animals of choice. Although experimenters typically used multiple species to counter the problem that interspecies variation was wide, rodents were the default option. The era of the 'lab rat' may be said to have begun in 1909, when a standard strain, the Wistar rat, was bred specifically for experimental use—the ancestor of the majority of laboratory rats used thereafter. The advantages were readily apparent: rats have a conveniently short generation time, reproduce easily, and are seen by the public as vermin and thus engender little sympathy, particularly those bred for the laboratory that have never been wild animals or pets. It is notable that illustrated propaganda from anti-vivisection groups rarely depicted rats, whereas pro-vivisection literature often did. The massive breeding programmes necessary to provide them in the large numbers required also had the desirable side effect of reducing intra-species variability, since the population became unnaturally genetically uniform due to inbreeding.

By the 1950s, LD50 testing was responsible for most animal deaths in the laboratory, and for a huge rise in the total number of experiments carried out. Though toxicity tests did appear in official statistics, the government dissembled by calling them 'simple injections', without adding '…of fatal poisons'. In fact, LD50 was almost bound to produce the maximum suffering possible, since the target dose was one that was only just fatal, perhaps after many days. Unlike the vivisection experiments of the nineteenth century, which were often public and involved mostly domestic animals whose sufferings were easily anthropomorphised, laboratory animals were experimented on in private, with bureaucratic efficiency, and the results reported in such a way that the animals were hardly even mentioned. Phrases in the academic literature such as 'the LD50 was determined' glossed over hundreds of slow, painful deaths. This routine, industrialised killing of creatures, without regard for suffering, was carried out not by medical visionaries but anonymous technicians, to whom the attribution of motives either of brutality or nobility of purpose would have seemed equally redundant.

Such was the confidence placed in LD50 testing that it was extended beyond pharmaceuticals to a bewildering range of domestic products, chemicals and cosmetics, though in many cases testing these for toxicity seems to have served little purpose. The BUAV took up the test case of the insecticide DDT, which was tested on a variety of domestic animals. Since an insecticide must obviously be poisonous, and since DDT would not in the real world be given to either animals or humans, why, they asked, were the tests needed at all? D.W. Jolly, the veterinary surgeon in charge, replied glibly that it was necessary to test any potentially dangerous chemical, though he added that he personally disliked the work and was reluctant to perform it. In its defence, he produced not the classic utilitarian argument but the bureaucrat's customary excuse for any misdeed: the tests had, he said, been 'planned by a committee', thus, presumably, absolving him, and anyone else, from personal responsibility. The fact that the authorities 'demand' such tests, replied the BUAV, only showed how foolish the system was, since the results were easily predictable.[46] Their objection was, however, brushed aside, and examples of similar senseless experiments—from injection of known poisons on the one hand to determining the LD50 of water on the other—might be supplied in abundance.

Testing on laboratory animals had now won such widespread scientific endorsement that its value had become practically unquestionable, not least because many of the leading figures in academic biomedicine had built their reputations on repetitive, protocol driven, quantitative experimentation, and continued to support it. Trevan, the inventor of the LD50 test, became a Fellow of the Royal Society, Research Director at the Wellcome Laboratories, advisor to the government, and Chairman of the RDS. His former assistant George Alexander Mogey (1917–2003) was Secretary of the Council for Postgraduate Medical Education, where he commemorated his earlier career in the laboratory by acquiring the car registration plate 'LD50'.[47]

The Sacred Cow of Science

In 1953, the LPAVS's position on medical science was succinctly set out in a review of Anthony Standen's book *Science is a Sacred Cow*: '... Standen shows the sacred cow as an unimpressive figure when she has a halo round her horns and is surrounded by white-coated figures bowing low, but he also shows that she remains just as good a cow, and gives as nourishing milk, when we treat her properly in her barn or in her meadow'.[48] Most anti-vivisectionists did not disdain science, but argued against excessive reliance upon it, and in particular against the requirement for every discovery to be 'validated' by experiments on animals. They tended, however, to ignore the rodents that made up the majority of the victims and to concentrate on saving domestic animals, especially dogs, though their efforts to get a dogs protection bill through parliament remained ineffectual. The first case of the 'liberation' of laboratory animals occurred in 1952, when an anti-vivisectionist released eight dogs from the kennels of a dealer. Ironically, considering the number of 'strays' and 'lost' dogs that were being kidnapped daily to supply laboratories, the dog-rescuer was convicted of stealing them, though he was conditionally discharged. The incident prompted the BUAV to start a campaign to raise money to buy up unwanted dogs, and so prevent them falling into the hands of laboratory suppliers.[49]

In an attempt to heal some of the divisions that beset the movement, a 'World Congress' of anti-vivisection societies met in London in 1954, with Risdon in the chair. He was the closest thing that British anti-vivisectionists had to a national leader, and his propaganda experience proved valuable in maintaining their public profile. He tried to improve long term support in the House of Commons by asking LPAVS members to 'badger' prospective parliamentary candidates about animal welfare issues, and contributed to radio discussions whenever he could, though he felt the BBC was biased in favour of vivisection and uncritically presented the government's position as authoritative.[50]

Chief among a dwindling number of anti-vivisection parliamentarians was Hugh Dowding, who had become a theosophist since his elevation to the House of Lords in 1943. In 1952, in a speech against animal experimentation, he rejected out of hand the defence of utility: '… even should it be conclusively proved that human beings benefit directly from the suffering of animals, its infliction would nevertheless be unethical and wrong'. In 1957, he attacked the secrecy surrounding animal research and summed up the regulatory system with military bluntness: '… a hollow sham, maintained to throw dust in the eyes of critics and to salve the conscience of the apathetic'.[51] His renewed calls for a government enquiry fell on deaf ears in parliament, and the RSPCA and Universities Federation for Animal Welfare

(UFAW, a graduate-only anti-vivisection society) added their voices to the appeal with scarcely more success. The RSPCA tried to meet the Home Secretary to tell him that five inspectors for millions of experiments was clearly inadequate, but he refused to receive their delegation. They also produced a leaflet, *Cruelty Within the Law*, which pointed out that the licensed experiments performed without anaesthetic included starvation, inoculation with virulent diseases, sleep deprivation, and exposure to poison gas. The Home Secretary's only concession was to appoint a sixth inspector—another doctor rather than the veterinarian the RSPCA had requested.[52]

Major C.W. Hume, founder and chairman of the UFAW, delivered a keynote speech in (1958) that stressed the historic virtue ethics argument, comparing experimenters who were thoughtless in their use of animals to First World War generals who coldly sacrificed their troops. Even if the latter's actions did ultimately lead to military victory, which must be the prime objective of any commander, their callous indifference to life would still have been wrong, on the grounds of both inhumanity and inefficiency. Hume, who was perhaps mindful, as a soldier, that the most reckless of commanders were often those who faced no personal risk, criticised experimenters for sacrificing animals for what they insisted were worthy causes, and yet declining to make any experiments upon themselves. The *Lancet* reprinted the speech with approval, exhorting experimenters to be more efficient and to reduce suffering whenever they could.[53]

Wishing 'to see laboratory techniques become more humane for the animals concerned', the UFAW commissioned the Oxford zoologist Dr William Russell to undertake a thorough study of the subject. Russell and his assistant Rex Burch published the results of their several years' work in (1959), as *The Principles of Humane Experimental Technique*, an influential report most notable for proposing the so-called 'three Rs': Replacement, Reduction, and Refinement of animals in laboratory experimentation.[54]

The NAVS, meanwhile, preferred to fight utilitarian science on its own terms by arguing that vivisection was not necessary for effective medical research. In the 1960s it published a series of short books to this effect by the theosophist and anti-vivisection doctor Maurice

Beddow Bayly (whose career at the Anti-Vivisection Hospital had ended so precipitately), the latest of which, *Clinical Medical Discoveries* (1961), described some of the many medical advances that had been made without vivisection. Bayly was the most prominent of the few doctors still working for the anti-vivisection cause in the post-war period, and his writings were lucid and well argued, but his lists of advances that had been made without animal experiments could be no more conclusive that the RDS's lists of advances made with them. How the development of medicine would have been different had vivisection never been permitted is a question of hypothetical history that is unlikely ever to be definitively answered.

The BUAV's latent pacifism resurfaced in the Cold War years, when it renewed its protests against the use of laboratory animals for military research, details of which were not declared in Home Office statistics for reasons of national security. Both the BUAV and the RSPCA noted with concern the use of monkeys and other animals in American rocket tests, and wanted to ensure these were not reproduced in Britain: according to the BUAV, the true objective of the 'conquest of space' was to achieve military supremacy by placing nuclear missiles in orbit.[55] The public, however, were mostly on the side of scientific progress, and watched developments in the 'space race' between the USSR and the West with interest.

In 1957, the Russian dog Laika (Barker) became world famous as the first living creature to orbit the earth. The Soviet government claimed she had been euthanised after 5 days in space, before her oxygen ran out, though she had actually died of overheating within a few hours of launch. Although the exact mode of Laika's death was not known in Britain until secret material was declassified in 2002, this had obviously been a lethal experiment upon a cooperative domestic animal, and it is significant that reports in the British press were overwhelmingly favourable, despite the experiment having been performed by a political rival and nominal enemy on the other side of the 'iron curtain'. The training of 'space dogs' included being confined in ever smaller cages and spun in centrifuges to accustom them to conditions inside a space capsule. It would not have taken much journalistic imagination to make a comparison between the fate of Laika and her fellow space dogs and that of the unwilling human victims of the relentless communist pursuit of technological and industrial superiority over the West. Instead, there was praise, without irony, for the 'selfless contribution' that dogs were making to scientific progress.[56] Indeed, if Laika had been any other species it seems unlikely that any protest would have been made at all, but some feeling that dogs were entitled to special consideration remained: the National Canine Defence League called on all dog owners to observe a minute's silence, and a few protestors gathered outside the Russian embassy, including the 79-year-old Lizzy Lind af Hageby.

The Littlewood Report and After

The RSPCA was still raising concerns over inadequate controls on vivisection in the 1960s: by this time there were over three million procedures annually, six thousand licensed vivisectors, and still only six inspectors, all medical men.[57] In May 1963, the Home Secretary finally responded to pressure and set up a committee, under the chairmanship of lawyer Sir Sydney Littlewood (1895–1967), with members drawn from science, the church, politics and anti-vivisection, to make a thorough review of the law on animal experimentation. Early on in its deliberations, the committee decided that 'vivisection' was no longer the appropriate word for the uses to which most laboratory animals were now being put. While the pro-vivisectionists on the committee may have preferred a more euphemistic term in order to avoid the visceral response that the suggestion of being cut up alive elicits, they were right to point out that the experiences of laboratory animals had changed beyond recognition since the 1876 Cruelty to Animals Act. The solitary physiologist who risked public disapproval to make great discoveries was a world away from the soulless, protocol-driven laboratories that consumed thousands of animals in 'routine' tests.

The committee received little response from the public, and had to rely instead on interviewing the editors of national newspapers to get a sense of public opinion. The editors confirmed that, apart from a few tireless correspondents who wrote into express the same pro- or anti-vivisection sentiments every time the subject was mentioned, they received few letters about it from their readers.[58] The public's desire for improved laboratory animal welfare legislation had long since passed. When the Littlewood report was completed, in 1965, it ran to 255 pages and made 83 recommendations. The report upheld the government's line that there was no overuse of animals and that the licensing system was adequate, though they did recommend that the 1876 Act, and its administration, be overhauled, and made some practical suggestions: the 'debarking' of laboratory dogs by cutting their vocal cords was to cease; Home Office inspectors were to have greater powers and better training; more inspectors were to be recruited; and the public were to be allowed to see animals under experiment.[59] The report was, however, never properly debated, and indeed it was 1971 before parliament discussed it at all. Anti-vivisection groups considered it a whitewash, and Risdon showed that public support could still be mobilised with a little effort by presenting a 300,000-signature petition of protest to parliament, but it was too late to make a difference.[60]

To meet the requirement for experimentation on an ever-larger scale, animals were still being illicitly supplied to laboratories. The RSPCA told the Littlewood committee that there was:

> A thriving trade in procuring and disposing of animals to hospitals and laboratories. But in all too many instances a certain duplicity is practised and members of the public are misled by vaguely-worded advertisements inserted in local newspapers and tending to create the impression that the dealers concerned are genuinely seeking to place unwanted animals with new owners.[61]

Even the RDS admitted that breeders and suppliers were struggling to keep pace with the burgeoning demand: speaking for the Society, Dr Lane-Petter complained of an 'embarrassing lack of animals in this country for trying out all manner of vital new drugs'.[62]

In 1967, the Medicines Control Agency was established, and by 1970, five times more experiments were being performed than in 1946, the great majority for regulatory purposes, and in particular, LD50 testing. Paradoxically, the methodological flaws that made LD50 an imperfect means of predicting human toxicity (differences in reaction between species; limited genetic diversity among rats and mice bred for the laboratory) only served to increase the number of animals used. What was needed, said the regulators, were more tests on an ever-greater variety of species. The thalidomide tragedy in 1959–1961 led to a redoubling of animal testing, which was made mandatory in 1969. Of course, it could never be established for certain that a drug was safe until it was given to patients, but the regulators required such large amounts of 'pre-clinical' animal toxicity data before researchers could even begin to test a drug on humans, that the *British Medical Journal* complained that over-regulation was delaying the introduction of new drugs.[63]

Conclusion

We come to the end of our chronological survey of the anti-vivisection movement at what can only seem an inauspicious period in its history. The total number of animals being used was at an all-time high, and anti-vivisection campaigners lacked the unity and the influence to translate a latent public dislike of vivisection into effective protest, still less to effect a change of heart where it mattered: in government, the medical profession and academia. Mindful of the great deal that remained to be done, one might be tempted to dismiss a century of anti-vivisection activity as having led nowhere. The movement's accomplishments, however, were far from negligible: imperfect and out-dated though the British legislation was, it was still the most comprehensive in the world, and for more than a 100 years the use of animals in scientific research had never been off the ethical and political agenda.

In no other country, over a sustained period, had so much time and effort been devoted to deliberating on the rights and wrongs of animal experimentation. Of course, there were ulterior motives on both sides, from anti-vivisection hospitals hoping to draw funds away from the voluntary sector, to research institutes whose hegemony depended on the supremacy of laboratory experimentation, and both were guilty of manipulating evidence, politicking, and sometimes downright intimidation; there was, however, at the heart of both pro- and anti-vivisection campaigns, a desire to do the right thing, and a firm belief in the importance of their own convictions.

Underlying their sometimes irreconcilable differences was a fundamental disagreement over what science was, or ought to be, since the anti-vivisection movement was founded on the premise that true progress could never come at the expense of cruelty, and so vivisection could not possibly benefit humanity, since it was intrinsically inhumane. It is a difference still to be resolved, and which keeps the opposing parties from achieving anything like mutual understanding. To many of the recipients of a 'scientific' education, anti-vivisection seems a misguided attempt to introduce sentiment and emotion into a sphere where they simply do not belong. To anti-vivisectionists, however, 'nothing which is ethically wrong can ever be scientifically right'.[64] Perhaps, having learned their history, even the most hardened experimentalist will grant them 'some credit for humanity'.[65]

Notes

1. 'Medical notes in parliament', *BMJ, 1* (1934), 1098.
2. Norah Elam, *The Medical Research Council: What it is and How it Works* (London: LPAVS, 1935) (Elam 1935).
3. Julie V. Gottlieb, *Feminine Fascism: Women in Britain's Fascist Movement, 1923–45* (London: I.B. Tauris, 2003), 299 (Gottlieb 2003).
4. Stuart, *Bloodless Revolution*, 442–444.
5. J.L. Risdon, *Black Shirt and Smoking Beagles: the Biography of Wilfred Risdon, an Unconventional Campaigner* (Scarborough: Wilfred Books, 2013), 340. Mosley replaced Risdon with William Joyce, 'Lord Haw-Haw', in 1934 (Risdon 2013).
6. Gottlieb, *Feminine Fascism*, 64 (2003) (Gottlieb 2003).
7. Richard Thurlow, *Fascism in Britain: a History, 1918–1945* (London: I.B. Tauris, 1998), 148. Kean, *Animal Rights*, 258, states that LPAVS members were 'totally committed' to anti-vivisection (Thurlow 1998).
8. Risdon, *Black Shirt*, 396 (2013) (Risdon 2013).
9. *Anti-Vivisection News-Sheet*, July 1940, 1.
10. 'Victory is ours' (editorial), *Anti-Vivisection News-Sheet*, July 1940, 3; 'We are not amused', *Anti-Vivisection News-Sheet*, July 1940, 19 (Victory is Ours 1940; We are not Amused 1940).

11. Guy Coleridge, 'Dog murder in Germany', *Anti-Vivisection News-Sheet*, July 1940, 19 (Coleridge 1940).
12. Nadja Durbach, *Bodily Matters: The Anti-Vaccination Movement in England, 1853–1907* (Durham: Duke University Press, 2005), 232 (Durbach 2005).
13. 'Vivisection—a depressed industry', *Animals' Defender*, *60* (1940), 1; Hopley, *Campaigning Against Cruelty*, 11 (Vivisection—A Depressed Industry 1940).
14. 'Very "hush-hush"', *Anti-Vivisection News-Sheet*, September 1940, 1; 'Our law allows this', *Animals' Defender*, *61* (1941), 1 (Very "Hush-Hush" 1940; Our Law Allows This 1941).
15. 'Blast!' (editorial), *Antivivisection News-Sheet*, September 1940, 2 (Blast 1940).
16. 'Estimate the suffering', *Animals' Defender*, *60* (1941), 1 (Estimate the suffering 1941).
17. M. Beddow Bayly, 'Recent experiments in British Laboratories', *Anti-Vivisection News-Sheet*, October 1953, 72 (Bayly 1953).
18. '"Interesting" experiments', *Animals' Defender*, 60 (1941), 1; Hopley, *Campaigning Against Cruelty*, 51 ("Interesting" Experiments 1941).
19. They also campaigned for a ban on the kosher method of killing, a not uncommon demand at the time: E.J.E., 'The History of Torture Through the Ages' (review), *Antivivisection News-Sheet*, October 1940, 2 (E.J.E 1940).
20. Letter, H. Marrian Perry to Sir Leonard, 10 July 1940, Well SA/RDS/C2.
21. Memo, 10 July 1940, Well SA/RDS/C2.
22. Memo from the honorary secretary of the RDS, September 1942, Well SA/RDS/C2.
23. RDS memoranda: 7 June 1943, 217; 20 January 1941, 207, Well SA/RDS/C2.
24. RDS archives, November 1945, 259, Well SA/RDS/C2.
25. RDS archives, 26 April 1946, 233, Well SA/RDS/C2.
26. *Times Law Reports*, *11* (1895), 541.
27. Peter Radan, 'Antivivisection and Charity', *Sydney Law Review*, *35* (2013), 519–539 (Radan 2013).
28. Bristol physiology department order books, Well GC/108/1; Risdon, *Black Shirt*, 346, 369.
29. Hopley, *Campaigning Against Cruelty*, 54–55.
30. Vyvyan, *The Dark Face*, 159.
31. Boria Sax, *Animals in the Third Reich: Pets, Scapegoats, and the Holocaust* (New York: Continuum, 2000) (Sax 2000).

32. A Universal Declaration of Animal Welfare was drafted in 2000 but has yet to be endorsed by the United Nations.
33. 'Deputation to the Home Secretary', *Animals' Defender*, April 1948, 47; Ryder, *Victims of Science*, 224 (Deputation to the Home Secretary 1948).
34. Ryder, *Victims of Science*, 226.
35. 'Do they ever say "no"?', *Animals' Defender*, March 1954, 46. I have been unable to discover evidence of a licence being refused under the 1876 Act (Do They Ever Say "No" 1954).
36. 'Atomic weapon experiments', *Animals' Defender*, *68* (1948), 1. The following year, the first historical account of the subject was published, E. Westacott's *A Century of Vivisection and Anti-Vivisection* (Ashingdon: C.W. Daniel, 1949) (Westacott 1949; Atomic Weapon Experiments 1948).
37. 'What happens at Harwell', *Animals' Defender*, January 1954, 1 (What Happens at Harwell 1954).
38. A.J. Eagleton, 'The standardization of tuberculin', *Lancet*, *1* (1921), 429–431 (Eagleton 1921).
39. J.H. Gaddum, 'John William Trevan, 1887–1956', *Biographical Memoirs of Fellows of the Royal Society*, 3 (1957), 273–288 (Gaddum 1957).
40. J.W. Trevan, 'The error of determination of toxicity', *Proceedings of the Royal Society of London*, *101* (1927), 483–514 (Trevan 1927).
41. 'The prohibition of vivisection', *Lancet*, *2* (1930), 1360.
42. Harry Eckstein, *Pressure Group Politics: The Case of the British Medical Association* (Stanford, CA: Stanford University Press, 1960), 75–78 (Eckstein 1960).
43. Marian Bielschowsky and H.N. Green, 'Fractionation, chemical properties and effective doses', *Lancet*, *2* (1943), 1531–1535 (Bielschowsky and Green 1943).
44. G.R. Cameron and R.F. Milton, 'Toxicity of tannic acid: an experimental investigation', *Lancet*, *2* (1943), 179–186 (Cameron and Milton 1943).
45. 'Antidote to arsenicals', *Lancet*, *2* (1945), 854–855.
46. 'Correspondence With a vivisector', *Animals' Defender*, June 1952, 7 (Correspondence With a Vivisector 1952).
47. Obituary, *BMJ* (2004), http://www.bmj.com/content/suppl/2004/04/15/328.7445.960-e.DC1, viewed 24 June 2016. Dwindling membership led the LPAVS to merge with the NAVS in 1957. Risdon became secretary of the merged organization, and worked towards unity with the BUAV up to his death in 1967, though as the BUAV remained

committed to total abolition as the only option, unity was never achieved: Risdon, *Black Shirt*, 496 (Obituary 2004).

48. 'Books reviewed', *Antivivisection News*, January 1953, 2 (Books Reviewed 1953).
49. Hopley, *Campaigning Against Cruelty*, 57–59.
50. Risdon, *Black Shirt*, 493, 659–668 (2013) (Risdon 2013).
51. Ryder, *Victims of Science*, 224–225.
52. Ryder, *Victims of Science*, 226.
53. C.W. Hume, 'Soldiers and laboratory animals: an analogy for experimental biologists', *Lancet*, *271* (1958), 424–426.
54. W.M.S. Russell and R.L. Burch, *The Principles of Humane Experimental Technique* (London, Methuen, 1959).
55. 'Those rocket tests', *Animals' Defender*, *72* (1952), 1 (Those Rocket Tests 1952).
56. Tacium, 'A history of anti-vivisection… Part I'.
57. Niven, *History of the Humane Movement*, 86.
58. John Bleby, 'The Littlewood Committee report on experiments on animals', *Journal of Small Animal Practice*, 7 (1966), 205–214 (Bleby 1966).
59. Ibid.
60. Risdon, *Black Shirt*, 498 (2013) (Risdon 2013).
61. *Report of the Departmental Committee on Experiments on Animals* (HMSO, 1965), 177 (HMSO 1965).
62. *The Anti-Vivisectionist*, July/August 1965, 44.
63. Bleby, 'The Littlewood Committee'.
64. 'Animals and us: quotations', *Quest*, 89 (2001), https://www.theosophical.org/publications/quest-magazine/42-publications/quest-magazinc/1325-animals-and-us-quotations, viewed 24 June 2016 (Animals and Us: Quotations 2009).
65. Robert Knox, 'Xavier Bichat: his life and labours; a biographical and philosophical study', *Lancet*, 2 (1854), 393–396 (Knox 1854).

References

Animals and Us: Quotations. (2009). *Quest*, 89. Retrieved June 24, 2016, from https://www.theosophical.org/publications/quest-magazine/42publications/questmagazine/1325-animals-and-us-quotations.

Atomic Weapon Experiments. (1948). *Animals' Defender, 68*, 1.

Bayly, M. B. (1953, October). Recent experiments in British Laboratories. *Anti-Vivisection News-Sheet*, 72.

Bielschowsky, M, & Green, H. N. (1943). Fractionation, chemical properties and effective doses. *Lancet, 2*, 1531–1535.

Blast! (Editorial). (1940, September). *Antivivisection News-Sheet*, 2.

Bleby, J. (1966). The Littlewood Committee report on experiments on animals. *Journal of Small Animal Practice, 7*, 205–214.

Books Reviewed. (1953, January). *Antivivisection News*, 2.

Cameron, G. R., & Milton, R. F. (1943). Toxicity of Tannic acid: An experimental investigation. *Lancet, 2*, 179–186.

Coleridge, G. (1940, July 19). Dog murder in Germany. *Anti-Vivisection News-Sheet*.

Correspondence With a Wivisector. (1952, June). *Animals' Defender*, 7.

Deputation to the Home Secretary. (1948, April). *Animals' Defender*, 47.

Do They Ever Say "No"?. (1954, March). *Animals' Defender*, 46.

Durbach, N. (2005). *Bodily matters: The anti-vaccination movement in England, 1853–1907*. Durham: Duke University Press.

Eagleton, A. J. (1921). The standardization of tuberculin. *Lancet, 1*, 429–431.

E.J.E. (1940, October). The history of torture through the ages (review). *Antivivisection News-Sheet*, 2.

Eckstein, H. (1960). *Pressure group politics: The case of the British Medical Association*. Stanford, CA: Stanford University Press.

Elam, N. (1935). *The medical research council: What it is and how it works*. London: LPAVS.

Estimate the Suffering. (1941). *Animals' Defender, 60*, 1.

Gaddum, J. H. (1957). John William Trevan, 1887–1956. *Biographical Memoirs of Fellows of the Royal Society, 3*, 273–288.

Gottlieb, J. V. (2003). *Feminine fascism: Women in Britain's fascist movement, 1923–1945* (p. 299). London: I.B. Tauris.

HMSO. (1965). *Report of the Departmental Committee on Experiments on Animals*, 177.

Hume, C. W. (1958). Soldiers and laboratory animals: An analogy for experimental biologists. *Lancet, 271*, 424–426.

"Interesting" Experiments. (1941). *Animals' Defender, 60*, 1.

Knox, R. (1854). Xavier Bichat: His life and labours: A biographical and philosophical study. *Lancet, 2*, 393–396.

Obituary. (2004). *BMJ*. Retrieved June 24, 2016, from http://www.bmj.com/content/suppl/2004/04/15/328.7445.960e.DC1.

Our Law Allows This. (1941). *Animals' Defender, 61,* 1.
Radan, P. (2013). Antivivisection and charity. *Sydney Law Review, 35,* 519–539.
Risdon, J. L. (2013). *Black shirt and smoking beagles: The biography of Wilfred Risdon, an unconventional campaigner*. Scarborough: Wilfred Books.
Russell, W. M. S., & Burch, R. L. (1959). *The principles of humane experimental technique*. London: Methuen.
Sax, B. (2000). *Animals in the Third Reich: Pets, scapegoats, and the holocaust*. New York: Continuum.
Those Rocket Tests. (1952). *Animals' Defender, 72,* 1.
Thurlow, R. (1998). *Fascism in Britain: A history, 1918–1945* (p. 148). London: I.B. Tauris.
Trevan, J. W. (1927). The error of determination of toxicity. *Proceedings of the Royal Society of London, 101,* 483–514.
Very "Hush-Hush". (1940, September). *Anti-Vivisection News-Sheet,* 1.
Victory is Ours (Editorial). (1940, July). *Anti-Vivisection News-Sheet,* 3.
Vivisection—A Depressed Industry. (1940). *Animals' Defender, 60,* 1.
We are not Amused. (1940, July). *Anti-Vivisection News-Sheet,* 19.
Westacott's, E. (1949). *A century of vivisection and anti-vivisection*. Ashingdon: C.W. Daniel.
What Happens at Harwell. (1954, January). *Animals' Defender,* 1.

8
Conclusion

I hope that what I have said respecting the exercise of humanity to animals, will awaken your attention to that virtue. Neither punishment, indeed, nor reward, are any where held out as inducements to its practice; but it is therefore not less a virtue, and you will have the satisfaction, at any rate, of doing good for its own sake, a thing, I fear, of not common occurrence in the present constitution of things.
James Lawson Drummond, Letters to a Young Naturalist (1831)

It might be thought that the last thing that twenty-first century Britain needs is more feeling for animals. The popular press is awash with sentimental animal stories of love and devotion and/or cruelty and neglect, designed to tug at our heartstrings or arouse angry indignation. Of course, we hardly expect scientists to be subject to such passions. Science is a privileged enclave from which normal emotional responses are excluded, and has been since at least the early-twentieth century, when it became acceptable for its practitioners to claim that, as Shaw stated ironically, 'as a Man of Science you are beyond good and evil'.[1] Thus, while no scientist wanted to perform vivisection, those who considered it necessary refused to allow personal feelings to get in the way. The ability to suppress one's natural sense of compassion became

A.W.H. Bates, *Anti-Vivisection and the Profession of Medicine in Britain*,
The Palgrave Macmillan Animal Ethics Series, DOI 10.1057/978-1-137-55697-4_8

something of a test for those embarking on a career in medical science, and they seem at times to have been proud of the objectivity they managed to achieve; or perhaps, as Vyvyan put it, 'scientists will go to any length to avoid feeling what they know'.[2]

Since the nineteenth century, the main justification for vivisection has been utility. The traditional Christian teachings that animals lack souls, and that human dominion over them is divinely ordained, certainly did not help their cause, but any tendency for these doctrines to encourage the exploitation of laboratory animals has to be weighed against the efforts of many dedicated anti-vivisection campaigners who were inspired by their Christian faith. The laboratory animal's tormentors were materialistic utilitarians, not Bible-believing Christians.

My judgement on their experiments, for what it is worth, is that the vast majority would have failed present day utilitarian criteria such as those proposed by Singer.[3] Of course, some were medically useful, a few led to very significant developments in medical practice, and only rarely (despite what anti-vivisectionists liked to claim) did extrapolation of results from animals to humans lead to dangerous error—for the most part, laboratory mammals tend to behave physiologically in a way very similar to ourselves. Most experiments on animals carried out during the period covered by this book were not, of course, groundbreaking scientific studies, but demonstrations, repeat experiments, and routine tests. With regard to novel investigative research on animals, however, the historical record does nothing to substantiate extreme views that either it reliably produced medical breakthroughs, or that no good ever came of it.

What the history of the anti-vivisection movement does demonstrate, is that utility has not always been the main issue, and that many early anti-vivisectionists ignored it altogether. Their motivation lay in their concerns that vivisection would exert a demoralising effect on individual experimenters, and on society as a whole. The potential benefits to medical knowledge, and whether the animals used were physiologically, intellectually, or spiritually comparable to ourselves, were issues of lesser importance than the feeling that inflicting pain on helpless creatures was a morally dangerous business. It was the fear that vivisection would promote a more brutal society that united people of diverse backgrounds in opposition to it, from the poor who feared being experimented on themselves, to the rich, who worried that the example of cruelty set by the professional classes might spread to the unlearned and precipitate them down a slippery slope to moral anarchy.

At a time when the opponents of vivisection concern themselves almost exclusively with the rights and interests of animals (a subject with its own lengthy history), it is salutary to recall that the radical Animals' Friend Society's five objections to vivisection did not mention animals at all: according to them, it was a moral failing, created public animosity against scientists, fostered cruelty towards humans, diverted charity away from human causes, and offended God. On these principals was built an anti-cruelty movement unequalled anywhere in the world.

Of the five objections, two might currently be accepted without demur: vivisection has certainly created animosity against scientists (some of whom have been the victims of violent attacks) and it probably diverts charitable efforts away from human causes (for some reason, it is anti-vivisectionists who tend to be blamed for this). The claim that vivisection promotes cruelty to humans is perhaps best regarded as unproven, though the link between cruelty to animals in general and violence towards humans is now well established. There has been no official pronouncement from any major religious denomination on whether vivisection offends God, despite the efforts, in recent years, of a growing number of animal theologians. What is curious is that the objection that vivisection is a moral failing on the part of the perpetrator, which was first on the list in the nineteenth century, is, nowadays, probably the most likely to be overlooked.

How did something that was once so important come to be so neglected? The declining interest in virtue ethics, especially in academic circles (where it is now enjoying something of a renaissance), has perhaps been partly responsible, as has an increased focus on the animals themselves, and in particular their rights and interests. So dominant has this approach become that it now seems somewhat strange to worry about the effect that vivisection has on us as humans.

One advantage of taking an anthropocentric view is that it does not matter whether animals have rights, or even feelings. Modern environmental ethics has, after all, been built on a foundation of human virtue: plants and landscapes do not have rights or feelings, but it is wrong to destroy them selfishly to serve one's own interests. When we hear of the environment being thoughtlessly damaged, we may well ask ourselves 'what sort of person would do a thing like that?'[4] It is the question that nineteenth-century anti-cruelty campaigners demanded of vivisectionists. At the very least, they expected them to undertake their work in a spirit of honesty, humility and mercy, and not be casual, uncaring, self-righteous or cruel.[5]

Apart from very rare cases of experimenters, notably Magendie, who did seem to be thoroughly heartless, the vast majority of scientists were, and are, determined to behave responsibly. They did not enjoy, and may positively have disliked, vivisection, and could suppress their natural emotional response to it only because a dispassionate attitude that would have been considered callous in everyday life was permitted, and even expected, among medical scientists. For a profession that allowed its practitioners to set conventional moral norms aside, Vyvyan's question—'To whom or what is a scientist responsible?'—became a crucial one.[6]

The practical answer was 'to him- or herself', because medical scientists, as educated people with privileged access to knowledge, were expected to self-regulate, an oxymoronic concept that led to the carte blanche conclusion that nothing could be cruel provided it was scientific. For many anti-vivisectionists, the exact reverse was true: morality came first, and nothing morally wrong could be scientifically right. For them, the vivisectors' claim that they were excused from moral guilt because they were engaged in science was an inversion of the proper order: the deep understanding of the world that constituted 'true' science would, they believed, preclude its possessors from trying to wrest nature's secrets out of her by brute force.[7]

We may now take it for granted that scientists are detached, objective, and unemotional, and that they are permitted to do things in the laboratory that would be socially unacceptable, illegal, or even damnable if done outside it, but in the nineteenth and early-twentieth centuries, when the philosophical and ethical rules of conduct for laboratory medicine were being laid down, it was not a foregone conclusion that amoral (or immoral) materialism would win out. In fact, the acceptance of animal experimentation in medicine represented an ethical break with the past, as the compassion and sensitivity that had characterised the medical gentleman were supplanted by the persona of the cool, impassive, white-coated medical scientist. Indeed, in a remarkable volte-face, emotion came to be seen as self-indulgent and unmanly, feelings as undesirable, and intuition as a methodological failing. Organizations such as the OGA that sought to preserve the role of the spirit and emotions in science became an increasingly marginalised voice, part of an alternative (sub)culture of utopian reformers, vegetarians, visionaries, and radicals.

The obvious heirs to this countercultural movement were the hippies of the 1960s and 1970s, with their ethos of pacifism, spirituality, syncretism and environmentalism, and there is enough common ground—the influence of transcendentalism, Eastern religions, Swedenborgianism, Unitarianism and theosophy, and the granting of equivalent legitimacy to laboratory experiments and subjective experience—to see the new age movement of the 1960s as a resurgence of the programme pursued by Oldfield and other reformers almost a century before, revived by a post-war generation after memories of the unfortunate association between the back-to-nature movement and National Socialism had faded. Anti-vivisection was revived too, though its wartime taint of disloyalty and subversion had perhaps not entirely been forgotten.

From the early history of British anti-vivisection emerge two points of relevance to us today: that medical practitioners thought from the first that vivisection was incompatible with the humane ethos of their profession, and that the objectivity of science was a contested construct. Medical practitioners in the nineteenth century *felt* that vivisection was wrong because it repelled them. They were prepared to accept emotions as evidence, and to situate their professional work in the wider context of their beliefs, something that the promoters of a morally neutral laboratory culture were determined to make unacceptable.

Theirs, of course, was the view that prevailed: there never were many medics who actually performed vivisection, but all were taught in medical schools that it was indispensable for knowledge, and that those who opposed it were enemies of science. To speak out was disloyalty, and medical students and young researchers (as I know from experience) went along with the culture of animal experimentation because to dissent was heresy. It may encourage future dissenters to note that the conception of science as beyond morality is a comparatively recent, debatable, and perhaps ephemeral, one. Possibly no one ever can truly reach a state where they could look upon vivisection unfeelingly, and if they could, they would have lost their humanity.

For ethicists, the most important lesson from history is that it *is* possible to construct a coherent and effective case against vivisection in which neither utilitarianism nor animal rights needs feature prominently!

Perhaps, in my lifetime, vivisection will be confined to history. Attitudes constantly change, and within living memory, experiments were carried out in the name of science (perhaps science is not such a civilising influence after all) that most scientists would find unacceptable, even abhorrent, today. Moral judgements cannot be reliably applied retrospectively; since the nineteenth century, the scope and influence of medical science has increased beyond all bounds, and there will always be fresh ethical challenges to be faced. It takes time to find the right answers, particularly when our capacity to do surpasses our capacity to know. The vigour with which our predecessors engaged in the vivisection debate was a sign of an impressive intellectual and moral commitment from participants on both sides to do the right thing. We owe them our gratitude, and their arguments our attention.

Notes

1. George Bernard Shaw, 'These scoundrels!,' *Sunday Express*, 7 August 1927 (Shaw 1927).
2. Vyvyan, *In Pity*, 20.
3. Singer, 'Animals and the Value of Life'.
4. Matt Zwolinski and David Schmidtz, 'Environmental virtue ethics: what it is, and what it needs to be', in Daniel C. Russell (ed.) *The Cambridge Companion to Virtue Ethics* (Cambridge: Cambridge University Press, 2012), 221–239, on p. 224 (Zwolinski and Schmidtz 2012).
5. Compare Oakley's discussion of induced abortion: 'Virtue ethics', 209.

6. Vyvyan, *In Pity*, 44.
7. Li, 'An unnatural alliance?'.

References

Drummond, J. L. (1831). On humanity to animals. *Edinburgh Philosophical Journal, 13*, 172–183.

Shaw, G. B. (1927, August 7). These scoundrels! *Sunday Express*.

Zwolinski, M., & Schmidtz D. (2012). Environmental virtue ethics: What it is, and what it needs to be. In D. C. Russell (Ed.), *The Cambridge companion to virtue ethics* (pp. 221–239, on p. 224). Cambridge: Cambridge University Press.

Chronology of Events

1792 Thomas Taylor publishes *A Vindication of the Rights of Brutes*
1809 Lord Erskine introduces an unsuccessful Cruelty to Animals Bill
1822 Richard Martin's Cruel and Improper Treatment of Cattle Act passed
1824 François Magendie gives vivisection demonstration in London; SPCA founded
1829 Anatomy murders in Edinburgh
1831 Marshall Hall publishes ethical guidelines for vivisectionists
1832 Anatomy Act
1833 Lewis Gompertz resigns from SPCA and founds Animals Friend Society
1835 Anti-cruelty law extended to domestic animals
1842 Etherington publishes *Vivisection Investigated and Vindicated*
1847 Marshall Hall publishes guidelines for vivisectors in the *Lancet*; Vegetarian Society founded
1852 Gompertz publishes *Fragments in Defence of Animals*
1858 Medical Act introduces medical registration
1859 Charles Darwin publishes *On the Origin of Species*

A.W.H. Bates, *Anti-Vivisection and the Profession of Medicine in Britain*,
The Palgrave Macmillan Animal Ethics Series, DOI 10.1057/978-1-137-55697-4

1860 Mary Tealby opens the Temporary Home for Lost and Starving Dogs in Holloway
1873 John Burdon-Sanderson publishes *Handbook for the Physiological Laboratory*
1874 Physiologist Éugène Magnan gives demonstration in Britain
1875 Attempted prosecution of Magnan for vivisection; first Royal Commission on Vivisection; Victoria Street Society (later the National Anti-Vivisection Society) founded by Frances Power Cobbe, who publishes *The Moral Aspects of Vivisection*; Archbishops of York and Dublin sign memorial against vivisection
1876 Cruelty to Animals Act ('Vivisection Act') passed; Physiological Society founded; London Anti-Vivisection Society Founded
1880 Anna Kingsford receives Paris MD, obtained without vivisection
1881 The International Medical Congress passes a resolution that vivisection by 'competent persons' should not be restricted
1882 Order of the Golden Age founded
1885 John Ruskin resigns his Oxford professorship in protest at vivisection
1891 National Canine Defence League founded; Henry Salt founds the Humanitarian League
1898 Frances Cobbe leaves the NAVS after it compromises on abolition, and founds the British Union for the Abolition of Vivisection; Oldfield opens first anti-vivisection hospital
1901 Stephen Coleridge publishes *The Metropolitan Hospitals and Vivisection*
1902 (Imperial) Cancer Research Fund Founded
1903 'Brown Dog' statue placed in Battersea; Lizzy Lind af Hageby and the Duchess of Hamilton found the Animal Defence and Anti-Vivisection Society; Lind af Hageby publishes *The Shambles of Science*; Professor Bayliss of UCL successfully sues Coleridge for libel; Battersea (National) Anti-Vivisection Hospital opens
1904 St Francis's Anti-Vivisection Hospital closes; OGA reconstituted
1905 Dogs Protection Bill first introduced in parliament

1906 Second Royal Commission on Vivisection begins; Dogs Act protects strays from vivisection; Dogs Protection Bill to ban all experiments on dogs is supported by a 300,000-signature petition but defeated in parliament
1907 Brown Dog riots begin
1908 Research Defence Society founded
1909 Wistar rat developed especially for experimental use
1910 Brown Dog statue removed
1911 National Insurance Act
1912 Second Royal Commission reports
1913 Medical Research Committee and Advisory Council founded; Dogs Protection Bill defeated in committee
1915 War Department Experimental Ground set up at Porton Down
1917 Association for the Advancement of Medical Research amalgamates with the RDS
1920 Medical Research Council receives royal charter; Humanitarian League closes down
1923 British Empire Cancer Campaign founded
1924 First Labour government
1926 University College professor acquitted of dog stealing; Major Charles Hume founds the University of London Animal Welfare Society
1927 BMA conference on research and animal experimentation suggests using strays for vivisection; LD50 testing developed
1928 Grove-Grady case: money given to help animals denied charitable status
1930 Joseph Kenworthy introduces a bill to ban spending public money on vivisection
1933 German government bans vivisection
1935 National Anti-Vivisection Hospital closes; Norah Elam publishes *The Medical Research Council, What It Is and How It Works*
1938 ULAWS becomes the Universities Federation for Animal Welfare (UFAW); OGA ceases activity in Britain
1939 Last official figures list over 900,000 animal experiments a year
1940 Norah Elam and Wilfred Risdon imprisoned
1941 Anti-Vivisection ruled not charitable

1942 Wilfred Risdon becomes secretary of LPAVS
1943 First research using LD50 published in Britain
1944 Draize test devised in USA
1946 National Health Service Act
1947 NAVS loses appeal to have its charitable status restored
1948 Universal Declaration of Human Rights
1950 Diseases of Animals Act
1952 First prosecution for liberation of laboratory animals
1954 World congress of anti-vivisection societies meets in London
1956 Therapeutic Substances Act passed
1957 The London and Provincial Anti-Vivisection Society amalgamates with the NAVS; Laika dies during space mission; NCDL campaigns against the use of dogs in space research
1959 William Russell and Rex Burch publish *The Principles of Humane Experimental Technique* and propose the three R's
1965 Littlewood Committee reports
1967 Medicines Control Agency established
1969 Testing of drugs on animals becomes mandatory
1971 Oxford philosophers publish *Animals, Men and Morals*

Bibliography

Bamwell, A. (1994). *Ecology in the 20th century: A history*. New Haven: Yale University Press.

Boddice, R. (2007). *A history of attitudes and behaviours toward animals in eighteenth- and nineteenth-century Britain: Anthropocentrism and the emergence of animals*. Lampeter: Mellen.

Boddice, R. (2011). Vivisecting major: A victorian gentleman scientist defends animal experimentation, 1876–1885. *Isis, 102,* 215–237.

DeMello, M. (2012). *Animals and society: An introduction to human-animal studies*. New York: Colombia University Press.

Feller, D. A. (2009). Dog fight: Darwin as animal advocate in the antivivisection controversy of 1875. *Studies in History and Philosophy of Biological and Biomedical Sciences, 40,* 265–271.

Giubilini, A., & Minerva, F. (2013). After-birth abortion: Why should the baby live? *Journal of Medical Ethics, 39,* 261–263.

Harrison, B. (1982). *Peaceable kingdom: Stability and change in modern Britain*. Oxford: Clarendon Press.

Hursthouse, R. (2001). *On virtue ethics*. Oxford: Oxford University Press.

Kete, K. (1994). *The beast in the boudoir: Pet keeping in nineteenth-century Paris*. Berkeley: University of California Press.

Klein, E., Burdon-Sanderson, J., Forster, M., & Brunton, T. L. (1873). *Handbook for the physiological laboratory*. London: J. and A. Churchill.

A.W.H. Bates, *Anti-Vivisection and the Profession of Medicine in Britain*,
The Palgrave Macmillan Animal Ethics Series, DOI 10.1057/978-1-137-55697-4

Li, C. (2012). An unnatural alliance? Political radicalism and the animal defence movement in late Victorian and Edwardian Britain. *EurAmerica, 42,* 1–43.

Linzey, A. (1999). *Animal gospel.* Louisville, KY: Westminster John Knox Press.

Merriam, G. (2008). *Virtue ethics and the moral significance of animals.* Ph.D. thesis, Rice University, TX.

Newton, D. E. (2003). *The animal experimentation debate: A reference handbook.* Santa Barbara, CA: ABC Clio.

Phillips, M. T., & Sechzer, J. A. (1989). *Animal research and ethical conflict: An analysis of the scientific literature: 1966–1986.* New York: Springer.

Richardson, R. (2001). *Death, dissection, and the destitute.* London: Phoenix Press.

Rupke, N. A. (Ed.). (1990). *Vivisection in historical perspective.* London: Routledge.

Russell, D. C. (Ed.). (2013). *The Cambridge companion to virtue ethics.* Cambridge: Cambridge University Press.

Sorenson, J. (Ed.). (2014). *Critical animal studies: Thinking the unthinkable.* Toronto: Canadian Scholars' Press.

Stepan, N. (1984). *The idea of race in science: Great Britain 1800–1960.* London: MacMillan.

Turner, J. (1980). *Reckoning with the beast: Animals, pain, and humanity in the Victorian mind.* Baltimore, MD: Johns Hopkins University Press.

Walters, K. S., & Portmess, L. (Eds.). (2001). *Religious vegetarianism: From Hesiod to the Dalai Lama.* New York: State University of New York Press.

Wynter, A. (1869). *Subtle brains and lissom fingers: Being some of the chisel-marks of our industrial and scientific progress, and other papers.* London: Robert Hardwicke.

Index

A

Abernethy, John 22
Alcott, Amos Bronson 70
Anaesthetics, in vivisection 6, 27
Anatomy Act, 1832 23, 27, 134
Anderson, Elizabeth Garrett 137
Anglican Church 47, 138, 149
Animal Defence and Anti-Vivisection Society 105, 139, 140, 170
Animals
- ability to feel pain 24, 48
- afterlife 8, 50, 57, 59
- rationality 49, 51, 57, 58
- rights 3, 4, 51, 71, 176, 200
- souls of 7, 43, 44, 47–50, 52, 58, 59, 85, 86, 112, 196

Animals' Friend Society 18, 19, 52, 197
Animals, Men and Morals (book) 3
Anthrax 141, 173
Anti-Semitism 89, 90
Anti-vaccination 9, 77, 88, 115, 118, 141, 172, 174, 176
Anti-vivisection
- character of its supporters 5, 7, 29, 31, 46, 57, 84, 108, 111, 146, 148, 178
- doctors and 17, 18, 20, 21, 24, 28, 53, 80, 108, 150, 199
- and feminism 15, 21, 82
- and pacifism 172, 184, 199
- petitions 14, 120, 143, 146, 147, 150, 152, 186
- 'shops' 140
- and social class 15, 16, 22, 29, 57, 107
- 'unpatriotic' 9, 88, 141, 171

Anti-Vivisection Committee, parliamentary 147

A.W.H. Bates, *Anti-Vivisection and the Profession of Medicine in Britain*,
The Palgrave Macmillan Animal Ethics Series, DOI 10.1057/978-1-137-55697-4

Anti-Vivisection Hospital, Battersea 8, 77, 80, 99, 122
Aquinas, Thomas 48
Aristotle 20, 48, 52
Association for the Advancement of Medical Research 28, 135, 137
Atheism 53
Atomic weapons testing 177

B

Back-to-nature movement 70, 82, 89, 90, 199
Bagehot, Walter 15
Banbury, Sir Frederick (Lord) 147, 148, 155
Band of Mercy 29
Barbauld, Anna Laetitia 48, 51
Battersea, district of London 80, 99, 100, 102, 106, 113, 115, 116, 119, 120, 124, 140
Bayliss, Sir William Maddock 136
Bayly, Maurice Beddow 114, 183, 184
Beard, Sidney Hartnoll 82, 90
Beaumont Animals Benevolent Society 144
Beevor, Charles Edward 135, 136
Bell, Ernest 82, 101
Bell, Robert 112
Bell, Sir John 104
Bennett, Sir William H. 103
Bentham, Jeremy 51
Bernard, Claude 19, 28, 29, 87, 138
Bioethics 2
Blackshirts. *See* Fascists, British Union of
Blundell, James 25, 47
Boatswain (dog) 43
Boddice, Rob 6
Body snatching 112, 133, 134, 156
Bowie, Alexander 102, 122
Brinson bath 113, 117
British Association for the Advancement of Science 22
British Empire Cancer Campaign 143
British Medical Association 74, 75, 106, 108, 111, 145, 147, 148, 150–153, 159, 177, 178
British Medical Journal 4, 21, 74, 117, 125, 187
British Union for the Abolition of Vivisection 108, 112, 118, 136, 137, 139, 140, 142, 145–147, 151, 152, 156–158, 172, 175, 177, 180–182, 184
Brown Dog affair 45, 105, 106, 115, 122, 135, 136
Browning, Robert 47
Brown Institute, London 136, 172
Burch, Rex 183
Burdett, Sir Henry 78, 79, 101, 109, 110, 124
Burdon-Sanderson, Sir John 26, 31, 136
Butler, Bishop Joseph 50
Byron, Lord 43

C

Calcutta, Black Hole of 51
Carnarvon, 3rd Earl of 19
Carpenter, William Benjamin 20
Carroll, Lewis (Charles Dodgson) 30
Carthew, Charles 77
Catholicism, Roman 46, 47, 49, 52, 53

Charity
anti-vivisection as 2, 9, 101, 104, 117, 121, 144, 145, 174–176, 197
and Metropolitan hospitals 79, 100, 104, 108, 122
Charity Organization Society 77–81
Christianity 5, 8, 44–50, 52, 53, 57, 59, 60, 72, 76, 82, 84, 85, 196
and animals 43–45, 47, 58, 72, 82, 84, 86, 196
Clauson, J. Earl 50
Clynes, J.R. 144
Cobbe, Frances Power 28, 31, 58, 108, 139, 172
Coleridge, Guy 171
Coleridge, Lord 101
Coleridge, Samuel Taylor 54, 56
Coleridge, Stephen 76, 78, 100, 101, 105, 120, 135, 136, 139
Concordium 70–72, 87
Cooper Perry, Sir Edwin 121
Coroners juries 18, 107, 113
Council for Postgraduate Medical Education 181
Cowherdites 72
Cromcr, Earl of 135
Cruel and Improper Treatment of Cattle Act, 1822 15
Cruelty to Animals Act, 1876 9, 19, 23, 26–29, 133–135, 150, 176, 185, 186
Culme-Seymour, Mary 115

D

Da Costa, Ronald 99, 100, 113
Dacre-Fox, Norah. *See* Elam
Darwin, Charles 21, 24, 29, 31, 56, 58, 71, 85
Origin of Species 44, 56
Darwinism 44, 69
Day, Sir John 27
Deontology 20
Dodgson, Charles. *See* Carroll, Lewis
Dogs Act, 1906 146, 154
Dogs Protection Bill 145, 146, 150, 152
Dornbusch, George 87
Douglas, C.H. 89
Douglas-Hamilton, Edith Annie 89
Dowding, Lord (Hugh) 6, 146, 171, 182
Druids, Ancient Order of 116
Drummond, James Lawson 19, 24, 47, 195

E

Eagleton, A.J. 178
Eastern philosophy 8, 59, 69, 86, 199
Edward VII 87, 105
Elam, Norah 150, 169–171
Emerson, Ralph Waldo 55
Erskine, Lord 51
Etherington, George 25
Evans, Lovatt 156, 157
Evolution, theories of 44, 45, 54, 55, 58, 59, 71, 85, 86

F

Fallows, John Prince 115
Fascism, British 9, 70, 90, 115, 170, 171
Fascists, British Union of 169, 171
Food Reform 70

Forster, Thomas 52, 53
Fox, George 50
Fremantle, Sir Francis 150, 174
French, Richard 10, 15
French Revolution 15
Frodsham, George (Bishop of Queensland) 149
Fur, wearing of 22, 111

G

General Medical Council 81
Gentleman, ethical conduct of 20, 31, 199
Geoffroy Saint-Hilaire, Étienne 55
Gill, Sir David 139
Gnosticism 86
Goethe, Johann Wolfgang von 54, 56
Golden Age, Order of the 8, 69, 71–73, 79, 80, 82–87, 89, 90, 199
Golden Dawn, Hermetic Order of the 80
Gompertz, Lewis 18, 25, 52
Grant, Robert 54
Green, Joseph Henry 54
Green Shirts. *See* Social Credit
Greenwood, G.G. 147
Griffith, Ellis 147
Grove-Grady case 145
Guerrier, Constance Edith 116
Guerrini, Anita 15
Gull, Sir William 31
Guy's Hospital 102

H

Hadwen, Walter 108, 137, 152, 157, 172
Haldane, J.B.S. 151
Hale, Sir Matthew 49
Hall, Marshall 25, 26
Hamilton, Lord Ernest 82, 101, 113, 115, 119–122
Harberton, Lord 78, 116
Harvey, William 24, 110
Henderson, Arthur 144
Herald of the Golden Age (periodical) 79, 83, 85
Hill, Leonard Erskine 136
Hills, Arnold Frank 74
Hinduism 45, 53, 99
Hitler, Adolf 172
Hoggan, George 28
Holism 4, 8, 54, 60, 88
Holland, Sydney (Lord Knutsford) 103, 104, 135, 150
Holwell, John Zephaniah 50
Homoeopathic Hospital, London 104, 105, 114
Hope, James 25
Horos, Laura and Theodore 80
Horsley, Sir Victor 135, 136
Hull, Robert 22, 47
Humanitarian League 71
Human Rights, Universal Declaration of, 1948 176
Hume, C.W. 183
Hunter, John 7, 24, 25
Hunting as 'sport' 43, 46, 111, 138
Hutchinson, Jonathan 30
Hydrophobia, Society for the Prevention of 136
Hydrophobia. *See* Rabies
Hyrtl, Josef 30

I

Imperial Cancer Research Fund 134, 143
International Medical Congress 6

J

Johnson, Samuel 20
Jolly, D.W. 181
Jones, Morgan 138

K

Kant, Immanuel 23
Kekewich, Sir George William 115
Kenworthy, Joseph 151, 178
Kibbo Kift 89
Kingsford, Anna 81, 86, 87, 112, 138
King's College Hospital 173
King's Fund 9, 77, 101, 103, 104, 107, 109, 110, 113, 115, 117–121, 124
Klein, Emanuel 27
Knox, Robert 21, 54, 55
Knutsford, Lord. *See* Holland, Sydney
Koch, Robert 30

L

Labour Party, British 139, 144, 151
Lady Margaret Hospital 80
Laika (dog) 184, 185
Lancet (periodical) 18, 80, 83, 88, 117, 120, 141, 173, 179, 183
Lansbury, Coral 45
LD50 177–181, 186
Lee, John Robert 121
Lee, Mr Justice 121
Lethal dose testing. *See* LD50
Levy, Joseph Hiam 115
Lewis, Lionel 18, 30, 52, 104
Lewis, Sir Thomas 150
Lichfield, 3rd Earl of 103
Lind af Hageby, Lizzy 105, 107, 136, 139, 142, 185
Linnaeus, Carl 44
Linzey, Andrew 4
Lister, Lord 105, 124
Littlewood Report 185, 186
Littlewood, Sir Sydney 185
Livery companies, City of London 119
Llangattock, Lord 78, 111, 138
London Anti-Vivisection Society 25, 101
London Hospital, The 76, 102, 103, 113
London and Provincial Anti-Vivisection Society 170–174, 181, 182
London School of Tropical Medicine 101
Lord Mayor of London 77, 104, 124
Lush-Wilson, Sir Herbert 119

M

Macdonald, Ramsay 144
Macmillan, Sir Frederick 140
Magendie, François 16, 17, 19, 20, 25, 198
Magnan, Éugène 23, 26
Maitland, Edward 112
Manning, Henry Cardinal 46, 47
Margaret Lodge 81
Margaret Manor 88, 89
Martin, Richard 15–18
Marx, Karl 24
Maynard, H.R. 116, 120

Medical Act, 1858 20
Medical Defence Union 80
Medical Research Council 136, 137, 143, 151, 153, 169, 179
Metempsychosis. *See* Transmigration of souls
Mogey, George Alexander 181
More, Henry 50
Morgan, Walter Vaughan 77
Morris, Richard 115
Mosley, Sir Oswald 170
Moulton, Fletcher (Lord) 135, 136

N

National Anti-Vivisection Hospital 100, 103, 104
National Anti-Vivisection Society 101, 108, 138, 183
National Canine Defence League 146, 150, 151, 154, 185
National Health Service 9, 124, 176
National Insurance Act, 1911 137
National Socialism 70, 90, 144, 170–172, 176, 199
Naturphilosophie 54
New age 5, 8, 57, 69, 70, 82, 84, 87, 89, 111, 170, 171, 199
New England 56, 70
Noailles, Countess de 116

O

Oldfield, Josiah 8, 69–82, 84–86, 88–90, 101, 111, 199
Oriolet Hospital 73, 74, 77, 78
Overton, Richard 50
Owen, Richard 54

P

Pacifism 5, 7, 8, 82
Paganism 8, 45
Paget, Stephen 135, 138, 141, 142
Pantheism 56, 60
Parkes, Sidney 122
Parliament, British 15, 28, 141, 143, 147, 148, 150, 152, 157, 177, 179, 182
Pasteur, Louis 30, 87, 102, 110, 139, 148
Pattison, Granville Sharp 53
Peaceable kingdom 84, 87
Peart, J.F. 117, 118
Perks, Robert Howell 83
Physiological Society, London 27, 135
Physiologists
  British 6, 9, 30, 133, 135, 151, 153, 156, 157, 175
  French 16, 17, 19, 25, 26
Physiology, experimental 27, 28, 30, 153
Pius IX, Pope 47
Plato 52, 54
Porton Down 141, 143, 156
Portsmouth, Countess of 78, 101, 116
Preece, Rod 45, 50
Prince of Wales (Edward VIII) 120
Pythagoras 50, 53
Pythagoreanism. *See* Transmigration of souls

Q

Quakers 19, 50

R

Rabies 110, 117, 136, 141, 148
Race, and health 90
Rats, experiments on 173, 179, 180, 187
Regan, Tom 45
Reid, Sir Robert 110
Research Defence Society 9, 59, 103, 133, 135–145, 148–150, 152, 153, 156–159, 174, 181, 184, 186
Risdon, Wilfred 170, 171, 174, 182, 186
Robbins, G.W.F. 100, 102, 103, 109, 112, 113, 140
Romanes, George 31
Royal Colleges, medical 27, 124, 158
Royal Commission on Vivisection, 1875 27
Royal Commission on Vivisection, 1906 134, 137
Royal Society of Medicine 148
Royal Veterinary School 145
RSPCA. *See* Society for the Prevention of Cruelty to Animals
Rupke, Nicolaas 10
Ruskin, John 43
Russell, William 183

S

Salt, Henry Stephens 71
Salter, Leopold 87
Sanden, Anthony 181
Saturday Fund 103
Schartau, Leisa 142
Science, nature of 5, 7, 13, 14, 21–24, 28, 31, 44, 46, 55, 57–59, 70, 71, 84–88, 106, 107, 111, 112, 122, 123, 125, 133, 134, 141, 149–152, 158, 175, 181–183, 185, 188, 196, 198–200
Scout Movement 89
Shaftesbury, 7th Earl of 28, 29, 46
Shaw, George Bernard 22, 152, 158, 195
Simon, John 6
Singer, Peter 3, 45, 196
Sinnett, A.P. 87
Sladen, E.S. 148
Smith, Robert Tweedy 115
Snowden, Philip 144
Social Credit movement 89
Socialism 71, 82, 122, 170
Society for the Prevention of Cruelty to Animals 16–19, 26, 45–47, 52, 90, 145, 157, 170, 183–186
Society for the Protection of Animals Liable to Vivisection. *See* Victoria Street Society
Society for the Suppression of Vice 45
South London Hospital for Women 116
Space exploration 9, 184
Spiritualism 5, 43, 57, 58, 60, 70
Stalin, Joseph 178
Starling, Ernest 135, 154–156
St Bartholomew's Hospital 99, 100, 102
Stevenson, Lloyd G. 56
St Francis, Hospital of 69, 75–80, 101, 109, 111
St Mary's Hospital, London 102
St Thomas's Hospital, London 102

Stuart, James Hamilton 113
Sunday Fund, Metropolitan Hospital 79, 101, 103–106, 109, 119
Swedenborgianism 199

T

Tail Waggers Club 145
Tansey, Tilli 134
Taylor, Thomas 51, 52, 71
Temperance 70, 104, 105, 114, 124
Tenterden, Lord 115, 116
Thalidomide 187
Theocratic Unity Temple 80
Theology of animals 7, 57, 86
Theosophical Society 86, 87, 89
Theosophy 5, 57, 86, 87, 89, 182, 183
Transcendentalism 8, 45, 53–57, 59, 60, 69, 70, 85, 199
  and beauty 55
Transmigration of souls 50–53, 59
Trevan, J.W. 178, 181
Tryon, Thomas 3
Tufnell, Thomas Jolliffe 26
Turner, S.C. 115
Tyerman, Daniel 49

U

Unitarianism 56, 199
Universities Federation for Animal Welfare 182, 183
University College London 53, 83, 105, 106, 135, 136, 142, 145, 153–155, 157, 158, 173, 179
University of London Animal Welfare Society 155
Utilitarianism 1–3, 17, 20, 23, 29, 30, 110, 123, 139, 175, 181, 183, 196, 200
Utopianism. *See* New age

V

Varney, Ernest 155, 157
Vegetarianism 53, 69, 70, 72, 73, 75, 81, 83
  as therapy 74, 75, 80, 83
  medical opposition to 83
Vegetarian Society 71, 72, 82, 87, 90, 101
Verney, Ernest 155, 156
Victoria, Queen 26, 27, 29, 104, 105, 120
Victoria Street Society 26, 29, 30, 43, 45–47, 75, 82, 86, 174
Virtue ethics 1, 7, 20–23, 183, 197
Vivisection
  of animals supplied by dealers 153–155, 157–159, 175, 182, 186
  bureaucracy facilitates 177, 180
  definition 1
  demoralizing 23, 29, 177, 196
  for teaching 27, 47, 76, 100–102, 107, 108, 114, 133, 151, 153, 158, 177
  human 7, 30, 100, 106, 107
  introduction to Britain 13
  link to violence 15, 21, 25, 70, 197
  and medical students 18, 19, 30, 106, 107, 137, 140, 158, 199
  methodological problems 23, 24, 186, 199

military 99, 141–143, 172, 174, 179, 182, 184
and social class 46, 71
of stray dogs 136, 146, 153, 157, 158, 175, 182
Vivisection Act. *See* Cruelty to Animals Act, 1876
Vivisectionists
character of 6, 7, 18, 20, 21, 111
prosecution of 26, 28
reluctant 30, 31, 181
Vyvyan, John 10, 14, 81, 86, 87, 176, 196, 198

W

Wachtmeister, Constance 87
Wakley, Thomas 18
Ward, Maidie Dudley 170
Wellcome laboratories 137, 175, 178, 181
Wells, H.G. 151, 152
Wesley, John 50
Wicca 89
Williams, Charles J.B. 25
Wolfe, Maynard Geraldine 116
Wollstonecraft, Mary 51
Woodcraft Chivalry, Order of 89
Wordsworth, William 56
World League Against Vivisection 139, 144
World soul 56, 59
Worthy, Fr John 49
Wynter, Andrew 24

Z

Zoophilist 46
Zuckerman, Lord 173